D0072818

RESEARCH IN
TECHNICAL
COMMUNICATION

RESEARCH IN TECHNICAL COMMUNICATION

A Bibliographic Sourcebook

Edited by
Michael G. Moran
and
Debra Journet

GREENWOOD PRESS
Westport, Connecticut • London, England

Library of Congress Cataloging in Publication Data

Main entry under title:

Research in technical communication.

Includes index.
1. Communication of technical information—Research—
Addresses, essays, lectures. 2. Technical writing—
Research—Addresses, essays, lectures. I. Moran,
Michael G. II. Journet, Debra.
T10.5.R47   1985   808'.0666   84-8977
ISBN 0-313-23431-0 (lib. bdg.)

Library of Congress Catalog Card Number: 84-8977
ISBN 0-313-23431-0

First published in 1985

Greenwood Press
A division of Congressional Information Service, Inc.
88 Post Road West, Westport, Connecticut 06881

Printed in the United States of America

10 9 8 7 6 5 4 3 2 1

284819

Contents

Figures

Preface

Research in Technical Communication demonstrates the vigorous and growing tradition of work done in technical and scientific communication. (Throughout this volume, the term "technical communication" or "technical writing" is generally used to include both technical and scientific communication; business writing, as a distinct area, is treated separately.) Although technical communication has been studied earlier, the past 15 years or so have seen increased and serious activity. While much of the earlier research tends to be pedagogical (and often anecdotal at that), recent research has become more scholarly, wide-ranging, and rigorous. This tradition of research, however, comes from a variety of fields, such as rhetoric, communication theory, literary theory, philosophy and the history of science, psychology, sociology, linguistics, and computer science. Because of its heterogeneous nature, research in technical communication is often difficult to assess in a coherent and unified manner. This volume presents essays that collect, in most cases for the first time, the diverse approaches this research has taken. *Research in Technical Communication* demonstrates—for researcher, teacher, and practitioner—the range of work already accomplished and the directions that seem most profitable and necessary for work in the future.

Perhaps the most pressing need enunciated in these essays is the need to erect a theoretical framework for the study of technical communication. Still in its relatively early stages of development, technical communication lacks a paradigm in which the merit or significance of discrete observations and generalizations can be accurately assessed. Without such a theoretical framework, research in technical communication will remain random, diffuse, and often academically unrespectable. The overriding conclusion most of the contributors to this volume reach is the necessity to construct that theory. This need has been cited for several years, but it still remains unfulfilled, except in a few, specific instances.

Research in Technical Communication offers what may become a basis from which researchers can begin to construct that theory. It outlines preliminary work done in articulating theoretical questions and demonstrates fruitful approaches and areas of study. The book begins with general concerns and progresses to particular applications. Part I consists of four chapters outlining larger theoretical ways to examine technical communication: humanistic approaches to technical communication, the history of technical communication, communication theory and technical writing, and the teaching of technical writing. Part II examines technical communication in relation to four traditional rhetorical concerns: invention, audience, modes of organization, and style. Part III, divided into three chapters, discusses specific types of technical communication: proposals, reports, and business correspondence. Part IV examines technical communication and related concerns, specifically, the use of the computer, oral communication and specialized forms of technical communication, notably, legal writing and writing for the government. The appendices offer guides to textbooks, style manuals, and the technical writing profession.

All chapters present a discussion of the most important research in their respective areas. Each chapter then concludes with a list of references, giving full citations for all sources mentioned, as well as, in some cases, other relevant work. The key to the abbreviations for the journals cited in the references follows the Preface.

The volume opens with a group of essays that provide overviews of extensive ways to study technical communication. These chapters demonstrate several of the general areas from which a comprehensive theory of technical communication may come. In the first chapter, "Technical and Scientific Writing and the Humanities," Philip M. Rubens explores one of the most potent of the general theoretical approaches: the examination of technical and scientific communication in terms of humanistic concerns. Rubens begins by examining the historical division between the "two cultures," as well as the possibilities of synthesis to be found in studies of the use of language, problems of ethics, and the nature of scientific concepts. More specific areas of interaction include, the relation of the humanities and engineering, the attempts to see science and literature as complementary activities, the question of values and ethics in science and technology, and the humanistic educational needs of science and technology students. Finally, Rubens turns his attention to the relation of science, technology, and rhetoric, an area of study ignored until recently, but now attracting much interest. Rubens examines the new concern with audience, persona, and rhetorical devices, such as metaphor, in scientific and technical writing. His essay demonstrates the rich possibilities which humanistic concerns and methodologies provide in the analysis of technical communication.

The following chapter, "The History of Technical and Scientific Writing" by Michael G. Moran, examines in more detail one humanistic approach to the evaluation of technical and scientific writing. While Moran sees historical analysis as a productive area of study, he also notes that there is no coherent background of material in the area and even no adequate definition of this important sub-discipline. Moran distinguishes the history of technical and scientific writing from related fields and, like many of the contributors to this volume, argues that the topic he treats centers on questions of rhetoric. Moran then examines material dealing with the rhetoric of scientific discourse in several historical periods: ancient, medieval, Renaissance, eighteenth, nineteenth, and twentieth century. Moran's chapter demonstrates the directions in which research into the history of technical and scientific writing might proceed and indicates the value such research will have.

In "Communication Theory and Technical Communication," George A. Barnett and Carol Hughes survey another group of theories that have had particular relevance to technical communication. Like other approaches explored in this volume, communication theory can be studied from a variety of perspectives—generated from both humanistic and scientific disciplines. Barnett and Hughes concentrate here on scientific theories based on empirical data. Their chapter makes the point, which is often made in this collection, that no single comprehensive theory exists to explain communication, particularly in regard to technical writing. Instead, Barnett and Hughes find a number of "middle-range theories" that offer a series of generalizations and syntheses of data. The essay describes several models of communication and then discusses six variables—source, message, channels, receivers, feedback, and environment—and their effect on technical communication.

In the last chapter in Part I, "Teaching Technical Writing," Anthony O'Keeffe examines one of the most thoroughly established areas of research in technical writing. Pedagogical applications have been reported for quite a while, and more recently, as O'Keeffe shows, these discussions of classroom activities have become increasingly rooted in solid theoretical work. O'Keeffe's chapter is ordered on a chronology of teaching technical writing. He begins by looking at material aimed at those getting started in teaching: basic references, attempts to define the essential characteristics of technical writing, and explorations of the double connection of technical writing with academic and professional worlds. O'Keeffe next examines the common undergraduate course: syllabus, organization, and special concerns such as audience analysis, graphics, or oral communication. The chapter then discusses program development after the basic course and concludes by looking at several special issues in the teaching of technical writing, particularly the debate about the relation of technical writing to the university curriculum. O'Keeffe shows the developing sophistication of pedagogical research and the contributions which work in composition and discourse theory have made to it.

The next part focuses on four topics that align technical communication, in some ways, with rhetoric and composition; the research cited also shows the contributions other disciplines must make. These approaches are among the most promising areas of research, and it is here that the demand for theoretical work is most evident.

Carolyn R. Miller's "Invention in Technical and Scientific Discourse: A Prospective Survey" clearly demonstrates the need for a pervasive theory of technical and scientific discourse as a rhetorical activity. As Miller argues, such a theory (based on a philosophy that sees science as persuasive rather than demonstrative) must exist before a discussion of the role of invention in technical and scientific writing can become meaningful. Lacking a coherent theory of technical and scientific discourse as argument, researchers must often look to other fields, as Miller does. She surveys work from diverse disciplines and integrates a good deal of material that is not always explicitly concerned with invention. Miller's wide-ranging research concerns itself with a broad view of invention—the process of inquiry and creation of ideas; a narrower view of invention—appropriate and effective use of existing knowledge; and particular applications, especially pedagogical. Her chapter shows both the contribution other fields can make to the study of technical and scientific communication, as well as the need to integrate technical and scientific communication into the rhetorical tradition itself.

Michael Keene and Marilyn Barnes-Ostrander's chapter, "Audience Analysis and Adaptation," looks at another central concern in communication and a major concern of theorists. Indeed, Keene and Barnes-Ostrander argue that, measured by duration or the number of adherents, an audience-centered view of discourse is the principal critical attitude of the Western world. Keene and Barnes-Ostrander place this concern with audience in a large historical context but concentrate on modern materials that are especially relevant to technical communication. They explore the role of audience within the dynamics of the communication situation by examining rhetorical and psychological models of communication. They then look at the interaction of audience with content, organization, style, and visuals. Finally, Keene and Barnes-Ostrander view approaches to teaching audience. Their chapter shows the range of study generated by this concern with readers, one of the most fruitful and diverse areas of research in technical communication.

In "Modes of Organization," Victoria M. Winkler surveys representative technical writing textbooks from the 1960s to the 1980s in terms of the way they recommend arranging material in scientific and technical memos and reports. She identifies three kinds of textbooks: general principle texts, which either ignore modes of organization or relegate them to secondary importance; structural model texts (the largest group), which are organized around the modes of discourse, primarily exposition; and alternative texts, which use patterns based on inventional models and a process approach to teaching writing. Her survey shows that both the first and second groups are more concerned with product than process and tend to present models prescriptively. The third group, alternative texts, focuses more on the process of writing, emphasizing inventional concerns. Winkler notes a gradual shift in attention from product to process, which she sees as part of our own paradigm shift. She recommends further research into alternative modes of organization that better explain the interactive, dynamic process of writing. In the second section of her chapter, Winkler examines recent research that has begun to "debunk" the traditional modes of organization.

In his essay on "Style in Technical Writing," Glenn J. Broadhead also points out the need to articulate a theoretical groundwork for research in technical communication. In this case, Broadhead shows the need for an adequate theoretical definition of style in technical writing, as well as a theoretical definition of technical writing itself in which questions of style are relevant. While Broadhead sees no adequate theory in existence at present, he argues that enough attention is being paid to style by theorists to suggest that the articulation of such a theory may not be far off. Like other contributors to this volume, Broadhead integrates technical writing studies with related fields of learning, to produce a wide-ranging coverage of stylistic considerations. The specific stylistic topics he considers include syntax (linguistic considerations that must underlie analysis of style), cohesion and punctuation (relations between different segments of a text), vocabulary (acceptable and unacceptable or prescribed and proscribed language), editorial conventions and usage (revision as part of the writer's process as well as the publishing process), and prescriptive approaches to style found in concepts of readability, usability, and rhetoric.

Part III treats specific forms of technical and business writing and presents many of the more traditional ways of studying technical communication. The authors of these chapters demonstrate the value of this work as well as the directions which future research should take. Specifically, they point out the need for empirical studies that test received wisdom and a new awareness of the rhetorical aspects of technical communication. The first of these chapters, Mark P. Haselkorn's "Proposals," argues strongly for empirical, replicatable studies that will deny or substantiate assertions commonly made about proposal writing. The vast majority of the work which Haselkorn surveys is "how to's" whose authority is usually the experience of the writer. Haselkorn also sees the need for more specific terminology that will allow us to distinguish between various kinds of proposals and recommendation reports. In looking at the work done on proposal writing, he divides his discussion into treatment of general studies on proposals, specific "how to's" by source and by need, textbooks and handbooks, studies that indicate the direction in which future research should proceed, and methods of teaching proposal writing.

The need for empirical testing of assertions is also demonstrated in Judith P. Stanton's chapter "Technical Reports." Although in many different technical fields reports may be written and used as primary means of communication, little important research has been conducted. Books in the field tend to reflect trends in other fields, such as readability, communication theory, and, most currently, problem-solving. Stanton argues that the area is ripe for more sophisticated research methodologies and for stronger, more effective textbooks and manuals. This need is intensified by the fact that many different sub-areas of business, government, and industry have developed specialized reports to meet specialized needs, and all of these deserve analysis. In addition, Stanton concludes, the area needs sounder pedagogical approaches to teaching students how to discover information, solve problems, and write effective reports to various audiences in various settings.

In "Business Letters, Memoranda, and Resumés," Mary Hurley Moran and

Michael G. Moran survey research about what are probably the most common kinds of documents people in business and industry produce. Given the importance of this kind of writing, they argue, little serious research has been done in the area. Instead, most of the research of the past 25 years has been redundant and derivative, based on cherished beliefs or "folk wisdom," rather than empirical studies. Moran and Moran review the best of this work, as well as more recent studies that suggest new trends. Research in the history of business correspondence, empirical studies that test established tenets of business correspondence, and studies that explore the rhetoric of business writing demonstrate the directions in which research into business correspondence might profitably go.

Part IV treats some of the related areas of study with which researchers in technical communication must deal. William L. Benzon's "Computing and the Future of Technical Communication" takes a broad look at the subject and identifies several areas where the computer is most likely to yield tools for technical communication. Benzon also surveys works in cognitive psychology, computational linguistics, and artificial intelligence which promise to produce insights into the process of technical communication. He concludes that technical communicators, because of their roles as writers of computer documentation and users of computer technology, are in a strong position to play a key role in the wise and human use of computer technology.

In "Oral Presentation and Presence in Business and Industry," Bertie E. Fearing briefly traces the history of research in oral communication to its roots in traditional rhetoric, as well as the contribution empirical research has made to speech criticism. In the major part of her essay, she surveys applied rhetorical theory, especially in light of three concerns: audience analysis, message analysis, and delivery analysis. Her research shows the complementary relation of traditional rhetorical precepts and quantitative research, the latter partially substantiating the former.

The last two chapters illuminate two special areas in technical communication which have certain unique problems and concerns. Russell Rutter's chapter on "Resources for Teaching Legal Writing" describes a field in its early stages of development. His survey of research on legal writing—legal training and legal forms, legal style and plain language laws, and resources for classroom teaching—shows a discipline that is often inadequately defined and poorly taught. As he argues, the main contribution which specialists can make is to identify legal writing as an area of study in its own right, separate from legal research and format, and to apply to this field methods developed by composition specialists.

In "Writing for the Government," Robert Scott Kellner makes sense out of the voluminous materials produced by the U.S. government, as well as other sources, that describe the requirements for writing for the government. Kellner looks specifically at style guides, and specifications and standards. Because much of the material he cites is not available in bookstores or libraries, he helpfully adds a section explaining how to obtain government publications.

The three appendices are included to help teachers, writers, and editors select textbooks and style manuals, as well as locate information about technical communication as a profession. In the first appendix, "Guide to Textbooks in Technical Communication," Susan Hilligoss surveys major textbooks in technical communication, discussing comprehensive texts, more specialized works—such as books written for specific fields, handbooks, and anthologies—and composition texts suitable for technical writing courses. She evaluates these works in terms of such considerations as their concern for audience, their attention to the writing process, their organization, and their format.

Appendix II, Caroline R. Goforth's "A Selection of Style Manuals," examines manuals useful in a wide variety of subject areas and types of writing, those useful in most technical writing, and those prepared for specific academic fields, kinds of writing, and publications. As Goforth points out, guides to style abound, and it is the writer's task to select the most appropriate, based on the writing assignment, the audience, and the writer's profession.

In the last appendix, "The Technical Writing Profession," Julie Lepick Kling looks at material concerning the professional definitions of both technical writers and editors, the professional status of the technical communicator, and the qualifications needed for a career in technical communication.

We hope this book, in collecting past research in technical communication, will prove useful to those who will develop its future. We would like to thank the contributors to the volume who often had to define their areas of study, as well as collect, synthesize, and evaluate research from an enormous range of sources. We would also like to acknowledge those who helped in this project from its inception to its conclusion: M. Thomas Inge and G. William Koon, past and present heads of Clemson's English Department; Marilyn Brownstein, acquisitions editor of Greenwood Press, Joyce Keenan, who helped regularize the reference lists; Martha Regalis, Larisa Garrison and Lewis R. Arrington, who compiled the indexes; and Jim S. Borck of Louisiana State University, who provided guidance and technology for preparation of the subject index.

Abbreviations

ABA J	*American Bar Association Journal*
ABCA Bul	*ABCA Bulletin*
Academe	*Academe: Bulletin of the AAUP*
Acad Manag J	*Academy of Management Journal*
ADE Bul	*ADE Bulletin*
Admin Manag	*Administration Management*
Admin Sci Q	*Administrative Science Quarterly*
Adv Comput	*Advances in Computers*
Adver Age	*Advertising Age*
Adv Manag J	*Advanced Management Journal*
Adv Sci	*Advancement in Science*
Aircraft Eng	*Aircraft Engineering*
Air Pol Cont Assoc J	*Air Pollution Control Association Journal*
Ala Law	*Alabama Lawyer*
Ala L Rev	*Alabama Law Review*
Albany L Rev	*Albany Law Review*
Alberta L Rev	*Alberta Law Review*
Am Behav Sci	*American Behavioral Sciences*
Ambio	*Ambio*
Am Bus	*American Business*
Am Doc	*American Documentation*
Am Educ	*American Education*

Am J Comput Linguist	*American Journal of Computational Linguistics*
Am J Soc	*American Journal of Sociology*
Am Psychol	*American Psychologist*
Am Sch	*American Scholar*
Am Sci	*American Scientist*
Am Soc Rev	*American Sociological Review*
Am Sp	*American Speech*
Am Vocat J	*American Vocational Journal*
Appl Ergon	*Applied Ergonomics*
Appl Psycholinguist	*Applied Psycholinguistics*
Appr J	*Appraisal Journal*
Architec Rec	*Architecture Record*
Assn Am Geog Ann	*Association of American Geographers Annals*
AV Comm Rev	*AV Communication Review*
Bal Sheet	*Balance Sheet*
Bankers Mag	*Bankers Magazine*
Bankers Month	*Bankers Monthly*
Banking	*Banking*
Behav Brain Sci	*The Behavioral and Brain Sciences*
Bell J Econ	*Bell Journal of Economics*
Best's Insur N	*Best's Insurance News*
Best's Insur N (Life Ed)	*Best's Insurance News (Life Edition)*
Best's Rev (L/H Ed)	*Best's Review (Life/Health Edition)*
Best's Rev (P/C Ed)	*Best's Review (Property/Casualty Edition)*
Biol Abstr	*Biological Abstracts*
Brit J Soc	*British Journal of Sociology*
Bul Atomic Sci	*Bulletin of the Atomic Scientist*
Bur Clear House	*Burroughs Clearing House*
Bus Auto	*Business Automation*
Bus Hist Rev	*Business History Review*
Bus Law	*Business Lawyer*
Bus Manag	*Business Management*
Bus Week	*Business Week*

Byte   *Byte*

Calif S B J   *California State Bar Journal*
CA Mag   *CA Magazine*
Can Bankers TCB Rev   *Canadian Bankers TCB Review*
Can Bus   *Canadian Business*
CASE Curr   *CASE Currents*
CCC   *College Composition and Communications*
CE   *College English*
CEDR Q   *CEDR Quarterly*
Chang Times   *Changing Times*
Chart Mech Eng   *Chartered Mechanical Engineer*
Chem Eng   *Chemical Engineering*
Chem Eng News   *Chemical and Engineering News*
Chem Soc Rev   *Chemical Society Review*
Chem Tech   *Chemical Technology*
Civ Eng   *Civil Engineering* (NY)
Class J   *Classical Journal*
Clearing House   *Clearing House*
Coal Age   *Coal Age*
Cog Psychol   *Cognitive Psychology*
Cog Therapy Res   *Cognitive Therapy Research*
Comm Mon   *Communication Monographs*
Comm Q   *Communication Quarterly*
Comm Res   *Communication Research*
Comm Sci Tech Info   *The Communication of Scientific and Technical Information*
Communication   *Communication*
Comput Auto   *Computers and Automation*
Comput Educ   *Computer and Education*
Computer   *Computer*
Computerworld   *Computerworld*
Comput Hum   *Computers and the Humanities*
Comput J   *Computer Journal*
Consumer Bul   *Consumer Bulletin*

Control Eng	*Control Engineering*
CPA J	*CPA Journal*
Cred Fin Manag	*Credit and Financial Management*
Curr Con	*Current Contents*
CS Speech J	*Central States Speech Journal*

Daedalus	*Daedalus*
Data Manag	*Data Management*
Datamation	*Datamation*
Director	*Director*
Drake L Rev	*Drake Law Review*
Dun's	*Dun's Review*

Educ Comm Tech J	*Educational Communication and Technology Journal*
Educ Inst TV	*Educational-Instructional TV*
Educ J Inst Dev Ind Law	*Education Journal of the Institute for the Development of India Law*
Educ Libr	*Education Libraries*
Educ Res Bul	*Education Research Bulletin*
Elect Eng	*Electronic Engineer*
Electron Power	*Electronics and Power*
Elem Engl	*Elementary English*
Eng Educ	*Engineering Education*
Engineering	*Engineering*
Eng J	*Engineering Journal*
Engl Educ	*English Education*
Engl J	*English Journal*
Engl Lang Teach J	*English Language Teaching Journal*
Engl Rec	*English Record*
Engl Stud	*English Studies*
Env Affairs	*Environmental Affairs*
Env Sci Tech	*Environmental Science and Technology*
Ergonomics	*Ergonomics*

Fed Aid Plan	*Federal Aid Planner*
Fed Home Loan Bank Board J	*Federal Home Loan Bank Board Journal*
Fed Proc	*Federation Proceedings*
Fin Ex	*Financial Executive*
Fla B J	*Florida Bar Journal*
Forbes	*Forbes*
Fortune	*Fortune*
Found Lang	*Foundations of Language*
Fueloil Oil Heat	*Fueloil and Oil Heat*
Fund Raising Manag	*Fund Raising Management*
GAO Rev	*GAO Review*
Gov Exec	*Government Executive*
Grants Mag	*Grants Magazine*
Harvard Bus Rev	*Harvard Business Review*
HCR	*Human Communication Research*
Health Educ	*Health Education*
Human Behav	*Human Behavior*
Human Fact	*Human Factors*
Human Relat	*Human Relations*
Human Res Manag	*Human Resource Management*
Hydrocarbon Process	*Hydrocarbon Processing*
IABC Bul	*IABC Bulletin*
IBM Syst J	*IBM Systems Journal*
Idaho L Rev	*Idaho Law Review*
IEEE Proc	*Proceedings of the IEEEE*
IEEE Spectrum	*IEEE Spectrum*
IEEE Trans Eng Manag	*IEEEE Transactions on Engineering Management*
IEEE Trans Eng Writ Speech	*IEEEE Transactions on Engineering Writing and Speech*
IEEE Trans Prof Comm	*IEEEE Transactions on Professional Communication*

Improv Coll Univ Teach	*Improving College and University Teaching*
Indus Distrib	*Industrial Distribution*
Indus Educ	*Industrial Education*
Indust Eng	*Industrial Engineering*
Indus Manag	*Industrial Management*
Indus Manag Rev	*Industrial Management Review*
Indus Mark	*Industrial Marketing*
Indus Mark Manag	*Industrial Marketing Management*
Indus Photo	*Industrial Photography*
Indus Train Int	*Industrial Training International*
Indus Week	*Industry Week*
Inform Stor Retrieval	*Information Storage Retrieval*
Infrosystems	*Infrosystems*
Inland Print/Amer Lith	*Inland Printer/American Lithographer*
Instr Sci	*Instructional Science*
Inter Aud	*Internal Auditor*
Int Manag	*International Management*
Int Soc Sci J	*International Social Science Journal*
Int Trade For	*International Trade Forum*
IRAL	*International Review of Applied Linguistics in Language Teaching*
IRE Trans Eng Writ Speech	*IRE Transactions on Engineering Writing and Speech*
Iron Age	*Iron Age*
J Abnorm Soc Psychol	*Journal of Abnormal and Social Psychology*
J Account	*Journal of Accountancy*
J Adver Manag	*Journal of Advertising Management*
J Adver Res	*Journal of Advertising Research*
J Aesth Art Crit	*Journal of Aesthetics and Art Criticism*
J Am Soc Inf Sci	*Journal of American Society for Information Sciences*
J Appl Comm Res	*Journal of Applied Communication Research*
J Appl Manag	*Journal of Applied Management*
J Appl Psychol	*Journal of Applied Psychology*

J Broad	*Journal of Broadcasting*
J Bus	*Journal of Business*
J Bus Comm	*Journal of Business Communication*
J Bus Educ	*Journal of Business Education*
J Coll Sci Teach	*Journal of College Science Teaching*
J Coll Univ Pers Assoc	*Journal of the College and University Personnel Association*
J Comm	*Journal of Communication*
J Comm Bank Lend	*Journal of Commercial Bank Lending*
J Consult Psychol	*Journal of Consulting Psychology*
J Creat Behav	*Journal of Creative Behavior*
J Dent Res	*Journal of Dental Research*
J Educ	*Journal of Education*
J Educ M	*Journal of Educational Measurement*
J Educ Psychol	*Journal of Educational Psychology*
J Educ Tech	*Journal of Educational Technology*
J Eng Educ	*Journal of Engineering Education*
J Exp Educ	*Journal of Experimental Education*
J Exp Psychol	*Journal of Experimental Psychology*
J Exp Psychol: Hum Learn Mem	*Journal of Experimental Psychology: Human Learning and Memory*
J Exp Psychol: Hum Perc Perf	*Journal of Experimental Psychology: Human Perception and Performance*
J Exp Soc Psychol	*Journal of Experimental Social Psychology*
J Hist Ideas	*Journal of the History of Ideas*
J Indus Teach Educ	*Journal of Industrial Teacher Education*
J Legal Educ	*Journal of Legal Education*
J Linguist	*Journal of Linguistics*
J Lit Seman	*Journal of Literary Semantics*
J Mark Res	*Journal of Marketing Research*
J Math Psychol	*Journal of Mathematical Psychology*
J Math Soc	*Journal of Mathematical Sociology*
Journ Q	*Journalism Quarterly*
J Per	*Journal of Personality*
J Pers Soc Psychol	*Journal of Personality and Social Psychology*
J Physiol	*Journal of Physiology*

J Psychol	*Journal of Psychology*
J Read	*Journal of Reading*
J Read Behav	*Journal of Reading Behavior*
J Rehab	*Journal of Rehabilitation*
J Res Dev Educ	*Journal of Research and Development in Education*
J Soc Psychol	*Journal of Social Psychology*
J Soc Res Admin	*Journal of the Society of Research Administrators*
J Sys Manag	*Journal of Systems Management*
J Tech Writ Comm	*Journal of Technical Writing and Communication*
Judicature	*Judicature*
J Val Inq	*Journal of Value Inquiry*
J Verb Learn Verb Behav	*Journal of Verbal Learning and Verbal Behavior*
Lang	*Language*
Lang Soc	*Language in Society*
Lang Speech Hear Serv Schools	*Language, Speech and Hearing Services in the Schools*
Lang Style	*Language and Style*
Linguist Phil	*Linguistics and Philosophy*
Linguistics	*Linguistics*
L Inst J	*Law Institute Journal*
LSA Bul	*LSA Bulletin*
Mach Des	*Machine Design*
Main Curr Mod Thought	*Main Currents in Modern Thought*
Manag Account	*Management Accounting*
Manag Ad	*Management Advisor*
Manag Methods	*Management Methods*
Manag Rev	*Management Review*
Manag Ser	*Management Services*
Manag Sci	*Management Science*
Manag World	*Management World*

Mat Res Stan	Materials Research and Standards
McGill L J	McGill Law Journal
Mech Eng	Mechanical Engineering
Med Phys	Medical Physics
Mem Cognition	Memory and Cognition
Mich B J	Michigan Bar Journal
Mich S B J	Michigan State Bar Journal
Minerva	Minerva
MLN	Modern Language Notes
Mo B J	Journal of the Missouri Bar
Mon L Rev	Monash University Law Review
NAASP Bul	NAASP Bulletin
NASPA J	NASPA Journal
Nation's Bus	Nation's Business
Nat Underw Life (Insur Ed)	National Underwriters Life (Insurance Edition)
Nature	Nature
New Direc Cont Educ	New Directions for Continuing Education
New Direc Inst Advanc	New Directions for Institutional Advancement
New Sci	New Scientist
New Statesman	New Statesman
Nurs Out	Nursing Outlook
Office	Office
Office Ex	Office Executive
Ohio North L Rev	Ohio Northern University Law Review
Oil Gas J	Oil and Gas Journal
Org Dynamics	Organizational Dynamics
Outdoor Comm	Outdoor Communication
Pacific Soc Rev	Pacific Sociological Review
Penn Speech A	Pennsylvania Speech Annual
Pers	Personnel
Pers Guid J	Personnel and Guidance Journal

Pers J	Personnel Journal
Petro Manag	Petroleum Management
Petro Ref	Petroleum Refiner
Philosophie et Logique	Philosophie et Logique
Phil Rhet	Philosophy and Rhetoric
Phil Soc Sci	Philosophy of the Social Sciences
Physics Educ	Physics Education
Physics Today	Physics Today
Plant Eng	Plant Engineer
Plas World	Plastics World
PMLA	Publications of the Modern Language Association
Poll Eng	Pollution Engineering
POQ	Public Opinion Quarterly
Prac Account	Practical Accountant
Printer's Ink	Printer's Ink
Product Eng	Product Engineer
Psychol Rep	Psychology Reports
Psychology	Psychology
Psychol Rev	Psychology Review
Public Works	Public Works
Pub Rel J	Public Relations Journal
Purchasing	Purchasing
Purch Mag	Purchasing Mag
Q J Speech	Quarterly Journal of Speech
Q J Speech Educ	Quarterly Journal of Speech Education
Railway Age	Railway Age
Read Res Q	Reading Research Quarterly
Real Est Today	Real Estate Today
Res Manag	Research Management
Res Policy	Research Policy
Rev Engl Stud	Review of English Studies
Rhetorician	Rhetorician

Rhet Rev	*Rhetoric Review*
Roy Bank Can Month N	*Royal Bank of Canada Monthly News*
RTE	*Research in the Teaching of English*
Russ Lang J	*Russian Language Journal*
SAE J	*SAE Journal*
Sales Manag	*Sales Management*
Sales Mark Manag	*Sales and Marketing Management*
S.A.M. Adv Manag J	*S.A.M. Advanced Management Journal*
Sat Rev	*Saturday Review*
Sci Am	*Scientific American*
Sci Educ	*Science Education*
Science	*Science*
Scientia	*Scientia*
Sci Mon	*Scientific Monthly*
Sec Manag	*Security Management*
Sigplan Notices	*Sigplan Notices*
Soc Forces	*Social Forces*
Soc Inq	*Sociological Inquiry*
Sociometry	*Sociometry*
Soc Sci Inform	*Social Sciences Information*
Soc Sci Res	*Social Science Research*
Soc Social Res	*Sociology and Social Research*
Speech Mon	*Speech Monographs*
Sp Libr	*Special Libraries*
S Speech J	*Southern Speech Journal*
Stud Angl Pos	*Studia Anglica Posnaniensa*
STWE Rev	*STWE Review*
STWP Rev	*STWP Review*
Style	*Style*
Supervision	*Supervision*
Supervisor	*Supervisor*
Sup Manag	*Supervisory Management*
Synthese	*Synthese*
Tappi	*Tappi*

Tech Comm	*Technical Communication*
Tech Cult	*Technology and Culture*
Tech Writ Teach	*Technical Writing Teacher*
TETYC	*Teaching English in the Two Year College*
Time	*Time*
TLS	*Times Literary Supplement*
Tool Manuf Eng	*Tool and Manufacturing Engineering*
Training	*Training*
Trusts Est	*Trusts and Estates*
U Richmond L Rev	*University of Richmond Law Review*
Visbl Lang	*Visible Language*
Voc Guid Q	*Vocational Guidance Quarterly*
Water Sew Works	*Water and Sewage Works*
W J. Speech Comm	*Western Journal of Speech Communication*
Word	*Word*
Word Study	*Word Study*
Yale Rev	*Yale Review*
Yale Sci Mag	*Yale Science Magazine*
Young Chil	*Young Children*

Part I

A Theoretical Examination of Technical Communication

Technical and Scientific Writing and the Humanities

PHILIP M. RUBENS

The origin of the supposed split between science and the humanities can, indeed, be found in Aristotle. In both the *Organum* and the *Analytica Posteriora*, he theorizes that there are two types of knowledge: knowledge of the certain, which includes all biology, logic, mathematics, and physics; and knowledge of the uncertain, which includes art, ethics, politics, and rhetoric. Furthermore, he argues that each kind of knowledge has a distinct method of reasoning. Certain knowledge depends on the syllogism or demonstration; uncertain knowledge relies on the enthymeme or dialectic.

That initial distinction remained intact even during the birth of the university system which mandated both the trivium (grammar, logic, and rhetoric) and the quadrivium (arithmetic, astronomy, geometry, and music) as basic courses of study for the liberal arts. By the time the university reached its present form, art, imaginative literature, and philosophy had also been added. These subjects formed the *literae humaniores*.

Natural philosophers, at the same time, were developing a new "hard" science based on objectivity, quantification, and a deterministic universe. Charles Coulston Gillispie in *The Edge of Objectivity* (1960) traces the evolution of modern science from Galileo to Einstein and maintains that the major factor in the creation of "hard" science was the development of mathematics. Specifically, he sees this movement as beginning with the introduction of geometry into the study of motion by Galileo and culminating with Newton's creation of the calculus. After this time experimentation, quantification, and objectivity become synonymous with science. This was true for Newton and physics in the seventeenth century, for Lavoisier and chemistry in the eighteenth century, and for Darwin and biology in the nineteenth century.

Coupled with the earlier distinctions for the types of knowledge, the basic differences in methodology and curriculum development literally forced natural philosophy (science) and the humanities to diverge. While that divergence is currently under considerable debate, this essay will assume that no resolution has been reached, though it will discuss the implications of the contemporary debate. As a consequence, the humanities will be defined as those fields that seek to affirm the intrinsic value of the individual and will include philosophy, literature, grammar, and rhetoric. Science will include all of those fields generally associated with experimental science—physics, chemistry, biology, and the like— as well as engineering in its broadest sense.

The basic assumption throughout this essay is that writing *models* experience, and, as a consequence, any aspect of "two-culture" philosophy that impinges on science, technology, the humanities, or the interrelation between these three has some impact on that central assumption. To address this impact, the essay explores such areas as (1) the clash between the humanities and science and technology; (2) the implications of the scientific/technological culture; and (3) the relation of all this material to scientific and technical communication in a humanistic mode.

In researching this field, the most complete general guide is the *Directory of Published Proceedings* (1981) which covers work done in the social sciences and the humanities from 1968 to the present. Barbara W. Hale's book, *The Subject Bibliography of the Social Sciences and Humanities* (1970), includes work performed prior to 1970; it can be supplemented by browsing through Rolland Elwell Stevens's *Reference Books in the Social Sciences and the Humanities* (1977). The most recent and fairly complete guide is Robert A. Rogers's *The Humanities* (1979).

Access to works dealing with technical and scientific communication, in general, can be found in A. H. Lytel's *Bibliography on Technical Writing and Related Subjects* (1958) and Russel Shank's *Bibliography of Technical Writing* (1958). Both of these works were updated, at least partially, by Frederick Van Veen's "An Index to 500 Papers Through 1962 on Engineering Writing and Related Subjects" (1963). Other relevant bibliographies include Lucille Mc-Clure, *Technical Writing* (1963); R. K. Hersch and H. V. Carlson, *An Annotated Bibliography on Technical Writing* (1966); Theresa A. Philler and colleagues, *An Annotated Bibliography on Technical Writing, Editing, Graphics, and Publishing* (1966); the Rutgers book, *Communication of Scientific and Technical Information* (1967); Donald H. Cunningham, "Bibliographies of Technical Writing Material" (1974); Dorothy H. Bankston, "1974 Bibliography of Technical Writing" (1975); Carolyn M. Blackman, "Technical Writing as a Cross-Cultural Field" (1976); Dennis E. Minor and L. F. Lynde, "Library Resource Materials for Technical Writing" (1976); Sarojini Balachandran, *Technical Writing* (1977); Helen V. Carlson and colleagues, *An Annotated Bibliography on Technical Writing, Editing, Graphics, and Publishing* (1982). Two bibliographies that will be of interest to teachers of technical writing are Donald H. Cunningham and Vivienne Hertz, "An Annotated Bibliography on the Teaching of Technical Writing" (1970) and Carolyn M. Blackman, "A Bibliography of Resources for Beginning Teachers of Technical Writing" (1977). Only two general bibliographies in rhetoric are useful for exploring this topic: James W. Cleary's *Rhetoric and Public Address* (1964) and Winifred Bryan Horner's *Historical Rhetoric* (1980). Two more general works of some importance are the United Nations, *Bibliography of Publications Designed to Raise the Standard of Scientific Literature* (1963) and the British Council, *Scientific and Technical English* (1973).

Values and ethics in science, technology, and the humanities can be explored through the annual bibliographies in *Isis*. In addition, Arthur J. Freed's *Some Ethical Problems of Science and Technology* (1964), Maxwell H. Goldberg's *Needles, Burrs, and Bibliographies* (1969), and Lynton K. Caldwell and colleagues' *Science, Technology, and Public Policy* (1972) offer good starting points. The most recent and comprehensive work in this area is Stephen H. Cutliffe's *Technology and Values in American Civilization* (1980).

Science and the Humanities: The Snow Controversy Revisited

While the split between science and the humanities can be traced back to antiquity, the most contemporary articulation can be found in Sir Charles Percy (C.P.) Snow's "The Two Cultures" (1956). Snow's position touched off a considerable, and hotly contested, debate that is still in progress. Essentially, he affirms the earlier division and takes the humanities to task for their role in maintaining the sense of division. It is also about this time that Jacob Bronowski began to write about Apollonians and Dyonisians, the Apollonians being those who look to the gods for machines and the Dyonisians those who see the gods as a source of well-being or human meaning. No matter how the split is described, there is little disagreement that such a division exists. The best discussion of this split can be found in David K. Cornelius and Edwin St. Vincent's *Cultures in Conflict* (1964).

Interestingly, even Snow builds on work that is nearly contemporaneous with his own. F.S.C. Northrop argues in *The Logic of the Sciences and the Humanities* (1948), in almost Aristotelian terms, that the basic difference between these two fields involves the one focusing on problems of facts and the other on problems of value. For the most part, however, two-culture commentators have been happy to demonstrate the impact that science has had on their respective fields without making value judgments. Howard Mumford Jones's "A Humanist Looks at Science" (1958), Harcourt Brown's *Science and the Creative Spirit* (1958), and Charles Angoff's *The Humanities in the Age of Science* (1968), all describe the influence of science on various areas of the humanities. Only Harold Gomes Cassidy's "The Problem of the Sciences and the Humanities" (1960) tries to assess any points that the two fields have in common. He maintains that both the humanities and science use the common intellectual tools of analysis, synthesis, and reduction. By understanding these similarities, he believes that the two fields can move closer together.

At the same time that Snow and his contemporaries were articulating the sense of division in their culture, other theorists were exploring the same principles that they saw as creating a sense of unity. Very much like Northrup, Cassius Jackson Keyser, in *Humanism and Science* (1931), tries to define both science and the humanities; he finds that the humanities can be defined as a philosophy centered in the value of the individual, but, at the same time, he finds that science cannot be as accurately defined. Perhaps it is this sense of uncertainty that provokes Oliver Leslie Reiser, *The Promise of Scientific Humanism* (1940), to suggest that the dualism of traditional Greek thought could be erased. Two more recent theorists—William Thomas Jones, *Science and Humanism* (1965), and Tad S. Clements, *Science and Man* (1968)—both outline ways in which this dualism could be eliminated. Jones sees the use of language and the problems of ethics as two areas of mutual concern and interest. Clements explores major scientific concepts, such as objectivity, and the social conditions within which a new ethos could emerge.

One major trend of contemporary thought that, though it lacks adequate definition, is suggestive for this essay focuses on those elements of humanism that may, indeed, offer valuable insights for science as well as call many scientific concepts into question. At the most formal level this trend includes such people as Thomas Kuhn, Larry Laudan, and Gerald Holton. Perhaps the best known of these, Thomas S. Kuhn, sees a kind of subjectivism at work in the selection of scientific objects of study in *The Structure of Scientific Revolutions* (1970). Ironically, his greatest detractor has been one of his students, Larry Laudan. In *Progress and Its Problems* (1978) Laudan sees this selection method as closer to contextual problem-solving that is necessary for progress. Science does require something beyond empiricism to test the commensurability of competing theories without lapsing into rationalism. Laudan claims that such an element plays an important role in selecting scientific studies. Gerald Holton in both *The Scientific Imagination* (1978) and *Thematic Origins of Scientific Thought* (1973) takes these assertions further by identifying the selection mechanism as a presupposition or "thema" that must both guide the individual work and earn acceptance. Scientific study, progress, and theory acceptance are thus linked to a private process of creation.

On the more informal side of this subject, there are any number of writers who have tried to explain the various aspects of the issue for a lay audience. Fritjof Capra, for instance, in *The Tao of Physics* (1977), outlines the many problems encountered in quantum mechanics that seem to defy our current view of the structure of the universe. Similar efforts can be found in Gary Zukav's *The Dancing Wu Li Masters* (1979) and Amaury de Reincourt's *The Eye of Shiva* (1981).

Humanism and a Technological Age

Surprisingly, not many works have been written on the relationship between the humanities and engineering. This is disturbing because, as Herbert A. Simon points out in *The Sciences of the Artificial* (1969), one of the hallmarks of engineering has been the fact that it represents the interface between science as pure research and the application of scientific principles for public uses. As a consequence, engineering has always exhibited a strong sense of ethical commitment. Be that as it may, very little has been written in this area.

David Lovekin and Donald Phillip Verene's work, *Essays in Humanism and Technology* (1978), sets the tone for this discussion because it asks the basic question: How can human values be maintained in a technological age? The answer as articulated by a number of writers seems to be that human values must be an integral part of a technological education. Both James A. Kent's "The Role of the Humanities and the Social Sciences in Technological Education" (1978) and Duncan Davies's *The Humane Technologist* (1976) take such a position, though Kent does so somewhat grudgingly and with some qualification.

Commentators in this area generally agree that technology will substantively change any culture. Daniel J. Boorstin's *The Republic of Technology* (1978) advances this view, as does William Graves Carleton's *Technology and Humanism* (1970). A slightly more avant-garde conception of the same topic is offered by John Jerome in *Truck* (1977), which is both more telling and better written than Robert M. Pirsig's *Zen and the Art of Motorcycle Maintenance* (1975).

Only two writers have explored the relationship between engineering and the humanities in depth. Harold Gomes Cassidy in "The Engineer" (1956) finds that the best engineers are those who *do* combine all three areas. Samuel Florman offers a similar view in *Engineering and the Liberal Arts* (1968). However, in a second work, *The Existential Pleasures of Engineering* (1976), Florman deviates from that position. In this piece, he berates the humanities for their inability to humanize and asserts that the study of humanist materials does little to improve the pragmatic needs of the engineer. An interesting contrast to this latter position can be found in the wonderfully articulate argument offered for the humanistic intent of technical writing by Carolyn Miller in "A Humanistic Rationale for Technical Writing" (1979).

Science, Technology, and Literature

There have been many attempts both to define the influence of science as a cultural force on literature and to try to develop a sense in which literature and science could be complementary pursuits. Thomas M. Sawyer, for instance, in "The Common Law of Science and the Common Law of Literature" (1970) points out that literature means more than fiction. It includes, in his view, legal documents, technical reports, and the like. The only difference between science and literature is that science describes the actions of seemingly inanimate nature, while literature explores human situations that science finds difficult to deal with.

Sawyer's point about this distinction is borne out by the works of Alexander Norman Jeffares, *Languages, Literature, and Science* (1959), and Duncan Davies, *The Language of Science and the Language of Literature* (1963). Aldous

Leonard Huxley goes even further in *Literature and Science* (1963) by considering the function, nature, and psychology of literature and science, as well as their potential for meaningful relationships.

Charles I. Glicksberg's "Science and the Literary Mind" (1950) builds on Huxley's work and maintains that the modern mind has been so permeated by scientific thought that it has influenced our conception of the world despite literary nay-saying. If our world has been remade by science, how do we feel about it? Sherwood Cummings attempts to answer that question in "Science in Fiction and Belle-Lettres" (1959). He finds that people are, indeed, not particularly happy about rapid change. But change even comes to literature. Stephen E. Fitzgerald, "Literature by Slide Rule" (1953), decries mechanical production of literary texts, in much the same vein that current writers are questioning the impact of the computer on creative productions. Herbert Dingle in *Science and Literary Criticism* (1949) worries about the impact of similar technology on critical scholarship, even though he proposes a kind of scientific methodology for examining texts.

Only two voices are raised to question the limits of scientific influence. B. Farrington, "Science and the Classics" (1961), maintains that there are discernible limits to this influence and suggests that studying the classics is beyond those limits. Marjorie Hope Nicolson in "Two Voices" (1963) raises issues on both sides of the question and leaves one without a clear explanation but with a nagging sense that all is not well. One interesting contrast to these writers, and an attack from *within* the literary community, can be found in Martin Green's *Science and the Shabby Curate of Poetry* (1964), in which he attacks the literati for their anti-scientific stand.

Even before Robert Oppenheimer quoted from the *Bhagavad Gita* at Alamagordo or Loren Eiseley began his long and distinguished writing career, poetry held a certain fascination for scientists. It is hardly surprising that a great deal of material has been written on this topic. From an historical perspective, I. A. Richards's *Science and Poetry* (1926) and Scott Buchanan's *Poetry and Mathematics* (1929, 1962) offer good general overviews, though Buchanan focuses more on Continental poetry. Marjorie Hope Nicolson's *The Breaking of the Circle* (1960) explores the influence of seventeenth-century mechanistic science on poetry of that period and offers perhaps the earliest treatment of scientific influence. Douglas Bush's *Science and English Poetry* (1950) focuses on the impact of Newtonian physics on eighteenth-century poetry as does D. J. Greene's "Smart, Berkeley, the Scientist, and the Poets" (1953). Peter Viereck, "The Poet in the Machine Age" (1949), studies the nineteenth-century reaction to moral issues of the burgeoning machine age, while J. Z. Fullmer, "Contemporary Science and the Poets" (1954), explores American poetry in relation to mid-twentieth-century science.

In much the same vein as the relation between other areas and science, poetry has explored the relationship to science. For the most part, critics come down squarely on either one or the other side of the two-culture issue. Hyatt Howe

Waggoner, for instance, in *The Heels of Elohim* (1950) sees poetry as a way for individuals to fulfill a need for myths to help them focus on values and humanity. Science does not afford this opportunity. Marjorie K. McCorquodale, "Poets and Scientists" (1965), also views the relationship in terms of contradictory models of reality, as do Harold Gomes Cassidy, "The Muse and the Axiom" (1963), and Eric Larrabee in "Science, Poetry, and Politics" (1953).

On the other side of the issue is a group of writers who either see complementary principles at work or discern potential bridges. Raymond J. Seeger, "Scientist and Poet" (1959), suggests such a bridge; he sees the interests and methods of both groups as partly overlapping and flexible, changing under changing conditions. Paul H. Oehser's "The Lion and the Lamb" (1955) explicates two complementary interests which, he claims, represent different facets of human intellection. This view is shared by Willard E. Arnett, "Poetry and Science" (1956), in which he maintains that both fields satisfy creative and curious elements in man in much the same way. A unique summary statement on this topic can be found in George Derfer's "Science, Poetry, and 'Human Specificity' " (1974), in which he interviews Jacob Bronowski concerning the scientist's conception of the relationship. Two final, and for our purposes, intriguing works are Mary Fran Buehler's *Poetry, Music, and Technical Writing* (1971) and M. J. Reddy's "Formal Referential Models of Poetic Structure" (1973). Both of these works explore the ways in which poetry is related to referential prose such as scientific or technical writing.

Science, Technology, and Ethics

Two schools dominate current thinking about values in science. One school advocates more human-oriented science with an emphasis on values; the second maintains that values will be incorporated into science as they emulate scientific method.

A good general description of this split can be discerned in the essays collected by Ervin Laszlo and James B. Wilbur in *Human Values and Natural Science* (1970). The standard work on ethics in science and technology is Abraham Edel's *Science and the Structure of Ethics* (1961). It is not surprising that the deepest commitment to more humanistic science should come from scientists of outstanding reputation. Jacob Bronowski in *Science and Human Values* (1965) as well as in *Magic, Science, and Civilization* (1978) makes just such a plea, as does Albert Einstein in "The Laws of Science and the Laws of Ethics" (1950). It is also not surprising that some writers feel the need to address the supposed split between the sciences and the humanities and its implications for ethics. Loren R. Graham, for instance, in *Between Science and Values* (1981) tries to allay fears founded on any split and asserts that science and ethics do interact successfully. Hiram Bentley Glass, *Scientific and Ethical Values* (1965), and Edward and Elizabeth Hutchings, *Scientific Progress and Human Values*

(1967), are not as optimistic. Their view is that the two-culture split is very real and has an adverse effect on ethics in science.

That perception is borne out, to some degree, by those writers who insist that ethics will be more productive as they become more scientific. Stephen Toulmin, "Can Science and Ethics Be Reconnected?" (1979), points out that achieving any kind of meaningful relationship is thwarted by the fact that science and ethics have lost touch during the past 100 to 150 years. As a consequence of this long-standing split, asserts Ralph Wendell Burhoe in *Science and Human Values in the 21st Century* (1971), it is possible that science will dominate the next century with very little attention paid to values. That split is exacerbated, according to Edward Walter, "Reasoning in Science and Ethics" (1976), by the fact that both fields employ different modes of reasoning; it is unlikely that they will be reconciled.

Based on these perceptions, Peter Caws, in *Science and the Theory of Value* (1967), maintains that value does not need to become thoroughly scientific, but that it will appropriate some of the methods of science. This view is shared by C. Judson Herrick, "Scientific Method and Human Values" (1946), though he tempers his assertions with the observation that science should be guided by the resulting human values. One final observer, Lawrence Cranberg, in "Ethical Code for Scientists" (1963), suggests that scientists and ethicists study the operating systems established by science for ethical self-regulation.

It seems that an inordinate amount of material has been written about ethics in science. This is ironic in that engineering has both a closer relationship to the end products of science *and* a highly developed code of ethics. For the most part, discussions of values in engineering focus on the need for engineers to perform moral acts that will not endanger the public and the necessity for truthful dealings with people in terms of written and oral communication.

Elena Cobian in "Moral Implications of the Scientific and Technological Revolution" (1978), for example, assesses the ways in which inaccurate information and irresponsible design have caused various problems, all of which have ethical importance and should have been addressed by the engineer. Actions such as these create a sense of schism in a culture like that described by Bruce O. Watkins in *Technology and Human Values* (1978). In contrast to this rather dismal view of engineeing ethics, Irene Taviss and Linda Silverman, *Technology and Values* (1969), and Ian G. Barbour, *Science and Secularity* (1970), find that there is a degree of interaction and all that is required for better ethical conduct is a more deliberate focus on the human aspects of engineering.

Not much work has been done in ethics in technical and scientific communication. Some work from journalism and general communication ethics such as Lee Thayer's *Communication* (1974) could prove valuable. Two other useful, and specific, pieces are Carolyn Miller's "Technology as a Form of Consciousness" (1978) and Philip M. Rubens's "Reinventing the Wheel" (1981). Both of these works tie language concerns common to technical and scientific communication to ethical concerns.

Science, Technology, and Education

Strangely enough, the early university did not quite know what to do with science. It was still a fairly ill-defined field. Yet, as Paul LaCroix points out in *Science and Literature in the Middle Ages and the Renaissance* (1978), both fields put their inevitable and special stamp even on the earliest of universities. Since these disciplines have shared the university from the onset, it is hardly likely that they will not continue to do so. The educational needs of both science and engineering students seem to depend, at least according to cultural commentators, on some form of union between the various disciplines.

Roy Niblett, for instance, in his book, *Science, the Humanities and the Technological Threat* (1975) asks that education remain balanced between science and the humanities. Joseph Jackson Schwab, *Science, Curriculum, and Liberal Education* (1978), carries that request further by pointing out that the modes of inquiry involved in reading and writing, two areas traditionally relegated to the humanities, are essential for study in all other fields. That concern is forwarded by a recent Commission on the Humanities report, *The Humanities in American Life* (1980), which calls for a continued emphasis on humanistic content in the college curriculum. Two final writers, José Ortega y Gasset, *The Mission of the University* (1944), and Julian Huxley, "Education and the Humanist Revolution" (1963), offer similar perspectives.

It is not surprising that some writers offer decidedly anti-humanistic viewpoints on science education. Boyd R. Keenan, *Science and the University* (1966), calls for the creation of models based on industrial experience for education in the sciences. In opposition, Hiram Bentley Glass in *Science and a Liberal Education* (1959), maintains that liberal education liberates the mind while a scientific education contracts it. More balanced views are offered by Philipp Frank, *Modern Science and Its Philosophy* (1949), who suggests that courses should relate philosophy and other humanistic content to science courses and vice versa, and John Ziman, *Teaching and Learning about Science and Society* (1980), who maintains that values are a necessary component of a science education and should be taught within the existing framework of the humanities.

In contrast to the treatment of ethics in the literature, more discussion has occurred in relation to technological education than science education. Sir Eric Ashby, perhaps the single most important figure in this discussion, has written on the subject for over two decades. In all three of his works—*Technology and the Academics* (1963), "Humanities for the Technologist" (1957), and *Adapting the University to a Technological Society* (1974)—he steadfastly advocates the importance of humanistic content in a technological curriculum. Hardy Cross's *Engineers and the Ivory Tower* (1952) also supports this position and suggests that such materials are necessary to help technologists understand the social responsibility of their work. Duncan Davies, *The Humane Technologist* (1976), offers still more support, as well as a fairly comprehensive study plan. The only dissenting voice to this line of reasoning is James A. Kent, "The Role of the

Humanities and the Social Sciences in Technological Education'' (1978), who maintains that the humanities play an extremely limited role in technological education and that they should adapt themselves to the technological university or leave.

Some work has been done in specific education areas germane to the focus of this essay. Deborah C. Andrews's ''An Interdisciplinary Course in Technical Communication'' (1976), E. Fred Carlisle's ''Teaching Scientific Writing Humanistically'' (1978), N. Ellman's ''The Two Cultures'' (1976), and Dennis E. Minor's ''An Integrated Technical Writing Course'' (1975), for instance, outline interdisciplinary approaches to teaching technical and scientific communication. Excellent advice on teaching report writing can be found in Herman A. Estrin's ''An Engineering Report Writing Course That Works'' (1968), J. C. Mathes and Dwight W. Stevenson's ''Completing the Bridge'' (1976), and Robert R. Rathbone's ''Cooperative Teaching of Technical Writing in Engineering Courses'' (1958). More specific writing tasks are addressed by such works as Merrill D. Whitburn's ''Audience'' (1980), R. John Brockmann's *Teaching Computer Documentation in Technical Communication* (1980), and Dorothy H. Bankston's ''Teaching the Detailed Description of a Mechanism,'' (1975).

Science, Technology, and Rhetoric

Until recently science, technology, and rhetoric have been a highly neglected area; however, with the current interest in exploring the nature of scientific methodology, more attention has been paid to this topic. The most general works in the field are Joseph Wilford Wenzel's ''The Rhetoric of Science'' (1963) and Philip C. Wander's 1976 work by the same title; though separated by 13 years, they take essentially the same positions. It has only been during the past decade, since Wander's article, that considerable attention has been focused on this area.

Walter B. Weimer's ''Science as a Rhetorical Transaction'' (1970), for instance, is the most recent article to look at the scientific method of inquiry as rhetorical in nature. Interestingly, his work echoes the earliest piece on rhetoric and science: Elbert W. Harrington's ''Rhetoric and the Scientific Method of Inquiry'' (1948). Another view on this topic is offered by Herbert W. Simons, ''Are Scientists Rhetors in Disguise?'' (1980), who claims that the characteristics of scientists and their method of discourse make their activity rhetorical. Gordon W. Hewes makes a similar case in ''An Explicit Formulation of the Relationship Between Tool-Using, Tool-Making, and the Emergence of Language'' (1973).

Other writers find that applying rhetorical analysis affords new perspectives on scientific texts. John Angus Campbell, for example, in ''Charles Darwin and the Crisis of Ecology'' (1974), finds additional levels of meaning in the text. S. Michael Halloran in ''The Birth of Molecular Biology'' (1984) makes similar discoveries by studying a particular case to show how certain scientists apprehend an idea or create an ethos. Two other works by Halloran, ''Technical Writing and the Rhetoric of Science'' (1978) and ''Ciceronian Rhetoric and the Rise of

Science'' (1982) (with Merrill D. Whitburn) are also both worth reading. Robert L. Corey's "The Persuasive Technical Proposal" (1975) looks at the role of rhetoric in a highly specialized communication situation.

Still other writers have tried to explore this topic from a historical perspective and offer ways in which that perspective can be used in teaching scientific and technical writing. William Powell Jones, for instance, in *The Rhetoric of Science* (1966), examines seventeenth- and nineteenth-century poetry in terms of the eighteenth-century's scientific enthusiasm and its cultural influence. More specific studies are offered by James P. Zappen, "Francis Bacon and the Rhetoric of Science" (1975), and James G. Paradis, "The Royal Society" (1981). Two other works assess the implications of traditional rhetoric for teaching: Thomas M. Sawyer's "Rhetoric in an Age of Science and Technology" (1972) and Andrea Lunsford's "Classical Rhetoric and Technical Writing" (1976).

Two major areas that rhetoric is concerned with are the audience and the persona of the writer. In terms of rhetorical interest in science and technical writing, this is an exceptionally new field. Most of the commentary has been written in the past half dozen years. Joseph Gusfield offers the earliest study of audience in "The Literary Rhetoric of Science" (1976). In that work he maintains that reports should be treated as literary texts; he demonstrates his theory by performing selective readings based on literary and rhetorical criticism. Michael A. Overington, "The Scientific Community as Audience" (1977), offers a slightly more selective interpretation of the relationship of rhetoric to science; he claims that science is rhetorical because scientific advance involves argumentation and persuasion before an audience. Finally, Collett B. Dilworth, in "Writing as a Moral Act" (1978), advocates an ethical stance toward audience based on the ethos that the writer assumes.

Persona has had similar attention. Paul Newell Campbell in "The *Personae* of Scientific Discourse" (1975) suggests that science only succeeds through a rhetorical approach to personality. Earl W. Britton's "Personality in Technical Writing" (1973) applies this perception to technical material, while Merrill D. Whitburn's "Personality in Scientific and Technical Writing" (1976) suggests that just as science has begun to recognize the subjective elements in its method of inquiry, so too must writing. Frank Walters's "Science, Rhetoric, and the Service Manual" (1980) supports Whitburn's contention and claims that even supposedly objective manuals reflect the author's personality.

Rhetoric Devices in Science and Technical Writing

The traditional view of scientific and technical explanation is that it is totally objective in nature. Recent works on the role of metaphor in the scientific method, however, have begun to influence the ways in which scientific and technical communication are perceived. Peter Alexander's work, *Sensationalism and Scientific Explanation* (1963), for example, offers ample evidence that the senses do play an important role in science. Alan E. Musgrave, "Explanation, Description, and Scientific Realism'' (1977), points out that realism, a mimetic representation of reality, is mediated by subjective influences. Both I. Scheffler, *Science and Subjectivity* (1967), and I. Mitroff, *The Subjective Side of Science* (1974), offer arguments for subjective elements in science writing. An additional work of general interest is R. B. Braithwaite's *Scientific Explanation* (1953).

Most of the research hinges on specific language elements found in scientific or technical writing and is based on works such as Gerald Holton's in scientific methodology. A work that precedes Holton, but takes a similar approach, is Walter Libby's "The Scientific Imagination" (1922), in which he reasons that some subjective elements must be present to help scientists establish a starting point for their work. A more recent piece, *Science and Imagination* (1967) by Warren Weaver, makes similar points.

The main problems seem to be how is this subjective or imaginative element expressed and what are its consequences? Holton calls them "thema" and relates them to the literary concept of metaphor. That perception has become the starting point for a great deal of commentary. Max Black, for instance, in *Models and Metaphors* (1962), claims that science's creation of models is analogous to the creation of metaphors and that the model is later translated into a metaphor appropriate for explaining the scientist's actions. Earl R. MacCormac, *Metaphor and Myth in Science and Religion* (1976), and Mary Hesse, *Models and Analogies in Science* (1966), offer like evidence. Such thinking is not confined to science. John Sterling Harris's "Metaphor in Technical Writing" (1975) finds similar forces at work in engineering writing.

Scientific and Technical Communication

Although there has been only one major attempt—Karl Pearson, *The Grammar of Science* (1911)—to create a general grammar for science writing, virtually every aspect of scientific and technical communication has been considered by writing theorists. Walter Edgar Floos in *Scientific Words* (1960), for instance, examines the ways in which scientists and engineers have created a highly specialized vocabulary. R. D. Huddleston examines the kinds of sentence and clause structures common to such writing in *Sentence and Clause in Technical English* (1968). At the upper level, Derek de Solla Price's "The Book as Scientific Instrument" (1967) looks at the ways in which the book has helped to advance scientific information. He echoes much that Elizabeth Eisenstein has to say in *The Printing Press as an Agent of Change* (1980), only in a very abbreviated version. Three attempts have been made to look at style in science writing: S. Aaronson's "Style in Scientific Writing" (1977), Colin B. Elliot's "Must Scientific English Be Dull?" (1976), and DeWitt Carter Reddick's *Literary Style in Science Writing* (1969). They all seem to agree that, contrary to expectations, scientific style contains figures of speech and a discernible personality. Both Northrop Frye, *The Anatomy of Criticism* (1971), and James Kinneavy, *A Theory of Discourse* (1971), also make general references to the relationships between science and/or referential writing and literary writing.

More detailed discussions of the specialized languages of science and engineering, however, concentrate specifically on certain features of these languages. Both Theodore H. Savory, *The Language of Science* (1958), and Patrick Meredith, *Instruments of Communication* (1966), provide extensive examinations of scientific language. General theories are offered by Charles L. Sanford's "Toward a Theory of Communication in the Sciences and the Humanities," and S. Ziemski's "Theoretical Assumptions of Science Communication" (1973). In addition to Edmund Andrews's *The History of Scientific English* (1947), two intriguing historical views can be found in Bruno Snell's "The Forging of a Language of Science in Ancient Greece" (1960) and Owen Hannaway's *The Chemist and the Word* (1975). The Hannaway work surveys the beginnings of chemistry as a science and details the impact of language on the ways in which the field developed. Snell's work focuses on ancient Greece. Both of these authors imply that certain areas of science developed in special ways because of the influence of the language that people chose to explain their work. That idea is forwarded by M. S. Peterson, *Scientific Thinking and Scientific Writing* (1961), and Albert Einstein, "The Common Language of Science" (1965). These writers insist that the special ways in which science is performed and the ways in which scientists think about their work influence their communication behaviors; as a consequence, the ways in which they communicate are unique and clearly distinct from public prose. One final work, however, Charles Sander Peirce's "Ideas, Stray or Stolen, About Scientific Writing" (1978), somewhat mediates that position. Peirce claims that science and rhetoric do belong together; he is especially fond of the ethics of terminology, which he claims sets the tone for this relationship.

Unlike scientific language, technical language has not received a great deal of attention. Carnot E. Nelson, however, takes a position very similar to Peirce's in *Communication Among Scientists and Engineers* (1970); that is, he sees this kind of specialized communication as inextricably bound up with more humanistic concerns. James R. Wright's "On Avoiding Ambiguity and Doublespeak in Technical Writing" (1975) also takes an ethical approach to technical communication. J.P.B. Allen and H. G. Widdowson's "Teaching the Communicative Use of English" (1974) sees the broader humanistic implications and manages to balance them quite well with the more pragmatic concerns of engineering. Marian S. Baumgold, *A Dialogue for the Decade* (1972), offers another call for humanistic concern in scientific and technical writing and reminds the reader that the end purpose of communication activities is to bring information and knowledge to people.

This humanistic concern has been voiced many times. The earliest articulation in this century is Philip McDonald's *English and Science* (1929). The most recent call comes from E. Garfield, *Essays of an Information Scientist* (1977), who argues that scientific information must be more human oriented. The logical place for that kind of orientation to occur is in the schools. Randolph Hoyt Hudson's fine collection of essays, *Technology, Culture, and Language* (1966), offers excellent peer models for science and technical students. Alfred M. Bork's *Science and Language* (1966) provides an excellent argument for the study of language by such students. He claims that although scientific thought and the materials under scientific consideration may be unique, they still require a thorough knowledge of language to work effectively. Bork believes that knowledge can come only from studying language in its full humanistic setting.

References

Aaronson, S. "Style in Scientific Writing." *Curr Con*, 2 (Jan. 1977), 6–15.

Alexander, Peter. *Sensationalism and Scientific Explanation*. London: Routledge, Kegan Paul, 1963.

Allen, J.P.B., and H. G. Widdowson. "Teaching the Communicative Use of English." *IRAL*, 12 (1974), 1–21.

Andrews, Deborah C. "An Interdisciplinary Course in Technical Communication." *Tech Comm* 23, No. 1 (1976), 12–15.

Andrews, Edmund. *The History of Scientific English*. New York: R. Smith, 1947.

Angoff, Charles, ed. *The Humanities in the Age of Science*. Rutherford, N.J.: Fairleigh Dickinson University Press, 1968.

Arnett, Willard E. "Poetry and Science." *J Aesth Art Crit*, 14 (1956), 445–52.

Ashby, Eric. *Adapting the University to a Technological Society*. San Francisco: Jossey-Bass, 1974.

———. "Humanities for the Technologist." *Nature*, 180 (1957), 624–27.

———. *Technology and the Academics*. New York: Macmillan, 1963.

Balachandran, Sarojini. *Technical Writing: A Bibliography*. Urbana, Ill.: American Business Communication Association, 1977.

Bankston, Dorothy H. "Teaching Detailed Description of a Mechanism." *Tech Writ Teach*, 2, No. 2 (1975), 14–15.

———, et al. "1974 Bibliography of Technical Writing." *Tech Writ Teach*, 3 (1975), 29–41.

Barbour, Ian G. *Science and Secularity: The Ethics of Technology*. New York: Harper, 1970.

Baumgold, Marian S., ed. *A Dialogue for the Decade: Humanists and Communicators*. Rensselaerville, N.Y.: Institute on Science and Man, 1972.

Black, Max. *Models and Metaphors*. Ithaca, N.Y.: Cornell University Press, 1962.

Blackman, Carolyn M. "A Bibliography of Resources for Beginning Teachers of Technical Writing." In *Programs in Technical and Professional Writing: Preparation for Beginning Teachers of Technical Writing*. Ann Arbor, Mich.: Department of Humanities, College of Engineering, University of Michigan, 1977, pp. 196–209.

———. "Technical Writing as a Cross-Cultural Field: A Personal Bibliography." *Tech Writ Teach*, 3 (1976), 84–91.

Boorstin, Daniel J. *The Republic of Technology: Reflections on Our Future Community*, New York: Harper, 1978.

Bork, Alfred M. *Science and Language: Selected Essays*. Boston: Heath, 1966.

Braithwaite, R. B. *Scientific Explanation*. London: Cambridge University Press, 1953.

British Council. *Scientific and Technical English: Specialised Bibliography B17*. London: English Teaching Information Centre, 1973.

Britton, Earl W. "Personality in Scientific Writing." *Tech Comm*, 20, No. 3 (1973), 9–11.

Brockmann, R. John. *Teaching Computer Documentation in Technical Communication*. Proceedings of the 27th International Technical Communication Conference, 1980, II, R85–R89.

Bronowski, Jacob. *Magic, Science, and Civilization*. New York: Columbia University Press, 1978.

———. *Science and Human Values*. New York: Harper, Row, 1965.

Brown, Harcourt. *Science and the Creative Spirit: Essays on the Humanistic Aspects of Science*. Toronto: University of Toronto Press, 1958.

Buchanan, Scott. *Poetry and Mathematics*. New York: Lippincott, 1962.

Buehler, Mary Fran. "Poetry, Music and Technical Writing." Proceedings of the 18th International Technical Communication Conference. San Francisco: Society for Technical Communication, 1971.

Burhoe, Ralph Wendell, ed. *Science and Human Values in the 21st Century*. Philadelphia: Westminster Press, 1971.

Bush, Douglas. *Science and English Poetry*. London: Oxford University Press, 1950.

Caldwell, Lynton K., et al., eds. *Science, Technology, and Public Policy: A Selected and Annotated Bibliography*. Bloomington: Indiana University Press, 1972.

Campbell, John Angus. "Charles Darwin and the Crisis of Ecology: A Rhetorical Perspective." *Q J Speech*, 60 (1974), 442–49.

Campbell, Paul Newell. "The *Personae* of Scientific Discourse." *Q J Speech*, 61 (1975), 391–405.

Capra, Fritjof. *The Tao of Physics: An Exploration of the Parallels Between Modern Physics and Eastern Mysticism*. New York: Bantam, 1977.

Carleton, William Graves. *Technology and Humanism*. Nashville, Tenn.: Vanderbilt University Press, 1970.

Carlisle, E. Fred. "Teaching Scientific Writing Humanistically: From Theory to Action." *Engl J*, 67, No. 4 (1978), 35–39.

Carlson, Helen V., et al. *An Annotated Bibliography on Technical Writing, Editing, Graphics, and Publishing, 1966–1980*. Washington, D.C.: Society for Technical Communication, 1982.

Cassidy, Harold Gomes. "The Engineer: A Blend of Scientist, Humanist, Technologist." *Yale Sci Mag*, 30 (1956), 4.

———. "The Muse and the Axiom." *Am Sci*, 51 (1963), 315–26.

———. "The Problem of the Sciences and the Humanities: A Diagnosis and a Prescription." *Am Sci*, 48 (1960), 383.

Caws, Peter. *Science and the Theory of Value*. New York: Random House, 1967.

Cleary, James W. *Rhetoric and Public Address: A Bibliography 1947–1961*. Madison: University of Wisconsin Press, 1964.

Clements, Tad S. *Science and Man: The Philosophy of Scientific Humanism*. Springfield, Ill.: Thomas, 1968.

Cobian, Elena. "Moral Implications of the Scientific and Technological Revolution." *Philosophie et Logique*, 20 (1978), 217–21.

Commission on the Humanities. *The Humanities in American Life: Report of the Commission on the Humanities*. Berkeley: University of California Press, 1980.

Corey, Robert L. "The Persuasive Technical Proposal: Rhetorical Form and the Writer." *Tech Comm*, 22, No. 4 (1975), 2–5.

Cornelius, David K., and Edwin St. Vincent. *Cultures in Conflict: Perspectives on the Snow-Leavis Controversy*. Chicago: Scott, Foresman, 1964.

Cranberg, Lawrence. "Ethical Code for Scientists." *Science*, 141 (1963), 1242.

Cross, Hardy. *Engineers and the Ivory Tower*. New York: McGraw-Hill, 1952.

Cummings, Sherwood. "Science in Fiction and Belles-Lettres." In *The Challenge of Science Education*. Ed. Josephy Slabey Roucek. New York: Philosophical Library, 1959.

Cunningham, Donald H. "Bibliographies of Technical Writing Material." *Tech Writ Teach*, 1, No. 2 (1974), 9–10.

——— and Vivienne Hertz. "An Annotated Bibliography on the Teaching of Technical Writing." *CCC*, 21 (1970), 177–86.

Cutliffe, Stephen H. *Technology and Values in American Civilization: A Guide to Information Sources*. Detroit: Gale Research, 1980.

Davies, Duncan. *The Humane Technologist*. London: Oxford University Press, 1976.

———. *The Language of Science and the Language of Literature, 1700–1740*. London: Sheed, Ward, 1963.

Derfer, George. "Science, Poetry and 'Human Specificity': An Interview with Jacob Bronowski." *Am Sch*, 43 (1974), 386–404.

Dilworth, Collett B., and Robert W. Resing. "Writing as a Moral Act: Developing a Sense of Audience." *Engl J*, 67, No. 8 (1978), 76–78.

Dingle, Herbert. *Science and Literary Criticism*. London: Nelson, 1949.

Directory of Published Proceedings. Series SSH. White Plains, N.Y.: Interdok, 1968–.

Edel, Abraham. *Science and the Structure of Ethics*. Chicago: University of Chicago Press, 1961.

Einstein, Albert. "The Common Language of Science." In *Classics in Semantics*. Eds. Donald E. Hayden and E. Paul Alworth. New York. Philosophical Library, 1965, pp. 323–26.

———. "The Laws of Science and the Laws of Ethics." In *Relativity—A Richer Truth*. Ed. Philipp Frank. Boston: Beacon, 1950.

Eisenstein, Elizabeth. *The Printing Press as an Agent of Change: Communications and Cultural Transformations in Early-Modern Europe*. Cambridge: Cambridge University Press, 1980.

Elliott, Colin B. "Must Scientific English Be Dull?" *Engl Lang Teach J*, 31 (1976), 29–34.

Ellman, N. "The Two Cultures: Exploring and Bridging the Gap." *Eng l Rec*, 65, No. 7 (1976), 55–56.

Estrin, Herman A. "An Engineering Report Writing Course That Works." *Improv Coll Univ Teach*, 16, (1968), 28–30.

Farrington, B. "Science and the Classics." *Nature*, 191 (1961), 1337–42.

Fitzgerald, Stephen E. "Literature by Slide Rule." *Sat Rev*, 14 Feb. 1953, p. 15, 54.

Floos, Walter Edgar. *Scientific Words: Their Structure and Meaning*. New York: Duell, 1960.

Florman, Samuel. *Engineering and the Liberal Arts*. New York: McGraw-Hill, 1968.

———. *The Existential Pleasures of Engineering*. New York: St. Martin's, 1976.

Frank, Philipp. *Modern Science and Its Philosophy*. Cambridge: Harvard University Press, 1949.

Freed, Arthur J. *Some Ethical Problems of Science and Technology: A Bibliography of Literature from 1955*. Washington, D.C.: U.S. Department of Commerce, 1964.

Frye, Northrop. *The Anatomy of Criticism*. Princeton, N.J.: Princeton University Press, 1971.

Fullmer, J. Z. "Contemporary Science and the Poets." *Science*, 119 (1954), 855–60.

Garfield, E. *Essays of an Information Scientist*. Philadelphia: ISI Press, 1977.

Gillispie, Charles Coulston. *The Edge of Objectivity: An Essay in the History of Scientific Ideas*. Princeton, N.J.: Princeton University Press, 1960.

Glass, Hiram Bentley. *Science and a Liberal Education*. Baton Rouge: Louisiana State University Press, 1959.

———. *Scientific and Ethical Values*. Chapel Hill: University of North Carolina Press, 1965.

Glicksberg, Charles I. "Science and the Literary Mind." *Sci Mon*, 70 (1950), 352–57.

Goldberg, Maxwell H., ed. *Needles, Burrs, and Bibliographies: Study Resources: Technological Change, Human Values, and the Humanities*. University Park: Pennsylvania State University, Center for Continuing Liberal Education, 1969.

Graham, Loren R. *Between Science and Values*. New York: Columbia University Press, 1981.

Green, Martin. *Science and the Shabby Curate of Poetry: Essays About Two Cultures*. New York: Norton, 1964.

Greene, D. J. "Smart, Berkeley, the Scientists and the Poets." *J Hist Ideas*, 14 (1953), 327–52.

Gusfield, Joseph. "The Literary Rhetoric of Science: Comedy and Pathos in Drinking Driver Research." *Am Soc Rev*, 41 (1976), 16–34.

Hale, Barbara W. *The Subject of Bibliography of the Social Sciences and Humanities*. Oxford: Pergamon, 1970.

Halloran, S. Michael. "The Birth of Molecular Biology: An Essay in the Rhetorical Criticism of Scientific Discourse." *Rhet. Rev*, 3 (1984), 70-83.

———. "Technical Writing and the Rhetoric of Science." *J Tech Writ Comm*, 8 (1978), 77–88; rpt. in *Technical Communication*, 27, No. 4 (1978), 7–10, 13.

———, and Merrill D. Whitburn. "Ciceronian Rhetoric and the Rise of Science: The Plain Style Reconsidered." In *The Rhetorical Tradition and Modern Writing*. Ed. James D. Murphy. New York: Modern Language Association, 1982, pp. 58–72.

Hannaway, Owen. *The Chemist and the Word: The Didactic Origins of Chemistry*. Baltimore: Johns Hopkins University Press, 1975.

Harrington, Elbert W. "Rhetoric and the Scientific Method of Inquiry." *University of Colorado Studies: Series in Language and Literature*, 1 (1948), 1–64.

Harris, John Sterling. "Metaphor in Technical Writing." *Tech Writ Teach*, 2, No. 2 (1975), 9–13.

Herrick, C. Judson. "Scientific Method and Human Values." *Am Sci*, 34 (1946), 239–45.

Hersch, R. K., and H. V. Carlson. *An Annotated Bibliography on Technical Writing*. Washington, D.C.: Society for Technical Communication, 1966.

Hesse, Mary. *Models and Analogies in Science*. Notre Dame, Ind.: University of Notre Dame Press, 1966.

Hewes, Gordon W. "An Explicit Formulation of the Relationship Between Tool-Using, Tool-Making, and the Emergence of Language." *Visbl Lang*, 7 (1973), 101–27.

Holton, Gerald. *The Scientific Imagination: Case Studies*. Cambridge: Cambridge University Press, 1978.

————. *Thematic Origins of Scientific Thought*. Cambridge, Mass.: MIT Press, 1973.

Horner, Winifred Bryan. *Historical Rhetoric: An Annotated Bibliography of Selected Sources in English*. Boston: G. K. Hall, 1980.

Huddleston, R. D., et al. *Sentence and Clause in Scientific English*. Washington, D.C.: Office of Scientific and Technical Information Report No. 5030, 1968.

Hudson, Randolph Hoyt. *Technology, Culture, and Language*. Boston: Heath, 1966.

Hutchings, Edward, and Elizabeth Hutchings, eds. *Scientific Progress and Human Values*. New York: Elsevier, 1967.

Huxley, Aldous Leonard. *Literature and Science*. New York: Harper, 1963.

Huxley, Julian. "Education and the Humanist Revolution." *Nature*, 197 (1963), 8–13.

Jeffares, Alexander Norman. *Languages, Literature, and Science: An Inaugural Lecture*. Cambridge: Leeds University Press, 1959.

Jerome, John. *Truck*. New York: Bantam, 1977.

Jones, Howard Mumford. "A Humanist Looks at Science." In *Science and the Modern Mind*. Ed. Gerald Holton. Boston: Beacon, 1958.

Jones, William Powell. *The Rhetoric of Science: A Study of Scientific Ideas and Imagery in Eighteenth-Century English Poetry*. Berkeley: University of California Press, 1966.

Jones, William Thomas. *Science and Humanism: Conflict and Reconciliation*. Berkeley: University of California Press, 1965.

Keenan, Boyd R. *Science and the University*. New York: Columbia University Press, 1966.

Kent, James A. "The Role of the Humanities and the Social Sciences in Technological Education." *Eng Educ*, 68 (1978), pp. 725–29.

Keyser, Cassius Jackson. *Humanism and Science*. New York: Columbia University Press, 1931.

Kinneavy, James. *A Theory of Discourse: The Aims of Discourse*. Englewood Cliffs, N.J.: Prentice-Hall, 1971.

Kuhn, Thomas S. *The Structure of Scientific Revolutions*. Chicago: University of Chicago Press, 1970.

LaCroix, Paul. *Science and Literature in the Middle Ages and the Renaissance*. New York: Ungar, 1978.

Larrabee, Eric. "Science, Poetry, and Politics." *Science*, 117 (1953), 395–99.

Laszlo, Ervin, and James B. Wilbur, eds. *Human Values and Natural Science*. New York: Gordon, Breach, 1970.

Laudan, Larry. *Progress and Its Problems: Towards a Theory of Scientific Growth*. Berkeley: University of California Press, 1978.

Libby, Walter. "The Scientific Imagination." *Sci Mon*, 15 (1922), 263–70.

Lovekin, David, and Donald Phillip Verene, eds. *Essays in Humanism and Technology*. Dixon, Ill.: Saux Valley College, 1978.

Lunsford, Andrea. "Classical Rhetoric and Technical Writing." *CCC*, 27 (1976), 289–91.

Lytel, A. H. *Bibliography on Technical Writing and Related Subjects*. Syracuse, N.Y.: General Electric Co., Electronics Laboratories, 1958.

McClure, Lucille. *Technical Writing: A Selected Bibliography*. Orlando, Fla.: Martin Marietta, 1963.

MacCormac, Earl R. *Metaphor and Myth in Science and Religion*. Durham, N.C.: Duke University Press, 1976.

McCorquodale, Marjorie K. "Poets and Scientists." *Bul Atomic Sci*, 21 (Nov. 1965), 18–20.

McDonald, Philip Bayand. *English and Science*. New York: Van Nostrand, 1929.

Mathes, J. C., and Dwight W. Stevenson. "Completing the Bridge: Report Writing in 'Real Life' Engineering Courses." *Eng Educ*, 67 (Nov. 1976), 154–59.

Meredith, Patrick. *Instruments of Communication: An Essay on Scientific Writing*. Oxford: Pergamon, 1966.

Miller, Carolyn. "A Humanistic Rationale for Technical Writing." *CE*, 40 (1979), 610–17.

———. "Technology as a Form of Consciousness: A Study of Contemporary Ethos." *CS Speech J*, 29 (1978), 228–36.

Minor, Dennis E. "An Integrated Technical Writing Course." *Tech Writ Teach*, 3 (1975), 21–24.

———., and L. F. Lynde. "Library Resource Materials for Technical Writing." *Tech Writ Teach*, 3 (1976), 135–43.

Mitroff, I. *The Subjective Side of Science*. The Hague: Mouton, 1974.

Musgrave, Alan E. "Explanation, Description, and Scientific Realism." *Scientia*, 112 (1977), 727–41.

Nelson, Carnot E., and Donald K. Pollock, eds. *Communication among Scientists and Engineers*. Lexington, Mass.: Heath, 1970.

Niblett, Roy, ed. *Science, the Humanities, and the Technological Threat*. London: University of London Press, 1975.

Nicolson, Marjorie Hope. *The Breaking of the Circle: Studies in the Effect of the "New Science" on Seventeenth-Century Poetry*. New York: Columbia University Press, 1960.

———. "Two Voices: Science and Literature." *Am Sci*, 51 (1963), 454–62.

Northrop, F.S.C. *The Logic of the Sciences and the Humanities*. New York: Macmillan, 1948.

Oehser, Paul H. "The Lion and the Lamb: An Essay on Science and Poetry." *Am Sci*, 43 (1955), 89–96.

Ortega y Gasset, José. *The Mission of the University*. Princeton, N.J.: Princeton University Press, 1944.

Overington, Michael A. "The Scientific Community as Audience: Toward a Rhetorical Analysis of Science." *Phil Rhet*, 10 (1977), 143–64.

Paradis, James G. "The Royal Society, Henry Oldenburg, and Some Origins of the Modern Technical Paper." Proceedings of the 28th International Technical Communication Conference, 1981, pp. E82–E86.

Pearson, Karl. *The Grammar of Science*. London: Black, 1911.

Peirce, Charles Sander. "Ideas, Stray or Stolen, About Scientific Writing." *Phil Rhet*, 11 (1978), 147–55.

Peterson, M. S. *Scientific Thinking and Scientific Writing*. New York: Reinhold, 1961.

Philler, Theresa A., et al., eds. *An Annotated Bibliography on Technical Writing, Editing, Graphics, and Publishing, 1950–1965*. Washington, D.C.: Society of Technical Writers and Publishers, 1966.

Pirsig, Robert M. *Zen and the Art of Motorcycle Maintenance*. New York: Bantam 1975.

Price, Derek de Solla. "The Book as Scientific Instrument." *Science*, 158 (1967), 102–104.

Rathbone, Robert R. "Cooperative Teaching of Technical Writing in Engineering Courses." *J Eng Educ*, 49 (Nov. 1958), 126–30.

Reddick, DeWitt Carter. *Literary Style in Science Writing*. New York: Magazine Publishers, 1969.

Reddy, M. J. "Formal Referential Models of Poetic Structure." In *Papers from the Ninth Regional Meeting*. Ed. C. T. Corum, et al. Chicago: Chicago Linguistic Society, 1973, pp. 263–66.

Reincourt, Amaury de. *The Eye of Shiva: Eastern Mysticism and Science*. New York: Morrow, 1981.

Reiser, Oliver Leslie. *The Promise of Scientific Humanism*. New York: Piest, 1940.

Richards, I. A. *Science and Poetry*. New York: Norton, 1926.

Rogers, Robert A. *The Humanities: A Selective Guide to Information Sources*. Littleton, Colo.: Libraries Unltd., 1979.

Rubens, Philip M. "Reinventing the Wheel: Ethics for Technical Communicators." *J Tech Writ Comm*, 11 (1981), 329–39.

Rutgers State University Graduate School of Library Service. *Communication of Scientific and Technical Information: A Bibliography*. New Brunswick, N.J.: Rutgers University Press, 1967.

Sanford, Charles L. "Toward a Theory of Communication in the Sciences and the Humanities." Unpublished Manuscript, Rensselaer Polytechnic Institute.

Savory, Theodore H. *The Language of Science: Its Growth, Character and Usage*. London: Deutsch, 1958.

Sawyer, Thomas M. "The Common Law of Science and the Common Law of Literature." *CCC*, 21 (1970), 337–41.

———. "Rhetoric in an Age of Science and Technology." *CCC*, 23 (1972), 390–98.

Scheffler, I. *Science and Subjectivity*. Indianapolis: Bobbs-Merrill, 1967.

Schwab, Joseph Jackson. *Science, Curriculum, and Liberal Education*. Chicago: University of Chicago Press, 1978.

Seeger, Raymond J. "Scientist and Poet." *Am Sci*, 47 (1959), 350–60.

Shank, Russel. *Bibliography of Technical Writing*. Columbus: Society of Technical Writers and Publishers, 1958.

Simon, Herbert A. *The Sciences of the Artificial*. Cambridge, Mass.: MIT Press, 1969.

Simons, Herbert W. "Are Scientists Rhetors in Disguise?: An Analysis of Discursive Processes Within Scientific Communities." In *Rhetoric in Transition: Studies in the Nature and Use of Rhetoric*. Ed. Eugene E. White. University Park, Pa.: Pennsylvania State University Press, 1980, pp. 115–130.

Snell, Bruno. "The Forging of a Language of Science in Ancient Greece." *Class J*, 56, No. 2 (1960), 50–60.

Snow, Sir Charles Percy. "The Two Cultures." *New Statesman*, 6 Oct. 1956, pp. 413–14.

Stevens, Rolland Elwell. *Reference Books in the Social Sciences and the Humanities*. Champaign, Ill.: Stipes, 1977.

Taviss, Irene, and Linda Silverman. *Technology and Values*. Cambridge: Harvard University Program on Technology and Society, 1969.

Thayer, Lee. *Communication: The Ethical and Moral Issues*. New York: Gordon, 1974.

Toulmin, Stephen. "Can Science and Ethics Be Reconnected?" *Hastings Center Report*, 9 (June 1979), 27–34.

United Nations. *Bibliography of Publications Designed to Raise the Standard of Scientific Literature*. Paris: United Nations Educational, Scientific, and Cultural Organization, 1963.

Van Veen, Frederick. "An Index to 500 Papers Through 1962 on Engineering Writing and Related Subjects." *IEEE Trans Eng Writ Speech*, 6 (1963), 50–58.

Viereck, Peter. "The Poet in the Machine Age." *J Hist Ideas*, 10 (1949), 88–103.

Waggoner, Hyatt Howe. *The Heels of Elohim: Science and Values in Modern Poetry*. Norman, Okla.: University of Oklahoma Press, 1950.

Walter, Edward. "Reasoning in Science and Ethics." *J Val Inq*, 8 (1976), 252–65.

Walters, Frank. "Science, Rhetoric, and the Service Manual." Proceedings of the 27th International Technical Communication Conference, 1980, W101–W108.

Wander, Philip C. "The Rhetoric of Science." *W J Speech Comm*, 40 (1976), 226–35.

Watkins, Bruce O. *Technology and Human Values: Collision and Resolution*. Ann Arbor, Mich.: Ann Arbor Science Publishers, 1978.

Weaver, Richard E. "Concealed Rhetoric in Scientistic Sociology." In *Scientism and Values*. Ed. Helmut Schoeck. Princeton, N.J.: Van Nostrand, 1960, pp. 85–99.

Weaver, Warren. *Science and Imagination*. New York: Basic, 1967.

Weimer, Walter B. "Science as a Rhetorical Transaction: Toward a Nonjustificational Conception of Rhetoric." *Phil Rhet*, 10 (1970), 1–20.

Wenzel, Joseph Wilford. "The Rhetoric of Science." Diss. University of Illinois 1963.

Whitburn, Merrill D. "Audience: A Foundation for Technical Writing Courses." In *Teaching Technical Writing: Teaching Audience Analysis and Adaptation*. Ed. Paul Anderson. Association of Teachers of Technical Writing Anthology No. 1. Morehead, Ky.: ATTW, 1980.

————. "Personality in Scientific and Technical Writing." *J Tech Writ Comm*, 6 (1976), 299–306.

Wright, James R. "On Avoiding Ambiguity and Doublespeak in Technical Writing." *TETYC*, 2, No. 4 (1975), 53–58.

Zappen, James P. "Francis Bacon and the Rhetoric of Science." *CCC*, 26 (1975), 244–47.

Ziemski, S. "Theoretical Assumptions of Science Communication." *Scientia*, 108 (1973), 781–87.

Ziman, John. *Teaching and Learning About Science and Society*. Cambridge: Cambridge University Press, 1980.

Zukav, Gary. *The Dancing Wu Li Masters: An Overview of the New Physics*. New York: Morrow, 1979.

The History of Technical and Scientific Writing

MICHAEL G. MORAN

The history of technical and scientific writing has not yet been written, so there exists no coherent body of material to cite. As the discussion below shows, we have only scattered pieces of scholarship that, when fitted together, do not yet make up a complete picture. What this means, of course, is that many projects need to be undertaken, most notably a major scholarly evaluation of technical and scientific writing from ancient times to the present.

We do not yet even have an adequate definition of this important sub-discipline. What is the study of the history of technical and scientific writing? It must first be distinguished from other closely related areas such as literary criticism, the history of science and technology, the philosophy of science, and the history of ideas. These disciplines often touch on questions related to the history of scientific and technical writing, but they do not define its center, for the essence of this subject concerns questions of rhetoric.

This essay, therefore, cites those articles and books that deal explicitly with the rhetoric of scientific discourse. Under this umbrella fall a number of studies including those of style, of organization and form, of audience adaptation, of readability, and of rhetorical strategy of technical and scientific writing from the earliest to the most contemporary examples. The discipline also includes studies of individual writers as well as studies of broad historical trends. Furthermore, it should raise questions about why technical and scientific writing changes and develops over time and why individual writers are motivated to write. Finally, it should ask who is the audience for this writing and how audience expectations influence its function and development.

Although quite a bit of work has been done on the history of scientific and technical writing, this scholarship has had little effect on teaching. No textbook seriously offers an historical perspective on scientific or technical writing. This, however, does not mean that teachers are not interested. In "When Technical Communicators Face the Past" (1978), Stephen L. Gresham reports that almost all participants surveyed at the 24th International Technical Communication Conference (ITCC) session entitled "An Informal History of Technical Communication in America" believed that the historical perspective was important and deserved more attention. In "From Aristotle to Einstein" (1981), Gresham reports on how he uses the writing of earlier scientists in his classroom, and Robert E. Masse and Patrick M. Kelley, in "Teaching the Tradition of Technical and Scientific Writing" (1977) explain how they teach the great works in the history of science to give their students a sense of the past. There is, then, a growing interest in the area.

Only one earlier bibliography devoted entirely to the subject is now in print: R. John Brockmann's "Bibliography of Articles on the History of Technical Writing" (1983). This useful article lists 36 basic sources that form an introductory core of readings. The present essay builds on Brockmann's by covering technical and scientific writing in the following historical periods: ancient, medieval, and Renaissance; seventeenth century; and eighteenth, nineteenth and twentieth centuries.

Ancient, Medieval, and Renaissance

There are apparently no complete studies of technical and scientific writing in the ancient world, although a few articles do touch on ancient writers. Walter James Miller's "What Can the Technical Writer of the Past Teach the Technical Writer of Today?" (1961) surveys twelve technical writers of the past who can still teach the twentieth-century writer. From the ancient world, Miller discusses Vitruvius, the architect for Augustus Caesar who wrote *Ten Books on Architecture*, a treatise for master builders, and Frontinus, the Roman water commissioner who wrote *Aqueducts of Rome*, which Miller calls the first information report. Miller goes on to discuss Renaissance, eighteenth-, nineteenth-, and twentieth-century technical writers who deserve continued study.

In two other general surveys, Joel J. Shulman also briefly discusses ancient writers. In "The Anonymous Technical Writer in History" (1960), he explores the problems of identifying the many figures who either wrote anonymously or have had works spuriously attributed to them. In Babylon, for instance, scientific texts were written laboriously on clay tablets that did not allow room for the writer's or scribe's name, and Hippocrates, the ancient physician, received credit for many works written long after his death. In "Technical Writers Who Became Famous as Scientists" (1960), Shulman discusses ancient writers who became famous not for original research but for collecting the work of others and communicating it convincingly. The Egyptian Ahmose, author of the Rhind papyrus (which is the first treatise on mathematics), was probably a scribe who compiled the work of other, more innovative thinkers. Euclid, Shulman claims, was less an innovator than a great synthesizer. Both articles continue to discuss writers from other periods.

The most interesting study of ancient rhetoric and its relationship to science writing is Elbert W. Harrington's *Rhetoric and the Scientific Method of Inquiry* (1948). Though dated, this monograph explores the degree to which ancient Greek and Roman rhetoricians' systems of invention are consistent with modern inquiry based on the scientific method. Harrington argues that both Plato and Aristotle (especially the latter) built a healthy skepticism into their methodologies while Latin theorists such as Cicero, Quintillian, and Longinus did not contribute much to scientific invention. Harrington also discusses later English rhetorical theories from the Renaissance to the nineteenth century.

Little work has been done on medieval technical writing, another area that is ripe for further investigation. Much fascinating research could shed light on proto-science, such as alchemy, which continued to exert an influence on science and scientific discourse through the eighteenth century.

The writer of the Middle Ages who has received the greatest scholarly attention is Geoffrey Chaucer, who, in addition to his literary productions, wrote what is generally considered the first technical tract in English, the *Treatise on the Astrolabe* (1391). Chaucer wrote the treatise for his ten-year-old son, Lewis.

The first article on the work, William A. Freedman's "Geoffrey Chaucer, Technical Writer" (1961), argues that Chaucer followed now-accepted good rules of writing, such as writing clear, precise, well-organized prose directed at and adapted to a given audience (a ten year old). Edmond A. Basquin in "The First Technical Writer in English" (1981) continues this argument by discussing Chaucer's five-part method of organization, his general method of exposition, and his stylistic devices. George Ovitt in "A Late Medieval Technical Directive" (1981) attempts to give a balanced view by pointing out weaknesses in the treatise; specifically, he points out that the description is not clear and that the definitions lack precision. He also notes that the work is an important bridge between the earlier medieval alchemical tradition and the new empiricism of the fourteenth and fifteenth centuries.

The most thorough article to date on the *Astrolabe* is Carol S. Lipson's "Descriptions and Instructions in Medieval Times" (1982). This piece examines the foreign-language sources upon which Chaucer based his treatise and places it within the tradition of early technical manuals. One of Chaucer's innovations, for instance, was the use of a preface to the entire piece that gives its purpose, audience, and significance. Lipson maintains that contemporary writers can learn much from Chaucer's approach to manual writing.

One area of technical writing in the Middle Ages that has been explored is the rise and development of business letters. As Luella M. Wolff argues in "A Brief History of the Art of Dictamen" (1979), letter writing was part of the liberal arts curriculum in medieval universities. Called *dictamen prosaicum* or *ars dictaminis*, the art developed in Italian universities as complicated interactions grew between church and state. *Dictamen* reached its apex at the University of Bologna in about 1200 A.D and spread from there throughout Europe. By the end of the thirteenth century, however, the need for precise legal documents arose, notaries took over the job of letter writing, and the art died. In "The

Earliest Business Letters in English" (1980), Malcolm Richardson expands Wolff's research by tracing letter writing in England. *Dictamen* was originally church-oriented because most literate people were associated with this institution. With the rise of business activity, however, the laity needed to write more letters, and by 1400 a scribe class had developed to handle correspondence in Latin and French. After that date, English began to replace these languages and by 1420, English-language letters had become common. These letters mixed business and personal material and were formal and rigid in style and tone.

One of the most innovative articles on late medieval and Renaissance scientific style is James Stephens's "Style as Therapy in Renaissance Science" (1983). Since Renaissance scientists mistrusted the human mind because it was associated with superstitions and old values, Stephens argues, they used popular images and allusions that they knew were false to communicate their new scientific discoveries to a skeptical, often hostile audience. These falsehoods soothed the readers' troubled minds by offering them familiar images and points of reference. Stephens traces three distinct historical stages in the period's scientific prose. In the first, Paracelsus developed a bombastic style that used alchemical images to bridge the growing gap between science and religion. In the second, Sir Francis Bacon, who criticized Paracelsus's obscure style, used classical references in his scientific rhetoric. In the third, Galileo used Christian allusions. From 1500 to 1700, scientific writing moved away from the obscure bombast of Paracelsus to the clearer prose of Bacon and Galileo.

Seventeenth Century

As the above discussion suggests, it is a mistake to think that science "began" in the early seventeenth century with the philosophical works of Sir Francis Bacon. Many earlier figures anticipated Bacon's emphasis on experimentation and close observation of nature. Nevertheless, Bacon remains a seminal figure in the philosophy of science, and the seventeenth century must be viewed as the century when the new empiricism became a powerful tool for advancing humankind's understanding of the natural world. It is also the period that has received the most attention from historians of scientific discourse.

Although Bacon's rhetorical commentaries are generally examined for their comments on the plain, unadorned style, two articles by James P. Zappen analyze these works for other concerns related to scientific discourse. In "Francis Bacon and the Rhetoric of Science" (1975), Zappen argues that the philosopher was not just interested in the plain style. In *The Advancement of Learning* Bacon not only criticizes the flowered prose of Cicero's Renaissance followers, but he also develops a comprehensive theory of the communication process based on subject and audience analysis. In "Francis Bacon and the Topics" (1977), Zappen argues that Bacon's criticism of the classical topics of Aristotle, Cicero, and Quintillian led to the modern view that they are conventional forms for organizing discourse rather than places to discover content. Furthermore, in *The Advancement of*

Learning and *De Argumentio Scientiarum* (1623), Bacon argues for a new method of invention based on the gradual development of a body of knowledge built by moving from experiments to axioms and back to experiments. Bacon thus rejects the role of traditional scholastic logic in the search for truth.

Although Bacon himself did not write in the plain style, he argued for it and therefore became, in the eyes of the scientists associated with the Royal Society later in the century, the symbol and inspiration for the movement toward an unadorned, accurate, mathematical prose. The reasons for the rise of this distinctive style, which became one of the cardinal principles of the Society, have elicited much debate.

Richard F. Jones in the classic article "Science and English Prose Style in the Third Quarter of the Seventeenth Century" (1930) distinguishes between the plain style of Bacon's followers in the Royal Society, such as John Wilkins, William Petty, Thomas Sprat, and others, and the plain style of what Morris W. Croll, in *Attic and Baroque Prose Style* (a volume of his early essays collected in 1966), calls the Anti-Ciceronians. Jones attributes the plain style, which lacked rhetorical flourish, directly to the rise of science, an argument he continues in "Science and Language in England of the Mid-Seventeenth Century" (1971) and "Science and Criticism" (1951). Croll, on the other hand, attributes this style to a general suspicion of elaborate prose which affected not only scientific but also critical and religious prose. In "Reviews of R. F. Jones's 'Science and English Prose Style in the Third Quarter of the Seventeenth Century' " (1971), both Croll and R. S. Crane attack Jones. Croll notes that the Royal Society's views were merely an extension of those of the earlier Anti-Ciceronian movement, while Crane points out that Jones's argument could not explain the general movement in all prose of the century toward a plainer, simpler style.

Other scholars have tried to resolve the controversy. Joan Bennett in "Science and the Plain Style" (1971) shows that Thomas Hobbes, as well as Bacon, mistrusted rhetoric and called for the precise, mathematical use of language. Moreover, she claims, this attitude affected many non-scientists of the period. The seminal discussion of the issue, however, is Robert Adolph's *The Rise of Modern Prose Style* (1971). Arguing that both Croll and Jones are inaccurate, Adolph attributes the rise of the plain style to a pervasive sense of utilitarianism that began with Bacon and was picked up by Thomas Sprat, Joseph Glanvill, and other members of the Royal Society. James R. Bennett's anthology *Prose Style* (1971) contains parts of Jones's, Adolph's, and Joan Bennett's work, and R. John Brockmann's "A Reformed Writer in 1676" (1982) shows that between the 1661 and the 1676 editions of *Variety of Dogmatizing* Glanvill simplified his prose in accordance with the new tenets of the Royal Society for a simpler, less adorned style.

The Royal Society had an important influence on the development of scientific discourse, a point James G. Paradis makes in "The Royal Society, Henry Oldenburg, and Some Origins of the Modern Technical Paper" (1981). Paradis traces the influence of Oldenburg, the first editor of the Royal Society's *Phil-*

osophical Transactions (founded in 1665), on the development of the modern scientific paper. The Royal Society insisted that scientific language use words that represent "single, agreed upon entities" (p. E–83). Oldenburg followed this requirement when he translated, edited, and created brief articles out of foreign and domestic correspondence. The short, pithy paper, free from stylistic adornment, became the norm for scientific prose.

In three articles, Merrill D. Whitburn discusses the implications of seventeenth-century scientific prose for the contemporary teacher and researcher. In "The Plain Style in Technical Writing" (1978), he argues that the heritage of the plain style can be detrimental to the contemporary student who has trouble with self-expression. In "The Past and Future of Scientific and Technical Writing" (1977), he discusses Sprat's *History of the Royal Society* (1667) and concludes that technical writing research should follow Sprat's scientific method of experimenting, forming principles, and testing them. Finally, in "Personality in Scientific and Technical Writing" (1976), he discusses Glanvill's translation of Fontenelle's "A Plurality of Worlds," which is a humorous discussion of scientific matters between Fontenelle and a Countess. Since the Countess lacks a scientific background, Fontenelle must use many techniques of audience adaptation which contemporary students could well utilize.

In "Bacon, Linnaeus and Lavoisier" (1983), James G. Paradis discusses how scientists saw the need for developing flexible scientific vocabularies designed to meet the needs of new realities that science defined. Bacon, Paradis argues, was the first to call for language reform and to develop a language system that connected words to observable reality. Linnaeus worked out many of the problems Bacon faced by constructing a botanical system of nomenclature that functioned as a tool for exploring reality. Lavoisier, the eighteenth-century French chemist, performed a similar function for chemistry by creating generic names for chemicals.

Although most of the work on seventeenth-century scientific writing has focused on Bacon and the members of the Royal Society, Michael H. Markel has commented on Sir Thomas Browne, an English physician of the century who did not write in the plain style. By examining *Pseudodoxia Epidemica*, Markel shows that Browne analyzes and addresses his audience, moves smoothly between abstractions and details, and strives to meet his ethical responsibilities by communicating true information.

Eighteenth, Nineteenth, and Twentieth Centuries

A good background for the study of eighteenth-century technical and scientific prose is Wilbur Samuel Howell's *Eighteenth Century British Logic and Rhetoric* (1971). In this volume, Howell argues that the logic and rhetoric of the period responded to the new science by gradually moving toward inductive methods that replaced the Scholastic systems emphasizing syllogistic reasoning and the classical topics. Donald W. Bush, Jr., in "Lessons from the 18th Century"

(1982) briefly shows how George Campbell's *Philosophy of Rhetoric* (1776) and Hugh Blair's *Lectures on Rhetoric and Belles Lettres* (1783) emphasized the importance of sentence structure and its effects on scientific style.

Another good background source is Donald Davie's little book, *The Language of Science and the Language of Literature* (1963). This slim volume outlines the effect of scientific language on literature—including philosophical and political writing—during the early decades of the eighteenth century. Davie shows how Samuel Johnson's *Dictionary* introduced many technical and scientific terms into the general vocabulary and how the satirists used the language of science to attack the materialism of natural science.

Joseph Priestley, the English chemist who isolated oxygen and influenced Lavoisier, has received some attention. Della A. Whittaker in "Priestley's Personal Style" (1979) shows how the scientist used personalized touches when discussing his experiments. He wrote using "I," expressed his emotional reactions to his discoveries, and informally discussed the work of fellow scientists. By describing all of the experiment, including his failures and blind alleys, Priestley achieved true objectivity, Whittaker concludes. Chester A. Lawson in "Joseph Priestley and the Process of Cultural Evolution" (1954) finds a generalized pattern of thought embedded in Priestley's scientific writing. This pattern consists of five steps in which Priestley begins with a belief that gives rise to a hypothesis which he then tests, compares the results of the tests with the hypothesis, doubts his findings if a discrepancy exists between the two, and develops a new belief that he again tests. The process, Lawson argues, advances knowledge from the known to the unknown. Michael G. Moran in "Joseph Priestley, William Duncan, and Analytic Arrangement in 18th-Century Scientific Discourse" (1984) shows that this method was known in eighteenth-century logic as analytic arrangement, that Priestley discusses it in *A Course of Lectures on Oratory and Criticism* (1777), and that he uses it in his scientific prose. The method possesses persuasive value because the readers are more likely to accept a conclusion if they have seen all steps in the discovery process leading up to it.

Erasmus Darwin's *The Botanical Garden* and *The Temple of Nature*, two late eighteenth-century poems that discuss new scientific developments, have been discussed by Geoffrey L. Scott in "The Scientific Poetry of Erasmus Darwin" (1982). Although they are written in heroic couplets and use poetic allusions, they possess many qualities of sound technical writing. They strive for technical accuracy, support the theoretical with the concrete and visual, use the active voice, and assume a didactic tone appropriate for a general audience. They are also in the tradition of the scientific poem that includes Hesiod's *Works and Days*, Edmund Spenser's *Shepherd's Calendar*, John Dyer's *The Fleece*, and James Grainger's *The Sugar Cane*.

William E. Rivers in "Lord Chesterfield on the Craft of Business Writing" (1979) examines this writer's comments to his son on the importance of business correspondence. Chesterfield insisted that awareness of basic principles such as clarity and sensitivity to audience needs was important to well-written letters, and he advocated wide reading to improve style.

American technical and scientific writers of the eighteenth-century have also received some attention. In "Technical Writing in America" (1981), Michael E. Connaughton discusses scientific and technical writing in America from the seventeenth century to 1815. During this period, scientific writers changed from amateurs, many of whom were clergymen, to professional scientists. This shift was marked by the founding of the *American Philosophical Society Transactions* which took the first faltering steps toward establishing a standard of scientific writing in the United States. Although it never developed into a first-rate publication, it laid the groundwork for more specialized instruments of science such as the *American Mineralogical Journal* of the early nineteenth century. Although clearly a preliminary report, Connaughton's article points the way to systematic research into the development of scientific writing in the United States.

Other studies have concentrated on individual technical writers in eighteenth-century America. As Joel J. Shulman argues in "Cotton Mather, America's First Great Technical Writer" (1963), Mather was the first American scientist of any stature. He was the first of his nation to be elected to the Royal Society on the basis of his scientific work. Although not a brilliant scientist, he was a talented technical writer who worked hard to communicate scientific findings. As Shulman shows, Mather contributed to technical writing by editing the work of other scientists, using new statistical methods of testing, supporting ideas with experimental evidence, and reporting on new material.

The eighteenth-century American writer who has received the most attention is Benjamin Franklin. In "America's First Great Technical Writer" (1962), Charles C. Hargis, Jr., notes that Franklin advocated good writing and recognized that his talents in that area contributed to his international reputation. In "Benjamin Franklin's Contributions to the Development of Technical Communication" (1977), Stephen L. Gresham argues that Franklin's pragmatic attitude toward writing grew from his general philosophical stance. Franklin influenced other scientific writers of his day, formatted his papers well, and adapted his prose to his audience. His writing can still serve as a model for twentieth-century technical writers. John A. Brogan in "Lessons from Benjamin Franklin" (1965) describes how Franklin learned to write using imitations of models, and Elizabeth Tebeaux in "Franklin's *Autobiography*" (1981) discusses how Franklin's use of tone, persona, simple sentences, and clear longer sentences still exemplify good technical writing.

Some work has been done on nineteenth-century technical and scientific writers. Donald W. Bush, Jr., in "The Diction of Sir Humphrey Davy" (1978) discusses the strengths of Davy's five-page description of his safety lamp (1816). He organizes the piece according to problem-solution, gives a personal history of his own efforts to maintain reader interest, and uses concrete language. Mary M. Lay in "A Classical Example of a Procedure" (1980) analyzes John Snow's 1824 "The Prevention of Cholera" to show how Snow establishes a clear purpose and analyzes audience needs. Shari A. Kelley and Patrick M. Kelley in "Sir Charles Lyell" (1980) discuss a short passage from *Elements of Geology* to show how Lyell communicated successfully with a diverse and often hostile audience. In "Moby Dick" (1981), Deborah Kilgore discusses *Moby Dick* as a classic of technical literature because of its detailed expositions on the science and technology of whaling.

In "The Technical Writer as Naturalist" (1979), Wayne A. Losano discusses one late eighteenth- and two nineteenth-century naturalists who wrote influential books on their travels. William Bartram's *Travels* (1791) is filled with romantic, inflated diction and describes in lavish detail many of the creatures he found. Henry Walter Bates's *The Naturalist on the Rivers Amazon* (1876) expresses the author's personal reactions and romantic inclinations in ways contemporary scientists cannot. Finally, Charles Darwin's *The Voyage of the Beagle* (1860) is less ornate and effusive than the first two but still expresses the author's personal opinions and observations. Losano concludes that scientific writing has unfortunately lost a gentility that made reading these accounts enjoyable.

Deborah C. Andrews and William D. Andrews in "Nineteenth Century American House Pattern Books" (1981) discuss another sub-genre of scientific and technical prose. As technology developed and affluence increased in nineteenth-century America, more families wanted homes. Books such as Andrew Jackson Downing's *Architecture of Country Homes* (1850) were published to teach non-experts how to build and maintain pre-designed houses.

In the twentieth century, technical and scientific writing has developed in several interesting directions. As Richard W. Ferguson shows in " 'Fear God and Take Your Own Part!' " (1980), America at the turn of the century had a holistic view of society that emphasized subordination of private needs to the greater good. This value system was expressed in the technical writing of the period when writers such as N. Hawkins in *Maxims and Instructions for the Boiler Room* (1903) and Charles C. Oliver in *The Miller and Milling Engineer* (1913) insisted that readers consider their work in larger social contexts.

The scientific writings of Einstein and George Washington Carver have been analyzed. In "The Relativity of Communication" (1980), Michael J. Baresich discusses Einstein's ability to adapt his discussions of a subject as complicated as relativity to various audiences. In "On the Electrodynamics of Moving Bodies" (1905), Einstein addresses an expert audience by using mathematical formulas and no background information. In *The Meaning of Relativity* (1922), he addresses a more general audience composed of scientists from various areas. In this book, Einstein attempts to put his theories in larger context but does not define general scientific terms. In *Relativity* (1952), addressed to a general, lay audience, he assumes only basic knowledge, withholds difficult material, and uses concrete illustrations. In "George Washington Carver and the Art of Technical Communication" (1979), Stephen L. Gresham examines Carver's work and finds that it exemplifies sound writing fundamentals. During the late nineteenth and early twentieth century, Carver wrote from his laboratory at Tuskegee numerous agricultural bulletins directed at poor, uneducated Alabama farmers. Many of these papers are minor masterpieces that establish a clear purpose, engage a difficult audience successfully, use a clear, instructional style, and follow rhetorical modes. In addition, Carver manages to address many of the problems of local farmers, educate them broadly by introducing historical information, and champion the benefits of technology.

Several articles address larger issues in twentieth-century technical and scientific writing. Richard M. Weaver in "Concealed Rhetoric in Scientistic Sociology" (1970) argues that much sociological writing pretends to be scientific when it actually is rhetorical. True scientific writing, Weaver maintains, is "concerned only with facts and the relationships between them" (p. 141). Rhetoric, on the other hand, is concerned with personal values and not facts alone. Sociologists work in the realm of human value systems and political choices, not the realm of the objective facts of natural science. Professionals in the field, Weaver concludes, should call themselves "social philosophers" so that they can overtly practice rhetoric.

Values also play a role in another kind of scientific writing, as Steven L. Del Sesto argues in "The Science Journalist and Early Popular Magazine Coverage of Nuclear Energy" (1981). With the advent of nuclear energy in the 1940s, journalists and technical writers had to popularize its peacetime uses after the horror of Hiroshima and Nagasaki. The 1940s and 1950s saw a flood of sensational, grandiose, and fantastic claims for the new energy source that emphasized its contribution to medicine, transportation, industry, and agriculture. At the time of these excesses, scientific journalism was in its infancy, and Del Sesto argues that now such writers must not only report but also criticize technological and scientific developments. Yuri V. Novozhilov and Jacques G. Richardson make a similar point in "Fifty Years After the Death of Flammarion" (1976). Author of *L'Astronomie Populaire* (1879), Flammarion was the first popularizer of scientific ideas. In the twentieth century, the science writers and popularizers form a distinct profession that must consider scientific advances in relation to the larger social good and a system of human values.

In a related issue, Debra Journet in "Rhetoric and Sociobiology" (1984) agrees with Thomas S. Kuhn in *The Structure of Scientific Revolutions* (1970) that scientific theories are human constructions that scientists support using rhetorical strategies. She reviews the debate over E. O. Wilson's *Sociobiology* (1975). A group of scientists writing in *The New York Review of Books* as well as other places attacked the last chapter, in which Wilson applies sociobiological theory to humans. Journet shows how both Wilson and his antagonists use classical rhetorical strategies to support their cases.

Finally, two articles on the academic discipline of technical writing have recently appeared. Richard W. Schmelzer in "The First Textbook on Technical Writing" (1977) argues that Ray Palmer Baker's 1924 *The Preparation of Technical Reports* (revised in 1936) was the first textbook in the field. In an impressively researched article entitled "The Rise of Technical Writing Instruction in America'' (1982), Robert J. Connors presents evidence that the honor goes to T. A. Rickard's *A Guide to Technical Writing* (1908). Connors goes on to trace the development of technical writing programs from their birth in engineering schools to their uneasy adoptions by English departments.

Conclusion

The works discussed in this chapter are just a beginning. They do little more than scratch the surface of the rich store of research potential which the history of technical and scientific writing offers. If this essay functions as a rough guide for future researchers in this important field, it will have served its purpose. The study of this discipline's history offers more than the discovery of dusty facts. Instead, as Stephen L. Gresham comments in "When Technical Communicators Face the Past" (1978), "an awareness of one's past clarifies one's view of the present and elevates one's expectations of the future" (p. 11).

References

Adolph, Robert. *The Rise of Modern Prose Style*. Cambridge, Mass.: MIT Press, 1971.

Andrews, Deborah C., and William D. Andrews. "Nineteenth Century American House Pattern Books: A Rhetorical Analysis." Proceedings of the 28th International Technical Communication Conference, 1981, pp. E–1–4.

Baresich, Michael J. "The Relativity of Communication: Albert Einstein as Technical Writer." *J Tech Writ Comm*, 10 (1980), 125–32.

Basquin, Edmond A. "The First Technical Writer in English: Geoffrey Chaucer." *Tech Comm*, 28, No. 3 (1981), 22–24.

Bennett, James R., ed. *Prose Style: A Historical Approach Through Studies*. San Francisco, Calif.: Chandler, 1971.

Bennett, Joan. "Science and the Plain Style." In *Prose Style: A Historical Approach Through Studies*. Ed. James R. Bennett. San Francisco, Calif.: Chandler, 1971, pp. 78–85. Also appeared as "An Aspect of the Evolution of Seventeenth Century Prose." *Rev Engl Stud*, 17 (1941), 281–97.

Brockmann, R. John. "Bibliography of Articles on the History of Technical Writing." *J Tech Writ Comm.*, 13 (1983), 155–65.

———. "A Reformed Writer in 1676." *Tech Comm*, 29, No. 2 (1982), 48.

Brogan, John A. "Lessons from Benjamin Franklin, America's First Great Technical Writer." *IEEE Trans Eng Writ Speech*, EWS–8, (June 1965), 3–7.

Bush, Donald W., Jr. "The Diction of Sir Humphrey Davy." *Tech Comm*, 25, No. 1 (1978), 32.

———. "Lessons from the 18th Century." *Tech Comm*, 29, No. 3 (1982), 64.

Connaughton, Michael E. "Technical Writing in America: A Historical Perspective." ERIC ED (1981) 199 733 and in *Technical Writings Past, Present and Future*. Ed. J. C. Mathes and Thomas E. Pinelli. Hampton, Va.: National Aeronautics and Space Administration, 1981, pp. 31–42.

Connors, Robert J. "The Rise of Technical Writing Instruction in America." *J Tech Writ Comm*, 12 (1982), 329–52.

Croll, Morris W. *Attic and Baroque Prose Style: The Anti-Ciceronian Movement*. Ed. J. Max Patrick, et al. Princeton, N.J.: Princeton University Press, 1966.

————, and R. S. Crane. "Reviews of R. F. Jones's 'Science and English Prose Style in the Third Quarter of the Seventeenth Century.' " In *Seventeenth Century Prose*. Ed. Stanley E. Fish. New York: Oxford University Press, 1971, pp. 90–93.

Davie, Donald. *The Language of Science and the Language of Literature, 1700–1740*. London: Sheed, Ward, 1963.

Del Sesto, Steven L. "The Science Journalist and Early Popular Magazine Coverage of Nuclear Energy." *J Tech Writ Comm*, 11 (1981), 315–27.

Ferguson, Richard W. " 'Fear God and Take Your Own Part!': Ethical Imperatives and Technical Writing—Some Turn-of-the-Century Examples." Proceedings of the 27th International Technical Communication Conference, 1980, pp. W–195–97.

Freedman, William A. "Geoffrey Chaucer, Technical Writer." *STWP Rev*, 8 (Oct. 1961), 14–15.

"The General Manager's Mail, 1879." *Bus Hist Rev*, 40 (1966), 369–71.

Gresham, Stephen L. "Benjamin Franklin's Contributions to the Development of Technical Communication." *J Tech Writ Comm*, 7 (1977), 5–13.

————. "From Aristotle to Einstein: Scientific Literature and the Teaching of Technical Writing." In *Courses, Components, and Exercises in Technical Communication*. Ed. Dwight W. Stevenson. Urbana Ill.: National Council of Teachers of English (NCTE), 1981, pp. 87–93.

————. "George Washington Carver and the Art of Technical Communication." *J Tech Writ Comm*, 9 (1979), 217–25.

————. "Harvesting the Past: The Legacy of Scientific and Technical Writing in America." Proceedings of the 24th International Technical Communication Conference, 1977, pp. 306–08.

————. "When Technical Communicators Face the Past." *Tech Comm*, 25 No. 3 (1978), 8–9, 11.

Hargis, Charles C., Jr. "America's First Great Technical Writer." *STWP Rev.*, 9 (Jan. 1962), 12–13.

Harrington, Elbert W. *Rhetoric and the Scientific Method of Inquiry: A Study of Invention*. University of Colorado Studies: Series in Language and Literature, No. 1. Boulder, Colo.: University of Colorado Press, 1948.

Howell, Wilbur Samuel. *Eighteenth-Century British Logic and Rhetoric*. Princeton, N.J.: Princeton University Press, 1971.

Jones, Richard Foster. "Science and Criticism." In *The Seventeenth Century: Studies in the History of English Thought and Literature from Bacon to Pope*. Ed. Francis R. Johnson, et al. Stanford, Calif.: Stanford University Press, 1951, pp. 41–71.

————. "Science and English Prose Style in the Third Quarter of the Seventeenth Century." *PMLA*, 45 (1930), 977–1009.

————. "Science and Language in England of the Mid-Seventeenth Century." In *Seventeenth Century Prose*. Ed. Stanley E. Fish. New York: Oxford University Press, 1971, pp. 94–111.

Journet, Debra. "Rhetoric and Sociobiology." *J Tech Writ Comm*, 14 (1984), 339–50.

Kelley, Shari A., and Patrick M. Kelley. "Sir Charles Lyell: Geologist and Technical Communicator." *Tech Comm*, 27, No. 2 (1980), 40.

Kilgore, Deborah. "Moby Dick: A Whale of a Handbook for Technical Writing Teachers." *J Tech Writ Comm*, 11 (1981), 209–16.

Kuhn, Thomas S. *The Structure of Scientific Revolutions*. 2nd ed. Chicago: University of Chicago Press, 1970.

Lawson, Chester A. "Joseph Priestley and the Process of Cultural Evolution." *Sci Educ*, 38 (1954), 267–76.

Lay, Mary M. "A Classical Example of a Procedure." *Tech Comm*, 27, No. 4 (1980), 40.

Lipson, Carol S. "Descriptions and Instructions in Medieval Times: Lessons to Be Learnt from Geoffrey Chaucer's Scientific Instruction Manual." *J Tech Writ Comm*, 12 (1982), 243–56.

Losano, Wayne A. "The Technical Writer as Naturalist: Some Lessons from the Classics." *J Tech Writ Comm*, 9 (1979), 227–37.

Markel, Michael H. "The Rhetorical Principles of Sir Thomas Browne." *Tech Comm*, 26, No. 1 (1979), 8–9.

Masse, Roger E., and Patrick M. Kelley. "Teaching the Tradition of Technical and Scientific Writing." In *Technical and Professional Communication*. Ed. Thomas M. Sawyer. Ann Arbor, Mich.: Professional Communications Press, 1977, pp. 79–87.

Miller, Walter James. "What Can the Technical Writer of the Past Teach the Technical Writer of Today?" *IRE Trans Eng Writ Speech*, EWS–4 (Dec. 1961), 69–76. Also in *The Teaching of Technical Writing* Ed. David H. Cunningham and Herman A. Estrin. Urbana: NCTE, 1975, pp. 198–216.

Mitchell, John H. "Whitehead on Style." *Tech Comm*, 25, No. 3 (1978), 40.

Moran, Michael G. "Joseph Priestley, William Duncan, and Analytic Arrangement in 18th-Century Scientific Discourse." *J Tech Writ Comm*, 14 (1984), 207–15.

Novozhilov, Yuri V., and Jacques G. Richardson. "Fifty Years After the Death of Flammarion, The Science Popularizer." *J Tech Writ Comm*, 6 (1976), 89–96.

Ovitt, George. "A Late Medieval Technical Directive: Chaucer's *Treatise on the Astrolabe.*" Proceedings of the 28th International Technical Communication Conference, 1981, pp. E–78–81.

Paradis, James G. "Bacon, Linnaeus, and Lavoisier: Early Language Reform in the Sciences." In *New Essays in Technical and Scientific Communication: Research, Theory, Practice*. Ed. Paul V. Anderson, R. John Brockmann, and Carolyn R. Miller. Farmingdale, N.Y.: Baywood, 1983, pp. 200–24.

———. "The Royal Society, Henry Oldenburg, and Some Origins of the Modern Technical Paper." Proceedings of the 28th International Technical Communication Conference, 1981, pp. E–82–86.

Richardson, Malcolm. "The Earliest Business Letters in English: An Overview." *J Bus Comm*, 17, No. 3 (1980), 19–31.

Rivers, William E. "Lord Chesterfield on the Craft of Business Writing: The Relations of Reading and Writing." *J Bus Comm* 17, No. 1 (1979), 3–12.

Schmelzer, Richard W. "The First Textbook on Technical Writing." *J Tech Writ Comm*, 7 (1977), 51–54.

Scott, Geoffrey L. "The Scientific Poetry of Erasmus Darwin." *Tech Comm*, 29, No. 3 (1982), 16–20.

Shulman, Joel J. "The Anonymous Technical Writer in History." *STWP Rev*, 7 (Jan. 1960), 22–26.

———. "Cotton Mather, America's First Great Technical Writer." *STWP Rev*, 10 (Apr. 1963), 20–22.

————. "Technical Writers Who Became Famous as Scientists." *STWP Rev*, 7 (July 1960), 17–21.

Stephens, James. "Style as Therapy in Renaissance Science." In *New Essays in Technical and Scientific Communication: Research, Theory, Practice*. Ed. Paul V. Anderson, R. John Brockmann, and Carolyn R. Miller. Farmingdale, N.Y.: Baywood, 1983, pp. 187–99.

Tebeaux, Elizabeth. "Franklin's *Autobiography*—Important Lessons in Tone, Syntax, and Persona." *J Tech Writ Comm*, 11 (1981), 341–49.

Weaver, Richard M. "Concealed Rhetoric in Scientific Sociology." In *Language Is Sermonic*. Baton Rouge, La.: Louisiana State University Press, 1970, pp. 139–58.

Whitburn, Merrill D. "The Past and the Future of Scientific and Technical Writing." *J Tech Writ Comm*, 7 (1977), 143–49.

————. "Personality in Scientific and Technical Writing." *J Tech Writ Comm*, 6 (1976), 299–306.

————. "The Plain Style in Technical Writing." *J Tech Writ Comm*, 8 (1978), 349–58.

Whittaker, Della A. "Priestley's Personal Style." *Tech Comm*, 26, No. 3 (1979), 28.

Wolff, Luella M. "A Brief History of the Art of Dictamen: Medieval Origins of Business Letter Writing." *J Bus Comm*, 16, No. 2 (1979), 3–11.

Zappen, James P. "Francis Bacon and the Rhetoric of Science." *CCC*, 26 (1975), 244–47.

————. "Francis Bacon and the Topics." Proceedings of the 24th International Technical Communication Conference, 1977, pp. 309–12.

Communication Theory and Technical Communication

GEORGE A. BARNETT AND CAROL HUGHES

Communication is the process by which information is exchanged between two or more systems existing within a common environment. These systems may be individuals, social organizations, animals, or machines. Information is generally defined as patterned matter or energy (David K. Berlo, *The Process of Communication* [1960]), which reduces the uncertainty in the future behavior of the interacting systems (Claude Shannon and Warren Weaver, *The Mathematical Theory of Communication* [1949]; Norbert Weiner, *Cybernetics* [1949]; Norbert Weiner, *The Human Use of Human Beings* [1954]; and J. R. Pierce, *Symbols, Signals and Noise* [1961]). When the system includes people, meaning may be attributed to the information.

Technical communication represents a sub-set of these activities, limited by (1) the content of subject matter of the information (Gordon H. Mills and John A. Walter, *Technical Communication* [1978]; Thomas E. Pearsall, *Teaching Technical Writing* [1975]; Patrick M. Kelley and Roger E. Masse, "A Definition of Technical Writing" [1977]; John S. Harris, "On Expanding the Definition of Technical Writing" [1978]; Margaret D. Blickle and Martha E. Passe, *Readings for Technical Writers* [1963]), (2) the style in which it is presented (Robert Hays, "What Is Technical Writing?" [1961]; A. J. Kirkman, "The Communication of Technical Thought" [1970]; Edmund P. Dandridge, Jr., "Notes Towards a Definition of Technical Writing" [1975]), (3) its function or purpose (Reginald O. Kapp, *The Presentation of Technical Information* [1957]; W. Earl Britton, "What Is Technical Writing?" [1965]; Donald Ross, Jr., "A Theory of the Function of Technical Writing" [1981]), and (4) the context in which it is used (Carolyn R. Miller, "Rules, Context, and Technical Communication"

The authors would like to thank David L. Carson, Carolyn R. Miller, Craig Harkins, Elaine Lewis, Charles Petrie, and many other people who helped in the preparation of this manuscript. A special note of thanks is due to Marian Deutschman for the preparation of the graphics.

[1980]). Without getting embroiled in the controversy over the definition of technical communication, for purposes of this chapter, we will consider technical communication to be communication about science, engineering (technology), and business (public or private) presented in a simple, objective, impartial, clear, and precise style. Generally, it occurs within the context of formal organizations whose functions are to deal with scientific or technical material or to disseminate information to the public. The function of technical communication is to present information in such a manner that the audience can draw one and only one meaning from the communication—the meaning intended by the communicator. The goal of technical communication is to present information with the greatest possible fidelity.

This chapter will review the theories and research about communication which have particular relevance to that sub-set of issues that fall under the rubric of technical communication. We will focus particularly on those notions that concern the fidelity of information exchange or communication effectiveness. As a result, this chapter will deal with its subject matter in a prescriptive manner. That is, we will make general recommendations about how practitioners of technical communication should proceed in order to maximize the likelihood of effective communication.

As a field of inquiry, communication has evolved from a variety of academic disciplines in both the humanities and sciences (natural and social). They range from rhetoric, speech, English, journalism, law, and linguistics at the humanistic end of the spectrum through the social sciences (anthropology, political science, sociology, economics, psychology) and management, to electrical engineering and computer and systems science at the scientific end. Communication cuts across all these fields. While its focus is the process and effects of information exchange, all these orientations have provided perspectives to analyze the process of communication. Because of the variety of perspectives from which communication may be studied, there is no single comprehensive theory or set of theories to explain communication (Aubrey Fisher, *Perspectives on Human Communication* [1978]). Possible exceptions may be Newton's laws of thermodynamics (Joseph Woelfel and Edward L. Fink, *The Measurement of Communication Processes* [1980]), Jean Piaget's (*Structuralism* [1970]) notion of structuralism, or general systems theory (Ludwig von Bertalanffy, *General Systems Theory* [1965]). These represent comprehensive theories that may encompass communication, but scholars are not universally agreed as to their role in the process.

What has emerged are a number of middle-range theories that are most often related to substantive communication issues (Robert I. Merton, *Social Theory and Social Structure* [1957]; Everett M. Rogers with F. Floyd Shoemaker, *Communication of Innovations* [1971]). Middle-range theories are midway in specificity or generality between observable data and grand theory. They represent a series of generalizations and syntheses of empirical findings. It is assumed that the development of middle-range theories will lead to more abstract and general theories as evidence accumulates and theoretical inferences are confirmed. Middle-range theories have the advantage of relating substantive observable phenomena to abstract theory. These operational foci are often lost when dealing with grand theory. For example, although prescriptions for communication behavior may be deduced from the laws of thermodynamics, such predictions are difficult, and, although heuristically interesting, not very useful for practitioners.

Examples of middle-range communication theories include Joseph Woelfel and Edward L. Fink's theory (1980), which describes the role of communication in attitude, social, and cultural change. At a comparable level, Everett M. Rogers with Floyd Shoemaker (1971) developed a theory to predict and explain the diffusion of innovations. Other theories in this category might be the cognitive consistency or balance theories (Fritz Heider, *The Psychology of Interpersonal Relations* [1956]; Theodore Newcomb, "An Approach to the Study of Communicative Acts" [1953]; Leon Festinger, *A Theory of Cognitive Dissonance* [1957]; Charles E. Osgood, George J. Suci, and Percy H. Tannenbaum, *The Measurement of Meaning* [1957]), social exchange theory (George C. Homans, "Social Behavior As Exchange" [1958]); Peter M. Blau, *Exchange and Power in Social Life* [1964]), Paul Watzlawick, Janet Bevin, and Don D. Jackson's theory of interpersonal relations (*Pragmatics of Human Communication* [1967]), and Elihu Katz and Paul Lazarsfeld's theory of media and interpersonal influence (*Personal Influence* [1955]). These are scientific theories based on empirical data. In this chapter, we will concentrate on the scientific theories of communication and on the research (which they have generated) that supports or refutes them. Other theories, based on humanistic perspectives, will be presented by the other authors in this volume.

To help organize the large quantity of scientific theories with implications for technical communication, we will begin with a discussion of a number of models of the communication process. This will allow us to identify categories of variables and the relationships among them. After reviewing the models, we will discuss the variables and the ways they influence the effectiveness of technical communication.

Models of Communication

Models are abstract representations of some aspects of theories (Nan Lin, *Foundations of Social Research* [1976]). They are classification systems that enable one to abstract and to categorize potentially relevant parts of processes (Gerald R. Miller, *Speech Communication* [1966]). They help establish the boundaries to the question, "What does communication entail?" and they provide structure for the components of the process (C. David Mortensen, *Communication* [1966]).

Models differ from theories in two ways. One, models do not contain epistemologic propositions linking concepts or variables. They only contain statements showing the relationship among concepts. Two, they lack the totality and complexity of theoretical statements. Models may represent a single proposition containing a limited number of concepts within a theoretical structure. Because models lack an epistemological demonstration and have only a partial structure, they may be considered "imperfect" theories. As such, they lack explanatory power because they have predictive power only for specific indicators.

Given these drawbacks, why construct models? Because of the universal and abstract nature of theories, they generally lack a specific operational focus. That is, how do we know the variables involved when we see them? Models provide this focus. They simplify the process of theory construction by facilitating the identification of the variables and relationships to consider when analyzing abstract phenomena such as technical communication. These graphic representations facilitate the use of the theoretical notions by practitioners by serving as behavioral guides.

Gerald R. Miller (1966) suggests that models of communication serve three major functions: an organizational or communication function; a heuristic or research-generating function; and an anticipatory or predictive function. A number of models of communication will be presented here. They should serve as a vantage point for identifying those concepts, variables, and relationships that affect the fidelity of information exchange. Thus, they should be considered when asking questions and interpreting observations about the technical communication process. These models provide a range of perspectives from which to view technical communication. They should serve as useful guides to practitioners in helping to specify their roles and responsibilities in relationship to clients and sponsoring organizations (Donna M. Hamlin and Craig Harkins, "A Model for Technical Communication" [1983]).

One of the earliest models of communication was developed by Harold D. Lasswell ("The Structure and Function of Communication in Society" [1948]):

Who

Says What

In Which Channel

To Whom and

With What Effect?

It is simple and graphic but lacks a number of elements necessary for an understanding of the communication process.

Claude E. Shannon and Warren Weaver in *The Mathematical Theory of Communication* (1949) developed the mathematical model of communication. It is presented in Figure 1. The model was developed for Bell Laboratories to describe communication over a mediated device such as the telephone. It represents an advance over previous models because it differentiates between the information source and the transmitter and the receiver and destination. In the case of technical communication, the source may be an engineer; the transmitter, a technical writer;

the receiver, the person who obtains the document; and the destination, the ultimate user. Each person adds noise to the communication process. This contributes distortion to the information transfer and may lead to a breakdown in communication. The Shannon-Weaver model lacks the critical notions of feedback—the exchange of information rather than the one-way transfer of it—and the context or environment in which the process takes place.

The SMCR model of communication proposed by David K. Berlo in *The Process of Communication* (1960) has many of the same faults of the earlier models. It is shown in Figure 2. It suggests a one-way flow of information from a source to a receiver without feedback, and it excludes the concept of noise. However, Berlo specifies those factors that influence the fidelity of communication and at which stage in the process these factors operate. For example, when considering the MESSAGE, he suggests that the *elements* of the message—its *content, structure, code,* and *treatment*—will influence its understanding by the receiver. Furthermore, while not explicitly discussing the context in which the process occurs, the model indicates that the source's and receiver's social system and culture, as well as the code system in which the message is constructed, do affect the fidelity of the communication process.

Rogers with Shoemaker in *Communication of Innovations* (1971) modified the Berlo model to make explicit the notion of the effects of communication on the diffusion of innovations. They state,

this SMCRE communication model corresponds closely to the elements of diffusion. (1) the receivers are the members of a social system; (2) the channels are the means by which the innovation spreads; (3) the message is a new idea; (4) the source is the origin of the innovation (an inventor, scientist, change agent, opinion leader, and the like); and (5) the effects are changes in attitudes, and overt behavior (adoption or rejection) regarding the innovation. (p. 19)

Bruce Westley and Malcolm MacLean's "A Conceptual Model for Communication Research" (1957), presented in Figure 3, has a number of important implications for technical communication. The model describes the ways in which individuals and organizations decide which messages are communicated and how they are modified or deleted in the process. Person(s) A receive(s) stimuli, X_1, from the environment. The process of reporting these events is imperfect. There are omissions and additions caused by selective perception and distortion resulting from bias in A. A then produces a message, X_1, and communicates it to C. C is an editor or gatekeeper. C selects the message, X_{11}, to communicate to the eventual audience, B, and modifies it as necessary. This decision is based upon the stimuli C receives from the environment, X_1, some of which may be the same as that A receives, X_3, and from audience feedback, f_{bc}. In the case of technical writing, A may be considered the writer, C the editor, and B the user of the document. X_1 represents the information A gathers from engineers, scientists, and other sources, which forms the basis of the technical document.

Figure 1
The Mathematical Model of Communication

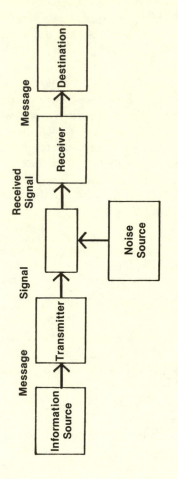

Source: The Mathematical Model of Communication by Claude E. Shannon and Warren Weaver, published by the University of Illinois Press, 1949, p. 98, is used with permission.

Figure 2
The SMCR Model of Communication

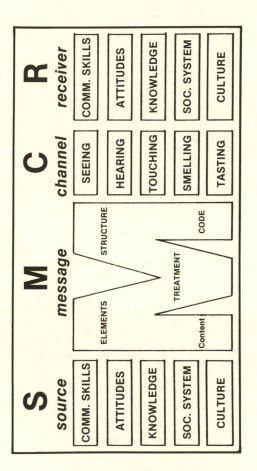

Figure 3
Conceptual Model for Communication Research

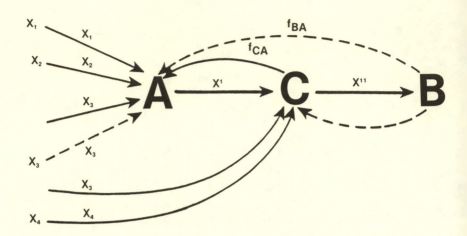

Source: Bruce Westley and Malcolm Maclean, "A Conceptual Model for Communication Research," *Journalism Quarterly* 34 (Winter 1957), p. 35. Used with permission.

Donna M. Hamlin and Craig Harkins developed "A Model for Technical Communication" (in press). It indicates that technical communication cuts across intrapersonal, interpersonal, small-group, organizational, intercultural and mass communication situations. It suggests that technical communication becomes increasingly difficult as one moves from intrapersonal to mass communication. Furthermore, Hamlin and Harkins suggest that technical communication deals with information from a number of different academic disciplines or topic areas, depending on the purpose. The model further differentiates technical communication from other communication by content, audience, and message complexity. The authors suggest that four disciplines have provided most of the information which has enabled technical communication to grow. They are (1) empirical research, (2) general semantics, (3) learning theory, and (4) modern rhetoric. As mentioned above, this chapter will deal with ideas from the first area only. Finally, the authors make explicit the values of the technical communicator.

We have presented only a limited set of models of communication. They have direct application to technical communication. Other models of communication have been proposed by Wilbur Schramm (*The Process and Effects of Mass Communication* [1954]; *Men, Messages, and Media* [1973]), Andrew T. Weaver and Ordean G. Ness (*The Fundamentals and Forms of Speech* [1957],) Elizabeth G. Andersch, Lorin C. Staats and Robert H. Bostrom (*Communication in Everyday Use* [1969]), Ray Eldon Hiebert, Donald F. Ungurait, and Thomas W. Bohn

(*Mass Media III* [1982]), and Melvin L. DeFleur and Sandra Ball-Rokeach (*Theories of Mass Communication* [1975]).

Everett Rogers and D. Lawrence Kincaid (*Communication Networks* [1981]) criticize the models presented above because they lead to seven biases. They are:

1. A view of communication as a linear, one-way act, rather than a cyclical, two-way process over time.
2. A source bias in these models: stress is placed on dependency rather than on the relationship of those who communicate and their fundamental interdependency.
3. A tendency to focus on the objects of communication as simple, isolated physical objects, at the expense of the context in which they exist.
4. A tendency to focus on the messages *per se* at the expense of silence and timing of messages.
5. A tendency to consider the primary function of communication to be persuasion rather than mutual understanding, consensus, and collective action.
6. A tendency to concentrate on the psychological effects of communication on separate individuals rather than on the social effects and the relationships among individuals within networks.
7. A belief in one-way mechanistic causation, rather than the mutual causation that characterizes human information systems, which are fundamentally cybernetic.

Many of these criticisms of models of communication also apply to the study and practice of technical communication. James L. Kinneavy's *A Theory of Discourse* (1971), the stimulus for much recent discussion within technical writing, has only four basic components: the person who encodes a message; the reality to which the message refers; the person who decodes the message; and the signal (language) that carries the message and unites the components of the process. Technical communication, generally, has been practiced as a one-way mechanistic process, concentrating on the production of isolated physical messages without considering the context in which they will be used or the social impact that results from them.

Recently, a number of theorists in technical communication have recognized these biases and have suggested corresponding modifications in practice. For example, George A. Barnett ("Applications of Communication Theory and Cybernetics to Technical Communication" [1979]) suggests that technical communication should be conceptualized as a cyclic cybernetic process that takes into account the environment of the user. Carolyn R. Miller ("A Humanistic Rationale for Technical Writing" [1979]) also considers environment, when she discusses technical communication as a rule-governed process. The rules are determined by the contexts in which technical communication occurs and are generated through the interactions of the audience and the writer within any given context. Others who have discussed the context in which technical documents are used include John S. Harris, "On Expanding the Definition of Technical Writing'' (1978) and Donald Ross, Jr., ''A Theory of The Function of Technical Writing'' (1981).

A number of writers have stressed the importance of knowing the users of the technical artifacts (George A. Barnett, ''Social System Homophily as a Function of Communication'' [1979]; Philip M. Rubens, ''Technical Communication'' [1981]). Generally, the process of communicating with the users begins with audience analysis (Thomas E. Pearsall, *Audience Analysis for Technical Writing* [1969]; Kenneth W. Houp and Thomas Pearsall, *Reporting Technical Information* [1969]). For a complete discussion of this topic, see ''Audience Analysis and Adaptation'' in this volume.

As an alternative to the biased models, Everett Rogers and D. Lawrence Kincaid (1981) propose the convergence model of communication. They stress the unity of information and action. All information is a consequence of action; through information processing, action may result in additional information. The model has no beginning or end. Only the mutually defining relationship among the parts gives meaning to the whole. When information is shared by two or more participants, information processing may lead to mutual understanding, agreement, and collective action.

One consequence of this model is that communication always implies a relationship, a mutual process of information-sharing among two or more people. Consequently, the analysis of the communication must take into account the interactants' differences and similarities, as well as changes in the relations between the technical writer and the user—both with one another and with the other individuals with whom they interact about the topics of the communications. Thus, the notion of context or environment in which communication takes place becomes increasingly important because it includes the interpersonal context.

One purpose of this discussion of models of communication is to help organize those factors that have impact on the technical communication process. The following review of the empirical communication theory discusses the variables and their relationship to the fidelity of information exchange. Based on the models presented above, the review is organized into sections that deal with *sources* (technical communicators), *messages, channels, receivers, feedback*, and the *context* or *environment* in which technical communication takes place. The effects of communication will not be explicitly discussed; we assume throughout that understanding, which leads to appropriate behavior, is the result of the communication process. While these factors will be presented as separate categories, remember that communication is a complex process with interacting components. Thus, while we have categorized the variables for presentation, it is very difficult to do so analytically and functionally. Accordingly, our organization is somewhat arbitrary.

Sources

We will discuss three aspects of sources and the way they affect technical communication. They are (1) source credibility; (2) the homophily or similarity between the source and receiver; and (3) information known about the source of technical documents, that is, technical communicators or writers.

It is generally recognized that the more credible the source of a message, the greater its effectiveness. Effectiveness is usually understood to be attitude change in the direction advocated by the source (Franklin S. Haiman, "The Effects of Ethos in Public Speaking" [1949]; Carl I. Hovland and Walter Weiss, "The Influence of Source Credibility on Communication Effectiveness" [1951]; Elliot Aronson and B. W. Golden, "The Effect of Relevant and Irrelevant Aspects of Communicator Credibility on Opinion Change" [1962]; Steven Bochner and Chester A. Insko, "Communicator Discrepancy, Source Credibility and Opinion Change" [1966]; Joseph Woelfel, Michael J. Cody, James R. Gillham, and Richard Holmes, "Basic Premises of Multidimensional Attitude Change Theory" [1980]). Source credibility, however, is a characteristic of the source *as perceived* by the receiver. It is part of the source's image and may vary among different communication situations. Usually, it is formed before the source and receiver enter the communication event (William J. McGuire, "Persuasion, Resistance and Attitude Change" [1973]).

Source credibility is a multi-dimensional construct. Early empirical research indicated that it is made up of three factors (David K. Berlo, "An Empirical Test of a General Construct of Credibility" [1961]; James B. Lemert, "Dimensions of Source Credibility" [1963]; James C. McCroskey, "Scales for the Measurement of Ethos" [1966]; Don A. Schweitzer and G. P. Ginsburg, "Factors of Communicator Credibility" [1966]). Recent research, however, suggests that the number of factors affecting credibility may be equal to the number of attributes used by receivers in evaluating the source (Michael J. Cody, John Marlier, and Joseph Woelfel, "An Application of the Multiple Measurement Model" [1975]; Michael J. Cody, "The Validity of Experimentally Induced Motions of Public Figures in Multidimensional Scaling Configurations" [1980]). The three factors are (1) authoritativeness—how reliable, informed, qualified (through title or profession), intelligent, or expert the source is perceived to be; (2) trustworthiness—how safe, honest, friendly, pleasant, and attractive the source is perceived to be; and (3) dynamism—how aggressive, forceful, bold, and energetic the source is perceived to be.

In technical communication, presentation of source attributes is generally minimized. The little information given usually refers to the source's credentials and title. Occasionally, pictures of the authors may be presented. Probably, they will be smiling and wearing business clothes. The credibility of most technical communication, however, is manifested in the message.

The evidence suggests that, although source credibility may be important in attitude change, it may detract from the fidelity of information exchange. William J. McGuire writes in "Persuasion, Resistance and Attitude Change" (1973):

There is evidence that source credibility factors affect attitude change via the yielding mediator rather than the attention and comprehension steps. While the source credibility effect tends to show up in ultimate change, the source variables tend not to be manifested in detectable differences in the extent of learning of the message contents,...[Messages] from unknown sources may be better learned than messages from sources known to be high or low in credibility (p. 230).

Effective communication occurs more easily when source and receiver are homophilous, or similar (Rogers with Shoemaker [1971]; Everett M. Rogers and Rekha Agarwala-Rogers, *Communication in Organizations* [1976]). The degree of homophily (similarity) or heterophily (difference) is determined by two factors (George A. Barnett, "Social System Homophily as a Function of Communication" [1974]). They are (1) objective or demographic homophily—similarity by age, sex, race, occupation, education, and so on; and (2) cognitive homophily—similarity in attitude, values, belief, culture, or knowledge. Members of homophilous dyads share common experiences, language, culture, and expertise. They are able to communicate more effectively because they can empathize with a person in a similar role or position in society. Rogers and Shoemaker (1971) cite a number of empirical studies which indicate that success in getting people to adopt technical innovations is a function of the change agents' homophily with their clients. Donn Byrne ("Attitudes and Attraction" [1969]) finds that receivers prefer sources to the extent that they are perceived as being similar, especially in the cognitive area (Milton Rokeach, *The Open and Closed Mind* [1960]). Thus, it appears that the effectiveness of a message may be enhanced by using what Kenneth Burke calls "the strategy of identification" in *A Grammar of Motives* (1962).

This implies that effective communication results from a source-receiver homophily. Actually, the reverse may be true (Barnett [1974]; D. Lawrence Kincaid, *The Convergence Model of Communication* [1979]; George A. Barnett and D. Lawrence Kincaid, "Cultural Convergence" [1983]).

Initially, the source and receiver may have little in common. By interacting, the source and receiver converge on a common cognitive framework of mutual understanding (Jürgen Habermas, *Communication and the Evolution of Society* [1979]). For example, the audiences for technical documents may know little or nothing about the topics before they begin to read. Furthermore, while it may be ideal to make the technical writer as homophilous as possible with the audience of a document, it may not be possible. The technical communicator and the audience are heterophilous by definition, at least to the extent that writers have the knowledge about what they are communicating and the receivers do not. This condition is called maximal homophily (William T. Liu and Robert W. Duff, "On Rogers' Homophily-Heterophily Concept of Communication" [1972]).

Who are the technical communicators? What sort of attitudes, beliefs, and values do they hold? What is their experience and expertise? George Barnett and David L. Carson ("Research on Defining the Profession of Technical Communication" [1980]) report that technical communicators perceive their profession as containing both scientific and humanistic elements. Technical writing/

communication serves as a bridge between these two orientations. The authors report a tension between the way technical communicators perceive themselves and the actual process of technical communication. Although one might expect the average technical writer to identify more closely with technology and the sciences than with humanistic matters, professionals, teachers, and students of technical communication perceive themselves as much closer to the humanities.

In a followup study, Barnett and Carson ("The Role of Communication in the Professional Socialization Process" [1983]) attempted to discover how this attitude set developed. They followed the socialization of one cohort of students through a graduate program in technical writing. This particular program once attracted students educated in either the sciences or engineering. Today, about half its students have undergraduate degrees in the humanities or social sciences. Barnett and Carson found a positive predisposition to the humanities—at the expense of science and technology—prior to students' entering the program. While the students' attitudes became more positive toward science and technology and increasingly congruent with professional technical communicators, the students still had more favorable attitudes toward the humanities when they completed the program.

These results suggest that for technical communication to achieve a proper balance between the humanities and sciences, practitioners must develop a more positive attitude toward technology. This may be achieved either through increased scientific and technical coursework in a technical communication program—at the expense of humanistic material—or through the recruitment of students previously educated in these areas. This would result in greater technical expertise about the subject matter which technical communicators deal with professionally as well as a greater degree of professionalism. The end result would be enhanced credibility for the source of technical communication. Furthermore, since the technical writer is also a receiver of information from scientists and engineers, education in these areas would make writers more homophilous with the ultimate source of the ideas about which they write. This would also improve the fidelity of the exchange of technical information.

Messages

David Berlo (1960) identifies five elements of messages that should be considered when analyzing communication. They are (1) content, (2) organization or structure, (3) code, (4) treatment, and (5) the elements of the message. Here we will discuss only two, organization and treatment. We assume that the content is the technical material, and the code system the source's and receiver's language. The elements of the message are words, sentences, paragraphs, pictures, tables, and other graphics. They vary, of course, with different channels.

The best way to organize a message depends on the culture in which the information is used. In Western societies, patterns of thinking and reasoning are linear or sequential (Clinton B. DeSota, "Learning a Social Structure" [1960];

Clinton B. DeSota, "The Predilection for Single Orderings" [1961]; Clinton B. DeSoto, M. London, and S. Handel, "Social Reasoning and Spatial Paralogic" [1965]). Linear processing characterizes all linguistic processing (reading and listening), as well as many sorts of problem-solving and reasoning activities (Roy Lachman, Janet L. Lachman, and Earl C. Butterfield, *Cognitive Psychology and Information Processing* [1979]; David E. Rumelhart, *Introduction to Human Information Processing* [1977]).

Thus, written and spoken messages should be organized in a linear fashion with a beginning, middle, and end. H. Marshall McLuhan (*Guttenberg Galaxy* [1962], and *Understanding Media* [1964]) has argued that this linear word-by-word arrangement of messages is true only for print media. As technical communication changes to make greater use of video and computer-based technologies, this manner of organization may prove less effective.

The optimal way to structure a message also depends on the audience. Factors such as their prior attitudes, education, commitment, skill in refutation, expectations of subsequent counterarguments, their attention and their level of arousal associated with the material all help dictate the best way to organize a message (C. David Mortensen, *Communication* [1972]). For example, should we present both sides of a technical issue—such as evidence in support of and against a technical decision, or the wrong way to complete a task as well as the proper method? Research by A. A. Lumsdaine and Irving L. Janis indicates that for highly educated audiences two-sided messages are more effective than one-sided ones ("Resistance to 'Counterpropaganda' Produced by One-sided and Two-sided 'Propaganda' Presentations" [1953]). However, for less educated audiences the opposite is true.

Before presenting the specific content of a message, a source should determine the audience's level of attention and the level of their anxiety or arousal associated with the material and the context in which it is presented. William J. McGuire ("Attitude Change" [1972]) points out that an intermediate level of anxiety is optimal for effectiveness. If there is too little or too much, comprehension will be lower (Susan Millman, "Anxiety, Comprehension and Susceptibility to Social Influence" [1968]; Arthur R. Cohen, "Situational Structure, Self-esteem and Threat-oriented Reactions to Power" [1959]; Stanley Lehmann, "Personality and Compliance" [1970]; Howard Leventhal, "Findings and Theory in the Study of Fear Communications" [1970]). This relationship is probably mediated by level of arousal, which determines the amount of attention "capacity" available at any time (Daniel Kahneman, *Attention and Effort* [1973]). Other sorts of motivations—for example, self-interest or curiosity—might function as well as anxiety. Thus, the first thing one should do is to structure the message to catch the attention of the audience and to manipulate their level of motivation or attention to the optimal level.

Research on the effects of order also has implications for technical communication. The theoretical assumption underlying this research is that message effectiveness depends upon the placement of arguments or material in a presentation. Three order strategies have been investigated: (1) climax, where the most important material is presented first; (2) anticlimax, where it is presented last; and (3) the pyramidal pattern, in which it is placed in the middle. The climactic or anticlimactic orders are more effective than the pyramidal arrangement, and most evidence suggests that the climax strategy is more effective than the anticlimax (Halbert E. Gulley and David K. Berlo, "Effect of Intercellular and Intracellular Speech Structure on Attitude Change and Learning" [1956]; Harvey Cromwell, "Relative Effect of Audience Attitudes of the First Versus the Second Argumentative Speech of a Series" [1950]; Howard Gilkinson, Stanley F. Paulson and Donald E. Sikkink, "Effects of Order and Authority in an Argumentative Speech" [1954]; Harold Sponberg, "The Relative Effectiveness of Climax and Anticlimax Order in an Argumentative Speech" [1946]).

Research on serial learning indicates that the relationship between order of presentation and learning is U-shaped (McGuire [1972]). Audiences tend to learn the initial material and the material presented at the end better than they learn the material in the middle. This would suggest an organizational schema where the important information—the conclusion—is presented initially, perhaps in the form of an abstract, and at the end, in a conclusion or summary. The body of the text is less important and may be filled with detail.

Recommendations about whether to present the conclusion first or last depend on when the information will be used. If it is to be used immediately after it is presented, the critical material should come at the end to take advantage of the effects of recency and short-term memory. The longer the delay after presentation the material will be used, the less effective the strategy. Learning diminishes rapidly over time (Philip C. Bossart and Francis J. Di Vesta, "Effects of Context, Frequency, and Order of Presentation of Evaluative Assertions on Impression Formation" [1966]; Abraham S. Luchins, "Experimental Attempts to Minimize the Impact of First Impression" [1957]; Abraham S. Luchins, "Definitiveness of Impression and Primacy-Recency in Communications" [1958]; C. W. Mayo and Walter H. Crockett, "Cognitive Complexity and Primacy-Recency Effects in Impression Formation" [1964]; Paul S. Rosenkrantz and Walter H. Crockett, "Some Factors Influencing the Assimilation of Disparate Information in Impression Formation" [1965]; Warner Wilson and Howard Miller, "Repetition, Order of Presentation, and Timing of Arguments and Measures as Determinants of Opinion Change" [1968]). Over longer periods of time, material presented first has at least as good a chance of being remembered as does material presented last.

Other researchers conclude that order of presentation affects such factors as attention, interest, comprehension, and recall. Robert G. Smith ("An Experimental Study of the Effects of Speech Organization upon Attitudes of College Students" [1951]) found that the most effective order in producing attitude change was (1) introduction, (2) transition, and (3) concluding information. Ernest Thompson ("An Experimental Investigation of the Relative Effectiveness of Organizational Structure in Oral Communication" [1960] and "Some Effects of Message Structure on Listener Comprehension'' [1967]) found that organized materials were recalled better than information presented in random order. Donald K. Darnell (''The Relation Between Sentence Order and Comprehension'' [1963]) tested whether a logical deductive order would be more effective than orders where the thesis sentence was placed in the middle. He concluded that organization made no difference in interest but did have a slight impact on retention. At a general level, research on learning and mnemonic processes indicates that comprehension and retention depend undeniably on organization (John R. Anderson and Gordon H. Bower, *Human Associative Memory* [1973]; Roy Lachman, Janet L. Lachman, and Earl C. Butterfield, *Cognitive Psychology and Information Processing* [1979] George Mandler, ''Organization and Memory'' [1967]; David E. Rumelhart, *Introduction to Human Information Processing* [1977]). That is, well-structured material is always understood and remembered better than unstructured material. On the other hand, results are equivocal about the exact ways in which the material should be structured.

William J. McGuire (1973) raises the question about how topics should be organized with respect to the relative desirability of the material. He has shown that there is greater total agreement over a whole range of topics if the desirable ones are presented first. He argues that the early contents reward and habituate the person for attending to the contents. When undesirable materials are presented first, they tend to punish paying attention in the beginning, so that the audience may not pay attention to the later material. McGuire's 1973 explanation depends on a stimulus-response learning theory, but his evidence is still useful. The technical communicator should determine the audience's attitudes and present material that they will agree with or find pleasant before the material they may find offensive. For example, difficult material should be placed after easy material. It may also be a good idea to begin a presentation with a bit of humor, although there is little empirical research relating humor to effectiveness; it might well be that, while enhancing attention to the communication situation, humor may hamper comprehension.

Technical communicators are often admonished to be selectively redundant. Repetition increases comprehension of the material (John Mathes and Dwight Stevenson, *Designing Technical Reports* [1976]). Joseph H. Bloom and Seth A. Goldstein, ''Experiments in Technical Writing'' (1960), found that reader retention increased with repetition of important facts and ideas, and that summaries that pick out, highlight, and orient readers to the important facts also improved reader comprehension and retention. They also found that redundancy across channels improved retention. Reader's retention improved when facts in the verbal presentation were highlighted by attention-getters such as underlining, capitalization, charts, and color.

How much redundancy is optimal for achieving an effective message? Joseph Woelfel and John Saltiel (''Cognitive Processes as Motions in a Multidimensional Space'' [1974]) argue that the relationship between repetition and effectiveness is linear. The more information one receives, the greater its effect. This conclusion is based on their earlier research (John Saltiel and Joseph Woelfel, "Inertia in Cognitive Processes" [1975]). However, William McGuire (1973), reviewing research by Ruth C. Peterson and L. L. Thurstone (*The Effect of Motion Pictures on the Social Attitudes of High School Students* [1933]), Arthur W. Staats ("Principles of the Attitude-Reinforcer-Discriminative System" [1968]), and John Bell Stewart (*Repetitive Advertising in Newspapers* [1964]) argues that, while repetition has an effect, "an increase in impact usually appears for one or two repetitions but quickly reaches an asymptote beyond which further repetitions have little effect" (p. 295).

There has been considerable research on the relation of evidence to message effectiveness (James C. McCroskey, "A Summary of Experimental Research on the Effects of Evidence in Persuasive Communication" [1969]). Raymond Cathcart ("An Experimental Study of the Relativeness of Four Methods of Presenting Evidence" [1955]) and Erwin B. Bettinghaus (*Message Preparation* [1966]) found that the use of authoritative evidence produced significantly more attitude change than was obtained without citing authorities. However, Gilkinson, Paulson, and Sikkink (1954) and Terry H. Ostermeier ("Effects of Type and Frequency of Reference and Perceived Source Credibility and Attitude Change" [1967]) did not find any advantage when citing authorities in support of claims. Furthermore, there have been a number of attempts to find any advantage in using statistical evidence (D. Costley, "An Experimental Study of the Effectiveness of Quantitative Evidence in Speeches of Advocacy" [1958]), authoritative quotations and pictures (Gerald A. Wagner, "An Experimental Study of the Relative Effectiveness of Varying Amounts of Evidence in a Persuasive Communication" [1958]), the number of citations (Dorothy I. Anderson, "The Effects of Various Uses of Authoritative Testimony in Persuasive Speaking" [1958]), the amount of commentary to increase the credibility of the cited authorities (Dorothy Anderson [1958]), and the proportion of satisfactory evidence or the number of irrelevant or internally inconsistent pieces of evidence (William R. Dresser, "Effects of 'Satisfactory' and 'Unsatisfactory' Evidence in a Speech of Advocacy" [1963]). In all cases, research supports the notion that evidence has no consistent, predictable effect on message effectiveness. The reason for these unanticipated findings, McCroskey (1969) argues, is that evidence interacts with the other factors in the communication situation, particularly the credibility of the source. Evidence may increase the effectiveness of a message when the source is only minimally or moderately credible.

In a review of the empirical literature on the diffusion and adoption of technical innovations, Everett Rogers and Floyd Shoemaker (1971) conclude that adoption of new products, practices, or ideas is a function of the relative advantages of the new idea; the compatibility of the innovation with the values, needs, and previously held ideas of the adopting audience; the complexity of the idea; its trialability; and its observability. Technical messages should state the advantages of new products, processes, or ideas. They should strive for compatibility with the audience's values and behavior, and should articulate how the innovation will satisfy user needs. The message should be simple. If possible, the message should include a way to allow the audience to try the innovation. For example, sample problems could be employed, requiring the audience to use the material they are learning. This would increase their involvement and thus their comprehension. Finally, the message should be observable, containing examples and graphics such as pictures, tables, and charts.

These recommendations contradict the prescriptions cited in the last paragraph. This contradiction may result because the earlier research was experimental using college students as the subjects. Rogers and Shoemaker (1971) review research generated in field surveys using members of the general public, often from less developed countries, to test the hypotheses.

Technical writers are continually reminded that correct style makes a difference in message effectiveness. Faulty grammar, poor organization, pauses, and other non-fluencies do produce poor ratings of speakers (McGuire [1973]), but their effect on message effectiveness is unclear. While David W. Addington (''Effects of Mispronunciations on General Speaking Effectiveness'' [1965]) reports that they do not reduce the persuasive impact of a message, Erwin P. Bettinghaus (''Operation of Congruity in an Oral Communication Setting'' [1961]) reports that delivery does relate to attitude change. Richard M. Davis (''Does Expression Make a Difference?'' [1976]) finds that for written technical materials, faulty grammar reduces comprehension, increases reading time, and reduces reader judgment of the author's competence as a writer and general credibility.

The technical communicator should strive to get the audience actively involved in and committed to the presented information because active participation is more efficacious than passive reading for adding material permanently to a person's cognitive repertory. Although Carl Hovland (*Order of Presentation in Persuasion* [1957]) did not find that an anonymous commitment had any impact on attitude change, Gerald R. Miller and Michael Burgoon (''Persuasion Research'' [1978]) report that a *public* commitment does affect the degree of attitude change. Their reason is that a public commitment is more ego-involving and active than is an anonymous commitment.

Given these conclusions, one would expect that were audiences to draw their own conclusions from the material, the communication would be more effective because drawing the conclusion requires more active participation by the receiver. However, explicitly stating the conclusions has sometimes been shown to be more efficacious (Carl I. Hovland and Wallace Mandell, ''An Experimental Comparison of Conclusion-Drawing by the Communicator and by the Audience'' [1952] and William J. McGuire, ''Inducing Resistance to Persuasion'' [1964]).

There is considerable research about how to present effective technical materials. George R. Klare (''Readable Technical Writing'' [1977]) describes how to make written technical materials readable. He argues that readable materials are more comprehensible. He begins with Rudolph F. Flesch's (''A New Readability Yardstick'' [1948]) research, which shows that readability is a function of the characteristics of words and sentences. He further specifies rules for producing readable messages:

1. Words of high frequency and familiarity increase readability.
2. Shorter words make reading easier and faster.
3. Words that have associative value (psychologically), calling up other words appearing later in the text, should be used.
4. Concrete words, rather than abstract words, make documents more readable.
5. Active verbs, instead of nominalized forms, improve readability.
6. Pronouns and anaphora (words or phrases that refer back to a previous word or unit of text) should be limited.
7. Sentences should be short. If writers are going to use conjunctions, they should use *and*, not *but, for,* or *because*.
8. Clauses should be short and sentence structure simple.
9. Active voice is more readable than passive voice.
10. Affirmative constructions are more readable than negative ones.
11. Statements produce better recall than questions.
12. Sentences with a great deal of word depth which require a great deal of commitment by the reader should be avoided.
13. Sentences with embedded words are less readable than embedded sentences.

There is contradictory evidence on some of these rules of thumb. For example, Bloom and Goldstein (1960) report that shorter words do not increase reading speed or comprehension. The psychological research on commitment suggests that audiences committed to learning a set of materials comprehend the material better than do non-committed audiences. Perhaps the writer should strive to produce—rather than to limit—reader commitment and involvement through a more difficult vocabulary and sentence structure.

Ulf F. Andersson argues in "Methods of Measuring Communication Results" (1971) that computational formulas, such as the Fog Index, do not measure clarity of communication. After we count the word length and number of words, affixes, and personal references, we still have no idea about how difficult it is to read the text. He suggests that other factors—such as the idea-chain in the text, its structure, and the concepts that are used to explain the idea—determine how difficult it will be to comprehend the material. Furthermore, he suggests that future research based on empirical measurement is needed to determine the factors that predict comprehension in technical texts. He suggests investigation of the following parameters:

1. Complexity of the structure and material.
2. Abstractness.

3. New concepts.

4. Need for background knowledge.

5. Workload during reading.

6. Time used.

7. Sensitivity to outside noise.

8. Longtime memory content.

V. A. Bram supports Klare's and Andersson's contentions, and reports in "Sentence Construction in Scientific and Engineering Texts'' (1978) that sentence structure has the greatest effect on readability.

The conclusions of the material on message variables and their impact on communication effectiveness are often contradictory because communication is a complex process involving the interaction of all the components described in the models. When research is conducted on a single component, such as the technical message, these other factors are not consistently taken into account. However, these exogenous factors continue to affect the communication situation. This results in inconclusive findings, so that any prescriptions should be viewed somewhat skeptically. Production of an effective message is contingent on the unique circumstances for which the message is produced. We share the attitude, expressed by Ulf Andersson (1971), that future empirical research is needed to better determine these interactions, so that guidelines can be established to help the technical communicator formulate effective materials.

Channels

A communication channel is a means of transmitting information to receivers. In "Channels and Audiences'' (1973), Wilbur Schramm categorizes or differentiates channels along six dimensions. They are described below:

1. The senses that are affected. Face-to-face communication makes possible the use of all senses, while the different media use a sub-set of these in combination to produce differential impacts on receivers (H. Marshall McLuhan, *Guttenberg Galaxy* [1962, *Understanding Media*, 1964]). For example, print media use only the visual channel, video and film use both the auditory and visual channels, and radio and sound recording use only the audio channel.

2. The opportunity for feedback. The chance for two-way exchange of information is maximal in face-to-face communication. Generally, interposing mass media restrict both the speed and the amount of feedback. For example, the telephone restricts non-verbal feedback to paralinguistic information. The impersonality of mass media organizations further discourages feedback from audiences of television, radio, newspapers, and magazines. Feedback is required, however, to ensure effective communication, or to understand transmitted information (Berlo [1960]; Daniel Katz and Robert H. Kahn, *The Social Psychology*

of Organizations (1978); Rogers and Agarwala-Rogers [1977]). Through feedback, receivers may secure clarification or additional information, thus allowing them to overcome social and psychological barriers of selective exposure, attention, and retention. As a result, when media are used for learning situations, as in technical communication, alternative feedback methods should be built in.

Currently, there is a great deal of excitement about new instructional technologies, and media systems with built-in, automated feedback mechanisms have been developed. They use video tape or disks and microcomputers, and provide feedback through computer-programmed and graded questions, which the student receives immediately after each program segment (learning module). Feedback is also given through verbal rewards, or by reporting material answered incorrectly (Philip Miller, "Responding to the New Television" [1981]). It is hoped that these technologies will succeed where educational television has failed (Philip Miller [1981]; Thomas R. Dargan, "Five Basic Patterns to Use in Interactive Flow Charts" [1982]; Nick Iuppa, "How Manufacturers Can Assist Users of Interactive Video" [1982]).

3. The amount of receiver control. For example, there is a great deal of control in interpersonal interaction. When using print, receivers can read at their own pace and re-read important or detailed sections. Receivers have little control over the broadcast media, however, unless they record the program on tape or disk. Schramm (1973) points out that the greater the user control, the greater the learning. Thus, the new technologies, such as interactive video tape/disk systems, are designed to maximize user control and involvement. Students can have modules repeated and can work at their own pace.

4. The type of message coding. Face-to-face interaction allows for the use of non-verbal codes. This is less true for video and film, and even less true for print. However, print seems to be better for conveying abstract ideas, while the audiovisual media are better for presenting concrete information.

H. Marshall McLuhan (1962, 1964) and Harold A. Innis (*Empire and Communications* [1950]; *The Bias of Communication* [1951] argue that the code system used in communication is in great measure determined by the channel. Print imposes a particular logic upon the organization of visual experience. It breaks down reality into discrete units—logically and causally related; linearly perceived; and abstracted from the wholeness, disorder, and multi-sensory quality of life. Empirical research, however, indicates that media type does not necessarily determine the way people process information (Edward Wilkus, Joseph Woelfel, George A. Barnett, and Norman Fontes, "McLuhan Hot and Cold" [1973]).

5. The multiplicative power. Mass communication systems can efficiently and rapidly reach large, physically dispersed audiences. Interpersonal channels can reach these audiences only with great effort and over relatively long periods of time.

6. Preservation of messages. An advantage of mass media is the absence of

a permanent record of face-to-face interaction. Traditionally, this advantage has been restricted to print. However, with video and audio tape and disk, this capacity has now been expanded to the electronic media.

There has been a great deal of research on the differential effects of channels (Bernard Berelson, Paul F. Lazarsfeld, and Robert N. McPhee, *Voting* [1954]; Elihu Katz and Paul F. Lazarsfeld, *Personal Influence* [1955]; Joseph T. Klapper, *The Effects of Mass Communication* [1960]; Melvin L. DeFleur and Sandra Ball-Rokeach, *Theories of Mass Communication* [1975]; George Comstock, Steven H. Chaffee, Nathan Katzman, and Donald Roberts, *Television and Human Behavior* [1978]). A summary of the social effects of the media is provided below.

1. Media have the power to focus attention and thus to direct interpersonal discussion. Maxwell E. McCombs and Donald L. Shaw ("The Agenda-Setting Function of the Mass Media" [1972]) label this the agenda-setting function of the media.

2. Media confer status (Paul F. Lazarsfeld and Robert K. Merton, "Friendship as Social Process" [1948]). People who appear in the media are viewed as important and highly credible.

3. Face-to-face communication is more effective for persuasion than are the audiovisual media (Joseph Woelfel and Donald Hernandez, "Media and Interpersonal Influence on Attitude Formation and Change" [1970]; Joseph Woelfel, John Woelfel, James R. Gillham, and Thomas L. McPhail, "Political Radicalization as a Communication Process" [1974]). Rogers with Shoemaker (1971) concludes from a number of studies that interpersonal communication is the most effective influence on adopting innovations, but that the mass media are more effective in creating knowledge and changing weak attitudes. Furthermore, they conclude that diverse information channels are far more effective in disseminating knowledge, while local media channels are more effective in persuading audiences. Among the media, electronic media are more effective than print for persuasion. However, as Joseph Klapper (1960) points out, "The relative power of the several media is thus, in real-life situations, likely to vary from one topic to another" (p. 109).

Steven Chaffee ("Mass Media Versus Interpersonal Channels" [1979]) has called the conflict over the relative effectiveness of mediated and interpersonal channels a "synthetic competition." He notes a number of intervening influences related to accessibility of the different channels and perceived credibility of sources. In other words, the relative effectiveness of interpersonal channels depends more on receivers' needs and perceptions than on channel effects *per se*.

4. A combination of face-to-face and mediated communication is likely to be more effective than either alone. For example, when instructional media are used in combination with study groups or radio forums, they tend to be more effective in producing learning and facilitating the adoption of new ideas. This is because interest in attendance and participation is encouraged by group pressure and social expectations. Thus, the channel becomes more credible because the

group believes the material is involving and important. In addition, the influence of the media is reinforced by the group.

5. A great deal of any social effect depends on the specific audience at any particular point in time (Bernard Berelson and George A. Steiner, *Human Behavior* [1964]; Wilbur Schramm, Jack Lyle, and Edwin B. Parker, *Television in the Lives of Our Children* [1961]). To design effective materials, the technical communicator must look at the receiver's social network and at demographic characteristics that mediate the effects of the information from the media (Katz and Lazarsfeld [1955]; Rogers and Kincaid [1980]). For example, channel use depends on socio-economic status (Comstock, Chaffee, Katzman, and Roberts [1978]). Jonathan Freedman and David Sears ("Selective Exposure" [1965]) report that better educated, wealthier individuals use print to a greater degree than do less educated and poorer individuals, who tend to use the broadcast media.

6. Audiences use the media differentially. Schramm (1973) points out that people use handy information sources. Furthermore, they use print media and the serious parts of audiovisual media, news programs, and educational television for information. George A. Barnett ("Bilingual Information Processing" [1976]) found that people perceive print primarily as an information source and use the electronic media primarily for entertainment. This may change, however, as new technologies become used for information storage and retrieval systems.

What are the implications of research on channel effects for technical communication? Technical communication has traditionally relied on the print media because they allow a great deal of receiver control. Print is good for communicating abstract ideas, and it can be efficiently disseminated to large, dispersed audiences. It allows for the physical preservation of the message. In addition, audiences have learned to rely on print for information. However, print media inhibit feedback, which is essential for ensuring comprehension. Print presents information using only the visual channel, which limits access to technical information for members of less educated groups and less literate societies.

Some educational psychologists argue that comprehension of certain materials may be improved by using channels other than print (J. J. Asher, *Sensory Interrelationships in the Automated Teaching of Foreign Languages* [1961]; M. A. May and A. A. Lumsdaine, *Learning from Films* [1958]). Furthermore, one way to increase comprehension is through the redundant presentation of material simultaneously over different channels. This requires the receiver to use more than one sense at a time. H. Marshall McLuhan (1964) points out that this results in greater involvement and thus greater comprehension. However, F. R. Hartman ("Single and Multiple Channel Communication" [1961]) warns that the use of multiple channels

may actually produce inferior learning because attention is divided and optimal learning is not possible in any of the channels. . . . Pictorial illustrations in many cases may distract rather than illustrate. . . . The tradition in the television message is to place the majority of the information in the verbal audio channel and to attract attention and illustrate it in the pictorial. Too often the picture is not properly related to the sound and a real barrier to effective communication is created by a tendency to focus attention on the picture when the message to be learned has been coded in the sound track. (p. 241)

In summary, technical communication should build mechanisms for feedback into the process, and use the channel most appropriate for the message, the receiver, and the effects desired for the technical materials. As with messages, the optimal channel for technical communication is contingent on the unique communication situation for which the message is created. This raises the question: What do we know about receivers and their patterns of seeking technical information?

Receivers

When analyzing a communication situation, one should consider factors about the audience such as their demographic and cultural background, prior attitudes, knowledge, and behavioral patterns, and the social system or environment in which they will use the information. Generally, the more similar the receivers and the source are in these ways, the easier and more effective the communication will be (Rogers with Shoemaker [1971]).

Knowledge about the receiver may be used to design more effective messages and deliver them via the most appropriate channel. William M. Carlson ("Engineering Information for National Defense" [1967]) summarized the implications of studies sponsored by the Defense Department by emphasizing that effective communication resulted when the information was keyed to the receiver. Consequently, technical communication should rely heavily on empirical audience analysis. George Barnett (1979) suggests that technical communicators investigate intended, actual, and potential audiences before the production of documents. This analysis should determine the needs the planned material will meet. If the materials are perceived as necessary, the analysis of the potential audience should identify their demographic characteristics, their level of expertise, along with the materials or people they currently use as information sources, and their suggestions about content and format for the new document. Barnett then suggests gathering feedback from the intended audience about the document before publication, to ensure that it meets the actual audience needs upon dissemination.

Technical communicators should also investigate patterns of information-seeking by scientists and engineers, the primary users of technical documents. This area has been reviewed by Bertita E. Compton ("Scientific Communication" [1973]), Charles Atkin ("Anticipated Communication and Mass Media Information Seeking" [1972]), Steven H. Chaffee, M. Jackson-Buck, J. Lewin, and B. Wilson ("The Interpersonal Context of Mass Communication" [1972]), and Charles W. Steinfield ("Explaining Managers' Use of Communication Channels for Performance Monitoring Implications for New Office Systems" [1981]). All these researchers conclude that people put little effort into information-seeking and will use the sources that are most accessible. Information is sought because it is socially rewarding and can be discussed in the users' interpersonal networks (James A. Danowski and Neal E. Cutler, "Political Information, Mass Media Use in Early Adulthood, and Political Socialization" [1977]).

A great deal of evidence indicates that scientists and engineers rely less on formal sources that require them to initiate information-seeking activities. For example, B. A. Lipetz (*Evaluation of the Impact of a Citation Index in Physics* [1964]) found that only a small proportion of physicists use citation indices. A. H. Rubenstein, R. W. Trueswell, G. J. Rath, and D. J. Werner ("Some Preliminary Experiments and a Model of Information-seeking Style of Research" [1966]) introduced a new information search service in 11 medical research organizations and received only 61 requests in a seven-week pilot period. Harold Van Cott and Robert Kincaide (*A Feasibility Study for Determining Requirements of Biological Information Services and Systems* [1967]) received less than 400 requests, generated by one-third that number of calls, in a biological science information clearinghouse; 5 percent of the scientists accounted for 25 percent of the requests. Harold Wooster (*Microfiche 1969—A User Study* [1969]) reports apathy and resistance by scientists when offered new information tools and resources such as microfiche. David B. Hertz and A. H. Rubenstein (*Team Research* [1953]) report that stimulating information rarely comes from written materials but from supervisors or colleagues. Herbert Menzel (*The Flow of Information Among Scientists* [1958]; "Sociological Perspectives in the Information-gathering Practices of the Scientific Investigator and the Medical Practitioner" [1966]; *Formal and Informal Satisfaction of the Information Requirements of Chemists* [1966]) demonstrates consistently the importance of interpersonal communication for the information-seeking behaviors of scientists in academic settings. Finally, William Carlson (1967) found that 70 percent of engineers in design and development research begin their information-seeking with informal (interpersonal) sources because formal sources tend to be less effective.

Conrad J. Kasperson ("An Analysis of the Relationship Between Information Sources and Creativity in Scientists and Engineers" [1978]) and Donna M. Hamlin ("Creativity in Organizations" [1978]) found differences among scientists and engineers based upon their information-seeking and usage patterns. These conclusions were based on individuals working in both academic and industrial settings. Both authors report that researchers viewed as creative or innovative by their peers tend to use a great quantity of widely variant information sources. Productive researchers used less variant and fewer sources. Non-productive individuals tended to do little information-seeking.

Bertita E. Compton ("Scientific Communication" [1973]) reports a study by the American Psychological Association (APA) indicating that a large and diverse number of books are used by psychologists but that few books are used by more than 1 percent of APA membership. The reason reported was that widely accessible media were viewed as carrying relatively "old" information, and that a multiplicity of media served a restricted audience with more up-to-date information. Timeliness was viewed as a problem. As a result, psychologists tended to rely on informal communication, which often took place at conventions or seminars. These preferences can affect the way audiences use technical communication and may even determine whether a specific message reaches its intended audience at all. Therefore, technical communication should devote greater attention to the patterns of social interaction and the use of informal communication channels by users of technical materials.

The theoretical and empirical literature on communication networks is extensive and has been reviewed in great detail by Rogers and Kincaid (1980). Basically, descriptions of the communication structure of a system are generated by examining the flows of information among the components of the system. These components may be individuals (Terrance L. Albrecht, "The Role of Communication in Perception of Organizational Climate" [1979]; Karlene H. Roberts and Charles A. O'Reilly III, "Organizations as Communication Structures" [1978]), small task groups (James A. Danowski, "Uniformity of Group Attitude-Belief and Connectivity of Organizational Communication Networks for Production, Innovation and Maintenance" [1980]), or entire formal organizations (Rolf T. Wigand, "Communication and Interorganizational Relationships Among Complex Organizations in Social Service Settings" [1976]). Formal mathematical procedures exist to calculate descriptive indices that may be used to predict a number of social implications (Richard D. Alba, "A Graph-theoretic Definition of a Sociometric Clique" [1973]; George A. Barnett, "Spatial Modelling of Social Networks with Applications to the Diffusion Process" [1979]; H. Russell Bernard and Peter D. Killworth, "On the Social Structure of an Ocean-going Research Vessel and Other Important Things" [1973]; Richard L. Breiger, S. A. Boorman, and P. Arabie, "An Algorithm for Clustering Relational Data with Application to Social Network Analysis and Comparison with Multidimensional Scaling" [1975]; William D. Richards, Jr., "Network Analysis in Large Complex Systems" [1974]). Some network analysis methods provide a graphic description or sociogram of the communication structure and define network roles (Richards [1974]; Gerald M. Goldhaber, Michael P. Yates, D. Thomas Porter, and Richard Lesniak, "Organizational Communication" [1978]). Such a sociogram is presented in Figure 4.

The theoretical assumption underlying network analysis is that individuals' positions in a system's communication structure determine their behaviors, attitudes, and knowledge. We will discuss the research on and implications of this approach which are relevant to users of technical communications.

Thomas J. Allen and Steven I. Cohen (*Information Flow in an R & D Laboratory* [1966]) found two groups in a research and development organization: a closely knit, highly interactive group of Ph.D.s and a less organized, less interactive, non-Ph.D. group. There was little information exchange among the groups. R. H. Maurice, Herbert Menzel, and Rolf Meyersohn ("Physicians' Information Levels as Affected by Milieu, Contact with Colleagues, and Current

Figure 4
Sociogram of the Communication Structure

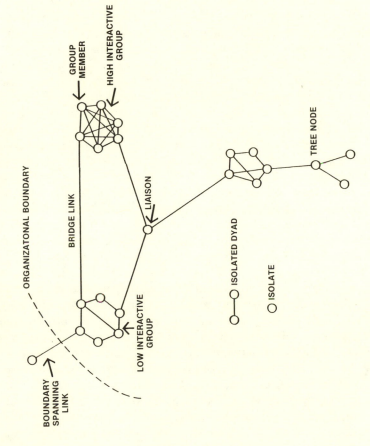

Awareness Activities'' [1966]) studied the social relationships and interactions among physicians and found that information levels were related to the amount and nature of social interaction in these groups. N. C. Mullins (''Social Networks Among Biological Scientists'' [1966]) discovered that communication clusters and linkages were based upon like orientations to research or use of similar methodological approaches rather than on a commonality of discipline or specialty. He also found that the social network often conveyed many of the newest ideas and unpublished findings.

Michael L. Tushman (''Special Boundary Roles in the Innovation Process'' [1977]; ''Work Characteristics and Subunit Communication Structure'' [1979]) focused on the need for innovative organizations to gather information from the external environment. He found that boundary spanners are dependent on the nature of the organization's research. The greater their task uncertainty, the greater their reliance upon external communication links. This research raises the following questions: How is the information communicated to others internal to the organization? Are the boundary spanners rewarded for going outside the organization for information? Are there gatekeepers or other bottlenecks which prevent the dissemination of this information to other members of the organization who need the information to complete their jobs? Or do boundary spanners perform liaison roles by keeping abreast of recent developments and translating them into usable forms for the other members of the organization? Menzel (1966) labels such individuals ''advisor colleagues.'' This role could be served by the technical communicator.

Thomas Allen and Steven Cohen (1966) examined the communication networks of users of technical materials in two research and development laboratories. They found that the structure resulted from the interaction of both the social relations and work structure. The individuals who were more central in the information flow, liaisons, provided the other members of the organization with information. They either made greater use of individuals outside the organization or read more literature than did other members of the laboratory.

James Danowski (1980) found that the optimal network structure varied with the function task groups performed. Those groups involved with the manifest productive task of the organization best performed their function when highly integrated. Those concerned with innovation required a great deal of boundary spanning and thus best performed their function when loosely interconnected.

The role of the technical communicator is different when materials are developed for internal consumption than when the materials are to be disseminated into the environment. This raises a further series of questions about where technical communicators fit into the communication structure of organizations and what role they should play in the structure. Indeed, this research implies that the technical communicator should be central rather than peripheral to the functioning of most organizations.

Because of the importance of information communication patterns in the dissemination of technical information, Diana Crane might describe organizations of scientists as *Invisible Colleges* (1972). They are informal groups of scientists from different academic disciplines investigating the same phenomenon. Patterns of communication corresponding to "invisible colleges" have been found using network analysis (Derek J. de Solla Price, "The Scientific Foundations of Science Policy" [1965]). Individuals often come together at conferences and seminars (Price [1965]; Mullins [1966]; Edwin B. Parker, *SPIRES* [1967]). Compton ("A Look at Conventions and What They Accomplish" [1966]) points out that attendance at these events appears to be particularly effective in conveying procedural information, supplying reinforcement and feedback, providing leads to archival sources, and facilitating the application of scientific knowledge (R. H. Orr, E. B. Coyl, and A. A. Leeds, "Trends Among Biomedical Scientists" [1964]).

Technical communicators should examine the activities surrounding these meetings and identity the behaviors of scientists and engineers—before, during, and after conventions—that lead to effective communication. Compton (1973) reports that pre-convention proceedings increase effectiveness in dissemination of information. She reports a study on annual meetings by the Johns Hopkins Center for Research in Scientific Communication, which found that only a limited audience attended those meetings. Research reported then was at an early stage in the dissemination process. The work was of recent inception, going back only 12 to 18 months prior to the convention. For the natural sciences, the research had first been reportable only six months before the meeting. The lag was even shorter for the social and behavioral sciences. Three-fourths to nine-tenths planned future publication, with little revision, of the reported findings. The authors answered program requests with reprints. Thus, conventions represent an important communication channel: they provide an avenue for early interpersonally based dissemination of information.

One final area concerns the use of new communication technologies such as computer networks, two-way interactive cable, satellite delivery systems, and video text (Roxanne Star Hiltz and Murray Turoff, *The Network Nation* [1978]). The research in this area is limited because of the newness of these technologies and because there is no workable video text system in the United States. Susan C. Freeman and Linton C. Freeman ("The Networkers Network" [1979]) and James A. Danowski ("A Methodology for a Network Based Content Analysis of Computer-mediated Communication" [1982]) have reported the initial findings of a National Science Foundation study on the use of computer networks for the communication of information by social scientists. Donald Case, Milton Chen, William Paisley, Ronald E. Rice, and Everett M. Rogers ("The Kentucky Green Thumb Videotext Experiment" [1982]) examined the use of an experimental video text system for the dissemination of agricultural information. Robert Epstein ("Down the Yellow Brick Road to the Computerized Office" [1982]; "The Wizardry of Measuring Users of Computer-based Office Systems" [1982]) examined the implications of telecommunications for organizational processes. Maureen Beninson, George A. Barnett, James DinKelacker, and Kimberly A.

Downing ("An Examination of the Diffusion Process" [1982]) examined automated ordering by computer and found that users preferred some intervening control by inputing the orders via terminal. So far, these studies are primarily descriptive, and their implications for professional communicators are unclear. As these technologies become more widely adopted for the communication of technical information, however, future research should be conducted.

Feedback

Feedback consists of messages sent by the receiver to the original source in response to the original message. Feedback makes possible the exchange of ideas. Thus, the goal of communication becomes understanding rather than a one-way flow or dissemination of information from source to receiver (Rogers and Kincaid [1980]). Feedback ensures effective communication—that is, the comprehension of ideas among individuals in a social network or formal organization (Berlo [1960]; Katz and Kahn [1978]; Rogers and Agarwala-Rogers [1976]).

George Barnett (1979) argues for a cybernetic approach to technical communication. Such an approach would build many feedback mechanisms into the process and change the role of users from passive readers to individuals actively involved in the preparation of documents that meet their needs. Feedback from users at the planning stage would help determine the specific document's function, content, and treatment. Upon dissemination, the audience should be solicited for feedback through mechanisms such as cards in the document which may be mailed to the source or surveys using book orders or library records to determine the sampling frame. Feedback to the following questions may be used to modify the document in order to improve its effectiveness:

1. How frequently do audience members consult technical materials?
2. How effectively does the document meet user needs?
3. Does the document meet the users' expectations?
4. How frequently is the document used, and for what purposes is it consulted?
5. How frequently do users supplement the use of the document by going to other sources?
6. Which other sources—documents and people—do users consult for the same information?
7. What additional information should the document contain?
8. What feedback can users offer on specific portions of the document?
9. What unanticipated feedback can users provide in response to open-ended questions?
10. What are the demographic and social characteristics of the actual users?

If the discrepancy between the document's goals and its use is significant, modifications should be made to correct these problems. This process may be refined and repeated over time until the document meets the user's needs. In this way, the focus of technical communication shifts from a one-way flow concentrating on message production to the exchange of ideas between the technical communicator and the user of the materials. With this change of focus will come a change in technical documents. They will be modular, thereby allowing easier modification as the need develops. The documents will be produced less expensively because they will be viewed not as permanent objects but rather as the product of the most recent interaction between the user and technical communicator. Finally, feedback will necessitate the development of computer-based technical materials because the production of permanent hard copy may not be appropriate or necessary.

Environment

The context or environment in which communication occurs has important implications for the technical communication process. The environment may produce noise that reduces the fidelity of information exchange. Noise is any signal or distracting disturbance that interferes with the reception of information (Claude Shannon and Warren Weaver, *The Mathematical Theory of Communication* [1949]). It is the ultimate limiter of communication, and it exists, if only in minuscule amounts, in all communication systems. Interference may result from a noisy channel, an unclear message, psychological factors with encoding or decoding, or any other aspect of the environment. When the disturbance is substantial, effective communication may be enhanced or recovered through an increase in redundancy.

Because the environments in which technical communication is produced and most often used are formal organizations, it may be fruitful for technical communication to examine formal organizations. There has been considerable theorizing and empirical research in organizational communication, and it has been reviewed in great detail by Gerald M. Goldhaber (*Organizational Communication* [1983]), Katz and Kahn (1978), R. Vincent Farace, Peter R. Monge, and Hamish M. Russell (*Communicating and Organizing* [1977]), and Everett M. Rogers and Rekha Agarwala-Rogers (1976). The basic notion underlying these theories is that formal organizations are information-processing systems (Lee Thayer, *Communication and Communication Systems* [1968]). Indeed, the coordination of the activities undertaken by members of any organization is made possible only through the communication of technical information. For an organization to survive, this information must meet three major functions:

1. The operational, production, or task-related function. For example, IBM's operational goal is manufacturing and servicing computer equipment and that of General Motors is manufacturing automobiles. Organizations must communicate technical information to their members to coordinate their behavior, making it possible to efficiently accomplish these goals.

2. The socio-emotional or maintenance function. Organizations must communicate human relations information to their employees to train them, indoctrinate them into the organizational culture, and provide information about health and other benefits, and about the rules for hiring, promotion, and firing.

3. The adaptive or innovative function. Organizations must communicate with their environment so that they can adapt to a changing world. Information must be gathered about competition, raw materials, labor, markets, general economic conditions, and scientific and technical innovations. This makes it possible for the organization to grow and to accomplish future societal needs. These activities are usually performed by units at the periphery of the organization, such as research and development laboratories, marketing departments, and planning groups.

Thus, organizations must gather and disseminate information both internally and with the environment; these external interactions may be with individuals or other organizations. Joanne E. Kapp and George A. Barnett ("Predicting Organizational Effectiveness from Communication Activities" [1983]), for example, found that organizational effectiveness was a direct function of the degree of both internal and external communication.

The communication of technical information among organizations is known as *technology transfer* and has been investigated by Thomas J. Allen ("Performance of Information Channels in the Transfer of Technology" [1966]), Samuel I. Doctors (*The Role of Federal Agencies in Technology Transfer* [1969]), and T. A. Jolly and J. W. Creighton (*Technology Transfer in Research and Development* [1975]). M. E. Essoglou ("The Linker Role in Technology Transfer" [1975]) identifies the following factors that may affect technology transfer:

Formal

1. Method of information documentation
2. The distribution system
3. The formal organization of the user
4. The selection process for projects

Informal

1. Capacity of the receiver
2. Informal linkers in the receiving organization
3. Credibility as viewed by the receiver
4. Perceived reward to the receiver
5. Willingness to be helped

These factors correspond to those reviewed throughout this chapter.

Effective communication may also be hindered by distractions within the organization. One area that has received considerable attention is information load—both underload and overload (Farace, Monge, and Russell [1977]). In overload situations, the receiver may not give enough attention to critical messages; the source may not take the time to prepare an effective message. In underload situations, the interactants may be unaccustomed to dealing with information and ignore it because the information may be perceived as not being for them.

Organizational communication suggests that managers should pay special attention to information processes within their systems. With the adoption of office automation systems, data-based management, and computer networks, managers have the opportunity to design systems to ensure effective communication. How one does this is not obvious. According to contingency theory, the optimal organizational communication structure is contingent on the organization's tasks, its environment, and rates of technological change (Paul R. Lawrence and Jay W. Lorsch, "Differentiation and Integration in Complex Organizations" [1967]; Jay R. Galbraith, *Designing Complex Organizations* [1973] and *Organization Design* [1977]). The optimal design of any organization should match its information needs and processing system. Generally, the greater the environmental uncertainty (the difference between the information known and that which is needed), the greater member integration required. However, as Danowski (1980) has pointed out, this may not be true for boundary spanners, those individuals who gather information from the environment.

In summary, technical communicators should consider the environment in which the process takes place—generally, a formal organization. They should seek information about the users' positions in the organizational structure, their information load relative to their processing capabilities, the other materials they use, and the other people they communicate with. They should make the same considerations about themselves. What are the technical communicators' environments? What are their positions in the communication structure? Do they receive all the information needed to complete assigned tasks? Ideally, technical communicators should serve the role of liaison, gathering information from the widest possible number of sources, processing it, and communicating it in the most effective manner to those who need it to complete their tasks. In the future, we see a changing role for technical communicators, one in which they will be recognized as liaisons.

Summary and Conclusions

This chapter provides only a cursory overview of communication theory and corresponding empirical research with applications for the technical communication process. We have excluded certain research areas which others assigned to the same task might have discussed. For example, we ignored linguistics. Clearly, theory from different perspectives would be useful.

We have stated some implications as facts, but they should be viewed somewhat skeptically. Deductions from theories generated for other purposes may lead to erroneous conclusions. In this case, much of the communication theory we cite was developed with persuasion rather than fidelity of information exchange as the central focus. Thus, future research is necessary to apply these and other theories specifically to technical communication.

Finally, we live in a rapidly changing world characterized by new technologies and increased contact between many different societies, each with its own unique culture and language. Scientific and technical information grows at an exponential rate (Derek J. de Solla Price, *Science Since Babylon* [1975]). Currently, the annual number of scientific papers is between 1.5 and 2 million (Anthony Liversidge, "Why Einstein Is Overrated" [1982]). Future research is needed which considers the role of new communication technologies in the process of technical communication. Will these technologies allow users of scientific and technical information to deal effectively with the potential overload? Can they be designed to deal more effectively with the information needs and behavioral patterns of users? One important aspect of the design process is the effective technical communication of the information stored in the electronic data systems. Research is needed on how intercultural communication affects or alters the process of technical communication. For example, Mark T. Palmer and George A. Barnett ("A Method to Determine Quality of Translation," [in press]) have proposed studying the translation of technical materials.

In conclusion, what has emerged is an implicit middle-range theory of technical communication. Effective technical communication is a function of the degree of learning that results from using the materials. This learning is a result of the technical material's ability to arouse attention and to be comprehended and recalled. These are a function of various characteristics of the *source, message, channel*, and *receiver*, the amount and type of *feedback*, and the *environment* in which the technical materials are created and used. Clearly, future research is needed to define these relationships more explicitly. A model suggested by this theory is presented in Figure 5.

In the future, our world will be increasingly dependent on technology and, therefore, on effective technical communication. To ensure that this need is met, empirical research is required. This research should be based on sound theories in which fidelity of information exchange is the central focus.

References

Addington, David W. "Effects of Mispronunciations on General Speaking Effectiveness." *Speech Mon*, 32 (1965), 159–63.

Alba, Richard D. "A Graph-theoretic Definition of a Sociometric Clique." *J Math Soc*, 3 (1973), 1–13.

Albrecht, Terrance L. "The Role of Communication in Perception of Organizational Climate." In *Communication Yearbook 3*. Ed. Dan Nimmo. New Brunswick, N.J.: Transaction, 1979, pp. 343–48.

Allen, Thomas J. "Performance of Information Channels in the Transfer of Technology." *Indus Manag Rev*, 8 (1966), 87–98.

———, and Steven I. Cohen. *Information Flow in an R & D Laboratory*. Cambridge, Mass.: Sloan School of Management, MIT, 1966.

Figure 5

Model of Middle Range Theory of Technical Communication

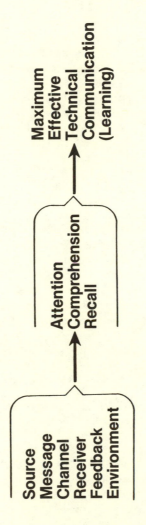

Source
Message
Channel
Receiver
Feedback
Environment

Attention
Comprehension
Recall

Maximum
Effective
Technical
Communication
(Learning)

Andersch, Elizabeth G., Lorin C. Staats, and Robert H. Bostrom. *Communication in Everyday Use.* 3rd ed. New York: Holt, Rinehart, Winston, 1969.

Anderson, Dorothy I. "The Effects of Various Uses of Authoritative Testimony in Persuasive Speaking." Thesis Ohio State University, 1958.

Anderson, John R., and Gordon H. Bower. *Human Associative Memory.* New York: Wiley, 1973.

Andersson, Ulf F. "Methods of Measuring Communication Results." *J Tech Writ Comm*, 1 (1971), 109–13.

Aronson, Elliot, and B. W. Golden. "The Effect of Relevant and Irrelevant Aspects of Communicator Credibility on Opinion Change." *J Pers*, 30 (1962), 135–46.

Asher, J. J. *Sensory Interrelationships in the Automated Teaching of Foreign Languages.* Washington, D.C.: U.S. Office of Education, 1961.

Atkin, Charles. "Anticipated Communication and Mass Media Information Seeking." *POQ*, 36 (1972), 188–99.

Barnett, George A. "Applications of Communication Theory and Cybernetics to Technical Communication." *J Tech Writ Comm*, 3 (1979), 337–47.

————. "Bilingual Information Processing: The Effects of Communication on Semantic Structure." Diss. Michigan State University, 1976.

————. "Social System Homophily as a Function of Communication." International Communication Association, New Orleans, April 1974.

————. "Spatial Modeling of Social Networks with Applications to the Diffusion Process." International Communication Association, Philadelphia, May 1979.

————, and David L. Carson. "Research on Defining the Profession of Technical Communication: A Bridge to Professional Understanding." Proceedings of International Technical Communication Conference. Minneapolis: Society for Technical Communication (STC), 1980, II, R29–33.

————, and David L. Carson. "The Role of Communication in the Professional Socialization Process." International Communication Association, Dallas, May 1983.

————, and D. Lawrence Kincaid. "Cultural Convergence: A Mathematical Theory." In *International Communication Theory: Current Perspectives.* Ed. William Gudykunst. Beverly Hills, Calif.: Sage, 1983, pp. 171–94.

Beninson, Maureen, George A. Barnett, James W. DinKelacker, and Kimberly A. Downing. "An Examination of the Diffusion Process: Automated Ordering in the Pharmaceutical Industry." International Communication Association, Boston, May 1982.

Berelson, Bernard, Paul F. Lazarsfeld, and Robert N. McPhee. *Voting: A Study of Opinion Formation in a Presidential Campaign.* Chicago: University of Chicago Press, 1954.

————, and George A. Steiner. *Human Behavior: An Inventory of Research Findings.* New York: Harcourt, Brace, World, 1964.

Berlo, David K. "An Empirical Test of a General Construct of Credibility." Speech Association of America, New York, 1961.

————. *The Process of Communication.* New York: Holt, Rinehart, Winston, 1960.

Bernard, N. Russell, and Peter D. Killworth. "On the Social Structure of an Oceangoing Research Vessel and Other Important Things." *Soc Sci Res*, 2 (1973), 145–84.

Bettinghaus, Erwin P. *Message Preparation: The Nature of Proof.* Indianapolis: Bobbs-Merrill, 1966.

————. "Operation of Congruity in an Oral Communication Setting." *Speech Mon*, 28 (1961), 131–42.

Blau, Peter M. *Exchange and Power in Social Life*. New York: Wiley, 1964.

Blickle, Margaret D., and Martha E. Passe, eds. *Readings for Technical Writers*. New York: Ronald, 1963.

Bloom, Joseph H., and Seth A. Goldstein. "Experiments in Technical Writing." *Prod Eng*, 31 (1960), 55.

Bochner, Steven, and Chester A. Insko. "Communicator Discrepancy, Source Credibility and Opinion Change." *J Pers Soc Psychol*, 4 (1966), 614–21.

Bossart, Philip C., and Francis J. Di Vesta. "Effects of Context, Frequency, and Order of Presentation of Evaluative Assertations on Impression Formation." *J Pers Soc Psychol*, 4 (1966), 538–44.

Bram, V. A. "Sentence Construction in Scientific and Engineering Texts." *Comm Sci Tech Info*, 34 (1978), 3.

Breiger, Richard L., S. A. Boorman, and P. Arabie. "An Algorithm for Clustering Relational Data with Application to Social Network Analysis and Comparison with Multidimensional Scaling." *J Math Psychol*, 12 (1975), 328–83.

Britton, W. Earl. "What Is Technical Writing?" *CCC*, 16 (1965), 113–16.

Burke, Kenneth. *A Grammar of Motives*. New York: Meredian, 1962.

Byrne, Donn. "Attitudes and Attraction." In *Advances in Experimental Social Psychology 4*. Ed. Leonard Berkowitz. New York: Academic, 1969, pp. 36–89.

Carlson, William M. "Engineering Information for National Defense." In *Engineering Societies and Their Literature Programs*. New York: Engineers Joint Council, 1967, pp. 150–61.

Case, Donald, Milton Chen, William Paisley, Ronald E. Rice, and Everett M. Rogers. "The Kentucky Green Thumb Videotext Experiment: Uses, Impacts and Evaluation." International Communication Association, Boston, May 1982.

Cathcart, Raymond. "An Experimental Study of the Relativeness of Four Methods of Presenting Evidence." *Speech Mon*, 22 (1955), 227–33.

Chaffee, Steven H. "Mass Media Versus Interpersonal Channels: The Synthetic Competition." Speech Communication Association, Austin, Tex., Nov. 1979.

————, M. Jackson-Buck, J. Lewin, and B. Wilson. "The Interpersonal Context of Mass Communication." In *Current Perspectives in Mass Communication Research*. Ed. F. Gerald Kline and Philip J. Tichenor. Beverly Hills, Calif.: Sage, 1972, pp. 95–120.

Cody, Michael J. "The Validity of Experimentally Induced Motions of Public Figures in Multidimensional Scaling Configurations." In *Communication Yearbook 4*. Ed. Dan Nimmo. New Brunswick, N.J.: Transaction, 1980, pp. 143–64.

————, John Marlier, and Joseph Woelfel. "An Application of the Multiple Attribute Measurement Model: Measurement and Manipulation of Source Credibility." Annual Meeting of the Mathematical Psychology Association, West Lafayette, Ind., Aug. 1975.

Cohen, Arthur R. "Situational Structure, Self-esteem and Threat-oriented Reactions to Power." In *Studies in Social Power*. Ed. Dorwin Cartwright. Ann Arbor: University of Michigan Press, 1959, pp. 35–52.

Compton, Bertita E. "A Look at Conventions and What They Accomplish." *Am Psychol*, 21 (1966), 176–83.

————. "Scientific Communication." In *Handbook of Communication*. Ed. Ithiel de

Sola Pool, Wilbur Schramm, Frederick W. Frey, Nathan Maccoby, and Edwin B. Parker. Chicago: Rand-McNally, 1973, pp. 755–78.

Comstock, George, Steven H. Chaffee, Nathan Katzman, and Donald Roberts. *Television and Human Behavior*. New York: Columbia University Press, 1978.

Costley, D. "An Experimental Study of the Effectiveness of Quantitative Evidence in Speeches of Advocacy." Thesis University of Oklahoma, 1958.

Crane, Diana. *Invisible Colleges: Diffusion of Knowledge in Scientific Communities*. Chicago: University of Chicago Press, 1972.

Cromwell, Harvey. "Relative Effect of Audience Attitudes of the First Versus the Second Argumentative Speech of a Series." *Speech Mon*, 17 (1950), 105–22.

Dandridge, Edmund P., Jr. "Notes Towards a Definition of Technical Writing." In *The Teaching of Technical Writing*. Ed. Donald H. Cunningham and Herman A. Estrin. Urbana: National Council of Teachers of English, 1975, pp. 15–20.

Danowski, James A. "A Methodology for a Network Based Content Analysis of Computer-mediated Communication: An Illustration with a CBBS Computer Conference." In *Communication Yearbook 6*. Ed. Michael Burgoon. Beverly Hills, Calif.: Sage, 1982, pp. 905–24.

———. "Uniformity of Group Attitude-belief and Connectivity of Organizational Communication Networks for Production, Innovation and Maintenance." *HCR*, 6 (1980), 299–308.

———, and Neal E. Cutler. "Political Information, Mass Media Use in Early Adulthood, and Political Socialization: Seeking Clarity Through Cohert Curves." In *Strategies for Communication Research*. Ed. Paul M. Hirsch, Peter V. Miller, and F. Gerald Kline. Beverly Hills, Calif.: Sage, 1977, pp. 205–30.

Dargan, Thomas R. "Five Basic Patterns to Use in Interactive Flow Charts." *Educ Indust TV* 14 (June 1982), 31–34.

Darnell, Donald K. "The Relation Between Sentence Order and Comprehension." *Speech Mon*, 30 (1963), 97–100.

Davis, Richard M. "Does Expression Make a Difference?" *Tech Comm*, 23, No. 2 (1976), 6–9.

DeFleur, Melvin L., and Sandra Ball-Rokeach. *Theories of Mass Communication*. New York: Longman, 1975.

DeSota, Clinton B. "Learning a Social Structure." *J Abnorm Soc Psychol*, 60 (1960), 417–21.

———. "The Predilection for Single Orderings." *J Abnorm Soc Psychol*, 62 (1961), 16–23.

———, M. London, and S. Handel. "Social Reasoning and Spatial Paralogic." *J Pers Soc Psychol*, 2 (1965), 513–21.

Doctors, Samuel I. *The Role of Federal Agencies in Technology Transfer*. Cambridge, Mass.: MIT Press, 1969.

Dresser, William R. "Effects of 'Satisfactory' and 'Unsatisfactory' Evidence in a Speech of Advocacy." *Speech Mon*, 20 (1963), 302–306.

Epstein, Robert. "Down the Yellow Brick Road to the Computerized Office." International Communication Association, Boston, May 1982.

———. "The Wizardry of Measuring Users of Computer-based Office Systems." Office Automation Conference, San Francisco, Apr. 1982.

Essoglou, M. E. "The Linker Role in Technology Transfer." In *Technology Transfer in Research and Development.* Ed. J. A. Jolly and J. W. Creighton. Monterey, Calif.: Naval Postgraduate School, 1975, pp. 1–16.

Farace, R. Vincent, Peter R. Monge, and Hamish M. Russell. *Communicating and Organizing.* Reading, Mass.: Addison-Wesley, 1977.

Festinger, Leon. *A Theory of Cognitive Dissonance.* New York: Harper, 1957.

Fisher, B. Aubrey. *Perspectives on Human Communication.* New York: Macmillan, 1978.

Flesch, Rudolph F. "A New Readability Yardstick." *J Appl Psychol,* 32 (1948), 221–33.

Freedman, Jonathan L., and David O. Sears. "Selective Exposure." In *Advances in Experimental Social Psychology-2.* Ed. Leonard Berkowitz. New York: Academic, 1965, pp. 58–97.

Freeman, Susan C., and Linton C. Freeman. "The Networkers Network: A Study of the Impact of a New Communication Medium on Sociometric Structure." Seminar on Network Analysis, East-West Communication Institute, Honolulu, Jan. 1979.

Galbraith, Jay R. *Designing Complex Organizations.* Reading, Mass.: Addison-Wesley, 1973.

———. *Organization Design.* Reading, Mass.: Addison-Wesley, 1977.

Gilkinson, Howard, Stanley F. Paulson, and Donald E. Sikkink. "Effects of Order and Authority in an Argumentative Speech." *Q J Speech,* 40 (1954), 183–92.

Goldhaber, Gerald M. *Organizational Communication.* 3rd ed. Dubuque, Iowa: William C. Brown, 1983.

———, Michael P. Yates, D. Thomas Porter, and Richard Lesniak. "Organizational Communication: 1978." *HCR,* 5 (1978), 76–96.

Gulley, Halbert E., and David K. Berlo. "Effect of Intercellular and Intracellular Speech Structure on Attitude Change and Learning." *Speech Mon,* 23 (1956), 288–97.

Habermas, Jürgen. *Communication and the Evolution of Society.* Boston: Beacon, 1979.

Haiman, Franklin S. "The Effects of Ethos in Public Speaking." *Speech Mon,* 16 (1949), 190–202.

Hamlin, Donna M. "Creativity in Organizations: A Preliminary Investigation." Thesis Rensselaer Polytechnic Institute, 1978.

———, and Craig Harkins. "A Model for Technical Communication." *J Tech Writ Comm,* 13, No. 1 (1983), pp. 57–81.

Harris, John S. "On Expanding the Definition of Technical Writing." *J Tech Writ Comm,* 8 (1978), 133–38.

Hartman, F. R. "Single and Multiple Channel Communication: A Review of Research and a Proposed Model." *AV Comm Rev,* 9 (1961), 235–62.

Hays, Robert. "What Is Technical Writing?" In *The Teaching of Technical Writing.* Ed. Donald H. Cunningham and Herman A. Estrin. Urbana: National Council of Teachers of English, 1961, pp. 3–8.

Heider, Fritz. *The Psychology of Interpersonal Relations.* New York: Wiley, 1956.

Hertz, David B., and A. H. Rubenstein. *Team Research.* New York: Columbia University, Department of Industrial Engineering, 1953.

Hiebert, Ray Eldon, Donald F. Ungurait, and Thomas W. Bohn. *Mass Media III: An Introduction to Modern Communication.* New York: Longman, 1982.

Hiltz, Roxanne Star, and Murray Turoff. *The Network Nation: Human Communication via Computer.* Reading, Mass.: Addison-Wesley, 1978.

Homans, George C. "Social Behavior As Exchange." *Am J Soc,* 63 (1958), 597–600.

Houp, Kenneth W., and Thomas Pearsall. *Reporting Technical Information*. 3rd Ed. Encino, Calif.: Glencoe, 1977.

Hovland, Carl I., ed. *Order of Presentation in Persuasion*. New Haven: Yale University Press, 1957.

——, and Wallace Mandell. "An Experimental Comparison of Conclusion-Drawing by the Communicator and by the Audience." *J Abnorm Soc Psychol*, 47 (1952), 581–88.

——, and Walter Weiss. "The Influence of Source Credibility on Communication Effectiveness." *POQ*, 15 (1951), 635–50.

Innis, Harold A. *The Bias of Communication*. Toronto: University of Toronto Press, 1951.

——. *Empire and Communications*. London: Oxford University Press, 1950.

Iuppa, Nick. "How Manufacturers Can Assist Users of Interactive Video." *Educ Indust TV*, 14 (June 1982), 27–30.

Jolly, T. A., and J. W. Creighton. *Technology Transfer in Research and Development*. Monterey, Calif.: Naval Postgraduate School, 1975.

Kahneman, Daniel. *Attention and Effort*. Englewood Cliffs, N.J.: Prentice-Hall, 1973.

Kapp, Joanne E., and George A. Barnett. "Predicting Organizational Effectiveness from Communication Activities: A Multiple Indicator Model." *HCR*, 9 (1983), 239–54.

Kapp, Reginald O. *The Presentation of Technical Information*. New York: Macmillan, 1957.

Kasperson, Conrad J. "An Analysis of the Relationship Between Information Sources and Creativity in Scientists and Engineers." *HCR*, 4 (1978), 113–119.

Katz, Daniel, and Robert H. Kahn. *The Social Psychology of Organizations*. New York: Wiley, 1978.

Katz, Elihu, and Paul F. Lazarsfeld. *Personal Influence: The Part Played by People in the Flow of Mass Communication*. New York: Free Press, 1955.

Kelley, Patrick M., and Roger E. Masse. "A Definition of Technical Writing." *Tech Writ Teach*, 4 (1977), 94–97.

Kincaid, D. Lawrence. *The Convergence Model of Communication*. East-West Communication Institute Paper Series, No. 18, Honolulu, 1979.

Kinneavy, James L. *A Theory of Discourse: The Aims of Discourse*. Englewood Cliffs, N.J.: Prentice-Hall, 1971.

Kirkman, A. J. "The Communication of Technical Thought." In *The Engineer and Society*. Ed. E. G. Semier. London: Institute of Mechanical Engineers, 1970, pp. 180–85.

Klapper, Joseph T. *The Effects of Mass Communication*. New York: Free Press, 1960.

Klare, George R. "Readable Technical Writing: Some Observations." *Tech Comm*, 24, No. 2 (1977), 1–5.

Lachman, Roy, Janet L. Lachman, and Earl C. Butterfield. *Cognitive Psychology and Information Processing*. Hillsdale, N.J.: Erlbaum, 1979.

Lasswell, Harold D. "The Structure and Function of Communication in Society." In *Communication of Ideas*. Ed. Lyman Bryson. New York: Institute for Religious and Social Studies, 1948, pp. 37–51.

Lawrence, Paul R., and J. W. Lorsch. "Differentiation and Integration in Complex Organizations." *Admin Sci Q*, 12 (1967), 1–47.

Lazarsfeld, Paul F., and Robert K. Merton. "Friendship as Social Process." In *Freedom and Control in Modern Society*. Ed. Monroe Berger. New York: Octagon, 1948.

Lehmann, Stanley. "Personality and Compliance: A Study of Anxiety and Self-esteem in Opinion and Behavior Change." *J Pers Soc Psychol*, 15 (1970), 76–86.

Lemert, James B. "Dimensions of Source Credibility." Association for Education in Journalism, Aug. 1963.

Leventhal, Howard. "Findings and Theory in the Study of Fear Communications." In *Advances in Experimental Social Psychology-5*. Ed. Leonard Berkowitz. New York: Academic, 1970, pp. 119–86.

Lin, Nan. *Foundations of Social Research*. New York: McGraw-Hill, 1976.

Lipetz, B. A. *Evaluation of the Impact of a Citation Index in Physics, AIP/DRP C1–3*. New York: American Institute of Physics, 1964.

Liu, William T., and Robert W. Duff. "On Rogers' Homophily-Heterophily Concept of Communication." Unpublished manuscript, 1972.

Liversidge, Anthony. "Why Einstein Is Overrated: Interview with Derek J. de Solla Price." *Omni*, Dec. 1982, pp. 88–102, 136.

Luchins, Abraham S. "Definitiveness of Impression and Primacy-Recency in Communications." *J Soc Psychol*, 48 (1958), 275–90.

———. "Experimental Attempts to Minimize the Impact of First Impression." In *The Order of Presentation in Persuasion*. Ed. Carl I. Hovland. New Haven: Yale University Press, 1957, pp. 62–75.

Lumsdaine, A. A., and Irving L. Janis. "Resistance to 'Counterpropaganda' Produced by One-sided and Two-sided 'Propaganda' Presentations." *POQ*, 17 (1953), 311–18.

McCombs, Maxwell E., and Donald L. Shaw. "The Agenda-Setting Function of the Mass Media." *POQ*, 36 (1972), 176–87.

McCroskey, James C. "Scales for the Measurement of Ethos." *Speech Mon*, 33 (1966), 65–72.

———. "A Summary of Experimental Research on the Effects of Evidence in Persuasive Communication." *Q J Speech* 55 (1969), 169–76.

McGuire, William J. "Attitude Change: The Information-processing Paradigm." In *Experimental Social Psychology*. Ed. Charles G. McClintock. New York: Holt, Rinehart, Winston, 1972, pp. 108–41.

———. "Inducing Resistance to Persuasion." In *Advances in Experimental Social Psychology*. Vol. I. Ed. Leonard Berkowitz. New York: Academic, 1964, pp. 191–229.

———. "Persuasion, Resistance and Attitude Change." In *Handbook of Communication*. Ed. Ithiel de Sola Pool, Frederick W. Frey, Wilbur Schramm, Nathan Maccoby, and Edwin B. Parker. Chicago: Rand-McNally, 1973, pp. 216–52.

McLuhan, H. Marshall. *Guttenberg Galaxy*. Toronto: University of Toronto Press, 1962.

———. *Understanding Media*. New York: McGraw-Hill, 1964.

Mandler, George. "Organization and Memory." In *Psychology of Learning and Motivation*. Vol. I. Ed. Kenneth W. Spence and Janet Taylor Spence. New York: Academic, 1967, pp. 327–72.

Mathes, John, and Dwight Stevenson. *Designing Technical Reports*. Indianapolis: Bobbs-Merrill, 1976.

Maurice, R. H., Herbert Menzel, and Rolf Meyersohn. "Physicians' Information Levels as Affected by Milieu, Contact with Colleagues, and Current Awareness Activities." Subcommittee on Medical Sociology, Sixth World Congress of Sociology, Evian, France, Sept. 1966.

May, M. A., and A. A. Lumsdaine. *Learning from Films*. New Haven: Yale University Press, 1958.

Mayo, C. W., and Walter H. Crockett. "Cognitive Complexity and Primacy-Recency Effects in Impression Formation." *J Abnorm Soc Psychol*, 68 (1964), 335–38.

Menzel, Herbert. *The Flow of Information Among Scientists—Problems, Opportunities and Research Questions*. New York: Columbia University, Bureau of Applied Social Research, 1958.

————. *Formal and Informal Satisfaction of the Information Requirements of Chemists*. New York: Columbia University, Bureau of Applied Social Research, 1966.

————. "Sociological Perspectives in the Information-gathering Practices of the Scientific Investigator and the Medical Practitioner." In *Bibliotheca Medica: Physician for Tomorrow, Dedication of the Countway Library of Medicine*. Boston: Harvard University Medical School, 1966, pp. 25–36.

Merton, Robert I. *Social Theory and Social Structure*. New York: Harper, 1957.

Miller, Carolyn R. "A Humanistic Rationale for Technical Writing." *CE*, 40 (1979), 610–17.

————. "Rules, Context, and Technical Communication." *J Tech Writ Comm*, 10 (1980), 149–58.

Miller, Gerald R. *Speech Communication: A Behavioral Approach*. Indianapolis: Bobbs-Merrill, 1966.

————, and Michail Burgoon. "Persuasion Research: Review and Commentary." In *Communication Yearbook 2*. Ed. Brent D. Ruben. New Brunswick, N.J.: Transaction, 1978, pp. 27–45.

Miller, Philip. "Responding to the New Television: Education and Interactive Video." Unpublished manuscript, Massachusetts Educational Television, June 1981.

Millman, Susan, "Anxiety, Comprehension and Susceptibility to Social Influence." *J Pers Soc Psychol*, 9 (1968), 251–56.

Mills, Gordon H., and John A. Walter. *Technical Communication*. 4th ed. New York: Holt, Rinehart, Winston, 1978.

Mortensen, C. David. *Communication: The Study of Human Interaction*. New York: McGraw-Hill, 1972.

Mullins, N. C. "Social Networks Among Biological Scientists." Diss. Harvard, 1966.

Newcomb, Theodore. "An Approach to the Study of Communicative Acts." *Psychol Rev*, 60 (1953), 393–404.

Orr, R. H., E. B. Coyl, and A. A. Leeds. "Trends Among Biomedical Scientists: Meetings and Travel." *Fed Proc*, 23 (1964), 1146–54.

Osgood, Charles E., George J. Suci, and Percy H. Tannenbaum. *The Measurement of Meaning*. Urbana, Ill.: University of Illinois Press, 1957.

Ostermeier, Terry H. "Effects of Type and Frequency of Reference and Perceived Source Credibility and Attitude Change." *Speech Mon*, 34 (1967), 137–44.

Palmer, Mark T., and George A. Barnett. "A Method to Determine Quality of Translation." In *International and Intercultural Communication Annual 8*. Ed. William Gudykunst. Beverly Hills, Calif.: Sage, in press.

Parker, Edwin B. *SPIRES (Stanford Physics Information Retrieval System 1967 Annual Report)*. Stanford, Calif.: Institute for Communication Research, Stanford University, 1967.

Pearsall, Thomas E. *Audience Analysis for Technical Writing*. Beverly Hills, Calif.: Glencoe, 1977.

———. *Teaching Technical Writing: Methods for College English Teachers*. Washington, D.C.: Society for Technical Communication, 1975.

Peterson, Ruth C., and L. L. Thurstone, *The Effect of Motion Pictures on the Social Attitudes of High School Students*. Chicago: University of Chicago Press, 1933.

Piaget, Jean. *Structuralism*. New York: Basic, 1970.

Pierce, J. R. *Symbols, Signals and Noise: The Nature and Process of Communication*. New York: Harper, 1961.

Price, Derek J. de Solla. *Science Since Babylon*. New Haven: Yale University Press, 1975.

———. "The Scientific Foundations of Science Policy." *Nature*, 206 (1965), 233-38.

Richards, William D., Jr. "Network Analysis in Large Complex Systems." International Communication Association, New Orleans, Apr., 1974.

Roberts, Karlene H., and Charles A. O'Reilly III. "Organizations as Communication Structures: An Empirical Approach." *HCR*, 4 (1978), 283-93.

Rogers, Everett M., and Rekha Agarwala-Rogers. *Communication in Organizations*. New York: Free Press, 1976.

———, and D. Lawrence Kincaid. *Communication Networks: Toward a New Paradigm for Research*. New York: Free Press, 1981.

———, and F. Floyd Shoemaker. *Communication of Innovations: A Cross-Cultural Approach*. 2nd Ed. New York: Free Press, 1971.

Rokeach, Milton. *The Open and Closed Mind*. New York: Basic, 1960.

Rosenkrantz, Paul S., and Walter H. Crockett. "Some Factors Influencing the Assimilation of Disparate Information in Impression Formation." *J Pers Soc Psychol*, 2 (1967), 397-402.

Ross, Donald, Jr. "A Theory of the Function of Technical Writing?" *Tech Writ Teach*, 9 (1981), 3-9.

Rubens, Philip M. "Technical Communication: Notes Toward Defining a Discipline." In *Technical Writing: Past, Present, and Future*. Technical Memorandum 81966. Ed. J. C. Mathes and Thomas E. Pinelli. Washington, D.C.: National Aeronautics and Space Agency, Mar. 1981.

Rubenstein, A. H., R. W. Trueswell, G. J. Rath, and D. J. Werner. "Some Preliminary Experiments and a Model of Information-seeking Style of Researcher." National Conference on the Administration of Research, Miami, Oct. 1966.

Rumelhart, David E. *Introduction to Human Information Processing*. New York: Wiley, 1977.

Saltiel, John, and Joseph Woelfel. "Inertia in Cognitive Processes: The Role of Accumulated Information in Attitude Change." *HCR*, 1 (1975), 333-44.

Schramm, Wilbur. "Channels and Audiences." In *Handbook of Communication*. Ed. Ithiel de Sola Pool, Frederick W. Frey, Wilbur Schramm, Nathan Maccoby, and Edwin B. Parker. Chicago: Rand-McNally, 1973, pp. 116-40.

———. *The Process and Effects of Mass Communication*. Urbana, Ill.: University of Illinois Press, 1954.

———. *Men, Messages, and Media*. New York: Harper, 1973.

———, Jack Lyle, and Edwin B. Parker. *Television in the Lives of Our Children*. Stanford, Calif.: Stanford University Press, 1961.

Schweitzer, Don A., and G. P. Ginsburg. "Factors of Communicator Credibility." In

Problems in Social Psychology. Ed. C. W. Backman and Paul F. Secord. New York: McGraw-Hill, 1966, pp. 94–102.

Shannon, Claude, E., and Warren Weaver. *The Mathematical Theory of Communication.* Urbana, Ill.: University of Illinois Press, 1949.

Smith, Robert G. "An Experimental Study of the Effects of Speech Organization upon Attitudes of College Students." *Speech Mon*, 18 (1951), 291–391.

Sponberg, Harold. "The Relative Effectiveness of Climax and Anticlimax Order in an Argumentative Speech." *Speech Mon*, 13 (1946), 35–44.

Staats, Arthur W. "Principles of the Attitude-Reinforcer-Discriminative System." In *Psychological Foundations of Attitudes.* Ed. Anthony G. Greenwald. New York: Academic, 1968, pp. 33–66.

Steinfeld, Charles W. "Explaining Managers' Use of Communication Channels for Performance Monitoring Implications for New Office Systems." International Communication Association, Minneapolis, May 1981.

Stewart, John Bell. *Repetitive Advertising in Newspapers: A Study in Two Products.* Boston: Harvard University, Division of Research, 1964.

Thayer, Lee. *Communication and Communication Systems.* Homewood, Ill.: Irwin, 1968.

Thompson, Ernest. "An Experimental Investigation of the Relative Effectiveness of Organizational Structure in Oral Communication." *S Speech J*, 26 (1960), 59–69.

———. "Some Effects of Message Structure on Listener Comprehension." *Speech Mon*, 34 (1967), 51–57.

Tushman, Michael L. "Special Boundary Roles in the Innovation Process." *Admin Sci Q*, 22 (1977), 587–605.

———. "Work Characteristics and Subunit Communication Structure: A Contingency Analysis." *Admin Sci Q*, 24 (1979), 82–98.

Van Cott, Harold P., and Robert Kincaide. *A Feasibility Study for Determining Requirements of Biological Information Services and Systems.* Final Report AIR F–57–11/67–TR–7. Washington, D.C.: American Institute for Research, 1967.

Von Bertalanffy, Ludwig. *General Systems Theory.* New York: Braziller, 1965.

Wagner, Gerald A. "An Experimental Study of the Relative Effectiveness of Varying Amounts of Evidence in a Persuasive Communication." Thesis University of Southern Mississippi, 1958.

Watzlawick, Paul, Janet Bevin, and Don D. Jackson. *Pragmatics of Human Communication.* New York: Norton, 1967.

Weaver, Andrew T., and Ordean G. Ness. *The Fundamentals and Forms of Speech.* Indianapolis: Bobbs-Merrill, 1957.

Weiner, Norbert. *Cybernetics.* Cambridge, Mass.: MIT Press, 1949.

———. *The Human Use of Human Beings: Cybernetics and Society.* Garden City, N.Y.: Doubleday, 1954.

Westley, Bruce, and Malcolm Maclean. "A Conceptual Model for Communication Research." *Journ Q*, 34 (1957), 31–38.

Wigand, Rolf T. "Communication and Interorganizational Relationships Among Complex Organizations in Social Service Settings." International Communication Association, Portland, Oreg., Apr. 1976.

Wilkus, Edward, Joseph Woelfel, George A. Barnett, and Norman Fontes. "McLuhan Hot and Cold: An Empirical Test." Unpublished research report, Department of Communication, Michigan State University, 1973.

Wilson, Warner, and Howard Miller. "Repetition, Order of Presentation, and Timing of Arguments and Measures as Determinants of Opinion Change." *J Pers Soc Psychol*, 9 (1968), 184–88.

Woelfel, Joseph, Michael J. Cody, James R. Gillham, and Richard Holmes. "Basic Premises of Multidimensional Attitude Change Theory." *HCR*, 6 (1980), 153–67.

————, and Edward L. Fink. *The Measurement of Communication Processes: Galileo Theory and Method*. New York: Academic, 1980.

————, and Donald Hernandez. "Media and Interpersonal Influence on Attitude Formation and Change." Unpublished Research Report, Department of Sociology, University of Illinois, 1970.

————, and John Saltiel. "Cognitive Processes as Motions in a Multidimensional Space." Unpublished manuscript. East Lansing, Mich.: Michigan State University, Department of Communication, 1974.

————, John Woelfel, James R. Gillham, and Thomas L. McPhail. "Political Radicalization as a Communication Process." *Comm Res*, 1 (1974), 243–63.

Wooster, Harold. *Microfiche 1969—A User Study*. AFOSR–69–184TR. Washington, D.C.: Air Force Office of Scientific Research, 1969.

Teaching Technical Writing

ANTHONY O'KEEFFE

While all good teachers are scholars, they also resemble the poet whom Robert Frost contrasts with the scholar: they get much of their best knowledge "in and out of books," and let "what will stick to them like burrs where they walk in the fields." The teaching of any skill is, after all, a human transaction, and so it is a thing of limited orderliness. An essay such as the one that follows, while making an immediate appeal to the teacher's sense of the useful, must also address his or her fundamental intuition that the essence of good teaching lies somehow beyond all our schematic methods and theorizings. It cannot settle for a mere businesslike ranging of "pedagogical concerns"—an inadequate abstraction to derive from that rich situation we face in the classroom. It achieves what good it can by making us attend to that ongoing commerce between experience and abstraction, to an enriching process rather than a set of categories. It is hoped that the array of ideas and arguments offered by the writers cited here will demonstrate that commerce.

The "mild boredom of order" of which Walter Benjamin spoke, in commenting on a friend's well-arranged library, is always going to shadow the bibliographical essay. But nowhere is order more helpful. This chapter is structured around a simple chronology of learning, and acting upon, the basics of technical writing teaching. The first section covers material that helps one get started: the important anthologies, journals, and bibliographies; the essential characteristics of technical writing, and its practitioners; its double connection with the academic and professional worlds. The second section examines the basic introductory course in technical writing—its syllabus and structure, the writing skills aimed at, and the established assignments through which they can be practiced. Then the third section moves beyond that first course into the development of a full program of courses and the fundamental research needed to give it coherent intellectual grounding. The final section takes up a few special issues in teaching technical writing, issues generated by the development of an academic identity for technical writing.

Getting Started

Five anthologies are essential to any solid library in technical writing pedagogy. Three of these present essays on a variety of issues, practical and theoretical, in the field. The earliest, *The Teaching of Technical Writing* (1975), edited by Donald H. Cunningham and Herman A. Estrin, gathered several now classic articles on how to define, teach, and research technical writing. In 1978, Baywood Press began its Technical Communications Series with *Directions in Technical Writing and Communication*, edited by Jay R. Gould. Like the Cunningham-Estrin volume, this work covers topics with both direct and indirect bearing on teaching practices: defining technical writing, classifying its basic forms, evaluating it, and assessing its place in the larger academic/professional scheme of things. Baywood's second series collection, *New Essays in Technical and Scientific Communication* (1983), edited by Paul V. Anderson, R. John Brockmann, and Carolyn R. Miller, shows a more obviously theoretical orientation. It provides a clear and necessary introduction to complex issues which are likely to set the early research agenda for technical writing: the use and impact of empirical research, the nature of technical writing readability, interdisciplinary approaches to technical writing, historical perspectives, wider definitions. The two other anthologies focus more single-mindedly on classroom practices and possibilities. They are Thomas M. Sawyer's *Technical and Professional Communication* (1977) and Dwight W. Stevenson's *Courses, Components, and Exercises in Technical Communication* (1981). For pure, practical classroom advice, the best anthology of the five is Stevenson's; its twenty-one articles, divided in roughly equal number among the title's three categories, offer invaluable, detailed suggestions on structuring courses and their individual assignments.

A handful of academic and professional journals provide several kinds of aid to the technical writing teacher. The *Journal of Technical Writing and Communication* and *The Technical Writing Teacher* most directly continue and advance the issues raised by the five anthologies. One should complement their basically academic viewpoint by consulting two journals more closely tied to professional communications concerns: the *IEEE Transactions in Professional Communication*, published by the Institute of Electrical and Electronics Engineers, and *Technical Communication*. Trafficking helpfully between the academic and professional spheres is *Engineering Education*; and essential to understanding the larger context of university writing programs and theory within which technical writing operates are *College English* and *College Composition and Communication*.

Carolyn M. Blackman's "A Bibliography of Resources for Beginning Teachers of Technical Writing" (1977) offers some telling introductory comments about the problems technical writing faces in establishing itself as a coherent field of inquiry. These comments are followed by an annotated list of organizations, conferences, meetings, and institutes on technical communication, periodicals, articles, and bibliographies. Since its Fall 1975 issue (with interruptions in 1979 and 1980), *The Technical Writing Teacher* has published an annual bibliography covering new books (and their reviews); theory, pedagogy, and research; the standard technical writing forms; technical correspondence, graphics, and speech; and other bibliographies. And in the first 1979 issue of the *Journal of Technical Writing and Communication*, Karen A. Edlefsen published an annotated bibliography covering that journal's first seven years.

As a practiced art, technical writing has a long history; as a formal discipline, however, it is relatively young and so, healthily unsettled. Its definition remains an open question, one that has sparked some thoughtful, important articles. The most complex and suggestive of these is David N. Dobrin's "What's Technical About Technical Writing?" (1983), an essay best approached after grasping those fundamental answers that have preceded Dobrin's own. Read in combination, W. Earl Britton's "What Is Technical Writing?" (1975) and James W. Souther's "Writing Is for *Other* People" (1979) establish the ground of debate. Britton covers briefly four criteria by which technical writers have sought to define their field: by subject matter, by linguistic character, by the thought process demanded, and by purpose. He concentrates on purpose as the best standard for generating a definition of direct use to writers and teachers. He identifies the essence of technical writing with the "effort of the author to convey one meaning and only one meaning" (p. 11). Souther's article provides a concise statement of those elements that establish technical and scientific writing as a separate academic discipline. His list of a dozen basic concepts for technical writing is particularly helpful in giving the reader a strong sense of the specifics that lie behind the debate's more generalized arguments. For a truly clear grasp of the issues that Dobrin confronts, one should read as well: Robert Hays's "What Is Technical Writing" (1975); Edmund P. Dandridge, Jr.'s style-oriented "Notes Toward a Definition of Technical Writing" (1975); John A. Walter's "Technical Writing" (1977); and John Sterling Harris's "On Expanding the Definition of Technical Writing" (1978).

Dobrin's argument (in mere caricature) is as follows: Writers who have attempted to define technical writing fall into two classes: those who look at texts, at the writing as a product; and those who look at the act which produces texts, the process of "technically writing." Dobrin cites the definition from Walter—built upon recurring rhetorical modes and formats, specialized vocabulary and objective style, and technical content—as typical of the product approach; he cites Harris—"Technical writing is the rhetoric of the scientific method" (p. 229)—as typical of the process approach. Both definitions, when pushed for the details they logically imply, yield contradiction, impreciseness, and confusion. Dobrin sees their hidden flaws as inevitably deriving from the theory of language that underlies both, a theory they share despite their superficially different angles of approach. Their essential assumptions about language are "universalist." The universalist starts from the fundamental belief that "a sentence can mean a particular thing and that precisely that meaning can be understood" (Dobrin, p. 234). Language *can*, if kept properly objective, become a "windowpane" allowing one to see a reality universally available, without language, to the rationally inquiring mind. Language can be the collection of data that reality is. Dobrin, by contrast, is a "monadist"—one for whom knowledge and language are not separable. The essential monadist assumption is that "one knows in language"; and since "there is no way of knowing without language—a human construct—there can be no privileged access to the world" (pp. 237–238). Language cannot ever become the pure windowpane, for the strategies by which the universalist strives to make it so—objectivity, quantification, univocality—are simply the "axiomatic fictions" of one interpretive community; for the monadist, every instance of writing is "a way of thinking and establishing human relations in a group" (p. 242). From his complex examination of the universalist/ monadist duality, Dobrin demonstrates three ways in which the universalist approach has led technical writing, *as practiced*, into difficulties: by oversimplifying and misunderstanding how we may translate technical information for the varying groups who demand it, by underestimating the technical writer's responsibility for and relation to such information, and by reinforcing a mistaken sense of technical writing's identity and durability. From his monadist foundation, he offers this elegantly simple, suggestive definition: "Technical writing is writing that accommodates technology to the user" (p. 242). Such a definition, according to Dobrin, "shifts attention to where it should be shifted, to technological practices" (p. 247). It derives from, and more clearly reveals, the intimate connection of technical writing with technology—which is itself, naturally, not simply "an array of tools and procedures" but "a way that people, machines, concepts, and relationships are organized" (p. 243). We are given, in the end, a wider, more challenging, less bleakly formulaic definition of technical writing—one that both reminds us of what technical writing shares with all writing, and still clarifies its specialized identity as a kind of writing.

The technical writing teacher is, of course, concerned about these ideas on a pragmatic as well as a theoretical level and will be curious to know what implication technical language's common bond with all writing, and its specialized identity, has for classroom practice. Dennis E. Minor's "A Concept of Language for Technical Writing Students" (1978) offers an immediately useful answer. Minor recommends that such students be taught a concept of language centered on three functions: *generative* (establishing and clarifying a subject in such a way as to provoke further discussion of it); *substantive* (defining the subject's terms and supporting the discussion with researched evidence); and *conclusive* (clarifying the natural limits set upon the discussion by the other two functions). His article demonstrates each function by example and makes a solid case for their integration in teaching technical report writing. Several articles can help sharpen the teacher's sense of what technical writing is by showing how it developed. Handy to start with are three relatively brief essays: W. Earl Britton's "Some Effects of Science and Technology Upon Our Language" (1970), Thomas M. Sawyer's "Rhetoric in an Age of Science and Technology" (1972), and Donald Ross, Jr.'s "A Theory of the Function of Technical Writing" (1981). Indispensable, however, is Walter James Miller's "What Can the Technical Writer of the Past Teach the Technical Writer of Today?" (1975), an illuminating and scholarly essay that traces technical writing's "line of descent" from the Romans Vitruvius and Frontinus down through Herbert Hoover and aviation engineer Arthur E. Raymond. Miller's catalogue, and his analysis of it, clearly demonstrate technical writing's potential for variety and excellence. Stephen Gresham's "From Aristotle to Einstein" (1981) shows how to realize Miller's ideas in effective classroom assignments. More limited in focus, but also useful, is "Teaching the Tradition of Technical and Scientific Writing," by Roger E. Masse and Patrick M. Kelley (1977), which presents ways to reinforce Miller's argument by use of the Great Books series.

A natural supplement to knowing the chief characteristics of technical writing is knowing those of technical writers. "Why Engineers and Scientists Write As They Do," by G. E. Schindler, Jr. (1967), identifies a dozen stylistic features of technical style (at the sentence level), providing a compact guide to the kind of writing one can expect from technically trained students—and the kinds of practice they will need. Terry C. Smith's "What Bugs Engineers Most About Report Writing" (1976) is particularly valuable in clarifying those problems seen as important by practicing writers. Jack Selzer's "The Composing Processes of an Engineer" (1983) shows in detail how one professional writer (here a transportation engineer) works through his typical writing tasks; this case study has definite implications for classroom practice, and Selzer attends carefully to them.

Most teachers getting started in technical writing will know a good deal about writing in general and are likely to turn to the articles considered so far in this section for information about the unfamiliar, about the distinctive character of technical writing. But it is also helpful to recognize what is familiar in such writing and what already useful knowledge we bring to the teaching of it. Stephen M. Halloran's "Classical Rhetoric for the Engineering Student" (1971) emphasizes the inherent practicality of the classical rhetorical framework and shows how its systematic nature can make a strong appeal to the technical student's usual habits of mind—giving that student a fresh and perhaps more comprehensible picture of how writing works. Andrea A. Lunsford extends Halloran's ideas in "Classical Rhetoric and Technical Writing" (1976), and suggests ways in which classical rhetoric can help in the technical writing classroom. A strong article directed at engineers themselves is J. Richard Johnson's "Communications—the Engineer's Job" (1975), which argues that engineers fail as communicators by approaching writing superficially and underestimating both its difficulties and its worth. Johnson offers helpful solutions to these two problems.

Many teachers find themselves making the transition from traditional writing or literature courses into technical writing. Two articles—Charles R. Stratton's

"Technical Writing" (1979) and David N. Dobrin's "What's Difficult About Teaching Technical Writing" (1982)—offer some good general advice on that switch. Anyone curious to understand at least schematically the state of current theory in the teaching of writing should consult James A. Berlin's "Contemporary Composition" (1982). James L. Kinneavy's *A Theory of Discourse* (1971) is the classic attempt at a comprehensive survey of writing theory and practice. It cannot, of course, be described even summarily here, and should be absorbed slowly and completely; but the technical writing teacher may wish to begin by consulting its long chapter on "reference discourse."

Technical writing is a discipline strongly rooted in two worlds. It draws its matter and methods from both the university and professional practice. A fundamental sense of what this duality means to the technical writing teacher can be gleaned from William E. McCarron's "In the Business World and in Academe" (1980). McCarron suggests what skills our society will demand from the college-trained writer, and how classical rhetoric can help answer that demand without compromising academic convictions about writing's value and standards as a field of study. In "Teaching the Teacher What Government and Industry Want from Technical Writing" (1977), Paul V. Anderson shows how teachers can supplement a theoretical knowledge of technical writing with practical experience—and why this is important.

In neglecting technical writing's professional ties, one may fail to teach newly required skills or to teach currently needed skills well. Two articles worth consulting for information on this issue are Richard W. Schmelzer's "Technical Writing in the Eighties" (1974) and R. John Brockmann's "Taking a Second Look at Technical Communications Pedagogy" (1980). No one teacher can, of course, master every field in which his or her technical students will operate, and this limits just how "professional" a technical writing course can become. An established way to confront this difficulty without weakening the usefulness of the course is for the teacher to function as an uninformed but seriously inquisitive audience for the student's expert writing. Robert L. Brown and William E. McCarron, in "Writing Technical Reports for an Uninformed Audience" (1975), provide some good exercises designed to show the student how to make technical subjects accessible to such an audience. A range of suggestions on this topic is supplied by the December 1982 issue of the *IEEE Transactions on Professional Communication*, given over entirely to the special topic "Interpreting Technology for the Nonspecialist." The issue covers how such interpretation can be done in speech as well as writing, and offers a nine-page "Bibliography of Writings on Writing."

The Common Undergraduate Course

The common undergraduate technical writing course is a heterogeneous affair. While many schools restrict its enrollment to upperclassmen with a solid grounding in their majors, others do not, and so one may find oneself teaching the course to every level of student. It is likely one's students will be drawn from a wide range of scientific and technical fields, which will in their turn confront one with a range of specialized formats and technical criteria. Making the course work as a complex whole demands knowing some fundamental choices in (1) organization of the syllabus, (2) the actual writing tasks involved, and (3) the classically established assignments by which they are learned.

Vigorous common sense marks Marion K. Smith's "What Should Be Taught in the Technical Writing Course?" (1977), which is a useful starting point for discussing the technical writing syllabus. Smith realistically assesses the limitations natural to a general introductory course, the ways these affect our objectives (pushing us toward "training" more than "educating"), and the resources available for the job. A solid complement to Smith is Patricia Wright's "Five Skills Technical Writers Need" (1981), which carries the discussion beyond pure language skills to those areas (such as graphic presentation, task analysis of how readers will use a report) important to a technical document's success. Gerald J. Alred's "Developing a Technical Writing Theory and Pedagogy Course in an English Department" (1980) outlines (for the not often rich English Department) one course designed to begin training new teachers of technical writing. The essay emphasizes those rigorous scholarly criteria that must underlie such a course, and it suggests, in a solid syllabus, the range of skills that must be taught.

A number of informative course overviews offering both a rationale and a scheme of assignments have been published. The advent of *The Technical Writing Teacher* guarantees that more will continue to appear. As a brief, clear introduction to the basic one-semester course, John A. Walter's "Confessions of a Teacher of Technical Writing" (1975) is indispensable—and apt to remain so. Walter sketches out the convictions underlying his syllabus, and gives a week-by-week course outline. Twenty-five years of experience lie behind his discussion, but Walter has not forgotten what it feels like to begin teaching technical writing. This double sensitivity makes the article thoroughly human and convincing. Dennis E. Minor's "An Integrated Technical Writing Course" (1975) recommends structuring a course so that each assignment leads toward and contributes to a final long report. Particularly interesting is his suggestion of following that report with a short popular article on its topic and findings. In "Developing Assignments for Scientific and Technical Writing" (1977), James W. Souther stresses more single-mindedly than Walter or Minor the idea that assignments "must have more than a logical and pedagogical purpose. They must also have dimensions of reality" (p. 261). Souther is careful to explain the situational and functional criteria by which much technical writing is generated and measured, and to suggest effective assignments in line with them.

A handful of articles on teaching the basic course in the two-year college focuses the essential issues. Roy A. McGalliard's "The Function and Content of Technical Writing in the Two-Year College" (1977) defines technical writing's special aims within the community college and provides a syllabus meant to realize them. "Preparing to Teach a Technical Writing Course in the Two-Year College" (1979), by Nell Ann Pickett, beyond listing basic course materials and resources, offers two thought-provoking questionnaires, one of which is meant to help determine the needs of the college's technical departments, the other to establish student backgrounds within the course. A pair of articles by David E. Fear—"Notes on Coping with Heterogeneous Community College Technical Writing Courses" and "Relevancy and Revision" (1975)—are doubly useful in that a good deal of what they offer as appropriate for the community college classroom is serviceable on almost any level at which the basic course is taught.

Because a variety of levels is possible even within the basic course, selection of an appropriate textbook demands some care. Thomas L. Warren's "Technical Writing Textbook Selection" (1974) demonstrates how to make that selection systematically. But should the chance arise to teach technical writing to students of a single discipline, one may have trouble finding a sufficiently specialized textbook. "Compiling Mini-Texts for Specialized Technical Writing Courses" (1979) by Laurie G. Kirszner shows how one may then assemble a "textbook" from materials grounded in the students' discipline. The article's two appendices offer an example of a course outline built around such a text and list the preliminary materials for a technical writing course that Kirszner taught to pharmacy students. There are, of course, ways to supplement a traditional textbook, whether in a generalized or specialized introductory course, and Wayne A. Losano's "*Scientific American* in the Technical Writing Course" (1981) shows how a single well-written journal can aid in teaching a range of technical writing skills.

Most textbooks will, to varying degrees, stress the connections of technical writing with the professional world in which it operates. It may help in organizing a course and choosing a text to know something of that world's expectations. Here two articles written by professionals are especially helpful, giving a detailed picture of both the kind of writing done in technical fields and the determining context in which it is done: "The Demands of Industry on the Technical Writer" (1975) by David M. McLean, and "Written Technical Communication Involves More Than Writing" (1977) by Cliff Tierney, Thomas J. Miranda, and Robert E. Wilson. A third article, Charles E. Van Hagen's "The Long and Short of Technical Writing Courses" (1971) considers technical writing completely outside of the academic context and clarifies professional writing standards in describing a variety of possible on-the-job courses, running from a one-day seminar to a semester-long class. Useful as a specific example of how one course was taught is Max Weber's "Teaching an Effective Course in Technical Writing in Private Industry" (1975).

Some issues that are irrelevant when organizing many university courses are commonly raised in connection with technical writing: team teaching, alternative classroom practices, and cassette grading. Sawyer's *Technical and Professional Communication* contains two important articles that discuss how technical writing teachers can draw upon the expertise of those outside their field: "Toward Teaching a New Engineering Professionalism" (1977) by Ben F. Barton and

Marthalee S. Barton, and "Technical Communication" (1977) by Victoria M. Winkler. Both argue forcefully the natural connection between good analytical thinking and good communications in engineering, and they assess realistically the problems and advantages of cooperative teaching. While both are also geared to senior level courses, they make suggestions that could profitably be adapted for use at lower levels. Why such cooperation should begin early is carefully explained by Ruth Mitchell in "Shared Responsibility" (1981). Her examination balances a sense of technical writing's distinctive character with a sense of what ties it to the larger discipline of writing. She then derives several principles to establish the necessity of interdepartmental cooperation. Alternative classroom practices in technical writing tend to be concerned with making students work together, a reflection of later on-the-job conditions. Charles R. Stratton's "A Project Team Approach to Technical Writing in the Classroom" (1973), and Gerald J. Gross's "Group Projects in the Technical Writing Course" (1981) furnish a basic introduction to cooperative assignments, their procedures, benefits, and problems. Ken Kiyama and Ellen Nold, in "Engineering Students Teach Each Other to Write" (1979), describe the Stanford School of Engineering's Communications Project, in which well-qualified engineering students work as writing tutors in undergraduate engineering courses. Finally, the procedure of cassette grading—recommended by several technical writing theorists as a means of creating a real, reactive audience for the writer, and of providing more extensive correction—is comprehensively examined in a collection of essays edited by Charles R. Stratton. His *Teaching Technical Writing* (1979) is Anthology No. 2 in a series published by the Association of Teachers of Technical Writing; its essays, drawn from several journals, are listed separately in this chapter's references.

In the technical writing classroom, we teach in part by applying familiar and universal writing standards (clarity, development, coherence, mechanical accuracy) to a specialized content. And that content does affect how we apply those standards—the details by which each is realized, what emphasis each receives. For example, in technical writing format tends to play a larger role in establishing coherence than it does in many other kinds of writing; mechanical accuracy often involves numbers and tables, as well as grammar; clarity will often depend upon graphical elements, in addition to accurate vocabulary and apt style. All such differences find general expression in a specially intense concern with audience analysis and adaptation. Clearly, to teach technical writing well demands not just that we work to develop a basic grasp of technical subject matter, but also that we extend and adjust our understanding of how good writing is generated and measured.

Several essays lay the basic groundwork for that effort. Herbert B. Michaelson's "Structure, Content, and Meaning in Technical Manuscripts" (1968) provides a concise analysis of the overall qualities that distinguish a well-written technical report. He recommends three general criteria—readability and intelligibility, effective expression, logical development of technical concepts—and demonstrates in detail how they may be met. Michaelson is especially helpful on the connections between structure and content, and on the variety of purposes possible in technical writing. Patricia A. Sullivan, in "Teaching the Writing Process in Scientific and Technical Writing Classes" (1980), fills a gap common in the textbooks; she carefully describes strategies for teaching the student how to *generate* those ideas for which the texts provide formats. Sullivan presents a flexible five-step procedure by which individual assignments may be carried out. She illustrates it with four sample topics: title writing, introductions, resumés, and instructions. Useful as a complement to her essay is an article which she cites (and advances the work of): Dennis R. Hall's more theoretical "The Role of Invention in Technical Writing" (1976). Victoria M. Winkler's "The Role of Models in Technical and Scientific Writing" (1983) examines the two key models (structural and inventional) that inform our teaching, and shows that we must understand how they determine the effectiveness of our classroom practices and how they can be used well in combination. Finally, "Completing the Bridge" (1976), by J. C. Mathes and Dwight W. Stevenson, argues that we can and should close that natural distance between classroom and industrial communications activities, by sharpening our sense of the differences in audience and purpose mandated by those different contexts. Mathes and Stevenson offer procedures to help with this task and discuss ways to carry them out.

There are few important discussions of technical writing—its content, its forms, its intentions—that do not consider its relationship with audience. Whether composed to explain or instruct or advise, technical writing is most often writing that leads to a decision and an action; it is writing that will be *used* by the reader. And so the technical writer must give special attention to that reader's needs and abilities. Anthology No. 1 from the Association of Teachers of Technical Writing, *Teaching Technical Writing* (edited by Paul V. Anderson, 1980), offers five essential articles that speak purely to the topic. Four deal with what Anderson describes as a traditional but intensifying trend: "advising students (and other writers) to learn about their reader in greater detail than was thought necessary in the past." The fifth, a compact annotated bibliography, clarifies an emerging trend: "an increasing desire to discover what other disciplines [such as psychology and sociology] can teach technical writing about audience analysis and adaptation" (p. v). Anderson's anthology provides invaluable suggestions on how we can, in fundamental, general ways, make audience analysis a part of the technical writing course; this effort leaves the collection little space to develop detailed individual assignments to teach the student a fully informed awareness of audience. One of the best places to begin pursuing information about such assignments is Elizabeth Tebeaux's "Getting More Mileage Out of Audience Analysis" (1982). The article furnishes specific methods for keeping audience analysis in continual focus throughout the technical writing course, and provides informative examples of student work resulting from such methods. "Analysis of the Same Subject in Diverse Periodicals" (1982), by Annette N. Bradford and Merrill D. Whitburn, describes an assignment ideal for both in-class discussion and an out-of-class essay. It is completely sketched in, with useful questions and illustrations. Narrower in their focus, but helpful in developing the concept specifically, are an essay by Gretchen H. Schoff—"Writing for John Q. Public" (1981)—and one by Nancy Roundy—"Team-Teaching Technical Writing" (1982).

The best way to introduce students to the primary concerns and procedures of technical writing, so that they can logically build upon their first knowledge, is the issue of another Association of Teachers of Technical Writing anthology (No. 3) and of several notable articles. *Teaching Technical Writing* (1979), edited by Merrill D. Whitburn, brings together five essays that report theoretical models and practical exercises useful in giving impetus and direction to an entire semester's work. This collection can be well supplemented by three independent articles. Dean G. Hall's "Technical Writing Class" (1981) offers a more whimsical, though no less forceful and convincing, approach than the anthology pieces. Through an in-class exercise based on the construction (and active exchange) of paper airplanes, Hall shows how one may quickly convince students (a) that technical writing is often tougher and more time-consuming than the process it explains, (b) that audience awareness is a central fact of technical writing's existence, and (c) that Britton's one-meaning standard is an excellent working measure to keep in mind in beginning to produce technical documents. "Readings in Technical Writing" (1975), by Steve Gresham and Carey Kaltenbach, moves beyond the first day, through the first two weeks of the semester, with an assignment made to help the student "form a working understanding of technical writing before being immersed in it" (p. 4). The essay recommends distributing to the class a four-category selected bibliography (a sample is included), concerning the theory of technical writing, its practice, its history as a discipline, and its special professionalism. Students then report individually, or through a panel discussion, on their readings. In either case they gain a direct overview of their new subject, becoming directly involved in examining its nature and making a start on developing a professional attitude. Finally, an article by Patricia A. Sullivan and David D. Roberts, "A Case for Diagnosis in Technical Writing" (1981), addresses one way to solve, at the start of the course, a problem commonly faced by the *teacher*. The variety of student majors and abilities with which the instructor of an introductory technical writing class is usually faced can explode the assumptions behind a well-planned syllabus. The diagnostic exercise Sullivan and Roberts suggest (a memo on the student's expected communications needs in his or her field) can provide sound guidelines for structuring the course, while leading the class directly into common introductory ideas about technical writing.

All good writing shares such common and interdependent qualities as clarity, coherence, and logically developed structure. How these qualities may be demonstrated to one's students in connection with the special content of technical writing is, in a sense, the unifying subject of all our pedagogical theorizing. And, artificial as it may be to consider any of these qualities in isolation, it is also necessary and helpful, especially in the introductory course. That clarity which technical writing pursues at the level of word choice and sentence structure is George R. Klare's subject in "Readable Technical Writing" (1977), a basic introduction to what help readability formulas can provide the writer. Both past and current practice in technical writing have leaned heavily upon metaphor for clarity, and John Sterling Harris's "Metaphor in Technical Writing" (1975) shows its continuing practicality. The narrow topic of Thomas N. Huckin's "Teaching the Use of English Articles to Nonnative Speakers in Technical Writing Classes" (1981) disguises a methodology (instruction through flow diagrams) that merits widespread attention. Coherence begins to be a central issue on the paragraph level, and here Jack Selzer's "Another Look at Paragraphs in Technical Writing" (1980) offers useful advice, grounded in contemporary research and theory, on improving the student's grasp of paragraph uses and construction. A helpful pragmatic supplement to Selzer is Thomas L. Kent's "Six Suggestions for Teaching Paragraph Cohesion" (1983). Fundamental teaching strategies for the larger issues of overall document structure are clarified in Paul V. Anderson's "Organizing Is Not Enough!" (1981). Anderson's essential point is that the technical writer must provide both organization *and* clear signals (by additions to the text or rearrangements of it) of how that organization works. A good selection of examples amplifies Anderson's discussion. In "Revising Functional Documents" (1983), Linda Flower, John R. Hayes, and Heidi Swarts examine how complex, expository federal regulations are revised to serve functional purposes—those, for example, of readers interested in acting in compliance with such regulations, or applying for services offered under them. The essay, a model of how empirical research can yield durable classroom theory and practice, isolates the "scenario principle": "that functional prose should be structured around a *human agent* performing *actions* in a particularized *situation*" (p. 42). The traditional tasks we associate with general document evaluation and revision are compactly presented in two solidly argued essays: E. F. Boomhower's "Producing Good Technical Communications Requires Two Types of Editing" (1975), and Mary Fran Buehler's "Creative Revision" (1976).

As technical writing developed into an academic field, certain assignments became established as essential. Most introductory courses (and many advanced ones) will teach the student about writing technical definitions and instructions; they will teach the efficient use of library resources, the fundamentals of graphics, and the elements of effective oral communication; and they will teach the writing of the abstract, the formal proposal, and the major report. Essays about all of these assignments will appear, of course, in this chapter's References, but it would be helpful for most teachers to have some of the better articles on these assignments listed here by type.

Definitions and instructions are often taught in connection with such larger topics as proposal or major report writing. Still, it can be useful to begin by covering them independently. Two articles that do this well are Elizabeth Tebeaux's "Using the Extended Definition Paper to Teach Organization" (1980), and Donald H. Cunningham and John H. Mitchell's "Teaching the Writing of Instructions" (1981).

Making the library a productive source of information (even inspiration) concerns the technical writing teacher immediately in the introductory course. Four articles offer excellent aid here: "The Information Resources Report" (1979), by Bernard Krimm; "The Importance of Following Up Library Instruction" (1979), by Elizabeth Tebeaux; "Teaching *Science Citation Index* for a Library Orientation" (1979), by Eileen Pritchard; and "Using Technical Information Resources" (1981), by Maurita Peterson Holland and Leslie Ann Olsen.

Technical illustration is a topic of book-length complexity, but one can, in the basic course, convey at least a rudimentary sense of its uses and procedures. The most wide-ranging introduction to graphics is provided by an *IEEE Transactions Professional Communication* Special Issue on the topic (June 1982). It can be well supplemented by these four articles: "Visual/Graphic Aids for the Technical Report" (1979), by Robert Cury; "Technical Illustration" (1981), by Charles E. Beck and William J. Wallisch, Jr.; "Using Computer Printouts to Teach Analysis and Graphics" (1981), by Elizabeth Tebeaux; and "A Primer on Tables and Figures" (1983), by Alan G. Gross.

Effective oral communication of technical information, whether in the daily on-the-job context of individual conversation and small-group discussion, or the more formal context of a public technical speech, is as important in most technical fields as effective written communication. Again a Special Issue of the *IEEE Transactions in Professional Communication*, this one on "Public Speaking For Engineers and Scientists" (March 1980), provides a diversified introduction. An exceptional single-article introduction is William E. McCarron's "Oral Briefing Versus Technical Report" (1981). Also helpful are Herman A. Estrin and Edward J. Monahan's "Effective Oral Presentation of Scientific and Technical Information" (1978), and Peter M. Schiff's "Speech" (1980).

The abstract, proposal, and formal report are naturally interdependent forms in technical writing, and one should read of them with a sense of that connectedness in mind. Essential background on the abstract can be gathered from Melvin F. Orth's "Abstracting for the Writer" (1972), Andrew A. Sekey's "Abstract, Conclusions and Summaries" (1973), and Andrew K. Clark's "The Abstract Way to Concrete Writing" (1981). Like the abstract, the proposal teaches much about technical writing in general. How it does so is well argued by Dennis E. Minor's "Teaching the Technical Writing Proposal" (1979) and George F. Kennedy's "Teaching Formal Proposals" (1983). The formal report might best be viewed not so much as a separate technical writing form as a particular integration, as variable as the circumstances out of which it grows, of all the diverse forms we teach. Perhaps partly for that reason, one will find few articles focused exclusively on the major report (most often approached full-scale through textbooks). For a basic sense of what such reports entail one can, however, turn to the best articles written on classroom assignments that simulate professional communications activities. Five useful essays on the subject are: "Writing as

Engineers and Writing in Class'' (1977), by Peter R. Klaver; "A Simulated Writing Experience" (1979), by James E. Spears; and, the articles in Stevenson's *Courses, Components, and Exercises in Technical Communication* (1981), "Communication Strategy in Professional Writing," by Linda S. Flower, "A Professional Scenario for the Technical Writing Classroom," by Lawrence J. Johnson, and "The Case Method" by Ben F. Barton and Marthalee S. Barton.

After the First Course

In his 1978 essay, "Mapping the Unexplored Area," Dwight W. Stevenson asserted that, as an academic discipline, technical writing had reached the point where it could "shift its attention from defending itself to developing itself" (p. 194). Increases in enrollment and in the number of technical writing programs obviously bear Stevenson out in one way. But more meaningful corroboration comes from the intellectual activity which is answering those new demands. In two areas—the topics of this section—technical writing is developing that coherence essential to an academic discipline: program and course development, and fundamental research.

Stevenson's article goes on from its primary assertion to demonstrate the range of courses necessary in a technical writing program, and to suggest a framework by which they can be integrated. He generates a matrix based upon four possible audiences (self, one, homogeneous many, diverse many) and three purposes (to inform, to affect, to effect). Within this matrix, we can isolate the proper instructional objectives of individual courses; considering the matrix as a whole, we can analyze the underlying logic of an entire program. The skills and information a program would have to teach in order to produce a qualified professional in technical writing is the focus of Marguerite F. D'Amico's "Educating the Technical Communicator" (1971). D'Amico considers the difficulties in founding a curriculum that must draw upon a double background in the sciences and in communications, and she recommends a basic core of study in science and technology, theoretical and practical communications, and social/behavioral psychology. James W. Souther's "The Expanding Dimensions of Technical Writing" (1971) reports briefly on what its author learned from setting up a Master's program in Medical and Technical Communication. While narrower in scope than Stevenson's or D'Amico's essay, this article does offer a good look at how specific programs are created. More importantly, it shows that "the ingredients for a professional technical communications education are all around us on campus" (p. 187)—a point not often enough realized by those searching for the resources around which to build a program.

A fully developed program means choices in course content and classroom method beyond those available in the introductory course. One effective and popular way of leading the student from basic understanding into the larger dimensions of technical writing has been the interdisciplinary course. In "An Interdisciplinary Course in Technical Communication" (1976), Deborah C. Andrews describes the logistics, content, and results of an advanced interdisciplinary course taught at Ohio State University, combining technical writing with metallurgical engineering. Andrews analyzes the basic problems any technical writing course entails, recommends ways by which to solve them, and shows how the design and materials of that course sought to embody those solutions. Anita Brostoff's "The Functional Writing Model in Technical Writing Courses" (1981) presents another significant approach suited to teaching technical writing within the advanced context of the technical course. Brostoff and her colleagues at Carnegie-Mellon University have isolated four central concepts relevant to both individual student writing problems and the general demands of a given technical field: (1) the organizing idea; (2) the reader's frame of reference; (3) forecasting—openly predicting a document's organization and sequence; and (4) continuous forecasting—openly showing a document's line of reasoning. An innovative and unusual essay, David Hamilton's "Interdisciplinary Writing" (1980), tackles interdisciplinary thinking within the fundamental process of invention. Hamilton teaches science writing through what he terms serious parodies of science, empirical problems that can be solved with simple supplies—and exacting thought. By these he can demonstrate to students with a variety of expertise the intimate and necessary relationship between language and scientific work. Finally, "Teaching Technical Communication at the Graduate Level" (1983), by Janet H. Potvin and Robert L. Woods, explains how team teaching can work at the highest levels of technical study.

Textbooks and anthologies such as Mathes and Stevenson's *Designing Technical Reports* (1976), and Debra Journet and Julie Lepick Kling's *Readings for Technical Writers* (1984), seem to be the best sources to consult in order to understand the content and procedures of technical writing, both at and beyond the introductory level. Few authors would try to treat so complex a topic as the advanced course within the limitations of a journal essay. Still, several articles cited earlier in this chapter—by Mathes and Stevenson (1976), by Stevenson (1978), and by D'Amico (1971)—clarify some of the options available to the upper courses. Two further essays give extremely valuable descriptions of what the syllabuses for particular advanced courses can be. Thomas M. Sawyer's "A Syllabus for a Course in Scientific and Technical Communication" (1973) describes the make-up of a senior course in technical writing for students of Michigan's College of Engineering. Robert Scott Kellner's "A Necessary and Natural Sequel" (1982) argues for a course in which technical writing skills are completed by a detailed knowledge of language editing, formats, graphics, layout and design, and publications production.

Two teaching strategies that may be adapted to the basic level but are possibly more useful beyond it are the discipline-specific course and the writing/tutoring center designed for technical students. John H. Mitchell's "Three Prescriptive Approaches to Teaching Factual Communications" (1976) gives a brief overview of three upperclass courses geared to particular majors: expository writing for Environmental Design majors; technical writing for engineers; and technical writing for MBA candidates. Of particular value here, Mitchell provides a text, description, and philosophy for each course. Two solid brief articles on courses geared to Engineering Technology students appear in Sawyer's *Technical and Professional Communication* (1977): Terrence J. Glenn and Marcus M. Green's "Educational Objectives for an Engineering Technology Technical Writing Course," and Harriet Hogan's "A Technical Writing Course for Engineering Technical Students." Also worth consulting is the article by Kirszner (1979) cited earlier. Jennie Skerl's "A Writing Center for Engineering Students" (1980) describes the organization and procedures of Rensselaer Polytechnic's writing center. Skerl reports briefly on some typical case studies and calls attention to two important ways in which the technical writing lab differs from most others: style replaces grammar as the central skill taught, and tutors specially qualified in technology and pedagogy (as well as writing) are essential. Muriel Harris, in "Supplementary Writing Instruction for Engineering Students" (1983), explains the innovative self-paced course in writing instruction developed at Purdue's writing lab for students who have completed freshman English but still lack the skills to do well in technical writing. The course is addressed, through self-instruction modules, to eight key deficiencies common to technical students who just got by at the freshman level, and so arrive at upperclass writing courses still unprepared.

In 1980, Paul V. Anderson affirmed that technical communication is really not one discipline but three: the profession of technical communication; its teaching; and its theory. Anderson's article was titled "The Need for Better Research in Technical Communication," and it suggested that the second and third of those disciplines must substantially improve their research activities. They needed to generate research that could give them a more coherent sense of their individual identities and that could be translated into informed, effective practice.

To some extent, the beginnings of such research had preceded Anderson's argument, especially in the teaching of technical writing. Here solid primary work has begun to be done in three important areas: theoretical models, audience response, and writer behavior.

James L. Kinneavy's *A Theory of Discourse* (1971) remains the essential book-length grounding in the issues and ideas from which a systematic framework in the theory of writing pedagogy can be built. The most useful compact account of its immediate relevance to technical writing is Elizabeth Harris's "Applications of Kinneavy's *Theory of Discourse* to Technical Writing" (1979). Harris demonstrates that Kinneavy's thought (1) can help clarify what technical writing is; (2) offers a theory of pragmatic writing procedures flexible and complete enough to answer questions inaccessible to the usual approach to technical writing by modes; (3) provides an intellectual depth often lacking in writing courses; and (4) brings new unity to technical writing's diverse concerns with audience. More narrowly focused, Steven Walton Lynn's "Kinneavy, Mathes, Mumford, and Lynn" (1980) supplies one practical example of Kinneavy's usefulness to a common technical writing mode. But to see how Kinneavy's larger concerns look when approached primarily from the technical writing perspective, one should consult Stevenson's "Toward a Rhetoric of Scientific and Technical Discourse" (1977). Stevenson cautions us that when undertaking our research, we keep in mind three salient criteria: that scientific and technical rhetoric be inductively developed; that it look to all rhetorical considerations (such as invention, arrangement); and that its results be constantly tested in actual writing situations.

Research into the connected ideas of audience response to technical writing, and audience analysis by the technical writer, is a complex area to which two articles provide a useful introduction. The first is Ruth Mitchell and Mary Taylor's "The Integrating Perspective" (1979), which proposes a teaching framework grounded in what research among psychology, linguistics, and the social sciences can tell us about communications effectiveness—a framework centered on writing as "a means of acting upon a receiver" (p. 250). The second is Richard M. Davis's "Experimental Research in the Effectiveness of Technical Writing" (1975). Davis reports on an experiment to determine, with a range of audiences, how variables within a 3,800-word technical description affected reader comprehension. The results allow him to isolate certain elements of a communication whose manipulation directly affects comprehensibility. A valuable continuation of Davis's inquiry can be found in Lester Faigley and Stephen Witte's "Topical Focus in Technical Writing" (1983), which analyzes an experiment to discover whether assigning topics to grammatical subject positions affects reader perception and recall of material. In this case the results indicate ways to teach writing that will help the reader grasp the topic clearly, and they suggest readability criteria beyond measures of vocabulary and sentence-length analysis. Readability occupies a distinct place in the larger discussion of audience, and two articles in *New Essays in Technical and Scientific Communication* bring us up to date on the current state of its theory. Jack Selzer's "What Constitutes a 'Readable' Style?" (1983) presents a strong challenge to the traditional valuation of readability formulas, and outlines research opportunities in the field. Thomas N. Huckin's "A Cognitive Approach to Readability" (1983) samples recent research in cognitive psychology that has direct bearing on readability assessment.

The actual (rather than theoretically "prescribed") methods by which writers generate their documents promise to furnish technical writing one of its most creative and demanding areas of empirical research. Articles cited earlier in this chapter, by Schindler (1967) and Selzer (1983), find a useful supplement in "Studying Writing in Non-Academic Settings" (1983), by Lee Odell, Dixie Goswami, Anne Herrington, and Doris Quick—an essay admittedly notable more in opening and establishing research avenues than in confirming already verified conclusions. Finally, Janice Lauer's "Heuristics and Composition" (1970) argues the importance of grounding any metatheory of rhetoric in what psychology can teach us of cognition and creativity, and supplies in her article a "Psychological Bibliography on Heuristics."

Some Special Issues

Technical writing has only lately attained full academic standing. Its oldest traditions reach back not into the long history of debate on the university's purpose and curricula, but into long-established and mostly practical human pursuits for which accurate communication has been a central need. In taking on new identity as an academic discipline, it has brought into an unaccustomed context the living core and spirit of those traditions. But within that context it becomes, quite naturally, an element of the old and honorable and never finally resolved debate about the aims of education. As a fresh element, technical writing has much to offer the university; as a keeper of flexible and informed intellectual standards, the university has much to offer technical writing. Both can profit by confronting what is unfamiliar, maybe even disconcerting, in the other.

The general exchange between technical writing's traditions of action and the academy's traditions of contemplation will be complex, many-directional, and continually open-ended. What must be recognized in the early stages of this exchange are those special concerns within the university curriculum that technical writing at once becomes entangled in. By virtue of being a form of writing, technical writing inevitably attaches to an already long-studied university subject. And so it must in some way define itself in relation to (which can, of course, mean against) the liberal arts framework out of which writing has been taught and theorized about.

This issue has immediate, pragmatic implications; how it is decided upon will determine whom we choose to put into the technical writing classroom and exactly what we expect them to do there. The most succinct and clear-headed expression of the argument for keeping technical writing separate from the usual liberal arts context is "Technical Writing" (1979), by J. C. Mathes, Dwight W. Stevenson, and Peter Klaver. Their conclusion that engineering faculty alone should teach the course is based on three assumptions: that English departments would mistakenly approach technical writing out of their traditional concern with affective communication; that they would base their teaching on inapplicable principles of classical rhetoric and writer self-awareness; and that English teachers are essentially undertrained in the teaching of writing. Those assumptions are arguable; Mathes had himself challenged them seven years earlier in "Rhetoric and the Engineering Approach" (1972). But the questions they raise cannot be blankly dismissed. In terms of classroom practice, two valuable answers come from Carolyn R. Miller's "A Humanistic Rationale for Technical Writing" (1979) and Elizabeth Harris's "In Defense of the Liberal Arts Approach to Technical Writing" (1982). Miller demonstrates the positivist presuppositions that have grounded the purely technical approach to writing. She shows how they cripple technical writing in the common classroom areas of evaluation, invention, and audience analysis. Harris points out ways in which the traditional humanistic understanding of language is more truly attuned to the widest dynamics of written communication and avoids the limitations of a completely "practical" perspective. In terms of theoretical analysis (provided also in part by Miller and Harris), David Hamilton's "Writing Science" (1980) makes an eloquent case for "an awareness of writing's creative force upon science itself," for seeing writing as "an integral act of science" (p. 32). Important to remember, however the debate unfolds, is that each side is honestly concerned with more than its own academic aggrandizement. The smug mean-spiritedness of such an article as John H. Mitchell's "It's a Craft Course" (1976) will not serve technical writing's cause. Two sensible, moderate articles remind us of just how importantly the two sides are connected: Thomas M. Sawyer's "The Common Law of Science and the Common Law of Literature" (1975), and Jay R. Gould's "Bringing Teachers of Technical Writing and Teachers of Literature Closer Together" (1979).

What all this can mean when focused in a limited question can be clearly seen in the arguments that set technical writing against freshman composition. In "The Trouble with Technical Writing Is Freshman Composition" (1975), W. Earl Britton advocates replacing the usual freshman English course with technical writing, which he sees as teaching more precise and real-world communication skills. The strongest direct response to this position is Merrill D. Whitburn's "Against Substituting Technical Writing for Freshman English" (1975). Whitburn unmasks some key errors in Britton's perceptions of freshman composition, and suggests how the two courses can be fitted into a logical sequence. C. G. Bruckmann seeks to reconcile the two positions in "What Is in a Name?" (1976), arguing that they are not really in essential conflict. Bruckmann emphasizes the different concerns which technical writing and freshman English address, the different problems they seek to cure, and, like Whitburn, he suggests how the two courses can be designed to work in concert. Precisely how that integration might proceed is described in detail by Elizabeth Tebeaux in "Technical Writing Is *Not* Enough" (1980). Beyond the specific recommendations it provides, her essay (like Sawyer's and Gould's, just cited) again helpfully reminds us of the necessary points of cooperation between distinct but interdependent parties of thought within the university.

The benefits of cooperation are clearly visible in one university venture that has become of increasing importance to students: internships. Esther M. Gloe's "Setting Up Internships in Technical Writing" (1983) is the best basic guide to the subject. It gives an essential bibliography, an overview of available programs, ways to go about finding employers, and the standard problems and successes of internship. "Internships in Technical Writing" (1977), by Leon C. Hull, examines a graduate-level internship program with the U.S. Naval Underwater Systems Center, reporting on the problems which both student and sponsor face in any limited employment/learning situation. Finally, for information on how to create an internship program solely from resources within the university, James P. Zappen's "A Mini-Internship in a Professional Writing Course" (1977) is invaluable.

The topic of internship leads us naturally back into that professional world where technical writing lives the largest portion of its life. And perhaps we should be recalled, in the end, to the great goods that history has put in technical writing's charge. Jacques Richardson's "What the Public Needs to Know About Science and Technology" (1981) brings us the global overview of a writer who edits UNESCO's quarterly journal *Impact of Science on Society*. He lays before us eight key areas, from Feeding the World and Natural Resources, to Energy, Absorbing Military Research into the Civil Sector, and the Environment. He convinces us of the technical writer's fundamental significance in bringing us information by which we can consciously preserve our world. To ignore such truth, to slight the medium that makes it available to us, is to risk unconscious collaboration with our own extinction.

References

Alred, Gerald J. "Developing a Technical Writing Theory and Pedagogy Course in an English Department." *J Tech Writ Comm*, 10 (1980), 337–45.

Anderson, Paul V. "Background and Resources for New Teachers of Technical Writing." *J Tech Writ Comm*, 7 (1977), 223–33.

———. "The Need for Better Research in Technical Communication." *J Tech Writ Comm*, 10 (1980), 271–82.

———. "Organizing Is Not Enough!" In *Courses, Components, and Exercises in Technical Communication*. Ed. Dwight W. Stevenson. Urbana: National Council of Teachers of English (NCTE), 1981, pp. 163–84.

———. "Teaching the Teacher What Government and Industry Want from Technical Writing." In *Technical and Professional Communication*. Ed. Thomas M. Sawyer. Ann Arbor: Professional Communication Press, 1977, pp. 65–78.

———, ed. *Teaching Technical Writing: Teaching Audience Analysis and Adaptation*. Anthology No. 1, Association of Teachers of Technical Writing, 1980.

———, R. John Brockmann, and Carolyn R. Miller, eds. *New Essays in Technical and Scientific Communication: Research, Theory, Practice*. Farmingdale, N.Y.: Baywood, 1983.

Andrews, Deborah C. "An Interdisciplinary Course in Technical Communication." *Tech Comm*, 24, No. 1 (1976), 12–15.

———. "Teaching Writing in the Engineering Classroom." *Eng Educ*, 66 (1975), 169–74.

Barton, Ben F., and Marthalee S. Barton. "The Case Method: Bridging the Gap Between Engineering Student and Professional." In *Courses, Components, and Exercises in Technical Communication*. Ed. Dwight W. Stevenson. Urbana: NCTE, 1981, pp. 22–33.

———. "Toward Teaching a New Engineering Professionalism: A Joint Instructional Effort in Technical Design and Communication." In *Technical and Professional Communication*. Ed. Thomas M. Sawyer. Ann Arbor: Professional Communication Press, 1977, pp. 119–28.

Beck, Charles E., and William J. Wallisch, Jr. "Technical Illustration." In *Courses, Components, and Exercises in Technical Communication*. Ed. Dwight W. Stevenson. Urbana: NCTE, 1981, pp. 122–31.

Berlin, James A. "Contemporary Composition: The Major Pedagogical Theories." *CE*, 44 (1982), 765–77.

Blackman, Carolyn M. "A Bibliography of Resources for Beginning Teachers of Technical Writing." In *Technical and Professional Communication*. Ed. Thomas M. Sawyer. Ann Arbor: Professional Communication Press, 1977, pp. 49–64.

Boomhower, E. F. "Producing Good Technical Communications Requires Two Types of Editing." *J Tech Writ Comm*, 5 (1975), 277–81.

Bradford, Annette N., and Merrill D. Whitburn. "Analysis of the Same Subject in Diverse Periodicals: One Method for Teaching Audience Adaptation." *Tech Writ Teach*, 9 (1982), 58–64.

Britton, W. Earl. "Some Effects of Science and Technology Upon Our Language." *CCC* 21 (1970), 342–46.

———. "The Trouble with Technical Writing Is Freshman Composition." In *The Teaching of Technical Writing*. Ed. Donald H. Cunningham and Herman A. Estrin. Urbana: NCTE, 1975, pp. 70–74.

———. "What Is Technical Writing?" In *The Teaching of Technical Writing*. Ed. Donald H. Cunningham and Herman A. Estrin. Urbana: NCTE, 1975, pp. 9–14.

Brockmann, R. John. "Taking a Second Look at Technical Communications Pedagogy." *J Tech Writ Comm*, 10 (1980), 283–91.

Brostoff, Anita. "The Functional Writing Model in Technical Writing Courses." In *Courses, Components, and Exercises in Technical Communication*. Ed. Dwight W. Stevenson. Urbana; NCTE, 1981, pp. 65–73.

Brouse, Albert J. "Clarity in Science Writing Is Not Enough." *J Tech Writ Comm*, 1 (1971), 73–78.

Brown, Robert L., and William E. McCarron. "Writing Technical Reports for an Uninformed Audience." *Tech Writ Teach*, 3 (1975), 1–7.

Bruckmann, C. G. "What Is in a Name? Freshman English or Technical Writing." *J Tech Writ Comm*, 6 (1976), 187–93.

Buehler, Mary Fran. "Creative Revision: From Rough Draft to Published Paper." *IEEE Trans Prof Comm*, 19, No. 2 (1976), 26–32.

Clark, Andrew K. "The Abstract Way to Concrete Writing." *J Tech Writ Comm*, 11 (1981), 131–38.

Corey, Jim. "Assignment: Journal Analysis—A Paradigm for Technical Writing." *Tech Writ Teach*, 8 (1981), 80–82.

Corey, Robert L. "Rhetoric and Technical Writing: Black Magic or Science?" *Tech Comm*, 26, No. 4 (1978), 2–6.

Covington, David H., and Hugh F. Keedy. "A Technical Communication Course Using Peer Evaluation of Reports." *Eng Educ*, 69 (1979), 417–19.

Cunningham, Donald H., and Herman A. Estrin, eds. *The Teaching of Technical Writing*. Urbana: NCTE, 1975.

———, and John H. Mitchell. "Teaching the Writing of Instructions." In *Courses, Components, and Exercises in Technical Communication*. Ed. Dwight W. Stevenson. Urbana: NCTE, 1981, pp. 136–43.

Cury, Robert. "Visual/Graphic Aids for the Technical Report." *J Tech Writ Comm*, 9 (1979), 287–91.

D'Amico, Marguerite F. "Educating the Technical Communicator." *J Tech Writ Comm*, 1 (1971), 11–16.

Dandridge, Edmund P., Jr. "Notes Toward a Definition of Technical Writing." In *The*

Teaching of Technical Writing. Ed. Donald H. Cunningham and Herman A. Estrin. Urbana: NCTE, 1975, pp. 15–20.

Davis, Richard M. "Experimental Research in the Effectiveness of Technical Writing." In *The Teaching of Technical Writing*. Ed. Donald H. Cunningham and Herman A. Estrin. Urbana: NCTE, 1975, pp. 109–22.

————. "Technical Writing in Industry and Government." *J Tech Writ Comm*, 7 (1977), 235–42.

Dobrin, David N. "What's Difficult About Teaching Technical Writing." *CE*, 44 (1982), 135–40.

————. "What's Technical About Technical Writing?" In *New Essays in Technical and Scientific Communication*. Ed. Paul V. Anderson, R. John Brockmann, and Carolyn R. Miller. Farmingdale, N.Y.: Baywood, 1983, pp. 227–50.

Douglas, George H. "The Common Diseases of Technical Writing." *J Tech Writ Comm*, 4 (1974), 37–46.

————. "The Informational Sketch—A Major Vice of the Technical Writer." *J Tech Writ Comm*, 12 (1982), 7–13.

Edlefsen, Karen A. "An Annotated Bibliography of the *Journal of Technical Writing and Communication*." *J Tech Writ Comm*, 9 (1979), 69–94.

Estrin, Herman A. "Six Innovative Methods of Teaching Technical Writing." *J Tech Writ Comm*, 9 (1979), 185–95.

————, and Edward J. Monahan. "Effective Oral Presentation of Scientific and Technical Information." In *Directions in Technical Writing and Communications*. Ed. Jay R. Gould. Farmingdale, N.Y.: Baywood, 1978, pp. 57–68.

Faigley, Lester, and Stephen Witte. "Topical Focus in Technical Writing." In *New Essays in Technical and Scientific Communication*. Ed. Paul V. Anderson, R. John Brockmann, and Carolyn R. Miller. Farmingdale, N.Y.: Baywood, 1983, pp. 59–68.

Fear, David E. "Notes on Coping with Heterogeneous Community College Technical Writing Courses." In *The Teaching of Technical Writing*. Ed. Donald H. Cunningham and Herman A. Estrin. Urbana: NCTE, 1975, pp. 34–38.

————. "Relevancy and Revision." In *The Teaching of Technical Writing*. Ed. Donald H. Cunningham and Herman A. Estrin. Urbana: NCTE, 1975, pp. 86–94.

Flower, Linda S. "Communication Strategy in Professional Writing: Teaching a Rhetorical Case." In *Courses, Components, and Exercises in Technical Communication*. Ed. Dwight W. Stevenson. Urbana: NCTE, 1981, pp. 34–46.

————, John R. Hayes, and Heidi Swarts. "Revising Functional Documents: The Scenario Principle." In *New Essays in Technical and Scientific Communication*. Ed. Paul V. Anderson, R. John Brockmann, and Carolyn R. Miller. Farmingdale, N.Y.: Baywood, 1983, pp. 41–58.

Ford, Arthur L. "Technical Writing and the Liberal Arts School." *J Tech Writ Comm*, 9 (1979), 271–79.

Geonetta, Sam C. "Increasing the Oral Communication Competencies of the Technological Student: The Professional Speaking Method." *J Tech Writ Comm*, 11 (1981), 233–44.

Gloe, Esther M. "Setting Up Internships in Technical Writing." *J Tech Writ Comm*, 13 (1983), 7–27.

Gould, Jay R. "Bringing Teachers of Technical Writing and Teachers of Literature Closer Together." *J Tech Writ Comm*, 9 (1979), 173–83.

————, ed. *Directions in Technical Writing and Communication*. Farmingdale, N.Y.: Baywood, 1978.

Gresham, Stephen. "From Aristotle to Einstein: Scientific Literature and the Teaching of Technical Writing." In *Courses, Components, and Exercises in Technical Communication*. Ed. Dwight W. Stevenson. Urbana: NCTE, 1981, pp. 87–93.

Gresham, Steve, and Carey Kaltenbach. "Readings in Technical Writing: An Orientation Workshop." *Tech Writ Teach*, 2 (1975), 4–8.

Gross, Alan G. "A Primer on Tables and Figures." *J Tech Writ Comm*, 13 (1983), 33–55.

Gross, Gerald J. "Group Projects in the Technical Writing Course." In *Courses, Components, and Exercises in Technical Communication*. Ed. Dwight W. Stevenson. Urbana: NCTE, 1981, pp. 54–64.

Hairston, Maxine. "The Winds of Change: Thomas Kuhn and the Revolution in the Teaching of Writing." *CCC*, 33 (1982), 76–88.

Hall, Dean G. "Technical Writing Class: Day One." In *Courses, Components, and Exercises in Technical Communication*. Ed. Dwight W. Stevenson. Urbana: NCTE, 1981, pp. 159–62.

Hall, Dennis R. "The Role of Invention in Technical Writing." *Tech Writ Teach*, 4 (1976), 13–24.

Halloran, Stephen M. "Classical Rhetoric for the Engineering Student." *J Tech Writ Comm*, 1 (1971), 17–24.

Hamilton, David. "Interdisciplinary Writing." *CE*, 41 (1980), 780–96.

————. "Writing Science." *CE*, 40 (1979), 32–40.

Harris, Elizabeth. "Applications of Kinneavy's *Theory of Discourse* to Technical Writing." *CE*, 40 (1979), 625–32.

————. "In Defense of the Liberal Arts Approach to Technical Writing." *CE*, 44 (1982), 628–36.

Harris, John Sterling. "Metaphor in Technical Writing." In *The Teaching of Technical Writing*. Ed. Donald H. Cunningham and Herman A. Estrin. Urbana: NCTE, 1975, pp. 192–97.

————. "On Expanding the Definition of Technical Writing." *J Tech Writ Comm*, 8 (1978), 133–38.

————. "So You're Going to Teach Technical Writing: A Primer for Beginners." *Tech Writ Teach*, 2 (1974), 1–6.

Harris, Muriel. "Supplementary Writing Instruction for Engineering Students." *Eng Educ*, 73 (1983), 311–13.

Hays, Robert. "What Is Technical Writing?" In *The Teaching of Technical Writing*. Ed. Donald H. Cunningham and Herman A. Estrin. Urbana: NCTE, 1975, pp. 3–8.

Holland, Maurita Peterson, and Leslie Ann Olsen. "Using Technical Information Resources." In *Courses, Components, and Exercises in Technical Communication*. Ed. Dwight W. Stevenson. Urbana: NCTE, 1981, pp. 115–21.

Huckin, Thomas N. "A Cognitive Approach to Readability." In *New Essays in Technical and Scientific Communication*. Ed. Paul V. Anderson, R. John Brockmann, and Carolyn R. Miller. Farmingdale, N.Y.: Baywood, 1983, pp. 90–108.

————. "Teaching the Use of English Articles to Nonnative Speakers in Technical Writing Classes." In *Courses, Components, and Exercises in Technical Communication*. Ed. Dwight W. Stevenson. Urbana: NCTE, 1981, pp. 210–23.

Hull, Keith N. "An Assignment for All Seasons." *Tech Writ Teach*, 7 (1980), 60–63.

————. "Notes from the Besieged, or Why English Teachers Should Teach Technical Writing." *CE*, 41 (1980), 876–83.

Hull, Leon C. "Internships in Technical Writing: A Sponsor's View." *Tech Comm*, 25, No. 1 (1977), 7–9.

Hunt, Russell A. "Technological Gift-Horse: Some Reflections on the Teeth of Cassette-Marking." *CE*, 36 (1975), 581–85.

IEEE Tran Prof Commun: Special Issue on Interpreting Technology for the Nonspecialist. 25, No. 4 (1982).

————. Special Issue on Making Information More Usable through Graphics. 25, No. 2 (1982).

————. Special Issue on Public Speaking for Engineers and Scientists. 23, No. 1 (1980).

Johnson, J. Richard. "Communications—the Engineer's Job." In *The Teaching of Technical Writing*. Ed. Donald H. Cunningham and Herman A. Estrin. Urbana: NCTE, 1975, pp. 50–57.

Johnson, Lawrence J. "A Professional Scenario for the Technical Writing Classroom." In *Courses, Components, and Exercises in Technical Communication*. Ed. Dwight W. Stevenson. Urbana: NCTE, 1981, pp. 3–21.

Journet, Debra, and Julie Lepick Kling. *Readings for Technical Writers*. Glenview, Ill.: Scott, Foresman, 1984.

Kellner, Robert Scott. "A Necessary and Natural Sequel: Technical Editing." *J Tech Writ Comm*, 12 (1982), 25–33.

Kennedy, George F. "Teaching Formal Proposals: A Versatile Minicourse in Technical Writing." *J Tech Writ Comm*, 13 (1983), 123–37.

Kent, Thomas L. "Six Suggestions for Teaching Paragraph Cohesion." *J Tech Writ Comm*, 13 (1983), 269–74.

Kinneavy, James L. *A Theory of Discourse: The Aims of Discourse*. Englewood Cliffs, N.J.: Prentice-Hall, 1971.

Kirszner, Laurie G. "Compiling Mini-Texts for Specialized Technical Writing Courses." *Tech Writ Teach*, 6 (1979), 95–98.

Kiyama, Ken, and Ellen Nold. "Engineering Students Teach Each Other to Write." *Eng Educ*, 69 (1979), 334–37.

Klare, George R. "Readable Technical Writing: Some Observations." *Tech Comm*, 25, No. 2 (1977), 1–5.

Klaver, Peter R. "Writing as Engineers and Writing in Class: Simulation as Solution and Problem." In *Technical and Professional Communication*. Ed. Thomas M. Sawyer. Ann Arbor: Professional Communication Press, 1977, pp. 155–66.

Krimm, Bernard. "The Information Resources Report: A Method for Integrating Library Instruction with Technical Writing Courses." *Tech Writ Teach*, 7 (1979), 35–38.

Lauer, Janice. "Heuristics and Composition." *CCC*, 21 (1970), 396–404.

Leesley, M. E., and M. L. Williams. "Improving the Writing of Freshman Chemical Engineers." *Eng Educ*, 69 (1979), 337–39.

Losano, Wayne A. "*Scientific American* in the Technical Writing Course." In *Courses, Components, and Exercises in Technical Communication*. Ed. Dwight W. Stevenson. Urbana: NCTE, 1981, pp. 94–99.

Lufkin, James M. "The Case Against Teaching Technical Writing in College." *Tech Comm*, 21, No. 1 (1973), 5–6.

Lunsford, Andrea A. "Classical Rhetoric and Technical Writing." *CCC*, 27 (1976), 289–91.

Lynn, Steven Walton. "Kinneavy, Mathes, Mumford, and Lynn: Teaching the Classificatory Mode in Technical Writing." *J Tech Writ Comm*, 10 (1980), 115–24.

McCarron, William E. "In the Business World and in Academe: The English Teacher in the 1980s." *CE*, 41 (1980), 812–21.

———. "Oral Briefing Versus Technical Report: Two Approaches to Communication Problems." In *Courses, Components, and Exercises in Technical Communication*. Ed. Dwight W. Stevenson. Urbana: NCTE, 1981, pp. 144–56.

McGalliard, Roy A. "The Function and Content of Technical Writing in the Two-Year College." In *Technical and Professional Communication*. Ed. Thomas M. Sawyer. Ann Arbor: Professional Communication Press, 1977, pp. 9–16.

McLean, David M. "The Demands of Industry on the Technical Writer." In *The Teaching of Technical Writing*. Ed. Donald H. Cunningham and Herman A. Estrin. Urbana: NCTE, 1975, pp. 145–52.

Marder, Daniel. "Technical Reporting Is Technical Rhetoric." *Tech Comm*, 26, No. 4 (1978), 11–13.

Masse, Roger E., and Patrick M. Kelley. "Teaching the Tradition of Technical and Scientific Writing." In *Technical and Professional Communication*. Ed. Thomas M. Sawyer. Ann Arbor: Professional Communication Press, 1977, pp. 79–87.

Mathes, J. C. "Rhetoric and the Engineering Approach: Three Maxims." *J Tech Writ Comm*, 2 (1972), 119–27.

———, and Dwight W. Stevenson. "Completing the Bridge: Report Writing in Real Life Engineering Courses." *Eng Educ*, 66 (1976), 154–58.

———, and Dwight W. Stevenson. *Designing Technical Reports: Writing for Audiences in Organizations*. Indianapolis, Ind.: Bobbs-Merrill, 1976.

———, Dwight W. Stevenson, and Peter Klaver. "Technical Writing: The Engineering Educator's Responsibility." *Eng Educ*, 69 (1979), 331–34.

Michaelson, Herbert B. "Structure, Content, and Meaning in Technical Manuscripts." *Tech Comm*, 16, No. 2 (1968), 15–18.

Miller, Carolyn R. "A Humanistic Rationale for Technical Writing." *CE*, 40 (1979), 610–17.

Miller, Walter James. "What Can the Technical Writer of the Past Teach the Technical Writer of Today?" In *The Teaching of Technical Writing*. Ed. Donald H. Cunningham and Herman A. Estrin. Urbana: NCTE, 1975, pp. 198–216.

Minor, Dennis E. "A Concept of Language for Technical Writing Students." *J Tech Writ Comm*, 8 (1978), 43–51.

———. "An Integrated Technical Writing Course." *Tech Writ Teach*, 3 (1975), 21–24.

———. "A Structure for the Problem-Solving Paper." *Tech Writ Teach*, 10 (1982), 8–11.

———. "Teaching the Technical Writing Proposal." *Tech Writ Teach*, 7 (1979), 24–27.

Mitchell, John H. "Educators Cannot Go It Alone." *Tech Comm*, 21, No. 1 (1973), 4–5.

———. "It's a Craft Course: Indoctrinate, Don't Educate." *Tech Writ Teach*, 4 (1976), 2–6.

———. "Three Prescriptive Approaches to Teaching Factual Communications." *Tech Writ Teach*, 4 (1976), 7–13.

Mitchell, Ruth. "Shared Responsibility: Teaching Technical Writing in the University." *CE*, 43 (1981), 543–55.

———, and Mary Taylor. "The Integrating Perspective: An Audience-Response Model for Writing." *CE*, 41 (1979), 247–71.

Moger, Susan, and Robert G. Wlezien. "Using Current Technological Issues in a Writing Course for Engineers." *Eng Educ*, 73 (1983), 316–18.

Odell, Lee, Dixie Goswami, Anne Herrington, and Doris Quick. "Studying Writing in Non-Academic Settings." In *New Essays in Technical and Scientific Communication*. Ed. Paul V. Anderson, R. John Brockmann, and Carolyn R. Miller. Farmingdale, N.Y.: Baywood, 1983, pp. 17–40.

Oreovicz, Frank S. "A Writing Instructor's Best Friend: The Word Processor." *Eng Educ*, 73 (1983), 376–78.

Orth, Melvin F. "Abstracting for the Writer." *IEEE Trans Prof Comm*, 15, No. 2 (1972), 43–44.

Pavelich, Joan L. "Organizing Special Classes for Foreign Students in the Technical Writing Course." *Tech Writ Teach*, 5 (1978), 55–58.

Pearsall, Thomas E. "Current University Programs in Technical Communication." *Tech Comm*, 23, No. 1 (1975), 16–18.

Pickett, Nell Ann. "Preparing to Teach a Technical Writing Course in the Two-Year College." *Tech Writ Teach*, 7 (1979), 2–7.

Potvin, Janet H., and Robert L. Woods. "Teaching Technical Communication at the Graduate Level: An Interdisciplinary Approach." *J Tech Writ Comm*, 13 (1983), 235–46.

Pritchard, Eileen. "Teaching *Science Citation Index* for a Library Orientation." *J Tech Writ Comm*, 9 (1979), 297–301.

Ramsey, Richard Davis. "Technical Writing, Stylistics, and TG Grammar." *J Tech Writ Comm*, 7 (1977), 333–45.

Richardson, Jacques. "What the Public Needs to Know About Science and Technology: A Report to the Club of Vienna." *J Tech Writ Comm*, 11 (1981), 303–13.

Robinson, Patricia A. "Technical Writing Workshops: An Alternative to Lectures." *Eng Educ*, 73 (1983), 314–15.

Ross, Donald, Jr. "A Theory of the Function of Technical Writing." *Tech Writ Teach*, 9 (1981), 3–9.

Roundy, Nancy. "Team-Teaching Technical Writing: Audience Analysis and the Lab Report." *Eng Educ*, 72 (1982), 395–96.

Sachs, Harley. "Rhetoric, Persuasion, and the Technical Communicator." *Tech Comm*, 26, No. 4 (1978), 14–15.

Samuels, Marilyn Schauer. "Scientific Logic: A Reader-Oriented Approach to Technical Writing." *J Tech Writ Comm*, 12 (1982), 307–28.

Sawyer, Thomas M. "The Common Law of Science and the Common Law of Literature." In *The Teaching of Technical Writing*. Ed. Donald H. Cunningham and Herman A. Estrin. Urbana: NCTE, 1975, pp. 185–91.

———. "It Is Easy to Communicate Electronically; It Is Hard to Communicate Electronics." *J Tech Writ Comm*, 8 (1978), 121–31.

———. "Rhetoric in an Age of Science and Technology." *CCC*, 23 (1972), 390–98.

———. "A Syllabus for a Course in Scientific and Technical Communication." *Tech Writ Teach*, 2 (1973), 17–23.

———, ed. *Technical and Professional Communication: Teaching in the Two-Year*

College, Four-Year College, Professional School. Ann Arbor: Professional Communication Press, 1977.

Schiff, Peter M. "Speech: Another Facet of Technical Communication." *Eng Educ*, 71 (1980), 180–81.

Schindler, G. E., Jr. "Why Engineers and Scientists Write As They Do—Twelve Characteristics of Their Prose." *IEEE Trans Prof Comm*, 10 (1967), 27–32.

Schmelzer, Richard W. "Technical Writing in the Eighties." *J Tech Writ Comm*, 4 (1974), 165–70.

Schoff, Gretchen H. "Writing for John Q. Public: The Challenge in Environmental Writing." In *Courses, Components, and Exercises in Technical Communication*. Ed. Dwight W. Stevenson. Urbana: NCTE, 1981, pp. 194–204.

Sekey, Andrew A. "Abstract, Conclusions and Summaries." *IEEE Trans Prof Comm*, 16 (1973), 25–26.

Selzer, Jack. "Another Look at Paragraphs in Technical Writing." *J Tech Writ Comm*, 10 (1980), 293–301.

———. "The Composing Processes of an Engineer." *CCC*, 34 (1983), 178–87.

———. "What Constitutes a 'Readable' Technical Style?" In *New Essays in Technical and Scientific Communication*. Ed. Paul V. Anderson, R. John Brockmann, and Carolyn R. Miller. Farmingdale, N.Y.: Baywood, 1983, pp. 71–89.

Shimberg, H. Lee. "Ethics and Rhetoric in Technical Writing." *Tech Comm*, 26, No. 4 (1978), 16–18.

Sides, Charles H. "Heuristics or Prescription: Synthesis Rather Than Choice." *J Tech Writ Comm*, 11 (1981), 115–120.

———. "What Should We Do with Technical Writing?" *Eng Educ*, 70 (1980), 743–44.

Skerl, Jennie. "A Writing Center for Engineering Students." *Eng Educ*, 70 (1980), 752–55.

Smith, Marion K. "What Should Be Taught in the Technical Writing Course?" In *Technical and Professional Communication*. Ed. Thomas M. Sawyer. Ann Arbor: Professional Communication Press, 1977, pp. 39–47.

Smith, Terry C. "What Bugs Engineers Most About Report Writing." *Tech Comm*, 24, No. 4 (1976), 2–6.

Souther, James W. "Developing Assignments for Scientific and Technical Writing." *J Tech Writ Comm*, 7 (1977), 261–69.

———. "The Expanding Dimensions of Technical Writing." *CCC*, 22 (1971), 185–87.

———. "Writing Is for *Other* People." *Tech Writ Teach*, 6 (1979), 38–42.

Spears, James E. "A Simulated Writing Experience." *Eng Educ*, 69 (1979), 342–43.

Stevenson, Dwight W., ed. *Courses, Components,and Exercises in Technical Communication*. Urbana: NCTE, 1981.

———. "Mapping the Unexplored Area: Developing New Courses and Coherent Programs in Technical Communication." *J Tech Writ Comm*, 8 (1978), 193–206.

———. "Toward a Rhetoric of Scientific and Technical Discourse." *Tech Writ Teach*, 5 (1977), 4–10.

Stratton, Charles R. "The Electric Report Card: A Follow-Up on Cassette Grading." *J Tech Writ Comm*, 5 (1975), 17–22.

———. "A Project Team Approach to Technical Writing in the Classroom." *Tech Comm*, 21, No. 2 (1973), 9–11.

————, ed. *Teaching Technical Writing: Cassette Grading.* Anthology No. 2, Association of Teachers of Technical Writing, 1979.

————. "Technical Writing: What It Is and What It Isn't." *J Tech Writ Comm*, 9 (1979), 9–16.

Sullivan, Patricia A. "Teaching the Writing Process in Scientific and Technical Writing Classes." *Tech Writ Teach*, 8 (1980), 10–16.

————, and David D. Roberts. "A Case for Diagnosis in Technical Writing." *J Tech Writ Comm*, 11 (1981), 35–43.

Tebeaux, Elizabeth. "Getting More Mileage Out of Audience Analysis—A Basic Approach." *J Tech Writ Comm*, 12 (1982), 15–24.

————. "Grade Report Writing with a Check Sheet." *Tech Writ Teach*, 7 (1980), 66–68.

————. "The Importance of Following Up Library Instruction." *J Tech Writ Comm*, 9 (1979), 27–32.

————. "Technical Writing is *Not* Enough." *Eng Educ*, 70 (1980), 741–43.

————. "Using Computer Printouts to Teach Analysis and Graphics." *J Tech Writ Comm*, 11 (1981), 13–22.

————. "Using the Extended Definition Paper to Teach Organization." *J Tech Writ Comm*, 10 (1980), 3–10.

Tierney, Cliff, Thomas J. Miranda, and Robert E. Wilson. "Written Technical Communication Involves More Than Writing." *Technical and Professional Communication.* Ed. Thomas M. Sawyer. Ann Arbor, Mich.: Professional Communication Press, 1977, pp. 93–98.

Titen, Jennifer. "Applications of Rudolf Arnheim's *Visual Thinking* to the Teaching of Technical Writing." *Tech Writ Teach*, 7 (1980), 113–18.

Van Hagan, Charles E. "The Long and Short of Technical Writing Courses." *IEEE Trans Prof Comm*, 21, No. 14 (1971), 68–75.

Van Veen, Frederick. "The Training of Technical Writers: A Viewpoint from Industry." *Tech Comm*, 21, No. 1 (1973), 2–4.

Walter, John A. "Confessions of a Teacher of Technical Writing." In *The Teaching of Technical Writing.* Ed. Donald H. Cunningham and Herman A. Estrin. Urbana: NCTE, 1975, pp. 95–101.

————. "Some Shibboleths In the Teaching of Technical Writing." *J Tech Writ Comm*, 1 (1971), 127–37.

————. "Technical Writing: Species or Genus?" *J Tech Writ Comm*, 7 (1977), 243–50.

Warren, Thomas L. "Technical Writing Textbook Selection." *Tech Writ Teach*, 2 (1974), 21–28.

Weber, Max. "Teaching an Effective Course in Technical Writing in Private Industry." *Tech Writ Teach*, 3 (1975), 8–20.

West, Gregory K., and Patricia Byrd. "Technical Writing Required of Graduate Engineering Students." *J Tech Writ Comm*, 12 (1982), 1–6.

Whitburn, Merrill D. "Against Substituting Technical Writing for Freshman English." In *The Teaching of Technical Writing.* Ed. Donald H. Cunningham and Herman A. Estrin. Urbana: NCTE, 1975, pp. 75–79.

————, ed. *Teaching Technical Writing: The First Day in the Technical Writing Course.* Anthology No. 3, Association of Teachers of Technical Writing, 1979.

Winkler, Victoria M. "The Role of Models in Technical and Scientific Writing." In *New*

Essays in Technical and Scientific Communication. Ed. Paul V. Anderson, R. John Brockmann, and Carolyn R. Miller. Farmingdale, N.Y.: Baywood, 1983, pp. 111–22.

————. "Technical Communication: A Cooperative Venture." In *Technical and Professional Communication*. Ed. Thomas M. Sawyer. Ann Arbor: Professional Communication Press, 1977, pp. 107–18.

Woods, Donald R., and Irwin A. Feuerstrin. "On Teaching Technical Communication." *Eng Educ*, 70 (1980), 745–49.

Workun, Arthur E. "Speech for the Technician: A Bibliography." *J Tech Writ Comm*, 4 (1974), 331–39.

Wright, Patricia. "Five Skills Technical Writers Need." *IEEE Trans Prof Comm*, 24, No. 1 (1981), 10–16.

Zappen, James P. "A Mini-Internship in a Professional Writing Course." In *Technical and Professional Communication*. Ed. Thomas M. Sawyer. Ann Arbor: Professional Communication Press, 1977, pp. 129–37.

Part II

Technical Communication and Rhetorical Concerns

Invention in Technical and Scientific Discourse: A Prospective Survey

CAROLYN R. MILLER

Invention is a concept that makes sense only within a certain type of rhetorical theory, one that prevailed in classical times and is now being revived. It is a theory of rhetoric as concerned with substance as well as with form, with wisdom as well as with eloquence, with the relationships between minds as well as between words. Invention is the art of discovering proofs or arguments, of the things to say and the ways to say them in given situations. To Aristotle, it was central to rhetoric, as suggested by his definition of rhetoric as "the faculty of discovering in the particular case the available means of persuasion" (*Rhetoric* I, 2). A recent definition that retains the same spirit is that of Richard Young ("Invention" [1976]): "Every writer," he says, "confronts the task of making sense of events in the world around him or within him...and of making what he wants to say understandable and believable to particular readers" (p. 1).

Because theories of rhetoric have not been stable in Western thought, some questions have only recently become askable; among these are questions concerning the nature and role of invention in technical and scientific discourse. Historically, rhetoric has not included technical and scientific discourse, and there have been periods when it did not include an important notion of invention either. Consequently, the subject of this review is likely to strike some readers as self-contradictory, others as problematic, and those who are familiar with the literature on technical and scientific discourse as just about non-existent. So we will begin by explaining the approach to the subject as a whole, first outlining the preconditions for even considering it—that is, the requisite conceptions of rhetoric, science, and technology —then exploring how to conceive of invention in those fields, and finally sketching out a system for organizing the material that follows.

In classical treatments of rhetoric, scientific discourse was excluded because its end was seen as very different from that of rhetoric: science concerns the certain, the demonstrably true, whereas rhetoric concerns the probable, matters of opinion. The mode of discourse appropriate to science was dialectic, not rhetoric. Charles W. Kneupper and Floyd D. Anderson review the classical formulations of rhetoric with special focus on invention and the relationship between rhetoric and the "scientific" or knowledge-productive fields of philosophy, politics, mathematics, and so on. ("Uniting Wisdom and Eloquence" [1980]). S. Michael Halloran also reviews the sources of the dichotomy between rhetoric and scientific discourse in "Technical Writing and the Rhetoric of Science" (1978). He points specifically to the metaphor of *topoi*, which Aristotle used to suggest that rhetoric and science argue "in different places, before different sorts of audiences" (p. 80). He goes on to suggest that a Renaissance variation on the dichotomy is equally responsible for the current situation. After Peter Ramus removed invention from the curriculum in rhetoric, handing it over to dialectic, the study and practice of rhetoric emphasized style and verbal ornamentation. Consequently, the makers of the early scientific revolution perceived rhetoric as an obstacle in the effort to observe and describe reality directly. In "A Humanistic Rationale for Technical Writing" (1979), Carolyn R. Miller reviews these developments briefly with attention to their legacy in current pedagogy.

There has been one systematic contemporary attempt to deal with invention in technical and scientific discourse, by James L. Kinneavy in *A Theory of Discourse* (1971). He describes such discourse as "referential," one of four primary types based on four possible aims. For each type, Kinneavy characterizes its nature, logic, organization, and style, likening the "logic" to invention. Thus, the logic of referential discourse involves factuality, comprehensiveness, surprise value, discovery procedures, and scientific induction and deduction. But he does not deal with the fundamental rift between rhetoric and science, and even reaffirms it by assigning them to two different aims and discussing them separately as referential and persuasive discourse. First, then, before we can consider the matter of invention we need theories of both rhetoric and science that involve each other. And the dichotomy between rhetoric and science is being challenged, from both sides. Several essays have helped establish the rhetorical nature of science in the rhetorical literature: Philip C. Wander, "The Rhetoric of Science" (1976); Michael A. Overington, "The Scientific Community as Audience" (1977); Walter B. Weimer, "Science as a Rhetorical Transaction" (1977); and Herbert W. Simons, "Are Scientists Rhetors in Disguise?" (1980). Another relevant trend in the rhetorical literature has been to argue that rhetoric is the means by which knowledge is created. There are several variations on this view of rhetoric as epistemic: some argue that all knowledge is rhetorically constructed; others that only social, as opposed to technical, knowledge is. The original statement of this position is in Robert L. Scott, "On Viewing Rhetoric as Epistemic" (1967); also see his "On Viewing Rhetoric as Epistemic" (1976). For a convenient review of this literature, see Michael C. Leff, "In Search of Ariadne's Thread" (1978); for the argument distinguishing technical from social knowledge, see Thomas B. Farrell, "Knowledge, Consensus, and Rhetorical

Theory'' (1976); for an extreme statement of the view that rhetoric is ''the advocacy of realities,'' see Barry Brummett, ''Some Implications of 'Process' or 'Intersubjectivity' '' (1976).

On the other side, the thrust of recent work in the philosophy and history of science is that scientific knowledge is not a matter of logical demonstration and that scientists do, indeed, engage in argumentation in the effort to win adherence to their claims, claims that can be, at best, highly probable. Thomas S. Kuhn's work has played perhaps the most important role in establishing science as a rhetorical enterprise. His *The Structure of Scientific Revolutions* (1970) describes the history of science in terms of the changing patterns of group commitments and the intellectual adherence those commitments represent. Scientific ''progress'' is a process of mind-changing achieved through argumentation in situations in which there can be no absolute proof just because prior commitments prevent agreement on the terms of the debate. But Kuhn is by no means the only philosopher or historian of science who makes room for rhetoric. Stephen Toulmin's work, particularly his *Human Understanding* (1972), also addresses the issue of conceptual change and the problem of rational choice. In renouncing what he calls ''universal epistemic principles,'' Toulmin must ask what are the processes and criteria for preferring one account of the world to another. In addition to Kuhn and Toulmin, other philosophers of science of the ''Weltanschauung'' school have dealt with the consequences of the decay of positivist science in the early and mid-twentieth century. These developments are summarized in Frederick Suppe's comprehensive introduction to *The Structure of Scientific Theories* (1977). More recently, in *Philosophy and the Mirror of Nature* (1979), Richard Rorty has challenged the view of knowledge as accurate representation, arguing that ''we understand knowledge when we understand the social justification of belief'' (p. 170).

Even to begin to speak of invention in scientific discourse, then, requires both a particular philosophy of science (and an accompanying epistemology) and a particular rhetorical theory, neither of which has prevailed historically. To see scientific discourse as rhetorical, one must see the task of science as constructive and persuasive, not as descriptive and demonstrative. To speak of invention in technical discourse, however, requires additional thought, for there is no comparable tradition to draw upon—probably because technology does not have the clear epistemic implications that science does and because discourse has had a major role to play in technology only recently. Much contemporary work has simply presumed there to be no important difference between technical and scientific discourse, especially the pedagogical literature. See, for example, John S. Harris's definition of technical writing as the rhetoric of the scientific method (''On Expanding the Definition of Technical Writing'' [1978]). Yet there is a growing body of literature devoted to discussing the nature and philosophy of technology as distinct from science. A useful collection of this literature is Carl Mitcham and Robert Mackey's *Philosophy and Technology* (1972). In this work, Henryk Skolinowski distinguishes science from technology on the basis of their goals: in science the investigation of a given reality, in technology the creation of reality according to human designs; I. C. Jarvie uses Gilbert Ryle's distinction between *knowing-that* and *knowing-how—knowing-that* must be a proposition put in symbolic form, while *knowing-how* is inarticulable, the mastery of technique; Mario Bunge argues that technology is the application of scientific laws to practical action. Important work by Lewis Mumford, Jacques Ellul, Lynn White, and Friedrich Dessauer also appears in this collection.

Another general collection of work on technology is in the special issue of *Daedalus* on Modern Technology: Problem or Opportunity. N. Bruce Hannay and Robert E. McGinn argue that the characteristic output of science is knowledge sought for general understanding of the natural world and that the output of technology consists of material products and systems for production and control created for the purpose of expanding the realm of practical human possibility ("The Anatomy of Modern Technology" [1980]). Michael Polanyi (*Personal Knowledge* [1964]) also makes the point that "technology teaches action"; we see this in particular when "it speaks in imperatives" (p. 176). Technology consists in turning facts to advantage, and advantage is determined by social and economic conditions. He points out that a statement is of value to science if it corresponds to facts, is relevant to an established scientific system, and bears on a subject of interest; a statement is of value in technology if it reveals an effective and ingenious operational principle that achieves substantial advantage (p. 187). A related view is that of Edwin T. Layton, who observes that thinking in technology "is intimately associated with the needs and values of a community" ("Technology as Knowledge" [1974], p. 40). Stephen Toulmin says that science has explanatory goals and technology practical goals (*Human Understanding* [1972]).

According to one line of thinking, we might assign a very small role to the rhetoric of technology, for inarticulate know-how does not seem to require discourse. But modern technology is very much a communal enterprise that inevitably requires articulation and symbolization. We must see technology as including managerial and social support systems that are necessary for development and application (Harvey Brooks, "Technology, Evolution, and Purpose" [1980]) and require team invention: "As invention and innovation have become less the achievement of the heroic individual and more the accomplishment of an integrated team of specialists, the locus has moved from the individual workshop to the organization's headquarters, laboratory, and plant" (Hannay and McGinn, "The Anatomy of Modern Technology" [1980], p. 40). Invention, design, application, marketing—all require communication. In "What's Technical About Technical Writing?" (1983), David N. Dobrin has defined technical writing as "writing that accommodates technology to the user," a definition reminiscent of Donald C. Bryant's definition of rhetoric as the adjusting of ideas to people and people to ideas ("Rhetoric" 1953). It focuses on the role of rhetoric as mediator in technology, as opposed to essential goal in science; rhetoric must mediate between product and user, designer and developer, engineering and marketing, subsidiary and headquarters, industry and regulatory agency. This is a broad definition but a useful one. It illustrates two things: first, the danger in trying to distinguish too sharply between technical discourse and business communication (or management communication or organizational communication), and second, the motivational scene in which technical rhetoric takes place, the scene that supplies the premises and materials for reasoning. It is in the corporate-industrial environment that technical discourse is invented. Kenneth Burke points up the centrality of this environment to contemporary rhetoric: "Our identification with these two great unwieldy leviathans—technology and the state—is central to the rhetorical situation as we now confront it" ("The Rhetorical Situation" [1973], p. 270).

With these approaches to rhetoric, science, and technology established as preconditions, we may turn back to the problem of invention. When Ramus assigned invention to the study of dialectic rather than rhetoric, he was reflecting a cautionary statement of Aristotle's that when we stray too far into the specific propositions of an area of inquiry we cease to practice rhetoric and begin to practice a specific discipline. This troublesome issue has been in the background of the unfriendly relations between science and rhetoric for most of their mutual lifetimes. Francis Bacon stated the problem in a widely quoted passage:

The invention of speech or argument is not properly an invention: for to invent is to discover that we know not, and not to recover or resummon that which we already know; and the use of this invention is no other but out of the knowledge whereof our mind is already possessed, to draw forth or call before us that which may be pertinent to the purpose which we take into our consideration (*Works*, III, 389).

According to Lisa Jardine in *Bacon* (1974), throughout his work Bacon stresses the distinction between discovery and invention. He adopts as fundamental to his scheme of knowledge the Ciceronian distinction between invention and judgment, but to Bacon invention remained the selection of received knowledge rather than, as Richard McKeon suggests it was for Cicero, the art of discovering new arguments and of uncovering new knowledge through argument ("The Method of Rhetoric and Philosophy" [1966]). Thomas Hobbes, however, equated rhetorical invention and the method of reason or science; James P. Zappen's discussion of Hobbes emphasizes his thinking on these issues ("Aristotelian and Ramist Rhetoric in Thomas Hobbes's *Leviathan*," [1983]). Among the many works on rhetoric in the Renaissance, several are of particular relevance to the development of scientific rhetoric: in addition to Jardine's book, James Stephens, *Francis Bacon and the Style of Science* (1975), Wilbur Samuel Howell, *Logic and Rhetoric in England* (1956), and James P. Zappen, "Science and Rhetoric from Bacon to Hobbes" (1979).

In his survey of the history of rhetorical invention, Elbert W. Harrington sees as central to the history of invention this problem of the soundness of ideas ("Rhetoric and the Scientific Method of Inquiry" [1948]). Invention can be seen, he says, either as an attempt to be wise as well as eloquent or as a scheme for finding arguments for a particular occasion; he calls these, respectively, the broad and narrow views of invention. Similarly, Richard Young's definition, quoted earlier, reflects this bipartite nature of invention, assigning it both a cognitive and a communicative dimension. Harrington argues for the broad view of invention, suggesting that scientific inquiry is an appropriate correlate of rhetoric in a scientific age. Similarly, McKeon argues that in a technological age, invention and discovery should be joined in an art that concerns itself with substantive change in the world ("The Uses of Rhetoric in a Technological Age" [1971]). Kneupper and Anderson also believe that it is a minimal invention theory that rests on the retrieval of information or experiences and a more powerful one that makes invention central to the processes of inquiry and the discovery of new knowledge. Richard Young also clearly prefers this broad view, and he suggests that pre-writing and tagmemic invention in particular extend the scope of the composing process to include problem-solving and inquiry, activities that are otherwise viewed as the concern of logic and substantive disciplines. Essentially, these are arguments for the reintegration of wisdom and eloquence, a goal sought by Cicero. (Kneupper and Anderson's essay traces the search in classical theory and practice for such a union). This approach contravenes the approaches of Aristotle, Ramus, and Bacon by requiring invention to include the substance of discourse. The implications for this review are that the processes of scientific inquiry and technological problem-solving become aspects of invention in technical and scientific discourse, rather than processes antecedent to discourse. Science and technology are the substance of such discourse, and invention must comprehend them.

This provides direction for an inquiry into invention in technical and scientific discourse, and it suggests a corollary: invention in these special fields of discourse must be different from invention in general. In his general survey of invention for the field of composition, Young describes four major heuristic systems. The point of these is that they can be applied to any rhetorical problem; in Janice Lauer's terms, they are "transcendent," or "non-data-conditioned" ("Toward a Metatheory of Heuristic Procedures" [1979]). Similarly, Aristotle's *Rhetoric* presents a system of invention that is appropriate for any of the occasions for public oratory that Aristotle identified. Rhetoric finds its proofs in "common places," the universal and common *topoi*. For discourse in particular fields of knowledge, Aristotle held, the argument uses "special *topoi*," the particular propositions belonging to the subject matter at hand. These *topoi*, or places of invention, are field-dependent, in Stephen Toulmin's terms (*The Uses of Argument* [1958]). The systems of invention described by Aristotle and Young are field-invariant, being applicable to any discourse (because of their supposed basis in human nature). Technical and scientific discourse, therefore, may make as much use of these systems as any other discourse; indeed, much of the work in the pedagogical literature draws from one or another of these field-invariant systems. But it may also be that we should look for systems of special *topoi* peculiar to scientific disciplines and, perhaps, to the rhetorical environments in which technical discourse is conducted.

The concept of *topoi* as the places in which one finds the substance of argument, or proofs, has a complex history. Kneupper and Anderson discuss the role of topics in classical invention, and Karl R. Wallace, in *"Topoi* and the Problem of Invention" (1972), discusses modern attempts to use the *topoi*, with particular emphasis on Perelman's work. Sara Leopold discusses the problems of devising modern sets of *topoi*, both common and special, in "Polanyi's 'Tacit Knowledge' and the Problem of Invention" (1979). James A. Kelso points out that rhetorical analysis of a scientist's theoretical claims must focus on *topoi*, which he describes as the epistemological assumptions and ontological concepts used to formulate a theory ("Science and the Rhetoric of Reality" [1980]). According to Wallace, what underlies all topical schemes are points of view toward knowing and learning and toward using what is known and learned. A set of modern topics "will reflect what is considered necessary to the acquisition of that knowledge which is productive of ready and effective communication" (p. 392). Evidently, then, *topoi* may be productive of invention both narrowly conceived and broadly conceived; that is, they can generate both new knowledge and appropriate ways of expressing knowledge. Ideally, what *topoi* produce are "good reasons," which Wallace, in another essay, defines as statements "offered in support of an *ought* proposition or a value-judgement" ("The Substance of Rhetoric" [1963], p. 247). He characterizes rhetoric as the art of finding and effectively presenting good reasons, which embrace both the substance and processes of practical reasoning. Good reasons constitute a *topoi* of values—the desirable, the obligatory, the admirable. Herbert W. Simons has suggested that good reasons provide the basis of scientific objectivity in a conception of science in which objectivity is unavailable through empirically based demonstration ("Are Scientists Rhetors in Disguise?" [1980]).

The study of invention in technical and scientific discourse, conceived in this way, leads in many different directions. In most of these directions what one finds is work that is not overtly *about* invention, or even in many cases about rhetoric. Research and scholarship in rhetoric have yet to pay much explicit attention to technical and scientific discourse, except in quite general terms, and work in technical writing has yet to take rhetorical theory seriously, for reasons alluded to earlier. Much of the work discussed in the following pages, therefore, is only potentially relevant to invention; and because the search was made widely, but perhaps not wisely, in diverse fields, there are undoubtedly omissions and inept selections. The bibliography should be taken as suggestive, as heuristic, not as authoritative. It should also be pointed out that invention is treated in yet another broad sense here. In much current literature in composition, invention is treated as a conscious process, as the pre-writing stage that a writer goes through deliberately. The treatment here is different in two ways. First, as discussed in this essay invention encompasses all the means by which writers come to their matter, whether consciously and systematically or intuitively and routinely. Invention involves more than heuristic devices; it involves presuppositions, premises, values, inspiration, work activities—anything that leads to or is taken as a "good reason" for belief. Second, not only examinations of writing as process but also criticism of writing as product are considered instructive about invention. Critical inferences about sources of argument and types of appeals can illuminate the effects of inquiry and expression upon each other in ways that the observation of heuristic procedures in action cannot.

This survey divides the material into three major areas. The first is concerned with the broad view of invention—the process of inquiry and the creation of ideas, the way in which scientists or problem-solvers in a technical environment make sense of the world around them. The second is concerned with the narrower view of invention—the appropriate and effective use of existing knowledge; the work here generally speaks to the constraints and conditions on expression and presentation, *topoi* relevant to the persuasive effect on an audience. The analysis of audience, of course, is an important aspect of invention, one that will not be covered here, except indirectly, because it is the subject of another essay in this collection. The third area covers work on practical applications, teaching methods, and explicit heuristics that have been developed for use in technical and scientific discourse.

Scientific Inquiry and Technical Problem-solving

The question of how scientific knowledge is created has long been subject to speculation. The philosophy of science has much to offer the student of scientific discourse, but its technicality and diversity can prove daunting; for this reason, a full review will not be possible here. One central distinction made early in this century will be helpful in applying this work to the problem of invention because it mirrors the two aspects of invention mentioned above as the broad and narrow views. It is the distinction between the context of discovery and the context of justification, originally made by Hans Reichenbach in *Experience and Prediction* (1938). In doing this, he provided a way for philosophers of science to bypass certain aspects of the scientific process by simply declaring them off limits to philosophy. The context of discovery, the intellectual environment in which ideas originate, he said, is the province of psychology and sociology; the context of justification, the intellectual environment in which ideas are rationally tested and supported, is the province of philosophy and epistemology. Philosophy's traditional propensity for logical analysis led to the conclusion that *post facto* justifiability was essential to the nature of science, while the actual process of creation was irrelevant. The question of whether there can be a "logic of discovery" was answered in this way by Reichenbach and later in the same way by Karl Popper in *The Logic of Scientific Discovery* (1959). These versions of scientific method, the same versions that exclude rhetoric, cannot deal with the origin of ideas and do not care to deal with the intellectual process of inquiry.

This is the rigorous view; fortunately, there are other, more helpful viewpoints.

Less rigorous theories characterize scientific method as simply a systematic version of the normal operation of human intelligence. Aristotle describes the acquisition of scientific knowledge as a universal cognitive process: scientific knowledge arises from demonstration, that is, deductions from premises; premises are arrived at through an intuitive induction from sense perceptions that have been generalized into experience. In this way, according to Aristotle, we arrive at knowledge of things that cannot be other than they are (*Posterior Analytics*, II, 19). Francis Bacon claims that his version of induction mirrors our natural apprehension of reality ("De Augmentis" in *Works*, I). This version of scientific method holds that universal principles can be attained by the recording, sifting, and tabulating of primitive sense perceptions. Lisa Jardine's discussion of Bacon's account of induction and of its relationship to rhetoric is especially instructive (*Francis Bacon* [1974], pp. 170 ff). Similarly, Thomas H. Huxley, in his essay, "The Method by Which the Causes of the Present and Past Conditions of Organic Nature Are to Be Discovered" (1907), claims that scientific method is nothing but the mind's "necessary mode of working." These accounts of scientific reasoning as simple deduction or induction locate the source of scientific ideas in the empirical world itself or in observation of it. The issue is whether new knowledge is deducible from old, inducible from observation, or created in a more complex way through an interplay of existing theory, hypothetical conjecture, and observation. Most philosophers now accept some version of this last, usually called the hypothetico-deductive view. Karl Popper's *The Logic of Scientific Discovery* (1959) is the standard statement of this view. In *The Art of the Soluble* (1967), P. B. Medawar gives a non-technical account of the hypothetico-deductive system and suggests that, ultimately, the "generative or elementary act in discovery is 'having an idea' or proposing a hypothesis." This is outside logic; it is a private event with an "inspirational" origin (pp. 147–55).

But other accounts go beyond this acquiescence to inspiration, accept the context of discovery, and attempt to explicate it. Thomas S. Kuhn questions the distinction between the context of discovery and the context of justification in his essay "Objectivity, Value Judgment, and Theory Choice" (in *The Essential Tension* [1977]). A helpful overview of the issue is Thomas Nickles's "Introductory Essay" (in *Scientific Discovery, Logic, and Rationality* [1980]). Frederick Suppe's critical introduction to *The Structure of Scientific Theories* (1977) provides a thorough overview of the technical issues on both sides of the question.

One of the earliest to examine the context of discovery seriously was Norwood Russell Hanson. Hanson proposed an account of scientific reasoning he called "retroduction," which involves reasoning backwards from anomalous observation (which must eventually prove to be the conclusion) to the premises and hypothesis that could lead to the previously anomalous conclusion. His account is intended to represent the actual reasoning process a scientist uses rather than a rational reconstruction of what justifies a conclusion once arrived at. Hanson's work is presented in full in *Patterns of Discovery* (1958) and is summarized in accessible form in *Observation and Explanation* (1971); retroduction is explicated in some detail in "Notes Toward a Logic of Discovery" (1965). Hanson believed that there can be a logic of discovery because of what he calls the "theory-laden" nature of observation and accepted knowledge. It is this background of accepted knowledge that makes one hypothesis seem more reasonable than another, that establishes "*criteria* in virtue of which one can distinguish *good* reasons from *bad* reasons" (*Observation and Explanation*, p. 64).

Marx W. Wartofsky calls the traditional accounts of science the "no-theory" theory of discovery because they aim at the mathematization of scientific knowledge through logical relationships. He recommends an alternative tradition that he calls the heuristic tradition, which includes an *ars inveniendi*. He likens science to practical "tinkering" and suggests that the logic of discovery is to be found in the doing of science, in experimental practice, technological innovation: "in scientific judgment, then, the act of creation consists in imagining new ways of relating present facts, or of imagining *new facts* in such a way as to realize them by a mode of action" ("Scientific Judgment" [1980], p. 14). The emphasis on judgment acquired through practical action is similar to Michael Polanyi's discussion of the tacit knowledge acquired through action (*Personal Knowledge* [1964]). The acquisition of skill and the development of judgment (which he calls "conoisseurship") are learned by example and practice, not through precept or instruction. The knowledge so gained is inarticulable and "personal," and creates forms of intellectual commitment that can be seen to have heuristic potential (Ch. 4, "Skills"). A case study of scientific practice that illustrates the lack of logical structure in the context of discovery is Bruno Latour and Steve Woolgar's *Laboratory Life* (1979). Their account emphasizes the "utter confusion" of everyday scientific practice, the "seething mass of alternative interpretations" and disordered array of observations. Order is created after the fact and often serendipitously. "Having an idea," they suggest, "represents a summary of a complicated material situation" (p. 170). In an intellectual recounting, the idea may appear to be the product of inexplicable inspiration. However, the authors find that ideas can be recounted sociologically and attributed to specific sources, such as institutional requirements, group traditions, seminars, and particular discussions with colleagues.

Other writers have emphasized the role of "non-verbal" thinking, especially in technology. It could be noted that in Polanyi's discussion, tacit knowledge, which represents this same inarticulable thought, is what he calls the "art" of doing research—not the content of a discipline, but the technology of science. Perhaps the most famous statement on non-verbal thinking is that of Einstein, in his response to Jacques Hadamard's questionnaire sent to mathematicians. In *The Psychology of Invention in the Mathematical Field* (1949), Hadamard excerpts Einstein's comments: "The words or the language, as they are written or spoken, do not seem to play any role in my mechanism of thought. The psychical entities which seem to serve as elements in thought are certain signs and more or less clear images...[these elements] are, in my case, of visual and some of muscular type. Conventional words or other signs have to be sought for laboriously only in a secondary stage'' (pp. 142–43). Roy Dreistadt uses other evidence about Einstein's thinking—his reliance on visual imagery, thought experiments, fantasy, and analogy—to describe Einstein's thought style (''The Psychology of Creativity'' [1974]). Hadamard's book also discusses the role of the unconscious, the stage of preparation, and conscious work in mathematical discovery. His approach was inspired by Henri Poincaré's lecture, ''Mathematical Creation'' (1913), in which Poincaré used personal experience to highlight the role of the unconscious. Hadamard's book contains other anecdotal evidence. Percy W. Bridgman's ''Words, Meanings, and Verbal Analysis'' (1966) alludes to the importance of non-verbal thinking, especially in designing apparatus (p. 23), and Brooke Hindle's *Emulation and Invention* (1981) and Eugene S. Ferguson's ''The Mind's Eye'' (1977) are useful general discussions of the role of spatial and pictorial thinking in mechanical design and technology. In his essay ''A Function for Thought Experiments'' (*The Essential Tension* [1977]), Thomas S. Kuhn discusses the role of thought experiments in the generation of new knowledge. He argues that from thought experiments people learn about both their concepts and the world.

One of the greatest aids to the scientific imagination is the model. In Chapter 13 of *Models and Metaphors*, ''Models and Archetypes'' (1962), Max Black provides an authoritative discussion of the types of models that scientists use and the roles they play: scale models, analogue models (which reproduce structural relationships in a different medium), mathematical models (which do not explain, although they may appear to refer to an implied explanatory mechanism), and theoretical models (which do explain by representing a phenomenon not as *though* it were like the analogue, but as *being* the analogue). Mary Hesse's work extends Black's overview. Unlike some philosophers of science who hold that all models are merely heuristic and therefore dispensable within the context of justification, she suggests that models and metaphors do refer and describe, not merely inspire, in part because they can be used to predict. See her ''Scientific Models'' (1972) and ''The Explanatory Function of Metaphor'' (1980). In Kuhn's thought, the exemplar, or model problem and solution, serves both as teaching device for the acquisition of tacit knowledge and as concrete model that can provide analogues for later problems and good reasons for theory choice (''Objectivity, Value Judgment, and Theory Choice,'' in *The Essential Tension* [1977]).

Models are often expressed as analogies or metaphors, and these features of scientific language may themselves become grounds for further inquiry or good reasons for evaluating later developments. There is a small but growing literature on the use of metaphor and other figures of speech in science. Both William J.J. Gordon (''Some Source Material in Discovery-by-Analogy'' [1974]) and Roy Dreistadt (''An Analysis of the Use of Analogies and Metaphors in Science'' [1968]) provide comprehensive historical surveys of the uses of analogies and metaphors in science. James Stephens explores the functions of figurative language for early audiences of scientific discourse in ''Style as Therapy in Renaissance Science" (1983). W. H. Leatherdale's *The Role of Analogy, Model and Metaphor in Science* (1974) reviews opinion on the use of metaphor in science, from Bacon and Newton to contemporary scientists. Earlier opinion (Bacon, Newton, Berkeley, Locke) was that because words are unchangeable labels for things, metaphors were simply misleading misrepresentations in science. But Leatherdale finds that these linguistic models are explanatory because they can help to reformulate or reorder observations, and that there is no reason to proscribe them from scientific discourse. In "Analogy and Metaphor in Science, Poetry and Philosophy," Chaim Perelman characterizes the role of metaphor in science as heuristic and temporary; metaphor must eventually be supplanted by technical language (in *The New Rhetoric and the Humanities* [1979]). S. Michael Halloran and Annette N. Bradford, in "Figures of Speech in the Rhetoric of Science and Technology" (1984), remind us that proscription of metaphor is standard in technical writing texts but suggests that figures of speech are useful in scientific and technical discourse in part because "a theory more often than not turns out to be a figure of both thought and speech, pressed hard and elaborated in great detail." Their examples are drawn largely from the metaphoric language of molecular biology. Robert R. Hoffman reviews the attitudes of philosophers and scientists for and against the use of images and metaphors, defining *metaphor* as the linguistic expression, *model* as a physical representation, and *theory* as the mathematics or statements that the model and metaphor instantiate ("Metaphor in Science" [1980]).

Michael Polanyi, in *Personal Knowledge* (1964), points out the importance of language in intellectual creation in general:

To learn a language or to modify its meaning is a tacit, irreversible, heuristic feat; it is a transformation of our intellectual life, originating in our own desire for greater clarity and coherence, and yet sustained by the hope of coming by it into closer touch with reality. Indeed, any modification of an anticipatory framework, whether conceptual, perceptual or appetitive, is an irreversible heuristic act, which transforms our ways of thinking, seeing and appreciating in the hope of attuning our understanding, perception or sensuality more closely to what is true and right (p. 106).

Percy W. Bridgman discusses the importance of precise meaning to scientific language in "The Operational Aspect of Meaning" (1950–51). He suggests that because meaning is ultimately tied to action, defining scientific terms in terms of operations, rather than in terms of objects and properties, is the only way to achieve precision necessary for scientific communication. James Paradis's work on the history of scientific language shows that scientific innovation is fundamentally tied to linguistic innovation, and furthermore, that key scientists were aware of this link and insisted on it ("Bacon, Linnaeus, and Lavoisier" [1983]). Paradis finds that "to Bacon, Linnaeus, and Lavoisier,...inventing language became an essential methodology—the necessary accompaniment to inventing evidence through observation and experiment" (p. 101). Bacon's own discussion in the "New Organon" (in *Works*, I), which Paradis summarizes, should itself be read, especially his description of the faulty language of the marketplace and the detrimental effect it could have on intellectual inquiry. The attempts by Linnaeus and Lavoisier to develop nomenclatures that systematically relate concepts and phenomena successfully guided the subsequent development of the new sciences of biology and chemistry. Charles Bazerman indicates the argumentative role that technical language plays in "What Written Knowledge Does" (1981).

The conceptual framework within which a scientist works is said by the so-called "Weltanschauung philosophers of science" to have the primary effect on what new ideas are created and how they are reasoned about. It determines the standards of argumentation and supplies the materials of argumentation. The work in this area is characterized by a general concern to understand the phenomenon of conceptual change; it understands science as a thoroughly rhetorical enterprise, and it has much to offer the study of rhetorical invention. Major works are Thomas S. Kuhn's *The Structure of Scientific Revolutions* (1970), Stephen Toulmin's *Human Understanding* (1972), Ludwig Fleck's *Genesis and Development of a Scientific Fact* (1935; rpt. 1979), and Walter B. Weimer's *Notes on the Methodology of Scientific Research* (1979). Kuhn's work is the best known and so far the most influential. He discusses both the ways in which new ideas come into being and the ways they take hold and become part of the conceptual apparatus of a scientific community. This conceptual apparatus, or background of expectations, Kuhn originally called a "paradigm." It includes expectations induced by theory, instruments, and methods: "novelty emerges only with difficulty, manifested by resistance, against a background provided by expectation" (p. 64). However, Kuhn does suggest that during a period of crisis in a scientific field, certain forces help to loosen the grip of explanations that can no longer satisfactorily account for new observations: a crisis "simultaneously loosens the stereotypes and provide the incremental data necessary for a fundamental paradigm shift" (p. 89). Philosophical analysis, thought experiments, concentrated effort, and consequent proliferation of discoveries all help this process. Fundamental insights that lead to previously unanticipated explanations most often occur, he says, to workers who are less committed to the traditional framework, those either very young or very new to the field of work (p. 90). According to Kuhn, the "paradigm debate" that ensues cannot be settled by falsification or by direct comparison with nature; instead, "there is no standard higher than the assent of the relevant community" (p. 94), because each paradigm defines the terms of the debate and the standards of resolution differently. The kinds of arguments that help to resolve such debates, that serve as "good reasons" for a given scientist or a community at large, range from idiosyncrasies of personality and biography to a set of *topoi* that characterize the larger concerns of science in general. Kuhn discusses several: the solution by the new paradigm of the problems that led the old one to crisis, the prediction of phenomena that had not been suspected under the old one, appeals to the sense of the appropriate or the aesthetic qualities of a theory, and faith in the new paradigm's potential for future research. Kuhn emphasizes that these arguments are never compelling, either singly or in combination (pp. 155–59). Kuhn's work has been much discussed and criticized; one important collection of criticism is *Criticism and the Growth of Knowledge* (edited by Imere Lakatos and Alan Musgrave 1970); clarification and further development of Kuhn's own thought is collected in *The Essential Tension* (1977).

Stephen Toulmin, in *Human Understanding* (1972), portrays the process of conceptual change as a process of evolutionary selection that accounts for the presence of both diversity and rationality. In the absence of what he calls "universal epistemic principles," rationality is not equivalent to logic but is the process that permits change and judges concepts by their fitness to intellectual niches. One may explain conceptual change by seeing the intellectual selection process in terms either of reasons or of causes, that is in internal (disciplinary) or external (professional) terms. Within a discipline, occasions for change arise from the difference between the explanatory ideals and the current capacities of the discipline; this difference presents the discipline with scientific problems (p. 152). Conceptual variants arise, are debated, and judged within forums of discussion, which Toulmin identifies as professions. The continual growth of a science keeps the selection criteria in a state of evolution, with the result that the definition of what is a good reason, or what is to count as rational within a discipline, is continually in flux, continually in question. This means, says Toulmin, that whether some change has been made with adequate rational justification or whether it is the result of some intellectually irrelevant cause is never quite clear. According to this account, the problems, goals, capacities, and selection criteria that help to bring new concepts into being and to determine their fate are all functions of the current state of the discipline itself and are located in a profession, in its participants and institutions. These factors all contribute to the process of scientific inquiry and are ultimately part of the inventional equipment of a discipline. In *An Introduction to Reasoning*, Stephen Toulmin, Richard Rieke, and Allan Janik (1979) present this view of scientific discourse in simplified form as Chapter 14, "Argumentation in Science." They identify the types of claims, warrants, and backing used in the forums of scientific argumentation, deriving these from the problems, issues, and goals of the scientific enterprise. James P. Zappen demonstrates the ways these elements control the rhetoric of technical and scientific reports in "A Rhetoric for Research in Sciences and Technologies" (1983).

Ludwig Fleck's *Genesis and Development of a Scientific Fact,* originally published in German in 1935, had effectively no audience until Thomas Kuhn chanced across it in 1950 and encouraged others to read it; it was finally published in English in 1979. On the basis of an historical analysis of the scientific understanding of syphilis as a disease and the development of the Wasserman test, Fleck explains scientific knowledge not as a dual relationship between a knowing subject and an object but as involving a third element, the existing fund of knowledge. The carrier of the fund of knowledge Fleck calls a "thought collective," which is "a community of persons mutually exchanging ideas or maintaining intellectual interaction" (p. 39). The thought collective has a particular thought style, which determines the form and nature of new developments. Although members of a thought collective are rarely conscious of the prevailing thought style, it exerts a "compulsive force" on their thinking. Consequently, "all empirical discovery can...be construed as a supplement, development, or transformation of the thought style" (p. 92). In addition to this theoretical analysis, which bears some affinities to that of Kuhn, Fleck's discussion of the development of syphilis as a medical concept and of the Wasserman test for it provides useful case material for the study of scientific inquiry and invention.

Walter B. Weimer's *Notes on the Methodology of Scientific Research* (1979) provides a critique and overview of the rhetorical issues engaged in the confrontation between what he terms the non-justificationist (or rhetorical) account of science, represented by Kuhn and others, and the justificationist (or logical) account, which assumes that proof is attainable. Israel Scheffler's *Science and Subjectivity* (1967) includes a critique of Kuhn's work on the basis that standards of proof in paradigm debates are available which guarantee the objectivity of science; these include some of the very standards to which Kuhn himself alludes. Harriet Zuckerman's "Theory Choice and Problem Choice in Science" (1968) reviews current work in sociology and philosophy on cognitive change in science to determine areas of agreement and divergence. In the area of theory choice in scientific work, she finds little correspondence between the two disciplines in coverage and findings but finds better correspondence in the area of problem choice. Empirical sociological research finds that theory and concepts can preempt or control the attention of researchers in five ways that are supported by philosophical work: theoretical concepts can lead to inconsistent observations and to the conclusion that a line of research is not feasible, can constrain interpretation of observation, determine what is believed to be problematic, and divert attention to other problems (p. 75). Accepted concepts thus serve as heuristic devices in a negative sense by diverting and focusing attention. The work of Diana Crane (*Invisible Colleges* [1972]) and Derek J. de Solla Price ("Citation Measures of Hard Science, Soft Science, Technology, and Nonscience" [1970] among many others) explores the ways in which previous work influences current work through the processes of cumulation, or "contagion" as Crane calls it, and discontinuity, as evidenced in citation patterns.

A related but slightly different account is offered in the work of Gerald Holton on scientific genius and the scientific imagination (*Thematic Origins of Scientific Thought* [1973]; *The Scientific Imagination* [1978]). An historian, Holton began with an interest in "the nascent moment" of scientific discovery, in the personal struggle, rather than the public justification. He finds evidence of the crucial role played by preconceptions, motivations, intuition, luck, neglect, and stubbornness in important scientific developments. These elements constitute a third "dimension" of science in addition to the empirical and the logical, a dimension he calls the thematic. Themata arise both in individual predilections and in historical movements. They often come in antithetical pairs: atomism/continuun, evolution/devolution, hierarchy/unity, mathematics/models; others are symmetry, complementarity, and chirality. He believes that the "deep attachment of some scientists to certain over-arching themata may well be one of the chief sources of innovative energy" (*The Scientific Imagination*, p. xi). In his work on Einstein, for example, Holton finds many polarities in Einstein's thought which seemed to propel him into the central issues of the unresolved problems in the physics of his time. Themata are rarely explicitly acknowledged or argued about but serve as rhetorical *topoi* that may lead to powerful arguments or insights.

Aesthetic value is a *topos* mentioned in passing by Kuhn and others. A collection of essays edited by Judith Wechsler, *On Aesthetics in Science* (1978), explores the role of aesthetic judgment in science and mathematics. Some of the aesthetic principles discussed are similar to Holton's themata (hierarchy and symmetry). Other essays discuss the role of visualization in the development of the quantum theory, the role of the unconscious in math, and the role of imagery in Darwin's thought, as evidenced in his notebooks, journals, and published writing. In her introductory essay, Wechsler refers to comments by Bohr, Dirac, Einstein, Heisenberg, and Poincaré that aesthetic judgment can be a decisive factor in accepting or rejecting a model or theory. Max Wertheimer's *Productive Thinking* (1959) compares two traditional theories of thinking (traditional logic and associationism) with gestalt learning as a way of comprehending structural features, groupings, and dynamic relation operations; there are chapters on Galileo's discovery of the law of inertia and Einstein's discovery of special relativity. The psychology of the individual scientist is the subject of Ian Mitroff's *The Subjective Side of Science* (1974), which, through an extensive case study of scientists studying the moon rocks from the Apollo missions, contends that the public account of science and scientific procedure fails to capture aspects of scientific rationality that are beyond logic. The general argument is similar to the arguments made by the major sources cited in this section, but the case material substantiates these claims and documents the process of conceptual change in an unprecedented and thorough way, in part because it is based on access to unfolding events rather than on historical materials. Two other influences on scientific inquiry have been suggested but are not developed at length: national character or "styles of mind," suggested by Pierre Duhem in a comparison of French and British physics in *The Aim and Structure of Physical Theory* (1962), and the nature of particular disciplines themselves, suggested by D. W. Theobald in "Some Considerations on the Philosophy of Chemistry" (1976). He claims that physics, chemistry, and biology use different types of concepts and different levels of organization, and have differing preferences for formal and quantitative explanations.

Conceptual change is a major result of scientific activity and a potential by-product of technological innovation. Both types of endeavor work through the process of problem-solving; the literature on problem-solving is important to the study of rhetorical invention in general, as Richard Young has suggested. Similarly, the literature on problem-solving in science and technology can illuminate the study of invention in these fields. Problem-solving can be conceived of both as a psychological phenomenon, in which individuals or groups engage in various activities to solve a problem, and as a social phenomenon, in which some social institution allocates resources to gain some innovation of social value.

Much of the work on individual problem-solving draws from introspective accounts, such as those of Henri Poincaré, Jacques Hadamard, and others cited above. These accounts typically list several stages; the most common account, perhaps derived from Poincaré, was popularized by Graham Wallas in *The Art of Thought* (1926) and was discussed at some length in Young, Becker, and Pike, *Rhetoric* (1970) and in Polanyi, *Personal Knowledge* ([1964] pp. 120–31). This account consists of four stages: preparation, incubation, illumination, and verification. Much of the literature on problem-solving is reviewed by John F. Feldhusen and Virginia Guthrie in "Models of Problem-Solving Process and Abilities" (1979). They cover information-processing models, human ability models, and creative models, and provide access to the most important work in each area, although none is specifically related to science or technology.

Most accounts of problem-solving include a preparatory stage when the problem itself must be perceived, identified, and defined. This stage is analogous to the doctrine of *stasis* in Greek and Roman rhetoric: the determination of the issue to be argued and the kinds of questions it raises, particularly with respect to law (see George A. Kennedy, *Classical Rhetoric* [1980]). A general discussion of problem-finding is found in J. W. Getzels, "Problem-Finding and the Inventiveness of Solutions" (1975). He suggests that this early stage is often the key to effective and inventive solutions for problems in practical affairs, science, art, and education. In "The Process of Problem Finding" (1969), William F. Pounds reports field work in which he attempted to discover how managers in a large technically based corporation acquired and defined the problems they dealt with. Drawing on theoretical work in the field of computer problem-solving, Pounds defines a problem as the difference between an existing situation and some desired situation. Managers "find" problems by comparing what they perceive to be the existing situation and some model that determines the desired situation: "The problem of understanding problem finding is therefore eventually reduced to the problem of understanding the models which managers use to define differences" (p. 5). Pounds found four kinds of models in use: historical patterns, planning projections, other people's models, and extra-organizational models. As a rule, the models used by these managers were naive and intuitive compared with the theoretical models used by engineers in the same company to define technical problems.

Indeed, one of the important areas of development in management theory today is the development of sophisticated modeling techniques for defining and solving management problems such as inventory, scheduling, and assembly-line balancing. The theoretical backgrounds of this work, in operations research, artificial intelligence, and computational complexity theory, are reviewed briefly by Herbert A. Simon in "On How to Decide What to Do" (1978), and some applications are mentioned in the next section of this essay. In *The Sciences of the Artificial* (1981), Simon points out that "uncertainty, computational complexity, and lack of operationality have been the principal barriers to extending operations research techniques to the upper levels of management. [Instead] heuristic search...is...the principal engine for human problem solving" (p. 36).

Simon and his co-workers have recently been interested in modeling (mimicking) human problem-solving behavior in computers, beginning with a General Problem Solver program and studies of chess playing and extending to such "semantically rich domains" as physics and engineering thermodynamics. This latter work represents the beginning of inquiry into technical problem-solving. Earlier, Simon had suggested that scientists use heuristic processes superior to those of everyday problem-solving, specifically that they possess superior techniques of observation and representation based on instrumentation and mathematics (*Models of Discovery* [1977], p. 291). He believes that scientific discovery in general is a form of problem-solving, and scientific processes can therefore be explained in terms of computer problem-solving theory, that is, with reference to pattern detection, heuristic searches, and comparison. In their study, "Expert and Novice Performance in Solving Physics Problems" (1980), Jill Larkin and colleagues found in thinking-aloud protocols of experts and novices four differences in their processes for solving a particular type of physics problem. First, the expert solved the problems much faster; second, the expert worked forward from givens and the novice worked backwards from unknowns in order to set sub-goals in the search; third, the expert apparently stored entire procedures and used them as units, while the novice recalled and worked with one step at a time; and fourth, the novice seemed to use a process of direct translation of the word problem into equations, while the expert seemed to generate a physical representation. In "Problem Solving in Semantically Rich Domains" (1977), R. Bhaskar and Herbert A. Simon use thinking-aloud protocols and parallel construction of computer programs to simulate the human processes revealed in the protocols. They conclude that even in technical domains such as engineering thermodynamics, people use strategies that are essentially similar to those observed for self-contained laboratory problems. Knowledge of thermodynamics enters into the process in several ways: the problem-solver can ignore some variables in the problem statement, check the units in the equations to detect errors, and evoke from memory equations containing variables that need to be found. The strategy combines a relatively content-free form of means-ends analysis with the stored semantic information by means of recognition mechanisms that recall the appropriate information or equations from memory. The reasoning that leads to medical diagnosis was studied through observation and controlled experiments by Arthur Elstein, Lee Shulman, and Sarah Sprafka (*Medical Prob-*

lem Solving [1978]). They present a heuristic that seems to help students solve medical problems.

The second type of study of problem-solving examines the effectiveness of problem-solving strategies in social contexts; these strategies, such as brainstorming, the Delphi method, and the nominal group technique, are organized procedures for encouraging creative problem-solving. Some of this work involves technical and scientific contexts. Brainstorming, originally developed by Alex F. Osborne in 1939 for use in his advertising agency (see his *Applied Imagination* [1953]), is a simple set of rules for encouraging the rapid generation of possible problem solutions. Donald W. Taylor, Paul C. Berry, and Clifford H. Block ("Does Group Participation When Using Brainstorming Facilitate or Inhibit Creative Thinking?" [1958]) found that individual work was superior to group participation with respect to the mean number of ideas produced, the mean number of unique ideas produced, and three measures of quality of solutions. The Delphi technique, developed at the RAND Corporation, was an attempt to provide structure to group problem-solving sessions so as to avoid the disadvantages of both confrontation and isolation and to obtain the most reliable consensus of a group of experts. The process consists essentially of a series of questions to isolated experts with controlled feedback about group opinion between questions. In "An Experimental Application of the Delphi Method to the Use of Experts" (1963), N. C. Dalkey and Olaf Helmer describe their initial use of the method with a panel of seven experts asked to estimate the number of bombs necessary to achieve a certain effect under certain conditions; they achieved increasing consensus through a series of five responses. Andrew H. Van de Ven and André L. Delbecq compare the methods and outcomes of three group decision procedures: unstructured groups, Delphi technique, and their own "nominal group technique," designed to provide structure to group problem-solving sessions for NASA engineers and citizens participating in social program planning. They find the Delphi and nominal group techniques equally effective and both more effective than unstructured groups, based on the quantity of unique ideas produced and the satisfaction of the participants. William E. Souder and Robert W. Ziegler provide a condensed view of problem-solving that has been or can be applied to technological innovation ("A Review of Creativity and Problem Solving Techniques" [1977]).

Other work on problem-solving in industry and research focuses on the types and sources of information sought during the problem-solving process. In "Studies of the Problem-Solving Process in Engineering Design" (1966), Thomas J. Allen provides a useful overview of the research program on the management of science and technology at MIT, as well as the specific methods and findings of one project. Three parallel R&D projects were compared on the basis of the quality of the solution, the number of alternatives considered, the duration and seriousness with which the alternatives were considered, and the information sources used by the engineers and scientists working on the problem. The sources sought depend upon the phase of the project itself and the problem-solving stage, and the time spent gathering information seems positively related to the quality of the solution. Much of Allen's work is compiled in *Managing the Flow of Technology* (1977), which also presents a great deal of data on the role of information and information sources in R&D. In "The Acquisition of Technical Information by R&D Managers for Problem Solving in Nonroutine Contingency Situations" (1979), William A. Fischer suggests that information-gathering is affected by the size of the firm, degree of technical familiarity with the problem, source of the information, and awareness of changes in the problem situation. Other work that explores the relationship of communication patterns to innovation in industry is reviewed in R. Rothwell and A. B. Robertson's "The Role of Communications in Technological Innovation" (1973). The variables typically examined in this type of research are the channels of communication, the organizational source, and the motivational origin of the idea (whether an idea arose in recognition of a need or in recognition of a new technical capability). In the studies reviewed by Rothwell and Robertson, personal contact is the most important channel for the transfer of information during innovation. The implication is that communication itself, and certain kinds of communication in particular, can serve a heuristic function. Other studies that make this connection are Donald C. Pelz and Frank M. Andrews's *Scientists in Organizations* (1966), which suggests that effective scientists both sought and received more contact with colleagues and that creative ability enhanced performance on new projects with free communication but seemed to impair performance in less flexible situations; D. W. Cravens's "An Exploratory Analysis of Individual Information Processing" (1970), which attempts to relate information-processing capabilities and preferences of decision-makers with features of the task itself and the relationship between the decision-maker and the decision task; and Michael J. Mahoney and Bobby G. DeMonbreun's "Psychology of the Scientist" (1977), which suggests that there is no significant difference in problem-solving efficiency between scientists and non-scientists and no significant difference in the tendency to rely on the logic of falsification.

Work on technological innovation provides insight into the criteria and directions of technological development and thus into the sorts of reasons that might be offered when arguing about such developments. Stephen Toulmin emphasizes that technological innovation is subject to both external, socio-economic factors and internal, professional factors (*Human Understanding*, pp. 367–68 [1972]). Henry Skolinowski, in "The Structure of Thinking in Technology" (1966), defines the criteria of technical progress as durability, reliability, sensitivity, speed, combinations of these, and the speed and cost of production. In "Creativity" (1976), Gerald G. Udell, Kenneth G. Baker, and Gerald S. Albaum describe a preliminary evaluation system for inventions to determine the likelihood of commercial success. There are five areas of evaluation, which form a similar set of general technological arguments: social utility, business risk, specific demand, market acceptance, and competition. Devendra Sahal's comprehensive study, *Patterns of Technological Innovation* (1981), finds that such innovation patterns are primarily physical and only secondarily socio-economic, that, in other words, the inner mechanism of innovation is largely technology-specific (pp. 13–14). Innovation is driven less by science or by social need than by what he calls "technological guideposts," which serve as exemplars or model solutions for incremental refinement and adaptation to different problems (pp. 33–36). The technology-specific features that govern the dynamics of development are the history or accumulated practical experience in a technology, and scaling, or the specific form appropriate for the adaptation of a technique to a task: "determining the appropriate scale of a technique for the performance of a given task is the very crux of research and development activity" (p. 307). Sahal's discussion is based on data from development in farm equipment, railroads, papermaking, petroleum refining, aircraft, and energy generation.

Contexts, Constraints, and Forums for Presentation

The narrow view of invention, as Harrington described it, concerns the search for arguments for a particular occasion, a search that may be thought of as guided by a concern more for eloquence—or perhaps effectiveness—than for wisdom. This is the more common version of rhetoric, understood as persuasion. It involves the need to understand one's audience and to seek more or less deliberately for proofs that the audience will accept as good reasons for assenting to one's claims. What becomes important at this point are the interests, knowledge, and values that rhetor and audience hold in common, the occasions in which they engage in discourse, the institutions and contexts that both motivate and constrain discourse.

Beyond the work on audience analysis covered elsewhere in this collection, there are several relevant areas of research that can illuminate these issues for scientific and technical discourse in particular. Sociologists and others have studied the values, norms, and procedures that characterize the scientific community; there are some diverse accounts of the rhetorical conditions in which scientists and technical people actually work; there is voluminous literature on the administrative and organizational contexts within which technical discourse is created and exists; and finally there are the beginnings of a literature on the broader social and cultural context within which scientific and technical discourse address social problems and public policy.

G. Nigel Gilbert observes that persuasion is crucial for science; it is the "process by which a scientist's research findings are transformed into accredited factual knowledge" ("The Transformation of Research Findings into Scientific Knowledge" [1976]). Gilbert identifies this process with the context of justification, rather than the context of discovery, although he does note that his concern is not with philosophical justification but with the justification "actually used by natural scientists to decide on the validity of claims to scientific knowledge" (p. 282). Gilbert argues that "the only public evaluation a knowledge claim receives occurs when it is cited as supporting evidence for further knowledge claims.'' The selection of which claims to cite is based on the research "models" from which researchers have learned about their research area and those that are current and considered valid within the research community. These become the basis of justification for the community. "Evaluation is therefore a process of deciding whether a knowledge claim is compatible with the family of models used within an area, the result of the decision being marked by the frequent citation of the claim by members of a research network" (p. 299). In this way, then, the intellectual substance that can provide heuristic force within the context of discovery provides persuasive force within the context of justification, so long as the models, concepts, and other aspects of intellectual substance are shared.

The disjunction between actual scientific work and the public accounting of it in published papers is reflected in P. B. Medawar's frequently quoted statement that "scientific 'papers'. . . [do] not merely conceal but actively misrepresent the reasoning that goes into the work they describe" (*The Art of the Soluble* [1967], p. 151). John Ziman's *Public Knowledge* (1968) sees scientific writing fundamentally as argument. He points to the rhetorical power of experimental method ("Seeing is believing") and to the persuasive force that the fact of publication possesses, indicating the imprimatur of an editor and a peer review system.

Analysis of the arguments in formal scientific literature has also been a recent project in the sociology of science. Charles Bazerman provides a detailed and comprehensive review of this literature, organizing it according to its relevance to rhetorical study ("Scientific Writing as a Social Act" [1983]). Stephen Yearley believes that "formal scientific papers should be regarded primarily as contributions to scientific debates" ("Textual Persuasion" [1981], p. 410). Karin D. Knorr-Cetina's *The Manufacture of Knowledge* (1981) is a detailed examination of the types of reasoning that scientists use and the ways their arguments gain force from the particular interests and requirements of scientific communities. In "The Birth of Molecular Biology" (1984), S. Michael Halloran examines the proofs used by James D. Watson and Francis Crick in their famous *Nature* paper; he argues that their style constitutes a powerful ethical appeal.

The relationship between rhetor and audience is the concern of ethics; the values by which this relationship is governed for scientists has come to be called the *ethos* of science. Karl R. Wallace, in "The Substance of Rhetoric" (1963), points out that the materials of discourse are "statements that are evoked by the need to make choices" (p. 241), that is, the "stuff" of rhetoric is ethics. The values that justify choices are consequently the concern of invention. Wallace points out that, although the choices and values in "expository" discourse, including that of scientists, are more remote and less apparent than those in persuasive discourse, even the scientist cannot escape the necessity of making choices: "His decisions are anchored in contexts governed by rules, conventions, and practices, whether they be those of the scientist or those of the non-scientist public" (p. 242). He notes that two values are fundamental to science: that knowledge itself is a good thing and that information is accurate and reliable.

Robert K. Merton's work in the sociology of science made of *ethos* a sociological commonplace. His early work on the relationship between Protestantism and institutional science led him to posit a "community of assumptions" that was mutually reinforcing. An essay in 1942, "The Normative Structure of Science," posited a general set of norms that governs the relationships of scientists. These are institutional values, both proscriptions and prescriptions, that scientists learn mostly from example and by inference from a "moral consensus" of scientists. These "institutional imperatives," Merton claimed, derive from the goals and methods of science; they are what make the extension of certified knowledge possible. The norms are therefore binding on scientists. This essay, as well as most of Merton's work in this area, is included in *The Sociology of Science* (1973); Norman Storer's "Introduction" is a useful historical review of the development of the sociology of science and Merton's role in its development.

Merton identified four institutional imperatives that he took to comprise the *ethos* of modern science: universalism, "communism," disinterestedness, and organized skepticism. Recently, this formulation has been subjected to some criticism, largely because there is no evidence of conscious commitment to its elements by scientists and because deviations are frequent. Some critics distinguish between social and cognitive (or technical) norms, between professed values and statistical norms, and between norms and counternorms. Merton himself suggested the notion of counternorms, and Ian Mitroff's lengthy case study of scientists studying rock samples from the moon provides empirical corroboration (*The Subjective Side of Science* [1974]). Thus, disinterestedness and skepticism are countered by strong commitment; universalism (or the judgment of claims according to universal standards) is balanced by particularism (the reliance on elite or personal standards); "communism," or communality, is balanced by secrecy, which prevents priority disputes and permits fuller verification of results before publication. The literature on norms, including the criticism, is reviewed in Robert A. Rothman, "A Dissenting View on the Scientific Ethos" (1972); Michael J. Mahoney, "Psychology of the Scientist" (1979); Michael Mulkay, "Norms and Ideology in Science" (1976); and Nico Stehr, "The Ethos of Science Revisited" (1978). In *Science and the Sociology of Knowledge* (1979), Mulkay observes that the *ethos* formulated by Merton is bound up with a positivist epistemology of science; Merton's norms explain how it is possible to achieve "statements of observable regularities, accurate within the technical limits of the time" (p. 24). If one treats the correspondence of scientific statements with observation as a social phenomenon that is subject to negotiation, the norms become themselves subject to social negotiation. If this is the case, Mulkay concludes, scientific knowledge is "inherently inconclusive" (p. 54) because claims are evaluated not by universal criteria but for their ability to meet the requirements of a particular context, that context being a particular problem-field. Scientific contexts usually present the following types of criteria: consistency with other knowledge claims and conformity to certain technical standards, such as quantitative precision, replicability, and range of evidence, which vary according to the prevailing standards of a particular field. Mulkay finally believes that the distinction between social and technical norms cannot be maintained and that all such norms are open to interpretation, negotiation, and change. They not only become the *topoi* for argument but are also subject to argument themselves.

Jacob Bronowski's *Science and Human Values* (1972) makes an argument similar to Merton's, that the goals and activities of science necessitate certain values, and further that science has promoted a set of values beneficial to the larger society, because "the scientific spirit is more human than the machinery of governments" (p. 70). He describes the values thus:

The society of scientists is simple because it has a directive purpose: to explore the truth. Nevertheless, it has to solve the problem of every society, which is to find a compromise between man and men. It must encourage the single scientist to be independent, and the body of scientists to be tolerant. From these basic conditions, which form the prime values, there follows step by step a range of values: dissent, freedom of thought and speech, justice, honor, human dignity and self-respect. (p. 68)

Most work on the *ethos* of technology has been in the form of social criticism that identifies it with ideology. In the thought of Jacques Ellul (*The Technological Society* [1964]) and Herbert Marcuse (*One-Dimensional Man* [1964]), technology as a system of control acquires social and political power through its control over action and thought. Daniel Bell grants to technology the same social power but sees it as a positive force, a new definition of rationality in terms of efficiency and optimization (*The Coming of Post-Industrial Society* [1976]). Jürgen Habermas distinguishes between purposive-rational action, which is promoted by technology and science, and symbolic interaction, which is required for the maintenance of social institutions. His ultimate claim is that with the institutionalizing of scientific and technical progress, this dualism vanishes, replacing personal and social values with the ideology of rationality ("Technology and Science as 'Ideology' " [1970]). In a similar critique, Carolyn R. Miller describes the self-effacing *ethos* that technology creates through the forms of action it generates ("Technology as a Form of Consciousness" [1978]). She points out that the closed-system thinking promoted by high-context technology precludes any notion of invention since anything discoverable within a closed system is a tautology.

Although there is no formal code of ethics for science, the American Association for the Advancement of Science has issued a report that surveys the ethical problems raised by the need of the scientific community for both freedom and responsibility (John T. Edsall, *Scientific Freedom and Responsibility* [1975]). It covers the conditions required for scientific freedom and responsibility; the problems encountered in highly competitive and heavily administered scientific work; some issues related to science and the public interest; some specific ethical problems in genetic, psychological, and fetal research; and the role of professional societies in ethical issues. The National Society of Professional Engineers does have a code of ethics, adopted in 1946, which covers the engineer's relations with other engineers, the public, clients and employers, and the profession. In addition, the National Council of Engineering Examiners has adopted a model law, intended to guide state boards of engineering registration in developing statutes involving the engineering profession. Both the code of ethics and the model law are reproduced in John D. Constance's *How to Become a Professional Engineer* (1978). Current problems in engineering ethics are explored in *Ethical Problems in Engineering* (1978), edited by Robert J. Baum and Albert Flores.

That scientific organizations should be more concerned with the implications of freedom and engineering organizations concerned with governmental regulation is instructive. The ethical issues are different for technologists and scientists, as are their goals and activities. The professional allegiances of the two groups differ, as Thomas J. Allen points out in "Roles in Technical Communication Networks" (1970); scientists generally engage in discipline-oriented work and technologists in mission-oriented work. In part, their conditions of employment are different and their professional allegiances are differently motivated. Scientists are usually employed by non-profit research organizations and owe professional allegiance to their discipline, to a research area or "invisible college" that is geographically dispersed. Technologists are usually employed by profit-making organizations to which their primary professional allegiance is owed. Scientists and technologists thus belong to different rhetorical communities and may be expected to use and assent to different sorts of arguments. The difficulties that scientists encounter within industrial organizations have been the subject of some commentary. William Kornhauser's *Scientists in Industry* (1963) studied the growing interdependence of the scientific professions and bureaucratic organizations. He found that the professional-level employee is often subject to conflicting sets of demands: to the profession and to the organization. The organization usually restricts the scientist's behavior, particularly the communication patterns that academic scientists take for granted; scientific developments become not part of the open literature but proprietary information to be protected by patents and trade secrecy. Frank Harrison, however, challenges the consensus of the available literature that the goals of scientists and their managers differ so widely. In "Goal Orientations of Managers and Scientists" (1980), he finds that the similarities greatly outnumber the differences in responses to a questionnaire on attitudes toward aspects of organizational management.

The effect of the working environment and work practices on rhetorical invention is an area about which only the sketchiest suggestions can be made. Scientific autobiographies, such as James D. Watson's *The Double Helix* (1968), provide some clues. Watson discusses in some detail the ways in which he and Francis Crick collaborated, the sources of the puzzle parts they fitted together in figuring out the structural model of DNA, and the pace and variety of laboratory work. Bruno Latour and Steve Woolgar's *Laboratory Life* (1979) also gives an intimate portrayal of scientific practice based upon detailed field observation of scientists at the Salk Institute. Analogous accounts of technological work are available in Richard L. Meehan's *Getting Sued and Other Tales of the Engineering Life* (1981) and in Tracy Kidder's *The Soul of a New Machine* (1981), an investigative account of the development of a new computer line in the lab of a major manufacturer. A case study that reveals the invention process of a single engineer is reported by Jack Selzer ("The Composing Processes of an Engineer" [1983]). The particular engineer studied, a manager in a consulting firm, spends about 80 percent of his composing time inventing and arranging. Invention techniques used include re-reading previous reports, analyzing client needs, making preliminary notes, consulting with colleagues, and establishing the criteria and knowledge of the audience. The role of collaboration in technical work is emphasized by N. Bruce Hannay and Robert E. McGinn ("The Anatomy of Modern Technology" [1980]) as well as the role of external contexts in providing not merely information but reasons for argument. They describe each of these contexts in some detail, explaining the influence of government policy and legal decision-making, market research, financial management, voter referenda, international relations, and other effects on the organization of the technological firm and the planning and conduct of its work.

Philip H. Abelson discusses the role of group interaction in the creative process, particularly in scientific research. He suggests that accounts emphasizing individual creativity and the process of illumination distort the importance of group judgment and motivation through group interaction ("Relation of Group Activity to Creativity in Science" [1965]). Other work emphasizes the influence of the organizational context in which scientific and technical work takes place. Thus, Harvey Brooks, in "Technology, Evolution, and Purpose" (1980), suggests that technology includes managerial and social supporting systems. Consequently, he says, "economies of scale have been a major driving force in the evolution of technology in the twentieth century" (p. 71), suggesting that this managerial concern has penetrated the processes and discourse of modern technology. More generally, N. R. Baker, J. Siegmann, and A. H. Rubenstein, in "The Effects of Perceived Needs and Means on the Generation of Ideas for Industrial Research and Development Projects" (1967), suggest that there is a relationship between a researcher's knowledge of organizational goals and needs and the generation of new ideas. In a survey about the development of 303 ideas in an idea generation group, knowledge of the organization's problems, needs, and opportunities helped to stimulate about 75 percent of the ideas. They conclude that because management has control over the perception of these problems and opportunities, the productivity of the researcher can be significantly influenced by research management.

The conditions under which discourse occurs are established not only by the disciplinary or technical concepts but also by a social and institutional framework. Thus, the organization that supplies the setting for technical and scientific rhetoric is of interest, especially to the study of technical communication, since technologists' discourse is more often constrained by the needs of the supporting corporation, agency, or institution. The body of literature on organization theory is therefore relevant to invention, in particular the branch that concerns itself with the ways organizations handle decision processes. The literature on problem-solving surveyed in the previous section informs the heuristic problem of determining what is right, what is new, and what is responsive to a problem; the literature on decision-making, although related, may be taken to inform the heuristic problem of determining what is acceptable and persuasive to an organizational audience or context. Charles Perrow's *Complex Organizations* (1979) provides a helpful introduction to the literature on organization theory. In summarizing the "neo-Weberian" model of organizations, Perrow points out that the premises of decision-making are more important than the process of decision-making or the capabilities of the individual who makes the decision. The premises are determined by the organization: they are found in the vocabulary or jargon of the organization; in the structure of communication; in the rules, regulations, and routines; in the selection criteria for personnel; and in other structural aspects of any organization.

A useful review of literature on decision-making in organizations with specific attention to information flow and communication networks is Terry Connolly's "Information Processing and Decision Making in Organizations" (1977), which emphasizes the effect of the "verbal" context on problem-definition, communication patterns, decision criteria, organizational structure, and thus on the entire decision-making process. Management reasoning is described in Toulmin, Rieke, and Janik's text, *An Introduction to Reasoning* (1979). They characterize it by its stress on the grounds for conclusions, that is, facts, databases, alternatives for action. Its warrants are often implicit, being based on organizational goals and values, such as profit, survival, efficiency; its backing is often provided by systems analysis and modeling.

Thomas J. Allen's work with R&D organizations suggested to him that bureaucratic organizations develop their own "coding schemes," that they interpret and structure problems and weigh criteria in their own way. This accounts for the negative relationship he found between the use of external information sources and project success (*Managing the Flow of Technology* [1977], pp. 135–36). Similarly, Susan Koch and Stanley Deetz, in "Metaphor Analysis of Social Reality in Organizations" (1981), suggest that "organizational discourse performs what can be called an 'epistemic' function" (p. 3), with both ostensive reference to events and activities and non-ostensive reference to the conceptual world. James G. March and Johan P. Olsen's view in *Ambiguity and Choice in Organizations* (1976) is similar; these authors say that an organization is a "set of procedures for argumentation and interpretation as well as for solving problems and making decisions" (p. 25). Harold Garfinkel's " 'Good' Organizational Reasons for 'Bad' Clinic Records" (1967) illustrates the ways in which the content and form of routine health clinic documents are invented, both when created and when subsequently used, by the prevailing interests and activities of the clinic itself.

In a case history of the management of a high-technology project in an R&D laboratory ("The Management of Ambiguity" [1979]), in which both management and technical decisions were followed over the course of nearly ten years by observation and interviews, Michael B. McCaskey finds that neither goals nor decisions can be described adequately except in historical terms: that is, arguments become apparent (or necessary) only over time. In the extreme case, a decision is "something invented after the occasion to explain how events evolved" (p. 42). McCaskey says, "In managing ambiguous situations, then, one invents in both directions. . . . In a confusing welter of possibilities, participants invent backward in time in order to see decisions and invent forward in time in order to see goals" (p. 43). The proofs of such inventions are to be found in the particular versions of symbolic organizational reality that the participants can agree on.

In large part, the project of this style of research has been to critique rational decision theory, the attempt by economists to predict economic behavior through a theory of rationality based in the calculation of self-interest. March and Olsen suggest that the theory of rational choice presupposes the pre-existence of purpose, the necessity of consistency, and the primacy of rationality (that is, ends-means calculations). In contrast, they find that choice situations within organizations provide occasions for more than rational calculation, and that "the ideas, beliefs and attitudes that participants come to hold are important outcomes of the process of decision making" (p. 55). They prescribe a sense of "playfulness," or "deliberate, temporary relaxation of rules" (p. 77) as a complement to rational decision processes. Their prescription includes five procedures intended to "suspend the operation of the system of reasoned intelligence" (p. 79) in order to introduce change: treat goals as hypotheses, treat intuition as real, treat hypocrisy as a transition between values and behavior, treat memory as an enemy, and treat experience as a theory. What they propose, in effect, are ways to encourage invention in situations that do not lend themselves to strict calculation.

The work of Herbert A. Simon has been central to this line of research. In early studies (see, for instance, Richard M. Cyert, Simon, and Donald B. Trow, "Observation of a Business Decision" [1956]), Simon realized that actual decision-making in business and industry did not conform to the rational economic models. His subsequent work has been, in part, an attempt to account for, model, and predict deviations from the rational model. The rational model is algorithmic; it provides a method that guarantees "correct" results. The decision processes of individuals and organizations, while not "rational" in this sense, Simon notes, are still "intelligent." Simon discusses his own work in general terms in *The Sciences of the Artificial* (1981) and in its relations to the related fields of operations research, artificial intelligence, and cognitive science in "On How to Decide What to Do" (1978). James G. March provides a comprehensive overview of work in the "decision sciences," with particular attention to where and why the rational theories of choice are inferior to learned and conventional behavior, in "Bounded Rationality, Ambiguity, and the Engineering of Choice" (1978). In *The Sciences of the Artificial*, Simon proposes topics for a curriculum in the theory of design, a program of relevance, he believes, for any professional "whose task is to solve problems, to choose, to synthesize, to decide" (p. 157). It includes such rhetorical-seeming topics as the limits on rationality in complex situations, the uses of data in planning (including feedback and prediction), identification of the client (or audience), limitations of time and space, and responses to changing situations. These curriculum topics are aspects of the design process that can be either tools or constraints; Simon proposes that by being made explicit they will become tools.

James March uses the term "technologies of reason" to describe the ways of making explicit the methods of decision-making, while Daniel Bell speaks of "intellectual technologies" (*The Coming of Post-Industrial Society* [1976], p. xvi). Bell defines these as the substitution of algorithms for intuitive judgment (p. 29); they become necessary, he says, because complex systems are counterintuitive. By formalizing a decision process, an algorithm becomes, in effect, a *topos*, or a set of *topoi*, for discourse relevant to the issues it applies to. The algorithm promises a proof. There appear to be two kinds of such "intellectual technologies," procedural and substantive; some appear to be useful in a variety of situations, regardless of the substantive issue being confronted; others are designed for specific types of decisions. Some are, in fact, algorithms, or calculation procedures, and some are heuristics, or guides to decision-making. In the following section only brief mention can be made of some of the more representative or available technologies. Thomas P. Ference in "Organizational Communications Systems and the Decision Process" (1970), proposes a five-stage decision procedure based on the communication framework within an organization: problem recognition, identification of the scope and scale of the problem, acquiring and integrating information, defining constraints, and comparing and selecting solutions to constraints and adapting one to the other. The detailed explanation suggests many sources of relevance and constraint for each of these stages, which function as aids to or limitations on invention. In *Decision Making* (1977), Irving L. Janis and Leon Mann provide a "decisional balance sheet" (p. 138), a grid with alternative courses of action on one axis and utilitarian gains and losses for self and others and approval and disapproval of self and others on the other axis. By providing a way of conceptualizing the elements that go into a decision, this tool becomes an aid to invention. Two other procedures widely used in complex organizations are the Program Evaluation and Review Technique (PERT) and Critical Path Management (CPM). A recent work by Edward J. Dunne and Laurence J. Klementowski ("An Investigation of the Use of Network Techniques in Research and Development Management" [1982]) reviews the use of PERT and CPM in aerospace R&D projects. Even though it is no longer required by the Department of Defense, PERT is still widely used because R&D managers find it one of the best planning methods available: It "forces thinking through the entire project from beginning to end. It results in a specific identification of the critical and noncritical elements of the overall project'' (p. 77). The technique thus governs subsequent planning and discourse about the project.

Substantive technologies, or lists of special *topoi*, are available in many areas of technical decision-making. For example, William G. Sullivan and Wayne Claycombe in ''Decision Analysis of Capacity Expansion Strategies for Electrical Utilities'' (1977) systematize common sources of argument in decisions made by power companies, such as availability of fuel contracts, satisfaction of siting requirements, and effectiveness of energy conservation measures. A decision tree suggests an optimal strategy for expansion over a given period of time. In ''An Empirically Derived New Product Project Selection Model'' (1981), Robert G. Cooper lists thirteen factors that have determined the success of newly developed products on the industrial market. He suggests using these factors as *topoi* for arguing the success of a proposed product: ''This step forward lends rigor and confidence to what has traditionally been a judgemental decision'' (p. 60).

In ''A Practical Tool for Improved Resource Allocation'' (1978) Tony J. Van Roy and Ludo F. Gelders review the literature on management methods for allocating resources to projects, including common priority rules for allocating resources. They present a new heuristic method which they claim is more widely applicable than some existing ones. Environmental decision-making is another area in which many attempts have been made to systematize complex problems. Mark B. Lapping reviews these in ''Environmental Impact Assessment Methodologies'' (1975), dividing them into four general types: the associated matrix method, the index value approach, computer models, and the generally inadequate and unsystematic descriptive resource analysis approach. In ''Environmental Impact Statements and Rhetorical Genres'' (1980), Carolyn R. Miller suggests that the legal significance of certain terms in the National Environmental Policy Act made them into *topoi* for Environmental Impact Statements. They serve, she says, not as places in which arguments may be found ''but places in which arguments *must* be found'' (p. 137) because of the interpretations by the courts. Other studies that describe the processes and methods of technical decision-making are Richard G. Head, ''The Sociology of Military Decision-Making'' (1973), Andrew M. Pettigrew, *The Politics of Organizational Decision-Making* (1973), and C. R. Shumway and colleagues, ''Diffuse Decision Making in Hierarchical Organizations'' (1975).

Technical argumentation and decision-making occur outside the administrative context, including, of course, the public and political arena. Here, too, the discovery of proofs is central to debate, yet there is no comprehensive or systematic treatment in the literature of the inventional aspects of technological controversy. Allan Mazur's book, *The Dynamics of Technical Controversy* (1981), comes closest. He examines in detail the disputes over fluoridation of water supplies and nuclear power, discovering that the same kinds of arguments were used in both disputes and on both sides of the issues. The most common arguments were the lack of evidence, the rejection of discrepant data, and the interpretation of ambiguous data to support one's own position. Mazur believes that the expert's own position is often attributable to non-technical factors, such as social influence. Similarly, a set of premises, or ideology, characterizes those who support and those who oppose any new technology. Proponents subscribe to three central beliefs: that there is an important need for the technology, that it is effective, and that it is safe. Opponents disagree by minimizing the problem, by questioning the efficacy of the technology, and by demonstrating its hazards. Furthermore, Mazur notes that the nature of a technology itself is a source of certain forms of argument: technologies that are very costly produce arguments about corporate profit and responsibility; military technology necessarily produces arguments about foreign policy; technologies that give low doses of stresses that are toxic at high doses produce arguments about dose-response curves and the responsibilities of regulatory agencies; technologies that cannot be adopted or rejected by individuals produce positions on individual rights and freedom of choice.

Another critique of public debate over technology is Randall L. Bytwerk's "The SST Controversy" (1979), in which he investigates the debate surrounding Congress's decision not to build the supersonic transport. As the first such decision against a new technology, Bytwerk believes that it marks a turning point in American public controversy, a point at which old arguments lose force and new ones develop. He observes that the burden of proof has shifted from those who oppose to those who favor a new technology; consequently, the nature and sources of proof will be different. In another study of the SST controversy, "Expert Advice in the Controversy About the Supersonic Transport in the United States" (1974), Ian D. Clark takes a dim view of the argument from authority: he finds that expert advice is rarely useful, is usually exploited to support political positions, and is seldom understood. His discussion of how to exploit expert advice is a somewhat cynical list of argumentative strategies that were used in the SST debate. In a study of another controversy over technology, the debate over the Food and Drug Administration's proposal to ban saccharin, Charles R. Bantz ("Public Arguing in the Regulation of Health and Safety" [1981]) suggests seven strategies that proponents can use to encourage "shared understanding" of an issue; these amount to a kind of Rogerian acknowledgment of the public's frame of reference and relative technological ignorance.

Often, the official argument in cases like these rests on the techniques of risk assessment. Two useful general discussions of how risk assessment is performed and how it is used in public policy debates are R. W. Kates, "Assessing the Assessors" (1977) and Chauncey Starr and Chris Whipple, "Risks of Risk Decisions" (1980). A sharp critique of the related field of technology assessment is given by B. Wynne in "The Rhetoric of Consensus Politics" (1975). The premises of the technology-assessment movement, according to Wynne, are that humans can control both nature and society and that knowledge is absolute and unchanging. These beliefs are the often unstated appeals underlying arguments based on technology assessment methods. At the heart of Wynne's critique is the assertion that technology assessment falsely assumes that science and politics can be cleanly distinguished. In a similar critique, Joseph R. Gusfield points out that both science and policy (what he calls the cognitive order and the moral order) are "invented," that they come to life by being dramatized. His Burkean analysis of the creation of the public problem of drunken driving takes the position that problems, crimes, and criminals are all social inventions that permeate public discourse (*The Culture of Public Problems* [1981]). Thomas B. Farrell and G. Thomas Goodnight, in "Accidental Rhetoric" (1981), examine the causes of what they consider to be failed technical communication. They suggest that the assumptions, procedures, expectations, and formats of technical communication are self-confirming, operating within undisturbed patterns. "The invention of advanced technology has had the unintended effect of technologizing rhetorical invention" (p. 277); as a consequence, the substance of communication is inaccessible to public comprehension and adjudication. Their indictment certainly suggests that whatever *topoi* are being used are not common ones. Similarly, Philip C. Wander suggests that science itself, particularly its technical language, becomes a major proof in public debate ("The Rhetoric of Science" [1976]).

Applications, Heuristics, Teaching Methods

Because invention as a rhetorical art has had no place in most thinking about technical and scientific discourse, there are scant resources for the teaching and application of the material covered in the previous sections of this review. In his history of the teaching of technical writing, Robert J. Connors attributes the general failure to teach invention to the lack of appropriately prepared teachers. In establishing the need for instruction in technical writing, engineering and technical schools cited the need for training in thinking and writing as a tool for technical work, but the teachers with literary backgrounds who eventually designed and controlled the courses were unable to address these needs ("The Rise of Technical Writing Instruction in America" [1982]). In addition, of course, such instruction reflected the general methods used in all writing instruction during the first half of the twentieth century. In "The Role of Models in Technical and Scientific Writing" (1983), Victoria M. Winkler briefly reviews recent discussions of the possibilities for the teaching of invention in the technical writing class and develops an explanation of the differences between the "product" and the "process" approaches to teaching writing based on the models of writing they presuppose. She recommends the process approach in technical writing pedagogy because it is based on an "inventional model" of the way the mind orders experience, and so includes both the processes that make technical and scientific writing distinctive (that is, scientific discovery and technical problem-solving) and the traditional structural (formal) models used by the product approach.

Material on the applications of invention can be organized as was the material in the previous sections: studies relevant to scientific and technical productivity and studies relevant to writing, both that intended for use by technical and scientific workers and that intended for the preparation of teachers or for use by students. In the first category are several works intended to improve the technical productivity or scientific creativity of technical or scientific workers. Alex F. Osborne's *Applied Imagination* (1953) and William J.J. Gordon's *Synectics* (1961), neither of which is confined to science and technology, are widely cited and adapted to scientific and technical contexts. G. Polya's *How to Solve It* (1957) discusses mathematical problem-solving and provides a "short dictionary of heuristic," including such entries as "look at the unknown," specialization, symmetry, wisdom of proverbs, analogy, "did you use all the data?" as well as entries on heuristic, heuristic reasoning, and modern heuristic. Fritz Zwicky's *Discovery, Invention, Research* (1969) is concerned with the potential contributions of science and technology to building a sound and stable world. Zwicky's general thesis is that each contribution will be more effective if pursued through what he calls the "morphological method," or "totality research," which amounts to a search for all possible solutions to a problem or all possible methods for solution. Finally, James L. Adams's *Conceptual Blockbusting* (1980) concerns the process of conceptualization, a major aspect of problem-solving that provides the problem-solver with more concepts to choose from. Through puzzles, examples, and systematic discussion, Adams aims to make the reader more aware of the creative process and the blocks that inhibit it. The book is based on instruction and research in the Design Division of the Stanford School of Engineering.

Other work addresses itself to the writing problems of technical and scientific professionals and students. For the professional, numerous articles of advice exist in the trade and professional journals. Many of these tend to discuss substance only in terms of the arrangement of sections in the completed discourse, but some include comments on what to write as well as how to organize, revise, document, and the like. A few of the more useful are noted here. Richard W. Dodge's "What to Report" (1962) describes the results of a survey of Westinghouse managers at all levels. It provides an extensive list of questions that managers want answered in the technical reports they read within each of five major technical areas of typical concern (technical problems, new projects and products, experiments and tests, materials and processes, and field troubles). These questions serve as heuristic *topoi* for report writers. Richard L. Larson's "How to Define Administrative Problems" (1962) is a kind of counterpart for managers themselves; it contends that management often fails both to understand the magnitude of a problem and to identify the reasons for its existence. Larson describes four common types of problems and suggests a systematic process for recognizing and articulating them clearly before attempting to solve them. The first chapters in two books about writing scientific and engineering papers and reports address the questions of what is publishable, that is, what constitutes a substantive addition to the discourse of these fields. Robert A. Day in *How to*

Write and Publish a Scientific Paper (1979) defines sufficiency of information for the primary scientific literature as that which permits potential readers to assess the observations made, repeat experiments, and evaluate intellectual processes. Herbert B. Michaelson's *How to Write and Publish Engineering Papers and Reports* (1982) urges the writer to assess the technical content of a manuscript by asking questions about utility to readers, originality, and whether the material is primarily conceptual, developmental, analytical, or descriptive. Subsequent chapters in both books allude to problems of content as they discuss issues of organization and style in more detail. H. Skolnik and L. F. McBurney discuss the functions of technical reports in a chemical R&D organization and the major types of reports that achieve these functions, including their major contents. Robert Hays's "Model Outlines Can Make Routine Writing Easier" (1982), while primarily concerned with arrangement, provides useful illustrations of the important contents of eleven typical kinds of technical reports. Mary M. Lay provides a detailed examination of the chronology, selection, and degree of detail appropriate for procedures, instructions, and specifications, with a series of questions to help guide the development of each ("Procedures, Instructions, and Specifications" [1982]). In their discussion of reader-based revision strategies for functional documents, Linda Flower, John R. Hayes, and Heidi Swarts make specific suggestions relevant to the content of such documents—fundamentally, that information should be structured around "human agents performing actions in particular situations." They suggest several specific ways to achieve this focus ("Revising Functional Documents" [1983]).

Work concerned with instruction in writing for students in science and technical fields, addressed either to their teachers or to students themselves, has recently begun to concern the problem of invention, as well as the writing process. The problem of invention is different for students than for working professionals, of course, because the student's situation is less likely to provide the sense of purpose, audience, and environment that actually constrain the substance of rhetoric by providing special *topoi*. For this reason, perhaps, several articles in the teaching literature have suggested the use of field-invariant heuristic aids to invention in technical writing. J. W. Allen, Jr. ("Introducing Invention to Technical Students" [1978]) discusses the difficulties of discussing invention in the technical writing class, ascribing them largely to the problem of distinguishing technical and scientific inquiry from rhetorical invention. He sees the processes as complementary and suggests that the tagmemic heuristic of Richard E. Young, Alton L. Becker, and Kenneth L. Pike is particularly appropriate for these students. Jeanne W. Halpern's "What Should We Be Teaching Students in Business Writing?" (1981) also suggests the use of the tagmemic heuristic's three perspectives—static, dynamic, and relative. Victoria M. Winkler, in "Creative Design and Rhetorical Inquiry" (1980), compares the process of engineering design and of rhetorical inquiry, using several versions of the problem-solving process in engineering textbooks and the tagmemic heuristic. The necessary shifting of roles from technical investigator to communicator suggests the utility of combining the process of technical investigation with the invention and arrangement aspects of the composing process. Ardner Cheshire, in "Teaching Invention" (1980), recommends the use of the common *topoi* developed by Frank D'Angelo from the classical *topoi* and recent work in cognitive psychology.

Others have commented that the special needs of technical writing instruction require different heuristic approaches. Several have focused on the problem-solving process as a source of heuristic potential. Michael G. Moran's "A Problem-Solving Heuristic" (1982) provides four problem-based questions that cover the major aspects of common business problems (problem identification, cause, structure, solution). More generally, Linda Flower and John R. Hayes ("Problem Solving Strategies and the Writing Process," [1977]) present a set of heuristic strategies for analytical writing based on the thesis that writing outside the classroom is goal oriented and that the strategies people use to achieve such goals can be abstracted and taught. Many of these strategies are also discussed in Flower's own text, *Problem-Solving Strategies for Writing* (1981). Discussion of the problem-solving process leads inevitably to the writing process itself. Patricia A. Sullivan's "Teaching the Writing Process in Scientific and Technical Writing Classes" (1980) advocates emphasizing the earlier stages of the writing process and provides examples of instructional approaches for teaching the thinking processes useful in preparing titles, introductions, resumés, and instructions. The course guide for the teaching of professional writing prepared at the Document Design Center also is organized around a "process model of document design," which provides, in the pre-writing stage, five topics of analysis: scope, purpose, audience, reader's task, and constraints (*Writing in the Professions* [1981], by Dixie Goswami and colleagues). David K. Farkas develops a set of questions he calls a heuristic of professional communication goals, designed around the problem of multiple goals students will encounter in their writing beyond the classroom. The six goals are types of needs a reader may have: to make a practical decision, to perform a task, to become aware of practical information, to respond with interest or satisfaction, to be motivated to do something, or to approve of the writer or writer's organization ("An Invention Heuristic for Business and Technical Communication" [1981]). A technique for making students aware of the goals and conditions of professional communication through simulated experience is described by Peter R. Klaver in "Build It Again, Sam" (1981).

In 1976, Dennis R. Hall published what was perhaps the first formal statement on the teaching of invention in technical writing ("The Role of Invention in Technical Writing"). He advocated less emphasis on form and more on competence in method, which he saw as an important point of connection between rhetoric and science. At that time, he said, "the most conspicuous failure of the current crop of technical writing books is the general avoidance of invention" (p. 18). The situation has improved only slightly since then. Most technical writing texts provide a superficial discussion of research methods, usually emphasizing library research over field and laboratory research, and subordinate any discussion of the functions and substance of documents to outlines of form and organization. J. C. Mathes and Dwight W. Stevenson's *Designing Technical Reports* (1976) is the most notable exception to these generalizations. Based soundly in organizational communication theory and organized around the design process, it places special emphasis on the early phase of that process: determining the function of the report in the system. Because each subsequent phase is constrained by these early decisions, invention is seen to permeate the entire report writing process. A similar but less elaborate presentation is given by James W. Souther and Myron L. White in their *Technical Report Writing* (1977). They also see the technical problem-solving process as a fundamental principle of report design, suggesting, first, attention to the communication problem (purpose, use, audience, information needs) and, second, analysis of alternatives in terms of the answers to the initial questions.

Two more recent books with similar approaches are intended for writers in government and management. Judson Monroe's *Effective Research and Report Writing in Government* (1980) is organized around a process that includes research and data analysis as well as writing. It suggests beginning the entire process with questions about the assignment, readers, subject, and analysis required. Monroe uses sets of reader questions to define common types of reports and provides other heuristic approaches to developing, analyzing, and organizing data and writing the report. Marya W. Holcombe and Judith K. Stein's *Writing for Decision Makers* (1981) is also organized around the writing process, with emphasis on identifying the reader's needs and using the problem-solving process to generate material for reports and memos. They provide examples and case studies to illustrate the heuristic methods they describe (most notably analysis "trees" and flowcharting). A final text illustrates the growing relationship between the teaching of technical writing and of general composition. In a chapter on "The Working World" in *Four Worlds of Writing*" (1981), Janice Lauer and colleagues begin their discussion of reports with advice to identify the problem and audience and to explore the problem with a version of the tagmemic heuristic. The text includes useful illustrations of how these modern versions of *stasis* and *topoi* can be used.

Conclusion

What stands out from the variety of material surveyed here, in a kind of negative relief, is the definitive influence of theory. Without a theory of technical and scientific discourse as argument, asking about invention in such discourse is an irrelevant—or foolish—undertaking. But with the beginning attempts to examine technical and scientific discourse as rhetoric, work that had seemed fragmented and unrelated acquires a new orientation, as though magnetized. A great deal of gap-filling and re-conceptualizing has yet to be done before invention in this area can be a coherent concept and before systematic and limited questions can be asked and rigorous answers found. To get started, it is tempting to import work from other fields, and this review attempts to suggest the potential benefits of doing so. But such borrowing should be done with care—with attention to the course of development, the assumptions, the conflicts and disagreements that characterize the field that is the source of the borrowed work. In turning to other fields and traditions for solutions to the initial problems in establishing an area of inquiry, one must be aware that one imports problems, as well as solutions, from other disciplines. Careful examination of the rhetorical tradition itself, which makes the concept of invention meaningful in the first place, is probably the safest and most promising way to begin.

References

Abelson, Philip H. "Relation of Group Activity to Creativity in Science." *Daedalus*, 94 (1965), 603–14.

Adams, James L. *Conceptual Blockbusting: A Guide to Better Ideas*. New York: Norton, 1980.

Allen, J. W., Jr. "Introducing Invention to Technical Students." *Tech Writ Teach*, 5 (1978), 45–49.

Allen, Thomas J. *Managing the Flow of Technology: Technology Transfer and the Dissemination of Technological Information Within the R&D Organization*. Cambridge, Mass.: MIT Press, 1977.

———. "Roles in Technical Communication Networks." In *Communication Among Scientists and Engineers*. Ed. Carnot E. Nelson and Donald K. Pollock. Lexington, Mass.: Heath, 1970, pp. 191–208.

———. "Studies of the Problem-Solving Process in Engineering Design." *IEEE Trans Eng Manag*, EM–13 (1966), 72–83.

Aristotle. *Posterior Analytics*. In *The Basic Works of Aristotle*. Ed. Richard McKeon. New York: Random House, 1941.

———. *The Rhetoric of Aristotle*. Ed. and trans. Lane Cooper. Englewood Cliffs, N.J.: Prentice-Hall, 1932.

Bacon, Francis. *Works of Francis Bacon*. 14 vols. Ed. James Spedding, Robert Leslie Ellis, and Douglas Denon Heath. London: 1859; rpt. Stuttgart, 1963.

Baker, N. R., J. Siegmann, and A. H. Rubenstein. "The Effects of Perceived Needs and Means on the Generation of Ideas for Industrial Research and Development Projects." *IEEE Trans Eng Manag*, 14 (1967), 156–62.

Bantz, Charles R. "Public Arguing in the Regulation of Health and Safety." *W J Speech Comm*, 45 (1981), 71–87.

Baum, Robert J., and Albert Flores, eds. *Ethical Problems in Engineering*. Troy, N.Y.: Rensselaer Polytechnic Institute, Center for the Study of the Human Dimensions of Science and Technology, 1978.

Bazerman, Charles. "Scientific Writing as a Social Act: A Review of the Literature of the Sociology of Science." In *New Essays in Technical and Scientific Communication: Theory, Research, and Practice*. Ed. Paul V. Anderson, R. John Brockmann, and Carolyn R. Miller. Farmingdale, N.Y.: Baywood, 1983, pp. 156–84.

———. "What Written Knowledge Does: Three Examples of Academic Discourse." *Phil Soc Sci*, 11 (1981), 361–87.

Bell, Daniel. *The Coming of Post-Industrial Society: A Venture in Social Forecasting*. New York: Basic, 1976.

Bhaskar, R., and Herbert A. Simon. "Problem-Solving in Semantically Rich Domains: An Example from Engineering Thermodynamics." *Cog Sci*, 1 (1977), 193–215.

Black, Max. *Models and Metaphors*. Ithaca, N.Y.: Cornell University Press, 1962.

Bridgman, P[ercy] W. "The Operational Aspect of Meaning." *Synthese*, 8 (1950–51), 251–59.

————. "Words, Meanings, and Verbal Analysis." In *Science and Language*. Ed. Alfred M. Bork. Boston: Heath, 1966, pp. 23–43.

Bronowski, Jacob. *Science and Human Values*. Rev. ed. New York: Harper, Row, 1965; rpt. New York, 1972.

Brooks, Harvey. "Technology, Evolution, and Purpose." *Daedalus*, 109, No. 1 (1980), 65–81.

Brummett, Barry. "Some Implications of 'Process' or 'Intersubjectivity': Postmodern Rhetoric." *Phil Rhet*, 9 (1976), 21–51.

Bryant, Donald C. "Rhetoric: Its Functions and Its Scope." *Q J Speech*, 39 (1953), 401–24.

Burke, Kenneth. "The Rhetorical Situation." In *Communication: Ethical and Moral Issues*. Ed. Lee Thayer. *Current Topics of Contemporary Thought*, vol. 10. New York: Gordon, Breach, 1973, pp. 263–75.

Bytwerk, Randall L. "The SST Controversy: A Case Study in the Rhetoric of Technology." *C S Speech J*, 30 (1979), 187–98.

Cheshire, Ardner. "Teaching Invention: Using Topical Categories in the Technical Writing Class." *Tech Writ Teach*, 8 (1980), 17–21.

Clark, Ian D. "Expert Advice in the Controversy About the Supersonic Transport in the United States." *Minerva*, 12 (1974), 416–32.

Connolly, Terry. "Information Processing and Decision Making in Organizations." In *New Directions in Organizational Behavior*. Ed. B. Staw and G. Salancik. Chicago: St. Clair, 1979, pp. 205–34.

Connors, Robert J. "The Rise of Technical Writing Instruction in America." *J Tech Writ Comm*, 12 (1982), 329–52.

Constance, John D. *How to Become a Professional Engineer*. 3rd ed. New York: McGraw-Hill, 1978.

Cooper, Robert G. "An Empirically Derived New Product Project Selection Model." *IEEE Trans Eng Manag*, EM–28 (1981), 54–61.

Crane, Diana. *Invisible Colleges: Diffusion of Knowledge in Scientific Communities*. Chicago: University of Chicago Press, 1972.

Cravens, D. W. "An Exploratory Analysis of Individual Information Processing." *Manag Sci*, 16 (1970), B–656–70.

Cyert, Richard M., Herbert A. Simon, and Donald B. Trow. "Observation of a Business Decision." *J Bus*, 29 (1956), 237–48.

Dalkey, N. C., and Olaf Helmer. "An Experimental Application of the Delphi Method to Use of Experts." *Manag Sci*, 9 (1963), 458–67.

Day, Robert A. *How to Write and Publish a Scientific Paper*. Philadelphia: ISI Press, 1979.

Dobrin, David N. "What's Technical About Technical Writing?" In *New Essays in Technical and Scientific Communication: Theory, Research, and Practice*. Ed.

Paul V. Anderson, R. John Brockmann, and Carolyn R. Miller. Farmingdale, N.Y.: Baywood, 1983, pp. 227–50.

Dodge, Richard W. "What to Report." *Westinghouse Engineer* (July-September 1962); rpt. Thomas L. Warren, *Technical Communication: An Outline*. Totowa, N.J.: Littlefield, Adams, 1978, pp. 111–17.

Dreistadt, Roy. "An Analysis of the Use of Analogies and Metaphors in Science." *J Psychol*, 68 (1968), 97–116.

———. "The Psychology of Creativity: How Einstein Discovered the Theory of Relativity." *Psychology*, 11 (Aug. 1974), 15–25.

Duhem, Pierre. *The Aim and Structure of Physical Theory*. Trans. Philip P. Wiener. New York: Atheneum, 1962.

Dunne, Edward J., Jr., and Lawrence J. Klementowski. "An Investigation of the Use of Network Techniques in Research and Development Management." *IEEE Trans Eng Manag*, EM–29 (Aug. 1982), 74–78.

Edsall, John T. *Scientific Freedom and Responsibility*. Washington, D.C.: American Association for the Advancement of Science, 1975.

Ellul, Jacques. *The Technological Society*. New York: Random House, 1964.

Elstein, Arthur, Lee Shulman, and Sarah Sprafka. *Medical Problem Solving: An Analysis of Clinical Reasoning*. Cambridge: Harvard University Press, 1978.

Farkas, David K. "An Invention Heuristic for Business and Technical Communication." *ABCA Bul*, 44, No. 4 (1981), 16–19.

Farrell, Thomas B. "Knowledge, Consensus, and Rhetorical Theory." *Q J Speech*, 62 (1976), 1–14.

———, and G. Thomas Goodnight. "Accidental Rhetoric: The Root Metaphors of Three Mile Island." *Comm Mon*, 48 (1981), 271–300.

Feldhusen, John F., and Virginia Guthrie. "Models of Problem-Solving Process and Abilities." *J Res Dev Educ*, 12 (1979), 22–32.

Ference, Thomas P. "Organizational Communications Systems and the Decision Process." *Manag Sci*, 17 (1970), B–83–96.

Ferguson, Eugene S. "The Mind's Eye: Nonverbal Thought in Technology." *Science*, 197 (1977), 821–36.

Fischer, William A. "The Acquisition of Technical Information by R&D Managers for Problem Solving in Nonroutine Contingency Situations." *IEEE Trans Eng Manag*, EM–26 (1979), 8–14.

Fleck, Ludwig. *Genesis and Development of a Scientific Fact*. Basel, 1935; rpt. Chicago: University of Chicago Press, 1979.

Flower, Linda. *Problem-Solving Strategies for Writing*. New York: Harcourt, 1981.

———, and John R. Hayes. "Problem-Solving Strategies and the Writing Process." *CE*, 39 (1977), 449–61.

———, John R. Hayes, and Heidi Swarts. "Revising Functional Documents: The Scenario Principle." In *New Essays in Technical and Scientific Communication: Theory, Research, and Practice*. Ed. Paul V. Anderson, R. John Brockmann, and Carolyn R. Miller. Farmingdale, N.Y.: Baywood, 1983, pp. 41–58.

Garfinkel, Harold. " 'Good' Organizational Reasons for 'Bad' Clinic Records." In *Studies in Ethnomethodology*, Englewood Cliffs, N.J.: Prentice-Hall, 1967, pp. 186–207.

Getzels, J. W. "Problem-Finding and the Inventiveness of Solutions." *J Creat Behav*, 9 (1975), 12–18.

Gilbert, G. Nigel. "The Transformation of Research Findings into Scientific Knowledge." *Soc Stud Sci*, 6 (1976), 281–306.

Gordon, William J. J. "Some Source Material in Discovery-by-Analogy." *J Creat Behav*, 8 (1974), 239–57.

————. *Synectics: The Development of Creative Capacity*. New York: Harper, 1961.

Goswami, Dixie, Janice C. Redish, Daniel B. Felker, and Alan Siegel. *Writing in the Professions: A Course Guide and Instructional Materials for an Advanced Composition Course*. Washington, D.C.: American Institutes for Research, 1981.

Gusfield, Joseph R. *The Culture of Public Problems: Drinking-Driving and the Symbolic Order*. Chicago: University of Chicago Press, 1981.

Habermas, Jürgen. "Technology and Science as 'Ideology.' " In *Toward a Rational Society: Student Protest, Science, and Politics*. Trans. Jeremy J. Shapiro. Boston: Beacon, 1970, pp. 81–122.

Hadamard, Jacques. *The Psychology of Invention in the Mathematical Field*. Princeton, N.J.: Princeton University Press, 1949.

Hall, Dennis R. "The Role of Invention in Technical Writing." *Tech Writ Teach*, 4 (1976), 13–24.

Halloran, S. Michael. "The Birth of Molecular Biology: An Essay in the Rhetorical Criticism of Scientific Discourse." *Rhet Rev*, 3 (1984), 70–83.

————. "Technical Writing and the Rhetoric of Science." *J Tech Writ Comm*, 8 (1978), 77–88.

————, and Annette N. Bradford. "Figures of Speech in the Rhetoric of Science and Technology." In *Classical Rhetoric and Modern Discourse*. Ed. Robert J. Connors, Lisa Ede, and Andrea Lunsford. Carbondale: Southern Illinois University Press, 1984, pp. 179–92.

Halpern, Jeanne W. "What Should We Be Teaching Students in Business Writing?" *J Bus Comm*, 18, No. 3 (1981), 39–53.

Hannay, N. Bruce, and Robert E. McGinn. "The Anatomy of Modern Technology: Prolegomenon to an Improved Public Policy for the Social Management of Technology." *Daedalus*, 109, No. 1 (1980), 25–53.

Hanson, Norwood Russell. "Notes Toward a Logic of Discovery." In *Perspectives on Peirce: Critical Essays on Charles Sanders Peirce*. Ed. Richard J. Bernstein. New Haven: Yale University Press, 1965, pp. 42–65.

————. *Observation and Explanation: A Guide to Philosophy of Science*. New York: Harper, 1971.

————. *Patterns of Discovery: An Inquiry into the Conceptual Foundations of Science*. Cambridge: Cambridge University Press, 1958.

Harrington, Elbert W. "Rhetoric and the Scientific Method of Inquiry." *University Colorado Studies in Language and Literature*, 1 (1984), 1–64.

Harris, John S. "On Expanding the Definition of Technical Writing." *J Tech Writ Comm*, 8 (1978), 133–38.

Harrison, Frank. "Goal Orientations of Managers and Scientists: An Illusory Dichotomy." *IEEE Trans Eng Manag*, EM–27 (Aug. 1980), 74–78.

Hays, Robert. "Model Outlines Can Make Routine Writing Easier." *Tech Comm*, 29, No. 1 (1982), 4–8.

Head, Richard G. "The Sociology of Military Decision-Making: The A-7 Aircraft." *Pacific Soc Rev*, 16 (1973), 209–27.

Hesse, Mary. "The Explanatory Function of Metaphor." In *Revolutions and Reconstruc-*

tions in the Philosophy of Science. Bloomington: Indiana University Press, 1980, pp. 111–24.

———. "Scientific Models" In *Essays on Metaphor*. Ed. Warren Shibles. Whitewater, Wis.: Language Press, 1972, pp. 169–80.

Hindle, Brooke. *Emulation and Invention*. New York: New York University Press, 1981.

Hoffman, Robert R. "Metaphor in Science." In *Cognition and Figurative Language*. Ed. Richard P. Honeck and Robert R. Hoffman. Hillsdale, N.J.: Erlbaum, 1980, pp. 393–423.

Holcombe, Marya W., and Judith K. Stein. *Writing for Decision Makers: Memos and Reports with a Competitive Edge*. Belmont, Calif.: Lifetime Learning, 1981.

Holton, Gerald. *The Scientific Imagination: Case Studies*. Cambridge: Cambridge University Press, 1978.

———. *Thematic Origins of Scientific Thought: Kepler to Einstein*. Cambridge: Harvard University Press, 1973.

Howell, Wilbur Samuel. *Logic and Rhetoric in England: 1500–1700*. Princeton, N.J.: Princeton University Press, 1956.

Huxley, Thomas H. "The Method by Which the Causes of the Present and Past Conditions of Organic Nature Are to Be Discovered, a Lecture to Working Men or Our Knowledge of the Causes of the Phenomena of Organic Nature." In *Darwiniana*. Vol. 2, Essays. London: Macmillan, 1907, pp. 358–90.

Janis, Irving L., and Leon Mann. *Decision Making*. New York: Free Press, 1977.

Jardine, Lisa. *Francis Bacon: Discovery and the Art of Discourse*. London: Cambridge University Press, 1974.

Kates, R. W. "Assessing the Assessors: The Act and Ideology of Risk Assessment." *Ambio*, 6 (1977), 247–52.

Kelso, James A. "Science and the Rhetoric of Reality." *C S Speech J*, 31 (1980), 17–29.

Kennedy, George A. *Classical Rhetoric and Its Christian and Secular Tradition from Ancient to Modern Times*. Chapel Hill: University of North Carolina Press, 1980.

Kidder, Tracy. *The Soul of a New Machine*. Boston: Little, Brown, 1981.

Kinneavy, James L. *A Theory of Discourse: The Aims of Discourse*. Englewood Cliffs, N.J.: Prentice-Hall, 1971.

Klaver, Peter R. " 'Build It Again, Sam': An Instructional Simulation Game." In *Courses, Components, and Exercises in Technical Communication*. Ed. Dwight W. Stevenson. Urbana: National Council of Teachers of English, 1981, pp. 185–93.

Kneupper, Charles W., and Floyd D. Anderson. "Uniting Wisdom and Eloquence: The Need for Rhetorical Invention." *Q J Speech*, 66 (1980), 313–26.

Knorr-Cetina, Karin D. *The Manufacture of Knowledge: An Essay on the Constructivist and Contextual Nature of Science*. Oxford: Pergamon, 1981.

Koch, Susan, and Stanley Deetz. "Metaphor Analysis of Social Reality in Organizations." *J Appl Comm Res*, 9 (1981), 1–15.

Kornhauser, William. *Scientists in Industry: Conflict and Accommodation*. Berkeley: University of California Press, 1963.

Kuhn, Thomas S. *The Essential Tension: Selected Studies in Scientific Tradition and Change*. Chicago: University of Chicago Press, 1977.

———. *The Structure of Scientific Revolutions*. 2nd ed. International Encyclopedia of Unified Science, 2, No. 2. Chicago: University of Chicago Press, 1970.

Lakatos, Imre, and Alan Musgrave, eds. *Criticism and the Growth of Knowledge*. Cambridge: Cambridge University Press, 1970.

Lapping, Mark B. "Environmental Impact Assessment Methodologies: A Critique." *Env Affairs*, 4 (1975), 124–34.

Larkin, Jill, John McDermott, Dorothea P. Simon, and Herbert A. Simon. "Expert and Novice Performance in Solving Physics Problems." *Science*, 208 (1980), 1335–42.

Larson, Richard L. "How to Define Administrative Problems." *Harvard Bus Rev*, 40 (1962), 68–80.

Latour, Bruno, and Steve Woolgar. *Laboratory Life: The Social Construction of Scientific Facts*. Beverly Hills, Calif.: Sage, 1979.

Lauer, Janice. "Toward a Metatheory of Heuristic Procedures." *CCC*, 30 (1979), 268–69.

———, Gene Montague, Andrea Lunsford, and Janet Emig. *Four Worlds of Writing*. New York: Harper, 1981.

Lay, Mary M. "Procedures, Instructions, and Specifications: A Challenge in Audience Analysis." *J Tech Writ Comm*, 12 (1982), 235–42.

Layton, Edwin T. "Technology as Knowledge." *Tech Cult*, 15 (1974), 31–41.

Leatherdale, W. H. *The Role of Analogy, Model and Metaphor in Science*. Amsterdam: North-Holland, 1974.

Leff, Michael C. "In Search of Ariadne's Thread: A Review of the Recent Literature on Rhetorical Theory." *C S Speech J*, 29 (1978), 73–91.

Leopold, Sara. "Polanyi's 'Tacit Knowledge' and the Problem of Invention." In *Rhetoric 78: Proceedings of Theory of Rhetoric, An Interdisciplinary Conference*. Ed. Robert L. Brown, Jr., and Martin Steinman, Jr. Minneapolis: University of Minnesota Center for Advanced Studies in Language, Style, and Literary Theory, 1979, pp. 241–50.

McCaskey, Michael B. "The Management of Ambiguity." *Org Dynamics*, 7 (1979), 31–48.

McKeon, Richard. "The Method of Rhetoric and Philosophy: Invention and Judgment." In *The Classical Tradition*. Ed. L. Wallach. Ithaca: Cornell University Press, 1966, pp. 365–74.

———. "The Uses of Rhetoric in a Technological Age: Architectonic Productive Arts." In *The Prospect of Rhetoric: Report of the National Development Project*. Ed. Lloyd F. Bitzer and Edwin Black. Englewood Cliffs, N.J.: Prentice-Hall, 1971, pp. 44–63.

Mahoney, Michael J. "Psychology of the Scientist: An Evaluative Review." *Soc Stud Sci*, 9 (1979), 349–76.

———, and Bobby G. DeMonbreun. "Psychology of the Scientist: An Analysis of Problem-Solving Bias." *Cog Therapy Res*, 1 (1977), 229–38.

March, James G. "Bounded Rationality, Ambiguity, and the Engineering of Choice," *Bell J Econ*, 9 (1978), 587–608.

———, and Johan P. Olsen. *Ambiguity and Choice in Organizations*. Bergen, Norway: Universitetsforlaget, 1976.

Marcuse, Herbert. *One-Dimensional Man*. Boston: Beacon, 1964.

Mathes, J. C., and Dwight W. Stevenson. *Designing Technical Reports: Writing for Audiences in Organizations*. Indianapolis: Bobbs-Merrill, 1976.

Mazur, Allan. *The Dynamics of Technical Controversy*. Washington, D.C.: Communications Press, 1981.

Medawar, P. B. *The Art of the Soluble*. London: Methuen, 1967.

Meehan, Richard L. *Getting Sued and Other Tales of the Engineering Life*. Cambridge: MIT Press, 1981.

Merton, Robert K. *The Sociology of Science: Theoretical and Empirical Investigations*. Chicago: University of Chicago Press, 1973.

Michaelson, Herbert B. *How to Write and Publish Engineering Papers and Reports*. Philadelphia, Pa.: ISI Press, 1982.

Miller, Carolyn R. "Environmental Impact Statements and Rhetorical Genres: An Application of Rhetorical Theory to Technical Communication." Diss. Rensselaer Polytechnic Institute, 1980.

————. "A Humanistic Rationale for Technical Writing." *CE*, 40 (1979), 610–17.

————. "Technology as a Form of Consciousness: A Study of Contemporary Ethos." *C S Speech J*, 29 (1978), 228–36.

Mitcham, Carl, and Robert Mackey, eds. *Philosophy and Technology: Readings in the Philosophic Problems of Technology*. New York: Free Press, 1972.

Mitroff, Ian. *The Subjective Side of Science*. New York: Elsevier, 1974.

Monroe, Judson. *Effective Research and Report Writing in Government*. New York: McGraw-Hill, 1980.

Moran, Michael G. "A Problem-Solving Heuristic." *Tech Comm*, 29, No. 3 (1982), 38.

Mulkay, Michael. "Norms and Ideology in Science." *Soc Sci Inform*, 15 (1976), 637–56.

————. *Science and the Sociology of Knowledge*. Controversies in Sociology. Vol. 8. Ed. T. B. Bottomore and M. J. Mulkay. London: Allen, Unwin, 1979.

Nickles, Thomas, ed. *Scientific Discovery, Logic and Rationality*. Boston Studies in the Philosophy of Science. Vol. 56. Dordrecht, Holland: Reidel, 1980.

Osborne, Alex F. *Applied Imagination: Principles and Procedures of Creative Problem Solving*. New York: Scribner's, 1953.

Overington, Michael A. "The Scientific Community as Audience: Toward a Rhetorical Analysis of Science." *Phil Rhet*, 10 (1977), 143–64.

Paradis, James. "Bacon, Linnaeus, and Lavoisier: Early Language Reform in the Sciences." In *New Essays in Technical and Scientific Communication: Theory, Research, and Practice*. Ed. Paul V. Anderson, R. John Brockmann, and Carolyn R. Miller. Farmingdale, N.Y.: Baywood, 1983, pp. 200–24.

Pelz, Donald C., and Frank M. Andrews. *Scientists in Organizations: Productive Climates for Research and Development*. New York: Wiley, 1966.

Perelman, Chaim. *The New Rhetoric and the Humanities: Essays on Rhetoric and Its Applications*. Dordrecht, Holland: Reidel, 1979.

Perrow, Charles. *Complex Organizations: A Critical Essay*. 2nd ed. Glenview, Ill.: Scott, Foresman, 1979.

Pettigrew, Andrew M. *The Politics of Organizational Decision-making*. London: Tavistock, 1973.

Poincaré, Henri. "Mathematical Discovery." In *Science and Method*. Trans. Francis Maitland. New York: Dover, 1952.

Polanyi, Michael. *Personal Knowledge: Towards a Post-Critical Philosophy*. Chicago, 1958; rpt. New York: Harper, 1964.

Polya, G. *How to Solve It: A New Aspect of Mathematical Method*. 2nd ed. Princeton, N.J.: 1945; rpt. Garden City, N.Y.: Doubleday, 1957.

Popper, Karl. *The Logic of Scientific Discovery*. New York: Basic, 1959.

Pounds, William F. "The Process of Problem Finding." *Indus Manag Rev*, 11 (1969), 1–19.

Price, Derek J. de Solla. "Citation Measures of Hard Science, Soft Science, Technology, and Nonscience." In *Communication Among Scientists and Engineers*. Ed. Carnot E. Nelson and Donald K. Pollock. Lexington, Mass.: Heath, 1970, pp. 3–22. 1970, pp. 3–22.

Reichenbach, Hans. *Experience and Prediction: An Analysis of the Foundations and the Structure of Knowledge*. Chicago: University of Chicago Press, 1938.

Rorty, Richard. *Philosophy and the Mirror of Nature*. Princeton, N.J.: Princeton University Press, 1979.

Rothman, Robert A. "A Dissenting View on the Scientific Ethos." *Brit J Soc*, 23 (1972), 102–108.

Rothwell, R., and A. B. Robertson. "The Role of Communications in Technological Innovation." *Res Policy*, 2 (1973), 204–25.

Sahal, Devendra. *Patterns of Technological Innovation*. Reading, Mass.: Addison-Wesley, 1981.

Scheffler, Israel. *Science and Subjectivity*. Indianapolis: Bobbs-Merrill, 1967.

Scott, Robert L. "On Viewing Rhetoric as Epistemic." *C S Speech J*, 18 (1967), 9–16.

———. "On Viewing Rhetoric as Epistemic: Ten Years Later." *CS Speech J*, 27 (1976), 258–66.

Selzer, Jack. "The Composing Processes of an Engineer." *CCC*, 34 (1983), 178–87.

Shumway, C. R., P. M. Maher, N. R. Baker, W. E. Souder, A. H. Rubenstein, and A. R. Gallant. "Diffuse Decision Making in Hierarchical Organizations: An Empirical Examination." *Manag Sci*, 21 (1975), 697–707.

Simon, Herbert A. *Models of Discovery*. Boston Studies in the Philosophy of Science. Vol. 54. Ed. R. S. Cohen and M. W. Wartofsky. Dordrecht, Holland: Reidel, 1977.

———. "On How to Decide What to Do." *Bell J Econ*, 9 (1978), 494–507.

———. *The Sciences of the Artificial*. 2nd ed. Cambridge: MIT Press, 1981.

Simons, Herbert W. "Are Scientists Rhetors in Disguise? An Analysis of Discursive Processes Within Scientific Communities." In *Rhetoric in Transition: Studies in the Nature and Uses of Rhetoric*. Ed. Eugene E. White. University Park: Pennsylvania State University Press, 1980, pp. 115–30.

Skolinowski, Henryk. "The Structure of Thinking in Technology." *Tech Cult*, 7 (1966), 371–83.

Skolnik, H., and L. F. McBurney. "Technical Reports and Decision-Making." *Chem Tech*, 1 (Feb. 1971), 82–85.

Souder, William E., and Robert W. Ziegler. "A Review of Creativity and Problem Solving Techniques." *Res Manag*, 20 (July 1977), 34–42.

Souther, James W., and Myron L. White. *Technical Report Writing*. 2nd ed. New York: Wiley, 1977.

Starr, Chauncey, and Chris Whipple. "Risks of Risk Decisions." *Science*, 208 (1980), 1114–19.

Stehr, Nico. "The Ethos of Science Revisited." *Soc Inq*, 48, No. 3–4 (1978), 172–96.

Stephens, James. *Francis Bacon and the Style of Science*. Chicago: University of Chicago Press, 1975.

————. "Style as Therapy in Renaissance Science." In *New Essays in Technical and Scientific Communication: Theory, Research, and Practice*. Ed. Paul V. Anderson, R. John Brockmann, and Carolyn R. Miller. Farmingdale, N.Y.: Baywood, 1983, pp. 187–99.

Sullivan, Patricia A. "Teaching the Writing Process in Scientific and Technical Writing Classes." *Tech Writ Teach*, 8 (1980), 10–16.

Sullivan, William G., and Wayne Claycombe. "Decision Analysis of Capacity Expansion Strategies for Electrical Utilities." *IEEE Trans Eng Manag*, EM–24 (1977), 139–44.

Suppe, Frederick, ed. *The Structure of Scientific Theories*. 2nd ed. Urbana: University of Illinois Press, 1977.

Taylor, Donald W., Paul C. Berry, and Clifford H. Block. "Does Group Participation When Using Brainstorming Facilitate or Inhibit Creative Thinking?" *Admin Sci Q*, 3 (1958), 23–47.

Theobald, D. W. "Some Considerations on the Philosophy of Chemistry." *Chem Soc Rev*, 5 (1976), 203–13.

Toulmin, Stephen. *Human Understanding: The Collective Use and Evolution of Concepts*. Princeton, N.J.: Princeton University Press, 1972.

————. *The Uses of Argument*. Cambridge: Cambridge University Press, 1958.

————, Richard Rieke, and Allan Janik. *An Introduction to Reasoning*. New York: Macmillan, 1979.

Udell, Gerald G., Kenneth G. Baker, and Gerald S. Albaum. "Creativity: Necessary, But Not Sufficient." *J Creat Behav*, 10 (1976), 92–103.

Van de Ven, Andrew H., and André L. Delbecq. "The Effectiveness of Nominal, Delphi, and Interacting Group Decision-Making Processes." *Acad Manag J*, 17 (1974), 605–21.

Van Roy, Tony J., and Ludo F. Gelders. "A Practical Tool for Improved Resource Allocation: The Dynamic Time Now Procedure." *IEEE Trans Eng Manag*, EM–25 (1978), 93–97.

Wallace, Karl R. "The Substance of Rhetoric: Good Reasons." *Q J Speech*, 49 (1963), 239–49.

————. "*Topoi* and the Problem of Invention." *Q J Speech*, 58 (1972), 387–95.

Wallas, Graham. *The Art of Thought*. New York: Harcourt, Brace, 1926.

Wander, Philip C. "The Rhetoric of Science." *W J Speech Comm*, 40 (1976), 226–35.

Wartofsky, Marx W. "Scientific Judgment: Creativity and Discovery in Scientific Thought." In *Scientific Discovery: Case Studies*. Boston Studies in the Philosophy of Science. Vol. 60. Ed. Thomas Nickles. Dordrecht, Holland: Reidel, 1980, pp. 1–16.

Watson, James D. *The Double Helix: A Personal Account of the Discovery of the Structure of DNA*. New York: New American Library, 1968.

Wechsler, Judith, ed. *On Aesthetics in Science*. Cambridge: MIT Press, 1978.

Weimer, Walter B. *Notes on the Methodology of Scientific Research*. Hillsdale, N.J.: Erlbaum, 1979.

————. "Science as a Rhetorical Transaction: Toward a Nonjustificational Conception of Rhetoric." *Phil Rhet*, 10 (1977), 1–29.

Wertheimer, Max. *Productive Thinking*. Enlarged ed. Ed. Michael Wertheimer. New York: Harper, 1959.

Winkler, Victoria M. "Creative Design and Rhetorical Inquiry: Report Writing Strate-
gies." Proceedings of the 27th International Technical Communication Confer-
ence, Minneapolis, May 14–17, 1980, II, W–89–W–97.
———. "The Role of Models in Technical and Scientific Writing." In *New Essays in
Technical and Scientific Communication: Theory, Research, and Practice*. Ed.
Paul V. Anderson, R. John Brockmann, and Carolyn R. Miller. Farmingdale,
N.Y.: Baywood, 1983, pp. 111–22.
Wynne, B. "The Rhetoric of Consensus Politics: A Critical Review of Technology
Assessment." *Res Policy*, 4 (1975), 108–58.
Yearley, Steven. "Textual Persuasion: The Role of Social Accounting in the Construction
of Scientific Arguments." *Phil Soc Sci*, 11 (1981), 409–35.
Young, Richard. "Invention: A Topographical Survey." In *Teaching Composition: 10
Bibliographical Essays*. Ed. Gary Tate. Fort Worth: Texas Christian University
Press, 1976, pp. 1–43.
Young, Richard E., Alton L. Becker, and Kenneth L. Pike. *Rhetoric: Discovery and
Change*. New York: Harcourt, Brace, 1970.
Zappen, James P. "Aristotelian and Ramist Rhetoric in Thomas Hobbes's *Leviathan*:
Pathos Versus Ethos and Logos." *Rhetorician*, (Spring 1983), 65–91.
———. "A Rhetoric for Research in Sciences and Technologies." In *New Essays in
Technical and Scientific Communication: Theory, Research, and Practice*. Ed.
Paul V. Anderson, R. John Brockmann, and Carolyn R. Miller. Farmingdale,
N.Y.: Baywood, 1983, pp. 123–38.
———. "Science and Rhetoric from Bacon to Hobbes." In *Rhetoric 78*. Ed. Robert L.
Brown, Jr., and Martin Steinman, Jr. Minneapolis: University of Minnesota,
Center for Advanced Studies in Language, Style, and Literary Theory, 1979, pp.
399–419.
Ziman, John. *Public Knowledge: The Social Dimension of Science*. Cambridge: Cam-
bridge University Press, 1968.
Zuckerman, Harriet. "Theory Choice and Problem Choice in Science." *Soc Inq*, 48
(1968), 65–95.
Zwicky, Fritz. *Discovery, Invention, Research: Through the Morphological Method*. New
York: Macmillan, 1969.

Audience Analysis and Adaptation

MICHAEL KEENE and MARILYN BARNES-OSTRANDER

Since the first recorded studies of the art of communication, audience has been a central concern of communicators. Audience is one of the four major elements that shape any kind of discourse. While these elements may be generally called the sender, the receiver, the message, and the subject, in different fields they bear different names. In the field of technical communication (also called professional rhetoric or information development), the sender has been variously called a writer, a technical communicator, or an information developer. The receiver (or audience) could be maintenance technicians, the general public, or the Secretary of Agriculture. The message might be a conceptual design report, a proposal, or user documentation. And the subject could range from the operation of computer terminals to the maintenance of airplanes. While all four elements are important, the subject of this chapter is the role of audience in technical communication.

Although we are aware of no comprehensive analysis of the interrelationships among these four elements of the communication situation in the field of technical communication, specialists in other areas of discourse theory have published studies both comprehensive and historical. Three of the best are James L. Kinneavy's *A Theory of Discourse* (1971), E. H. Gombrich's *Art and Illusion* (1960), and M. H. Abrams's *The Mirror and the Lamp* (1953). According to Abrams, various periods of history have emphasized one of the four elements of discourse over the others. The emphasis on audience, an emphasis that explains discourse as something made to affect readers, has its origin in classical rhetoric; it is the

*Grateful acknowledgment is made of the assistance of Professor Merrill Whitburn in every stage of this project. Grateful acknowledgment is also made to the Better English Fund of the University of Tennessee, established by the late Professor Emeritus John C. Hodges, which provided financial support for part of this research.

major critical attitude from the time Horace wrote the *Ars Poetica* (19-18 B.C.) through the eighteenth century.

Several factors have contributed to making emphasis on audience once again the major concern of theorists. These factors include the explosion of the mass media in this half of the twentieth century, the increasing awareness within the literary-critical community of the importance of reader response, and the growing attention among professional teachers of writing to audience-interaction models of rhetoric. Measured either by its duration or by the numbers of its adherents, the audience-centered view of discourse has been the principal critical attitude of the Western world.

A definitive bibliography of audience analysis and adaptation in the field of technical communication would place modern works within this rich historical context. Far from striving to be definitive in this article, we seek only to offer a selective, annotated bibliography of modern materials pertaining to audience analysis and adaptation, especially as they are relevant to technical communication. This selective listing represents our own choices of significant sources, with significance determined in part because a source is typical of a whole cluster of documents, in part because a source is a potential (or proven) cornerstone for future work, and in part because the source is original. We hope readers will bring to our attention any additional articles or books they feel should have appeared here.

To speak of what a human being is as a reader (or hearer) of technical communication is to speak of everything a human is. With audience as our topic, we actually have the whole range, depth, and complexity of the human condition to look at. Our search areas for this bibliography included the literatures of technical communication, rhetoric and composition, literary criticism, psychology, education, engineering, linguistics, and human factors engineering. Because audience affects every aspect of technical communication, we have chosen the following structure: the importance of audience analysis and adaptation; the role of audience in the dynamics of the communication situation; the impact of audience on content, organization, style, and visuals; and the teaching of audience analysis and adaptation.

The Importance of Audience Analysis and Adaptation

Audience analysis and adaptation are essential skills for any technical communicator. The attitude of audience awareness is the hallmark of a professional in the field. Within the response of an audience lies the final determination of the success or failure of any piece of technical communication. The audience (or rhetorical community) is a primary determiner of what needs to be said or left unsaid, of the message's structure, and of the concepts that the writer can successfully employ. The writer's awareness of audience affects every part of the writer's composing process. For all these reasons, audience has been the object of attention in textbooks and articles in several fields.

One way to measure the importance of audience is through its history in textbooks. In this century alone, as early as 1920, T. A. Rickard emphasized the importance of audience awareness: "In his technical writing he [the technical man] must keep in mind the human element; for he is recording himself not in the sand of the seashore, but on paper to be read by his fellows. Thus I come to a fundamental rule: REMEMBER THE READER" (*Technical Writing*, p. 11). Contemporary texts such as John M. Lannon's *Technical Writing* (1982) and Kenneth W. Houp and Thomas E. Pearsall's *Reporting Technical Information* (1980) give substantial coverage to audience. Arguably the most sophisticated text in the field, J. C. Mathes and D. W. Stevenson's *Designing Technical Reports* (1976), presents a unique method for audience analysis and adaptation, the egocentric bubble chart. The book's subtitle, *Writing for Audiences in Organization*, accurately depicts the thorough and useful treatment of audience it offers.

Books in other communication fields also emphasize audience. For instance, in *Persuasion* (1976), Herbert W. Simons thoroughly covers different theories of persuasion and their relationship to key attributes of the receiver. Two chapters of Henry M. Boettinger's *Moving Mountains* (1975) deal directly with audience analysis and adaptation. Four chapters of Peter Elbow's *Writing with Power* (1981) discuss in detail the writer's relationship with the audience.

In his comprehensive essay, "The Meanings of 'Audience' " (1982), Douglas B. Park describes the combination of the writer's awareness of the audience's needs with the ability to respond to those needs as a "field of awareness":

For a writer, operating comfortably within a set of conventions is often a matter simply of being on sure ground, of being able to conjure up the right kind of voice, of knowing intuitively that that voice and way of proceeding have "listeners." Such an intuitive sense is surely describable as a sense of audience; we describe the apparent absence of it in a piece of prose as a lack of a sense of audience. Yet that kind of intuitive grasp of convention is very little like a conscious focus on the imagined reactions of specific people. (p. 254)

J. H. Flavell spells out the basic stages of how people must learn to deal with audiences in "The Development of Inferences about Others" (1974): awareness of the *existence* of another's feeling, awareness of the *need* to address that feeling, an *inference* about how to address that feeling, and *application* of a change in behavior as a result of that inference (pp. 71–72). This model applies to all kinds of human communication, especially writing.

In "A Writer's Awareness of Audience" (1981), Carol Berkenkotter provides a deep exploration of the effects on a writer of the writer's awareness of audience. She discovers two ways of thinking about audience shared by writers in different disciplines: all form a rich representation of audience which plays a significant role in the development of the writer's goals, and most create individual rhetorical contexts or scenarios that also contribute in an important way to the writer's goal-making. In "Cognitive Egocentrism and the Problem of Audience Awareness in Written Discourse" (1978), Barry Kroll takes this explanation of "the constructive processes operative in the mind of the writer" farther, tracing audience awareness to the writer's level of cognitive development: "Writers who can decenter their perspective, taking the view of a hypothetical readership, are more likely to display audience awareness than writers who are embedded in their personal view of reality" (p. 79).

Susan Miller's "Rhetorical Maturity" (1979) sees the writer's movement from "egocentric, to explanatory, to persuasive discourse" as "a movement from the writer's assumption of union with an audience to the writer's recognition of another as audience, and finally to the writer's analysis of a distant, unfamiliar, universalized series of values as an audience" (p. 1). The implications of the beginning writer's natural tendency to assume a reader who mirrors the writer's identity are fully developed in Walter J. Ong's "The Writer's Audience Is Always a Fiction" (1977). Ong traces "the history of the ways in which readers have been called on to relate to texts before them" (p. 55). He also traces the way writers learn to create images of their readers (or to copy those images from earlier writers).

Several scholars have studied the effects on the writing process of a writer's awareness of audience. In "Writer Insensitivity to Audience—Causes and Cures" (1980), Marshall Atlas measured the differences between unskilled and skilled writers' responses to an assignment that required them to write a letter to a hostile audience. "Revision Strategies of Student Writers and Experienced Adult Writers" (1980), by Nancy Sommers, shows that experienced writers have two main concerns in their revising: form and readership. "The anticipation of a reader's judgment causes a feeling of dissonance when the writer recognizes incongruities between intention and execution, and requires these writers to make revisions on all levels" (p. 385). In "The Effect of Audience Considerations upon the Revisions of a Group of Basic Writers and More Competent Junior and Senior Writers" (1981), Janice N. Hays concludes that "those students who composed with a strong sense of audience and purpose were less concerned with lexical and scribal matters and more focused upon the ideas that they wished to convey than were writers without this involvement" (p. 1). Results consistent with those of Hays's study are found in Timothy D. Nolan's "A Comparative Study of the Planning, Implementation, and Evaluation Process of Audience-Committed Non-Directed Technical Writing Students" (1977).

The literature also contains practical demonstrations of the importance of audience. In "Applied Pragmatics in the Development of Technical Writing" (1981), Frances B. Emerson explains that audience is important in technical writing because the technical writer carries a degree of liability for any ineffective or misleading writing. John Maynard's "A User-Driven Approach to Better User Manuals" (1982) explains how user polls can guide writers in the production of more effective user manuals. In "User Edit" (1981), Marshall Atlas recommends the "user edit" as the simplest way to make a technical manual easier to use; by having an inexperienced user try to work with a machine with only its manual as a guide, one learns quickly where the manual's weak points are. "Making Written Information Fit Workers' Purposes" (1981), by Willia Diehl and Larry Mikulecky, describes the implications for technical writers of research into occupational literacy. By paying attention to workers' purposes and the nature of their uses of written materials, writers can create more usable material.

The sources described here show that the importance of audience analysis and adaptation extends from the broadest concerns of readers (such as the success or failure of a written document) to the psychological factors in the behavior of writers (such as how a writer's audience awareness shapes the writing process). The next section of this chapter places the important qualities of audience in their larger context, the dynamics of the communication situation.

The Role of Audience in the Dynamics of the Communication Situation

There is much more to discourse than sender, receiver, message, and subject; the interaction of these four elements forms a dynamic element that must also be considered. Without specific attention to the role of audience in the dynamics of the communication situation, no discussion of audience can be complete. There is little theoretical agreement about the most accurate or useful depiction of the communication situation. While limited studies of specific instances of communication abound, significant generalizations based on them are rare.

Alphonse Chapanis's "Words, Words, Words!" (1965) provides a good introduction to the importance of studying audience as a critical part of the communication situation. Chapanis sees three reasons for studying and improving written language: (1) words are the uniquely human form of communication; (2) our civilization is suffering from a deluge of words; and (3) reckoning with words is absolutely necessary in order for anyone to operate or learn to operate a machine. Chapanis sees practical research into real communication situations, necessarily involving real audiences, as the first step in improving the readability of documents. A full presentation of the complex nature of all communication situations appears in Richard M. Davis's "The Communication Situation—A Model and Discussion" (1974). Davis emphasizes the importance of the reader in each situation.

To define the limits of the communication situation requires one to define a theory of discourse. Of the several scholars who have attempted to do that, perhaps the best known as James L. Kinneavy. In *A Theory of Discourse* (1971), Kinneavy presents a thorough exploration of the aims (or purposes) of discourse. In his view, the aim is determined by the text, but for him "text" means much more than just the physical object and groupings of words before him. For Kinneavy (as for many later critics), "text" includes all of the human factors and situational factors associated with any document, including the writer's thoughts, the reader's thoughts, and the larger rhetorical context. Kinneavy divides aims into expressive, referential, literary, and persuasive. The sets of documents we typically refer to as "kinds" of writing (job application letters, minutes of meetings, and so on) can all be analyzed in terms of the various balances in these aims. Kinneavy explores the balance of the different aims of scientific discourse and pays special attention to the role of audience.

Some readers find one of Kinneavy's sources, Roman Jakobson's description of the factors and functions in communication, to be itself a more elegant description of the theoretical structure of discourse. As first presented in the Linguistics Society of America's 1956 Presidential Address, "Metalanguage as a Linguistic Problem" (1956), Jakobson describes the verbal model as involving six factors: an addresser and an addressee are connected by context, message, contact, and code. Each factor has paired with it a function of language: emotive language focuses on the addresser, conative language on the addressee, referential language on the context, poetic language on the message, phatic (ceremonial) language on the contact, and metalingual language on the code. Following Jakobson, one can analyze any discourse in terms of which of those factors or functions of the communication situation is foremost in the discourse, and then (with Kinneavy) trace the implications of the emphasis on that element.

A more traditional rhetorical view of discourse can be found in the collection of essays by Richard Weaver titled *Language Is Sermonic* (Richard L. Johannesen and colleagues [1970]). In Weaver's view, all language is fundamentally persuasive, and the most telling analysis of any piece of language is in those terms. Focusing on the connection between technical communication, persuasion, and audience opens to our field a wealth of research on persuasion. While the emphasis on all language as being fundamentally persuasive is not an exclusively current theory of discourse, like all other theories of discourse it places audience within the dynamics of the communication situation, and hence it is worthy of consideration here. One of the standard sources on this subject is Irving L. Janis and Carl Hovland's *Personality and Persuasibility* (1959). A more recent source typical of research in this area is "Language Intensity and Resistance to Persuasion" (1976), in which Lawrence J. Chase and Clifford W. Kelly review theory about use of language to bring about resistance to persuasion and test the relationship between language intensity and persuasion.

Contemporary theories of discourse pay specific attention to the reader's place in the communication situation. One such theory which is most amenable to both the teaching and the practicing of technical communication is James Britton's, whose description of the kinds of writing done by 5,000 schoolchildren in *The Development of Writing Abilities, 11-18* (1975) remains one of the few broadly based and detailed examinations of writing yet done. Britton and his group set out to define the range of possible relationships between writers and readers. They eventually arrived at ten categories for the writer's sense of audience and found that two of these categories accounted for 92 percent of the scripts. They found only scanty evidence that the audience in school writing adequately prepared students to write for a public audience. Audience is central both to the kind of writing students are prepared to do and to the kind they are not prepared to do. Many of Britton's articles have recently been brought together in *Prospect and Retrospect* (Gordon M. Pradl [1982]).

Other major figures in rhetoric, composition, and communication should also be considered with Britton. The works of James Moffett (especially *Teaching the Universe of Discourse* [1968]), Colin Cherry (especially *On Human Communication* [1978]), Kenneth Burke (especially *A Rhetoric of Motives* [1969]), Wayne Booth ("The Rhetorical Stance" [1963]), and Richard E. Young, Alton L. Becker, and Kenneth L. Pike (*Rhetoric* [1970]) operate on the same level of theory as Britton's. Each offers a distinctive and popular view of the dynamics of the communication situation, and each view carries with it specific implications for the role of audience.

In contrast to the rhetorical analyses of the communication situation and audience's role in it, another kind of model of communication begins by describing the qualities of humans as readers. The psychologist Carl Rogers has in several essays argued persuasively that fear is the biggest hurdle to be overcome for effective communication to take place. That point is especially clear in "Communication" (1961). Rogers's theories are interpreted by Maxine Hairston in *Contemporary Rhetoric* (1982). Hairston explains that communication which challenges its audience's *a priori* assumptions may lose its audience (and thus fail) simply through failing to deal with the audience's fears. She offers five principles of communication based on Rogers's theories to help writers deal successfully with such situations. Another specific approach to dealing with the audience's fears is offered in Norma Carr-Smith's "Overcoming Defensive Barriers to Communication" (1978), which makes the important distinction between defensive messages and supportive messages. Another transactional approach can be found in Otto Baskin and Sam J. Bruno's "A Transactional Systems Model for Communication" (1977).

The role of the writer's own apprehensions has also been examined in such studies as Edgar M. Richardson's "Research on Writing" (1981). By looking at writing done for distant versus familiar audiences, Richardson illuminates many of the issues surrounding audience and apprehension, and his bibliography is extensive.

Another psychological factor shared by writers and readers which also implies a whole theory of communication is problem-solving. Linda Flower and John Hayes have published a number of articles describing how the problem-solving characteristics of humans shape the communication situation. Audience figures largely in their work, especially in "Problem-Solving Strategies and the Writing Process" (1977). Linda Flower's *Problem-Solving Strategies for Writing* (1981) clearly connects the three key elements of writing, problem-solving, and audience. One of the most important concepts Flower and Hayes have developed for writers is the distinction between writer-based and reader-based prose, which then allows them to focus on the ways a text can be translated from the former to the latter.

Recently, the concept of rhetorical communities and their influence on particular aspects of communication has received attention. Perhaps most notable in this approach is Carolyn R. Miller, who argues persuasively in "A Humanistic Rationale for Technical Writing" (1979) for the rhetorical nature of the scientific community and explains its implications for technical communication. She sees language as a "persuasive version of experience" essential to winning the scientific community's assent, assent necessary for the scientific enterprise. Under this view, "whatever we know of reality is created by individual action and communal assent. Reality cannot be separated from our knowledge of it; knowledge cannot be separated from the knower; the knower cannot be separated from a community" (p. 615). The classification of audiences in technical writing becomes more than divisions among levels; the classification scheme must identify and explore communities. The writer's task is in large part one of learning how to make the text "belong" to its appropriate community.

In "Thomas Kuhn, Scientism, and English Studies" (1979), Patricia Bizzell studies the ways language communities (in particular the academic community) establish standards for thinking and acting. She points out the ways academic audiences may be manipulated through their own unconscious and unrealized expectations. Students can fail to adapt to teachers because the teachers have traits, standards, and values they themselves do not recognize. In " 'That Sunny Dome, Those Caves of Ice' " (1979), Alan C. Purves describes exactly such a situation. While he is speaking of a reader's response to creative literature, his point is equally true of anyone reading anything, including technical reports: "When people read, they seek to ascertain meaning which is guided by their belief in the intentionality of the writer, and they find significance, which has an experiential base and a critical one, the first founded in knowledge of external reality and the second in knowledge of literature" (p. 807). If we read Purves's "knowledge of literature" to include one's knowledge of the literature in one's field, regardless of what that field may be, we can see in his statement (and in the larger theories of Bizzell and Miller), a powerful description of the ways in which qualities of the audience determine the meaning (and success) of any document.

The school of literary criticism designated "reader response" has pursued the importance of Purves's view of audience. Borrowing from psychology, these critics discuss such aspects of the reader's mental make-up as story grammars, which are representations of readers' internalized expectations about the form of narratives. In "Psycholinguistics and Literature" (1978), Eugene R. Kintgen explains such grammars: "Readers develop these grammars from their own experience of stories and from what they know about causality and permissable or reasonable sequences of actions; they use them to guide their perception of stories by directing attention to what is to come, and signalling when some part of the story is complete" (p. 767). The concept of story grammars could easily be extended to include report grammars. In "Putting Readers in Their Places" (1980), Purves brings up two other aspects of the reader that could also be applied to technical communication: the readers' acquisition or development of an appropriate stance towards the text, and the readers' conscious cognitive act of examining their experiences of the text.

All such theories clearly have their own views of the communication situation's dynamics and thus their own roles for audience within that situation. Such theories about the behavior of readers during reading draw in part on the contemporary field of study known as psycholinguistics. The best introduction to that area remains the collection of essays in *Psycholinguistics and Reading* (1973), edited by Frank Smith. A more recent review of the field is *Psycholinguistics* (1979) by Dan Isaac Slobin. Readers who want even more material on readers' mental activities should turn to the works of Walter Kintsch, especially *The Representation of Meaning in Memory* (1974) and *Memory and Cognition* (1982).

David E. Rumelhart's *Introduction to Human Information Processing* (1977) is another comprehensive and clearly written discussion of the current view of the reading process. It supports with theory and empirical data the observation that linguistic comprehension is an interactive process depending not only on sensory input but also on the receptor's previous knowledge. Rumelhart discusses syntactic processing (using the augmented transition network model), semantic processing, and the role of context in both. He summarizes a number of studies in experimental psychology of special value to the student of reader comprehension processes. The book includes a glossary and an especially useful bibliography.

Many of the approaches described above can be viewed under the general heading of psychological approaches to audience and writing. An excellent summary of the important works in that area is Robert de Beaugrande's "Psychology and Composition" (1982). He describes the field of cognitive science, "a recently emerging field at the crossroads of psychology, linguistics, philosophy, computer science, anthropology, sociology, and education. Its goal is to create a unified science of cognition and communication, with the specific concerns of the several sub-disciplines forming an integrated whole" (p. 229).

Computers, too, can be audiences. One of the classes of languages in which we address computers is query languages, statements executed immediately upon entry from the terminal keyboard that specify the goal of a program but not its procedures. Such languages must balance the qualities of a human source against the qualities of a computer audience; the constraints upon the structure of such languages are discussed in S. L. Ehrenreich's "Query Languages" (1981).

One of the most important areas of activity for technical communicators is the study and writing of user documentation for computers. That communication situation has its own dynamics with profound implications for the user (and hence the writer) of such a manual. A good beginning in this area is K. D. Eason's "Understanding the Naive Computer User" (1976). Eason details the implications of four qualities of such users: (1) interest in the computer only as a means to accomplishing their particular goals, (2) interest only in the skills and knowledge necessary to accomplish their own computer-related tasks, (3) willingness to spend only enough time with the computer as is necessary to achieve their goals, and (4) ease with which they are intimidated or traumatized by computer malfunction or an unusual system response.

Audiences can differ in much more than education and job description. What of audiences composed of non-native speakers? As Dwight Stevenson explains in "Audience Analysis across Cultures" (1982), our failure to recognize such audiences is telling:

In what we have written we have signalled our cultural insularity by virtually ignoring the facts that in our technical communication programs throughout the country the non-native student population is very substantial (in many programs it exceeds 50%) and that among professionals around the world, English technical discourse is used as the international language of business and technology. English technical discourse is the "new Latin" or the "Esperanto"...; yet in our approaches to it—and specifically in our discussions of audience—there is almost no recognition of that fact whatsoever (p. 1).

According to Stevenson, the profession of technical communication needs "to recognize the extent to which multi-national corporations, international trade, and electronic means of communication create the need for a kind of audience awareness beyond any we have seriously looked at before" (p. 9).

Another issue properly addressed in this context is the role of audience in the information society as opposed to its role in the industrial society of the past. As fundamental changes occur in the nature of the society within which communication takes place, the role of audience in that communication will also change. The emergence of the information society and the nature of changes in communication caused by that emerging information society are detailed in the U.S. Congress's *Informational Technology and Its Impact on American Education* (1982). This topic is thoroughly discussed in William L. Benzon's "Computing and the Future of Technical Communication" elsewhere in this book.

The Role of Audience in Content, Organization, Style, and Visuals

Perhaps the major sources of information on the interaction of audience with content and organization are the leading textbooks in technical communication mentioned at the beginning of this chapter. Besides offering a view of the role of audience within the dynamics of the communications situation, research on the nature of language as persuasion offers insight into what kinds of content one should include in a document. In " 'And Thinking Makes It So' " (1980), Richard M. Perloff and Timothy C. Brock explain five factors that condition the audience's responses to content. (1) The long-range impact of persuasive messages is largely determined by the amount of initial cognitive processing by the audience during the message. (2) The audience's evaluation of the communicator impinges on the impact of the message. (3) The amount of the audience's involvement with the issue in a persuasive message also has an impact on the level of persuasion. (4) Distracting information also affects the degree of persuasion a message can elicit. (5) Individuals rate their own thoughts much more highly than those of others.

Learning theory offers another approach to determining the interaction between audience and persuasive content. A good summary of both the behaviorist and cognitivist positions and their implications for persuasive content appears in Judee K. Burgoon, Michael Burgoon, Gerald R. Miller, and Michael Summafrank's "Learning Theory Approaches to Persuasion" (1981). The article includes discussions of such disparate elements as the possibilities of reinforcement through repetition, the effects of increasingly vivid stimuli, the relative ease or difficulty of pro-and-con arguments compared to one-sided arguments, and the role of feedback.

More specific studies of the audience's comprehension of content in technical communication include David E. Kieras's "Thematic Processes in the Comprehension of Technical Prose" (1982). Kieras summarizes the results of a study of how readers identify the important content of technical prose. The author presents models of both the comprehension and the main idea identification processes, based on a theoretical framework utilizing both semantic and surface structures. As Thomas P. Johnson's "How Well Do You Inform?" (1982) shows, an important factor in the reader's recognition of main ideas is the author's cueing of those ideas. Johnson makes an important distinction between the "catalogical" writing done by most engineers, which handles details serially and fails to indicate which ones are more (or less) important, and analytical writing, which clearly distinguishes levels of importance among the various details and is thus preferable.

The literature of user documentation provides specific examples of adapting content to audience. Elizabeth Berry's "How to Get Users to Follow Procedures" (1982) suggests three basic criteria for descriptions of procedures: use an appropriate format, do not assume more knowledge of the system than the user possesses, and be fair to the user. Arlan Saunders's "Writing Effective Assembly Procedures" (1982) stresses the value of a number of techniques which dictate the document's content.

Discussions of organization patterns usually connect more directly to elements of traditional rhetoric than they do to specific audiences. As an aid to discovering subject matter, the *topoi* (topics) can be used: the common topics are definition, comparison, relationship, circumstance, and testimony. Edward P.J. Corbett's *Classical Rhetoric for the Modern Student* (1971) and George A. Kennedy's *Classical Rhetoric* (1980) are two standard sources on the subject. The persistence of elements of classical rhetoric in our own day can be seen in the organizational patterns our textbooks teach. The former invention *topoi* of definition, comparison, and so on now appear as patterns of organization, a relationship detailed by Frank D'Angelo in "Paradigms as Structural Counterparts of *Topoi*" (1980). The patterns seem to endure throughout history quite independently of changing audiences.

This century's concern with the way our minds reshape the world we perceive has led to proposals of new patterns of organization, patterns that putatively are based on fundamental qualities of the human mind as an information-processing system. The obvious has been suggested; perhaps the traditional patterns of definition, cause and effect, comparison, and so on have some fundamental status as mental filters through which we all unwittingly perceive reality. Frank D'Angelo's *A Conceptual Theory of Rhetoric* (1975) remains the central document in this argument. If this argument is valid, we can say the organizational patterns have some clear relationship to specific audiences because if one could prove the traditional patterns enjoy some special status as cognitive filters, it would indeed behoove writers to so organize their words.

In "The Ideal Orator and Literary Critic as Technical Communicators" (1983), Merrill D. Whitburn traces a similarly persistent pattern, the content outline, as an illustration of the way imitation of a successful model can override concerns of both audience and subject. Companies commonly outline the content of a successful document and use that outline as a guide to develop similar documents in the future. Whitburn argues that such outlines (and the people who persist in using them exclusively to determine structure) "focus on only part of the past communication situation (the work) and on only one facet of that part (its organization or content outline)" (p. 235). One recalls E. H. Gombrich's argument about the persistence of stock figures in visual art (in *Art and Illusion*, 1960, 1972), articles that connect form in written documents with visual form (such as Irvin Hashimoto, "Helping Students to Sort and Display Their Information" [1983]), and Walter J. Ong's argument in "The Writer's Audience Is Always a Fiction" (1977) that writers learn the audiences they envision primarily from imitating audiences created by earlier writers.

Contemporary views of organization which differ from the classical pattern and depart from the content outline approach to structure tend to come almost exclusively from academia. Francis Christensen's "A Generative Rhetoric of the Paragraph" (1965) draws attention to two dominant paragraph patterns, coordinate and subordinate. His approach, popularized in *Notes Toward a New Rhetoric* (1978) and *The Christensen Method* (1979), assigns numbers to the levels of structure in paragraphs, allowing one to trace the downshifting and upshifting that structure paragraphs.

In "The Grammar of Coherence" (1975), Ross Winterowd proposes a different set of relationships among sentences: coordination, observativity, causativity, conclusivity, alternativity, inclusivity, and sequence. His focus is then on the transitional units (T-units) which link these relationships. As with the other structural patterns presented here, the set of relationships can be used as an invention device, but the relationships themselves do not depend on audience at all.

Another classification for structural patterns is proposed by Richard Larson in "Toward a Linear Rhetoric of the Essay" (1971). Larson proposes a "linear" plan to complement such hierarchical models as Christensen's. The linear plan unfolds via a series of questions for writers to ask as they compose. Another structural grid keyed to questions is the tagmemic heuristic developed by Richard E. Young, Alton L. Becker, and Kenneth L. Pike in *Rhetoric* (1970). By using a nine-cell grid bordered by contrast, variation, and distribution along one axis and by particle, wave, and field along the other, a set of questions is generated for writers to answer concerning their topics. Gregory Bator's "The Impact of Cognitive Development upon Audience Awareness in the Writing Process" (1980) is a long exploration of the applications of this grid to adapting discourse to specific audiences.

More elaborate views of structure draw on contemporary cognitive theory. One of the most influential schemes is the propositional analysis model offered by Walter Kintsch, for example, in "Comprehension and Memory of Text" (1978). Among other things, the ranking of propositions in texts allows researchers to predict which specific propositions readers will recall. Kintsch also discusses the role of schemata, prototypes or norms of events that specify (in an imprecise fashion) what usually occurs in a given situation. Some recent studies suggest that text comprehension is based on schema. David E. Rumelhart and Andrew Ortony's "The Representation of Knowledge in Memory" (1977) discusses schema and connects them to the way metaphors work. A useful discussion of schema and other aspects that contribute to the establishment of meaning can be found in Martin Nystrand's "The Structure of Textual Space" (1982).

M.A.K. Halliday and Ruqaiya Hassan offer a view of structure based on elements that bind texts together in *Cohesion in English* (1976). In "An Analysis of Errors in Written Communication" (1982), Martin Nystrand explains cohesion ("continuity of text", p. 65) as one of several areas in which written communication can break down. Nystrand offers a thorough application of error analysis to writing, including a discussion of the role of audience in errors.

One other fruitful area for research into the interaction of structure and audience is the way a particular piece orders old versus new information. One study of this with specific reference to technical communication is Robert de Beaugrande's "Communication in Technical Writing" (1978). As de Beaugrande points out, the success of any document may be measured by the way it organizes old and new information into patterns that allow particular readers to understand it in light of their background. In "Defining Thematic Progressions and Their Relationship to Reader Comprehension" (1982), Barbara S. Glatt tests the principle of thematic progression (that given information should precede new information in sentences). She finds that "information ordered according to ab-ac and ab-bc (where the first letter in each pair represents the theme and initial sentence position, the second letter represents theme and noninitial sentence position, and repeated letters represent given information) will be easier to comprehend than the same information ordered according to ab-ca or ab-cb" (p. 102).

The interaction of style and audience has attracted tremendous attention in two related areas: complexity and readability. Research in both areas converges in computer text-critiquing systems, such as the IBM EPISTLE.

Studies of reader recall of text and the factors that control it examine many issues, from the role of reader motivation to the effects of individual words, sentence structures, and larger units of text. A convenient summary of many of these issues appears in Doris Aaronson's ''Performance Theories for Sentence Coding'' (1976). The study's own premise is that the task to which the reader is set (free versus serial recall) helps determine the type of perceptual coding the reader makes. Another study, ''Performance Theories for Sentence Coding'' (1976), by Doris Aaronson and Hollis Scarborough, provides empirical support for the idea that the perceptual coding of words and sentences is flexible, based on the reader's experience, and dependent on the reader's goal in reading.

More recent studies also reveal the effects of reader motivation and preparation on text recall. In ''Sentence Cueing and Effectiveness of Bizarre Imagery'' (1981), Keith A. Waller and Steven D. Cox conclude that recall for bizarre imagery (''The hen smoked the cigar'') versus non-bizarre imagery (''The horse ate the hay'') varies depending on whether the recall is free or cued (with the first two words provided). Other studies over the years have shown that the likelihood of recall varies inversely with structural complexity. In ''Grammatical Factors in Sentence Retention'' (1966), Edwin Martin and Kelyn Roberts show that the degree of embeddedness of items in various sentence structures affected recall in two ways. Structural complexity was seen to be inversely correlated with the likelihood of correct recall. When both length and complexity of the sentence were controlled, the type of sentence had little impact on recall.

One author who applies the varied and occasionally contradictory findings of such studies to technical communications is Robert de Beaugrande. In ''Information and Grammar in Technical Writing'' (1977), he discusses the effect on readers of such features as grammar, extended modifiers, and use of passives. Another author whose name appears often in the literature is Gene L. Piche. In ''Development in Syntactic and Strategic Aspects of Audience Adaptation Skills in Written Persuasive Communication'' (1979), Piche and Donald L. Rubin test the extent to which audience adaptation in syntax is a developmental tendency and the degree to which the use of various persuasive strategies is a measure of audience adaptation. In ''Audience and Mode of Discourse Effects on Syntactic Complexity in Writing at Two Grade Levels'' (1979), Marion Crowhurst and Piche find that contrasts in the age, intimacy, and power of the audience relative to the writer produce observed differences in the written text's syntactic complexity. They also find that such variations in syntactic complexity occur much later in writing than in speech.

In ''Names in Search of a Concept'' (1980), Lester Faigley sorts out some of the confusing terminology associated with this area of research. He points out that whether a descriptive model of writing is based on a sentence grammar (as most models measuring complexity are) or a meaning grammar (as models involving propositional analysis are), such models still fail to offer a complete picture:

These models...do not explain important conditions such as *coherence*, nor do they define the systematic relationships of a given text to its *context*. The effectiveness of a prose text depends in large part on its appropriateness to the communicative context. The description of the appropriateness of a given piece of prose requires pragmatic rules that specify the general knowledge and assumptions about discourse structure of the particular readers whom the text addresses (p. 299).

If complexity is a difficult issue, then readability may well be an impossible one. Yet readability is crucial to the interaction of style and audience. The literature on readability threatens to overwhelm all other stylistic approaches by its very quantity. It is too extensive to be more than mentioned here. While the several branches of the armed forces, IBM, General Motors, and the IRS (to name a few) computerize readability formulas as ways of testing their documents' effectiveness, it is difficult to find any two authors who agree on just what aspects of texts should be measured, or just what such formulas actually measure. The following discussion offers a brief summary of the major sources.

The three traditional names in readability are R. Gunning (*The Techniques of Clear Writing* [1952]), George R. Klare (*The Measurement of Readability* [1963]), and Rudolph Flesch (*The Art of Readable Writing* [1949]). Gunning's Fog Index counts average sentence length and percentage of polysyllabic words. George Klare is primarily a bibliographer of readability; his analysis of readability in *Know Your Reader* (1954) focuses on audience adaptation. Rudolph Flesch's Reading Ease Formula counts the average number of words per "unit of thought" (usually a sentence) and the average number of syllables per hundred words. A "Recalculated Flesch" scale (as in J. P. Kincaid and colleagues, *Derivation of New Readability Formulas for Navy Enlisted Personnel* [1975]) is popular in the military. Beginning in 1978, readability was required in service manuals (explained in J. D. Kniffin, "The New Readability Requirements for Military Technical Manuals" [1979]).

Names nearly as well known in readability are Edgar Dale and J. S. Chall ("A Formula for Predicting Readability" [1948]) and Edward Fry ("A Readability Formula That Saves Time" [1968]). The Dale-Chall formula counts the percentage of words not on Dale's list of 3,000 familiar words and the average number of words per sentence. Edward Fry's Readability Graph counts the total number of sentences in at least three 100-word passages, and the total number of syllables in each 100-word sample, and plots the results on a graph.

Others have developed somewhat different measures of readability. Perhaps the central name in recent readability research is John Bormuth (*Development of Readability Analysis* [1969]). Bormuth attempted to use 132 variables to come up with a comprehensive measure of readability and was forced to conclude that a measure with "economic practicality, face validity, and predictive accuracy" was at the time impossible. Bormuth's research did, however, help draw attention to the cloze procedures test for readability (W. L. Taylor, "Cloze Procedure" [1953]), which measures the reader's ability to replace words omitted from a text. More recent research (for example, T. A. Anderson, "Cloze Measures as Indices of Achievement Comprehension Learning from Extended Prose" [1974]) has focused on the cloze method. Another newer measure is the SMOG Index (G. H. McLaughlin, "Comparing Styles of Presenting Technical Information" [1966]), which arrives at a reading grade level by adding three to the square root of the number of polysyllabic words in a 30-sentence sample.

No formula for readability has been able to silence the critics of all such schemes. One of the big problems with such formulas is that they inevitably become prescriptive rather than descriptive and are used to write and revise documents rather than to compare them. In "Usefulness of Readability Formulas for Achieving Army Objectives" (1980), Richard P. Kern concludes that a text written to satisfy a targeted reading grade level (based on a readability formula) winds up focusing attention on meeting that level but not on organizing the material to meet the reader's information needs. Here we find that an initial focus on audience, which establishes such a norm as "8th grade level," winds up indirectly (and perversely) producing writing which defeats that very concern for audience.

Readability formulas have difficulty measuring the influence of reader motivation and background, the effect of many stylistic differences, the effect of tone, the effect of sentence logic, and the visual elements of the text. They also generally cannot satisfy Lester Faigley's objections to definitions of complexity, as described earlier. As S. Michael Halloran and Merrill Whitburn conclude in "Ciceronian Rhetoric and the Rise of Science" (1982), "Only one instrument has the power to analyze communication situations—the human mind. Efforts to quantify communication situations are inevitably either trivial or inconclusive because quantitative instruments will never be subtle or powerful enough for the task" (p. 18).

In the face of such obstacles, it is a testimony to the importance of readability that so much continues to be done in this area. Three disparate examples of current approaches to readability illustrate this. Arn Tibbetts's "Ten Rules for Writing Readably" (1982) explains how to achieve a readable style by proper handling of ideas, words, phrases, clauses, logic, syntax, and personality. Six essays in the *IEEE Transactions on Professional Communication* "Forum" (March 1981) cover the whole spectrum of uses of readability. Finally, IBM's experimental EPISTLE text-critiquing computer system (G. E. Heidorn and colleagues, "The EPISTLE Text-Critiquing System" [1982]) critiques the grammar and style of business letters, and is being refined to handle more difficult, semantically rooted errors.

The visual element of the text may be the aspect of the text that is most neglected, underused, or misused in technical communication. Whether it is typeface, graphics, or pictorial material, the visual element can be critical to the success of any text.

General discussions of the psychological significance of visual presentations of information can be found in E. H. Gombrich's *Art and Illusion* (1977), Rudolf Arnheim's *Visual Thinking* (1969), and Kurt Hanks and Larry Belliston's *Draw* (1977). The general source on when to use visuals, different typefaces, layout principles, color coding, and message intelligibility is Wesley E. Woodson's *Human Factors Design Handbook* (1981). It summarizes much of the research on these human factors in readable form. A similarly general source is Wilbert O. Galitz's *Human Factors in Office Automation* (1980). A number of specific studies have investigated the relative merits of verbal versus visual presentations of information in various applications. Patricia Wright's "Presenting Technical Information" (1977) is a comprehensive overview of graphical and textual presentation of material. Many different elements of text are covered, such as headings, type size, numerals, tables, charts, graphs, and illustrations. Harold R. Booher's "Relative Comprehensibility of Pictorial Information and Printed Words" (1975) tested two single-channel formats (verbal and pictorial) and four mixed-channel formats (various mixes of pictorial, print, and redundancy) as instructional systems. Minimum time and minimum errors in performance resulted from the formats containing relatively high pictorial content and low amounts of printed matter.

The use of flowcharts in instructions is one popular decision point for visual versus verbal presentations of information. Studies such as "The Simplification and Avoidance of Instruction" (C. P. Gane and colleagues [1966]), "Writing To Be Understood" (Patricia Wright [1971]), and "The Comprehensibility of Printed Instructions and the Flowchart Alternative" (Richard Kamman [1975]) all point to the desirability of using flowcharts.

When cost considerations are not overriding, the decision of whether to use color or black and white can be difficult. In "The Effect of IQ Level on the Instructional Effectiveness of Black-and-White and Color Illustrations" (1976), F. M. Dwyer found that simple line drawings in color were the most effective way of improving student achievement. Pictorial composition is another important issue studied in W. Niekamp's "An Exploratory Investigation in Factors Affecting Visual Balance" (1981).

The interaction of visuals and text can take the shape of visual cueing (such as underlining). Studies such as G. R. Klare and colleagues' "The Relationship of Patterning (Underlining) to Immediate Retention and to Acceptability of Technical Material" (1955), W. A. Hershberger and D. F. Terry's "Typographic Cueing in Conventional and Programmed Texts" (1965), and J. H. Crouse and P. Idstein's "Effects of Encoding Cues on Prose Learning" (1972) agree that a moderate amount of underlining aids in text comprehension. More recently, authors such as James Hartley ("Spatial Cues in Text" [1980]), David H. Jonassen ("Information Mapping" [1981]), and Dirk Wendt ("Improving the Legibility of Textbooks" [1982] have focused on more radical departures from the visual appearance of the traditional printed page as aids to comprehension. In 1981 *Visible Language* published a special double issue (Volume 15, Nos. 2 and 3) on visual cues in word recognition and reading.

The area of visuals attracting the most current attention is, of course, computer graphics. In *The Educational Effectiveness of Graphic Displays for Computer Assisted Instruction* (1978), N. V. Moore and L. H. Nawrocki seek to determine the state of the art for the instructional uses of graphics. They find that the addition of graphic instructional material does not guarantee an increase in instructional effectiveness, and there is no systematic way of determining just what conditions most invite the use of graphics. Thomas S. Tullis's "An Evaluation of Alphanumeric, Graphic, and Color Information Displays" (1981) evaluated four different types of CRT display formats and summarized a number of earlier studies. Tullis found no significant difference between color and black-and-white displays. He also found that graphic displays were superior to narratives, and that structural displays that separate and group logically related data were especially useful. Turner Whitted's "Some Recent Advances in Computer Graphics" (1982) summarizes the current state of computer graphics.

Two studies that cover a variety of visual elements of text are Frances J. Lauer's "Readability Techniques for Authors and Editors" (1976) and Walter Nash's "Layout and Rhetorical Pattern" (1980). Lauer summarizes research into the effects of various typefaces, locations on the page of important material, and location of captions. Nash discusses the graphology of text and layout as part of both the content and the communicative intent of discourse.

The Teaching of Audience Analysis and Adaptation

A growing body of useful literature exists on approaches to teaching audience analysis and adaptation. That literature is discussed here in three groupings: theories, approaches, and pedagogy. While there is certainly overlap among the three areas, the distinction is one of scope: theories (the most general area) imply the somewhat more specific approaches, which themselves lead to still more specific pedagogy.

A comprehensive theory that embodies teaching audience analysis and adaptation as the essential core for writing classes is Ruth Mitchell and Mary Taylor's "The Integrating Perspective" (1979). Mitchell and Taylor decry the two most typical approaches to teaching writing, which focus on the writer or the written product. They offer instead a focus on audience, the audience's response to the written product, and the community context within which the writer and the reader are working. They suggest these five criteria for evaluating instructional techniques:

> Does this method help the student accommodate his writing to an audience?
>
> Is she learning from it that her writing must affect a reader?
>
> Does the method help him understand how his writing will be evaluated?

Does it give her any information about her audience?

Is he learning how readers read so that he can both assist them and his own purpose by careful presentational strategy? (p. 257)

Donald M. Murray, a professional writer and teacher of writing, has always emphasized the importance of audience, from his seminal *A Writer Teaches Writing* (1968) to the essays collected in *Learning by Teaching* (1982). He consistently stresses the reader over one's shoulder, the "other self." In "Teaching the Other Self" (1982), he explains this internalized audience's functions: It tracks the writing activity that is taking place; it gives the writer's self distance from the text; it provides an evolving context for the writer; it articulates the process of writing; and it is the critic who continually looks at the writing to see if it works.

Similar to Taylor and Mitchell's "integrating" perspective is Barry Kroll's "interactionist" perspective (in "Developmental Perspectives and the Teaching of Composition" [1980]): "In the interactionist course, writing is presented as a dialectic between one's awareness of purpose (what the writer intends) and one's awareness of audience (how the reader will react), resulting in the creation of shared meanings—in short, as communication" (p. 752). Kroll's work epitomizes the cognitivist/developmental perspective which is gaining popularity among writing teachers. In its thrust (if not its vocabulary), his work is consistent with that of Mitchell and Taylor, Carolyn Miller, and Carol Berkenkotter mentioned earlier.

Approaches to teaching technical communication courses based on audience usually aim at changing the audiences of students' papers and changing the teacher's relationship to those papers. Four approaches often described in the literature directly address the issues of the kind of writing students do and the audiences for that writing: the use of second (expert) readers, writing across the curriculum, peer tutors, and case-study assignments. The four approaches are closely related.

The first approach, the use of second (expert) readers, or "technical advisors," has been popularized by Thomas M. Sawyer in such articles as "Examining Scientific and Technical Literature" (1975). The technical writing teacher works with a subject specialist in the student's own field. This reinforces both stylistic clarity and technical accuracy in the student's reports. By thus manipulating the report's audience, the designers of such courses hope to provide a rhetorical situation that better prepares students for the writing they will do outside of college.

As described by Toby Fulwiler and Art Young in *Language Connections* (1982) and by Karen Burke LeFevre and Mary Jane Dickerson in *Until I See What I Say* (1981), the writing across the curriculum approach tailors the kinds of writing students do to the demands of those students' particular disciplines. Since this approach involves teaching students to write for mechanical engineering professors, math professors, biology professors, as well as English professors, audience becomes a central concern.

The third approach, the use of peer tutors (the collaborative approach), is described among other places in Richard Gebhardt's "Teamwork and Feedback" (1980). In this approach, the student's work is assisted by feedback from other students at every stage of the writing process. Thus, the student learns first-hand the reality of readers.

The fourth approach is the case-study method, described among many other sources in David Tedlock's "The Case Approach to Composition" (1981) and Linda Woodson's *From Cases to Composition* (1982). Each writing case dictates a situational context within which the writer works, one that includes a specific audience. A similar approach is described in James W. Souther's "Developing Assignments for Scientific and Technical Writing" (1977).

In practice these four approaches combine in many useful ways. The STC publication, "How to Involve Students in Writing Actual Reports" (1980), by Joseph A. Rice, explains how to get students involved in writing projects around the campus, perhaps doing new user documentation for a computer or revising the description of a procedure. Combining elements of all four approaches, this technique puts students into writing situations very close to those they will meet outside college. In "Practical Work for Advanced Composition Students" (1980), Donald Stewart describes having the students in his advanced composition class grade the papers of his freshmen. As Stewart says, "Students always do better work when they are playing for keeps."

A number of specific techniques for teaching technical communication based on audience analysis and adaptation are recommended in such collections of essays as the Association of Teachers of Technical Writing's *Teaching Technical Writing* (1979) and *Teaching Technical Writing* (1980), Donald H. Cunningham and Herman A. Estrin's *The Teaching of Technical Writing* (1975), and Dwight Stevenson's *Courses, Components, and Exercises in Technical Communication* (1981). Many articles also suggest specific audience-centered teaching techniques and assignments. These include Merrill D. Whitburn's "The First Day in the Technical Writing Course" (1979), Elizabeth Tebeaux's "Getting More Mileage Out of Audience Analysis" (1982), David Carson's "Audience in Technical Writing" (1979), and Mary Coney's "The Use of the Reader in Technical Writing" (1978).

A last and important issue in the teaching of audience-centered technical communication classes is the role of human maturation in successful audience analysis and adaptation. The cognitivist/developmental perspective of the essays by Mitchell and Taylor, Kroll, Miller, and Berkenkotter is at least loosely based on Piagetian theory, and one of the central tenets of that theory is that the ability to see another's viewpoint is strongly age-related. If that is true, then the kind of audience-centered approach that might work with 17-year-old college freshmen could be quite different from the audience-centered approach that might work with college seniors, simply because the ages (and hence levels of maturation) of the students are different. This theory can be taken another way, and used to argue that teaching audience-centered writing courses not only measures growth on the scale from egocentric to sociocentric thought but also actively encourages that growth. A good explanation of these elements of Piagetian thought and their place in the language classroom may be found in Margaret Donaldson's *Children's Minds* (1979).

Conclusion

The published literature contains an abundance of material on the importance of audience and the teaching of audience analysis and adaptation. In other areas, such as style and structure, published materials tend to focus more on the mechanical aspects of technical communication (such as readability or the role of visual organizers) than on the human aspects (the nature of an audience's response).

Several other trends relevant to this topic deserve mention here. First, as teaching technical writing attracts more and more specialists, it can only move closer and closer to the kind of model described above by Ruth Mitchell and Mary Taylor. These specialists are increasingly able to take advantage of rich backgrounds as professional technical writers and editors, as scholars in the field of rhetoric, and as trained writing teachers. All three areas lead to an increased awareness of the importance of audience.

Second, the literature cited here shows the rapid growth of and change in our understanding of the nature of written language. While studies that treat writing as a secondary, derivative form of speech still appear, a growing number of articles and books (such as Martin Nystrand's *What Writers Know* [1982]) treat writing as a language all its own. Beyond that, writing is increasingly seen not as an isolated system of signs and conventions (a "second speech") but as a unique and uniquely human activity. Increasing attention is devoted to the special qualities of writers (such as the literature on writing apprehension), the special qualities of readers (such as the literature on rhetorical communities), and the interactions of those two sets of qualities with the formal aspects of language systems.

The third trend, less well-developed than the first two but especially interesting, is the changing character of the role of technical communicators in the information society. In addition to the traditional roles of technical communicators (writing, editing, publications production, problem-solving), technical communicators are increasingly being seen in the twin roles of information managers and information brokers. At that point the audience has ceased to say to the writer "organize this information for me and disseminate it in the right format to the right people" and has begun to say "*collect* this information, then organize it, then disseminate it." The change is a significant one in many ways; when the audience asks us different kinds of questions, we must be able to give different kinds of answers.

References

Aaronson, Doris. "Performance Theories for Sentence Coding: Some Qualitative Observations." *J Exp Psychol: Hum Perc Perf*, 6 (1976), 42–55.

———, and Hollis Scarborough. "Performance Theories for Sentence Coding: Some Quantitative Evidence." *J Exp Psychol: Hum Perc Perf*, 6 (1976), 56–70.

Abrams, M. H. *The Mirror and the Lamp*. New York: Oxford University Press, 1953.

Anderson, T. A. "Cloze Measures as Indices of Achievement Comprehension Learning from Extended Prose." *J Educ M*, 11 (1974), 83–92.

Arnheim, Rudolf. *Visual Thinking*. Berkeley: University of California Press, 1969.

Association of Teachers of Technical Writing (ATTW). *Teaching Technical Writing: The First Day in the Technical Writing Course*. Ed. Merrill Whitburn. ATTW, 1979.

———. *Teaching Technical Writing: Teaching Audience Analysis and Adaptation*. Ed. Paul V. Anderson. ATTW, 1980.

Atlas, Marshall. "User Edit: Making Manuals Easier to Use." *IEEE Trans Prof Comm*, 24, No. 1 (1981), 28–29.

———. "Writer Insensitivity to Audience—Causes and Cures." Annual Meeting of the American Educational Research Association, Boston, Mass., 7–11 Apr. 1980. ED 185 568.

Baskin, Otto, and Sam J. Bruno. "A Transactional Systems Model for Communication: Implications for Transactional Analysis." *J Bus Comm*, 15, No. 1 (1977), 64–73.

Bator, Gregory. "The Impact of Cognitive Development upon Audience Awareness in the Writing Process." Diss. University of Michigan, 1980.

Becker, Curtis A. "Semantic Context and Word Frequency Effects in Visual Word Recognition." *J Exp Psychol: Hum Perc Perf*, 5 (1979), 252–59.

Berkenkotter, Carol. "A Writer's Awareness of Audience." *CCC*, 32 (1981), 388–97.

Berry, Elizabeth. "How to Get Users to Follow Procedures." *IEEE Trans Prof Comm*, 25, No. 1 (1982), 22–25.

Bizzell, Patricia. "Thomas Kuhn, Scientism, and English Studies." *CE*, 40 (1979), 764–71.

Boettinger, Henry M. *Moving Mountains: Or the Art & Craft of Letting Others See Things Your Way*. New York: Macmillan, 1975.

Booher, Harold R. "Relative Comprehensibility of Pictorial Information and Printed Words—Proceduralized Instructions." *Human Fact*, 17 (1975), 266–77.

Booth, Wayne. "The Rhetorical Stance." *CCC*, 14 (1963), 139–45.

Bormuth, John. *Development of Readability Analysis*. Washington, D.C.: U.S. Office of Education, 1969.

Britton, James, et al. *The Development of Writing Abilities, 11–18*. London: Macmillan Education Ltd., 1975.

Burgoon, Judee K., Michael Burgoon, Gerald R. Miller, and Michael Summafrank. "Learning Theory Approaches to Persuasion." *HCR*, 7 (1981), 161–79.

Burke, Kenneth. *A Rhetoric of Motives*. Berkeley: University of California Press, 1969.

Carr-Smith, Norma. "Overcoming Defensive Barriers to Communication: A Transactional Analysis Approach." *ABCA Bul*, 41, No. 1 (1978), 12–15.

Carson, David. "Audience in Technical Writing." *Tech Writ Teach*, 7 (1979), 8–11.

Chapanis, Alphonse. "Words, Words, Words!" *Human Fact*, 7 (1965), 1–17.

Chase, Lawrence J., and Clifford W. Kelly. "Language Intensity and Resistance to Persuasion: A Research Note." *HCR*, 3 (1976), 82–85.

Cherry, Colin. *On Human Communication*. 3rd ed. Cambridge, Mass. MIT Press, 1978.

Christensen, Bonniejean. *The Christensen Method: Text and Workbook*. New York: Harper, 1979.

Christensen, Francis. "A Generative Rhetoric of the Paragraph." *CCC*, 16 (1965), 144–56; rpt. in Christensen and Christensen, 1978 (cited below), pp. 74–103.

―――, and Bonniejean Christensen. *Notes Toward a New Rhetoric: Nine Essays for Teachers*. New York: Harper, 1978.

Clevenger, Theodore. *Audience Analysis*. Indianapolis: Bobbs-Merrill, 1966.

Coney, Mary. "The Use of the Reader in Technical Writing." *J Tech Writ Comm*, 8 (1978), 97–106.

Corbett, Edward P. J. *Classical Rhetoric for the Modern Student*, 2nd ed. Oxford: Oxford University Press, 1971.

Crouse, J. H., and P. Idstein. "Effects of Encoding Cues on Prose Learning." *J Educ*, 63 (1972), 309–13.

Crowhurst, Marion, and Gene L. Piche. "Audience and Mode of Discourse Effects on Syntactic Complexity in Writing at Two Grade Levels." *RTE*, 13 (1979), 101–109.

Cunningham, Donald H., and Herman A. Estrin. *The Teaching of Technical Writing*. Urbana, Ill.: NCTE, 1975.

Dale, Edgar, and J. S. Chall. "A Formula for Predicting Readability." *Educ Res Bul*, 21 Jan. and 17 Feb. 1948, pp. 11–20, 37–54.

D'Angelo, Frank. *A Conceptual Theory of Rhetoric*. Cambridge, Mass.: Winthrop, 1975.

―――. "Paradigms as Structural Counterparts of 'Topoi'." *Lang Style*, 13 (1980), 41–51.

Davis, Richard M. "The Communication Situation—A Model and Discussion." *J Tech Writ Comm*, 4 (1974), 185–205.

De Beaugrande, Robert. "Communication in Technical Writing." *J Tech Writ Comm*, 8 (1978), 5–15.

―――. "Information and Grammar in Technical Writing." *CCC*, 28 (1977), 325–32.

―――. "Psychology and Composition: Past, Present, and Future." In *What Writers Know*. Ed. Martin Nystrand. New York: Academic, 1982, pp. 211–68.

Diehl, Willia, and Larry Mikulecky. "Making Written Information Fit Workers' Purposes." *IEEE Trans Prof Comm*, 24, No. 1 (1981), 5–9.

Donaldson, Margaret. *Children's Minds*. London: Croon Helm, 1979.

Dwyer, F. M. "The Effect of IQ Level on the Instructional Effectiveness of Black-and-White and Color Illustrations." *Comm Rev*, 24 (1976), 49–62.

―――. *A Guide for Improving Visualized Instruction*. State College, Pa.: Learning Services, 1972.

Eason, K. D. "Understanding the Naive Computer User." *Comput J*, 19 (1976), 3–7.

Ede, Lisa. "On Audience and Composition." *CCC*, 30 (1979), 291–95.

Ehrenreich, S. L. "Query Languages: Design Recommendations Derived from the Human Factors Literature." *Human Fact*, 23 (1981), 709–25.

Elbow, Peter. *Writing with Power*. New York: Oxford University Press, 1981.

Emerson, Frances B. "Applied Pragmatics in the Development of Technical Writing." *Tech Writ Teach*, 8 (1981), 63–68.

Faigley, Lester. "Names in Search of a Concept: Maturity, Fluency, Complexity, and Growth in Written Syntax." *CCC*, 31 (1980), 291–300.

Flavell, J. H. "The Development of Inferences about Others." In *Understanding Other Persons*. Ed. Theodore Mischel. Totowa, N.J.: Rowman, Littlefield, 1974.

Flesch, Rudolph. *The Art of Readable Writing*. New York: Harper, 1949.

Flower, Linda. *Problem-Solving Strategies for Writing*. New York: Harcourt, 1981.

————, and John R. Hayes. "The Cognition of Discovery: Defining a Rhetorical Problem." *CCC*, 31 (1980), 21–32.

————, and John R. Hayes. "Problem-Solving Strategies and the Writing Process." *CE*, 39 (1977), 449–61.

Fry, Edward. "A Readability Formula That Saves Time." *J Read*, 2 (1968), 513–16, 575.

Fulwiler, Toby, and Art Young, eds. *Language Connections: Writing & Reading Across the Curriculum*. Urbana: National Council of Teachers of English (NCTE), 1982.

Galitz, Wilbert O. *Human Factors in Office Automation*. Atlanta: Life Office Management Association, 1980.

Gane, C. P., et al. "The Simplification and Avoidance of Instruction." *Indus Train Int*, 1 (1966), 160–66.

Gebhardt, Richard. "Teamwork and Feedback: Broadening the Base of Collaborative Writing." *CE*, 42 (1980), 69–74.

Glatt, Barbara S. "Defining Thematic Progressions and Their Relationship to Reader Comprehension." In *What Writers Know*. Ed. Martin Nystrand. New York: Academic, 1982, pp. 87–104.

Gombrich, E. H. *Art and Illusion*. 5th ed. Princeton, N.J.: Princeton University Press, 1977.

Gunning, R. *The Techniques of Clear Writing*. New York: McGraw-Hill, 1952, 1968.

Hairston, Maxine. *Contemporary Rhetoric*, 3rd ed. Boston: Houghton Mifflin, 1982.

————. "Not All Errors Are Created Equal: Nonacademic Readers in the Professions Respond to Lapses in Usage." *CE*, 43 (1981), 794–806.

Halliday, M.A.K., and Ruqaiya Hassan. *Cohesion in English*. London: Longman, 1976.

Halloran, S. Michael, and Merrill Whitburn. "Ciceronian Rhetoric and the Rise of Science: The Plain Style Reconsidered." In *The Rhetorical Tradition and Modern Writing*. Ed. James J. Murphy. New York: Modern Language Association, 1982, pp. 58–72.

Hanks, Kurt, and Larry Belliston. *Draw: A Visual Approach to Thinking, Learning, and Communicating*. Los Altos, Calif.: Kaufmann, 1977.

Hartley, James. "Spatial Cues in Text." *Visbl Lang*, 14 (1980), 62–79.

Hashimoto, Irvin. "Helping Students to Sort and Display Their Information." *CE*, 45 (1983), 277–87.

Hasling, John. *The Message, the Audience, and the Speaker*. New York: McGraw-Hill, 1976.

Hays, Janice N. "The Effect of Audience Considerations upon the Revisions of a Group of Basic Writers and More Competent Junior and Senior Writers." Annual Meeting of the Conference on College Composition and Communication, Dallas, 26–28 Mar. 1981. ED 204–802.

Heidorn, G. E., et al. "The EPISTLE Text-Critiquing System." *IBM Syst J*, 21 (1982), 305–26.

Hershberger, W. A., and D. E. Terry. "Typographic Cueing in Conventional and Programmed Texts." *J Appl Psychol*, 49 (1965), 55–60.

Horace. *Ars Poetica*. In *Classical Literary Criticism*. Trans. and ed. T. S. Dorsch. Baltimore: Penguin, 1965.

Houp, Kenneth, and Thomas E. Pearsall. *Reporting Technical Information*, 4th ed. Encino, Calif.: Collier Macmillan, 1980.

IEEE Trans Prof Comm "Forum." PO 24, No. 1 (1981), pp. 43–54.

Jakobson, Roman. "Metalanguage as a Linguistic Problem." In *The Scientific Study of Language: Fifty Years of LSA, 1924–1973*. Ed. Anwar S. Dil. Abbotabad, Pakistan: Linguistics Research Group of Pakistan, 1975.

Janis, Irving L., and Carl Hovland. "An Overview of Persuasibility Research." In *Personality and Persuasibility*. Ed. Irving L. Janis and Carl Hovland. New Haven: Yale University Press, 1959, pp. 1–26.

Johanessen, Richard L., et al., eds. *Language Is Sermonic: Richard M. Weaver on the Nature of Rhetoric*. Baton Rouge, La.: Louisiana State University Press, 1970.

Johnson, Thomas P. "How Well Do You Inform?" *IEEE Trans Prof Comm*, 25 (1982), 5–9.

Jonassen, David H. "Information Mapping: A Description, Rationale and Comparison with Programmed Instruction." *Visbl Lang*, 15 (1981), 55–66.

Jones, David E. "Evidence for a Conceptual Theory of Rhetoric," *CCC*, 28 (1977), 333–37.

Kamman, Richard. "The Comprehensibility of Printed Instructions and the Flowchart Alternative." *Human Fact*, 17 (1975), 183–91.

Kapp, Reginald O. *Presentation of Technical Information*. New York: Macmillan, 1948.

Kennedy, George A. *Classical Rhetoric and Its Christian and Secular Tradition from Ancient to Modern Times*. Chapel Hill: University of North Carolina Press, 1980.

Kern, Richard P. "Usefulness of Readability Formulas for Achieving Army Objectives: Research and State-of-the-Art Applied to the Army's Problem." AN AD–A086 408/2. 1980.

Kieras, David E. "Thematic Processes in the Comprehension of Technical Prose." AD–A112 011/2. 1982.

Kincaid, J. P., et al. *Derivation of New Readability Formulas for Navy Enlisted Personnel*. Millington, Tenn.: Naval Air Station Memphis, 1975.

Kinneavy, James L. *A Theory of Discourse: The Aims of Discourse*. Englewood Cliffs, N.J.: Prentice-Hall, 1971.

Kintgen, Eugene R. "Psycholinguistics and Literature." *CE* 39 (1978), 755–69.

Kintsch, Walter. "Comprehension and Memory of Text." In *Linguistic Functions in Cognitive Theory*. Ed. W. K. Estes. Hillsdale, N.J.: Erlbaum, 1978, pp. 57–86.

———. *Memory and Cognition*. New York: Wiley, 1970, 1977.

———. *The Representation of Meaning in Memory*. Hillsdale, N.J.: Erlbaum, 1974.

Klare, George R. *The Measurement of Readability*. Ames: Iowa State University Press, 1963.

———, and Byron Buck. *Know Your Reader*. New York: Hermitage House, 1954.

———, et al. "The Relationship of Patterning (Underlining) to Immediate Retention and to Acceptability of Technical Material." *J Appl Psychol*, 39 (1955), 40–42.

Kniffin, J. D. "The New Readability Requirements for Military Technical Manuals." *Tech Comm*, 26, No. 3 (1979), 16–19.

Kroll, Barry. "Cognitive Egocentrism and the Problem of Audience Awareness in Written Discourse." *RTE*, 12 (1978), 269–81.

————. "Developmental Perspectives and the Teaching of Composition." *CE*, 41 (1980), 741–52.

————. *Explorations in the Development of Writing: Theory, Research, and Practice*. New York: Wylie, 1983.

————. *Exploring Speaking-Writing Relationships: Connections and Contrasts*. Urbana: NCTE, 1981.

Lannon, John M. *Technical Writing*, 2nd ed. Boston: Little, Brown, 1982.

Larson, Richard. "Toward a Linear Rhetoric of the Essay." *CCC*, 22 (1971), 140–46.

Lauer, Frances J. "Readability Techniques for Authors and Editors." *J Tech Writ Comm*, 6 (1976), 203–14.

LeFevre, Karen Burke, and Mary Jane Dickerson. *Until I See What I Say*. Burlington, Vt.: IDC Publications, 1981.

McLaughlin, G. H. "Comparing Styles of Presenting Technical Information." *Ergonomics*, 9 (1966), 257–59.

Martin, Edwin, and Kelyn Roberts. "Grammatical Factors in Sentence Retention." *J Verb Learn Verb Behav*, 5 (1966), 211–18.

Mathes, J. C., and D. W. Stevenson. *Designing Technical Reports: Writing for Audiences in Organizations*. Indianapolis: Bobbs-Merrill, 1976.

Maynard, John. "A User-Driven Approach to Better User Manuals." *IEEE Trans Prof Comm*, 25 (1982), 16–19.

Miller, Carolyn R. "A Humanistic Rationale for Technical Writing." *CE*, 40 (1979), 610–17.

Miller, Susan. "Rhetorical Maturity: Definition and Development." Annual Meeting of the Canadian Council of Teachers of English, Ottawa, Canada. 8–11 May 1979. ED 176 292.

Mitchell, Ruth, and Mary Taylor. "The Integrating Perspective: An Audience-Response Model for Writing." *CE*, 41 (1979), 247–72.

Moffett, James. *Teaching the Universe of Discourse*. Boston: Houghton Mifflin, 1968.

Moore, N. V., and L. H. Nawrocki. *The Educational Effectiveness of Graphic Displays for Computer Assisted Instruction*. U.S. Army Research Institute for the Behavioral and Social Sciences, Sept. 1978.

Morrisey, George L. *Effective Business and Technical Presentations*. Reading, Mass.: Addison-Wesley, 1975.

Murray, Donald M. *Learning by Teaching*. Montclair, N.J.: Boynton/Cook, 1982.

————. "Teaching the Other Self: The Writer's First Reader." *CE*, 33 (1982), 140–47.

————. *A Writer Teaches Writing*. Boston: Houghton Mifflin, 1968.

Nash, Walter. "Layout and Rhetorical Pattern." In *Designs in Prose*. Ed. Randolph Quirk. London: Longman, 1980, pp. 1–20.

Niekamp. W. "An Exploratory Investigation in Factors Affecting Visual Balance." *Educ Comm Tech J*, 29 (1981), 37–48.

Nolan, Timothy D. "A Comparative Study of the Planning, Implementation, and Evaluation Process of Audience-Committed Non-Directed Technical Writing Students." *Tech Writ Teach*, 4 (1977), 50–54.

Nystrand, Martin. "An Analysis of Errors in Written Communication." In *What Writers Know*. Ed. Martin Nystrand. New York: Academic, 1982, pp. 57–74.

————. "The Structure of Textual Space." In *What Writers Know*. Ed. Martin Nystrand. New York: Academic, 1982, pp. 75–86.

————, ed. *What Writers Know: The Language, Process, and Structure of Written Discourse*. New York: Academic, 1982.

Ong, Walter J. "The Writer's Audience Is Always a Fiction." In *Interfaces of the Word: Studies in the Evolution of Consciousness and Culture*. Ithaca: Cornell University Press, 1977, pp. 53–81.

Overington, Michael A. "The Scientific Community as Audience: Toward a Rhetorical Analysis of Science." *Phil Rhet*, 10 (1977), 143–64.

Park, Douglas B. "The Meanings of 'Audience'." *CE*, 44 (1982), 247–57.

Pearce, Clifton Glenn. "The Effect on Reader Comprehension of Report Parts, Organization in Paragraphing, and Use of Headings in a Long Business Report." Diss. Georgia State University, 1974.

Pearsall, Thomas E. *Audience Analysis for Technical Writing*. Beverly Hills, Calif.: Glencoe, 1969.

Perloff, Richard M., and Timothy C. Brock. " 'And Thinking Makes It So': Cognitive Responses to Persuasion." In *Persuasion: New Directions in Theory and Research*. Ed. Michael E. Roloff and Gerald R. Miller. Beverly Hills, Calif.: Sage, 1980, pp. 67–99.

Piche, Gene L., and Donald L. Rubin. "Development in Syntactic and Strategic Aspects of Audience Adaptation Skills in Written Persuasive Communication." *RTE*, 13 (1979), 293–316.

Powell, Kenneth B. "Readability Formulas: Used or Abused," *IEEE Trans Prof Comm*, 24 (1981), 43–52.

Pradl, Gordon M., ed. *Prospect and Retrospect: Selected Essays of James Britton*. Montclair, N.J.: Boynton/Cook, 1982.

Purves, Alan C. "Putting Readers in Their Places: Some Alternatives to Cloning Stanley Fish." *CE*, 42 (1980), 228–36.

————. "That Sunny Dome, Those Caves of Ice: A Model for Research in Reader Response." *CE*, 40 (1979), 802–12.

Rice, Joseph A. "How to Involve Students in Writing Actual Reports." Washington, D.C.: Society for Technical Communication, 1980.

Richardson, Edgar M. "Research on Writing: Apprehension, Quality, and Audience." Annual Meeting of the American Education Research Association, Los Angeles, 1981. ED 204 813.

Rickard, T. A. *Technical Writing*. New York: Wiley, 1920.

Rogers, Carl. "Communication: Its Blocking and Its Facilitation." In *On Becoming a Person*. Boston: Houghton Mifflin, 1961, pp. 329–77.

Rose, Mike. "Rigid Rules, Inflexible Plans, and the Stifling of Language: A Cognitivist Analysis of Writer's Block." *CCC*, 31 (1980), 389–401.

Rumelhart, David E. *Introduction to Human Information Processing*. New York: Wiley, 1977.

————, and Andrew Ortony. "The Representation of Knowledge in Memory." In *Schooling and the Acquisition of Knowledge*. Ed. Richard C. Anderson, et al. Hillsdale, N.J.: Erlbaum, 1977, pp. 99–135.

Saunders, Arlan. "Writing Effective Assembly Procedures." *IEEE Trans Prof Comm*, 25, No. 1 (1982), 20–21.

Sawyer, Thomas M. "Examining Scientific and Technical Literature." In *The Teaching of Technical Writing*. Ed. Donald H. Cunningham and Herman A. Estrin. Urbana: NCTE, 1975, pp. 139–42.

Simons, Herbert W. *Persuasion: Understanding, Practice, and Analysis*. Reading, Mass.: Addison-Wesley, 1976.

Slobin, Dan Isaac. *Psycholinguistics*. 2nd ed. Glenview, Ill.: Scott, Foresman, 1979.

Smith, Frank. *Psycholinguistics and Reading*. New York: Holt, Rinehart, Winston, 1973.

———. *Writing and the Writer*. New York: Holt, Rinehart, Winston, 1982.

Smith, William L., and M. Beverly Swan. "Adjusting Syntactic Structures to Varied Levels of Audience." *J Exp Educ*, 46, No. 4 (1978), 29–34.

Sommers, Nancy. "Revision Strategies of Student Writers and Experienced Adult Writers." *CCC*, 31 (1980), 378–88.

Souther, James W. "Developing Assignments for Scientific and Technical Writing." *J Tech Writ Comm*, 7 (1977), 261–69.

Stevenson, Dwight. "Audience Analysis Across Cultures." Unpublished manuscript, 1982.

———, ed. *Courses, Components, and Exercises in Technical Communication*. Urbana: NCTE, 1981.

Stewart, Donald. "Practical Work for Advanced Composition Students." *CCC*, 31 (1980), 81–83.

Taylor, W. L. "Cloze Procedure: A New Tool for Measuring Readability." *Journ Q*, 30 (1953), 415–33.

Tebeaux, Elizabeth. "Getting More Mileage Out of Audience Analysis—A Basic Approach." *J Tech Writ Comm*, 12 (1982), 15–24.

Tedlock, David. "The Case Approach to Composition." *CCC*, 32 (1981), 253–61.

Thayer, Lee. "On the Limits of Western Communication Theory." *Communication*, 4 (1979), 9–14.

Tibbetts, Arn. "Ten Rules for Writing Readably." *IEEE Trans Prof Comm*, 25, No. 1 (1982), 10–13.

Tullis, Thomas S. "An Evaluation of Alphanumeric, Graphic, and Color Information Displays." *Human Fact*, 23 (1981), 541–50.

U.S. Congress. Office of Technology Assessment. *Informational Technology and Its Impact on American Education*. OTA–CIT–187. Washington, D.C.: U.S. GPO, 1982.

Visible Language. 15, No. 2 (1981).

Visible Language. 15, No. 3 (1981).

Waller, Keith A., and Steven D. Cox. "Sentence Cueing and Effectiveness of Bizarre Imagery." *J Exp Psychol: Human Learn Mem*, 7 (1981), 386–92.

Wendt, Dirk. "Improving the Legibility of Textbooks: Effects of Wording and Typographic Design." *Visbl Lang*, 16 (1982), 88–93.

Whitburn, Merrill D. "The First Day in the Technical Writing Course." *Tech Writ Teach*, (1976), 115–18.

———. "The Ideal Orator and Literary Critic as Technical Communicators: An Emerging Revolution in English Departments." In *Essays on Classical Rhetoric and Modern Discourse*. Ed. Robert J. Connors, Lisa Ede, and Andrea Lunsford. Carbondale: Southern Illinois University, 1984, pp. 226–47.

Whitted, Turner. "Some Recent Advances in Computer Graphics." *Science*, 215 (1982), 767–74.

Wilkins, Keith A. "A Receiver-Bound Concept of Communication." *J Tech Writ Comm*, 4 (1974), 305–13.

Winterowd, Ross. "The Grammar of Coherence." In *Contemporary Rhetoric: A Con-*

ceptual Background with Readings. Ed. Ross Winterowd. New York: Harcourt, 1975.

Woodson, Linda. *From Cases to Composition*. Glenview, Ill.: Scott, Foresman, 1982.

Woodson, Wesley E., *Human Factors Design Handbook*. New York: McGraw-Hill, 1981.

Wright, Patricia. "Presenting Technical Information: A Summary of Research Findings." *Instr Sci*, 6 (1977), 93–134.

———. "Writing to Be Understood: Why Use Sentences?" *Appl Ergon*, 2 (1971), 207–209.

Young, Richard E., Alton L. Becker, and Kenneth L. Pike. *Rhetoric: Discovery and Change*. New York: Harcourt, Brace, 1970.

Modes of Organization

VICTORIA M. WINKLER

An examination of the modes of organization leads us back to George Campbell's *Philosophy of Rhetoric* (1776), William B. Cairn's *The Forms of Discourse* (1896), and Alexander Bain's *English Composition and Rhetoric* (1866). These early works identify the modes and describe them. In reviewing the literature from the 1890s to the 1960s, we find that the traditional modes of organization—description, narration, exposition, and argumentation—have been widely accepted, adopted, and taught without being questioned until recently. Consequently, there is little or no research on the modes *per se*. The most fruitful way for teachers of technical communication to trace the history of the modes is to examine their use in textbooks, especially technical, business, and scientific writing textbooks. This essay, therefore, will use as its research base the textbooks themselves.

By tracing the modes of organization through the texts, we can see how the traditional modes have been narrowed to exposition and how description and narration are often subordinated to exposition. As we move into the late 1960s and early 1970s, we witness a paradigm shift in the teaching of writing. This shift from a product to a process approach to teaching writing is presaged in some of the technical writing texts, and it calls for a reevaluation of the role of the traditional modes of organization. The modes are not abandoned, but they are viewed as heuristics rather than as algorithms. The emergent research by James Britton, James Kinneavy, and James Moffet (cited below) proposes alternatives to the traditional modes, new ways of expanding our view of organizational patterns as "structural models" or conceptual frameworks whose use must be coordinated with, and sometimes subordinated to, inventional concerns such as audience and purpose. The alternative organizational schemas to supplement the static modes with dynamic process models provide technical communication scholars with a new field of inquiry and a fertile new area for research.

This chapter surveys a representative sample of technical and business writing texts in order to identify the arrangement patterns they recommend for organizing information in scientific and technical memos and reports. The first section, on use of the modes of discourse in technical writing texts, identifies these modes. We can then characterize the texts into three major types and discuss the pedagogical and theoretical implications of these texts for teachers of technical writing.

The procedure to select texts for examination consisted of a random sample of 150 books from Gerald J. Alred, Diana C. Reep, and Mohan R. Limaye's *Business and Technical Writing* (1981). The original sample was supplemented by 25 of the more popular contemporary texts and articles. The works cited in the essay are representative of the kinds of treatment the modes of organization are given in most technical and business writing textbooks. They help us to generalize about how the modes are reflected in and have influenced the teaching of technical and business writing.

In "Modes of Discourse" (1976), Frank J. D'Angelo describes the changing attitudes toward the traditional modes of discourse (description, narration, exposition, and argumentation) by rhetoricians and composition theorists. Most of the alternative modes of organizing information that D'Angelo mentions are not yet widely used in basic composition courses, and they are only beginning to be discussed by teachers of technical and business writing. These alternative methods of organizing discourse derive from a process approach to teaching writing and are drawn primarily from the work of Leo Rockas (*Modes of Rhetoric* [1964]), James Moffett (*Teaching the Universe of Discourse* [1968]), and James Kinneavy (*A Theory of Discourse* [1971]). The implications of their reclassifications of the modes of discourse will be discussed in the second section, on debunking the traditional modes of organization.

Historically, description, narration, exposition, and argumentation—the four traditional categories or "modes" of discourse—evolved from the period when rhetoric broadened its realm of inquiry from persuasive oratory to all forms of written discourse. We can trace them back to Campbell's *Philosophy of Rhetoric* (1776). Campbell identified four "ends of speaking": to enlighten the understanding, to please the imagination, to move the passions, and to influence the will. Campbell's categories are based on the aims or purposes of oratory, not on the orations (products) themselves. These categories are given a more familiar ring when Alexander Bain applies them to written discourse and identifies five "forms": description, narration, exposition, oratory, and poetry.

In *English Composition and Rhetoric* (1866), Bain states that all writing can be classified on the basis of form. Therefore, in discussing the modes of organization, we are exploring a universe of discourse which includes a particular *form*, that is, the contour of structure of discourse as distinguished from its substance; the *kind*, class or category it belongs to; and the *type*, genus or genre it derives from or represents. Classifying discourse according to form is part of a long tradition that began in the 1880s with Bain and William B. Cairns (*The Forms of Discourse* [1886]) and continues into the 1980s in most technical writing texts. Both Bain and Cairns relate the forms of discourse to the three faculties of the mind (understanding, volition, and perception) and to the aims of discourse (to inform, to persuade, and to please). D'Angelo does not dismiss Bain's and Cairns's attempts to relate the forms of discourse to the faculties of the mind as naive because Bain was using the most current associational psychology of his day in postulating these connections. Even today, Janet Emig (*The Composing Process of Twelfth Graders* [1971]), Janice Lauer ("Heuristics and Composition," [1970]), and Linda Flower and colleagues ("A Process Model of Composition" [1980]) are building cases for writing as a mode of knowing. These contemporary theorists also claim that the plans or strategies for organizing discourse may reveal not only "what" writers know but also "how" they know.

We need much more information before we can draw any final conclusions about the relationships between the processes of thought and the patterns of organization. What we should note, however, are the results for teaching writing that linking the modes of organization with the thought processes have had: the modes of discourse have dominated writing texts for the past 100 years; they have been accepted without question; they have been a hallmark of the product approach to teaching writing; and in many cases they have been taught prescriptively. Because of their *ex cathedra* status, D'Angelo ends his article on the modes of discourse with the following admonition:

Whether the modes of discourse are taken as genres, as aims, as attitudes, or as conventions, they must not be thought of as unchangeable and immutable archetypes. They are rather a cluster of changing conventions classified for specific purpose. At its best, the modes of discourse approach to writing forces us to attend more closely to differences in rhetorical purpose, attitudes, values, and audience. At its weakest, it may develop into a mere formalism, with undue emphasis on static conventions, rather than with a more proper emphasis on the processes of discourse. (p. 135)

Use of the Modes of Discourse in Technical Writing Texts

In the "Introduction" to his annotated bibliography, Gerald J. Alred states that increased demand for business instruction and the widespread adoption of the typewriter were the two most important factors contributing to the proliferation of business writing textbooks over the last 100 years. According to Alred, the increasing number of technical writing textbooks resulted from the professional education of engineers and scientists and the need after World War II for technical writers who could produce "a myriad of publications related to the maintenance, construction, and operation of highly technical equipment" (p. 4). But it was not until the 1950s that books exclusively devoted to pedagogy in business and technical writing appeared, and not until the 1970s that collections of articles about teaching business and technical writing appeared. Among the collections of articles are Donald H. Cunningham and Herman A. Estrin's *The Teaching of Technical Writing* (1975), Thomas M. Sawyer's *Technical and*

Professional Communication (1977), George H. Douglas's *The Teaching of Business Communication* (1978), and Paul V. Anderson, R. John Brockmann, and Carolyn R. Miller's *New Essays in Technical and Scientific Communication* (1983). Because the technical writing profession was established after World War II, most of the texts mentioned in this essay will have been written within the past 35 years. Most of these texts fall into three categories with respect to their use of the modes of discourse:

1. General principles texts. These texts either ignore the modes of organization or relegate them to secondary importance by concentrating on elements of style and diction.

2. Structural model texts. These texts, which make up the largest category, are organized around the modes of discourse. Many deal exclusively with exposition and the methods of exposition (definition, description, process, classification and partition, and so on). They also provide models of letter, memo, and report types.

3. Alternative texts. These texts use alternative organizational patterns based on inventional models and the process approach to teaching writing.

The remainder of this section will discuss each of these three categories of technical writing texts.

Most of the general principles texts provide prose descriptions about different forms of writing, but they do not provide many organizational outlines. They make use of specimen texts, but these specimens are often expected to speak for themselves. In most cases, bad examples are followed by good examples, and explanations of editing changes are found at the sentence or paragraph level. General principles texts concentrate on style and diction, and they are full of helpful hints, nifty ideas, and memorable phrases. They reflect the product approach to teaching technical and scientific writing and rely on the experience and advice of practitioners of the art. Their concern is with editing and revising rather than planning and writing. Clifford E. Baker's *A Guide to Technical Writing* (1961) and David W. Ewing's *Writing for Results in Business, Government, and the Professions* (1974) are examples of such texts. Reginald O. Kapp's *The Presentation of Technical Information* (1957), which has been considered a "classic," is composed of four lectures originally given at University College, London. Kapp describes what industry wants and discusses the need for "functional" English. He defines "functional" English as telling what the discourse is about (definition); making it easy to understand (using logic, connectives, and building word bridges); and making it easy to remember (relevance, timing, "beacon" words, repetitions, analogies, and so on).

Some authors distill a certain number of principles or use gimmicks to arouse their readers' interest and to differentiate their texts from other general principles texts. Robert Gunning's books, *New Guide to More Effective Writing in Business and Industry* (1963), *The Technique of Clear Writing* (1968), and *What an Executive Should Know About the Art of Clear Writing* (1968) are organized around ten principles for clear writing and what the author calls lowering the

"Fog Index." Most of these books focus on making writing more readable by concentrating on style, diction, and sentence length. Rudolf Flesch and A. H. Loss's *The Way to Write* (1955) provides students with standard principles, interesting prose descriptions, and numerous pictures and cartoons to maintain the reader's interest, but it includes no detailed organizational patterns. Flesch's later, better known books, *How to Write Plain English* (1979) and *Rudolf Flesch on Business Communication* (1974) teach writers how to apply his readability index to revise their work to meet Plain English standards.

Special texts that are designed for a student in a specific discipline or that specialize in a certain type of writing can fall either into the category of general principles texts or structural models texts. The following examples are organized according to general principles. Bruce Joplin and James W. Pattillo's *Effective Accounting Reports* (1969) concentrates on matters of style and general rhetorical principles. The authors do examine special types of accounting reports, such as financial statements, decision-making aids, sales and distribution reports, credit-collection reports, purchase department reports, personnel and payroll reports, status reports, and inventory reports. However, since most of these reports have prescribed forms, the authors provide examples and discuss filling out the forms properly rather than discuss the principles involved in designing reports. The same is true of Jennie M. Palen's *Report Writing for Accountants* (1965). The emphasis in this text is on style, tone, and format specifications (such as headings, captions, and sequencing). Palen adds audit reports and balance sheets to the report types covered. The kinds of arguments about "form" in these texts deal with form *literally* as the following example illustrates:

Accountants have always disagreed on the matter of form. It has been the English accountant's practice to place capital and liabilities on the left side of the sheet, assets on the right. . . . The American accountant lists assets on the left side, then shows, on the right, outstanding liabilities . . . and . . . contributed capital and retained earnings . . . (p. 47)

As the examples illustrate, the general principles texts either ignore the modes of discourse or subordinate them to matters of grammar and style. Most of these are product-oriented texts that do more talking about writing and revision than teaching students how to compose.

The structural model texts generally devote a major portion of the text either to discussing the four modes of discourse or concentrating on the expository mode. In texts that concentrate on exposition, a number of chapters are devoted to the "methods" of exposition, such as definition, description, narration, process, classification and partition, induction and deduction. The authors of these texts often subordinate narration and description to exposition, leading us to question the status of the four traditional modes. In these texts, the modes and mini-modes are often presented as general structural models to help students see the relationships between the parts of the discourse. In some cases, these structural models are almost "generic," consisting of Introduction, Body, Conclusions; in other texts, the models are presented in outline form and may detail up to five levels of specificity in structuring a discourse.

In examining the structural model texts used in teaching technical and scientific writing, we find more similarities than differences. The major differences concern the detail with which these texts present the structural models for arranging content into traditional patterns. Inevitably, these texts begin with an introductory chapter defining technical or scientific writings, specifying the audiences for whom the book was intended, and forecasting what will be covered in the text. Sometimes they even include information about the communication process. The next section either reviews the four discourse modes or concentrates on exposition and definition. This section often deals with mini-modes such as comparison, process segments, evaluation, classification and partition, definition, and the logic of organizing information in these mini-modes. The third section often reviews specific types of technical discourse including letters (inquiry, complaint, application, transmittal, and so forth), memos, informal reports, and formal reports (recommendation reports, status reports, feasibility reports, proposals, and so on). The fourth section deals with style and grammar. Some texts have a grammar and usage handbook at the end or a series of specimen reports to serve as good examples.

These texts make use of detailed patterns, usually in the form of topic outlines, for organizing information in scientific and technical discourse. The organizational patterns can provide outlines for the entire discourse or for specific sections of a long report. In "The Role of Models in Technical and Scientific Writing" (1983), Victoria M. Winkler calls these organizational patterns "structural models." The structural models help writers arrange information in conventional, acceptable formats for everything from technical articles to production or recommendation reports. The use of structural models, which is the dominant characteristic of the product approach to writing, leads to an emphasis on style and correctness of the finished product. Authors of scientific and technical writing textbooks recognize that reliance on structural models stems from their usefulness as pedagogical tools for identifying the parts of a discourse and indicating how to sequence information. These models help writers to control the subject matter by providing conceptual frameworks to suggest possible arrangement patterns and by serving as checklists for ensuring that the writer has not overlooked something.

The assumption governing the textbook authors' preoccupation with structural models, according to Dennis R. Hall, is that "the writer is teeming with information and that the writer's principal, if not exclusive, problems are matters of clear and concise statement and of ordering statements in one of several appropriate forms" ("The Role of Invention in Technical Writing" [1976], 19). These texts usually include a chapter on audience, but only in the latest texts do audience and purpose become dominant factors in shaping technical discourse.

In Herman M. Weisman's *Technical Report Writing* (1975), for example, the author is writing for technicians, engineers, and scientists who have to report on their work. He assumes that the content is given and that the writers have already defined their purposes. He includes no chapter dealing with audience. In his other book, *Basic Technical Writing* (1980), Weisman divides the text into five parts. Part I contains the introduction and chapters on the history and theory of technical writing, the communication process, and writing style. Part II deals with fundamentals, that is, basic expository techniques such as definition, description, explanation of process, and analysis. Part III examines technical report writing generally and explains the scientific method, investigative procedures, basic organization, format, writing, and illustrating. Part IV, on shorter technical forms, covers technical papers, articles, correspondence, proposals, and oral reports. Part V is a usage, punctuation, and grammar handbook. The appendices review requirements for progress and final reports and provide examples of the writing forms covered in the text.

Clarence A. Andrews's *Technical and Business Writing* (1975) begins by reviewing sentence patterns, paragraphs, letters/memos, and the retrieval of technical information. He then has chapters on standards, properties, specifications; definitions; technical descriptions; instructions; technical reports (general, informal, and formal); and magazine writing. The early chapters teach by example without much discussion or outlines of the arrangement patterns. In the later chapters, Andrews uses more structural models. The chapter on instructions, which the author calls "How-to-do-it Information," includes the following outline:

1. Before you write
      Know your subject
      Gather materials
      Analyze your subject

2. Writing and Illustrating Technical Instructions
      Labeling
      Table of Contents
      Introduction
      Parts list
      List of materials
      Aids for the reader (headings, forecasts, and so on)
      Operating details
      Possible difficulties
      Warranty notice
      Quality control

Andrews's early chapters, dealing with specific kinds of writing, as the previous example illustrates, read more like a laundry list than a structural model based on rhetorical principles. In later chapters, Andrews returns to more conventional arrangement patterns. For example, in discussing laboratory reports, he lists the following model:

Introduction:	Purpose
	Problem
	Scope
Apparatus	
Procedures	
Body:	Data
	Interpretation
Conclusion	
Recommendations	

In the informal report chapter, laboratory reports are covered again, but this time the narrative nature of the lab report is stressed.

In L. O. Guthrie's *Factual Communication* (1948), Chapter 4 emphasizes the need for outlining information to determine the relationship of the parts to the whole and to check for logical consistencies. Guthrie concentrates on exposition and provides structural models in the form of outlines for definitions, objective descriptions, explaining a process, explaining by classification, investigative reports, and business letters. Similarly, in *The American Technical Writer* (1960), C. V. Wicker and W. P. Albrecht state that they have tried "to write a book that emphasizes rhetorical principles and illustrates their application in various forms of professional writing" (p. v). They define "objective writing" as good expository writing with practical intent. In their treatment of the structural models, the authors discuss and provide examples of the four modes of discourse (narration, description, exposition, and argumentation), but they blur the distinction between these modes by stating that the modes may be blended in a piece of prose so that it is hard to separate them. This "blending" or conflation is not explained either in terms of the overall rhetorical purpose of the discourse or the secondary purposes of the individual sections. The fact that these modes rarely appear in pure form and that they are sometimes used for purposes contrary to or different from their obvious stated purposes points out another major difficulty in relying too heavily on the traditional modes. In Chapter 3, which deals with the organization of objective exposition, Wicker and Albrecht state that "through analysis of his subject, the writer should seek a principle of organization inherent in the material itself." They appear to be advocating subject matter structuring based on classification and partition, but they do not provide the writer with strategies to discover this "inherent" organizational principle. Later, they discuss subject matter structuring and logical patterns, providing their readers with examples of each, but they do not teach the readers how to decide whether subject matter structuring would be appropriate in specific cases (based on the audience's needs and the writer's rhetorical purpose). Nor do they discuss whether the most evident *logical* pattern is the best *psychological* pattern to use for structuring a specific discourse.

In addition to the four traditional modes of discourse, Wicker and Albrecht review and cite examples of pragmatic organizing principles such as chronological order, spatial relationships, causal methods, two types of comparison, and inductive and deductive methods, but they do not provide outlines of these arrangement patterns. The section titled "Principles of Technical Writing" contains chapters on definition, analysis, analysis of mechanisms and processes, evaluation, and standards and specifications. In the chapter on definition, the authors combine analysis and definition, telling the reader that both are thought processes: "Analysis and definition, therefore, are simultaneous and correlative: sound analysis rests upon sound definition; sound definition depends upon sound analysis (91)." Such statements reinforce Bain's and Cairns's connections between the forms of discourse and thought processes and provide examples of the typical tautological dicta that appear in many technical writing texts. The chapters on definition, analysis, analysis of mechanisms, and evaluation, standards, and specifications, however, do provide detailed arrangement patterns and sufficient examples for students to use as models for their own reports and memos.

The section on interpretation in Wicker and Albrecht's text deals with how the mind arrives at the most probable inferences from a set of data (p. 159). The authors state that interpretation is the application of logic to life, but that interpretation also requires experience, observation, analysis, expert training and knowledge, clear thinking (the principles of logic), and insight (common sense, intuition, and imagination). This leads them into a discussion of logical thinking and logical fallacies and a review of statistical and literary interpretation. A summary of the rules of interpretation reveals a list of "musts": the interpreter must reason logically; seek the highest degree of probability; use insight, common sense, objectively controlled imagination, and intuition; and *think of his reader's need for information and ability to understand* (my emphasis). As this example illustrates, the reader's needs are considered as an afterthought toward the end of the book rather than as a primary organizing and selecting principle, and the models are often taught prescriptively. The reason for devoting so much attention to Wicker and Albrecht's text here is that it is typical of the *better* technical writing texts using structural models. There are few differences between it and many texts produced in the 1970s and 1980s.

Other similar texts include Robert E. Tuttle and C. A. Brown's *Writing Useful Reports* (1965). Tuttle and Brown, however, provide a set of heuristic questions to help writers decide when to deviate from the standard structural models (pp. 13–14). They also present the idea of the "three-level report," which goes to supervisors, executives, and administrators. These authors advocate a two-component structure for reports composed of the executive summary and discussion components. Thomas P. Johnson's major premise in *Analytical Writing* (1966) is that writers must not merely "list," but also analyze and interpret. He advocates using the inverted pyramid, a deductive structure, for organizing reports, and he provides simple structural outlines. In *Effective Technical Writing and Speaking* (1974), Barry T. Turner also advises structuring reports using the inverted pyramid form for visit reports, progress reports, investigative reports, and procedures manuals. He graphically documents the difference between the investigation to generate the content of discourse and the finished report format. Turner states that the procedure for the investigation consists of

1. Defining the problem.
2. Gathering the facts.
3. Analyzing the facts.
4. Determining the results.

In structuring a report, the information gathered during the investigation is arranged differently. The report follows this arrangement pattern:

1. A statement of the objective.
2. A summary of the results.
3. An analysis of the results and their implications.
4. A detailed account of the investigation.

More recently (1982), Marilyn Schauer Samuels restated Turner's argument for deductively structuring reports in "Scientific Logic."

Gordon H. Mills and John A. Walter's *Technical Writing* (1978) is one of the most comprehensive of the texts using structural models and concentrating on exposition. The organization of the text follows the psychological order of the composing process more closely than do most of these texts, with the chapter including definition, description, classification, and interpretation before the chapter on introductions and conclusions. The section on the various types of reports provides structural outlines that often have five levels of specificity, considerably more detail than the other texts. The authors do make use of some heuristic questions to help writers gather the information necessary for process descriptions. In the section on evaluation, they provide writers with three variations of persuasive formats and an informative format for an entire discourse. However, these persuasive structural models are simply presented without much commentary, and it is assumed that the writers will know when to use each one. There is no comprehensive discussion of rhetorical purpose and of how determining and stating the purpose of a discourse can help the writer select an appropriate structure from the choices the authors present. Although Mills and Walter seem to advocate a *de facto* management summary for longer reports, they do not separate it from the discussion component.

Joseph N. Ulman, Jr., and Jay R. Gould's *Technical Reporting* (1972) combines many of the best features of the Mills and Walter text and introduces the idea of a Foreword and Summary after the Table of Contents in formal reports. The structural model for designing a Foreword includes (1) a general orientation to the report, expanding on the title, and a brief statement of purpose; (2) an optional statement telling who authorized the report; (3) an acknowledgment of help; (4) pertinent comments about the report; and (5) a reference to other related reports or future reports (pp. 72–73). Ulman and Gould also indicate that the Foreword may be replaced by a letter of transmittal. This marks one of the earliest structural models for the executive or management summary and results in a deductively structured two-component report. (Most two-component reports present preliminaries and a summary in the first component and a discussion of the particulars and appendix material in the second component.) Ulman and Gould even advocate the use of the two-component report for memorandum reports. They also seem to have created the category they call "service reports," which includes survey, progress, trip, conference, and trouble reports (p. 51). In *Technical Report Writing Today* (1973), Steven Pauley also includes an "introductory summary" and marks it as an advance in the structure of reports. Pauley includes a section on manuals, identifying four types of manuals: assembly, operation, service, and maintenance. However, the structural model for manuals that Pauley provides is merely a sketchy outline.

On the other hand, Thomas F. Walton's *Technical Manual Writing and Administration* (1968) includes a section on the procedural and special purpose manuals. Walton provides detailed structural outlines of what should be included and designates proper sequencing of information. Most of these manuals are arranged as process segments or classification/partition segments, although the author does not call this information to the reader's attention. Walton provides procedures for designing and writing the manuals, including information on outlining both tasks and steps in the process. He also offers a section discussing standard specifications, such as the MIL Standards, and provides examples of the standards. The outlines move deductively from the scope to the details and are designed for the entire manual. Segment outlines are not presented. Since the only organizational outlines presented are those for the entire manual, the tendency would be to use these outlines prescriptively. Had the author discussed the types of segments that usually appear in manuals and the functions of those segments, students would be able to generate their own outlines or modify the general outlines to meet specific product or audience needs.

Kenneth W. Houp and Thomas E. Pearsall's *Reporting Technical Information* (1980) provides more detailed structural models for organizing prose components and various report types. The introductory section includes a chapter on audience based on Thomas E. Pearsall's *Audience Analysis for Technical Writing* (1969). Another chapter deals with rhetorical modes. However, this text does not include the writer's purpose as an important structuring component.

John M. Lannon's *Technical Writing* (1979) is concerned with exposition and devotes one section to organizational strategies such as summarizing, defining, classification, and partition, and one section to the types of reports and letters. The arrangement patterns that Lannon presents are general, and he makes use of the "generic" Introduction-Body-Conclusion format, which he consistently uses for nearly all report types. Lannon also includes a chapter on audience, but he incorporates audience concerns throughout the text. He introduces the notion of the writer's intention or purpose as an important factor for the writer to consider in making decisions about form and the selection and arrangement of content.

Ann A. Laster and Nell Ann Pickett's *Occupational English* (1977) stresses exposition and provides detailed structural models for organizing information for writing instructions, process segments, descriptions of mechanisms, and extended definitions. In the analysis and classification, analysis through partition, and analysis through cause-and-effect sections, as in the other chapters of their text, the general principles for designing the analysis segment are given, followed by the extended procedural outline (structural model). The worksheets provided for the students serve as planning and organizing heuristics, and the exercises allow the students practice in thinking, planning, and assembling data. Since the text is designed for two-year college students, some exercises would be inappropriate for advanced technical writing classes, but the general principles and structural models offer excellent reference information for designing report segments. The chapter on long reports is weak because not enough information is presented on the design of the body of these reports. References to the earlier chapters dealing with segment outlines and discussions of how these segments could be arranged to form the body of longer reports would strengthen this section.

George C. Harwell's *Technical Communication* (1960) concentrates on exposition. Chapter 3 describes the methods of exposition: explication, description, definition, and narration. Harwell's structural models are very simple, and no detailed outlines are provided; however, Harwell stresses that the selection of information should be based on the reader's needs, and that the author's purpose should be stated. Many early texts which discuss purpose confuse the purpose of the investigation with the rhetorical purpose (or what response the writer wants from the reader), but this book marks a change in focus for early 1960 texts. Harwell also provides a chapter on ordering information pragmatically. In addition to the standard formats for the methods of exposition, Harwell suggests arranging the content according to the order of occurrence, order of descending importance, order of ascending importance, combination sequences, and departing from the Basic Method. In this chapter, the author simply cites the ordering principle and example; however, there is little explanation or rationale for selecting among these ordering principles. The rest of the text covers types of reports with simple structural models.

Walter E. Oliu, Charles T. Brusaw, and Gerald J. Alred's *Writing That Works* (1980) is a later text that includes a chapter on pragmatic arrangement patterns. In discussing these patterns, the authors present specific content outlines and the passages generated from the outlines. It is obvious, however, that the outlines were really constructed from the finished discourse. They do provide students with a skeletal view of the structure of the discourse specimen that they are examining, but we could question how transferable these specific outlines will be when the students compose their own memos, letters, and reports. No general structural patterns are presented here. The authors deal only with exposition and the methods of exposition. Chapter 5, entitled "Writing for Special Purposes," covers instructions, explaining a process, description, comparison, division and classification, definition, cause and effect, and persuasion. These are mostly segments rather than entire discourses, and again, no generic outlines are given to guide the students in preparing their reports. The only general outline the authors present is in the chapter on formal reports, but they overlook the Body, Conclusions and Recommendations sections. They divide the formal report into three sections:

Front Matter	*Body*	*Back Matter*
Title page	Introduction	Bibliography
Abstract	Footnotes	Appendices
Table of Contents	Heads	Glossary
List of Figures	References	
List of Tables		
Preface		
Abbreviations and		
Symbols (p. 274)		

Sidney W. Wilcox's *Technical Communication* (1962) differs from the standard structural model texts because Wilcox includes formulaic models, similar to algebraic formulas, as algorithms (not heuristics) for report writers. For example, the model for writing technical descriptions is:

$$T = N + (G + O) + (Snd) + F$$

where T = technical description

N = name of object

G = general impression

O = orientation of object to reader

S = subdivisions

n = number of subdivisions

d = necessary details to be included about each of the subdivisions

F = function or use

These algebraic models might serve as useful mnemonic devices for students whose interests and inclinations run toward the formulaic. The models convey the impression that technical writing is more objective, mechanical, and quantifiable than most of us would be willing to admit, but they also oversimplify the selection and arrangement process. The same criticism arises concerning Wilcox's text, as with so many others: there is more description of the finished product than explanation of how to compose.

In summary, the structural model texts from 1960 to 1980 rely heavily on exposition, often presenting description and narration as "methods" of exposition. These texts are more concerned with product than process. They assume that the content is given and that all the writer has to do is organize it in a conventional way. Therefore, they present the structural models prescriptively and provide information on editing and revising the early drafts. These texts largely ignore audience and the writer's purpose. They do not emphasize how audience and purpose can be used as pre-writing considerations to help the writer make informed choices about which structural models to apply or which models to combine or revise in arranging information in memos and reports. If they do mention audience, their comments consist of admonitions to avoid jargon, make the writing clear, use headings, and use "beacon" words to help readers remember the major points. Most of these texts advocate a one-component structure for reports and memos.

In reviewing these texts, we also witness an evolutionary change in the teaching of technical writing from a product to a process approach. In 1965, Tuttle and Brown generate some questions as heuristics for deciding when to deviate from the conventional structural models. They recommend a three-level report to meet the needs of specific audiences, and they propose a two-component report structure. Johnson (1966) and Turner (1974) recommend arranging reports deductively. Ulman and Gould (1972) reinforce the two-component structure by providing models for designing the Foreword and Summary segments. They also suggest using the letter of transmittal as a management summary and extending the two-component structure to memorandum reports. Houp and Pearsall add a chapter on audience in their second edition (1973), and Lannon (1979) incorporates both audience and purpose.

These changes, which emerged piecemeal over the past 20 years, are now beginning to crystallize. They parallel the resurgent interest in rhetorical invention and the movement from product to process by composition theorists. For more information about rhetorical invention and the process approach to teaching writing, refer to Richard Young's "Invention: A Topographical Survey" (1976) and "Paradigms and Problems: Needed Research in Rhetorical Invention" (1978).

The alternative texts provide alternative organizational patterns or a shift in focus from the product to a process approach to teaching writing. These texts use many of the same structural models we find in the product texts, but the authors of the alternative texts use these models as heuristics and subordinate the models to the demands of audience and purpose.

In 1976, J. C. Mathes and Dwight W. Stevenson published *Designing Technical Reports*. Mathes and Stevenson based their text on rhetorical principles and engineering design principles. The text is divided into three sections: designing, writing, and editing reports. The first section provides students with systematic procedures for analyzing their audiences and determining and stating their purposes. The authors state that the purpose of a report can be either informative or persuasive. After students have determined their purpose, they select a basic structure for the reports that will help them to accomplish that purpose with a certain audience. The authors present three structural models for discourse based on whether the writer's purpose is to persuade or to inform: the rhetorical purpose outline (persuasive), the intellectual problem-solving outline (informative), and the subject-matter outline (informative). Once writers have chosen an appropriate basic design for their reports, they can then begin writing report segments. The authors provide structural models for persuasive descriptive, comparative, cause and effect, and question and answer segments. The segment outlines they present are not as comprehensive as those we find in other texts, nor are they as detailed; however, they are presented as suggestions, not prescriptions. Mathes and Stevenson's focus is different from that of most of the other texts: they spend more time on pre-writing and writing, that is, teaching students the *process* of composing. To teach process, they rely on guides and checklists that suggest arrangement patterns, guide students through the pre-writing stage of composing, and identify the rhetorical choices writers must make at various stages in the composing process. Their approach to editing is also different. Rather than including a grammar and usage handbook, the authors provide chapters on contextual and single-sentence editing. Again, their advice to writers is to make informed choices throughout the revision process, and they provide students with the tools to make these choices.

Mathes and Stevenson advocate a two-component structure for reports: an opening component and a discussion component. The opening component consists of heading information, a Foreword, and a Summary. The discussion component consists of a self-sufficient detailed discussion section and appendices (if necessary).

Ingrid Brunner, J. C. Mathes, and Dwight W. Stevenson use the same focus and many of the same principles in *The Technician As Writer* (1980). This text is designed for students in two-year and community colleges and uses case studies and numerous annotated examples. Chapter 5, "Arranging the Discussion," includes sections on general-to-particular order, descending order of importance, and segment outlines for persuasive, problem/solution, cause/effect or effect/cause, comparison and contrast, analysis, description, process, and investigative segments. The segment outlines are more comprehensive than those in the original Mathes and Stevenson text.

Perhaps the most dramatic example of the transition from a product to a process approach to teaching technical writing can be made by comparing the first (1978) and second (1982) editions of Thomas E. Pearsall and Donald H. Cunningham's *How to Write for the World of Work*. The first edition teaches students about "occupational writing," whereas the second edition talks about "transactional writing." The term "transactional writing" is taken from James Britton's report on *The Development of Writing Abilities* (1979) among 11 to 18 year olds. Both editions concentrate on short report, letter, and memorandum formats, but the second edition stresses that the structural models used for these discourse types should be considered as suggestions and not as prescriptions. Although audience is mentioned in the first edition, it is more thoroughly integrated, chapter by chapter, in the second edition. Moreover, the audience's needs become more important as a structuring principle in the second edition. No real emphasis is placed on the writer's purpose in the first edition, while in the second edition, the writer's purpose or objective is discussed and integrated into the chapters, and becomes a second major structuring principle. This new emphasis on audience and purpose increases the amount of space devoted to pre-writing considerations in the second edition. The introductory chapter includes analyzing the audience, setting objectives (purpose), checking and gathering information, planning the organization, planning graphics, and offers tips on writing and revising. Another important change in the second edition is the inclusion of a section on persuasion in the section on causal analysis. Persuasion seems to carry the stigma of irrational emotional appeals and propaganda to Pearsall and Cunningham, and they appear uncomfortable talking about persuasion in the section on analytical reports. They do not seem to be ready to go as far as Mathes and Stevenson, who indicated that, although there may be a variety of purposes for writing, the primary purpose of a given piece of discourse is either informative or persuasive. Rather than presenting structural models in outline form, Pearsall and Cunningham discuss the elements of various models in prose paragraphs. They then annotate the examples, pointing out and commenting on the basic structural elements. Although the basic report structure advocated by Pearsall and Cunningham has the look of a one-component structure, the information they place in the letter of transmittal could serve as an executive summary. In the structural model for the letter of transmittal, the authors include: (1) explaining the authorization or occasion for the report, (2) restating the title, (3) explaining the features of the report that are of special interest, and (4) acknowledging special assistance (p. 120). The third element, features of interest, does not specify problem/purpose, summary of results, and conclusions/recommendations, but the specimen transmittal letter (p. 122) states the purpose and presents the findings. The Preface repeats these two items. Consequently, the authors have modified the one-component structure, but they have not fully made the transition to a two-component structure.

These alternative texts still make use of exposition, the "methods" of exposition, and structural models, but the emphasis has changed. These texts are moving closer to a process approach to writing by adding inventional concerns at the pre-writing stage and devoting more time to the pre-writing and writing stages of the composing process.

The changes that we see in these three texts mark the beginning of our own paradigm shift. We need research into alternative modes of organization that will explore our expanding fields of inquiry and help us to design new models to help writers plan and produce more effective discourse. The problems with the traditional modes become more apparent as we move from product to process approaches because we are now calling on the traditional static modes to describe and explain interactive dynamic processes.

The following section will explore some of the shortcomings of the traditional modes.

Debunking the Traditional Modes of Organization

In *The Development of Writing Abilities (11–18)* (1979), James Britton discusses the history of the four modes of discourse and reflects on how the modes have become so much a part of our thinking that we accept them without question. However, Britton identifies five shortcomings of the modes of discourse that are leading rhetoricians and composition theorists to question the modes' usefulness in teaching students how to write. The shortcomings that Britton cites include:

1. The four modes of discourse "are derived from an examination of the finished products of professional writers, from whose work come both the categories and the rules for producing instances of them. The tradition is profoundly prescriptive and shows little inclination to observe the writing process: its concern is with how people *should* write, rather than how they do" (p. 4).
2. The taxonomy of the modes is a weakness because the modes, "supposedly based on the purpose or intention of a given piece of writing, are seen only in terms of the intended effect upon an audience. Yet narrative can scarcely be seen as an intention in the same sense as persuasion or exposition might be" (pp. 4–5). A narrative might be used in fiction to describe, in a factual account to explain, or in an advertisement to persuade.
3. The four modes are not equal in status. "If it is the intention of a given discourse to persuade or to explain, then on this criterion the narrative and descriptive categories can be conflated with the other two. . . . Only by giving narrative and description sharply distinctive *functions* could the system be made consistent and workable" (p. 5).
4. "If we attempt to use the categories, not for prescriptive purposes (for example, narrative is a category and this is how to narrate well), but as a sorting system which throws light on development, then it rapidly becomes apparent that many pieces of writing employ one mode to fulfill the functions of another" (p. 5).
5. "The system obliges us to assume that we are dealing with four major writing activities which correspond to fundamental mental activities, and that though we may encounter them only in an impure state, the pure forms exist as ideals" (p. 5). Description is the most problematic of the forms because we almost never see it in its "pure form," but instead as subordinated to one of the other modes.

After discussing the five weaknesses of the traditional modes of discourse, Britton calls for the development of a new model that will demonstrate the relationship between the development of writing and the development of thinking.

Such a model will have to focus on the *processes* involved in writing, and might well emerge from psychological and linguistic studies in child development. This process model will have to include the strategies writers use to accomplish their purposes with a particular audience in a particular context. To determine which strategies would be most effective, writers must understand their audiences and what motivates them, and they must have a clear idea of their purpose in writing. Britton states that "the strategies a writer uses must be the outcome of a series of interlocking choices that arise from the context within which he writes and the resources of experience, linguistic and non-linguistic, that he brings to the occasion" (p. 9).

The categories or modes of discourse that Britton's model encompasses provide a process model that places individual pieces of writing along a continuum from transactional to expressive to poetic modes. Teachers of technical writing would probably be most interested in teaching students to move from the expressive to the transactional mode. The transactional mode involves participation in the world's affairs; it is writing to get something done. For example, informing is a way of participating; it is a type of transaction. Britton states that "as expressive writing changes to meet the demands of this task [informing], it will become more explicit: that is, it will supply more of the context, will reflect a concern for accurate and specific reference; it will seek the kind of organization that most effectively carries out such a task, and will exclude the personal, self-revealing features that might interfere with it" (p. 83). Transactional writing, therefore, is writing to get things done: to inform, to advise, to persuade, or to instruct.

Transactional writing can be broken down into two sub-categories: informative and conative. Britton sub-divides conative writing into regulative and persuasive, and he borrows from James Moffet's *Teaching the Universe of Discourse* some of the sub-divisions for informative writing: recording, reporting, generalized narrative or descriptive information, three levels of analogic information (or generalizations), and tautologic (or theoretical) information.

The implications of Britton's process model for teaching technical writing have not yet been thoroughly explored. Britton's model raises some interesting questions about how we should sequence learning tasks and assignments in the technical writing classroom if we want to match the assignments to the development of the student's thought processes. It certainly would place the focus on audience and the function of a piece of writing and employ more planning and goal setting than many of our current scientific and technical writing texts. The strategies the writer chooses for selecting and organizing the content would be governed by the situational context, the audience's needs, and the writer's purpose. To bring novice writers to the level of mature writers would require that we assess the writing plans and strategies that our students come with and devise lessons to help them develop and practice the more sophisticated plans used by mature writers.

But Britton's model is not the only alternative to the traditional modes of organization. Leo Rockas in *Modes of Rhetoric*, James Moffett in *Teaching the Universe of Discourse*, and James Kinneavy in *A Theory of Discourse* provide us with other categorizations.

Rockas reclassifies the modes into four categories with two sub-divisions under each category, a concrete and an abstract sub-division. He attempts to move away from the traditional static configuration of the modes to a hierarchical arrangement which he believes parallels the processes of the mind. An outline of his system appears below:

Modes of Rhetoric
    I.   The Static Modes
          A. Description
          B. Definition
    II.   The Temporal Modes
          A. Narration
          B. Process
    III. The Mimetic Modes
          A. Drama
          B. Dialogue
    IV.   The Mental Modes
          A. Reverie
          B. Persuasion

The static, temporal, and mental modes would be of most interest to teachers of technical writing. Rockas's alternative, however, does not seem as promising as the models of Moffett or Kinneavy.

Moffett proposes four categories in his scale of abstraction representing the relationship of a writer to his topic: *recording*, a running account of what is immediately present in the writer's environment (such as a spoken sports commentary or talk-aloud protocol); *reporting*, writing about the past as a reliable informant using observable events and scenes rather than generalizations; *generalizing*, drawing lower level generalizations; *theorizing*, developing propositions or discussing the relationships between propositions. Moffett's categories eliminate some of the difficulties with the traditional modes, and he posits his categories as a tool for distancing the writer from the material. Moffett's model may help the writer define his role and stance, but we must still relate Moffett's model to reader-based prose.

Kinneavy's entire reclassification model is well known, but the section that is of immediate interest to technical writing teachers is his variation of the expository mode. Since most technical writing texts focus on exposition and the "methods" of exposition, Kinneavy's observations are particularly apposite. Kinneavy notes that exposition is generally reserved for informative or scientific discourse. As such, it is generally juxtaposed with creative writing. This juxtaposition fosters the impression that only literary writing is creative. Moreover, it confuses a *mode* of discourse with an *aim* of discourse. Referential discourse is the category in Kinneavy's system that replaces the expository mode. In defining the organization of reference discourse, Kinneavy states that purpose or aim should be the dominant structuring principle. Reference discourse will also be influenced by the medium in which it occurs and the subject matter. In his reclassification of the modes of discourse, Kinneavy provides what appears to be a consistent and comprehensive system that describes, explains, and might even predict the strategies and plans a writer can employ in composing effective scientific or technical discourse.

Which of these reclassification systems or what permutations of these systems we find useful in teaching technical writing is still to be seen. The reclassification models of Britton, Moffett, and Kinneavy seem better suited to the process approach to writing than do the traditional modes. They provide the writer with an array of informed choices for designing discourse based on the audience's need and the writer's purpose. Moreover, these schemas serve as heuristics, which are applied at the planning, writing, and revision stages. As such, they are inherent in the *process* of writing rather than derived from the finished product and used almost exclusively in the revision stage.

Robert J. Connors provides a historical survey of the modes of discourse, citing the changes in texts that reflect the changes in theories of composing in "The Rise and Fall of the Modes of Discourse" (1981). Connors, like Britton, concludes that the weakness of the modes of discourse is that they do not really help students learn to write: "In our time, the modes are little more than an unofficial descriptive myth, replaced in theory by empirically derived classifications of discourse and in practice by the 'methods of exposition' and other non-modal classes" (p. 454). Connors states that Moffett and Britton are providing us with the important theoretical classification schemas for the future. And he singles out the advance these two schemas have over the modes: "They are based on the writer's purposes, the ends of his or her composing, rather than merely being classifications of written discourse" (p. 454).

The possible application of Britton's, Kinneavy's or Moffett's models to teaching technical writing provides a whole new area for inquiry. Elizabeth Harris applies Moffett's and Kinneavy's models to "how-to" discourse in "A Theoretical Perspective on 'How-to' Discourse" (1983). Elizabeth Tebeaux, in her research on the organizational communication process, has learned that the *medium* for producing reports has changed, requiring corresponding changes in how we view the audiences, the situational context, and the dissemination of reports. Her findings have direct bearings on what we incorporate in our process models in the writing classroom, and they are reported in "Keeping Technical Writing Relevant (Or, How to Become a Dictator)" (1983). Tebeaux states that we must teach students dictation, and to do so we must first teach them to compose sentence outlines. Second, we must teach them to structure their dictated memos and reports deductively. Her findings show that the dictated discourse should be short and divided into three parts: the main idea/problem, supporting material, and indications of what readers should do or what attitudes they should adopt. Since the distribution of these dictated memos and reports will be by electronic mail, they will replace traditional memos and letters. If this is so, we will have to re-think the validity of our current informal report and letter forms.

As these two essays suggest, the move from product to process approaches to teaching writing is affecting our inventional models, our structural models, and our teaching styles. It is forcing us to articulate and reexamine the assumptions underlying much of our composing theory and pedagogy. David N. Dobrin attempts such a redefinition of technical writing in "What's Technical about Technical Writing?" (1983). Dobrin redefines technical writing as "writing that accommodates technology to the user" (p. 242).

The alternative texts and articles by Harris, Tebeaux, and Dobrin indicate that we are finally heeding the advice of James W. Souther ("Design That Report!" [1951]):

It seems that we need to shift our emphasis from the exactness of the finished product to the activity of writing. We need to help students reach the finished product; moreover, we should criticize the work from the point of view of how well it achieves its purpose and fits the situation rather than merely correcting it in a grammatical vacuum (p. 228).

References

Alred, Gerald J., Diana C. Reep, and Mohan R. Limaye. *Business and Technical Writing: An Annotated Bibliography of Books, 1880–1980*. Metuchen, N.J.: Scarecrow, 1981.

Anderson, Paul V., R. John Brockmann, and Carolyn R. Miller, eds. *New Essays in Technical and Scientific Communication: Research, Theory, Practice*. 2d ser. Farmingdale, N.Y.: Baywood, 1983.

Andrews, Clarence A. *Technical and Business Writing*. Boston: Houghton Mifflin, 1975.

Bain, Alexander. *English Composition and Rhetoric. A Manual*. New York: Appleton, 1866.

Baker, Clifford E. *A Guide to Technical Writing*. New York: Pitman, 1961.

Britton, James, et al. *The Development of Writing Abilities (11-18)*. London: Macmillan Education, 1979.

Brunner, Ingrid, J. C. Mathes, and Dwight W. Stevenson. *The Technician As Writer: Preparing Technical Reports*. Indianapolis: Bobbs-Merrill, 1980.

Cairns, William B. *The Forms of Discourse*. Boston: Ginn, 1886.

Campbell, George. *Philosophy of Rhetoric*. 1776; rpt. New York: Harper, 1875.

Connors, Robert J. "The Rise and Fall of the Modes of Discourse." *CCC*, 32 (1981), 444–55.

Cunningham, Donald H., and Herman A. Estrin, eds. *The Teaching of Technical Writing*. Urbana: National Council of Teachers of English (NCTE), 1975.

D'Angelo, Frank J. "Modes of Discourse." In *Teaching Composition: 10 Bibliographical Essays*. Ed. Gary Tate. Fort Worth: Texas Christian University Press, 1976, pp. 111–35.

Dobrin, David N. "What's Technical About Technical Writing." *New Essays in Technical and Scientific Communication: Research, Theory, Practice*. Ed. Paul V. Anderson, et al. 2nd ser. Farmingdale, N.Y.: Baywood, 1983, pp. 227–50.

Douglas, George H. ed. *The Teaching of Business Communication*. Champaign, Ill.: American Business Communication Association, 1978.

Emig, Janet. *The Composing Process of Twelfth Graders*. No. 13. Urbana: NCTE, 1971.

Ewing, David W. *Writing for Results in Business, Government and the Professions*. New York: Wiley, 1974.

Flesch, Rudolf. *How to Write Plain English: A Book for Lawyers and Consumers*. New York: Harper, 1979.

————. *Rudolf Flesch on Business Communication: How to Say What You Mean in Plain English*. New York: Barnes, Noble, 1974.

————, and A. H. Loss. *The Way to Write*. 2nd ed. New York: McGraw-Hill, 1955.

Flower, Linda, et al. "A Process Model of Composition." In *Cognitive Processes in Writing*. Ed. L. W. Gregg and E. R. Steinberg. Hillsdale, N.J.: Erlbaum, 1980.

Gunning, Robert. *New Guide to More Effective Writing in Business and Industry*. Boston: Industrial Education Institute, 1963.

————. *The Technique of Clear Writing*. Rev. ed. New York: McGraw-Hill, 1968.

————. *What an Executive Should Know About the Art of Clear Writing*. Chicago: Dartnell, 1968.

Guthrie, L. O. *Factual Communication: A Handbook of American English*. New York: Macmillan, 1948.

Hall, Dennis R. "The Role of Invention in Technical Writing." *Tech Writ Teach*, 4 (1976), 19–23.

Harris, Elizabeth. "A Theoretical Perspective on 'How-to' Discourse." In *New Essays in Technical and Scientific Communication*. Ed. Paul V. Anderson et al. 2nd ser. Farmingdale, N.Y.: Baywood, 1983, pp. 139–55.

Harwell, George C. *Technical Communication*. New York: Macmillan, 1960.

Hayes, John R., and Linda Flower. "A Process Model of Composition." In *Cognitive Processes in Writing*. Ed. L. W. Gregg and E. R. Steinberg. Hillsdale, N.J.: Erlbaum, 1980.

Houp, Kenneth W., and Thomas E. Pearsall. *Reporting Technical Information*. 4th ed. Encino, Calif.: Glencoe, 1980.

Johnson, Thomas P. *Analytical Writing: Handbook for Business and Technical Writing*. New York: Harper, 1966.

Joplin, Bruce, and James W. Pattillo. *Effective Accounting Reports*. Englewood Cliffs, N.J.: Prentice-Hall, 1969.

Kapp, Reginald O. *The Presentation of Technical Information*. New York: Macmillan, 1957.

Kinneavy, James. *A Theory of Discourse: The Aims of Discourse*. Englewood Cliffs, N.J.: Prentice-Hall, 1971.

————, John Cope, and J. W. Campbell. *Writing—Basic Modes of Discourse*. Dubuque, Iowa: Kendall/Hunt, 1976.

Lannon, John M. *Technical Writing*. Boston: Little, Brown, 1979.

Laster, Ann A., and Nell Ann Pickett. *Occupational English*. 2nd ed. San Francisco: Canfield, 1977.

Lauer, Janice. "Heuristics and Composition." *CCC*, 21 (1970), 396–404.

Mathes, J. C., and Dwight W. Stevenson. *Designing Technical Reports: Writing for Audiences in Organizations*. Indianapolis: Bobbs-Merrill, 1976.

Mills, Gordon H., and John A. Walter. *Technical Writing*. 4th ed. New York: Holt, Rinehart, Winston, 1978.

Moffett, James. *Teaching the Universe of Discourse*. Boston: Houghton Mifflin, 1968.

Oliu, Walter E., Charles T. Brusaw, and Gerald J. Alred. *Writing That Works: How to Write Effectively on the Job*. New York: St. Martin's, 1980.

Palen, Jennie M. *Report Writing for Accountants*. Englewood Cliffs, N.J.: Prentice-Hall, 1965.

Pauley, Steven. *Technical Report Writing Today*. Boston: Houghton Mifflin, 1973.

Pearsall, Thomas E. *Audience Analysis for Technical Writing*. Beverly Hills, Calif.: Glencoe, 1969.

————, and Donald H. Cunningham. *How to Write for the World of Work*. Rev. ed. New York: Holt, Rinehart, Winston, 1982.

Rockas, Leo. *Modes of Rhetoric*. New York: St. Martin's, 1964.

Samuels, Marilyn Schauer. "Scientific Logic: A Reader-Oriented Approach to Technical Writing." *Tech Writ Comm*, 12 (1982), 307–28.

Sawyer, Thomas M., ed. *Technical and Professional Communication in the Two- and Four-Year School*. Ann Arbor, Mich.: Professional Communication Press, 1977.

Souther, James W. "Design That Report!" 1951; rpt. in *Technical and Professional Writing: A Practical Anthology*. Ed. Herman A. Estrin, New York: Harcourt, Brace, 1963, pp. 225–29.

Tebeaux, Elizabeth. "Keeping Technical Writing Relevant (Or, How to Become a Dictator)." *CE*, 45, (1983), 174–83.

Turner, Barry T. *Effective Technical Writing and Speaking*. London: Business Books, 1974.

Tuttle, Robert E., and C. A. Brown. *Writing Useful Reports: Principles and Applications*. New York: Appleton-Century-Crofts, 1965.

Ulman, Joseph N., Jr., and Jay R. Gould. *Technical Reporting*. 3rd ed. New York: Holt, Rinehart, Winston, 1972.

Walton, Thomas F. *Technical Manual Writing and Administration*. New York: McGraw-Hill, 1968.

Weisman, Herman M. *Basic Technical Report Writing*. 4th ed. Columbus, Ohio: Merrill, 1980.

————. *Technical Report Writing*. 2nd ed. Columbus, Ohio: Merrill, 1975.

Wicker, C. V., and W. P. Albrecht. *The American Technical Writer: A Handbook of Objective Writing*. New York: American Book, 1960.

Wilcox, Sidney W. *Technical Communication*. Scranton, Pa.: International Textbook, 1962.

Winkler, Victoria M. "The Role of Models in Technical and Scientific Writing." In *New Essays in Technical and Scientific Communication: Research, Theory, and Practice*. Ed. Paul V. Anderson, et al. 2nd ser. Farmingdale, N.Y.: Baywood, 1983, pp. 111–22.

Young, Richard. "Invention: A Topographical Survey." In *Teaching Composition: 10 Bibliographical Essays*. Ed. Gary Tate. Fort Worth: Texas Christian University Press, 1976, pp. 1–44.

————. "Paradigms and Problems: Needed Research in Rhetorical Invention." In *Research on Composing*. Ed. Charles R. Cooper and Lee Odell. Urbana: NCTE, 1978, pp. 29–47.

Style in Technical and Scientific Writing

GLENN J. BROADHEAD

Between 1945 and 1981, well over 1,500 articles and books appeared that presented theories of style or that analyzed the style of non-fiction discourse. To the extent that technical writing might share some features of all written composition and differ in other features, most of these 1,500 articles are relevant to the present survey, with a few hundred of them specifically devoted to stylistic elements in business, industrial, professional, and scientific writing. Until the last decade or so, however, little interaction occurred between the various approaches. Writing in 1977, Joseph Williams could still claim that, while most literature and composition teachers in English departments know much about stylistic and other elements in fiction and literature, they know little about the writing in industry or government ("Linguistic Responsibility"). And on the other side, commentaries on style in technical writing have only recently begun to draw significantly on theoretical and empirical studies in other fields—with the exception of too-often simplistic references to "readability" studies, and not always to the best of those.

Because of this general lack of interdisciplinary perspective, and also because there has been no comprehensive bibliography of style in technical writing, the following survey of scholarship will aim for comprehensiveness rather than detailed description of single works in order to facilitate the growing trend toward greater integration of technical writing studies with a greater range of related fields of learning. For this reason, the first main section—on the theoretical background—will constitute an extended rationale for the organization of the remaining five sections. The next four sections will deal with four of the variable features by which style is achieved: syntax, cohesion and punctuation, vocabulary, and editorial conventions and usage. The final section will discuss prescriptive approaches to technical style (readability, usability, and rhetoric.)

Theoretical Background

Dictionary definitions and the literature about technical writing suggest four main "meaning-groups" for the various senses in which "style" is used—"groups" not in the sense of logically discrete and consistent categories to describe a single body of facts but rather in the sense of overlapping phenomena to which people have applied the word.

The first of these groups might be called behavioral applications of the term—or, for the sake of convenience, "behavioral style," which may involve either substantive actions ("Notre Dame ran the clock out and settled for a tie; that's their style") or the manner of acting ("Evonne doesn't just play tennis; she plays with style") or both. This distinction between "doing something" and "the way in which something is done" appears to be less a distinction between two kinds of phenomena than one between two points of view. That is, "doing something" may be viewed as a discrete thing or act (for example, "playing tennis" as opposed to "reading a book") or as a thing or act consisting of discrete parts (for example, "holding a tennis racquet," "swinging a tennis racquet," "running," "calling shots," "smiling," "harassing the line judge," "not harassing the line judge"), each of which might be divided and again divided, until "manner" becomes not "a way of doing something" but rather "doing one batch of things instead of another batch." In any case, since writing may be conceived of as a process as well as a product, "style" has been applied to actions (behavior) such as thinking ("cognitive style") and production of discourse ("composing style"). A second meaning-group, applied mainly to printed or written matter, might be called "presentational style," involving matters of physical make-up or appearance (layout, typeface, graphics, paper quality). A closely related third group of meanings is applied to "editorial" aspects, comprised of an editor's decisions about conventions of format, arrangement, documentation, punctuation, spelling, usage, and the like. A fourth meaning-group may be called "discourse style," which involves sentence structure and length, paragraph structure and length, vocabulary, usage, punctuation, and so forth. While these four kinds of applications of "style" are not adequate as a theoretical breakdown of style itself (because of cross-categorizing of factors such as headings, punctuation, or paragraph length), all of them have been treated as relevant to "technical writing style."

Most frequently, however, "style" has referred to editorial conventions and to various linguistic features of discourse. Since editorial conventions are treated in this volume's appendix on style guides, this survey of scholarship will focus on elements of discourse style. Some attention will also be given to the ways these elements affect and are affected by behavioral, presentational, and editorial matters. But even given this restricted scope, to what aspects of language does the term "style" apply? What is style? This question is crucial, for with some definitions of the term, the notion of "technical writing style" is nonsensical, and with others, the idea of "style in technical writing," though not inconceivable, is roughly parallel to the idea of "snowballs in hell."

This need for an adequate theoretical definition is noted in Edward P.J. Corbett's bibliographic survey of style for composition teachers, "Approaches to the Study of Style" (1976), which recommends two "overview" articles. The first is Louis T. Milic's "Theories of Style and Their Implications for the Teaching of Composition" (1965), which makes a fundamental distinction between "monistic" and "dualistic" theories. Milic identifies with the "organic" approach of Benedetto Croce (in literary criticism) and the "general semantics" approach of S. I. Hayakawa (in linguistics). In his highly polemical article, Milic argues that, by rejecting any distinction between style and meaning, monistic theories are pedagogically useless—unless rhetorical instruction is to be "reduced" to exercises in sensitivity training, morality, and other aspects of personal development. Only a dualistic theory—that is, only the belief that "one thing can be said in different ways"—provides a tenable concept on which to build an art or science of rhetoric.

In the second overview article, Nils Erik Enkvist ("On Defining Style" [1964]), like Milic, rejects monistic theories because they are inconvenient for his purpose (teaching English to non-native speakers). He discriminates six dualistic approaches among literary critics and linguists, and each approach has been echoed or approximated in discussions of technical writing.

For example, discussions of style as (1) "a shell surrounding a pre-existing core of thought or expression" include W. K. Wimsatt, Jr.'s "Verbal Style" (1950), which defines style as "iconic" qualities, both "logical" and "counter-logical," that technical writing would appear to avoid; Michael Riffaterre's "Criteria for Style Analysis" (1959), which considers style as an "emphasis," either "expressive, affective or aesthetic"; and John E. Carroll's "Technical Writes and Wrongs" (1979), which views style as a creative, "free expression" that does not appear in "fact"-oriented technical writing.

Style conceived as (2) "the choice between alternative expressions" appears in Richard Ohmann's "Prolegomena to the Analysis of Prose Style" (1969), where style is treated as the result of perceptual and linguistic selection from "modes of experience and habits of feeling." Jane R. Walpole's "Style as Option" (1980) views style as "the sum of all the linguistic and rhetorical choices a writer makes." And Frank J. D'Angelo's "The Art of Paraphrase" (1979) is based on the premise that roughly "the same thing" may be expressed in different ways.

Style conceived as (3) "individual characteristics" of the writer appears to figure positively in Merrill D. Whitburn's "The Plain Style in Scientific and Technical Writing" (1978) and negatively in John H. Mitchell's "Basic Writing Concepts for Scientists and Engineers" (1980), though it is not clear whether "personality" or "self-expression" is actually synonymous with "style" in their remarks. Style as an interplay between the linguistic structure of the text and the perceptual or cognitive mental set of the reader is presented in Eugene R. Kintgen's "Reader Response and Stylistics" (1977).

Style as (4) "deviation from a norm" is set forth in Charles E. Osgood's

"Some Effects of Motivation on Style of Encoding" (1971), where style is conceived of as an individual's deviations from a situational norm (itself a deviation from the overall norm of frequencies of variable features in the whole language). This individualistic orientation has been often used in criticism of literary works but appears not to have been applied to technical writing—with the possible exception of articles that equate style with usage, and thus treat deviation from conventional patterns as stylistic errors.

Style as (5) "collective characteristics" (for example, "Romantic style," "seventeenth-century style") is assumed informally by class offerings in perhaps every college and university in the United States. However, its theoretical adequacy has been strongly questioned by Louis T. Milic's "Against the Typology of Styles" (1967) and by Robert Cluett's *Prose Style and Critical Reading* (1976). Still, some such idea seems implicit in three very diverse approaches: David Merrill's "Psychology of Communication" (1967), which treats style as the linguistic and behavioral habits of persons conforming to various social roles or cognitive sets; David Shapiro's "Speech Characteristics of Rigid Characters" (1977), which defines style as verbal cues of "psychological condition," such as "neurotic styles"; and Willard D. Reel's "Project Literacy" (1964), which distinguishes between pre-World War I and post-World War I styles of scientific writing.

Style as (6) "those relations among linguistic entities that are statable in terms of wider spans of text than the sentence" is most clearly evident in Archibald A. Hill's "Beyond the Sentence" (1958) and Frank J. D'Angelo's "Style as Structure" (1974), both of which relate linguistic features to larger units such as paragraphs, sections, and whole texts. A concern for style in this sense also appears to underlie Larry Selinker's "On the Use of Informants in Discourse Analysis" (1979), Carolyn R. Miller's "Rules, Context, and Technical Communication" (1980), Alan M. Perlman's "Some Linguistic Components of Tone" (1981), and Michael Millard's "On the Improvement of the Style of Technical Writing" (1972).

Having noted these six approaches, Enkvist adopts a working definition that, roughly paraphrased, treats style as the configuration of variable features (phonological, grammatical, lexical) found in a given context. For example, items such as the words "interface" or "breadboard" occur with determinable frequencies in various contexts, as, for example, computer sales literature, popular science journals, newspapers, nursery tales, or eighteenth-century mock epic poetry. Just as these two words might occur in each of these contexts from high to low frequency, so other features might also occur in varying proportions—features such as passive voice construction, Latinate vocabulary, rhyme, meter, usage errors, and the like. As configurations of such features become "appropriate" (likely) or "inappropriate" (unlikely) in particular contexts, group and individual styles emerge. Whether they emerge from necessity (that is, the nature of the subject or the context), from choice based on rhetorical principles or personal preference, or from idiosyncratic or transcendental impulse is irrelevant to the statistical probabilities of occurrence. Although the cause of variation might be important to the teaching of writing, it is not so to stylistic description.

But even given this working definition of style, the scope of this survey still depends upon an adequate definition of "technical writing." Perhaps because of historical and economic factors concerning the academic home for instruction about technical writing, many attempts to define this variety of discourse have ended up describing an academic discipline or department, as in James W. Souther's "Writing Is for Other People" (1979) or Charles R. Stratton's "Technical Writing" (1979). Noting this difficulty in defining technical writing, Elizabeth Harris ("Applications of Kinneavy's *Theory of Discourse* to Technical Writing" [1979]) describes four kinds of approach: definition by subject area, as in Gordon H. Mills and John A. Walter's *Technical Writing* (1978); definition by "linguistic" description, as in A. J. Kirkman's "The Communication of Technical Thought" (1963); definition "in terms of logic," as in Reginald O. Kapp's *The Presentation of Technical Information* (1957); and definition "in terms of purpose broadly conceived," as in W. Earl Britton's "What Is Technical Writing?" (1965). Borrowing from James L. Kinneavy's *A Theory of Discourse* (1971), Harris goes on to define technical writing by its "aim" as a form of "referential" writing distinguished by its "organization, logic, and style." As Ben F. Barton and Marthalee S. Barton point out in "What Is Technical Writing?" (1981), many of these definitions rely on errors of bias, outdated epistemology, false binary opposition, and unsystematic assignment of definitional properties. Yet another strategy for definition is provided by Richard B. Vowles's "Language, Logic, and Creative Engineering" (1954), which defines technical writing as the writing found within a particular communication net—that is, the "large industrial group," or "that hierarchy which ranges from the theoretical scientist through the director to the supervisor of the pilot plant and, in another direction, to the public relations department" (p. 455). This network presumably also extends into the university, the research center, and the government.

The consequence of Vowles's definition is that a great variety of audiences, discourse types, purposes, aims, and (consequently) styles are to be found within the network. Indeed, remarks on the variability of style in technical fields caused by these factors have echoed over the thirty years since Vowles's essay, as, for example, in M. L. Feistman's "Engineering Writing 'Up or Down' " (1959), which notes some dangers in overadapting material to various audiences; in Joseph Racker's "Selecting and Writing to the Proper Level" (1959), which describes five varieties of reader within the industrial system; in James M. Lufkin's "Generalization and the Interpretation of Science and Technology" (1972), which illustrates some dangers of assuming that all readers desire only details without generalizations; in Thomas L. Warren's "Style in Technical Writing" (1979), which outlines the influence of the writer's subject matter, the characteristics of the audience, and the purpose of the message; in J. C. Mathes and Dwight W. Stevenson's *Designing Technical Reports* (1976), which recommends an "egocentric" analysis of potential readership; and in William Diehl and Larry Mikulecky's convincing statement of the need to analyze an audience and adapt to it with visual cues and textual signals ("Making Written Information Fit Workers' Purposes" [1981]). Some differences between "technical" and "business" writing are outlined in Paul M. Zall's "The Three-Horned Dilemma" (1978) and in Donna Stine and Donald Skarzenski's "A Comparison of Technical Writing and Business Communication Courses" (1978).

In sum, then, an adequate theory of style in technical writing does not appear to be in general use at present, although the attention paid to technical writing by theorists such as Robert de Beaugrande, Michael P. Jordan, Patricia Wright, and Joseph Williams suggests that such a definition is not far off. The influence of these four writers may be seen in the subsequent sections of this survey, which, based upon Enkvist's working definition, will examine scholarship and lore dealing with some of the variable features of style in technical writing and with prescriptions for style based upon them.

Variable Features of Style: Syntax

Beginning in the late 1950s, Richard Ohmann re-focused literary criticism upon syntactic elements of fiction and poetry, drawing upon Noam Chomsky's early works (later presented in *Aspects of the Theory of Syntax* [1965]) to buttress his claims that sentence structure is one of the primary determinants of a writer's style, and that generative-transformational grammar is the best tool for stylistic analysis of sentences ("Literature as Sentences" [1969]; "Generative Grammars and the Concept of Literary Style" [1969]). Calls for a similar linguistic focus on technical writing began in the early 1960s, as with Harold Wooster's "A Web of Words" (1963), and have continued into recent years with Richard David Ramsey's "Technical Writing, Stylistics, and TG Grammar" (1977) and Dennis E. Minor's "A Concept of Language for Technical Writing Students" (1978). For a sense of trends in linguistics, composition, and related fields that are relevant to technical writing, however, nothing is more serviceable than Robert A. de Beaugrande's series of articles and books—in particular, "Information and Grammar in Technical Writing" (1977), "Linguistic Theory and Composition" (1978), *Text, Discourse, and Process* (1980), and *Text Production* (1982). Together, these incorporate and extend many of the concepts and methods used by the studies described in this section on syntax and in subsequent sections.

In a critique of articles dealing with syntax—"Scientific English" (1976)—Donald Porter reviews previous attempts at a "linguistic characterization" of the "language of science" and finds them "surprisingly careless." He criticizes Leonard Bloomfield's *Linguistic Aspects of Science* (1938) for vagueness and C. L. Barber's "Some Measurable Characteristics of Modern Scientific Prose" (1962) for being based on an analysis of too few features in a seriously inadequate sample. His criticism does not extend, however, to *Sentence and Clause in Scientific English* (1968), by R. D. Huddleston, R. A. Hudson, E. D. Winter, and A. Henrici—a study of 27 texts of 5,000 words each, distributed among three "strata": high (specialist journals), middle (undergraduate textbooks), and low ("popular works addressed to the intelligent and well-informed layman"). Because this work is linguistic rather than stylistic, it presents considerable difficulties for the non-linguist or for anyone unfamiliar with the work of M.A.K. Halliday, particularly his three-part series on "Transitivity and Theme" (1967–68). In that series of articles, Halliday sketches part of a complicated "systemic" approach to language, whereby sentences and larger elements are analyzed into various "networks"—a clause system network, a "nominal group (noun phrase) system network," and so on. These interlocking networks allow Halliday to achieve a variety of "degrees of delicacy" in the analysis of prose, partly because "meaning" takes on several meanings. From the point of view of transitivity, for example, a sentence consists of one or more clauses that create meaning in the usual sense of stating a proposition:

> John saw the play yesterday.

But from the point of view of theme, a sentence also has a text-oriented meaning or significance, in that the first part of the sentence repeats information that is "given" in a previous sentence or segment, while the second part of the sentence offers "new" information. For example, two sentences might have the same propositional or experiential meaning but have different significance in the transitive system:

> John saw the play yesterday.
> Yesterday, John saw the play.

Taken as isolated propositions, both sentences assert the same concept; they differ in their role within the elements of discourse larger than the clause or sentence. The first might be appropriate to a context related to the question, "When did John see the play?" The second might be appropriate to a context related to the question, "What did John do yesterday?" Such differences in textual (as opposed to propositional) meaning are well marked by intonation patterns in everyday speech, and are also signalled by subtle structural patterns within and between sentences in written discourse. Thus, style becomes another aspect of meaning—again, text meaning or significance or appropriateness, rather than experiential meaning. Syntactic variations such as transformations to passive voice are not mere conventions or decorations, but functional parts of the language system.

Halliday's approach thus seems to present a linguistic resolution to some of the difficulties raised by the style/meaning dichotomy. Moreover, it ties in nicely with Ohmann's influential "Prolegomena" essay (1969), which attempts to define style as the linguistic manifestation of a primary "perceptual" or "mental" style by which one creates "meaning" from the flux of life: one person might characteristically perceive causal relations, while another might perceive metaphoric ones, and as writers select from the available linguistic resources of a given language in order to express what they perceive or "mean," a "style" emerges that could be described linguistically and that could be unique to one writer or common to a group of writers with similar habits of perceiving and thinking. By offering a powerfully descriptive instrument that is conformable with Ohmann's comprehensive, unifying theory, Halliday has set a very high standard for the linguistic description that must underpin analyses of style.

Whatever the virtues of Halliday's approach, however, it remains the case that much of *Sentence and Clause in Scientific English* is incomprehensible to the uninitiated. The most easily recoverable (and stylistically useful) information includes a discussion of several varieties of passive voice construction (with tables of verbs showing their respective percentages of active and passive forms), an analysis of various techniques of cohesion, a layman's introduction to the use of statistics in grammatical description, and a contrastive study of linguistic structures in the three "strata" of scientific texts mentioned earlier.

Another book-length study is Myrna Gopnik's *Linguistic Structures in Scientific Texts* (1973), which examines short, self-contained articles from the proceedings of a biological research organization. Even in such a restricted sample, Gopnik finds three types of texts: the "controlled experiment," the "hypothesis verification," and the "technique-descriptive." Each type has characteristic linguistic features, such as parenthetical structures, "law-like sentences," adverbs of time, or comparative forms. Since Gopnik's goal is a "decomposition" of the texts into their primary clauses, her study, like that of Huddleston and colleagues, is not an easily accessible description of style in scientific writing, but it is useful as a source of data for such description.

Another limitation of the studies by Gopnik and by Huddleston is that they deal only with scientific writing, so that the assumption that "scientific writing" is actually different from (say) "humanities writing" goes untested. This problem is addressed to some extent by Glenn J. Broadhead, James A. Berlin, and Marlis Manley Broadhead's "Sentence Structure in Academic Prose and Its Implications for College Writing Teachers" (1982), which analyzes 26 aspects of syntax in 64 "high stratum" academic journals representing four areas: humanities, social sciences, natural sciences, and engineering. In "Toward Defining 'Good' Writing" (1981), Randall R. Freisinger and Bruce T. Petersen report preliminary results from a long-range project aimed at providing a comprehensive analysis of many kinds of writing in the communication network of American business. This pioneering project will greatly assist subsequent research into the neglected areas noted by Williams at the beginning of this survey.

Comparative studies involving fewer stylistic features (mainly sentence length) include Henry Kucera and W. Nelson Francis's *Computational Analysis of Present-Day American English* (1962), which provides information about sentence length and variability in a very wide range of fields, from scientific/scholarly books to fiction to "do-it-yourself" manuals. Differences in sentence length and complexity in informal memos by scientists as opposed to engineers are discussed in Winford E. Holland and Bette A. Stead's "Exploring the Scientist-Engineer Conflict" (1972), the results of which suggest the positive correlation that Dona M. Kagan describes in "Syntactic Complexity and Cognitive Style" (1980). Another sentence-length study with a fairly broad range is Henrietta J. Tichy's "Engineers Can Write Better" (1954), an early demonstration (based on articles in *Chemical Engineering Progress* and the *New York Times*) that many of the stylistic prescriptions based on "readability" (described in the final section of this article) are oversimple and misleading. Tichy claims that variability in sentence length is much more important than average length, since length must be influenced by the nature of the reader, the subject matter, and the type of writing (the context of the message), as well as by the demands of variety and emphasis.

The variety of types of structures used by scientific/technical writers is reviewed by Glenn J. Broadhead's "Sentence Skills for Technical Writers" (1981), which draws on the "generative rhetoric" approach of Francis Christensen (*Notes Toward a New Rhetoric* [1978]) and Lester L. Faigley ("Generative Rhetoric as a Way of Increasing Syntactic Fluency" [1979]) and on the sentence-combining approach of John C. Mellon ("Issues in the Theory and Practice of Sentence-Combining" [1979]) and Donald A. Daiker, Andrew Kerek, and Max Morenberg ("Sentence-Combining and Syntactic Maturity in Freshman English" [1978]). Such structures are, of course, susceptible to misuse. Both Muriel Harris ("Mending the Fragmented Free Modifier" [1981]) and Charles R. Kline, Jr., and W. Dean Memering ("Formal Fragments" [1977]) show that most sentence-fragment errors are conscious or unconscious attempts to use free modifiers (especially in final position, after the independent clause they modify). In all of these Christensen-oriented articles, the norm of "complexity" or "sophistication" is implied—a norm made explicit in Charles R. Stratton's "Analyzing Technical Style" (1979), which holds that "generally, and up to a point, the more structurally complex a sentence is, the more effective it is as a tool of communication." In direct response to Stratton, Don Bush's "Does Sophistication Equal Excellence?" (1980) notes the problems of overly complex sentences and paragraphs. Other Christensen-oriented approaches to adult writing include John Chard's "The Incidence of Sentence Openers in Selected Technical or Scientific Periodicals and Journals" (1975) and Anthony Wolk's "The Relative Importance of the Final Free Modifier" (1970).

Besides these "macro-syntactic" studies that deal with punctuated word-groups within a sentence, attention has also been directed to "micro-syntax"—the relations between elements within clauses and free modifiers. For example, the need to fill key grammatical points with semantically important words is described in Gordon Coggshall's "Using the Core Sentence to Edit Poorly Written Technical Manuscripts" (1980) and in Peter Burton Ross's "Slash for Quick Editing" (1977). The problem of nominalization—of saying, for instance, "the man effected a change in the room" instead of "the man changed the room"—is discussed in Donald C. Freeman's "Phenomenal Nominals" (1981) and in Herman R. Struck's "Recommended Diet for Padded Writing" (1954). Among articles treating various other micro-syntactic features are Della A. Whittaker's "Remember the Tradition?" (1977) which discusses pronominalization and tenses; Larry Selinker and Louis Trimble's "Formal Written Communication and ESL" (1974), tenses; Knud Sorensen's "Some Observations on Pronominalization" (1981), pronouns; Milla Bayuk's "Grammatical Calisthenics in Scientific Russian Translations" (1978), common word-forms and methods of phrasing; and Mohan R. Limaye's "Improving Technical and Bureaucratic Writing" (1981), absence of grammatical signal-words in "telegraphic" style.

One feature of syntax—the passive voice construction—has received extensive comment, much of which is briefly abstracted in Thomas L. Warren's two-part "The Passive Voice Verb" (1981). The use of passive voice in technical writing has long had its supporters and detractors. Among the latter, Elizabeth Tebeaux's "What Makes Technical Writing Bad?" (1980) treats passive voice as a stylistic fault leading to other forms of pomposity and wordiness. She traces this effect to the "elegant" use of the passive voice brought about by the dominance of the Normans during the middle English period, in which the decay of inflections was accompanied by a heavy borrowing of French nouns and their accompanying prepositions (for example, "his accumulation of riches" rather than "his riches"). In a similar vein, Julia P. Stanley ("Passive Motivation" [1975]) claims that, disregarding its forced uses, passive voice is generally used (consciously or unconsciously) to evade responsibility—a motive also ascribed to bureaucratic use of passive voice by Walker Gibson in *Tough, Sweet and Stuffy* (1966). But passive voice has found defenders as an aid to accuracy (when the agent is unknown), to cohesion or flow of ideas (when the "acted upon" has just been discussed, and thus makes the flow of ideas easier to perceive when it appears as the grammatical subject), to tact (when the reader was the agent responsible for an unwelcome result), and to various other legitimate rhetorical and stylistic decisions—most notably by John M. Coetzee's "The Rhetoric of the Passive in English" (1980), Jane R. Walpole's "Why Must the Passive Be Damned?" (1979), Emmon W. Bach's "In Defense of Passive" (1980), and Don Bush's summary and application of Walpole's article to technical writing, "The Passive Voice Should Be Avoided—Sometimes" (1981). Also of interest is Richard David Ramsey's "Grammatical Voice and Person in Technical Writing" (1980), which finds that, among English university students at least, the passive voice is less effective in communicating information but is received positively by some students and negatively by others.

Variable Features of Style: Cohesion and Punctuation

Systematic study of stylistic features concerned with relations between different segments of a text began with two articles by Zellig S. Harris on "Discourse Analysis" (1952), some features of which are applied to composition by

George Goodin and Kyle Perkins in "Discourse Analysis and the Art of Coherence" (1982). Other notable contributions to discourse analysis include Teun A. van Dijk's *Text and Context* (1977), Herbert H. Clark and Susan E. Haviland's "Comprehension and the Given-New Contract" (1977), John R. Searle's *Speech Acts* (1969), and Frantisek Danes's "Functional Sentence Perspective and the Organization of the Text" (1974). Applications of these and other works to composition and technical writing have been initiated by Robert de Beaugrande's "Information and Grammar in Technical Writing" (1977), Winifred B. Horner's "Speech-Act and Text-Act Theory" (1979), and William J. Vande Kopple's "Functional Sentence Perspective, Composition, and Reading" (1982).

The most complete treatment of cohesion from a linguistic point of view is M.A.K. Halliday and Ruqaiya Hasan's *Cohesion in English* (1976), which gives very full breakdowns of the kinds of logical relations between elements in a text and of the linguistic means of signalling such relationships. Other discussions of these relationships include the revision of Christensen by Willis L. Pitkin, Jr., in "Discourse Blocks" (1969), W. Ross Winterowd's "The Grammar of Coherence" (1970), and Ellen W. Nold and Brent E. Davis's "The Discourse Matrix" (1980). Theoretical and practical analyses of the techniques by which such relationships are signalled in texts include E. K. Lybbert and D. W. Cummings's "On Repetition and Coherence" (1969), Alan M. Lesgold's "Pronominalization" (1972), Richard Braddock's "The Frequency and Placement of Topic Sentences in Expository Prose" (1974), Kurt M. Marshek's "Transitional Devices for the Writer" (1975), Eugene O. Winter's "A Clause-Relational Approach to English Texts" (1977), Jan W. Broer's "Linking While Writing" (1978), Mohan R. Limaye's "Improving Technical and Bureaucratic Writing" (1981), W. Earl Britton's "AND—The Simplest Connective" (1981), and Michael P. Jordan's "Some Associated Nominals in Technical Writing" (1981). Some of the effects of such techniques have been traced by Stephen P. Witte and Lester Faigley in "Coherence, Cohesion, and Writing Quality" (1981).

For purposes of cohesion and emphasis, technical writing appears to use titles and headings to the fullest. These, of course, may be conceived of as free modifiers that have been fully detached from the sentence and that, like all free modifiers, provide information and signal relationships between segments of the text. Representative works on effective titles include Rhys Samuel's "Let's Use Our Heads" (1958), Robert A. Kennedy's "Writing Informative Titles for Technical Literature" (1964), Abdul Aziz's "Article Titles for Tools of Communication" (1974), F. L. Scheffler, H. H. Schumacher, and J. F. March's "The Significance of Titles, Abstracts, and Other Portions of Technical Documents for Information Retrieval" (1974), and Jan W. Broer's "On Two Active-Reader Stimulants" (1977). Helpful studies of the use of headings include Ely Kozminsky's "Altering Comprehension" (1977), Jeremy J. Foster's "The Use of Visual Cues in Text" (1979), and Richard Showstack's "Discourse Punctuation" (1980). Many aspects of layout and its cohesive interaction with discourse style are treated in the anthology *Processing of Visible Language 2*, edited by Paul

A. Kolers and colleagues, (1980)—particularly the essays by L. J. Chapman and Alan Stokes ("Developmental Trends in the Perception of Textual Cohesion"), Wayne L. Shebilske ("Structuring an Internal Representation of Text"), and Robert H. W. Waller ("Graphic Aspects of Complex Texts").

Showstack's and Waller's shared analogy between headings or graphic features and punctuation might seem odd since punctuation is very often presented as a list of "mechanical rules" to be observed for the sake of correctness. But as Christensen pointed out (*Notes*), punctuation is a means of dividing strings of syntactic structures into notional or rhetorical units, thereby making it easier to understand relationships between ideas expressed in different structures. Clarity-oriented guidelines for punctuation have appeared in Theodore M. Bernstein's "Punctuation" (1977), and an excellent treatment of cohesive aspects of syntax and its relevant punctuation appears in J. C. Mathes's "Contextual Editing" (1976), a version of material also included in Mathes and Dwight W. Stevenson's *Designing Technical Reports* (1976). Book-length studies include Eric Partridge's *You Have a Point There* (1955) and H. Shaw's *Punctuate It Right* (1963). Further stylistic implications of punctuation—mainly in literary works—are covered in James R. Bennett's "Punctuation and Style" (1977).

Variable Features of Style: Vocabulary

Studies of the vocabulary—or, more broadly, the diction—of technical writing involve seven main areas: overviews of diction, word structure (etymology, coining, definitions), word hordes (lists of acceptable or characteristic words), jargon, sexism, figurative language (tropes, figures of speech, humor), and miscellaneous aspects.

A technically oriented overview of conventional aspects of diction is presented in Mary C. Bromage's "A Matter of Wording" (1963). Bromage deals with standard distinctions between concrete and abstract, short and long, correct and incorrect, few and many, apt and trite, direct and mechanical, objective and subjective, and general and special. In addition, Gibson A. Cederborg's "Engineering Writing to Eliminate Gobbledygook" (1957) covers redundancy, superfluity, vitiated verbs, slipshod synonyms, indecisiveness, verbosity, and showiness. Longer studies include W. E. Flood's *Scientific Words* (1960), T. H. Savory's *The Language of Science* (1967), Lancelot Hogben's *The Vocabulary of Science* (1970), A. Mandell's *The Language of Science* (1974), and Stig Johansson's *Some Aspects of the Vocabulary of Learned and Scientific English* (1978).

Brief reviews of the issues related to the coining of scientific terms are presented in Charles E. Whitmore's "The Language of Science" (1955), which holds that the adoption of new terms is more a matter of chance than of conformity with the dictates of logic, attractiveness, or even, upon occasion, clarity. Arthur Lewis Caso's "The Production of New Scientific Terms" (1980) describes six categories of processes by which new terms are created: semantic change, morphophonemic change, functional change, composition, neologizing or borrowing, and such miscellaneous processes as folk etymologizing, loan translation, anagramming, back-formation, and concatenation. One of three problems related to coinings is illustrated in J. J. Brown's "Stop Coining Words" (1955), which argues against the coining of new words when old ones are available. As Whitmore notes, however, such attempts to prescribe usage rather than accept what is used are rarely successful; writing in 1955, for example, Brown urges writers to use "automatism" rather than "automation." Another problem—use of technical definitions where common lexical definitions would be appropriate—is treated in Sidney I. Landau's "Of Matters Lexicographical" (1974). Finally, Landau's "Popular Meanings of Scientific and Technical Terms" (1980) examines the kinds of problems that occur when technical terms are introduced into common use.

Unnecessary or otherwise inappropriate use of technical terms has provoked two approaches to establishing scientific and technical "word hordes." One is to list terms and phrases (whether technical or common) that should not be used, as in Daniel A. McDonald's "Be a Better Writer (Don't Use Dirty Words)" (1977), which exemplifies the hit-list approach of many usage prescriptivists. The other is to list terms and phrases that may be used while unlisted words are excluded. A prime example of this "controlled English" approach is Bernt W. von Glasenapp's description of "Caterpillar Fundamental English" (1972)—that is, the limited vocabulary established by the Caterpillar Tractor Company for use in its manuals. The controlled approach has been defended more recently in John Kirkman's "Heroism or Hocus-Pocus?" (1981) and in Joseph M. Kleinman's "A Limited-Word Technical Dictionary for Technical Manuals" (1982). Both approaches, along with the stylistic prescriptions of some "readability" proponents (to be discussed in the final section of this article), appear to have influenced the Carter Administration's "Plain English" program to make government documents more accessible to a wider range of readers. A number of aspects of the Plain English movement in government, law, and business are presented in *Drafting Documents in Plain Language* (1979), edited by Duncan A. MacDonald. A two-part historical review of this movement is presented in H. Lee Shimberg's "Clarifying Federal Regulations by Using Plain English" (1980, 1981).

To speak of prescription and proscription regarding the vocabulary of science and technology is inevitably to speak of jargon, one of the favorite targets of style critics, though it also has its defenders. Good jargon—jargon used to edify or save time—is allowed in technical writing by Joseph D. Elder's "Jargon—Good and Bad" (1954), D. T. McAllister's "Is There Accepted Scientific Jargon?" (1955), and the many special-field dictionaries that, like Kate C. Ornsen's "The Petroleum Chemist's Vernacular" (1954), introduce the uninitiated to technical terms of an area. Techniques of defining necessary technical terms for non-specialist readers are presented in W. Earl Britton's "What to Do About Hard Words" (1964). Bad jargon—jargon used to astonish or exclude, whether intentionally or not—is, of course, nearly universally decried, as in Stuart Chase's excoriation of "Gobbledygook" (1978), Max S. Marshall's "Jogging the Jargon" (1964), Ernest L. Boyer's "Jargon in Government" (1980), and Charles T. Brusaw's "Dismantling the Tower of Babel in Computer Documentation" (1980). In "Training Tomorrow's Writers" (1975), John Paul Kowal continues the amusing "buzzword generator" tradition, in which terms from three or more lists are randomly combined to produce a phrase that sounds "technical," such as "synchronized third-generation trade-offs."

Another set of proscribed language forms has arisen through the movement to eliminate sexist expressions. Some of the most convincing scholarship in this movement focuses on the personal pronouns—the dilemma of filling in the blank in, say, "Everyone should bring——own book." For example, Ann Bodine's extensively researched, historically oriented study of "Androcentrism in Prescriptive Grammar" (1975) traces the social and cultural causes of the nineteenth-century castigation of the long-used singular "they," and also discusses problems with the "sex-indefinite" or generic "he" and the allegedly ameliorative "he or she." The generic "he" is also analyzed by Wendy Martyna's "What Does 'He' Mean?" (1978). Martyna concludes that "We ought to eliminate a term which is routinely replaced by 'she,' 'they,' and 'he and she,' depending on what it is we're talking about, how we are saying it, and whether we are male or female" (p. 322). Specific stylistic and substantive guidelines for pronouns and other troublesome matters are presented in Patricia A. Billingsley and Neil A. Johnson's "Nonsexist Use of Language in Scientific and Technical Writing" (1979).

Ever since Thomas Sprat opposed the ornamental rhetoric of exornation to the "scientific" plain style—that is, ever since perspicuity replaced amplitude as the governing norm for the transmission of ideas—few scholars have dared to challenge the belief that technical writing avoids what W. Earl Britton has called the "charms of style": allusion, assonance, alliteration rhythm, cadence, harmony, humor, and, in general, all of the stylistic expressions of a pleasant and attractive manner of personality ("Personality in Scientific Writing" [1972]). Brief studies of specific functions of tropes and figures of speech include John B. Colby's "Models for Technical Communicators" (1981), illustrating uses of metaphor, simile, and analogy; and Robert Schoenfeld's "Human Dimensions for Inanimate Objects?" (1981), arguing that "Table 1 shows" is permissible while "Table 1 argues" is not. The role of metaphor in conceiving and expressing scientific theories has been extensively examined, as is evident in Robert R. Hoffman's wide-ranging survey, "Metaphor in Science" (1980). But the use of tropes and figures of speech as a rhetorical tool—and hence as an element of style—has pretty much been neglected, though this may begin to be rectified as reports from recent professional conferences make their way into print.

A number of miscellaneous aspects of vocabulary relevant to technical writing style have also been treated: acronyms, in Roy V. Hughson's "Initials, Acronyms, and Chaos" (1969) and Gerald F. Williamson's "Avoid Dirty Acronym

Pollution Today'' (1973); confusing homonyms, in Sarah Montoya's "Word Watching" (1980); malaprops, in Louis Foley's "Malapropism Becomes Commonplace" (1976); cliches, in Robert L. Dean's "Cliches in Full-Scale Production" (1951); and loaded terms, in Barbara G. Cox and Charles G. Roland's "How Rhetoric Confuses Scientific Issues" (1973).

Variable Features of Style: Editorial Conventions and Usage

Those aspects of writing that are the concern of the editor as well as the writer range from arrangement (as when journal editors require segmentation of the text into sections on introductory material, purpose, methods, results, and discussion), to cohesion (as when editors specify rules about the use of headings, typeface, and graphics), to linguistic style (as when copy editors revise a writer's text for conciseness or clarity), and to presentational conventions (as when editors require footnotes rather than endnotes, APA rather than MLA reference formats, or words rather than numerals to denote numbers). Overviews of editing and editorial style include H. Lee Shimberg's general introduction to *Technical Communication*'s special issue on technical editing (volume 28, number 4, Fourth Quarter 1981), Ruth M. Power's "Who Needs a Technical Editor?" (1981), and Robert Scott Kellner's "A Necessary and Natural Sequel" (1982). Since current style guides are listed in an appendix to this volume, the present survey will be limited to the editing process, editorial norms and problem areas, development of company style guides, and the effects of editorial style.

The editing process begins, of course, not with a separate reviewer but with writers themselves—and not always after a "rough draft" has been readied for "polishing." Rather, the thinking-writing-revising sequence appears to be more of a looping or spiralling motion than a mere linear sequence of steps from A to C: A1 leads to B1 leads to A2 leads to C1 leads to A3, and so on. In this respect, the "protocol analysis" technique described by John R. Hayes and Linda S. Flower ("Identifying the Organization of Writing Processes" [1980]) has encouraged empirical studies of revision such as Nancy Sommers's "Revision Strategies of Student Writers and Experienced Adult Writers" (1980) and Lester L. Faigley and Stephen Witte's "Analyzing Revision" (1981). The Faigley article is particularly valuable for its breakdown of revision into "surface" changes (both "formal" and "meaning-preserving") and "text-base" changes (involving both "microstructure" and "macrostructure").

Just as revision is conceptually but rarely practically distinct from other "steps" in the writing process, and is therefore implemented through a variety of "styles" of revision, the editing process varies according to the type of publication, the complexity of the generation/composing process, and, in some cases, the cognitive style of the writer. Among studies analyzing the editing process, Pauline Snure's "Editing and Production of Scientific and Technical Journals" (1961) focuses mainly on academic or research publications, while James W. McCafferty's "Constructive Editing" (1971) emphasizes company-generated material, as does Ronald S. Blicq's " 'Editing' Guidelines for Supervisory Engineers" (1976). A step-by-step "levels-of-edit" approach used at Cal Tech's Jet Propulsion Laboratory is described by Mary Fran Beuhler's "Creative Revision" (1976), which documents both the kinds of personnel involved in editing and the consequent types of editing (for example, substantive, policy, language, mechanical style, format, integrity, copy clarification). Nuts-and-bolts rules for low-level editing are provided by Ruth H. Turner's "Thirty-six Aids to Successful Proofreading" (1979).

Norms for these editing processes are presented in Mary Fran Beuhler's "Situational Editing" (1980), which recommends a relativistic "rhetorical" approach rather than "programmatic" or "rule-following" goals indiscriminately applied to all writing contexts. Don Bush's "Content Editing, an Opportunity for Growth" (1981) similarly recommends attention to meaning as well as to "correct" copy. Other normative concerns are voiced in Lola Zook's "Editing and the Editor" (1981), H. Lee Shimberg's "Editing Authors' Style" (1981), and Harold F. Osborne's "Intuition, Integrity, and the Decline of Editing" (1981).

Ideally, writers as well as editors should have internalized such norms in order to apply them to the production of specific texts. A useful tool for this purpose is the company style guide—a reasoned list of choices related to editorial style for a particular organization or operational unit. A number of articles are available to assist in the development of these specialized manuals, including R. M. Reid's "A Writer's Cookbook" (1960), Ethaline Cortelyou's "Building an Organization Style Manual for Technical Reports" (1961), Barbara Holaday's "Go Write a Style Guide" (1967), and Della A. Whittaker's "Teaching Students to Prepare Their Own Style Guides" (1979).

A major benefit of such guides is described by Luther C. Sparks, Jr., in "The Style Guide as a Cost Reduction Tool" (1974). Empirical studies of the effect of editorial style upon readers have been conducted by Richard M. Davis ("Sloppy Typing and Reproduction in a Written Technical Message" [1972]) and Robert D. Dycus ("The Relative Effectiveness of Proposal Approaches" [1975]; "The Effect of Proposal Appearance on the Technical Evaluation Scoring of Government Proposals" [1977]). Earlier research in this area is reviewed by Paul Gardner Ronco's *Characteristics of Technical Reports That Affect Reader Behavior* (1964).

Editors and style guides traditionally emphasize usage, and articles and letters on this subject have appeared frequently in journals dealing with business and technical writing and in many professional and trade journals as well. In the 1950s and 1960s, these tended to express concern about the overall quality of writing (engineering writing in particular) because of supposed violations of "correct grammar." This earlier attitude, typified by A. J. Kirkman's "Standards of English in Science and Technology" (1962), is voiced now mainly by ESL-oriented writers, as in Hiroshi Ohta's "Language Barriers in Japan" (1979), Yoshihaki Shinoda's "Pitfalls for Japanese Specialists in English Technical Writing" (1980), or Arthur Hughes and Chyrssoula Lascaratou's "Competing Criteria for Error Gravity" (1982). The Hughes article reports varying attitudes toward errors in English by three sets of evaluators: non-native (Greek) speakers of English, who emphasize violations of usage rules; native-speaking lay persons, who emphasize intelligibility; and native-speaking teachers, whose evaluations generally reflect a balance between correctness and intelligibility.

This balanced or relativistic point of view occurs frequently in criticism of technical writing, as in Richard C. Gerfen's "Fallacies in Rhetoric" (1964), Bergen Evans's "The Changing English Language" (1967), James M. Luflin's "The Gulf Between Correctness and Understanding" (1976), or Don Bush's "How to Handle Grammatical Dogma" (1980). A recent influence on the trend toward relativism is the ESL-generated approach of "error analysis," particularly as presented by Mina Shaughnessy's *Errors and Expectations* (1977), Barry M. Kroll and John C. Schafer's "Error Analysis and the Teaching of Composition" (1978), and David Bartholomae's "The Study of Error" (1980), all of which attribute error in part to conflicting language systems or mental processes (rather than to laziness or stupidity), so that usage and other errors can be dealt with systematically and effectively.

This trend toward relativism, however, has been accompanied by a recognition that usage is an important stylistic variable, as Robert M. Gorrell notes in "Usage as Rhetoric" (1977). Empirical studies of error recognition and attitudes toward error suggest that teachers are more sensitive to usage errors than students or non-teachers (Jack R. Cameron, "The Sensitivity of Speakers of Standard English to Usage" [1968]; Lewis J. Poteet, "Minnesota Freshmen and Ten Controversial Linguistic Forms" [1969]; Henry B. Slotnick and W. Todd Rogers's "Writing Errors" [1973]; and Sidney Greenbaum and John Taylor's "The Recognition of Usage Errors by Instructors of Freshman Composition" [1981]). At the same time, some studies have shown considerable importance assigned to correctness by persons in business and the professions (Edward Anderson, "Language and Success" [1981]; Maxine Hairston, "Not All Errors Are Created Equal" [1981]; Donald Ross, Jr., "A Brief Note on How Writing Errors Are Judged" [1981]). The most comprehensive survey of current values is *Attitudes to English Usage* (1970), by W. H. Mittins and colleagues.

Some notion of the relative importance of various errors can be gained by observing various compendia of deviations, such as Thomas E. Connolly's "Some Major Pitfalls in Technical Writing" (1958), Jay R. Gould's "Ten Common Weaknesses in Engineering Reports" (1963), John H. McKeehan's "The Inarticulate Engineer" (1966), Glenn W. Kerfoot's "Tips on Technical Writing" (1977), Melvin F. Orth's "Striking Out" (1978), Hilary Jones's "I Believe in Basic English" (1980), and Fern Rook's ongoing series, "Slaying the English Jargon," which appears in *Technical Communication* from 1980 on.

Full-length, comprehensive treatments include Bergan Evans and Cornelia Evans's *A Dictionary of Contemporary American Usage* (1957), Roy H. Copperud's *American Usage* (1970), and Theodore M. Bernstein's *Miss Thistlebottom's Hobgoblins* (1971).

Prescriptive Approaches to Style: Readability, Usability, Rhetoric

The "readability" approach began as a means of ranking school textbooks according to levels of reading difficulty, as in Edgar Dale and Jeanne S. Chall's "The Concept of Readability" (1949). Such ranking is achieved by quantitative analysis of a sample of the text, measuring such factors as sentence length, word length, word familiarity, and "human interest" (as measured by, say, proper nouns or personal pronouns). Common measurement formulas include those reported in Rudolf Flesch's *How to Test Readability* (1951), Robert Gunning's *How to Take the Fog Out of Writing* (1964), Edward B. Fry's "A Readability Formula That Saves Time" (1968), G. Harry McLaughlin's "SMOG Grading" (1969), Wilson L. Taylor's "Cloze Procedure" (1953), and John R. Bormuth's "The Cloze Readability Procedure" (1968). Six of these formulas may now be calculated by computer in FORTRAN, as reported by Jeanne G. Barry, "Computerized Readability Levels" (1980); and a "Computer Readability Editing System" (1981) has been reported by J. Peter Kincaid and colleagues. The most comprehensive survey of the varieties and applications of readability formulas is George R. Klare's *The Measurement of Readability* (1963), which may be supplemented by John Gilliland's *Readability* (1972) and by Klare's own updates, "Assessing Readability" (1974–1975) and "A Second Look at the Validity of Readability Formulas" (1976). General introductions directed toward technical writing include Stewart Docter's "Testing the Readability of Engineering Writing" (1961), Andrew K. Clark's "Readability in Technical Writing" (1975), Eleanor M. Schenck's "Technical Writer-Readability Formulas and the Nontechnical Reader" (1977), and, preeminently, George R. Klare's "Readable Technical Writing" (1977).

At its best, the "readability" approach is a helpful tool for adapting specific information to a specific audience for a specific purpose, as illustrated in George R. Klare and Byron Buck's *Know Your Reader* (1954), which may be the most useful application of readability formulas to the writing process. But the relativistic precepts of readability can easily be perverted to stylistic absolutes. Undoubtedly the greatest influence on the development in technical writing of an absolute norm of style called "readability" is Rudolf Flesch, who marketed his early research—"A New Readability Yardstick" (1948)—in a number of popular how-to-do-it books. For each relative factor of readability, Flesch assigned an absolute norm in his books and in such trade journal articles as "How to Write for Today's Busy Readers" (1951) and "Shirt-Sleeve English in One Easy Lesson" (1958): if different texts are read at different speeds, the text that is read most quickly is always the best; if some words are more familiar than others, familiar words are best; if some words promote reader identification while others do not, familiar words are best; if speech registers range from formal to colloquial, colloquial is best. Flesch's method of determining readability and his main stylistic applications may be found in *How to Test Readability* (1951), *A New Way to Better English* (1958), and *How to Be Brief* (1962). A Fleschly school soon arose in technical writing circles, starting with John A. Miller's "Technical Writing" (1948) and Robert L. Shurter's "Let's Take the Strait Jacket Off Technical Style" (1952) and continuing to the present, with several current textbooks appealing to Flesch's authority.

In the 1960s, however, Flesch's dominance in readability began to be challenged by Gunning, whose Fog Index may now be more frequently invoked than the Flesch "reading ease" or "human interest" indices. Recent endorsements of the Fog Index appear in Charles H. Vervalin's "Checked Your Fog Index Lately?" (1980) and Douglas Mueller's "Put Clarity in Your Writing" (1980). Mueller's work is especially interesting because of his claim that the Gunning-Mueller Clear Writing Institute "owns" ten cliches about simple style. While the Gunning-Mueller rules would undoubtedly improve much technical writing, they, too, are often oversimplified when applied indiscriminately to all writing situations. For example, John J. Heldt's graphic aid for figuring the Fog Index claims to measure "Quality in Writing" (1976), not just simplicity or brevity.

Evaluations of the readability approach to writing and editing are numerous. Antagonistic responses began almost as soon as Flesch's works began to become popular, as in J. Harold Janis's "Business Writing Isn't All Rules, Dr. Flesch" (1951), William H. Whyte, Jr.'s "The Prose Engineers" (1952), Stephen E. Fitzgerald's "Literature by Slide Rule" (1953), Martin V.H. Prince's "It Ain't Necessarily So" (1955), and John S. Fielden's "Writing Papers for Readability" (1959). Most of these early attacks are suspicious of quantification as an analytic tool for the study of prose and appeal to the time-honored strategies of taste and hard work as means of achieving true readability. More recently, Bertram Bruce, Andee Rubin, and Kathleen Starr, in "Why Readability Formulas Fail" (1981), have attacked the formulas on other grounds, citing the formulas' lack of consideration of all relevant influences on comprehension, their lack of statistical validity and reliability, and their ineffectiveness as guides for revising existing texts. Evaluations that offer qualified recommendations of readability formulas as guides to writing and editing include Janice C. Redish's "Understanding the Limitations of Readability Formulas" (1981), Kenneth B. Powell's "Readability Guides Are Helpful If . . . " (1981), Daniel L. Plung's "Readability Formulas and Technical Communication" (1981), and Jeanne C. Barry's "Computerized Readability Levels" (1981), which confusingly bears the same title as her 1980 article on computer programs. All of the 1981 articles just mentioned appear in the *IEEE Transactions on Professional Communication* for March of that year, making that issue an ideal starting point for information about readability formulas in technical writing.

Despite their shortcomings, readability formulas have also been used frequently as tools for measurement or evaluation of style in technical writing. Readability-oriented research has been conducted for training movies (William Allen, "Readability of Instructional Film Commentary" [1952]), for 17 "reports in the field of science" (Harry F. Arader, "Sentence and Word Length in Scientific Writing" [1956]), for articles in *Industrial and Engineering Chemistry*

(Robert J. Roth, "How Readable Is Chemical Literature?" [1956]), for "18 arbitrary categories of literature" (William F. Kwolek, "A Readability Survey of Technical and Popular Literature" [1973]), for journalistic versus academic journals in the field of metallurgy (David M. Locke and Alan K. Stewart, "Comparative Analysis of Technical Literature" [1973]), and for industrial education textbooks (Andrew K. Clark, "Readability of Industrial Education Textbooks" [1978]).

In sum, "readability" is well entrenched in the literature about technical writing—as a technique for audience analysis, as a set of norms based on that technique, and as a general equivalent for "good" or "clear" or "simple" writing. Its main limitations are that it fails to take into account the varying characteristics of audience needs and wishes; it ignores important aspects of linguistic structure and cohesion discussed in the section above on syntax; and it does not consider the ultimate goal of style in writing—which is not merely to achieve speed, ease, or personal involvement, but rather to create understanding or comprehension of the information in the text. For these reasons, readability as a stylistic norm has been challenged at two levels: first, at the level of presentational style, by proponents of "usability"; second, at the level of discourse style, by critics who for the most part view technical writing as a particular application of traditional rhetorical principles, though many of these have been influenced by recent developments in composition theory.

With the development of the "usability" perspective, understanding and comprehension have received much attention, particularly among cognitive psychologists, whose work is reviewed by Walter Kintsch in *Memory and Cognition* (1977). Rhetorical and stylistic applications of this psychological literature have been presented in many essays by Patricia Wright and her associates. In "Feeding the Information Eaters" (1978), Wright reviews a great deal of this material in support of her call for an integration of "pure and applied research on language comprehension." A major step in such integration is presented in her essay "Usability" (1980), in which she offers the "usability" approach as an alternative not only to readability formulas but also to models of the reading process and to psycholinguistic models. Defining "comprehension" as "the user's interaction with written information," Wright holds that understanding and use of a text are affected by four processes in the reader. The first of these are "perceptual and attentional processes," involving legibility (M. A. Tinker, *Legibility of Print* [1963]; H. Spencer, *The Visible Word* [1969]), language (T. G. Bever, "The Cognitive Basis for Linguistic Structures" [1970]; Herbert H. and E. V. Clark, *Psychology and Language* [1977]), and layout (Patricia Wright, "Presenting Information in Tables" [1970]). Usability is also affected by "decision," "memory," and "response" processes. Wright reviews the literature for each of these types as well in the usability essay, which reflects her own substantial contributions in "Writing to Be Understood" (1971), "Written Information" (1973, with F. Reid), and "Five Skills Technical Writers Need" (1981). Thus, several tasks are necessary to achieve usability: finding out about the readers, finding out how to present the text, and finding out if the text is adequate for readers' use. In short, the criterion of usability encompasses all of the meaning-groups related to "style," from linguistic and editorial features to manner of overall presentation. In addition to Wright's surveys, James Hartley's "Eighty Ways of Improving Instructional Text" (1981) exemplifies the usability approach in an essay that is at once wide ranging and concise.

In regard to discourse style, prescriptive alternatives to readability are presented with two main problems. The first is the dominance of vocabulary in subjective analyses of style. In "Mistaking Subject Matter for Style" (1981), Gary Sloan, for example, has noted the strong influence of subject matter on recognition of famous literary styles; and in *The Philosophy of Composition* (1977), E. D. Hirsch, Jr., has similarly noted that evaluations of style are largely dependent on the familiarity of the vocabulary and ideas. Second, even when prescriptions are implemented, subjective evaluators do not always appreciate them. In an experiment conducted by Rosemary L. Hake and Joseph M. Williams, and reported in "Style and Its Consequences" (1981), English teachers gave higher grades to a "pretentious, wordy" passage than to its simple, concise counterpart. Even though tests show the latter to be easier to process, and even though the latter more closely observes the norms of traditional rhetoric, the nominal style seemed to be more "believable" since that is the way most official prose looks, whether in education, government, or business. If this believability factor is evidenced in the judgments of all readers, and not just of teachers, then it constitutes a significant caveat for conventional claims about clarity, conciseness, correctness, and the like.

These three qualities, as noted earlier, have long dominated the prescriptions of those urging a "simple" style for technical writing, as in John H. Mitchell's "Basic Writing Concepts for Scientists and Engineers" (1980). This "plain style" tradition is generally held to have originated in the scientific revolution of the seventeenth century; but its tenets suggest an equally likely origin in the nineteenth- and twentieth-century textbooks and handbooks of what has been called "current-traditional rhetoric." In this respect, there is little to distinguish the concerns and precepts of many present-day textbooks from earlier prescriptive essays such as Donald M. Crawford's "On Engineering Writing" (1945), John R. Baker's "English Style in Scientific Papers" (1955), or Herman M. Weisman's "Problems in Technical Style, Diction, and Exposition" (1959).

But while the ideal of a simple style based on the norms of clarity, conciseness, and correctness continues to exert a great influence, and while it has undoubtedly helped improve the prose of many bewildered writers as they sought to deal with the problem of conveying information in the midst of the "knowledge explosion" that followed World War II, this modern version of the plain style has been challenged in three ways.

First, as noted in the section on usage, the norm of correctness, along with its hip-shot condemnations of "errors," has been put into a broader perspective by essays such as "Why Engineers and Scientists Write as They Do" (1975), by George E. Schindler, Jr. The twelve features he considers—many of which are frequently considered faults—are (1) length, (2) passive voice, (3) nominalization, (4) preference for "which" over "that," (5) underpunctuation, (6) lack of grammatical focus on key ideas, (7) avoidance of "inanimate action" (personification), (8) use of pleonasms—"more words than are necessary to express a thought," (9) multiple adjectives, particularly stacked-up nouns, (10) Latinate rather than Anglo-Saxon vocabulary, (11) false notions of correctness based on analogy, and (12) "mixed verbosity and conciseness." In Freda F. Stohrer's "Style in Technical Writing" (1981), too, many apparent faults found in some technical writing are treated as appropriate expressions necessitated by the subject matter or the audience. Some of these faults may at worst reflect a conflict between two competing stylistic norms—a conflict discussed in Daniel Marder and Dorothy Margaret Guinn's "Defensive Aesthetics for the Technical Writer" (1982).

Second, the norm of a simple style has been challenged by the rise of audience analysis—a fuller recognition that varying kinds of readers need to be addressed by different kinds of technical writing within the information network of industrial technology. H. R. Clauser's "Writing Is for Readers" (1961) is an early instance of this point of view; Marshall Keith's "Informal Writing" (1967) is another. Other relevant articles have been mentioned in previous sections.

Third, the excesses of some "simplicity" prescriptivists have been challenged by the recognition that grammatically primitive sentences are inadequate to achieve the goals of clarity, conciseness, and accuracy in all but a few situations in which technical information must be conveyed. When seekers of technical information have high reading ability, relatively demanding verbal styles may be tolerated or even appreciated. As Dona M. Kagan notes in "Syntactic Complexity and Cognitive Style" (1980), an intimate connection exists between ways of perceiving and thinking and ways of constructing sentences, and persons with particular cognitive styles may naturally seek out discourse that is less limited than that prescribed by the plain style. Furthermore, as Joseph M. Williams notes in a touchstone article mentioned earlier ("Defining Complexity" [1979]), so-called complex sentences are in many cases highly "processed" structures that demand less organizing and interpreting by readers: some kinds of complex writing make for easier comprehension by readers at all levels of reading skill. Articles that reflect this growing awareness of the role of complexity in technical style include Gertrude Taylor Smith's "Differences in the Thinking-Writing Process" (1972), Thomas L. Warren's "Style in Technical Writing" (1979), Merrill D. Whitburn's "The Plain Style in Scientific and Technical Writing" (1976), and Marvin Rabinovitch's "Technical Writing's Last Stand" (1980).

In sum, prescriptions about style—whether based on readability, usability, or rhetoric, and whether promoting norms of simplicity, complexity, or a middle ground—demonstrate the same characteristics noted in earlier sections of this survey: in the absence of precise, generally adopted definitions, there have been and continue to be a great number of conflicting approaches to style in technical writing. On the whole, this condition would appear to bode well. In "The Need for Better Research in Technical Communication" (1980), Paul V. Anderson has justly lamented the fact that technical writing research and lore have been overly concerned with style, to the detriment of studies into invention, arrangement, argumentation, audience analysis, discourse analysis, and other important aspects of composition. But, with only a seeming paradox, it might now be argued that because of the vigorous infusion of ideas from these new areas of inquiry, the study of style in technical writing has begun afresh.

References

Allen, William. "Readability of Instructional Film Commentary." *J Appl Psychol*, 36 (1952), 164–68.

Anderson, Edward. "Languages and Success." *CE*, 43 (1981), 807–17.

Anderson, Paul V. "The Need for Better Research in Technical Communication." *J Tech Writ Comm*, 10 (1980), 271–82.

Arader, Harry F. "Sentence and Word Length in Scientific Writing." *J Eng Educ*, 46 (1956), 560–62.

Aziz, Abdul. "Article Titles as Tools of Communication." *J Tech Writ Comm*, 4 (1974), 19–21.

Bach, Emmon W. "In Defense of Passive." *Linguist Phil*, 3 (1980), 297–341.

Baker, John R. "English Style in Scientific Papers." *Nature*, 176 (1955), 851–52. Rpt. in *Science*, 123, (1956), 713–14, 720–21.

Barber, C. L. "Some Measurable Characteristics of Modern Scientific Prose." In *Contributions to English Syntax and Philology*. Ed. Frank Behre. Gothenburg: Almqvist, Wiksell, 1962, pp. 21–43.

Barry, Jeanne G. "Computerized Readability Levels." *IEEE Trans Prof Comm*, PC–23, No. 2 (1980), 88–90.

———. "Computerized Readability Levels." *IEEE Trans Prof Comm*, PC-24, No. 1 (1981), 45–46.

Bartholomae, David. "The Study of Error." *CCC*, 31 (1980), 253–68.

Barton, Ben F., and Marthalee S. Barton. "What Is Technical Writing? Prolegomenon to a Contextual Definition." In *Technical Communication: Perspectives for the Eighties*. Ed. J. C. Mathes and Thomas E. Pinelli. Washington, D.C.: NASA, 1981, pp. 3–14.

Bayuk, Milla. "Grammatical Calisthenics in Scientific Russian Translation." *Russ Lang J*, 32 (1978), 31–35.

Bennett, James R., et al. "Punctuation and Style: An Annotated Bibliography." *Style*, 11 (1977), 119–35.

Bernstein, Theodore M. *Miss Thistlebottom's Hobgoblins: A Careful Writer's Guide to Taboos, Bugbears, and Outmoded Rules of English Usage*. New York: Farrar, Straus, Giroux, 1971.

Buehler, Mary Fran. "Controlled Flexibility in Technical Editing: The Levels-of-Edit Concept at JPL." *Tech Comm*, 24, No. 1 (1977), 1–4.

———. "Creative Revision: From Rough Draft to Published Paper." *IEEE Trans Prof Comm*, PC-19, No. 2 (1976), 26–32.

————. "Situational Editing: A Rhetorical Approach for the Technical Editor." *Tech Comm*, 27, No. 3 (1980), 18–22.

Bever, T. G. "The Cognitive Basis for Linguistic Structures." In *Cognition and Development of Language*. Ed. R. J. Hayes. New York: Wiley, 1969.

Billingsley, Patricia A., and Neil A. Johnson. "Nonsexist Use of Language in Scientific and Technical Writing." *IEEE Trans Prof Comm*, PC-22, No. 4 (1979), 193–98.

Blicq, Ronald S. " 'Editing' Guidelines for Supervisory Engineers." *IEEE Trans Prof Comm*, PC-19, No. 2 (1976), 33–37.

Bloomfield, Leonard. *Linguistic Aspects of Science*. In *The International Encyclopedia of Unified Science*. Ed. Otto Neurath, et al. No. 5. Chicago: University of Chicago Press, 1938.

Bodine, Ann. "Androcentrism in Prescriptive Grammar: Singular 'They,' Sex-Indefinite 'He,' and 'He or She.' " *Lang Soc*, 4 (1975), 129–46.

Bormuth, John R. "The Cloze Readability Procedure." *Elem Engl*, 44 (1968), 429–36.

Boyer, Ernest L. "Jargon in Government: Symptoms, Causes, and Cures." *Tech Comm*, 27, No. 2 (1980), 4–5, 12.

Braddock, Richard. "The Frequency and Placement of Topic Sentences in Expository Prose." *RTE*, 8 (1974), 287–302.

Britton, W. Earl. "And–The Simplest Connective." *Proceedings 4th STWE Convention*. Washington, D.C.: Society for Technical Writers and Editors, 1957, pp. 15–19. Rpt. in *Tech Comm*, 28, No. 2 (1981), 19–22.

————. "Personality in Scientific Writing." Proceedings of the 19th International Technical Communication Conference. Washington, D.C.: Society for Technical Communication, 1972, pp. 71–76.

————. "What Is Technical Writing?" *CCC*, 16 (1965), 1–4.

————. "What to Do About Hard Words." *Tech Comm*, 11, No. 3 (1964), 13–16.

Broadhead, Glenn J. "Sentence Skills for Technical Writers." *J Tech Writ Comm*, 11 (1981), 139–50.

————, James A. Berlin, and Marlis Manley Broadhead. "Sentence Structure in Academic Prose and Its Implications for College Writing Teachers." *RTE*, 16 (1982), 225–40.

Broer, Jan W. "Linking While Writing—Do You or Don't You?" *J Tech Writ Comm*, 8 (1978), 217–25.

————. "On Two Active-Reader Stimulants: Multiple Titles and Inverse Writing—Maximizing a Figure of Merit for Your Publication." *J Tech Writ Comm*, 7 (1977), 151–57.

Bromage, Mary C. "A Matter of Wording." *J Account*, 115, No. 1 (1963), 59–62.

Brown, J. J. "Stop Coining Words." *Control Eng*, 2, No. 3 (1955), 48–49.

Bruce, Bertram, Andee Rubin, and Kathleen Starr. "Why Readability Formulas Fail." *IEEE Trans Prof Comm*, PC-24, No. 1 (1981), 50–52.

Brusaw, Charles T. "Dismantling the Tower of Babel in Computer Documentation." *J Tech Writ Comm*, 10 (1980), 133–39.

Bush, Don. "Content Editing, an Opportunity for Growth." *Tech Comm*, 28, No. 4 (1981), 15–18.

————. "Does Sophistication Equal Excellence?" *Tech Comm*, 27, No. 3 (1980), 61–63.

————. "How to Handle Grammatical Dogma." *Tech Comm*, 27, No. 1 (1980), 14–15.

————. "The Passive Voice Should Be Avoided—Sometimes." *Tech Comm*, 28, No. 1 (1981), 19–20, 22.

Cameron, Jack R. "The Sensitivity of Speakers of Standard English to Usage." *RTE*, 2 (1968), 24–31.

Carroll, John E. "Technical Writes and Wrongs." *Electron Power*, 25 (1979), 256–58. Rpt. in *IEEE Trans Prof Comm*, PC-23, No. 2 (1980), 68–71.

Caso, Arthur Lewis. "The Production of New Scientific Terms." *Am Sp*, 55 (1980), 101–11.

Cederborg, Gibson A. "Engineering Writing to Eliminate Gobbledygook." *Mach Des*, 29, No. 5 (1957), 80–82.

Chapman, L. J., and Alan Stokes. "Development Trends in the Perception of Textual Cohesion." In *Processing of Visible Language 2*. Ed. Paul A. Kolers, M. E. Wrolstad, and H. Bouma. New York: Plenum, 1980, pp. 219–26.

Chard, John. "The Incidence of Sentence Openers in Selected Technical or Scientific Periodicals and Journals." *J Tech Writ Comm*, 5 (1975), 91–98.

Chase, Stuart. "Gobbledygook." In *The Practical Craft*. Ed. W. Keats Sparrow and Donald Cunningham. Boston: Houghton Mifflin, 1978, pp. 62–70.

Chomsky, Noam. *Aspects of the Theory of Syntax*. Cambridge, Mass.: M.I.T. Press, 1965.

Christensen, Francis, and Bonniejean Christensen. *Notes Toward a New Rhetoric*. 2nd ed. New York: Harper, 1978.

Clark, Andrew K. "Readability in Technical Writing—Principles and Procedures." *IEEE Trans Prof Comm*, PC-18, No. 2 (1975), 6–70.

————. "Readability of Industrial Education Textbooks." *J Indus Teach Educ*, 16, No. 1 (1978), 13–23.

Clark, Herbert H., and E. V. Clark. *Psychology and Language*. New York: Harcourt, 1977.

————, and Susan E. Haviland. "Comprehension and the Given-New Contract." In *Discourse Production and Comprehension*. Ed. R. O. Freedle. Norwood, N.J.: Ablex, 1977, pp. 3–37.

Clauser, H. R. "Writing Is for Readers." *STWP Rev*, 8 (1961), 12–17.

Cluett, Robert. *Prose Style and Critical Reading*. New York and London: Teachers College Press, 1976.

Coetzee, John M. "The Rhetoric of the Passive in English." *Linguistics*, 18 (1980), 199–201.

Coggshall, Gordon. "Using the Core Sentence to Edit Poorly Written Technical Communication." *Tech Comm*, 27, No. 1 (1980), 19–23.

Colby, John B. "Models for Technical Communicators: Figures of Speech." *Tech Comm*, 28, No. 3 (1981), 64.

Connolly, Thomas E. "Some Major Pitfalls in Technical Writing." *IRE Trans Eng Writ Speech*, EWS-2, No. 2 (1958), 22–25.

Copperud, Roy H. *American Usage: The Consensus*. New York: Van Nostrand, 1970.

Corbett, Edward P.J. "Approaches to the Study of Style." In *Teaching Composition: Ten Bibliographical Essays*. Ed. Gary Tate. Fort Worth: Texas Christian University Press, 1976, pp. 73–109.

Cortelyou, Ethaline. "Building an Organization Style Manual for Technical Reports." *STWP Rev*, 8, No. 2 (1961), 28–32.

Cox, Barbara G., and Charles G. Roland. "How Rhetoric Confuses Scientific Issues." *IEEE Trans Prof Comm*, PC–16, No. 3 (1973), 140–42.

Crawford, Donald M. "On Engineering Writing." *Mech Eng*, 67 (1945), 607–609.

Daiker, Donald A., Andrew Kerek, and Max Morenberg. "Sentence Combining and Syntactic Maturity in Freshman English." *CCC*, 29 (1978), 36–41.

Dale, Edgar, and Jeanne S. Chall. "The Concept of Readability." *Elem Engl*, 26 (1949), 19–26.

Danes, Frantisek. "Functional Sentence Perspective and the Organization of Text." In *Papers on Functional Sentence Perspective*. Ed. F. Danes. The Hague: Mouton, 1974, pp. 106–28.

D'Angelo, Frank G. "The Art of Paraphrase." *CCC*, 30 (1979), 255–59.

———. "Style as Structure." *Style*, 8 (1974), 322–64.

Davis, Richard M. *An Experimental Approach to Effective Industrial Communications*. Kettering, Ohio: R. M. Davis, 1962.

———. "Experimental Research in the Effectiveness of Technical Writing." *IEEE Trans Eng Writ Speech*, EWS–10, No. 2 (1967), 33.

———. "Sloppy Typing and Reproduction in a Written Technical Message—An Experiment." *J Tech Writ Comm*, 2 (1972), 43–55.

Dean, Robert L. "Cliches in Full-Scale Production." *Chem Eng News*, 29, No. 27 (1951), 2729.

de Beaugrande, Robert A. "Information and Grammar in Technical Writing." *CCC*, 28 (1977), 325–32.

———. "Linguistic Theory and Composition." *CCC*, 29 (1978), 134–40.

———. *Text, Discourse, and Process*. Norwood, N.J.: Ablex, 1980.

———. *Text Production: Toward a Science of Composition*. Norwood, N.J.: Ablex, 1982.

Diehl, William, and Larry Mikulecky. "Making Written Information Fit Workers' Purposes." *IEEE Trans Prof Comm*, PC-24, No. 1 (1981), 5–9.

Docter, Stewart. "Testing the Readability of Engineering Writing." *IRE Trans Eng Writ Speech*, EWS–4, No. 3 (1961), 91–96.

Dycus, Robert D. "The Effect of Proposal Appearance on the Technical Evaluation Scoring of Government Proposals." *J Tech Writ Comm*, 7 (1977), 285–93.

———. "The Relative Effectiveness of Proposal Approaches—An Experimental Study." *Tech Comm*, 22, No. 1 (1975), 9–11.

Elder, Joseph D. "Jargon—Good and Bad." *Science*, 119 (1954), 536–38.

Enkvist, Nils Erik. "On Defining Style." In *Linguistics and Style*. Ed. N. E. Enkvist, J. Spencer, and M. J. Gregory. London: Oxford University Press, 1964.

Evans, Bergen. "The Changing English Language." Proceedings of the 1966 Institute in Technical and Industrial Communications. Fort Collins, Colo.: ITIC, 1967, pp. 63–72.

———, and Cornelia Evans. *A Dictionary of Contemporary American Usage*. New York: Random House, 1957.

Faigley, Lester L. "Generative Rhetoric as a Way of Increasing Syntactic Fluency." *CCC*, 30 (1979), 176–81.

———, and Stephen Witte. "Analyzing Revision." *CCC*, 32 (1981), 400–14.

Feistman, M. L. "Engineering Writing 'Up or Down.' " *IRE Trans Eng Writ Speech*, EWS-2, No. 1 (1959), 22–23.

Fielden, John S. "Writing Papers for Readability." *Mech Eng*, 81, No. 3 (1959), 46.

Fitzgerald, Stephen E. "Literature by Slide Rule." *Sat Rev*, 36 (14 Feb. 1953), pp. 15–16, 53–54.

Flesch, Rudolf. *How to Be Brief: An Index to Simple Writing*. New York: Harper, 1962.

———. *How to Test Readability*. New York: Harper, 1951.

———. "How to Write for Today's Busy Readers." *Ptr Ink*, 235 (29 June 1951), 31–32.

———. "A New Readability Yardstick." *J Applied Psychol*, 32 (1948), 221–33.

———. *A New Way to Better English*. New York: Harper, 1958.

———. "Shirt-Sleeve English in One Easy Lesson." *Ptr Ink*, 231 (30 June 1950), 25–26.

Flood, W. E. *Scientific Words—Their Structure and Meaning*. Des Moines: Meredith, 1960.

Foley, Louis. "Malapropism Becomes Commonplace." *J Tech Writ Comm*, 6, No. 2 (1976), 129–33.

Foster, Jeremy J. "The Use of Visual Cues in Text." In *Processing of Visible Language 1*. Ed. Paul A. Kolers, M. E. Wrolstad, and H. Bouma. New York: Plenum, 1979, pp. 189–203.

Freeman, Donald C. "Phenomenal Nominals." *CCC*, 32 (1981), 183–88.

Freisinger, Randall R., and Bruce T. Petersen. "Toward Defining 'Good' Writing: A Rhetorical Analysis of Words, Sentences, and Paragraphs in 16 Industrial Scripts." In *Technical Communication: Perspectives for the Eighties*. Ed. J. C. Mathes and Thomas E. Pinelli. Washington, D.C.: NASA, 1981, pp. 291–304.

Fry, Edward B. "A Readability Formula That Saves Time." *J Read*, 2 (1968), 513–16, 575.

Gerfen, Richard C. "Fallacies in Rhetoric." *STWP Rev*, 11 (July 1964), 6–9.

Gibson, Walker. *Tough, Sweet and Stuffy: An Essay on Modern American Prose Style*. Bloomington: Indiana University Press, 1966.

Gilliland, John. *Readability*. London: University of London Press, 1972.

Goodin, George, and Kyle Perkins. "Discourse Analysis and the Art of Coherence." *CE*, 44 (1982), 57–63.

Gopnik, Myrna. *Linguistic Structures in Scientific Texts*. The Hague: Mouton, 1973.

Gorrell, Robert M. "Usage as Rhetoric." *CCC*, 28 (1977), 20–25.

Gould, Jay R. "Ten Common Weaknesses in Engineering Reports." *Chem Eng (NY)*, 70, No. 21 (1963), 210, 212, 214.

Greenbaum, Sidney, and John Taylor. "The Recognition of Usage Errors by Instructors of Freshman Composition." *CCC*, 32 (1981), 169–74.

Gunning, Robert. *How to Take the Fog Out of Writing*. Chicago: Dartnell, 1964.

Hairston, Maxine. "Not All Errors Are Created Equal: Nonacademic Readers in the Professions Respond to Lapses in Usage." *CE*, 43 (1981), 794–806.

Hake, Rosmary L., and Joseph M. Williams. "Style and Its Consequences: Do as I Do, Not as I Say." *CE*, 43 (1981), 433–51.

Halliday, M.A.K. "Notes on Transitivity and Theme in English: Part 1." *J Linguist*, 3 (1967), 37–81.

———. "Notes on Transitivity and Theme in English: Part 2." *J Linguist*, 3 (1967), 199–244.

————. "Notes on Transitivity and Theme in English: Part 3." *J Linguist*, 4 (1968), 179–215.

————, and Ruqaiya Hasan. *Cohesion in English*. London: Longmans, 1976.

Harris, Elizabeth. "Applications of Kinneavy's *Theory of Discourse* to Technical Writing." *CE*, 40 (1979), 625–32.

Harris, Muriel. "Mending the Fragmented Free Modifier." *CCC*, 32 (1981), 175–82.

Harris, Zellig S. "Discourse Analysis." *Lang*, 28 (1952), 1–30.

————. "Discourse Analysis: A Sample Text." *Lang*, 28 (1952), 474–94.

Hartley, James. "Eighty Ways of Improving Instructional Text." *IEEE Trans Prof Comm*, PC–24, No. 1 (1981), 17–27.

Hayes, John R., and Linda S. Flower. "Identifying the Organization of Writing Processes." In *Cognitive Processes in Writing: An Interdisciplinary Approach*. Ed. Lee Gregg and Erwin Steinberg. Hillsdale, N.J.: Erlbaum, 1980 pp. 3–30.

Heldt, John J. "Quality in Writing." *Quality*, 15, No. 8 (1976), 78.

Hill, Archibald A. "Beyond the Sentence." *Introduction to Linguistic Structures*. New York: Harcourt, Brace, 1958, pp. 406–17.

Hirsch, E. D., Jr. *The Philosophy of Composition*. Chicago: University of Chicago Press, 1977.

Hoey, Michael. *Signalling in Discourse*. Discourse Analysis Monograph No. 6. Birmingham: English Language Research, University of Birmingham, 1979.

Hoffman, Robert R. "Metaphor in Science." In *Cognition and Figurative Language*. Ed. Richard P. Honeck and Robert R. Hoffman. Hillsdale, N.J.: Erlbaum, 1980, pp. 393–423.

Hogben, Lancelot. *The Vocabulary of Science*. New York: Stein, Day, 1970.

Holaday, Barbara. "Go Write a Style Guide." *Tech Comm*, 14, No. 3 (1967), 20–23.

Holland, Winford E., and Bette A. Stead. "Exploring the Scientist-Engineer Conflict: A Form and Content Analysis of Their Written Communication." *IEEE Trans Prof Comm*, PC–15, No. 4 (1972), 119–23.

Horner, Winifred B. "Speech-Act and Text-Act Theory: 'Theme-ing' in Freshman Composition." *CCC*, 30 (1979), 165–69.

Huddleston, R. D., R. A. Hudson, E. D. Winter, and A. Henrici. *Sentence and Clause in Scientific English*. London: Communication Research Centre, Department of General Linguistics, University College London, 1968.

Hughes, Arthur, and Chryssoula Lascaratou. "Competing Criteria for Error Gravity." *Eng Lang Teach J*, 36 (1982), 175–82.

Hughson, Roy V. "Initials, Acronyms, and Chaos." *Chem Eng (NY)*, 76, No. 26 (1969), 106, 108.

Janis, J. Harold. "Business Writing Isn't All Rules, Dr. Flesch." *Ptr Ink*, 236 (10 Aug. 1951), 31–32.

Johansson, Stig. *Some Aspects of the Vocabulary of Learned and Scientific English*. *Gothenburg Studies in English*. Vol. 42. Goeteborg, Sweden: Acta Universitatis Gothoburgensis, 1978.

Jones, Hillary. "I Believe in Basic English." *IEEE Trans Prof Comm*, PC–23, No. 1 (1980), 34–37.

Jordan, Michael P. "Short Texts to Explain Problem-Solution Structures—And Vice Versa." *Instr Sci*, 9 (1980), 221–52.

————. "Some Associated Nominals in Technical Writing." *J Tech Writ Comm*, 11 (1981), 251–63.

Kagan, Dona M. "Syntactic Complexity and Cognitive Style." *Appl Psycholinguist*, 1 (1980), 111–22.

Kapp, Reginald O. *The Presentation of Technical Information*. New York: Macmillan, 1957.

Keith, Marshall. "Informal Writing: Milestone or Millstone?" *IEEE Trans Eng Writ Speech*, EWS–10, No. 2 (1967), 39–40.

Kellner, Robert Scott. "A Necessary and Natural Sequel: Technical Editing." *J Tech Writ Comm*, 12 (1982), 25–33.

Kennedy, Robert A. "Writing Informative Titles for Technical Literature—An Aid to Efficient Information Retrieval." *IEEE Trans Eng Writ Speech*, EWS–7, No. 1 (1964), 4–5.

Kerfoot, Glenn W. "Tips on Technical Writing." *IEEE Trans Prof Comm*, PC–20, No. 1 (1977), 17–19.

Kincaid, J. Peter, James A. Aagard, John W. O'Hara, and Larry K. Cottrell. "Computer Readability Editing System." *IEEE Trans Prof Comm*, PC–24, No. 1 (1981), 38–41.

Kinneavy, James L. *A Theory of Discourse: The Aims of Discourse*. Englewood Cliffs, N.J.: Prentice-Hall, 1971.

Kintgen, Eugene R. "Reader Response and Stylistics." *Style*, 11 (1977), 1–18.

Kintsch, Walter. *Memory and Cognition*. New York: Wiley, 1977.

Kirkman, A. J. "The Communication of Technical Thought." *Chart Mech Eng*, 10 (1963), 594–99. Rpt. in *The Engineer and Society*. Ed. E. G. Semler. London: Institute of Mechanical Engineers, 1970.

———. "Standards of English in Science and Technology." *Nature*, 196 (1962), 807–809.

Kirkman, John. "Heroism or Hocus Pocus?" *Tech Comm*, 28, No. 2 (1981), 43–47.

Klare, George R. "Assessing Readability," *Read Res Q*, 1 (1974–1975), 62–102.

———. *The Measurement of Readability*. Ames: Iowa State University Press, 1963.

———. "Measures of the Readability of Written Communication: An Evaluation." *J Educ Psychol*, 43 (1952), 385–99.

———. "Readable Technical Writing: Some Observations." *Tech Comm*, 24, No. 2 (1977), 1–3, 5.

———. "A Second Look at the Validity of Readability Formulas," *J Read Behav*, 8 (1976), 129–52.

———, and Byron Buck. *Know Your Reader—The Scientific Approach to Readability*. New York: Hermitage, 1954.

Kleinman, Joseph M. "A Limited-Word Technical Dictionary for Technical Manuals." *Tech Comm*, 29, No. 1 (1982), 16–19.

Kline, Charles R., Jr., and W. Dean Memering. "Formal Fragments: The English Minor Sentence." *RTE*, 11 (1977), 97–110.

Kolers, Paul A., M. E. Wrolstad, and H. Bouma, eds. *Processing of Visible Language 2*. New York: Plenum, 1980.

Kowal, John Paul. "Training Tomorrow's Writers." *J Tech Writ Comm*, 5 (1975), 181–85.

Kozminsky, Ely. "Altering Comprehension: The Effect of Biasing Titles on Text Comprehension." *Mem Cognition*, 5 (1977), 482–90.

Kroll, Barry M., and John C. Schafer. "Error Analysis and the Teaching of Composition." *CCC*, 29 (1978), 242–48.

Kucera, Henry, and W. Nelson Francis. *Computational Analysis of Present-Day American English*. Providence, R.I.: Brown University Press, 1962.

Kwolek, W. F. "A Readability Survey of Technical and Popular Literature." *Journ Q*, 50 (1973), 255–64.

Landau, Sidney I. "Of Matters Lexicographical: Scientific and Technical Entries in American Dictionaries." *Am Sp*, 49 (1974), 241–44.

———. "Popular Meanings of Scientific and Technical Terms." *Am Sp*, 55 (1980), 204–209.

Lesgold, A. M. "Pronominalization: A Device for Unifying Sentences in Memory." *J Verb Learn Verb Behav*, 11 (1972), 316–23.

Limaye, Mohan R. "Improving Technical and Bureaucratic Writing." *J Tech Writ Comm*, 11 (1981), 23–33.

Locke, David M., and Alan K. Stewart. "Comparative Analysis of Technical Literature." *J Tech Writ Comm*, 3 (1973), 205–16.

Lufkin, James M. "Generalization and the Interpretation of Science and Technology." *IEEE Trans Prof Comm*, PC–15, No. 4 (1972), 108–11.

———. "The Gulf Between Correctness and Understanding." *IEEE Trans Prof Comm*, PC–19, No. 1 (1976), 4–6.

Lybbert, E. K., and D. W. Cummings. "On Repetition and Coherence." *CCC*, 20 (1969), 35–38.

McAllister, D. T. "Is There Accepted Scientific Jargon?" *Science*, 121 (1955), 530–32.

McCafferty, James W. "Constructive Editing." In *Handbook of Technical Writing Practices*. Ed. Stello Jordan, Joseph M. Kleinman, and H. Lee Schimberg. New York: Wiley-Interscience, 1971, II, 909–24.

McDonald, Daniel A. "Be a Better Writer (Don't Use Dirty Words)." *J Tech Writ Comm*, 7 (1977), 183–90.

MacDonald, Duncan A., ed. *Drafting Documents in Plain Language*. New York: Practising Law Institute, 1979.

McKeehan, John H. "The Inarticulate Engineer (A Communications Dilemma)." *IEEE Trans Eng Writing Speech*, EWS–9, No. 2 (1966), 48–50.

McLaughlin, G. Harry. "SMOG Grading—A New Readability Formula." *J Read*, 12 (1969), 639–47.

Mandell, A. *The Language of Science*. Washington, D.C.: National Science Teachers Association, 1974.

Marder, Daniel, and Dorothy Margaret Guinn. "Defensive Aesthetics for the Technical Writer." *J Tech Writ Comm*, 12 (1982), 35–42.

Marshall, Max S. "Jogging the Jargon." *Improv Coll Univ Teach*, 12 (1964), 216–18.

Marshek, Kurt M. "Transitional Devices for the Writer." *IEEE Trans Prof Comm*, PC–18, No. 4 (1975), 320–22.

Martyna, Wendy. "What Does 'He' Mean? Use of the Generic Masculine." *J Comm*, 28 (1978), 131–38.

Mathes, J. C. "Contextual Editing: The First Step in Editing Sentences." Proceedings of the 23rd International Technical Communication Conference. Washington, D.C.: Society for Technical Communication, 1976, pp. 21–25.

———, and Dwight W. Stevenson. *Designing Technical Reports*. Indianapolis: Bobbs Merrill, 1976.

Mellon, John C. "Issues in the Theory and Practice of Sentence Combining: A Twenty-Year Perspective." In *Sentence Combining and the Teaching of Writing*. Ed.

Donald A. Daiker, Andrew Kerek, and Max Morenberg. Studies in Contemporary Language, No. 3. Akron, Ohio: L & S Books, University of Akron, 1979, pp. 1–38.

Merrill, David. "Psychology of Communication." Proceedings of the 1966 Institute in Technical and Industrial Communications. Fort Collins. Colo.: ITIC, 1967, pp. 26–31.

Milic, Louis T. "Against the Typology of Styles." In *Essays in the Language of Literature*. Ed. Samuel R. Levin. Boston: Houghton Mifflin, 1967, pp. 425–50.

———. "Theories of Style and Their Implications for the Teaching of Composition." *CCC*, 16 (1965), 66–69. Rpt. in *Contemporary Essays on Style*. Ed. Glen A. Love and Michael Payne. Glenview, Ill.: Scott, Foresman, 1969, pp. 15–20.

Millard, Michael. "On the Improvement of the Style of Technical Writing." *J Tech Writ Comm*, 2 (1972), 147–53.

Miller, Carolyn R. "Rules, Context, and Technical Communication." *J Tech Writ Comm*, 10 (1980), 149–58.

Miller, John A. "Technical Writing—An Easily Acquired Skill." *Civ Eng (NY)*, 18 (May 1948), 43–44, 80.

Mills, Gordon H., and John A. Walter. *Technical Writing*. 4th ed. New York: Holt, 1978.

Minor, Dennis E. "A Concept of Language for Technical Writing Students." *J Tech Writ Comm*, 8 (1978), 43–51.

Mitchell, John H. "Basic Writing Concepts for Scientists and Engineers." *Tech Writ Teach*, 8 (1980), 3–6.

Mittins, W. H., Mary Salu, Mary Edminson, and Sheila Coyne. *Attitudes to English Usage*. London: Oxford University Press, 1970.

Montoya, Sarah. "Word Watching: One Word or Two?" *IEEE Trans Prof Comm*, PC–23, No. 3 (1980), 133–35.

Mueller, Douglas. "Put Clarity in Your Writing." *Hydrocarbon Process*, 60 (1980), 143. Rpt. in *IEEE Trans Prof Comm*, PC–23, 4 (1980), 173–78.

Nold, Ellen W., and Brent E. Davis. "The Discourse Matrix." *CCC*, 31 (1980), 141–52.

Ohmann, Richard. "Generative Grammars and the Concept of Literary Style." In *Contemporary Essays on Style*. Ed. Glen A. Love and Michael Payne. Glenview, Ill.: Scott, Foresman, 1969, pp. 133–48.

———. "Literature as Sentences." In *Contemporary Essays on Style*. Ed. Glen A. Love and Michael Payne. Glenview, Ill.: Scott, Foresman, 1969, pp. 149–57.

———. "Prolegomena to the Analysis of Prose Style." In *Contemporary Essays on Style*. Ed. Glen A. Love and Michael Payne. Glenview, Ill.: Scott, Foresman, 1969, pp. 177–90.

Ohta, Hiroshi. "Language Barriers in Japan: An Economist's View." *Int Soc Sci J*, 31 (1979), 79–85.

Ornsen, Kate C. "The Petroleum Chemist's Vernacular." *Am Doc*, 5 (1954), 218–22.

Orth, Melvin F. "Striking Out: Poor Style and Grammar Still Abound in Technical Writing." *IEEE Trans Prof Comm*, PC–21, No. 2 (1978), 44–47.

Osborne, Harold F. "Intuition, Integrity, and the Decline of Editing." *Tech Comm*, 28, No. 4 (1981), 21–26.

Osgood, Charles E. "Some Effects of Motivation on Style of Encoding." In *Style in*

Language. Ed. T. A. Sebeok. Cambridge, Mass.: M.I.T. Press, 1971, pp. 293–306.

Partridge, Eric. *You Have a Point There*. London: Hamish Hamilton, 1955.

Perlman, Alan M. "Some Linguistic Components of Tone." *Tech Comm*, 28, No. 2 (1981), 12–15.

Pitkin, Willis L., Jr. "Discourse Blocks." *CCC*, 20 (1969), 138–48.

Plung, Daniel L. "Readability Formulas and Technical Communication." *IEEE Trans Prof Comm*, PC–24, No. 1 (1981), 52–54.

Porter, Donald. "Scientific English: An Oversight in Stylistics?" *Stud Angl Pos*, 8 (1976), 77–87.

Poteet, Lewis J. "Minnesota Freshmen and Ten Controversial Linguistic Forms." *RTE*, 3 (1969), 62–69.

Powell, Kenneth B. "Readability Guides Are Helpful If. . . . " *IEEE Trans Prof Comm*, PC–24, No. 1 (1981), 43–52.

Power, Ruth M. "Who Needs a Technical Editor?" *IEEE Trans Prof Comm*, PC–24, No. 3 (1981), 139–40.

Prince, Martin V.H. "It Ain't Necessarily So—Short Words and Simple Sentences Are Not Necessarily the Clue to Clarity and Readability." *Chem Eng News*, 33, No. 34 (1955), 3513.

Rabinovitch, Marvin. "Technical Writing's Last Stand." *Tech Comm*, 27, No. 3 (1980), 23–25, 54.

Racker, Joseph. "Selecting and Writing to the Proper Level." *IRE Tran Eng Writ Speech*, EWS–2, No. 1 (1959), 16–21.

Ramsey, Richard David. "Grammatical Voice and Person in Technical Writing: Results of a Survey." *J Tech Writ Comm*, 10 (1980), 109–13.

———. "Technical Writing, Stylistics, and TG Grammar." *J Tech Writ Comm*, 7, (1977), 333–45.

Redish, Janice C. "Understanding the Limitations of Readability Formulas." *IEEE Trans Prof Comm*, PC–24, No. 1 (1981), 46–48.

Reel, Willard D. "Project Literacy." *IEEE Trans Eng Writ Speech*, EWS–7, No. 3 (1964), 3–8.

Reid, R. M. "A Writer's Cookbook." *STWE Rev*, 7, No. 2 (Apr. 1960), 29–31.

Riffaterre, Michael. "Criteria for Style Analysis." *Word*, 15 (1959), 154–74.

Ronco, Paul Gardner. *Characteristics of Technical Reports that Affect Reader Behavior—A Review of the Literature*. Springfield, Va.: Clearinghouse for Federal Scientific and Technical Information, 1964.

Rook, Fern. "Slaying the English Jargon: About the Hyphen." *Tech Comm*, 28, No. 1 (1981), 27.

———. "Slaying the English Jargon: Apropos of Apostrophes." *Tech Comm*, 28, No. 2 (1981), 29.

———. "Slaying the English Jargon: Being Personable with Personal Pronouns." *Tech Comm*, 27, No. 3 (1980), 39.

———. "Slaying the English Jargon: Pedantry and Passives." *Tech Comm*, 27, No. 4 (1980), 29.

———. "Slaying the English Jargon: Sense About Tense." *Tech Comm*, 28, No. 4 (1981), 46.

———. "Slaying the English Jargon: The (?) Dictionary." *Tech Comm*, 28, No. 3 (1981), 42.

———. "Slaying the English Jargon: Three Little Words." *Tech Comm*, 27, No. 2 (1980), 29.

———. "Slaying the English Jargon: To Comma or Not to Comma." *Tech Comm*, 27, No. 1 (1980), 35.

Ross, Donald, Jr. "A Brief Note on How Writing Errors Are Judged," *J Tech Writ Comm*, 11, No. 2 (1981), 163–73.

Ross, Peter Burton. "Slash for Quick Editing." *Tech Comm*, 24, No. 3 (1977), 11–14.

Roth, Robert J. "How Readable Is Chemical Literature?" *Am Doc*, 7 (1956), 215–21.

Samuel, Rhys. "Let's Use Our Heads." *IRE Trans Eng Writ Speech*, EWS–1, No. 2 (1958), 13–17.

Savory, T. H. *The Language of Science—Its Growth, Character and Usage.* Rev. ed. London: Deutsch, 1967.

Scheffler, F. L., H. H. Schumacher, and J. F. March. "The Significance of Titles, Abstracts, and Other Portions of Technical Documents for Information Retrieval." *IEEE Trans Prof Comm*, PC–17, No. 1 (1974), 1–8.

Schenck, Eleanor M. "Technical Writer-Readability Formulas and the Nontechnical Reader." *J Tech Writ Comm*, 7 (1977), 303–307.

Schindler, George E., Jr. "Why Engineers and Scientists Write as They Do—Twelve Characteristics of Their Prose." *IEEE Trans Prof Comm*, PC–18, No. 1 (1975), 5–10.

Schoenfeld, Robert. "Human Dimensions for Inanimate Objects?" *IEEE Trans Prof Comm*, PC–24, No. 4 (1981), 182–83.

Searle, John R. *Speech Acts: An Essay in the Philosophy of Language.* Cambridge: Cambridge University Press, 1969.

Selinker, Larry. "On the Use of Informants in Discourse Analysis and 'Language for Specialized Purposes.' " *IRAL*, 17 (1979), 189–215.

———, and Louis Trimble. "Formal Written Communication and ESL." *J Tech Writ Comm*, 4 (1974), 81–91.

Shapiro, David. "Speech Characteristics of Rigid Characters." *Lang Style*, 10 (1977), 262–69.

Shaughnessy, Mina. *Errors and Expectations.* New York: Oxford University Press, 1977.

Shaw, H. *Punctuate It Right.* New York: Barnes, Noble, 1963.

Shebilske, Wayne L. "Structuring an Internal Representation of Text." In *Processing of Visible Language 2.* Ed. Paul A. Kolers, M. E. Wrolstad, and H. Bouma. New York: Plenum, 1980, pp. 227–39.

Shimberg, H. Lee. "Clarifying Federal Regulations by Using Plain English, Part 1." *Tech Comm*, 27, No. 2 (1980), 6–12.

———. "Clarifying Federal Regulations by Using Plain English, Part 2." *Tech Comm*, 28, No. 2 (1981), 6–18.

———. "Editing Authors' Style—A Few Guidelines." *Tech Comm*, 28, No. 4 (1981), 31–35.

———. "Special Issue on Technical Editing: Introduction." *Tech Comm*, 28, No. 4 (1981), 4.

Shinoda, Yoshiaki. "Pitfalls for Japanese Specialists in English Technical Writing." *J Tech Writ Comm*, 10, (1980), 103–107.

Showstack, Richard. "Discourse Punctuation: The Next Stage of Printing." *IEEE Trans Prof Comm*, PC–23, No. 3 (1980), 143–47.

Shurter, Robert L. "Let's Take the Strait Jacket Off Technical Style." *Mech Eng*, 74 (1952), 649–50.

Sloan, Gary. "Mistaking Subject Matter for Style." *CE*, 43 (1981), 502–507.

Slotnick, Henry B., and W. Todd Rogers. "Writing Errors: Implications About Student Writers." *RTE*, 7 (1973), 387–98.

Smith, Gertrude Taylor. "Differences in the Thinking-Writing Process." *J Tech Writ Comm*, 2 (1972), 19–32.

Snure, Pauline. "Editing and Production of Scientific and Technical Journals." Proceedings of the 1961 Institute in Technical and Industrial Communication. Fort Collins, Colo.: ITIC, 1961, pp. 25–35.

Sommers, Nancy. "Revision Strategies of Student Writers and Experienced Adult Writers." *CCC*, 3 (1980), 378–88.

Sopher, H. "Discourse Analysis: The Hierarchic Structure of Meaning-Content." *J Lit Seman*, 8 (1979), 100–108.

Sorensen, Knud. "Some Observations on Pronominalization." *Engl Stud*, 62 (1981), 146–55.

Souther, James W. "Writing Is for Other People." *J Tech Writ Comm*, 6 (1979), 38–42.

Sparks, Luther C., Jr. "The Style Guide as a Cost Reduction Tool." *J Tech Writ Comm*, 4 (1974), 217–21.

Spencer, H. *The Visible Word*. London: Thames Drawing Office Ltd., 1968.

Stanley, Julia P. "Passive Motivation." *Found Lang*, 13, (1975), 25–39.

Stine, Donna, and Donald Skarzenski. "A Comparison of Technical Writing and Business Communication Courses." *J Tech Writ Comm*, 6 (1978), 15–18.

Stohrer, Freda F. "Style in Technical Writing." *TETYC*, 7 (1981), 217–22.

Stratton, Charles R. "Analyzing Technical Style." *Tech Comm*, 26, No. 3 (1979), 4–8.

———. "Technical Writing: What It Is and What It Isn't." *J Tech Writ Comm*, 9 (1979), 9–16.

Struck, Herman R. "Recommended Diet for Padded Writing." *Science*, 119, (1954), 522–25.

Taylor, Wilson L. "Cloze Procedure: A New Tool for Measuring Readability." *Journ Q*, 30 (1953), 415–33.

Tebeaux, Elizabeth. "What Makes Bad Technical Writing Bad? A Historical Analysis." *IEEE Trans Prof Comm*, PC–23, No. 2 (1980), 71–76.

Tichy, Henrietta J. "Engineers Can Write Better: The Long and Short of It." *Chem Eng Progress*, 50 (1954), 206–13.

Tinker, M. A. *Legibility of Print*. Ames: Iowa State University Press, 1963.

Turner, Ruth H. "Thirty-Six Aids to Successful Proofreading." *IEEE Trans Prof Comm*, PC–22, No. 1 (1979), 19–20.

Vande Kopple, William J. "Functional Sentence Perspective, Composition, and Reading." *CCC*, 33 (1982), 50–63.

van Dijk, Teun A. *Text and Context*. London: Longman, 1977.

Vervalin, Charles H. "Checked Your Fog Index Lately?" *IEEE Trans Prof Comm*, PC–23, No. 2 (1980), 87–88.

von Glasenapp, Brent W. "Caterpillar Fundamental English." Proceedings of the 19th International Technical Communication Conference. Washington, D.C.: Society for Technical Communication, 1972, pp. 81–85.

Vowles, Richard B. "Language, Logic, and Creative Engineering." *CE*, 15 (1954), 454–59.

Waller, Robert H.W. "Graphic Aspects of Complex Texts: Typography as Macro-Punctuation." In *Processing of Visible Language 2*. Ed. Paul A. Kolers, M. E. Wrolstad, and H. Bouma. New York: Plenum, 1980, pp. 241–53.

Walpole, Jane R. "Style as Option." *CCC*, 31 (1980), 205–12.

———. "Why Must the Passive Be Damned?" *CCC*, 30 (1979), 251–54.

Walter, John A. "Usage and Style in Technical Writing: A Realistic Position." In *The Practical Craft: Readings for Business and Technical Writers*. Ed. W. Keats Sparrow and Donald H. Cunningham. Boston: Houghton Mifflin, 1978, pp. 90–98.

Warren, Thomas L. "The Passive Voice Verb: A Selected, Annotated Bibliography—Part I." *J Tech Writ Comm*, 11 (1981), 271–86.

———. "The Passive Voice Verb: A Selected, Annotated Bibliography—Part II." *J Tech Writ Comm*, 11 (1981), 373–89.

———. "Style in Technical Writing." *Tech Writ Teach*, 6 (1979), 47–49.

Weisman, Herman M. "Problems in Technical Style, Diction, and Exposition." Proceedings of the 1959 Institute in Technical and Industrial Communication. Fort Collins, Colo.: ITIC, 1959, pp. 31–41.

Whalen, Thomas H. "Total English Equals Writing Competence." *RTE*, 3 (1969), 52–61.

Whitburn, Merrill D. "The Plain Style in Scientific and Technical Writing." *J Tech Writ Comm*, 8 (1978), 349–58.

Whitmore, Charles E. "Language of Science." *Sci Mon*, 80 (1955), 185–91.

Whittaker, Della A. "Remember the Tradition?" *J Tech Writ Comm*, 7 (1977), 191–95.

———. "Teaching Students to Prepare Their Own Style Guides." *J Tech Writ Comm*, 6 (1979), 103–105.

Whyte, William H., Jr. "The Prose Engineers." *J Comm*, 2 (1952), 6–10.

Williams, Joseph M. "Defining Complexity." *CE*, 40 (1979), 595–609.

———. "Linguistic Responsibility." *CCC*, 39 (1977), 8–17.

Williamson, Gerald F. "Avoid Dirty Acronym Pollution Today (ADAPT)." *J Tech Writ Comm*, 3 (1973), 47–50.

Wimsatt, W. K., Jr. "Verbal Style: Logical and Counterlogical." *PMLA*, 65 (1950), 5–20.

Winter, Eugene O. "A Clause-Relational Approach to English Texts: A Study of Some Predictive Lexical Items in Written Discourse." *Instr Sci*, 6 (1977), 1–92.

Winterowd, W. Ross. "The Grammar of Coherence." *CE*, 31 (1970), 828–35.

Witte, Stephen P., and Lester Faigley. "Coherence, Cohesion, and Writing Quality." *CCC*, 32 (1981), 189–204.

Wolk, Anthony. "The Relative Importance of the Final Free Modifier: A Quantitative Analysis." *RTE*, 4 (1970), 59–68.

Wooster, Harold. "A Web of Words." Proceedings of the 1963 Institute in Technical and Industrial Communication. Fort Collins, Colo.: ITIC, 1963, pp. 1–16.

Wright, Patricia. "Feeding the Information Eaters: Suggestions for Integrating Pure and Applied Research on Language Comprehension." *Instr Sci*, 7 (1978), 249–312.

———. "Five Skills Technical Writers Need." *IEEE Trans Prof Comm*, PC–24, No. 1 (1981), 10–16.

———. "Presenting Information in Tables." *Appl Ergon*, 1 (1970), 234–42.

————. "Presenting Technical Information: A Survey of Research Findings." *Instr Sci*, 6 (1977), 93–134.

————. "Usability: The Criterion for Designing Written Information." In *Processing of Visible Language 2*. Ed. Paul A. Kolers, M. E. Wrolstad, and H. Bouma. New York: Plenum, 1980, pp. 185–205.

————. "Writing to Be Understood: Why Use Sentences?" *Appl Ergon*, 2 (1971), 207–209.

————, and F. Reid. "Written Information: Some Alternatives to Prose for Expressing the Outcomes of Complex Contingencies." *J Appl Psychol*, 57 (1973), 160–66.

Zall, Paul M. "The Three-Horned Dilemma: Technical Writing, Business Writing, and Journalism." In *The Practical Craft*. Ed. W. Keats Sparrow and Donald Cunningham. Boston: Houghton Mifflin, 1978, pp. 14–21.

Zook, Lola. "Editing and the Editor: Views and Values." *Tech Comm*, 28, No. 4 (1981), 5–9.

Part III

Specific Types of Technical Communication

Proposals

MARK P. HASELKORN

In the most general terms, a written proposal is a document in which the writer offers something beneficial to the reader in exchange for something in return. The writer (or writers and the organization they represent) may offer to conduct research, develop systems, construct equipment, improve services, repair damage, or increase profits. In return, the reader (or readers and the organization they represent) will provide funding, payment, equipment, and other support. The proposal situation may arise out of a need stated by the reader, a need recognized by the writer, or a need negotiated and developed by both.

Proposals fall into six categories: (1) applications for government grants, (2) bids for government contracts, (3) applications for foundation grants, (4) applications for corporate grants, (5) bids for commercial contracts, and (6) internal proposals (where writer and reader are members of the same organization). The first five of these categories can be grouped under the heading of "formal proposals" while the sixth, internal proposals, can also be called "informal." Unfortunately, not all works on proposal writing fit neatly into these six categories.

There are a number of other ways that authors focus their writing about proposals. Instead of concentrating on the source and type of support, an author may focus on the need—that is, proposal writing in education, in university research, in health, for libraries, and so on. Or the writer may focus on what is to be done—that is, research proposals, evaluation proposals, development proposals. Some authors address aspects of the proposal writing process—that is, writing problem statements, constructing budgets, finding sources, and so forth. Other writers may attempt to focus on proposal writing in general, making statements appropriate for the type of work being written—that is, textbook, handbook, workbook. Finally, two other types of works on proposal writing are research on proposal writing and teaching of proposal writing.

Almost all works written on proposal writing, however they segment and focus the general field, are "how-to's" of some kind. These "how-to's" come from various sources: government evaluators and directors, successful proposal writers, scholars and teachers of technical writing, scholars and teachers of business writing, managers in business and industry, and people who combine these areas of experience. Despite the wide diversity of advice given in these "how-to's," they share one thing in common: the authority for the advice given is the experience and knowledge of the author. This is an inherent weakness in all of these works since there is no research to verify the claims of these "how-to's." This weakness, the failure to back up proposal writing advice by subjecting this advice to empirical tests, is a general symptom of technical writing research.

In discussing the sources available in proposal writing, the works may be divided into the following six major categories:

1. General "How-to's"
2. Specific "How-to's" by Source and Type
3. Specific "How-to's" by Need
4. Textbooks and Handbooks
5. Empirical Research
6. Teaching

Before beginning the discussion of specific works, a few general questions must be answered.

First, where does the general proposal situation end and proposal *writing* begin? The general proposal situation can be divided into pre-proposal, proposal writing, and the post-proposal phases. The pre-proposal phase includes activities such as getting and developing project ideas, locating sources, and establishing connections; the post-proposal phase includes activities such as negotiating a contract, managing the funded project, disseminating results, and reapplying for additional funds. Some aspects of these "pre-" and "post-" phases have an impact on the actual writing of the various application sections. For example, the pre-proposal analysis that goes into matching a project idea with an appropriate funding source is a part of the audience analysis so crucial to any effective writing. Other aspects of these "pre-" and "post-" phases, such as contract negotiations and program management, are not as relevant here. Therefore, while some works that focus on the "pre-" and "post-" phases of proposal writing have been included, this was done only where the work related to the writing process itself. A work that does nothing but list grant sources has not been included, while a work that discusses how to "pitch" to various grant sources has been covered.

A second question is, where does proposal writing end and other report writing begin? The most troublesome distinction here is between internal or informal proposals and recommendation reports. Some authors include organizational recommendations for, say, a new company procedure under their proposal sections. Frank Smith, in "Engineering Proposals" (1971), attempts to clarify the distinction by saying that proposals say "here's what I'll do for you over a given period of time for a certain price," while reports transmit information and make recommendations in response to questions and needs within the company. While useful, it seems that this distinction blurs in technical situations where writers, having investigated some problem, write to their managers recommending (proposing?) that funds be allocated for some project they will undertake to rectify the situation. Works whose authors have chosen to call such recommendation reports "proposals" (internal or informal) have been included in this chapter.

The phrase "proposal writing" is itself a potential source of confusion. In use, "proposal writing" is somewhat ambiguous. Some writers use "proposal writing" to mean only grant application writing. Others use it to mean only the writing of commercial bids. This essay avoids defining "proposal writing" in either of these restricted ways.

Finally, a note on handbooks. The handbooks placed in the "Textbooks and Handbooks" section are those general handbooks of business and/or technical writing which, like the textbooks, devote a section to proposal writing. Some handbooks, however, are devoted solely to proposal writing or even some aspect of proposal writing. These will be placed in relevant sections, based on their content and orientation.

General "How-to's"

General "how-to's" will be discussed in three groups: works that cover proposal writing in the broad sense; works that treat general proposals as grant proposals; and works that treat general proposals as contract bids.

Very few works attempt to treat proposals in the broad sense, and of those that do try, none includes the internal proposal in its coverage. Among the best of the general works is Jill Ammon-Wexler and Catherine Carmer's *How to Create a Winning Proposal* (1976), which covers all formal proposal writing situations. This book has a business and industry orientation, treating proposals as one of the primary means of acquiring new business. Despite its broad scope (government grants and contracts, commercial contracts, and private foundation grants), the information is extremely practical, including planning, proposal components, and step-by-step writing of the application. The book is best on the actual writing steps, with a detailed breakdown of the technical, management, and pricing components of a proposal.

Also extremely good is Harold Zallen and Eugenia M. Zallen's *Ideas Plus Dollars* (1976). This book has well-developed "pre-" and "post-" writing sections and integrates these well with the actual application writing. While the scope is limited to government and foundation grants and government contracts, this is one of the few works to give detailed tips on writing the preliminary proposal, a brief initial proposal for informal review. The formal proposal is seen as the final evolution of a dialogue begun with the preliminary proposal. Examples are given of proposals based on specific guidelines (NASA), and general guidelines are given for situations in which no specific guidelines are provided. This general outline covers Title Page, Abstract, Table of Contents, Problem, Objectives, Procedures, Evaluation, Dissemination, Resources, Budget, and Appendices. Tips are give on each section.

While Roy J. Loring and Harold Kerzner's *Proposal Preparation and Management Handbook* (1982) mentions all formal proposals, it focuses on a management system for proposals that would be useful primarily in business and industry. True to this orientation, the book pays special attention to commercial contract bids. As does Ammon-Wexler, Loring sees proposals as a device for generating income in an organization. The book looks carefully at what goes into a proposal, dividing it into Technical, Management, and Cost sections. (A warning—the citations in Loring's bibliographies are consistently wrong and incomplete. He even errs in citing his own articles!)

Thomas E. Jordan's *Proposal Writing* (1976) is less significant than the works mentioned thus far; yet it takes a nice approach to general proposal writing by dividing proposals according to types of work to be done. Thus it covers *research* proposals, *development* proposals, and *evaluation* proposals, giving tips on strategy, preparation steps, and management for each type. Not all possibilities are covered, and this work is more relevant for grant writing than for contract proposals.

Far more works focus on general grant writing (government, foundation, corporate) than do those that cover proposal writing in the broad sense. To many writers, "proposal writing" equals "grant writing." In general, the more limited focus makes these works more successful.

Probably the best known and most comprehensive book is Virginia P. White's *Grants* (1975). This book covers the entire grant situation, from "What is a grant?" to the post-application phases. Sources are discussed from government, foundations, and business. The application itself is also covered along with advice, largely strategy, on writing the proposal. Particularly helpful to the writer is a discussion of how grants get awarded. White provides an excellent general guide to both public and private grant seeking.

Audrey Richards's *Grantwriter's Handbook* (1979–80) covers ground similar to White's book, but focuses more on the writing of the proposal itself. A collection of articles, forms, writing tips, checklists, training exercises, resources, and criteria gives proposal writers everything they should need in a practical form. Perhaps even more detailed is Daniel L. Conrad's *The Grants Planner* (1979), which takes a workbook approach to how organizations can get government, foundation, and corporate grants. Conrad takes a systems approach to grant writing; provides charts, guides, and checklists; and is very practical.

Grantsmanship (1978) is a brief but useful guide to the general grant situation. It focuses mainly on pre-writing activities (defining goals, locating donors, writing letters of inquiry) but it also has a section on preparing formal proposals. "Post-" activities such as reporting results are also covered. Louis A. Urgo's *Models for Money* (1978) is another useful guide that covers only government and foundation applications but focuses more on actual writing than does *Grants-manship*. After an opening section on how to approach agencies, Urgo provides writing tips, evaluation criteria, and a chapter of model proposals that is the heart of the book. Models include an equipment proposal in education, a staffing proposal in the arts, a museum proposal, a renewal request, and a proposal for expansion of services.

J. Meyer's *Writing Action Proposals* (1976) defines "action" proposals as those that develop ideas for providing direct or indirect services to a designated group of people. Meyer does not, therefore, cover research proposals, nor does he include corporate grants. He divides the writing phase into Problem, Objectives, Procedures and Target Group, Program Evaluation, Future Funding, Budget, and Appendices, and provides a sample budget.

The most influential article on grant writing is Norton J. Kiritz's "Program Planning and Proposal Writing" (1982–83). This oft-cited article appears in three places other than that cited here, and an expanded version is available through the Grantsmanship Center (publishers of the influential *Grantsmanship Center News* which provides vital information on grants for both the public and private sector). Kiritz divides proposal writing into a seven-step format, after which a summary is written. The steps are: (1) Introduction, (2) Problems Statement or Assessment of Need, (3) Program Objectives, (4) Methods, (5) Evaluation, (6) Budget, and (7) Future Funding. Many other works adopt this model and refer to the advice Kiritz provides on writing each section.

A number of other articles cover various aspects of the general grant writing situation. B. Clayton's "The Other Side of Proposal Writing" (1982) presents strategies for "pitching to the catcher" in grant proposals, Tim Whalen ("Grant Proposals" [1982]) also stresses understanding audience needs, and provides a checklist and rating scale to help writers. In "The Art of Persuasion" (1978), Lois DeBakey and Selma DeBakey focus on "logic and language," including ways to draft and revise the proposal and the choice of language. Richard G. Maybee's "A Process Approach to Proposal Development" (1981) provides a systematic plan for developing a proposal that has four major phases: concept development, proposal writing, funding agency review, and project operation. In "Use of Sponsor's Evaluation Criteria in Writing Proposals" (1980), Gerald V. Teague points out how proposal writers can learn what to include in an application by studying the Proposal Evaluation Criteria section of a grant announcement. Finally, Lawrence E. Schlesinger and Nhuyen Nhan's "Project Proposals" (1975) presents a framework for assessing a research project grant proposal.

Works on general contract proposal writing describe how to respond to a Request for Proposals (RFP) from business or the government. Accordingly, there is a strong commercial orientation to these works. A number of studies come directly out of proposal writing groups in industry, including groups at General Electric, TRW, Honeywell, and Sylvania Electronics Systems. Overall, there are fewer works on contract bids than on grant proposals.

Best of all is "Engineering Proposals" (1971) by Frank Smith. While Smith focuses on commercial proposals, he takes the time to locate this type of proposal within the context of general proposal writing. He then gives a practical discussion—complete with examples, charts, and forms—of how to respond to RFPs. Smith covers kinds (systems proposal, hardware or production proposal, research and development proposal, and service proposal), preparation (the team, the schedule, costs, proposal development, and security), content (front matter, technical proposal, business-management proposal, cost-and-contract proposal, back matter), and role of the technical writer (author, editor, coordinator) in engineering proposals. It all comes across as hints from a man who has been there (and still is).

A number of articles show the business and industry orientation of contract proposal writing. Sylvia Walker's "What to Do Until the Proposal Writer Comes" (1977) describes how organizational managers can best help the professional proposal writer with whom they will be working. In "Strong Proposals Make Easy Going" (1980), David K. Williams focuses on the pre-writing stage in an organization; he provides charts and discussion designed to show how careful planning and preparation will increase funding possibilities. Finally, David Englebret ("Storyboarding" [1972]) shows how a project team will benefit by using the storyboard technique (borrowed from TV advertising) to plan and prepare proposals.

Specific "How-to's" by Source and Type

As stated earlier, a breakdown of proposals by source and type yields six distinct categories: government grants, government contracts, foundation grants, corporate grants, commercial contracts, and internal proposals. There are several works dedicated solely to each of these categories.

Of the books dealing with government grants, Howard Hillman's *The Art of Winning Government Grants* (1977) is particularly useful. Hillman follows a basic format in all his works. (He has written other books on foundation grants, corporate grants, and internal reports and proposals.) Hillman breaks down the overall grant process into why they give, who they give to, what they give, how they give, who you are, research, developing contacts, writing, and follow through. His writing section consists mainly of a few tips and a few samples. The work also contains extensive grant sources.

Not suprisingly, the government provides information in this area. The *Catalog of Federal Domestic Assistance Annual* is an annual publication of the Office of Management and Budget (OMB) which provides detailed information of government programs for domestic assistance. Of particular interest to writers is a section on application procedures, including a checklist. Another work which, despite its name, focuses exclusively on OMB grants is L. Michael Tompkins's *The First... Universal Grants Management Handbook...in English* (1977). This work outlines the OMB grant procedure with discussion of key sections.

Philip Des Mairas's *How to Get Government Grants* (1977) is a good general guide covering "pre-" (process and policy, agencies and programs, types of grants), writing (applications and proposals, budget writing), and "post-" (grant reporting, organizing grant operations) phases of the grant procedure. Of particular interest are three case studies of successful grants from the National Institute of Mental Health (NIMH), the National Endowment for the Humanities (NEH), and the National Science Foundation (NSF).

A Budget Primer by Craig E. Daniels is a workbook that focuses exclusively on budget writing for federal grant proposals. It includes discussion, worksheets, and sample budget forms from NSF and Health Education and Welfare. Diane Duca's "New Strategy for Writing Proposals Now Necessary" (1982) also has a particular focus, that of writing successful grants to the Reagan Administration, given its efforts to reduce expenditures. Far more general is "Developing the Successful Grant Proposal" (1973), which attempts to describe the thought processes that generate ideas for proposals, and outlines the writing techniques that should follow.

A surprising number of books do a good job of describing how organizations can attract new business by responding to government RFPs. Mary Jo Hall's *Developing Skills in Proposal Writing* (1977) is particularly good because it presents a practical model for proposal development, followed by a detailed guide to the actual writing process, complete with sample forms, samples of successful proposals, and sample review criteria. Each section of the proposal is discussed in detail with practical tips included. Help is also given in constructing budget, personnel, and facilities descriptions.

Another very practical work with good attention to how the proposal should be written is Robert D. Guyton and Thomas R. Schaeffer's *Prerequisites for Winning Government R&D Contracts* (1970). This book deals separately with solicited versus unsolicited proposals, and also treats technical and cost components as two distinct proposals. According to Guyton and Schaeffer, technical evaluation of a proposal project goes on separately from pricing. Technical and cost proposal writing is equally distinct, the technical proposal following strict guidelines (introduction, objective, technical description of the proposed program, management, background and qualifications, personnel, and corporate resources) but the cost proposal requiring more information than attention to how it should be presented.

Yet another practical guide to developing winning proposals for government contracts is Herman Holtz and T. Schmidt's *The Winning Proposal* (1981). The book covers three main phases of the process, two "pre-" (audience analysis and formulation of approach) and one the actual writing. Proposal writing is seen as a problem in marketing. The general proposal is presented as consisting of introductory gambits (general attention-getters), technical arguments (arguments that you have the best approach or are best qualified), program proposed (staff, tasks, schedule, specification of deliverable items and services), qualifications and experience (suitability of your organization to carry out the project), and appendices. Written last but coming first are a title page, executive summary, and letter of transmittal. Tips are also given for following mandated formats, developing management plans, and writing persuasively.

Holtz also has an earlier book, *Government Contracts* (1979), with much specific "how-to" information, though the central strategy is still to sell the government on the proposal. Information includes ways to prepare and submit bids, methods of evaluation, proposal formats, and packaging. Development of the proposal is traced from idea to submission and evaluation. Clear writing is stressed, but little is presented on the writing of particular proposal sections. Robert B. Greenly's *How to Win Government Contracts* (1983) is similar to Herman Holtz's *Government Contracts* in that it too gives selling strategies, traces case studies, and presents "how-to" guidance from the plan through the writing to the post-proposal negotiations. Greenly, however, places more emphasis on the actual writing of sections.

W. James Popham's "Key Decision Points in a Contractor's Response to an RFP" (1980) and Jeffrey P. Davidson and Barry D. Rosenberg's "Contract Proposals" (1980) are two articles that present strategies for responding to government RFPs. Popham focuses on two decisions—whether to respond and how to respond—while Davidson and Rosenberg attempt to break down both the proposal segments and the writing preparation phase.

Foundation grant proposals differ enough from government grant proposals to warrant special attention. Foundations, for example, generally do not provide a prescribed application format. It is not surprising, therefore, that a number of works focus exclusively on seeking grants from foundations.

Joseph Dermer has a series of books on getting money from foundations. *How to Raise Funds from Foundations* (1979), which focuses on pre-writing concerns, complements his earlier work, *How to Write Successful Foundation Presentations* (1974), which focuses on the writing phase itself. *How to Raise Funds from Foundations* relies mainly on examples, and besides the formal proposal, it covers the appointment letter, the appeal, the letter of renewal and special presentations. Dermer's latest work is *A Guide to Foundation Fund Raising Under the Reagan Administration* (1982).

As mentioned, Howard Hillman has devoted one of his series of books to foundation fund raising. *The Art of Winning Foundation Grants* (1975) follows the format presented for Hillman's government grant book. Proposal writing is placed in the context of the entire grant seeking process. The writing chapter contains a few samples, but consists mostly of brief tips. An entire sample proposal is presented.

The Foundation Library Center's *Some Suggestions by Foundations on the Preparation of Proposals* (1969) is somewhat dated but is still useful. The work is a compilation of hints from major foundations on the content, timing, and submission of applications. In a similar but far more limited vein, Bill Somerville's "Where Proposals Fail" (1982) is a series of brief tips on what *not* to do, written by the director of a foundation.

Two other articles focus on foundation proposals. Betty E. McGuire's "Plain English" (1981) talks about the language of foundations, with suggestions on beginning and drafting the proposal. "A Winning Strategy" (1980) by Sandra A. Glass focuses on pre-writing concerns and advises far more cultivation of foundations before submission of the proposal.

Very few works cover only the corporate grant proposal. In truth, Hillman's *The Art of Winning Corporate Grants* (1980) is very similar to his other two books on winning government and foundation grants: the same format, some examples, brief tips, and a full-blown sample proposal. The primary distinctions are in the area of institutional need. The strategies for impressing a profit-oriented corporation are often different from those needed when addressing a non-profit foundation or the government.

Interestingly, Susan L. Washburn's "Stalking the Corporate and Foundation Dollar" (1980) discusses just this question of the similarities and differences in seeking grants from corporations and foundations. Comparisons between the two are made in the areas of institutional need, types of research, avenues of approach, proposal writing, types of giving, local support, and follow-up.

Commercial contracts, the situation of a proposal from engineer/contractor to owner, is given significant attention by industry. Many works, as we have seen, cover government contracts as well, but some focus solely on the commercial bid. Most of these are articles in traditional engineering journals.

Roy J. Loring has two such articles in *Chemical Engineering*: "The Proposal Manager's Work" and "Cost of Preparing Proposals" (both 1970). The first is written to the owner, telling about the role of the proposal manager in owner/contractor relationships. While the primary purpose of "The Proposal Manager's Work" is to clear up misunderstandings, the article does divide the bid package into technical, commercial, and cost components and also classifies types of bids—order-of-magnitude bids (made without detailed engineering data), approximate bids (made without detailed engineering data but prorated from previous similar projects), and definite bids (made with well-defined engineering data). The last-named article is a guide to help the contractor prepare a detailed proposal budget. "Engineering Proposals" (1965) by Steele Morris is another article in a traditional engineering journal. It tells how to blend engineering and salesmanship in the preparation of a commercial contract proposal. The article stresses the importance of writing since the proposal must often stand alone, but it discusses general strategies and evaluation criteria rather than specific parts.

Morris's article is old, but David L. Caldwell's "Techniques and Practices of Proposal Writing" (1959) is even older. Still, its discussion of contract bids in the chemical and petroleum industry has some interest. Caldwell discusses concepts such as persuasion, definition, and organization within the context of a proposal from engineer/contractor to owner. Some general tips and techniques are included, but the writing section is simplistic, relying on buzz words like "accuracy," "brevity," "clarity," and "explicitness."

Finally, Stephen A. Kliment's "Writing for Marketing Impact" (1977) tells design professionals how to, among other things, write commercial proposals that sell.

As indicated earlier, internal proposals is a potentially confusing category. The inclusion of reports in Hillman's *The Art of Writing Business Reports and Proposals* (1981) again points out the difficulty in avoiding confusion between informal proposals and other types of reports. For example, Harold K. Mintz's "Memos That Get Things Moving" (1981) discusses reports that are intended to achieve action on the part of the reader; yet what he suggests in terms of strategy and presentation is applicable to internal proposals as well. (Mintz's article is representative of many other works that make a similar identification of proposals and reports.)

The textbooks and handbooks section (below) includes works that begin to focus squarely on the internal/informal proposal as a distinct type. In an article that also seems to do this, "To Get What You Need" (1980), James E. Barr argues that written internal proposals are the most effective means of requesting equipment, supplies, programs, and other needs. Yet even in stressing the importance of these internal proposals, Barr refers to them as *formal written proposals*. It is hoped that as writers become more aware of the possible proposal writing situations, the formal/informal distinction will become clearer.

Specific "How-to's" by Need

In writing about proposals, many authors speak to audiences with support needs in specific areas. The areas covered in this section are education, university research, health, libraries, social services, and other fields.

It is amazing how many short works exist to tell educators how best to apply for government and foundation grants. This undoubtedly reflects the importance of federal funding to the operation of educational institutions, but it also reflects the proclivity of educators to write and publish, the naïveté of educators in the area of proposal writing, and the eagerness of educational journals and information exchanges to accept works on this topic.

The content of most of these works on educational proposals tends to be restatements of the advice given in the general "how-to's," but directed to particular audiences. The level of sophistication is very low, since the primary audience seems to be people who have never tried proposal writing before. Overall, the following works are not recommended for people interested in general proposal research, except as a significant source of popularly held notions about proposal writing.

Many of the works on proposal writing for educators are guides generated by local agencies, institutions, and workshops primarily for local, specific needs. Funding for vocational and technical education is an extremely popular topic. The Kentucky State Department of Education has both a handbook to tell how to seek vocational educational funds from the state and federal governments (*A Guide for the Development of Proposals, Progress, and Final Reports* [1976]) and the proceedings of a conference to give vocational educators practical training in writing proposals (Floyd L. McKinney and E. Norman Sims, *Proceedings of a Series of Workshops* [1974]). Pennsylvania's Department of Education also has a report from a workshop to help vocational educators seek federal funds (Ernest L. Peters, *Workshop in Proposal Writing* [1972]), while West Virginia's Department of Education has a detailed guide to preparation and submission of applications for funds to support vocational education (*Procedural Guide for Writing Proposals* [1968]). Florida's Division of Vocational Education of the Department of Education has a two-book series for vocational educators, guiding them all the way from planning a proposal to managing the successful project (Nancy Grasser and Cynthia Halderson, *Guide to Proposal Writing, Book 1 and Book 2* [1981]). While these books are for beginners, they are far better than the simplistic and mechanical handbook for preparing research and development projects in vocational-technical education put out by Tennessee's Board for Vocational Education (Edwin E. Lamberth, *Preparing Research and Development Proposals* [1973]).

Indiana's Board of Vocational and Technical Education did something a little more innovative and far more constructive than introductory guides and workshops. *Indiana Vocational-Technical Education Research and Service Center. Final Report* (1979) reports the results of an assessment of 60 vo-tech proposals from the previous year and, among other conclusions, finds that the content of documents is consistently less effective than the format. This is not surprising, given that so many works present simplistic advice on how to mechanically construct a proposal.

Some works are directed to community college educators. Boston University's *Guidelines for the Proposal Writer* (1969) gives the usual mechanics, strategy, logic, and style of proposal writing arising from a Kellog-sponsored workshop. As in the vo-tech area, this emphasis on mechanics seems to have done little good, since Edward Robings's "Proposal Writing" (1971) presents suggestions from a proposal evaluator arising from the general inadequacy of community college proposals. Unfortunately, most of Robings's suggestions do not directly focus on the actual writing of the proposal.

For elementary school educators there is Carol M. Anderson's *Proposal Writing* (1974) which gives the specific procedure for Title III, ESEA proposals by focusing on the case of one successful elementary school, and Clement A. Seldon and Robert N. Maloy's "Public School Grant Writing" (1981) which similarly describes the success of a grant writing office in a Massachusetts school district. For secondary school principals and faculty, David E. Rawnsley's "Proposal Writing Made Palatable" (1979) presents a proposal writing checklist.

Other educational areas are not without their introductory works on proposal writing. Carol Sterling's *Arts Proposal Writing* (1982) is a workbook-type, step-by-step set of instructions for arts educators. *Proposal Writer's Handbook* (1973) is HEW's guide to "pre-", writing, and "post-" concerns for special education proposal writers. For the speech educator, there is Carol A. Esterreicher and

Ralph J. Haw's "Writing Funding Proposals for Speech-Language Staff Development Projects" (1982), which focuses on a proposal management procedure used in a Utah school district. For science educators, there is "Requesting Support for Science Programs" (1976) by Wendell F. McBurney and Doris H. Merritt. Donald Clark's "Planning for Block Grants" (1982) is a brief tip for industrial educators, telling them that if they recognize the similarities between a mass production project and block grant funding, their project proposals will be easier to generate.

Finally, a number of works on proposal writing are directed to educators in general. Most are guides and introductory works similar to those written for specific audiences. These works can present detailed, step-by-step procedures (Gerald V. Teague and Betty S. Heathington, *The Process of Grant Proposal Development* [1980]); focus on various possible proposal writing outlines (Henry T. Gayley, *How to Write for Development* [1981]); focus on evaluation criteria (*How to Know That You Have Met Federal Teachers Centers Application Criteria* [1981]); give tips on packaging (Carmen L. Battaglia, "How to Ask for Federal Funding" [1977]); present proposal writing exercises (Howard F. Alvir, *A Systematic Approach to Proposal Writing* [1976]); report results of specific proposal development training projects (Robert L. Alford, *Interinstitutional Program for Proposal Development* [1981]); present alternative management systems to streamline proposal development (Frederick G. Knirk, "Systematic Alternatives to Proposal Preparation" [1975]); or give general strategy tips on the entire proposal writing process (Peter J. Hampton, "Writing the Funding Proposal" [1973]; Dave Honchalk, "For Those Who Help Themselves" [1981]).

It would be interesting to investigate whether a connection exists between the great number of works on educational proposal writing and the reported low quality of educational proposals.

The works on university research are generally of a higher quality than those for educational development. Here authors tend to speak to a more sophisticated, better focused, and highly motivated audience. David R. Krothvohl's *How to Prepare a Research Proposal* (1977) is a much consulted work, particularly useful for the actual writing of proposals. Although it is aimed primarily at those seeking funding for behavioral science research, it is often cited by proposal writers in other areas. This is primarily because of its careful section-by-section presentation of the research proposal problem statement, discussion of related research, statement of objectives, procedure, facilities, budget, and abstract. Not only does Krothvohl give a helpful discussion of proposal research design, but he also provides a detailed, practical checklist for preparing the proposal.

Also useful, though directed toward new proposal writers, is Robert E. McAdam, Michael Maher, and John F. McAteer's *Research and Project Funding for the Uninitiated* (1982). This work covers developing the idea and actual proposal writing for those seeking external research funding in colleges and universities. Similarly to Krothvohl, McAdam and colleagues break down proposal writing into problem, related studies, objectives, procedure, evaluation and dissemination, personnel, facilities, budget, and appendices (resumés, bibliographies, reprints, charts and tables, letters). There is a particularly good discussion of budget considerations.

Less good is Patricia R. Orlich and Donald C. Orlich's *The Art of Writing a Successful R&D Proposal* (1977). Here the actual discussion of writing the proposal sections is sketchy and not well focused, though it covers the standard parts. Perhaps the problem is that Orlich and Orlich's earlier guide, *Writing a Successful Research Grant Proposal* (1975), was directed primarily to vocational educators and combined discussion of proposals for research, demonstration, and development. Even more poorly focused is Howard P. Alvir's *A Detailed Sample* (1975), which jumps from research to curriculum development, from grant to contract.

The government has its own sourcebook for higher education: Audrey Richards's *The Complete Grants Sourcebook for Higher Education* (1980). While this is primarily a directory of funding sources, it also has a section on how to seek grant support. The work follows the usual three-part division of ''pre-'' (focus on organization preparation), actual proposal writing, and ''post-'' followup. In addition, Washington has sponsored *Helpful Hints for External Funding Proposal Development* (Harold Harty and Robert Seibel [1973]) which includes a sample proposal, and *Educational Research Development and Evaluation* (Patrica B. Campbell and colleagues [1981]), which reports on a workshop for professionals, designed to increase participants' skills in project development, proposal writing, and research and evaluation methodology.

Universities often provide their own research proposal guides. These tend to be directed toward those with little or no experience in writing proposals for sponsored research. As such, they give skeletal breakdowns of the process that are comprehensive but superficial. They also contain information that pertains only to grant seeking at their particular institution. Three such representative works are *Proposal Preparation Guide* (1971, Case Western Reserve University), *Proposal Writer's Guide* (1975, University of Michigan), and *A Manual on Proposal Writing & Research Techniques* (Linda E. Brown [1976] Texas Southern University).

Some works focus on student proposals for academic research. Lawrence F. Locke and Waneen Myrick Spirduso (*Proposals That Work* [1976]) follow Krothvohl's ideas, but gear them to graduate students writing research proposals for theses and dissertations. The book is very useful and gives much attention to the planning stage and a number of sample proposals. In ''The Campus Bread Game'' (1974), Ernest J. Scalberg suggests that student-initiated projects would be more successful at securing funding if students were given more experience in proposal writing. These student-oriented works offer a unique perspective on proposal writing.

A few works provide grant writing help for health professionals. Harry A. Sultz and Francis S. Sherwin's *Grant Writing for Health Professionals* (1981) has the most general scope. Placed between ''pre-'' (cultivating sponsors) and "post-" (review process and site visit) sections is a writing section that contains detailed discussion and examples of proposal sections (problem, objectives, method, evaluation, budget, and appendices). Unfortunately, attempts to handle tone and style rely on simple do's and dont's. More closely focused on public health concerns is Liane Reif-Lehrer's *Writing a Successful Grant Application* (1982). This is a close examination of the NIH grant, but the only samples provided are of summary statements. For dental researchers, A. S. Bleiweis's "Preparation of the Grant Proposal" (1981) is a brief "how-to" for the NIH grant. For nurses, Dorothy L. Sexton's "Developing Skills in Grant Writing" (1982) discusses "pre-" (planning the budget), "post-" (the review process), and application writing concerns.

Only a few works focus on grants for libraries, but two of them are significant. Richard W. Boss's *Grant Money and How to Get It* (1980) is the best work on grantsmanship for librarians. It has a "pre-" section of sources, assessment of chance, and so on, and an extensive writing section with a detailed breakdown of the proposal into title page, compliance and exemption forms, abstract, contents, statement of need, objectives, methodology, qualifications, dissemination, evaluation, budget, and appendix. Also useful but less detailed in its treatment of actual writing is Emmett Corry's *Grants for Libraries* (1982). Corry divides his work by what the grant is for: media program, college and university library, public library, and so forth, and spends considerable time covering pre-writing concerns. His writing section is more general than Boss's, however, dividing the proposal into abstract, introduction, problem, objectives, methods and procedures, evaluation, budget, and summary.

The primary author in the area of social services grantsmanship is Armand Lauffer, who has a nine-volume series to improve child placement practices, *Sage Human Services Guides*. Volume 1, *Grantsmanship* (1977), is devoted entirely to discussion of gaining government support for child placement projects, but Volume 6, *Resources for Child Placement and Other Human Services* (1979), is also particularly useful in both identifying and interacting with social service agencies. Especially fascinating is Chapter 11, which describes a simulation game called RFP in which players attempt to gain "Resources for Permanence" by filling out grant proposal forms in response to detailed "Requests for Proposals." In *How to Raise Money for Kids* (1978), Anne Burr Dodge presents a general guide to proposal writing for social service organizations, with heavy emphasis on finding the appropriate source. In "Finding the Green" (1980), Mary E. Nolan offers fund raising and proposal writing hints to directors of early childhood programs.

There remain a few areas with works covering their particular fund raising needs. Easily the most significant work is Virginia P. White's *Grants for the Arts* (1980), which covers grant seeking in the arts in the same manner that her highly successful *Grants* (1975) covered the general grant seeking process. The book contains extensive sections on "pre-", writing, and "post-" concerns, with special attention to sources for grants in the arts.

In the area of community development, Terry Marshall's *How to Write Proposals for State, Federal and Private Funds* (1977) is the second of a series of three books designed to help rural Americans improve their communities. This handbook contains considerable information from major components of the proposal and detailed discussion of the preparation, submission, and followup process, to when to use a consultant. Another work directed to community development is "The Secret of Successful Proposals" (1980), which argues that state, county, and local governments should adopt practices used successfully by private sector firms in their search for federal funding.

For occupational researchers there is *A Guide for the Preparation of Proposals in Occupational Research, Development, and Training* (1969). This work, however, is dated (research priorities for 1966–67 are presented) and focuses primarily on proposals to the state of Delaware.

Textbooks and Handbooks

The textbooks and handbooks included in this section are works in technical or business writing that devote some segment of their coverage to proposal writing. This coverage may be as much as an extensive chapter or as little as a brief paragraph.(Not all existing texts and handbooks have been examined.) What follows is a representative sample, and it should not be assumed, therefore, that all works omitted from this discussion exclude the proposal. It is worth noting, however, that many texts on business or technical writing have no coverage of proposal writing. Oddly, works that devote so much time to reporting the results of research often ignore the primary means of acquiring this type of work.

Technical writing textbooks are the most likely to treat proposal writing in the broad sense presented earlier in this chapter. Anne Eisenberg's *Effective Technical Communication* (1982) is particularly good in this sense. When she states that proposals "solicit new business, compete for research money, bid for a government contract, and justify a new expenditure, typically for equipment" (p. 235), she covers commercial contracts; government, foundation, and corporate grants; government contracts; and internal proposals all in one sentence. Her chapter on preparing proposals discusses proposal segments (problem, objectives, procedure, evaluation, follow-up, qualifications, budget, abstract, and summary), examines proposal audiences, and has good, though limited, exercises. Guidelines for NSF and NIH proposals are given, along with a sample research proposal.

Leslie A. Olsen and Thomas N. Huckin's *Principles of Communication for Science and Technology* (1983) is also effective. It mentions all types of proposals but pays special attention to the internal, short informal proposal. The work discusses the formal proposal, both long and short, and gives a sample short formal proposal; it is best, however, on the informal proposal, and includes a sample short informal proposal for an in-house computer demonstration.

Thomas E. Pearsall and Donald H. Cunningham's *How to Write for the World of Work* (1978) includes a chapter that covers general proposal writing, but the authors do not include the informal proposal in their definition of "proposal." The chapter uses the solicited versus unsolicited distinction, presents brief writing tips and appropriate content, and has samples related to NSF and educational funding. Also quite general is Kenneth W. Houp and Thomas E. Pearsall's proposal chapter in *Reporting Technical Information* (1980), which has a breakdown consisting only of Introduction, Body, Conclusion, and Attachments. Discussion of particulars in each of these sections helps overcome this generality. The focus is essentially commercial, and the chapter presents a sample short, unsolicited, proposal letter.

A number of technical writing textbooks focus on proposals as bids for government and commercial contracts. James Miles, Donald Bush, and Allin Kaplan see the proposal as securing new business through contracts, and in *Technical Writing* (1982) they take a nice story approach to a sample case leading to a student proposal. This proposal chapter also uses the solicited versus unsolicited distinction (most texts do, for it seems to be an easy distinction for a general text). It divides the proposal into a technical section (introduction, statement of work, technical approach), management section (project orientation, resumés, facilities, related experience, schedules) and cost section (prices, qualifications, and so on).

Theodore A. Sherman's proposal coverage in *Modern Technical Writing* (1966) also focuses on commercial bids. He uses the major versus minor instead of the standard formal versus informal distinction, but he does a good job of emphasizing the importance of proposal writing. He presents a sample proposal by Texas Instruments to study solid-state instrumentation techniques.

Not all technical writing texts give adequate coverage to proposal writing. Joseph A. Alvarez's *The Elements of Technical Writing* (1980) is quite weak, attempting to cover general proposal writing in three pages. Two of these pages are a sample informal proposal to recommend construction that fits squarely into the confusing grey area between the internal proposal and recommendation report.

David E. Fear's (*Technical Communication* [1981]) coverage is sketchy, breaking the proposal into a layman part and a technical part. A sample commercial construction proposal is included. Willis H. Waldo (*Better Report Writing* [1965]) has a short section on the research and technical report, with a focus on commercial bids.

Herman M. Weisman's *Basic Technical Writing* (1980) is one of the few technical writing texts to cover grant proposals, but the chapter is brief and sketchy. Most of it is a sample proposal for an information and technology transfer program.

Some technical writing texts place a distinct student emphasis on proposal writing. In *Technical Writing* (1978), Deborah C. Andrews and Margaret D. Blickle create a student involvement that would be particularly useful in the classroom. Their central theme is how to be persuasive, and they carry this out using student research proposals as a focus. Good exercises and sample organizational charts are included. John M. Lannon's popular *Technical Writing* (1982) also has a student emphasis, but in this case it leads to some confusion. The chapter presents a three-part proposal process: (1) Client Need (2) Proposal (3) Client Decision. Yet much of the rest of the chapter does not fit this outline, especially the use of student proposals for thesis research. The short sample of an internal, unsolicited proposal seems close to a recommendation report, and Lannon's definition that a proposal is an "offer to do something or *suggestion for action*" (p. 429) [my emphasis] adds to this confusion.

Business writing textbooks tend to focus on internal proposals if they include proposal writing at all. In discussing proposals, many business writing texts focus on simplistic tips about keeping them simple and straightforward, and they will even mention grammar, usage, punctuation, and capitalization. Mary A. DeVries (*Guide to Better Business Writing* [1981]) does this in a four-paragraph section on proposals. *Business Communications* (William C. Himstreet and Wayne Murlin Baty [1981]) is only slightly better in discussing proposals and recommendations primarily in letter form.

Other business writing texts with limited proposal coverage include *Business Communication Dynamics* (Bobbye Sorrels Persing [1981]) which has a fairly extensive example of a research and development proposal; *Communicating in Business* (Richard Hatch [1977]) which has a sample research proposal broken down into background, problem, goals, research plan, and cost sections; *Business Report Writing* (Phillip V. Lewis and William H. Baker [1978]) which has a sample internal research proposal with brief hints on writing each section; *Writing and Communicating in Business* (J. Harold Janis [1973]) which, again, has a brief section with a sample internal proposal; and *Communication for Management and Business* (Norman B. Sigband [1976]) which barely mentions proposals. Fortunately, there are some exceptions to this weak coverage of proposal writing in business writing texts.

In *Communication at Work* (1977) Roger P. Wilcox has a 68-page chapter on writing effective proposals and reports. His focus is on internal proposals to persuade managers to give authorization for projects and equipment. Wilcox spends more time on logic than do authors of most works, discussing how to go from objective, real world facts to convincing subjective judgments and proposals. Herta A. Murphy and Charles E. Peck have two sections in *Effective Business Communications* (1976)—one on short informal reports and proposals and one on formal proposals, by which they mean commercial bids. They present samples of an internal proposal to get a project accepted and an external proposal to get work for the company. Louis J. Visco (*The Manager as an Editor* [1981]) also uses this internal/external distinction in his discussion of the manager's role in the proposal writing process. For Visco, external proposals mean bids for government and commercial contracts. The chapter divides the external proposal into summary, problem statement, statement of work, technical approach, program management, program schedule, and program cost. David W. Ewing (*Writ-*

ing for Results [1979]) focuses on internal proposals for new projects but also includes the government contract proposal under his ''report patterns.'' He follows the common technical/management/cost breakdown of proposal writing and includes a number of examples.

In general, technical writing texts are far better sources for information on proposal writing than are business writing and communication texts.

Unlike textbooks, handbooks, by their very nature, attempt to treat a subject in a brief, mechanistic way; yet the importance of proposal writing and the need for handy references on it can be seen in the extensive treatment handbooks often give.

In *The Business Writing Handbook* (1981), William C. Paxson devotes a major section to proposals. He gives a general definition that covers all proposals save the internal; makes the solicited versus unsolicited distinction; gives a basic format; emphasizes the sales approach; and presents two samples, one commercial (to relocate an antenna) and one social (to study police-community relations).

Most handbooks focus on proposal writing for contracts in response to government and commercial RFPs. R. S. Blicq's *Guidelines for the Report Writer* (1982) contains a useful chapter on ''Suggestions and Proposals'' which presents the pieces of a formal contract proposal and what goes into them, along with internal proposals that he breaks into ''semi-formal'' and informal. Harry E. Chandler's chapter in *Technical Writers Handbook* (1983) covers both company response to RFPs and unsolicited proposals to do research financed in and out of the company. Chandler presents sample formats from major companies, and divides the contract proposal into introduction, summary, statement of problem, technical discussion, and program plan. He also includes a random sampling of proposal reader criticisms that consist of useless pithy phrases like ''often too wordy . . . theme or message sometimes difficult to follow or find'' (p. 234).

Robert W. Bly and Gary Blake (*Technical Writing* [1982]) focus on proposals for the company which is attempting to provide services, products, or ideas to potential buyers at a specific cost, usually in response to an RFP. The brief section divides these proposals into technical and cost segments, sometimes with an executive summary. Earl G. Bingham's (*Pocketbook for Technical and Professional Writers* [1982]) proposal section also focuses on responses to RFPs, and it breaks down the proposal into summary, contents, introduction, technical discussion, tasks, project organization, schedules, costs, and qualifications. Bingham also tries to distinguish between reports and proposals by claiming that reports chronicle past accomplishments while proposals suggest future tasks. (This would make all recommendations into proposals.)

The Research and Report Handbook (1981) by R. Moyer, E. Stevens, and R. Switzer has a chapter on proposals with very little text, most of it being a sample commercial proposal. Charles T. Brusaw, Gerald J. Alred, and Walter E. Oliu's *The Business Writer's Handbook* (1976) also has a brief section divided into two parts, one for the government contract proposal and the other for the sales (commercial) contract proposal. There are brief samples in each part. Finally, Siegfried Mandel's *Writing for Science and Technology* (1970) has a proposal writing chapter that defines a proposal as a "request for a contract to do a certain job." He covers the contract proposal in detail, including drawings and Bill of Material. Most of the chapter is a sample proposal to the Air Force for radar analysis of bird movements, but there are comments on the sample.

Empirical Research

While very little empirical research is conducted in the area of proposal writing, there is just enough to show what proposal writing research can do and how desperately it is needed. In addition to empirical research, case studies will be included in this section.

The preceding overview of well over 100 works essentially describes "how-to's." Contained in these "how-to's" are literally thousands of tips, suggestions, and instructions on how to write proposals. In each case, the authority behind the authors' advice is their experience and knowledge. How can we know which advice is effective and, when there are disagreements, who is correct?

In 1953, communication researchers asserted that two-sided communication (with both supportive and refutational defense) is superior to one-sided communication (with just supportive defense). Over 20 years later, Robert D. Dycus decided to test this widely accepted principle. He placed 27 experienced government proposal evaluators in a room and had them rank mock proposals using both one-sided and two-sided arguments. Dycus ("Relative Efficacy of a One-sided vs. Two-Sided Communication in a Simulated Government Evaluation of Proposals" [1976]) found that evaluation scores, while in the predicted direction, did not differ significantly and failed to substantiate the advantage of two-sided communication.

With so much proposal writing strategy asserted by so many authors primarily on the basis of personal experience, the testing of these assertions is clearly a wide-open area for research in proposal writing. Only when this research is conducted and verified will we be able to describe confidently those conventions most effective in the various types of proposal writing.

Another effort to verify effective proposal features is Kjell R. Knudsen's *Emphasis in Educational Research* (1974), which analyzed some 3,000 proposals submitted for research grants in education in an effort to identity research features that seem to receive priority.

Other research studies focus on the attitudes and assumptions of proposal writers. In "Proposal Preparation, Negotiation and Award" (1976), Arthur B. Jebens reports the results of a study to determine the impact of federal agency requirements on proposal preparation. Among the communication difficulties Jebens found was that the difference between grand and contract was not clear (a problem that authors of works about proposal writing share). William E. Loadman and Desmond Cook's study of the proposal writing perceptions of educational researchers ("Developing and Assessing Instrumentation to Reflect Perceptions and Attitudes Toward Proposal Development and Funding" [1982]) also identifies many misconceptions among proposal writers, though many perceptions are identified as truths as well. Perceptions are also grouped according to sex and previous experience.

A final piece of research worth mentioning, though not directly related to proposal writing, is Gerald V. Teague and Betty S. Heathington's study of the cost-efficiency of proposal preparation in colleges and universities ("Proposal Applications" [1979]). They found that proposals represented a return ten times over the initial investment.

While case studies are not empirical research, when well done they are another effective form of research into the workings of and factors affecting fund raising. Far and away the best book of this type is Virginia P. White's *Grant Proposals That Succeeded* (1983). This work focuses on federal grant writing, adding at the end a section on federal contracts by Teague and another on approaching foundations and corporations by Hennessey. Most of the book, however, is a series of detailed case studies including historical background on the types of grants, history and development of the project, proposal preparation, and post-proposal activities. Part I of White's book covers research grants and includes biomedical science (NIH), social science (NIMH), and engineering (NSF). Part II covers training grants and includes curriculum development (CETA), applied social research (NIHM), and a health advocacy master's program (Florence V. Burden Foundation). Part III covers the arts and includes youth involvement in opera (three California foundations), an art exhibition (NEA), a movie (the Film Fund), and theater for rehabilitation (Ford Foundation). Part IV is on the humanities and presents a proposal for a sequence of interdisciplinary humanistic courses (NEH).

Other case studies are far less ambitious or effective. *Proposal Writer's Swipe File III* (1981), edited by Susan Ezell and colleagues, is more a collection of models than of case studies, primarily from foundation grants. C. H. Knoblauch's "Intentionality in the Writing Process" (1980) presents a case of proposal writing by executives in a large consulting firm.

Teaching

This final section covers a number of articles on the teaching of proposal writing. Those articles either present the advantages of using proposals in the writing classroom, or tell how proposal writing should be taught.

Josep S. Horobetz ("No Chapter on Proposal Writing" [1978]) calls the teaching of proposal writing a mini-course in itself since it incorporates all the techniques of technical writing. He also provides a sample outline of how to teach proposals. Similarly, G. E. Kennedy ("Teaching Formal Proposals" [1983]) points out the advantages of teaching formal proposals, including the practical benefits to the student and the extensive use of technical writing techniques. Bill

G. Rainey ("Proposal Writing" [1974]) complains that proposal writing instruction is neglected and offers suggestions for developing courses on proposal writing. Mary Ellen Campbell ("Proposal Writing" [1981]) points out how proposal writing can create student interest in business, while Dennis E. Minor ("Teaching the Technical Writing Proposal" [1979]) simply makes suggestions on how to teach the writing of technical proposals.

Last, and best, is Frank Smith's "Education for Proposal Writers" (1976) which nicely shifts the focus from the proposal to the writer. Smith describes the work done by proposal writers in the aerospace industry and suggests how educational institutions could better prepare students for this work.

Conclusion

Works on proposal writing, taken as a whole, form a large body of advice on what constitutes a successful proposal in each of its types. This advice is organized in a number of ways, mainly by type of proposal and area of need. Unfortunately, no matter how it is organized, this advice shares one common feature—it is in dire need of objective verification since it is based on the personal experience and expertise of the authors.

Future work in proposal writing should consist of empirical studies that test, claim by claim, the large amount of advice already in print. The task is great since research like that conducted by Dycus is arduous and must be replicated. Such research, however, is the only way we can confidently claim to know which proposal writing conventions are the most effective.

References

Alford, Robert L. *Interinstitutional Program for Proposal Development.* 1981, ERIC ED 204454.

Alvarez, Joseph A. *The Elements of Technical Writing.* New York: Harcourt, 1980.

Alvir, Howard P. *A Detailed Sample of the Minute Analysis and Planning That Precedes the Final Draft of a Request for Research Grant.* 1975. ERIC ED 115753.

———. *A Systematic Approach to Proposal Writing.* 1976. ERIC ED 123655.

Ammon-Wexler, Jill and Catherine Carmer. *How to Create a Winning Proposal.* Santa Cruz, Calif.: Mercury Communications, 1976.

Anderson, Carol M. *Proposal Writing: A Strategy for Funding and Curriculum Improvement. A Practicum Report.* 1974. ERIC Ed 089451.

Andrews, Deborah C., and Margaret D. Blickle. *Technical Writing: Principles and Forms.* New York: Macmillan, 1978.

Barr, James E. "To Get What You Need—Supply the Facts." *Bal Sheet*, 62 (1980), 75–78, 93.

Battaglia, Carmen L. "How to Ask for Federal Funding." *Am Ed*, 13, No. 6 (1977), 6–9.

Bingham, Earl G. *Pocketbook for Technical and Professional Writers.* Belmont, Calif.: Wadsworth, 1982.

Bleiweis, A. S. "Preparation of the Grant Proposal." *J Dent Res*, 60 (1981), 294.

Blicq, R. S. *Guidelines for the Report Writer*. Englewood Cliffs, N.J.: Prentice-Hall, 1982.

Bly, Robert W., and Gary Blake. *Technical Writing: Structure, Standards, and Style*. New York: McGraw-Hill, 1982.

Boiler Room Proposal Writing. Minneapolis: Honeywell DSD Communications Department, 1972.

Boss, Richard W. *Grant Money and How to Get It: A Handbook for Libraries*. New York: Bowker, 1980.

Brakely, George A., Jr. *Tested Ways to Successful Fund Raising*. New York: AMCOM, 1980.

Brown, Linda E. *A Manual on Proposal Writing & Research Techniques*. Houston: Texas Southern University Urban Resources Center, 1976. ERIC ED 135063.

Brusaw, Charles T., Gerald J. Alred, and Walter E. Oliu. *The Business Writer's Handbook*. New York: St. Martin's, 1976.

Caldwell, David L. "Techniques and Practices of Proposal Writing." In *Writing in Industry*. Vol. I. Ed. Siegfried Mandel. New York: Plenum, 1959, pp. 53–63.

Campbell, Mary Ellen. "Proposal Writing: An Effective Way to Peak Student Interest in Business." *ABCA Bul*, 44, No. 4 (1981), 30–32.

Campbell, Patricia B., et al. *Educational Research Development and Evaluation: A Training Curriculum*. 1981, ERIC ED 220469.

Catalog of Federal Domestic Assistance Annual. Washington, D.C.: U.S. Office of Management and Budget (annual).

Chandler, Harry E. *Technical Writers Handbook*. Metals Park, Ohio: American Society for Metals, 1983.

Clark, Donald. "Planning for Block Grants." *Indus Educ*, 71, No. 6 (1982), 8, 11.

Clayton, B. "The Other Side of Proposal Writing—People." *Pers Guid J*, 60 (1982), 629–32.

Cohen, John M., and Terry Marshall. *How to Gather Information on Community Needs and Funding Sources. Resources for Rural Development Series: Handbook No. 1*, Ithaca, N.Y.: Cornell University, Department of Rural Sociology, 1976. ERIC ED 212397.

Conrad, Daniel L., et al. *The Grants Planner*. San Francisco: Public Management Institute, 1979.

Cook, D. F., and L. B. Blanton. *Writing to Win*. Scotia, N.Y.: General Electric Co. 1975.

Corry, Emmett. *Grants for Libraries*, Littleton, Colo.: Libraries Unltd, 1982.

Daniels, Craig E. *A Budget Primer and Worksheets for Proposal Writers*. Washington, D.C.: Association of American Colleges, 1979. ERIC Ed 201241.

Davidson, Jeffrey P., and Barry D. Rosenberg. "Contract Proposals: Sharing the Wealth with Uncle Sam." *J Appl Manag*, 5, No. 4 (1980), 10–11, 31.

DeBakey, Lois, and Selma DeBakey. "The Art of Persuasion: Logic and Language in Proposal Writing." *Grants Mag*, 1 (1978), 43–60.

Dermer, Joseph. *A Guide to Foundation Fund Raising Under the Reagan Administration*. New York: Public Service Materials Center, 1982.

———. *How to Raise Funds from Foundations*. 3rd ed. New York: Public Service Materials Center, 1979.

————. *How to Write Successful Foundation Presentations*. New York: Public Service Materials Center, 1974.

Des Marais, Philip. *How to Get Government Grants*. 2nd ed. New York: Public Service Materials Center, 1977.

"Developing the Successful Grant Proposal." *Federal Aid Planner* (Winter 1973), 10–16.

DeVries, Mary A. *Guide to Better Business Writing*. Piscataway, N.J.: New Century Publishers, 1981.

Dodge, Anne Burr. *How to Raise Money for Kids (Public and Private)*. Washington, D.C.: Coalition for Children and Youth, 1978. ERIC ED 160204.

Duca, Diane. "New Strategy for Writing Proposals Now Necessary." *Fund Raising Manag*, 12, No. 12 (1982), 58.

Dycus, Robert D. "Relative Efficacy of a One-Sided vs. Two-Sided Communication in a Simulated Government Evaluation of Proposals." *Psychol Rev*, 38 (1976), 787–90.

Eisenberg, Anne. *Effective Technical Communication*. New York: McGraw-Hill, 1982.

Englebret, David. "Storyboarding a Better Way of Planning and Writing Proposals." *IEEE Trans Prof Comm*, 15, No. 72 (1972), 115–18.

Esterreicher, Carol A., and Ralph J. Haws. "Writing Funding Proposals for Speech-Language Staff Development Projects." *Lang Speech Hear Serv Schools*, 13, No. 3 (1982), 163–71.

Ewing, David W. *Writing for Results in Business, Government, the Sciences, the Professions*. New York: Wiley, 1979.

Ezell, Susan, et al., eds. *Proposal Writer's Swipe File III*. Washington, D.C.: Taft Corp., 1981.

Fear, David E. *Technical Communication*. 2nd ed. Glenview, Ill.: Scott, Foresman, 1981.

Foundation Library Center. *Some Suggestions by Foundations on the Preparation of Proposals*. New York: Foundation Center, 1969.

Gayley, Henry T. *How to Write for Development: Better Communication Brings Bigger Dollar Results*. Washington D.C.: CASE Publications, 1981. ERIC ED 212203.

Glass, Sandra A. "A Winning Strategy: For Victory in the Home Stretch, Spend More Time Cultivating Foundations and Less Mailing Proposals." *CASE Curr*, 6, No. 5 (1980), 29–31.

Goodson, G., and S. Hart. *How to Storyboard*. San Mateo, Calif.: TRW Systems Group, 1970.

Grantsmanship: Money and How to Get It. 2nd ed. Published by editors of the *Annual Register of Grant Support*, Chicago, Ill.: Marquis, 1978.

Grasser, Nancy, and Cynthia Halderson. *Guide to Proposal Writing and Project Management in Vocational Education. Book 1: Planning a Proposal*. Tallahassee: Florida State Department of Education, Division of Vocational Education, 1981. ERIC ED 206819.

————. *Guide to Proposal Writing and Project Management in Vocational Education. Book 2: Project Management*. Tallahasee: Florida State Department of Education, Division of Vocational Education, 1981. ERIC ED 206820.

Greenly, Robert B. *How to Win Government Contracts*. New York: Van Nostrand, 1983.

A Guide for the Development of Proposals, Progress, and Final Reports. Frankfort: Kentucky State Department of Education, 1976. ERIC ED 115748.

A Guide for the Preparation of Proposals in Occupational Research, Development, and Training. Dover: Delaware Occupational Research Coordinating Unit, 1969. ERIC ED 022917.

Guidelines for the Proposal Writer (Report of the Community College Proposal Writers' Workshop; Boston University, December 14, 1968). Boston: Boston University School of Education, 1969. ERIC ED 031201.

Guyton, Robert D., and Thomas R. Schaeffer. *Prerequisites for Winning Government R&D Contracts.* Dayton, Ohio: Universal Technology Corp., 1970.

Hall, Mary Jo. *Developing Skills in Proposal Writing.* 2nd ed. Portland, Oreg.: Continuing Education Publications, 1977.

Hampton, Peter J. "Writing the Funding Proposal." *J Coll Univ Pers Assoc*, 24, No. 4 (1973), 57–63.

Harty, Harold, and Robert Seibel. *Helpful Hints for External Funding Proposal Development. Teacher Education Forum Series. Vol. 1, No. 12*, Bloomington: Indiana University School of Education, 1973. ERIC ED 096271.

Hatch, Richard. *Communicating in Business.* Chicago: SRA, 1977.

Hellwig, Susan A., and Jerry E. Mandel. *Funding Resources for the Communication Arts and Sciences.* Falls Church, Va.: Speech Communication Association, 1979. ERIC ED 177645.

Hillman, Howard. *The Art of Winning Corporate Grants.* New York: Vanguard, 1980.

———. *The Art of Winning Foundation Grants.* New York: Vanguard, 1975.

———. *The Art of Winning Government Grants.* New York: Vanguard, 1977.

———. *The Art of Writing Business Reports and Proposals.* New York: Vanguard, 1981.

Himstreet, William C., and Wayne Murlin Baty. *Business Communications: Principles and Methods.* 6th ed. Boston: Kent, 1981.

Holcombe, Marya W., and Judith K. Stein. *Writing for Decision Makers: Reports and Memos with a Competitive Edge.* Belmont, Calif.: Lifetime Learning Publications, 1981.

Holtz, Herman. *Government Contracts: Proposalmanship and Winning Strategies.* New York: Plenum, 1979.

———, and T. Schmidt. *The Winning Proposal: How to Write It.* New York: McGraw-Hill, 1981.

Honchalk, Dave, "For Those Who Help Themselves...Grants." *Outdoor Comm*, 11, No. 4 (1981), 6–10.

Horobetz, Joseph S. " 'No Chapter on Proposal Writing' does not equal 'No Proposal Writing.' " *Tech Writ Teach*, 5 (1978), 95–96.

Houp, Kenneth W., and Thomas E. Pearsall. *Reporting Technical Information.* 4th ed. New York: Macmillan, 1980.

How to Know That You Have Met Federal Teachers Centers Application Criteria: A Guidebook Providing Some Indicators of Federal Criteria. Providence, R.I.: National Teacher Center Resource Center, 1981. ERIC ED 206607.

Indiana Vocational-Technical Education Research and Service Center. Final Report. Crawfordsville, Ind.: New Educational Directions, 1979. ERIC ED 186604.

Janis, J. Harold. *Writing and Communicating in Business.* New York: Macmillan, 1973.

Jebens, Arthur B. "Proposal Preparation, Negotiation and Award: Analysis and Recommendations." *J Soc Res Admin*, 8, No. 1 (1976), 29–34.

Jordon, Thomas E. *Proposal Writing.* Lake Charles, La.: Phi Delta Kappa, 1976.

Kennedy G. E. "Teaching Formal Proposals—A Versatile Minicourse in Technical Writing." *J Tech Writ Comm*, 13 (1983), 123–37.

Kiritz, Norton, J. "Program Planning and Proposal Writing." In *Annual Register of Grant Support*. Chicago: Marquis Academic Media, 1982–83, pp. xv–xxii.

Kliment, Stephen A. "Writing for Marketing Impact: Letters, Brochures, Proposals." *Architec Rec*, 161 (1977), 71–73.

Knirk, Frederick G., et al. "Systematic Alternatives to Proposal Preparation." Annual Meeting of the American Educational Research Association, Los Angeles. 13–17 Apr. 1975. ERIC ED 202880.

Knoblauch, C. H. "Intentionality in the Writing Process: A Case Study." *CCC*, 31 (1980), 153–59.

Knudsen, Kjell R., et al. *Emphasis in Educational Research: a Description of Selected Substantive and Methodological Characteristics of Proposals in the 1973 National Institute of Education Field Initiated Studies Program*. Washington D.C.: National Institute of Education, 1974. ERIC ED 096193.

Krothvohl, David R. *How to Prepare a Research Proposal*. Syracuse, N.Y.: Syracuse University, 1977.

Lamberth, Edwin E. *Preparing Research and Development Proposals for Vocational-Technical Education*. Nashville: Tennessee State Board for Vocational Education, 1973.

Lannon, John M. *Technical Writing*. 2nd ed. Boston: Little, Brown, 1982.

Lauffer, Armand. *Grantsmanship*. Beverly Hills, Calif.: SAGE, 1977.

———. *Resources for Child Placement and Other Human Services*. Beverly Hills, Calif.: SAGE, 1979.

Lawe, Theodore M. *How to Secure and Manage Foundation and Federal Funds in the 1980's*. Dallas: MRDC Educational Institute, 1980. ERIC ED 210962.

Lefferts, Robert. *Getting a Grant: How to Write Successful Grant Proposals*. Englewood Cliffs, N.J.: Prentice-Hall, 1978.

Lesikar, Raymond. *Report Writing for Business*. 6th ed. Homewood, Ill.: Richard D. Irwin, 1981.

Lewis, Phillip V., and William H. Baker. *Business Report Writing*. Columbus, Ohio: Grid, 1978.

Loadman, William E., and Desmond Cook. "Developing and Assessing Instrumentation to Reflect Perceptions and Attitudes Toward Proposal Development and Funding." Annual Meeting of the American Educational Research Association. New York, 19–23 Mar. 1982. ERIC ED 220496.

Locke, Lawrence F., and Waneen Wyrick Spirduso. *Proposals That Work: A Guide for Planning Research*. New York: Teacher's College Press, 1976.

Loring Roy J. "Cost of Preparing Proposals." *Chem Eng*, 77, No. 25 (1970), 126–27.

———. "The Proposal Manager's Work." *Chem Eng*, 77, No. 18 (1970), 98–102.

———, and Harold Kerzner. *Proposal Preparation and Management Handbook*. New York: Van Nostrand, 1982.

McAdam, Robert E., Michael Maher, and John F. McAteer, *Research and Project Funding for the Uninitiated*. Springfield, Ill.: Thomas, 1982.

McBurney, Wendall F., and Doris H. Merritt. "Requesting Support for Science Programs: An Exercise in Thoughtful Persuasion." *J Coll Sci Teach*, 6 (1976), 85–88.

McGuire, Betty E. "Plain English: The Language of Foundations." *New Direc Inst Advanc*, No. 11 (1981), 41–47.

McKinney, Floyd L., and E. Norman Sims, eds. *Proceedings of a Series of Workshops on Writing Research and Development Proposals: A Final Report*. Frankfort: Kentucky State Department of Education, Bureau of Vocational Education, 1974. ERIC ED 130054.

Mandel, Siegfried. *Writing for Science and Technology*. New York: Delta, 1970.

———, and David L. Caldwell. *Proposal and Inquiry Writing: Analysis, Techniques, Practices*. New York: Macmillan, 1962.

Marshall, Terry. *How to Write Proposals for State, Federal and Private Funds. Resources for Rural Development Series: Handbook No. 2*. Ithaca, N.Y.: Northeast Regional Center for Rural Development, 1977. ERIC ED 212398.

Maybee, Richard G. "A Process Approach to Proposal Development." *New Direc Cont Educ*, 3, No. 12 (1981), 5–18.

Meyer, J. *Writing Action Proposals: A Practical Guide*. Houston: Center for Human Resources, University of Houston, 1976.

Miles, James, Donald Bush, and Allin Kaplan. *Technical Writing: Principles and Practices*. Chicago: SRA, 1982.

Minor, Dennis E. "Teaching the Technical Writing Proposal." *Tech Writ Teach*, 7 (1979), 24–27.

Mintz, Harold K. "Memos That Get Things Moving." In *Effective Communication on the Job*. 3rd ed. Ed. William K. Fallon. New York: AMACOM, 1981.

Mohrman, Kathryn. *Federal Grants: A Basic Handbook*. Washington, D.C.: Federal Resources Advisory Service, 1977.

Morgenstern, Ellen. "Grantsmanship: Proposal Targeting and Drafting." *Academe*, 66, No. 2 (1980), 114–17.

Morris, Steele. "Engineering Proposals." *Mach Des*, 37, No. 11 (1965), 164–68.

Moyer, R., E. Stevens, and R. Switzer. *The Research and Report Handbook—For Managers and Executives in Business, Industry, and Government*. New York: Wiley, 1981.

Murphy, Herta A., and Charles E. Peck. *Effective Business Communications*. 2nd ed. New York: McGraw-Hill, 1976.

Nazzaro, Jean, and William V. Schipper, eds. *Proposal Writer's Handbook: A Step-by-Step Process*. Washington, D.C.: National Association of State Directors of Special Education, 1976. ERIC ED 125218.

Nolan, Mary E. "Finding the Green ($$$) Funding Early Childhood Programs." *Young Chil*, 35, No. 3 (1980), 14–20.

Olsen, Leslie A., and Thomas N. Huckin. *Principles of Communication for Science and Technology*. New York: McGraw-Hill, 1983.

Orlich, Patricia R., and Donald C. Orlich. *The Art of Writing a Successful R&D Proposal*. Pleasantville, N.Y.: Redgrave, 1977.

———. *Writing a Successful Research Grant Proposal*. Olympia: Washington Research Coordinating Unit for Vocational Education, 1975. ERIC ED 112016.

Paxson, William C. *The Business Writing Handbook*. New York: Bantam, 1981.

Pearsall, Thomas E., and Donald H. Cunningham. *How to Write for the World of Work*. New York: Holt, Rinehart, Winston, 1978.

Perry, Guest. "Writing Proposals: Current Resources." *Educ Libr*, 6 (1981), 15, 25.

Persing, Bobbye Sorrels. *Business Communication Dynamics*. Columbus, Ohio: Merrill, 1981.

Peters, Ernest L. *Workshop in Proposal Writing. Final Report*. Harrisburg: Pennsylvania

State Department of Education. Bureau of Vocational, Technical, and Continuing Education, 1972. ERIC ED 072307.

Poe, Roy W. *The McGraw-Hill Guide to Effective Business Reports*. New York: McGraw-Hill, 1981.

Popham, W. James. "Key Decision Points in a Contractor's Response to an RFP." Annual Meeting of the American Educational Research Association, 7–11 Apr. 1980. ERIC ED 202898.

Procedural Guide for Writing of Proposals. Huntington, W. Va.: West Virginia State Department of Education, 1968.

Proposal Preparation Guide, Cleveland, Ohio: Case Western Reserve Office of Research Administration, 1971.

Proposal Writer's Guide. Ann Arbor, Mich.: University of Michigan, Division of Research Development and Administration, 1975.

Proposal Writer's Handbook. Minneapolis: Honeywell DSD Communications Department, 1973.

Rainey, Bill G. "Proposal Writing: A Neglected Area of Instruction." *J Bus Comm*, 11, No. 4 (1974), 30–39.

Rawnsley, David E. "Proposal Writing Made Palatable." *NASSP Bul*, 63, NO. 426 (1979), 60–66.

Reif-Lehrer, Liane. *Writing a Successful Grant Application*. Boston: Science Books, 1982.

Renner, Stan. *Introduction to the Stop Technique as Applied to Organizing and Writing Proposals*. SESW-S69. Sylvania Electronics Systems, Western Division, 1970.

Richards, Audrey, ed. *The Complete Grants Sourcebook for Higher Education*. Washington, D.C.: American Council on Education, 1980. ERIC ED 207477.

————, ed. *Grantwriter's Handbook*. Vol. II. San Francisco: Public Management Institute, 1979–80.

Rivers, William E., ed. *Business Reports: Samples from the "Real World."* Englewood Cliffs, N.J.: Prentice-Hall, 1981.

Robings, Edward. *Proposal Writing: Reactions of an Evaluator*. Los Angeles: L.A. Trade-Technical College, 1971. ERIC ED 070439.

Rugh, D. E., and R. E. Manning. *Proposal Management Using the Modular Technique*. Los Altos, Calif.: Peninsula, 1982.

Scalberg, Ernest J. "The Campus Bread Game: Guidelines for Student Proposals." *NASPA J*, 11, No. 4 (1974), 10–17.

Schlesinger, Lawrence E., and Nhuyen Nhan. "Project Proposals:- How to Assess." *J Rehab*, 41, No. 2 (1975), 29–31.

Schmidt, B. A. "Preparation for LCC Proposals and Contracts." *Proceedings of the Annual Reliability and Maintainability Symposium*, Salt Lake City, 1979, pp. 62–66.

"The Secret of Successful Proposals." *Gov Exec*, 12 No. 8 (1980), 40–41.

Seldon, Clement A., and Robert W. Maloy. "Public School Grant Writing: Educational Innovation in Times of Retrenchment." *Clearing House* 54, No. 7 (1981), 330–33.

Sexton, Dorothy L. "Developing Skills in Grant Writing." *Nurs Out*, 30, No. 1 (1982), 31–38.

Sherman, Theodore A. *Modern Technical Writing*. 2nd ed. Englewood Cliffs, N.J.: Prentice-Hall, 1966.

Shrivastava, P. "Preparation of Grant Proposals." *Med Phys*, 7 (1980), 444–45.

Sigband, Norman B. *Communication for Management and Business*. 2nd ed. Glenview, Ill.: Scott, Foresman, 1976.

Sliepcevich, Elena M., and Elaine M. Vitello. "A Selective Bibliography—Proposal Writing and Grant Sources." *Health Educ*, 9, No. 5 (1978), 5–7.

Smith, Frank. "Education For Proposal Writers." *J Tech Writ Comm*, 6 (1976), 113–22.

———. "Engineering Proposals." In *Handbook of Technical Writing Practices*, Vol. 1. Ed. Stella Jordon. New York: Wiley, 1971, pp. 493–579.

Somerville, Bill. "Where Proposals Fail." *The Grantsmanship Center News*, 10, No. 1 (1982), 24–25.

Sterling, Carol, et. al. *Arts Proposal Writing. A Sourcebook of Ideas for Writing Proposals for Any School Program. For People Who Thought They Couldn't Write a Proposal, or Wouldn't Ever Need to and for Those Who Didn't Even Realize They Had a Proposal to Make*. Princeton, N.J.: Educational Improvement Center-Central, 1982. ERIC ED 214860.

STOP—A Way of Managing Proposals. Minneapolis: Honeywell DSD Communications Department, 1972.

Sultz, Harry A., and Frances S. Sherwin. *Grant Writing for Health Professionals*. Boston: Little, Brown, 1981.

Teague, Gerald V. "Use of Sponsor's Evaluation Criteria in Writing Proposals." *CEDR Q*, 13, No. 1 (1980), 7–8.

———, and Betty S. Heathington. *The Process of Grant Proposal Development. Fastback 143*. Bloomington, Ind.: Phi Delta Kappa Educational Foundation, 1980. ERIC ED 187035.

———. "Proposal Applications: Are They Really Worth the Price?" *J Soc Res Admin*, 11, No. 1 (1979), 37–39.

Tompkins, L. Michael. *The First. . . Universal Grants Management Handbook. . . in English*. Citrus Heights, Calif.: La Grange Press, 1977.

Urgo, Louis A. *Models for Money: Obtaining Government and Foundation Grants Assistance*. 2nd ed. Boston: Spaulding, 1978.

Visco, Louis J. *The Manager as an Editor: Reviewing Memos, Letters, and Reports*. Boston: CBI Publishing Co., 1981.

Waldo, Willis H. *Better Report Writing*. New York: Reinhold Publishing Co., 1965.

Walker, Sylvia. "What to Do Until the Proposal Writer Comes Or Not at All." *Fund Raising Manag*, 8, No. 1 (1977), 53.

Washburn, Susan L. "Stalking the Corporate and Foundation Dollar." *New Direc Inst Advanc*, No. 7 (1980), 77–86.

Weisman, Herman M. *Basic Technical Writing*. 4th ed. Columbus, Ohio: Merrill, 1980.

Whalen, Tim. "Grant Proposals: A Rhetorical Approach." *ABCA Bul*, 45, No. 1 (1982), 36–38.

White, Virginia P., ed. *Grant Proposals That Succeeded*. New York: Plenum, 1983.

———. *Grants: How To Find Out About Them and What to Do Next*. New York: Plenum, 1975.

———. *Grants for the Arts*. New York: Plenum, 1980.

Wilcox, Roger P. *Communication at Work: Writing and Speaking*. Boston: Houghton Mifflin, 1977.

Williams, David K. "Strong Proposals Make Easy Going on Solicitation Road." *Fund Raising Manag*, 11 (1980), 20–23.

Williams, Don. *Writing Successful Proposals. School Accountability Series. Monograph 7.* Austin, Tex.: Learning Concepts, 1976. ERIC ED 133819.

Zallen, Harold, and Eugenia M. Zallen. *Ideas Plus Dollars: Research Methodology and Funding.* Norman, Okla.: Academic World I, 1976.

Technical Reports

JUDITH P. STANTON

Along with letters, the technical report is the most commonly assigned form of writing in technical and business writing courses, and it is a common form of written communication in business and industry. In general, the technical report represents and analyzes financial, management, or technical subjects of concern either to an organization itself or to its client. Often, such reports draw conclusions about the subject analyzed and recommend a course of action. Technical reports in more or less the form we produce them today have been around for decades; the term is so slippery and general, however, that most current theorists try to categorize reports anew. Yet they add little to Thomas Radford Agg and Walter L. Foster's rubrics—by subject, use, class, or type—set forth in *The Preparation of Engineering Reports* (1935). The form is so conservative that perhaps the last major change was already underway when Ralph U. Fitting, in *Report Writing* (1924), described the new "Double Report." In it, "two separate reports are submitted," the conventional long one, and a digest. At that time, the shorter report was variously called "brief report," "epitome," or "digested report." It seems to have been the equivalent of the modern executive summary and conclusions that appear at the beginning of reports.

In a more limited sense, the technical report is the engineering report of some length which provides a solution to an engineering problem with a view to what management needs to know. It is clear, however, from the articles and books examined for this essay, that many documents from other fields can be considered reports. These can be long or short, formal or informal, analytical or informational. When reports are classified according to subject, we find management, investigation, field, and trip reports; financial, accounting, and credit reports; design, research, test, or failure reports; and proposals, along with feasibility studies, preliminary and progress reports. What such a variety of reports has in common is a conventional pattern of organization, designed for efficient reading by readers with different needs. Depending on the complexity of the subject, these parts can be foreshortened or greatly extended. An abstract or summary comes first. It is sometimes followed by a more detailed executive or factual summary. An introduction usually explains the purpose of the report and may give its history or background. In most longer and many shorter reports, conclusions and recommendations are placed next, as near to the front and as easy to locate as possible. The longer discussion—whether it presents test results or analyzes a management problem—is relegated to the end, where it stands as reference material for those interested in reading it or technically qualified to evaluate it. It is variously called the body, discussion section, appendix, or annex.

Few of the works on technical reports do much more than superficially update this basic form. The technical report is perceived to be a workable, conventional form that has evolved into an efficient state and is too cumbersome and variable to admit of any experimentation. With the possible exception of Thomas E. Pearsall's *Audience Analysis for Technical Writing* (1969) and J. C. Mathes and Dwight Stevenson's presentation of audience analysis in *Designing Technical Reports* (1976), the technical report literature adapts ideas refined by researchers in other fields. For example, in books on reports written in the 1950s, readability formulas developed for the government were widely set forth as the main concern for report writers. Emerging communications theory began appearing, along with some attention to semantics, in books written in the 1960s. The problem-solving technique, developed by systems analysts, is the current trend and seems to be a good one, but the method has not been integrated into report writing theory. Nevertheless, it appears to be the only approach to the writing process that is likely to supersede some authors' lame and stultifying insistence on outlining as the invention method of choice.

In spite of some excellent publications, the field is ripe for research and improved textbooks and manuals. Few experiments have been carried out on arrangements of content, the interplay of content and physical design, or the interplay of text and graphics. Because of rapid technological change, few texts reflect the impact of the computer on organizations, on research done using data bases, or on our own writing using word processing, Most texts and guidebooks do not address the complex written interaction between government and its contractors and do not deal with the government's own definitions of and requirements for proposals, reports, and contracts. Even the best books draw most of their model reports from large national and international corporations. We need studies of reports put out by smaller businesses and organizations. We would also benefit from studies of the writing processes of experienced report writers working both singly and in groups.

Even though we need fresh approaches in this field, many usable books and articles have been written on technical and business reports. This bibliographical essay discusses studies on reports of all lengths, in all forms, and in most special fields other than law and medicine. The opening section introduces the reader new to technical writing to a half-dozen books that provide a balanced, up-to-date overview of types of reports with samples. The essay next takes up books on reports, with a section on reports in business and industry in general and separate sections on accounting reports and technical reports. This portion of the essay concludes with books on reports in a wider context, such as reports management and production. Articles on reports themselves and on pedagogical methods are treated in the two final sections.

Books to Consult for an Overview of Report Writing

The single most useful introduction to reports in Ron Blicq's new large-format book, *Guidelines for Report Writers* (1982). This "reference manual" provides sample reports from a range of professions. Informal reports presented include occurrence (incident), trip, inspection, progress, and short investigation reports. Semi-formal reports include test and lab reports, proposals, and investigation and evaluation reports. Traditional as well as alternative arrangements for formal reports are shown, and the book concludes with a chapter on working with report production teams. On each page of each sample report, interesting features are marked with a number keyed to explanatory comments on the facing page. The second chapter briefly covers reader analysis, purpose statements, and the pyramid technique as a heuristic for identifying "the most important information" and focusing the reader on it.

Two books afford a look at reports within organizations. Blicq's textbook *Technically Write* (1981) focuses on how the fictional firm, H. L. Winman and Associates, generates a variety of reports. Cases for students to solve as well as sample reports are plentiful. In both of his books, Blicq's reports tend to be answers to technical problems. In contrast, Marya W. Holcombe and Judith K. Stein's *Writing for Decision Makers* (1981) focuses on the human problems that often underlie technical ones. It leads readers to apply the "managerial skills you already have to your writing" and details a problem-solving approach—using analysis trees and flowcharts rather than outlining—as a means of arriving at a right answer and, at the same time, preparing the report. Two complex cases, one from engineering and one from business, are traced throughout the book as models for analyzing, drafting, writing, and re-writing a final report. A self-teaching book, with answers at the end, the book has cases, summaries, and bibliographies for each chapter. The authors also advocate some new approaches: background sections should be shortened and submerged into introductions; and figure and table titles should state the point of the figure. Editing others' work and reviewing for peers, subordinates, and superiors are also discussed.

Three textbooks, taken together, cover most report types. Raymond Lesikar's *Report Writing for Business* (1981) thoroughly reviews conventional business reports. Lesikar incorporates communication theory into his chapter on how reports are used in business. For instructors, he provides 41 cases, all new, as subjects for student reports. Kenneth W. Houp and Thomas Pearsall, in *Reporting*

Technical Information (1984), present reports from science and industry according to subject: in addition to the formal engineering report, which they call a "professional report," they devote a chapter each to the progress, feasibility, management, and physical research (scientific) report. Their discussion of library research and other means of gathering information and an appendix of on-line databases are up to date and useful. Finally, Mathes and Stevenson's *Designing Technical Reports* (1976) focuses on the typical engineering report for large corporations, contains interesting professional models and detailed checklists for finalizing reports, and thoroughly treats audience analysis and purpose statements. Its teachers' manual is excellent.

Reports In Business, Industry, And Government

In the last decade, more and more books on business writing have covered both letters and reports, and the notion of a "business report" has come to cover almost any form of communication that "reports" something to someone in an organization. What is a report in business? Most books present the long report pretty much as described above, but many include even standardized one-page trip-report forms as yet another kind of reporting situation. Of course, for the writer, the rhetorical problems are similar: the narrative of what happened must be sorted out from the analysis and classification of what the company needs to know. A business-centered text may make even more elaborate distinctions of form such as a memo report, a letter report, and an audit report in memo form. To add to the confusion, the titles of these books do not necessarily reflect their content. Some titles mention only "reports," yet treat letters; some name both but treat one or the other cursorily. Trying to ascertain standard business practice by surveying the trade and textbooks is difficult. In fact, business writers report information in letter and in memo form depending on their companies' typical practices. A report within an organization is likely to be couched in memo form, if short, or preceded by a cover or transmittal memo, if long. Reports sent outside the organization are more often in letter form.

This muddle of terminology notwithstanding, there are a number of useful books on the subject. In addition to his *Report Writing in Business*, Raymond Lesikar's tradebook for young executives, *How to Write a Report Your Boss Will Read and Remember* (1974), covers territory by emphasizing patterns of organization and audience adaptation. His bold, attractive graphics are easy to understand, and both his guide to formatting and his sample reports are instructive. His companion textbook, *Business Communication* (1980), treats reports thoroughly and letters briefly. The problems and case studies have been updated, and there are 11 pages of subjects for research reports.

Several older books have features of interest to writers and teachers. Conrad T. Berenson and Raymond R. Colton's *Research and Report Writing for Business and Economics* (1971) is a useful handbook, with guides to research sources, style, interview methods, and questionnaire design. William J. Gallagher's tradebook, *Report Writing for Management* (1969), discusses weighing evidence and interpreting data. This unusually literate and leisurely book is also sprinkled with pertinent anecdotes from the author's experiences. David M. Robinson's similarly titled 1969 text, *Writing Reports for Management Decisions*, is quite different and would probably still hold up for classroom use. Its well-considered textbook apparatus includes summaries at the ends of chapters, discussion questions, practice cases, and projects for study and practice. Another strength is Robinson's knowledge of the writer in business situations. The beginning technical writing instructor might also wish to review the many ways of classifying reports presented here: by time and frequency, by activity or subject, by degree of formality—for example, an informal weekly sales report. A further category, function, is divided into the informational report, the examinational report which presents and interprets, and the analytical report which presents solutions. Raymond A. Rogers's 32-page pamphlet, *How to Report Research and Development Findings to Management* (1973), examines the parts of reports and stages of writing them in as short a compass as possible.

Other books are less comprehensive but still useful. Robert L. Shurter, J. Peter Williamson, and Wayne G. Broehl's *Business Research and Report Writing* (1965) does explain older research methods and report types, but does not place reports in their organizational context. It does, however, have some statistical sophistication about presenting visual aids. Howard Hillman's recent tradebook, *The Art of Writing Business Reports and Proposals* (1981), might have a popular market, but it does not live up to its promising title. Most chapters consist of rather interesting tips, organized randomly. In 1963, Federal Electric Corporation published the only programmed text that this search found. *How to Write Effective Reports* packs in a good deal of standard information, but readers may find its informal coaxing a bit cloying.

Many tradebooks and textbooks on all kinds of business communication devote as much as a quarter of their pages to reports. Two tradebooks are Robert G. Weaver and Patricia C. Weaver's *Persuasive Writing* (1977) and William M. Parr's *Executive Guide to Effective Letters and Reports* (1976). Each is short on samples and on graphics. Textbooks include Herta A. Murphy and Charles E. Peck's *Effective Business Communication* (1976), which crowds good explanations and samples into three chapters. A much briefer but more readable treatment is Berle Haggblade's three chapters in *Business Communication* (1982). Norman B. Sigband's *Communication for Management and Business* (1976) has six chapters, one with a substantial annotated bibliography of business reference sources. With David N. Batman, Sigband recently wrote a text for beginning and community college students, *Communicating in Business* (1981). The six chapters on reports in William C. Himstreet and Wayne Murlin Baty's *Business Communications* (1977) include a useful model.

Accounting Reports

Accountants do not usually write the kind of management or analytical report that these books describe; yet many accounting students take all-purpose business and technical writing courses in spite of the fact that as CPAs and comptrollers they will "write" mainly financial statements. These statements consist largely of tabulated financial data—balance sheets, income, surplus, and consolidated statements accompanied by limited prose opinions and disclaimers in carefully constructed conventional language. In this modest amount of prose, accountants, internal and external auditors, and, most of all, students are adhering to a language fostered by the Federal Accounting Standards Board (FASB) in line with GAAP (generally accepted accounting practices). Most books avoid the subject, even though this historical form is commonplace.

Happily, several very good books shed light on accounting reports. The single most informative book is *Effective Accounting Reports* (1969) by Bruce Joplin and James W. Pattillo, both CPAs; Joplin is a consultant in state government and industry, and Pattillo is an accounting professor. This handsome, large-format book gives modest attention to composition but thoroughly addresses graphics, a major problem with so much data. It also emphasizes how to design reports to better reflect responsibility accounting (where it is made clear which manager or division is associated with notable profits, losses, and other trends) and exception reporting (where results that fall outside of set statistical boundaries are flagged for management's attention). Chapters also treat format, narrative portions, visual aids for oral presentation, graphics, and types of reports. Jennie M. Palen's 1955 *Report Writing for Accountants* details the responsibilities of independent auditors and explains how financial data are turned into a comprehensive financial statement. Four chapters discuss the opinion, which is a written statement, three discuss the prose comments, and four additional chapters treat clarity and word choice in both. Ronello B. Lewis's *Accounting Reports for Management* (1957) discusses how to improve the readability of the tables themselves. Using many fold-out illustrations, Lewis demonstrates how to emphasize key financial data easily lost in a sea of numbers. Two books that do not treat writing can broaden our knowledge about report content: George Demare's *A Handbook of Model Reports to Clients* (1964) and Leopold A. Bernstein's *Understanding Corporate Reports* (1974). Finally, in *Writing Audit Reports* (1979), Mary C. Bromage has authoritatively written the ultimate specialized book. While she gives only conventional advice on grammar and mechanics, all examples are from actual audit reports. Audience, organization, and design, the subjects of the later chapters, are intelligently treated, though non-specialists will find the prose rather heavy going.

What constitutes good writing in accounting has not been settled, and three articles attesting to that may be added to these books. In "Clear Writing" (1981), Angela Maniak, herself an internal auditor, emphasizes that the audit report must interpret data, not merely state findings. Two sides of a related argument have appeared in two leading accounting journals. Fred C. Foy argues in part that rounding figures is essential for clarity in "Accounting Reports Don't Have to Be Dull" (1973), and A.S.C. Ehrenberg defends precise figures in "Annual Reports Don't Have to Be Obscure" (1976).

Technical Reports

Books on technical report writing usually have several features in common—
little or no attention to letter writing, a discussion of the processes of gathering,
analyzing, and beginning to write up data, some treatment of grammar and
mechanics, and some samples. One category of such books is aimed at technical
and professional students outside of business, but is not strictly limited to engineers. A good number are suitable for advanced students and practicing professionals as well. W. Paul Jones's eighth edition of *Writing Scientific Papers and
Reports* (1981) emphasizes science, is thoroughly readable, and has useful samples, appendices, and updated information on databases for library research.
Russell Rutter and Karl E. Gwiasda's *Writing Professional Reports* (1977) is
appropriate for advanced technical students. Other durable textbooks are Houp
and Pearsall (1984) (discussed above), James W. Souther and Myron L. White's
Technical Report Writing (1977), Herman M. Weisman's *Technical Report Writ-
ing* (1975), Theodore A. Sherman and Simon S. Johnson's *Modern Technical
Writing* (1975), and J. N. Ulman and Jay R. Gould's *Technical Reporting* (1972).
Sherman and Johnson as well as Ulman and Gould each have more than 100
pages of samples with annotations on the facing page. Because of their samples,
Robert R. Rathbone and James B. Stone's *A Writer's Guide for Engineers and
Scientists* (1962) and David B. Comer and Ralph R. Spillman's *Modern Technical
and Industrial Reports* (1962) are still informative, though the Comer-Spillman
text is needlessly learned. Half of Rufus P. Turner's *Technical Report Writing*
(1971) contains specimens. William A. Damerest's *Clear Technical Reports*
(1972) shows sample pages typed rather than typeset, which provides more
realistic samples. This book should have been titled *Clear Technical Writing*,
however, for it also covers letters. Dwight E. Gray's *So You Have to Write a
Technical Report* (1970) succinctly reviews report parts but provides no examples. Good textbooks for beginning and community college students in technical
fields are Steven J. Pauley's *Technical Report Writing Today* (1979), John M.
Lannon's *Technical Writing* (1982), and Ingrid Brunner, J. C. Mathes, and
Dwight W. Stevenson's *The Technician as Writer* (1980). They provide sample
student reports.

Many books treat writing for engineers only. Although advanced, Mathes and
Stevenson's *Designing Technical Reports* is the best. For professionals, their
book is complemented by Herbert B. Michaelson's *How to Write and Publish
Engineering Papers and Reports* (1982). In spite of its title, it emphasizes papers
much more than reports. *Effective Communication for Engineers* (1975) collects
articles that originally appeared in *Chemical Engineering*. Of dozens of articles,
twelve are on reports and report visuals. The book reprints the Westinghouse
Survey on "What Managers Look for in Engineering Reports," as well as articles
on writing faster, writing processes, common weaknesses, R and D (research
and development) reports, and keeping laboratory notebooks. The articles on
visuals provide a good review of figures and charts, formatting, and using flow-

sheet symbols. Two 1964 books provide useful general background. Charles A. Ranous's *Communication for Engineers* (1964) devotes only two chapters to reports, but provides an overall background to the engineering profession and a context in which to see engineering report writing. Allen B. Rosenstein, Robert R. Rathbone, and William F. Schneerer's *Engineering Communication* (1964)—a collaboration by professors of engineering, English, and engineering graphics—attempts to place engineering reports and graphic design in the context of information theory.

Three books on report writing for engineers stress the mathematical side of engineering reports, a side neglected in more recent works. In their brief *Technical Report Standards* (1977), L. Harvill and Thomas L. Kraft, both engineers, devote a section to error discussion. The book is also a good short guide to report format and graphics for those who prefer generalized models. Dale Stroble Davis's *Elements of Engineering Reports* has an apparently unique chapter, on the "graphical presentation of engineering equations" (1963). The statistical emphasis of Fred H. Rhodes's *Technical Report Writing* (1961) is unusual in the field, although H. F. Glidden's 1964 *Reports, Technical Writing, and Specifications* devotes a chapter to mathematical, chemical, and graphical "languages."

Glidden also provides a chapter on specifications, with emphasis on legal considerations, samples of parts of specifications, and a glossary. Four other books cover this subject. Thomas S. Sawyer's *Specification and Engineering Writer's Manual* (1960) discusses the legal ramifications of specifications. Tyler G. Hicks's *Writing for Engineering and Science* (1961) and Clarence Andrews's *Technical and Business Writing* (1975) cover the subject from different angles. Hicks introduces military manuals and discusses standards, while Andrews discusses properties. Lionel D. Wyld's handbook *Preparing Effective Reports* (1967) reprints United States Army Engineer Command's "Standards for Technical Reports." It has usable exercises and some detail on tables, charts, and graphs.

Reports In A Wider Context

It is difficult to stay within the boundaries of a subject like technical reports, at least partly because the boundaries are unclear. Technical writers and writing teachers need to know in the most practical way that reports are much more variable and flexible than many textbooks lead us to believe. We need a broader background, if possible from both practical experience and books, simply to enable us to gauge how closely tradebooks and textbooks show us actual practice. A few books that are not about report *writing* address some interesting aspect of reports in the working world. Frank Gilmore, in *Formulation and Advocacy of Business Policy* (1970), looks at the strategies and methodical thinking behind a policy proposal, which is roughly equivalent to a management report. He notes that the nature of corporate planning has changed from the "sizing-up" approach of the 1920s to the 1950s to the current long-range planning where emphasis has shifted from "searching for problems" to formulating new policies. Unlike other books on business policy, Gilmore's interestingly shows how policy can evolve out of the report writing process. While he deals not at all with writing, audience, or report parts, he sees policy as deriving from an outline, which derives from a brief, which derives from managers working together at a planning stage.

In larger organizations, reports proliferate, almost promiscuously. John B. McMaster's 36-page booklet for the American Management Association, *The Network Reports System of Analysis and Control* (1977), discusses a method of reports management within a company. His proposed reports management program would prevent unneeded reports, get rid of obsolete ones, improve existing and needed ones, and add new ones more efficiently because executives could readily see the need for them. The system includes switching from a manual to a computer reports directory. Another study provides background, somewhat outdated, on how technical literature is produced within an organization. Emerson Clarke's *A Guide to Technical Literature Production* (1961) discusses the role of technical writers, the costs (very outdated) and types of literature, and recruiting and training writers. Malden Grange Bishop in *Billions for Confusion* (1963) harshly recounts his experiences with dishonesty and incompetency among technical writers for the government, especially the military. It is worth perusing for examples.

The federal government is the largest producer and consumer of technical reports. Judson Monroe's *Effective Research and Report Writing in Government* (1980) puts reports in the context of political concerns. More than most guides, it has a sense of writing as process, not product, and is very good on managing data, interpreting results, and handling statistics. Its brief bibliography gives sources on sampling and statistics. Anyone with a taste for being overwhelmed by the diversity of reports literature, its classification, and its retrieval may feast on *Use of Reports Literature* (1975) edited by Charles Peter Auger. It compiles various British and American sources of reports in aerospace, agriculture and food, biology and medicine, business and economics, education, nuclear energy, and science and technology applied in industry. In addition to discussing conventional indexes and new retrieval sources, a brief chapter on report writing reminds us of standards for report writing published by many government departments as well as the American National Standards Institute (ANSI). Their titles are self-explanatory: N. Brearly's "The Role of Technical Reports in the Scientific and Technical Community" (1973); the U.S. Federal Council for Science and Technology's *Guidelines to Format Standards for Scientific and Technical Reports Prepared by or for the Federal Government* (1968) and *The Role of the Technical Report in Scientific and Technical Communication* (1968); the U.S. Department of Transportation's *Format and Distribution Requirements for DOT Scientific and Technical Reports* (1972); *Format Requirements for Scientific and Technical Reports Prepared by or for the Department of Defense* (1973); and A. G. Hoshovsky's *Suggested Criteria for Titles, Abstracts, and Index Terms in Department of Defense Technical Reports* (1965). Two documents lie outside the federal government's domain: ANSI's *Guidelines for Format and Production of Scientific and Technical Reports* (1974) and the British Standards Institute's *Specifications for the Presentation of Research and Development Reports* (1972).

Business and Technical Reports and Reporting Systems

Two kinds of articles on reports will not be treated in this section—those on the annual report and those numerous, superficial one-to-two-page articles on how to write a better report in three to ten easy steps. The annual report has, perhaps properly, become the province of those trained in journalism and public relations. It is worth noting, at the same time, that the annual report receives much more attention in business journals of all kinds than do ordinary management and financial reports. Any volume of *Business Periodicals Index* will yield only about half a dozen articles on technical reports and reporting. But under the heading for individual fields—Construction Industry, Corporation, Insurance Companies, for example—there will usually be at least one to several dozen articles on producing annual reports. Moreover, under "Business," the subcategory "Reports to Government" lists many articles about reporting data to comply with increasing government regulations.

A word about the superficial articles on writing. They are as bad as bad can be, though usually well written, often clever, and sometimes produced by technical writing teachers. Most specialty journals, from *Supervisory Management* to *Oil and Gas Journal*, give over a page or two every few years to such articles. They are brief, formulaic, and provide little information on the difficult processes of analyzing a situation and writing about it. Considering that it takes most instructors a semester to teach their students basic concepts about logic, audience, readability, and format, it is hard to imagine these articles inspiring change in even sensitive professionals who might recognize their need to be retrained. These articles are included in the checklist not to perpetuate them but for the convenience of anyone interested in whatever work might have been done in a special field.

Nevertheless, for teachers of multidisciplinary technical writing courses or aspiring technical writers, a number of the articles from highly specialized journals offer specific information about what report writers really write. Several provide a most interesting look at reports in a larger context and address the problem of managing proliferating reports. William L. Kendig and Thomas D. Johnson's "Developing Systematic Reporting Structures" (1972) stresses inventory of current practices, interviewing report recipients, recommending changes, and preparing a coding system for old and new reports. P. Wulff's "Management Report Gets to All Management" (1970) describes a bi-weekly reporting system in a steel equipment company between a purchasing and a materials department that led to savings because the system made supply and inventory problems more obvious. Robert A. Lull, in "Reporting Results" (1973), explains how to set up a reporting system that prevents distorting such matters as productivity and quality control and reflects the actual situation. James Pattillo's "Communication Through Reports" (1969) describes communicating as a behavioral process and discusses how such matters as timing, setting, authority, and existing practice will affect readers' responses. Other articles, most in the *Journal of Systems Management*, discuss reports in an overall context: John Caldwell's "The Effective Report Crisis" (1975), Belden Menkus's "Effective Systems Reports" (1976), Joseph Wilkinson's "Effective Reporting Structures" (1976), and Edward W. Matlak's "Structured Report Programs" (1978).

About a dozen articles treat specialized accounting and other business reports. Michael J. Reiter's "Reports That Communicate" (1967) presents by kind and frequency three types of accounting reports—statistical, financial, and narrative. The misleadingly titled article, "Fight Paper Pollution, Stamp Out Reports" (1970), interviews Herbert Geisler, a management consultant, on how to handle financial reports. He stresses how to streamline reports to focus on profits, responsibility accounting, and exception reporting in order to make replanning easier: thus, writing a report is seen as an integral part of correcting a situation. R. I. Stevens's "Exception Reporting" (1974) and Robert L. Johnson's "Writing the Exception Report" (1969) are brief but useful. Johnson's article differentiates a shorter report from the longer expanded staff study, which is military in origin. Allen H. Seed, in "Improving the Effectiveness of Management Reports" (1969), suggests that management by objective strategies should be applied to report writing and stresses readability and responsibility accounting. Reading the narrative portions of financial reports is the concern of four studies: Arthur Harris Adelberg and Richard A. Lewis's "Financial Reports Can be Made More Understandable" (1980), Mary C. Bromage's "Wording the Management Audit Report" (1972), Michael Southgate's "Plessey Researches Financial Reporting" (1977), and Edward V. McIntyre's "Communicating Through Financial Reports" (1975). Of these, McIntyre's empirical study found that the verbal portions of financial reports, especially footnotes, need to be improved. Four other articles describe types of reports, the first two with examples: D. B. Tinsley and Conway T. Rucks's "Interim Reports" (1976), John O. Morris and Thomas R. Wilcox's "Well-Written Credit Reports" (1974), Richard L. Clark's "How to Prepare Inspection Reports" (1979), and Thomas R. Wotruba and Richard Mangone's "More Effective Sales Force Reporting" (1979).

As with the books already discussed, articles on technical rather than business writing show somewhat different concerns. Technical report articles, like the books, give more attention to information-gathering and practical approaches to on-the-job writing. For example, Alfred N. Weiner provides a brief checklist of information to record in a log for use in the subsequent project report—background, theory, process, equipment, operation, and other project data—in "Today's Records, Tomorrow's Reports" (1964). In his 1974 article, "Dear Diary," he adds to that list the following: drawings, math, experiments, tables, graphs, photos, expenses, and reference material. Several writers give different pre-writing strategies. In "How to Attack a Special Assignment" (1979), Margaret Drossel provides a flowchart to aid in problem analysis which is, in effect, highly structured pre-writing. Stephen L. Pitner's "Improve Your Method of Preparing a Technical Study" (1978) outlines a practical seven-step approach that includes identifying needs, alternatives, and possible sources early on. Donald R. Woods's "How to Outline Your Reports" (1964) uses the outline, shared with a supervisor early in the report writing stages, as a brainstorming method. James W. Hill's "Help Fight CDP (Communications Planning Deficiency)" (1979) offers a model "project planning sheet" to make report writing more efficient.

Since the variety of "standard" report types is growing, those treated in specialized journals can keep us up to date and are worth discussing in some detail. Robert E. Berry's "First Response Procedures for Hazardous Materials" (1980) reproduces a detailed two-page form that is a checklist of matters to be considered, consulted, or recorded when there has been a spill. It facilitates gathering for the final report the information now required by law. John Mueller's "How to Prepare an EIR" (1974) summarizes what Environmental Impact Reports contain, what they are likely to cost, and how consultants and the public can best be used in preparing one. Mueller sees EIRs as an unacknowledged planning tool and provides a copy of the California guidelines for EIRs. For the field of materials research, Ralph L. Darby and Walter H. Veazie describe "Writing a State-of-the-Art Report" (1968) and distinguish among the simple state-of-the-art reports, those that add a specific objective, and those combined with a feasibility report. The authors explore how the reports are compiled, with a step-by-step timetable, and explain how the reports may be used for research and development as well as for management decisions. Richard J. Matt's "The Case for Engineering Project Reports" (1968) discusses a reporting system to enable the different departments of a growing firm to keep track of their goals, projects, responsibilities, and engineering information. The article describes four forms that may be used for this task: Project Assignment Sheet, Project Status Report, Monthly Project Report, and Engineering Report. Robert W. Richards's "Engineering Reports" (1965) briefly reviews types of reports common in public works, such as progress and annual reports, and explains how they fit into a project from beginning to end. John C. Bumstead's "Concept of the Modern Engineering Report" (1962) outlines the contents of reports for water and sewage works. He lists conventional report parts and names three others special to the field: "Alternate Project and Costs," "Financing the Improvements," and "Legal and Policy Decisions." Finally, Robert G. Murdick's "Engineering and Research Reports" (1961) summarizes seven types of reports common in machine design with a view to timing, style, form, and distribution.

Other articles address typical writing problems. Thomas P. Johnson's four-article series includes "Organize the Report for Fast Writing, Easy Reading" (1969). Johnson offers a version of the pyramid structure for audience analysis and suggests using a cover sheet of "Report Highlights" to replace the conventional report parts. In "Ten Common Weaknesses in Engineering Reports"

(1963), Jay R. Gould examines, section by section, where reports are likely to be flawed, from the abstract to the references. Twenty years later, not much has changed. In 1960, *Petroleum Refiner* devoted a section called "Effective Technical Reporting" to five articles about reports, two of which are of interest here: Kathryn O'Keeffe's "Effective Technical Reporting" and John Walter's "Supplements to the Technical Report" which discusses report parts. In her three-article series, "The Language of Business" (1981–82), Cheryl Reimold covers first, assessing what managers need to know; second, applying a "Pyramid of Value" to determine the amount of technical detail for different report parts; and third, sorting out information appropriate for different report parts. Donald R. Woods's "Updating Our Approach to Written Communications" (1964) used a pyramid approach, exactly reversing Reimold's, to explain levels of readers and language.

Reports are also often discussed from a management perspective. B. C. Brookes's "Report Writing Improves with Morale" (1961) discusses management styles that can interfere with report writing. In "Communicating Technical Information" (1981), Herman Skolnik stresses that management must learn to ask for the reports it needs, as well as writers to write what is needed. In an earlier article with L. F. McBurney, Herman Skolnik discusses the relationship between "Technical Reports and Decision-Making" (1971). In "Effective Communication" (1973), Norman B. Sigband asserts that clarity in writing reports is related to promotability. Finally, after so many articles on so many aspects of report writing, it is a relief to find one with a fresh idea. Patricia Wright, in "Alternatives to Prose for Sharp, Hard-Hitting Reports" (1974), recommends and gives excellent examples of tables, logic trees, and short sentences; she states that the writer should consider using them *before* automatically turning to a standard report form.

Teaching Technical Reports

Beginning technical writing teachers may face the need to develop report writing courses, often coordinated with courses in the students' major. They may also need to come up with workable assignments, train students in advanced library research, help students generate report content and sort that content out into appropriate report parts, and finally evaluate the result. This section discusses articles on these topics. Given that working world reports come in a great variety of lengths, types, and purposes—and that report writing is a staple of technical writing courses—material on teaching the report itself is surprisingly scant, though it has recently increased.

What we should teach is a question rarely addressed systematically. Ellamaye VanFleet in "Determining the Content of a Collegiate Report Writing Course" (1971) studied 167 reports from two companies and interviewed 60 report writers and 28 report readers for answers. Even though her results are limited and could well be updated, they suggest a practical emphasis for curriculum development.

Briefly, she found that major textbooks were just adequate in reflecting practice and that writers need instruction in analyzing and interpreting data, planning shorter reports, writing report sections, and varying reports to suit needs. Writers had the least difficulty collecting data and designing graphics and the most difficulty explaining ideas. Readers were more concerned with adequacy of analysis and clarity than with any aspect of appearance. A brief 1976 *Business Week* article, "Teaching the Boss to Write," corroborates these findings when it stresses buried conclusions and lack of logic as writing problems. Noting the growing popularity of in-house seminars in writing, it also recommends that consultants include top executives in planning sessions. Joseph Baim thoughtfully discusses the consultant's role in his 1977 article, "In-House Training in Report Writing." He insists that course objectives be carefully designed in cooperation with management only after the consultant has analyzed typical company documents. For those developing college report writing courses, two articles discuss the difference between students' and professors' needs and assumptions and the needs of readers and writers in the working world: J. C. Mathes and Dwight W. Stevenson's "Completing the Bridge" (1976) and J. E. Baxter's "Technical Report Writing in Victoria, Australia" (1971). Herman Estrin's "Teaching Report Writing" (1968) describes a course that stresses masterpieces of English writing and has its students edit each other's reports.

Overall, appropriate teaching methodologies for these courses have rarely been tested or discussed. In 1980, Joan C. Kaltenbach described "The Effects of Two Teaching Methodologies on the Performance and Attitudes of Students in a Technical Report-Writing Course." One section, taught by traditional lectures with optional conferences, was successful for half the students, while the other, taught by individual conference with much use of outside examples, was successful for 87 percent. Further studies along these lines would be welcome, for this suggestive one-semester experiment lacked controls as well as an adequate sample. Robert D. Gisselman describes "A Nontraditional Report Writing Course" (1981) that, like Kaltenbach's, seems to work well with the motivated student that advanced technical writing courses attract. Although he begins with traditional lecture and discussion sessions, he relies mainly on conference/tutorials, emphasizing a great deal of practice in which students write in various forms. In his article, "Guided Design" (1972), David C. Sherrin describes a writing unit in an engineering course; he found that report writing improved when the unit was expanded from two to four class periods devoted to the content of the reports.

Report writing courses or course units are often designed by composition specialists in collaboration with professors in the students' majors. The most thorough review of strategies for such efforts is Janet H. Potvin and Robert L. Woods's "Teaching Technical Communication at the Graduate Level" (1983). They provide a selected review of the literature on the dynamics and administration of team-taught courses in general and some specific engineering courses. The components of their course are described in more detail than usual; a proposal, progress report, and oral presentation are tied into the formal report. In addition to discussing how to evaluate assignments, they enumerate both the advantages and limitations of such courses. Three briefer articles focus on particular courses. In "Team-Teaching Technical Writing" (1981), Nancy Roundy has chemical engineering students producing a major technical report based on research done in their Heat and Mass Transfer course. Harriet Hogan's "A Cooperative Course in Communication and Technology" (1980) emphasizes course content and provides a "report evaluation guide." Marilyn B. Silver's "Technical Report Writing in the Community College" (1982) describes how to design and implement cooperative courses. Her interdisciplinary course for dental hygiene students concludes with a final report.

For teachers of technical writing courses not overtly linked to the students' majors, directing students to interesting, workable report topics is a challenge, term after term. Here researchers have been resourceful. In "Increasing Student Involvement" (1982), William C. Sharbrough explains how his students generate their own topics working in groups in which they list, record, and vote on the ideas submitted. In "Questionnaires and Informal Reports" (1980), Diana Reep has students working in groups create questionnaires, give them to small populations, and write up the results in a short report. Robert R. Ledbetter uses "The Field Trip as a Means of Topic Selection" (1978). Developing an issue in an urban or semi-urban area, neighborhood, or industry impresses students with the actuality of reports and provides ample "raw material" for the student to gather, sort out, and analyze. Wayne Murlin Baty explains "Using the Critique as a Report-Writing Assignment" (1974). The students carefully analyze a paper that they have written for another course to see how it follows or violates principles of good writing discussed in class. Hilda F. Allred's students combine "The Campus Environment and Report Writing" (1976). They begin by working in brainstorming groups to isolate campus problems that they would like to analyze, research, and write up. Their research can include questionnaires and on-campus informational services. Juanita Williams Dudley's "Report Monopoly" (1977) is a game designed to teach principles of coherence and the document's effectiveness to decision-makers. Students have to wheel and deal to reassemble eight reports that have been cut up into self-contained units. Class discussion centers on why some reports are more effective than others, so that students learn about logic, coherence, and unity. Patricia J. Marcum in "An English Ph.D in the College of Business" (1977) divides her classes into committees in which students plan a business conference where they present oral reports. The committees are responsible for topics, publicity and scheduling, media, and evaluation and feedback. Several other articles describe report writing assignments: Ted Atkinson, "Doing Institutional Research to Teach the Long Report" (1983); Robert A. Kaftan, "The Long Report" (1981); Marlene Rosenfield, "Prove It" (1977); Bonny J. Stalnaker, "Documented Position Paper" (1978); and Thomas L. Warren, "Teaching Formal Technical Reports" (1982).

Students often arrive in report writing courses with limited skills to do research in their major field at the level necessary to produce a suitable report. Bernard Krimm and Stuart Glogoff in "The Information Resources Report" (1979) not only are quite detailed about the difficulties of the research itself but also describe an assignment in which students write an evaluative report about the library resources that they discover during a library exercise. Though not specifically tied to report writing, Virginia Allanson's "Library Instruction for Students in Technical Report Writing Classes" (1982) gives a plan for instructors and librarians to work together to give students effective classroom presentations followed by supervised library instruction. In "The Business Report" (1983), Vanessa Dean Arnold briefly describes several ways of gathering data for reports—secondary, or library, research; and primary research which may draw on survey, observational, and experimental data. James M. Lahiff's "Effective Research" (1974) explains a library exercise for business students. James T. Watt and Wade S. Hobbs give a model for "Research and Report Writing" (1979).

Whatever the course design or assignments, very little has been written on how students write individual report parts. An interesting article challenges our assumptions about following standard report form. Carol S. Lipson's "Theoretical and Empirical Considerations for Designing Openings of Technical and Business Reports" (1983) questions the efficacy of teaching students to be so redundant at the beginning of reports. She reviews what several major textbooks advise and what we know about repetition from studies in other fields, including speech, education research, and linguistics. Her article is an excellent starting point for some carefully designed empirical research on the subject. Even so, most attention has been given to openings. Robert A. Francis considers "A Good Title" (1974) to be the point of origin from which the rest of the report grows. Titles should have two elements—a subject and a narrowing agent which comments on the subject and forces students to be selective. Carefully devising titles can help students to partition the report by type, cause, example, location, and time, and so lead them to a well-outlined and developed report. In separate articles, David Roberts and Kitty O. Locker treat abstracts, not necessarily as they apply to reports. Roberts's "Teaching Abstracts in Technical Writing" (1982) recommends writing them "early and often" and provides a five-stage method, with examples, for teaching the informative abstract. His students first study abstracts by others, all write abstracts for the same published article, compare the results, write abstracts for articles they find in their fields, and finally write abstracts for their own reports. Noting that abstracting improves reading skills, Locker in "Teaching Students to Write Abstracts" (1982) distinguishes among descriptive, informative, and mixed abstracts, gives examples, describes in-class and followup assignments, and explains how to use outlining to derive content. Nancy Roundy gives "A Process Approach to Teaching the Abstract" (1982), and Frank C. Weightman explains how to construct "The Executive Summary" (1982). Marvin Swift's "Writing a Conclusion" (1981) is the only article found on the subject. Swift discusses how to differentiate among findings, conclusions, and recommendations.

Much of the report writer's task is finding and explaining the solution to a problem, a difficult task for students. M. P. Jordan's "Structured Information in Functional Writing" (1982) explains one problem-solving approach to help students write reports, using the topics "Situation-Problem-Solution-Evaluation" to guide their analysis. Along these lines, a more detailed set of questions to be applied to problems is given in Michael G. Moran's "A Problem-Solving Heuristic" (1982). Dennis E. Minor's "A Structure for the Problem-Solving Paper" (1982) explains how to keep expanding a general outline to break a problem down into all its parts. Examples are provided. Kenneth R. Mayer in "A Process/ Product Approach to Business Report Writing" (1979) describes how students follow a model report while writing their own. Jeanette W. Gilsdorf's students are taught to use "The Modified Sentence Outlines" (1982) for organization and format.

Everyone trained in literature who teaches technical writing knows the strain of trying to evaluate material about which we are often far from expert. On this subject, J. C. Mathes asserts that English teachers can judge content as well as form. Poor rhetoric, he argues in "Rhetoric and the Engineering Approach" (1972), signals poor technical knowledge, unscientific thinking, and lack of concern for engineering values. There are other issues in evaluation of reports. Barron Wells in "A Plan for Grading Formal Business Reports" (1977) divides the long report into stages. The introduction, review of research procedures, secondary data, primary data, and final summary, conclusion, and recommendations are submitted for comment during the term and are combined at the end of the semester for a final grade. Students receive useful feedback, and instructors' grading loads are lightened. One result of David H. Covington's "A Technical Communication Course Using Peer Evaluation of Reports" (1979) is the students' development of self-esteem as writers. Peer evaluation seems to be commonly used in report writing courses, and yet little attention is given to processes for making it work. Methods for teachers to use in evaluating students' work are presented by David L. Carson and John B. McTasney in "Grading Technical Reports with the Cassette Tape Recorder" (1973) and Elizabeth Tebeaux in "Grade Report Writing with a Check Sheet" (1980).

References

Adelberg, Arthur Harris, and Richard A. Lewis. "Financial Reports Can Be Made More Understandable." *J Account*, 149 (June 1980), 44–50.

Agg, Thomas Radford, and Walter L. Foster. *The Preparation of Engineering Reports*. New York: McGraw-Hill, 1935.

Allanson, Virginia. "Library Instruction for Students in Technical Report Writing Classes." *Tech Writ Teach*, 10 (Fall 1982), 45–47.

Allred, Hilda F. "The Campus Environment and Report Writing." *ABCA Bul*, 39 (June 1976), 20–23.

American National Standards Institute Specification Z39.18–1974. *Guidelines for Format and Production of Scientific and Technical Reports*. New York: ANSI, 1974.

Andrews, Clarence. *Technical and Business Writing*. Boston: Houghton Mifflin, 1975.

Arnold, Vanessa Dean. "The Business Report: A Basic Element in Basic Business Education." *J Bus Educ*, 58 (Jan. 1983), 157–60.

Atkinson, Ted. "Doing Institutional Research to Teach the Long Report." *ABCA Bul*, 46 (Mar. 1983), 10–11.

Auger, Charles Peter, ed. *Use of Reports Literature*. Hamden, Conn.: Archon, 1975.

Baim, Joseph. "In-House Training in Report Writing: A Collaborative Approach." *ABCA Bul*, 40 (Dec. 1977), 5–8.

Baker, Ray Palmer, and Almonte Charles Howell. *The Preparation of Reports: Scientific, Engineering, Administrative, Business*. New York: Ronald, 1938.

Ballard, Charles R. "Some Tips on Improving Your Report Writing." *Prac Account*, 13 (Nov. 1980), 43–47.

Baty, Wayne Murlin. "Using the Critique as a Report-Writing Assignment." *ABCA Bul*, 37 (Mar. 1974), 20–22.

Baxter, J. E. "Technical Report Writing in Victoria, Australia." *J Tech Writ Comm*, 1, No. 3 (1971), 223–27.

Benjamin, Flissy. "Impress Top Management with Your Written Reports." *Chemical Engineering*, 26 Mar. 1979, pp. 179–80. Reprinted in *IEEE Trans Prof Comm*, PC–22, No. 4 (Dec. 1979), 202–203.

Berenson, Conrad T., and Raymond R. Colton. *Research and Report Writing for Business and Economics*. New York: Random House, 1971.

Bernstein, Leopold A. *Understanding Corporate Reports: A Guide to Financial Statement Analysis*. Homewood, Ill.: Dow-Jones-Irwin, 1974.

Berry, Robert E. "First Response Procedures for Hazardous Materials." *Poll Eng*, 12 (Oct. 1980), 37–41.

Bishop, Malden Grange. *Billions for Confusion: The Technical Writing Industry*. Charlotte, N.C.: McNally, Loftin, 1963.

Black, Max. "Improving Nonpublic Company Financial Reports." *CPA J*, 45 (Oct. 1975), 76–77.

Black, T. W. "Tips on Writing Engineering Reports." *Tool Manuf Eng* 48 (Feb. 1962), 72–76.

Blickle, Margaret D., and Kenneth W. Houp. *Reports for Science and Industry*. 2nd ed. New York: Holt, Rinehart, Winston, 1961.

Blicq, Ron. *Guidelines for Report Writers: A Complete Manual for On-the-Job Report Writing*. Englewood Cliffs, N.J.: Prentice-Hall, 1982.

———. *Technically Write: Communication in a Technological Era*. 2nd ed. Englewood Cliffs, N.J.: Prentice-Hall, 1981.

Brearly, N. "The Role of Technical Reports in the Scientific and Technical Communities." *IEEE Trans Prof Comm*, PC–16, No. 3 (1973), 117–19.

British Standards Institute. *British Standard 4811:1972—Specifications for the Presentation of Research and Development Reports*.

Britt, Steuart Henderson. "Writing of Readable Research Reports." *J Mark Res*, 8 (May 1971), 262–66.

Bromage, Mary C. "Wording the Management Audit Report." *J Account*, 133 (Feb. 1972), 50–57.

————. *Writing Audit Reports*. New York: McGraw-Hill, 1979.

Brookes, B. C. "Report Writing Improves with Morale." *Engineering*, 3 Mar. 1961, pp. 315–16.

Brunner, Ingrid, J. C. Mathes, and Dwight W. Stevenson. *The Technician as Writer: Preparing Technical Reports*. Indianapolis: Bobbs-Merrill, 1980.

Bumstead, John C. "Concept of the Modern Engineering Report." *Water Sew Works*, 30 Nov. 1962, pp. R16–18.

Burgess, J. A. "File Now, Find Later." *Mach Des*, 28 Apr. 1966, pp. 176–80.

Caldwell, John. "The Effective Report Crisis." *J Sys Manag*, 26 (June 1975), 7–12.

Campfield, William L. "Primer on Reports That Persuade Managerial Action." *Adv Manag J*, 32 (July 1967), 69–73.

Carson, David L., and John B. McTasney. "Grading Technical Reports with the Cassette Tape Recorder: The Results of a Test Program at the United States Air Force Academy." *J Tech Writ Comm*, 3, No. 3 (1973), 131–44.

Cederborg, G. A. "Write Disciplined Reports, That Captivate Your Readers." *Chem Eng* 7 July 1975, pp. 98, 100.

Clark, Richard L. "How to Prepare Inspection Reports." *Hydrocarbon Process*, 57 (Feb. 1978), 159 and (Mar. 1978), 159. Reprinted in *IEEE Trans Prof Comm*, PC-22, No. 4 (Dec. 1979).

Clarke, Emerson. *A Guide to Technical Literature Production: A Concise Guide to Production Methods*. River Forest, Ill.: TW Publishers, 1961.

"Color Bolsters Technical Reports; Gulf Research and Development." *Indus Photo*, 10 (Jan. 1961), 30–31.

Comer, David B., and Ralph R. Spillman. *Modern Technical and Industrial Reports*. New York: Putnam, 1962.

Cooper, Bruce M. *Writing Technical Reports*. Baltimore: Penguin, 1964.

Covington, David H. "A Technical Communication Course Using Peer Evaluation of Reports." *Eng Educ*, 69 (Feb. 1979), 417–19.

"Critical Look at Report Writing." *Manag Rev*, 64 (Dec. 1975), 46–48.

Cury, Robert. "Visual/Graphic Aids for the Technical Report." *J Tech Writ Comm*, 9, No. 3 (1980), 287–91.

Damerst, William A. *Clear Technical Reports*. New York: Harcourt Brace, Jovanovich, 1972.

Darby, Ralph L., and Walter H. Veazie. "Writing a State-of-the-Art Report." *Mat Res Stan*, 8 (May 1968), 28–32.

Davis, Dale Stroble. *Elements of Engineering Reports*. New York: Chemical Publishing Co., 1963.

Demare, George. *A Handbook of Model Reports to Clients*. New York: Price, Waterhouse, 1964.

Devine, J. B. "Write Better Reports." *Tool Manuf Eng*, 53 (Sept. 1964), 73–74.

Dowst, Somerby. "Informal Correspondence Gets Results." *Purchasing*, 9 Jan. 1969, pp. 117.

Drossel, Margaret. "How to Attack a Special Assignment." *Chem Eng*, 16 July 1979, pp. 115–16, 118.

Dudley, Juanita Williams. "Report Monopoly: The Hottest Game in Town." *ABCA Bul*, 37 (Sept. 1977), 30–34.

Effective Communication for Engineers. New York: McGraw-Hill, 1975.

Ehrenberg, A.S.C. "Annual Reports Don't Have to Be Obscure." *J Account*, 142 (Aug. 1976), 88–92.

Estrin, Herman. "Teaching Report Writing." *Civ Eng*, 38 (Dec. 1968), 64–65.

Federal Council for Science and Technology. *The Role of the Technical Report in Scientific and Technical Communication*. Washington, D.C.: COSATI, 1968. PB–180–944.

Federal Electric Corporation. *How to Write Effective Reports*. Reading, Mass.: Addison-Wesley, 1963.

Fife, Jim, and William F. Carstens. *A Practical Approach to Writing*. Glenview, Ill.: Scott, Foresman, 1967.

"Fight Paper Pollution, Stamp Out Reports." *Indus Week*, Mar. 1970, pp. 36–40.

Fitting, Ralph U. *Report Writing*. New York: Ronald, 1924.

Foy, Fred C. "Accounting Reports Don't Have to Be Dull." *Harvard Bus Rev*, 51 (Jan.-Feb. 1973), 49.

Francis, Robert A. "A Good Title: Prescription for a Good Report." *ABCA Bul*, 37 (June 1974), 31–35.

Fuller, Don. "How to Write Reports That Won't Be Ignored." *Mach Des*, 11 Jan. 1979, pp. 76–79.

Gallagher, William J. *Report Writing for Management*. Reading, Mass.: Addison-Wesley, 1969.

———. *So You Have to Write a Report*. Cambridge, Mass.: Arthur D. Little, 1963.

Gilmore, Frank. *Formulation and Advocacy of Business Policy*. Ithaca, N.Y.: Cornell University, 1970.

Gilsdorf, Jeanette W. "The Modified Sentence Outlines: A Timesaving Report Format." *ABCA Bul*, 45 (Mar. 1982), 15–18.

Gisselman, Robert D. "A Nontraditional Report Writing Course: A Modest Proposal." *Tech Writ Teach*, 8 (Spring 1981), 62–65.

Glidden, H. F. *Reports, Technical Writing, and Specifications*. New York: McGraw-Hill, 1964.

Glover, John George. *Business Operational Research and Reports*. New York: American Book Co., 1949.

Gould, Jay R. "Ten Common Weaknesses in Engineering Reports." *Chem Eng*, 14 Oct. 1963, pp. 210, 212, 214.

Graves, H. F., and Lyne S. Hoffman. *Report Writing*. 4th ed. Englewood Cliffs, N.J.: Prentice-Hall, 1965.

Gray, Dwight E. *So You Have to Write a Technical Report: Elements of Technical Report Writing*. Washington, D.C.: Information Resources Press, 1970.

Gros, Ridley J. "Determining the Effectiveness of Selected Techniques Taught in Business Report Writing." *J Bus Comm*, 11 (Spring 1974), 21–27.

Haggblade, Berle. *Business Communication*. St. Paul: West Publishing Co., 1982.

Harvill, L., and Thomas L. Kraft. *Technical Report Standards: How to Prepare and Write Effective Technical Reports*. La Mesa, Calif.: Banner Books International, 1977.

Hays, Robert William. *Principles of Technical Writing*. Reading, Mass.: Addison-Wesley, 1965.

Herzog, Raymond E. "How to Write Reports That Bring Results." *Elect Eng* 28 (Dec. 1969), 33–34.

Hicks, Tyler G. "How to Write Reports That Get Read." *SAE J*, 68 (Nov. 1960), 75–79.

————. *Writing for Engineering and Science*. New York: McGraw-Hill, 1961.

Hill, James W. "Help Fight CPD [Communications Planning Deficiency]: Plan Your Report with Your Project—and Optimize the Quality of Each." *Sup Manag*, 24 (Dec. 1979), 8–14.

Hillman, Howard. *The Art of Writing Business Reports and Proposals*. New York: Vanguard, 1981.

Himstreet, William C., and Wayne Murlin Baty. *Business Communications: Principles and Methods*. 5th ed. Belmont, Calif.: Wadsworth, 1977.

Hine, Edward A. "Write in Style: Be Clear and Concise." *Chem Eng*, 22 Dec. 1975, pp. 40–52.

Hissong, Douglas W. "Write and Present Persuasive Reports." *Chem Eng*, 4 July 1977, pp. 131–32.

Hoer, Kenneth L. "How to Make Technical Reports Communicate." *SAE J*, 77 (Feb. 1969), 37–38.

Hogan, Harriet. "A Cooperative Course in Communication and Technology." *Tech Writ Teach*, 7 (Spring 1980), 108–12.

Holcombe, Marya W., and Judith K. Stein. *Writing for Decision Makers: Memos and Reports with a Competitive Edge*. Belmont, Calif.: Lifetime Learning Publications, 1981.

Holden, G. Fredric. "Dress Up Your Technical Reports." *Chem Eng*, 27 Dec. 1971, pp. 80–83.

Hoshovsky, A. G. *Suggested Criteria for Titles, Abstracts, and Index Terms in Department of Defense Technical Reports*. Office of Aerospace Research, AD–622 944 (1965).

Houlehen, Robert. "Writing Reports That Communicate." *Indus Week*, 22 Sept. 1975, p. 46.

Houp, Kenneth W., and Margaret B. Blickle. *Reports for Science and Industry*. 2nd ed. New York: Holt, Rinehart, Winston, 1961.

————, and Thomas Pearsall. *Reporting Technical Information*. 5th ed. Beverly Hills, Calif.: Glencoe, 1984.

"How to Write a Report," *Banking*, June 1976, pp. 43–44, 65, 68, 70.

Johnson, Robert L. "Writing the Exception Report." *Bus Auto*, 16 (Feb. 1969), 72, 74.

Johnson, Thomas P. "Organize the Report for Fast Writing, Easy Reading." *Chem Eng*, 30 June 1969, pp. 104–10.

Jones, W. Paul. *Writing Scientific Papers and Reports*. 8th ed. Rev. Michael L. Keene. Dubuque, Iowa: William C. Brown, 1981.

Joplin, Bruce, and James W. Pattillo. *Effective Accounting Reports*. Englewood Cliffs, N.J.: Prentice-Hall, 1969.

Jordan, M. P. "Structured Information in Functional Writing." *TETYC*, 9 (Fall 1982), 61–64.

Kaftan, Robert A. "The Long Report: A Comprehensive Model." *ABCA Bul*, 44 (Dec. 1981), 35–36.

Kaltenbach, Joan C. "The Effects of Two Teaching Methodologies on the Performance and Attitudes of Students in a Technical Report-Writing Course." *J Tech Writ Comm*, 10, No. 4 (1980), 323–27.

Kendig. William L., and Thomas D. Johnson. "Developing Systematic Reporting Structures." *Manag Ad*, Jan. 1972, pp. 20–26.

Kolins, Wayne. "Accounting and Auditing Reports: New Guidelines for Preparing Special Reports." *Prac Account*, 10 (Mar.-Apr. 1977), 45–47.

Krimm, Bernard, and Stuart Glogoff. "The Information Resources Report: A Method for Integrating Library Instruction with Technical Writing Courses." *Tech Writ Teach*, 7 (Fall 1979), 35–38.

Lahiff, James M. "Effective Research: The Route to Good Reports." *ABCA Bull*, 37 (Mar. 1974), 25.

Laird, J. P. "How to Start to Write a Report." *Prod Eng*, 23 Jan. 1961, pp. 46–47.

Lannon, John M. *Technical Writing*. 2nd ed. Boston: Little, Brown, 1982.

Ledbetter, Robert R. "The Field Trip as a Means of Topic Selection." *Tech Writ Teach*, 6 (Fall 1978), 22–23.

Lesikar, Raymond. *Business Communication: Theory and Practice*. 4th ed. Homewood, Ill.: Richard D. Irwin, 1980.

———. *How to Write a Report Your Boss Will Read and Remember*. Homewood, Ill.: Dow-Jones-Irwin, 1974.

———. *Report Writing for Business*. 6th ed. Homewood, Ill.: Richard D. Irwin, 1981.

Lewis, Ronello B. *Accounting Reports for Management*. Englewood Cliffs, N.J.: Prentice-Hall, 1957.

Lipson, Carol S. "Theoretical and Empirical Considerations for Designing Openings of Technical and Business Reports." *J Bus Comm*, 20 (Winter 1983), 41–53.

Locker, Kitty O. "Teaching Students to Write Abstracts." *Tech Writ Teach*, 10 (Fall 1982), 17–20.

Lull, Robert A. "Reporting Results: Get to Your Boss Before He Gets to You." *Sup Manag*, 18 (Mar. 1973), 9–14.

Lundborg, Louis B. "Selling Report Writing." *Indus Week*, 14 May 1979, p. 162.

McIntyre, Edward V. "Communicating Through Financial Reports: An Empirical Study." *J Bus Comm*, 12 (Spring 1975), 9–15.

McMahon, E. M., R. S. Birdwell, G. S. Cassell, and M. West. *Preparation of Technical Reports and Papers*. Kingsport, Tenn.: Tennessee Eastman Co., Research Laboratories, 1962.

McMaster, John B. *The Network Reports System of Analysis and Control*. New York: AMACOM, 1977.

Maniak, Angela. "Clear Writing: Rx for Foggy Audit Reports," *Inter Aud*, 38 (Aug. 1981), 44–50.

Mann, L., Jr. "Do They Read Your Reports? If Not, Here Are Some Simple Rules to Follow." *Plant Eng*, 15 (Mar. 1961), 130–32.

Marcum, Patricia J. "An English Ph.D in the College of Business." *ABCA Bul* 40 (Sept. 1977), 19–20.

Marschner, R. F., and J. O. Howe. "How to Train People to Write Better Reports." *Oil Gas J*, 27 Mar. 1961, pp. 94–96.

Mathes, J. C. "Rhetoric and the Engineering Approach." *J Tech Writ Comm*, 2, No. 2 (1972), 119–27.

———, and Dwight W. Stevenson. "Completing the Bridge: Report Writing in 'Real Life' Engineering Courses." *Eng Educ*, 67 (Nov. 1976), 150–53.

———. *Designing Technical Reports: Writing for Audiences in Organizations*. Indianapolis: Bobbs-Merrill, 1976.

Matlak, Edward W. "Structured Report Programs." *J Sys Manag*, 29 (Oct. 1978), 42–45.

Matt, Richard J. "The Case for Engineering Project Reports." *Mach Des*, 7 Nov. 1968, pp. 157–60.

Mayer, Kenneth R. "A Process/Product Approach to Business Report Writing." *ABCA Bul*, 42 (June 1979), 18-21.

Menkus, Belden. "Effective Systems Reports." *J Sys Manag*, 27 (Sept. 1976), 18–20.

Michaelson, Herbert B. *How to Write and Publish Engineering Papers and Reports*. Philadelphia: ISI Press, 1982.

Miller S. "Reports Worth Reading." *Env Sci Tech*, 14 (Apr. 1980), 376.

Minor, Dennis E. "A Structure for the Problem-Solving Paper." *Tech Writ Teach*, 10 (Fall 1982), 8–11.

Monroe, Judson. *Effective Research and Report Writing in Government*. New York: McGraw-Hill, 1980.

Moran, Michael G. "A Problem-Solving Heuristic." *Tech Comm* 29, No. 3 (1982), 38.

Morris, John O., and Thomas R. Wilcox. "Well-Written Credit Reports: A Successful Program." *J Comm Bank Lend* 56 (July 1974), 51–63.

Mueller, John. "How to Prepare an EIR [Environmental Impact Report]." *Chem Eng*, 21 Oct. 1974, pp. 39–43.

Murdick, Robert G. "Engineering and Research Reports," *Mach Des*, 31 Aug. 1961, pp. 70–75.

Murphy, Herta A., and Charles E. Peck. *Effective Business Communication*. 2nd ed. New York: McGraw-Hill, 1976.

Nelson, E. N. "Technical Presentations: To Enlighten or Obscure." *Air Pol Cont Assoc*, 27 (Jan. 1977), 22–25.

O'Keeffe, Kathryn. "Effective Technical Reporting: Put Life in Your Technical Report." *Pet Ref*, 39 (Dec. 1960), 109–15.

Palen, Jennie M. *Report Writing for Accountants*. Englewood Cliffs, N.J.: Prentice-Hall, 1955.

Parker, I. "Ten Ways to Make Your Reports and Publications Unreadable." *Engineering*, 218 (Feb. 1978), 145.

Parr, William M. *Executive's Guide to Effective Letters and Reports*. West Nyack, N.Y.: Parken, 1976.

Pattillo, James W. "Communication Through Reports." *Manag Account*, 51 (Oct. 1969), 19–22.

Pauley, Steven J. *Technical Report Writing Today*. 2nd ed. Boston: Houghton Mifflin, 1979.

Pearsall, Thomas E. *Audience Analysis for Technical Writing*. Beverly Hills, Calif.: Glencoe, 1969.

Petrolino, Bob. "Do-it-Yourself Editing." *Mach Des*, 9 Mar. 1972, pp. 93–94.

Piper, Henry Dan, and Frank E. Davie. *Guide to Technical Reports*. New York: Rinehart, 1958.

Pitner, Stephen L. "Improve Your Method of Preparing a Technical Study." *Chem Eng*, 24 Apr. 1978, pp. 105–106.

Potvin, Janet H., and Robert L. Woods. "Teaching Technical Communication at the Graduate Level: An Interdisciplinary Approach." *J Tech Writ Comm*, 13, No. 3 (1983), 235–46.

Quackenbos, H. M. "Creative Report Writing. Parts I and II." *Chem Eng*, 10 July 1972, p. 94; 24 July 1972, p. 146.

Ranous, Charles A. *Communication for Engineers*. Boston: Allyn, Bacon, 1964.

Rathbone, Robert R., and James B. Stone. *A Writer's Guide for Engineers and Scientists*. Englewood Cliffs, N.J.: Prentice-Hall, 1962.

Raudsepp, Eugene. "How to Write Effective Reports." *Mach Des*, 17 Dec. 1964, pp. 122–26.

Reep, Diana. "Questionnaires and Informal Reports: A Project for Freshman Technical Writing Students." *Tech Writ Teach*, 7 (Winter 1980), 74–75.

Reimold, Cheryl. "The Language of Business: The Technical Report." *Tappi*, 64 (Nov. 1981), 124; 65 (Jan. 1982), 60–61 and (Feb. 1982), 78–79.

Reiter, Michael J. "Reports That Communicate." *Manag Serv*, 4 (Jan, 1967), 27–30.

"Reports Production: Howard, Needles, Tammen and Bergendoff Style." *Civ Eng*, 36 (Oct. 1966), 54–55.

"Report Writer Helps Get Reports to Users." *Infosystems*, 27 (Apr. 1980), 92.

Rhodes, Fred H. *Technical Report Writing*. 2nd ed. New York: McGraw-Hill, 1961.

Richards, Robert W. "Engineering Reports: Prerequisite for Progress." *Public Works*, 96 (Dec. 1965), 101–102.

———. "A New Look at Engineering Reports." *Civ Eng*, 36 (Oct. 1966), 52–53.

Richards, Thomas O., and Ralph A. Richardson. *Technical Writing*. Detroit: Research Laboratories Division, General Motors Corp., 1941.

Roberts, David. "Teaching Abstracts in Technical Writing: Early and Often." *Tech Writ Teach*, 10 (Fall 1982), 12–16.

Robinson, David M. *Writing Reports for Management Decisions*. Columbus, Ohio: Merrill, 1969.

Rogers, Raymond A. *How to Report Research and Development Findings to Management*. New York: Pilot Industries, 1973.

Rosenfield, Marlene. "Prove It: Write Me a Persuasive Report." *ABCA Bul*, 40 (Sept. 1977), 20.

Rosenstein, Allen B., Robert R. Rathbone, and William F. Schneerer. *Engineering Communications*. Prentice-Hall Series in Engineering Design. Ed. James B. Reswick. Englewood Cliffs, N.J.: Prentice-Hall, 1964.

Roundy, Nancy. "A Process Approach to Teaching the Abstract." *ABCA Bul*, 45 (Sept. 1982), 34–38.

———. "Team-Teaching Technical Writing: A Practical Approach to a Practical Discipline." *Tech Writ Teach*, 9 (Fall 1981), 23–24.

Rutter, Russell, and Karl E. Gwiasda. *Writing Professional Reports: A Guide for Students*. Dubuque, Iowa: Kendall/Hunt, 1977.

Saalbach, W. F. "Written Report: How to Approach It." *Coal Age*, 78 (Sept. 1973), 102.

Saunders, Alta Gwinn, and Chester Reed Anderson. *Business Reports: Investigation and Presentation*. 2nd ed. New York: McGraw-Hill, 1940.

Sawyer, Thomas S. *Specification and Engineering Writer's Manual*. Chicago: Nelson-Hall, 1960.

Schultz, Howard, and Robert G. Webster. *Technical Report Writing: A Manual and Source Book*. New York: D. McKay, 1962.

Seed, Allen H. "Improving the Effectiveness of Management Reports." *Fin Ex*, 37 (Sept. 1969), 62–63, 65–67.

Sharbrough, William C. "Increasing Student Involvement: Using Nominal Grouping to Generate Formal Report Topics." *ABCA Bul*, 45 (June 1982), 44–45.

Sherman, Theodore A. *Modern Technical Writing*. 2nd ed. Englewood Cliffs, N.J.: Prentice-Hall, 1966.

————, and Simon S. Johnson. *Modern Technical Writing*. 3rd ed. Englewood Cliffs, N.J.: Prentice-Hall, 1975.

Sherrin, David C. "Guided Design: Design and Evaluation of an Instructional Unit in Technical Report Writing." *J Eng Educ*, 62 (Apr. 1972), 814–15

Shurter, Robert L., J. Peter Williamson, and Wayne G. Broehl, Jr. *Business Research and Report Writing*. New York: McGraw-Hill, 1965.

Sigband, Norman B. *Communication for Management and Business*. 2nd ed. Glenview, Ill.: Scott, Foresman, 1976.

————. "Effective Communication: Key to Promotion." *Chem Eng*, 80, No. 17 (1973), 122, 124, 126.

————. *Effective Report Writing: For Business, Industry, and Government*. New York: Harper, 1960.

————. "Writing Reports That Lead to Effective Decisions." *Sup Manag*, 15 (June 1970), 2–6.

————, and David N. Batman. *Communicating in Business*. Glenview, Ill.: Scott, Foresman, 1981.

Silver, Marilyn B. "Technical Report Writing in the Community College: An Interdisciplinary Approach." *Tech Writ Teach*, 9 (Spring 1982), 173–78.

Sklare, Arnold B. *Creative Report Writing*. New York: McGraw-Hill, 1964.

Skolnik, Herman. "Communicating Technical Information." *IEEE Trans Prof Comm*, PC–24, No. 2 (1981), 72.

————, and L. F. McBurney. "Technical Reports and Decision-Making." *Chem Tech*, Feb. 1971, pp. 82–85.

Smith, Charles B. "How to Write a Poor Report." *Appr J*, 41 (Apr. 1973), 254–59.

Smith, Marshall. "Improve Your Report Writing. Parts I, II, and III." *Sup Manag*, 13 (Dec. 1968), 2–5; 14 (Jan. 1969), 7–9; and (Feb. 1969), 15–18.

Smook, G. A. "Illustrative Techniques for Technical Reports." *Chem Eng*, 21 Feb. 1972, pp. 62–67.

Souther, James W., and Myron L. White. *Technical Report Writing*. 2nd ed. New York: Wiley, 1977.

Southgate, Michael. "Plessy Researches Financial Reporting." *Indus Mark*, 62 (Apr. 1977), 112, 114, 116.

Spaulding, William E. "The Anatomy of a Business Report." *Data Manag* 11 (July 1973), 16–20.

Stalnaker, Bonny J. "Documented Position Paper: A Useful Approach to Teaching the Formal Research Report." *ABCA Bul*, 41 (June 1978), 15–17.

Stevens, R. I. "Exception Reporting." *J Sys Manag*, 25 (May 1974), 37.

Stevens, Robley D. "Can You Write a Good Engineering Report?" *Petro Manag*, 34 (Mar. 1962), 32–33.

————. "You, Too, Can Write a Good Engineering Report." *Plant Eng*, 18 (Sept. 1964), 147.

Stratton, Charles R. "The Electric Report Card: A Followup on Cassette Grading." *J Tech Writ Comm* 5 (1975), 17–22.

Summers, W. "How to Present Interesting Reports." *Sup Manag*, 17 (Oct. 1972), 36–39.

Swift, Marvin. "Writing a Conclusion." *ABCA Bul*, 44 (Dec. 1981), 19–21.

"Teaching the Boss to Write." *Bus Week*, 25 Oct. 1976, pp. 56, 58.

Tebeaux, Elizabeth. "Grade Report Writing with a Check Sheet." *Tech Writ Teach*, 7 (Winter 1980), 66–68.

Tinsley, D. B., and Conway T. Rucks. "Interim Reports: A Neglected Aspect of Marketing Research." *J Bus Comm*, 13 (Winter 1976), 3–10.

Tschantre, M. A. *Preparation of Research and Engineering Reports*. Wilson Dam, Ala.: Tennessee Valley Authority, Division of Chemical Engineering, June 1950.

Turner, Rufus P. *Technical Report Writing*. Rev. ed. San Francisco: Rinehart, 1971.

Tuttle, Robert E., and C. A. Brown. *Writing Useful Reports: Principles and Applications*. New York: Appleton-Century-Crofts, 1956.

Tver, David F. "Do Your Reports Get Out-box Reviews?" *Hydrocarbon Process*, 46 (Aug. 1967), 167–70.

Ullman, J. N., and Jay R. Gould. *Technical Reporting*. 3rd ed. New York: Holt, Rinehart, Winston, 1972.

U.S. Department of Defense. MIL-STD-847A: *Format Requirements for Scientific and Technical Reports Prepared by or for the Department of Defense*. Alexandria, Va., 1973.

U.S. Department of Transportation. *Format and Distribution Requirements for DOT Scientific and Technical Reports*. Washington, D.C. DOT: 1972. PB–222 172/9.

U.S. Federal Council for Science and Technology, Committee on Scientific and Technical Information. *Guidelines to Format Standards for Scientific and Technical Reports Prepared by or for the Federal Government*. Washington, D.C.: [Clearinghouse for Federal Scientific and Technical Information, Springfield, Va.], 1968. PB– 180–600 (1968).

VanFleet, Ellamaye. "Determining the Content of a Collegiate Report-Writing Course." *J Bus Comm*, 8 (Spring 1971), 27–38.

Van Hagen, Charles E. *Report Writer's Handbook*. Englewood Cliffs, N.J.: Prentice-Hall, 1961.

Vinci, Vincent. "Ten Report Writing Pitfalls: How to Avoid Them." *Chem Eng*, 22 Dec. 1975, pp. 45–48.

"Visualize Your Reports." *Office*, Apr. 1974, pp. 116–17.

Wainright, Gordon. "Effective Report Writing." *Aircraft Eng* 40 (Apr. 1968): 35–37.

Waldo, Willis H. *Better Report Writing*. New York: Reinhold, 1965.

Walter, John. "Supplements to the Technical Report." *Petro Ref*, 39 (Dec. 1960), 116–20.

Warren, Thomas L. "Teaching Formal Technical Reports." *TETYC*, 8 (Winter 1982), 137–42.

Watt, James T., and Wade S. Hobbs. "Research and Report Writing: A Model of Their Interrelationships." *ABCA Bul* 42 (Sept. 1979), 22–25.

Weaver, Robert G., and Patricia C. Weaver. *Persuasive Writing: A Manager's Guide to Effective Letters and Reports*. Riverside, N.J.: Free Press, 1977.

Weightman, Frank C. "The Executive Summary: An Indispensable Management Tool." *ABCA Bul*, 45 (Dec. 1982), 3–5.

Weiner, Alfred N. "Dear Diary." *Indus Eng*, 6 (Nov. 1974), 22–24.

———. "How to Write a Report." *Plas World*, 24 (Jan. 1966), 48–49.

———. "Today's Records, Tomorrow's Reports." *Mach Des*, 27 Feb. 1964, pp. 117–18.

Weisman, Herman M. *Technical Report Writing*. 2nd ed. Columbus, Ohio: Merrill, 1975.

Weiss, Allen. "Beyond Mystery and Style." *Sup Manag*, 23 (Jan. 1978), 29–34.

Weiss, W. H. "Writing Reports Doesn't Need to Be Difficult." *Supervision*, 40 (Dec. 1978), 4–5.

Wells, Barron. "A Plan for Grading Formal Business Reports." *ABCA Bul*, 40 (Sept. 1977), 12.

Wilkinson, Joseph. "Effective Reporting Structures." *J Sys Manag*, 27 (Nov. 1976), 38–42.

Winfrey, Robley. *Technical and Business Report Preparation*. 3rd ed. Ames: Iowa State University Press, 1962.

Woods, Donald R. "How to Outline Your Reports." *Hydrocarbon Process*, 43 (Nov. 1964), 237–38.

———. "Updating Our Approach to Written Communications." *Eng J*, 47 (Oct. 1964), 43–45.

Woolsey, Gene. "On Learning Where to Begin, How to Listen, and Where to Stop." *IEEE Trans Prof Comm* PC–24, No. 4 (Dec 1981), 197–98.

Wotruba, Thomas R., and Richard Mangone. "More Effective Sales Force Reporting." *Indus Mark Manag*, 8 (June 1979), 236-45.

Wright, Patricia. "Alternatives to Prose for Sharp, Hard-Hitting Reports." *Mach Des*, 24 Jan. 1974, pp. 82–84.

"Write Reports That Get Action." *Hydrocarbon Process*, 45 (June 1966), 207–209.

Wulff, P. "Management Report Gets to All Management." *Purchasing*, 5 Mar. 1970, pp. 43–45.

Wyld, Lionel D. *Preparing Effective Reports*. New York: Odyssey, 1967.

Zall, Paul M. *Elements of Technical Report Writing*. New York: Harper, 1962.

Business Letters, Memoranda, and Resumés

MARY HURLEY MORAN and MICHAEL G. MORAN

Business and industry probably produce more pieces of business correspondence than any other kind of document. Even technicians working in the most obscure research laboratory must write letters and memoranda almost daily. If they need a new piece of equipment, they must write letters to the manufacturer to order it. If the equipment arrives damaged, they must write a letter of complaint. If they wish to communicate with their bosses in writing, they generally write a memo. If they want to get a better job, they must compose letters of application and resumés. While writing good reports, proposals, and manuals is an important skill, the ability to write sound, effective letters and memos is just as important because of the large number that the average business person produces in a professional lifetime.

Given this fact, a surprisingly small amount of serious research has been done on business correspondence. Most of the work published during the last 25 years has been redundant and derivative. Instead of designing innovative research projects, writers in the field have tended either to rely on a kind of folk wisdom handed down from generation to generation of writers or to depend on rather limited personal experience. This has led to a great deal of repetition in the published articles.

Some recent research, however, suggests that this trend is changing. New studies have recently appeared that begin to establish basic principles of writing letters and memos. Work has appeared, for instance, on the history of business letters, on innovative and tested methods of organizing them, and on various kinds of empirical studies that measure and evaluate the effectiveness of specific writing techniques. In short, the best of the new research suggests that we are moving toward a sounder rhetoric for business correspondence—but we still have a long way to go.

The present essay surveys the research done in the field since about 1960. Although we cite and discuss all research of note, we attempt to emphasize and identify those studies that appear to be the most innovative and useful. We have concentrated most of our attention on articles and books devoted exclusively to business correspondence, but, because of limitations of space, have not attempted to evaluate all of the business and technical writing books that have chapters or sections on the subject.

Several earlier bibliographies are currently in print, but these cover the entire field of business communication rather than limiting themselves to correspondence. Ruth M. Walsh's *Business Communication* (1973) covers the field in general and has many useful, lightly annotated references to material on letters and memos. Her 1980 *Business Communication*, compiled with Stanley J. Birkin, is more thorough, covering material published in the field in the 1960s and 1970s. This volume is difficult to use since the annotations are separated from the citations. Two other bibliographies are also useful: Mary Ann Bowman's "Books on Business Writing and Technical Writing in the University of Illinois Library" (1975); and Bowman and Joan D. Stamas's *Written Communication in Business* (1980), a selective listing of over 800 books and articles published between 1967 and 1977. The Bowman-Stamas volume pays particular attention to articles on teaching business communication.

This chapter and the References following it fall into three sections: business letters, memoranda, and job letters and resumés.

Business Letters

Only recently have scholars turned their attention to the history of business letters. Luella M. Wolff in "A Brief History of the Art of Dictamen" (1979) argues that letter writing became an important branch of the liberal arts curriculum in medieval universities. Developed in Italy, *dictamen prosaicum* or *ars dictaminis* emphasized the rhetoric of letter writing as the relationships between church and state grew more complicated and both the clergy and the laity had to interact on a daily basis. The specialization gradually waned with the development of complex, precise legal documents and notaries, who took over many functions of the letter writers. Malcolm Richardson, in "The Earliest Business Letters in English" (1980), expands Wolff's work by tracing the rise and fall of *dictamen* in England. As commerce became more important to the nation, the need for scribes grew, and during the fourteenth century, special courses in letter writing appeared at English universities. Richardson also discusses the collections of family business letters of the period that are still extant. In the eighteenth century, as William E. Rivers shows in "Lord Chesterfield on the Craft of Business Writing" (1979), literary figures such as Lord Chesterfield appreciated the importance of well-written business letters. Chesterfield emphasized to his son the need for clarity and audience awareness. He also argued that broad reading of good prose would help the business person write stronger letters. Finally, "The General Manager's Mail, 1879" (1966) excerpts from Marshall Monroe Kirkman's 1879 *Railway Review*, a handbook for railway managers, several letters of complaint which these administrators were expected to answer "with the prescience of a statesman and the facility of a schoolteacher" (p. 369). This suggests that the ability to answer the letter of complaint was recognized as an essential managerial skill as early as the nineteenth century. Since these are the only articles we found on the history of the business letter, it is clear that more research needs to be done on this interesting and important form of communication.

By far, the largest segment of articles on the business letter falls under the general category of "tips." Generally concerned with style, structure, and tone, these articles present a surprisingly consistent and redundant body of practical advice that amounts to a kind of folk wisdom based on tradition and blind faith rather than on research. These principles include such platitudes as personalizing letters by putting the writer's personality in them; avoiding clichés and business jargon; placing the most important information at the beginning; using the "you attitude"; using strong (or picture) verbs, short words, and short sentences; being brief and cutting to the point; selecting concrete words rather than abstract ones; constructing strong paragraphs; and organizing the letter carefully. Rather than discussing all of these articles, we will examine only a few of the outstanding ones and place the majority in a separate section of the References entitled "Tips on Writing Business Letters."

Several of these general articles stand out. Michael H. Murray's "If You Have Any Questions, Please Do Not Hesitate to Contact Us" (1975) suggests that writers should avoid jargon and "Biz-Eng," personalize letters, state points positively, organize with the reader's needs in mind, and be precise by using short paragraphs and simple words. Mary C. Bromage in "The Management of Communications" (1973) gives general advice for improving correspondence, such as using a vocabulary appropriate to the content and audience, using short, memorable sentences, and starting with the single most important point. In one of the most elegant overviews of letter writing, "Making Business Letters Interesting" (1970) (condensed as "Keep Your Letters Interesting" [1971]), writers are advised to read broadly to develop a wide sense of stylistic options, a welcome admonition given the hordes of writers advising simplicity. Cutting against the grain, J. Harold Janis in "Business Writing" (1965) defends the cliché by arguing that business writers use jargon for a reason. The business environment encourages a stereotyped, formal, and impersonal style, and many business situations require fuzzy statements. To change business writing, Janis concludes, one would have to change general business behavior.

Several general books on writing letters merit special mention here. Leslie Llewellyn Lewis's *The Dartnell Business-Letter Deskbook* (1969) is a well-produced book filled with excellent and practical advice for writing all kinds of common business letters. It is notable for its exceptional sample letters. William M. Parr's *Executive's Guide to Effective Letters* (1976) discusses most kinds of common letters while emphasizing how to motivate readers. Luther A. Brock's *How to Communicate by Letter and Memo* (1974), though shorter than the others, is filled with excellent advice, as is L. E. Frailey's *Handbook of Business Letters*

(1965). A good recent book is Ferd Naugheim's *Letter Perfect* (1982), which uses a particularly strong reader-oriented approach and emphasizes difficult letters for awkward situations. Finally, Herman W. Weisman's *Technical Correspondence* (1968) covers all aspects of business and technical letters and is geared to the needs of the practicing professional engineer and scientist.

As might be expected, the sales letter has received quite a bit of attention from researchers. Patrick Monaghan's *Writing Letters That Sell* (1968), though now somewhat dated, maintains that all letters should sell and discusses techniques for writing practically all kinds of letters using a selling edge. In "Take a Letter, Plain and Simple" (1981), Michael G. Hardy makes a similar point by arguing that all letters, like sales letters, must get the reader (1) to take action and (2) to respond in the writer's favor. Sales letters should get attention, create interest, present information, sustain interest, and close effectively. One of the most elegant discussions of sales letters is "Letters That Sell" (1974) which emphasizes principles such as knowing the reader and product before writing, selling with ideas by using proof and reasons, and personalizing the letters even when using formulaic techniques.

Other articles offer similar tips on writing the sales letter effectively. In "Letters You'll Be Proud Of" (1958), Richard H. Morris advises salespeople that they should have a sincere desire to help their fellow human beings and want to write strong, natural, courteous, commonsensical, and creative letters. Ted Pollock in "How Letters Can Multiply Your Sales Wallop" (1959) lists all the ways sales letters can help the salesperson: they can arouse the reader's interest in the product, clinch sales, arrange followup visits, get testimonials from happy customers, ask for leads, convey special offers, and keep in touch with customers. Pollack gives numerous examples of letters that accomplish these functions. Michael Lipman in "How to Sell with the Written Word" (1961) points out that letters must appeal to the underlying, deep desires of readers to be successful. Bob Stone in "Here Are Some Ways You Can Write a Better Sales Letter" (1972) and in "20 Ways to Upgrade Your Sales Letters" (1968) gives practical advice about composing sales letters. Writers should make extensive notes before writing copy, organize the notes, discover effective leads, isolate one big idea with sales appeal, use various hooks and appeals such as testimonials, and so forth. Sig Rosenblum in "Ten Secrets of Better Sales Letters" (1977) offers similar advice.

An interesting and useful series of articles on sales letters is Robert B. Hanford's "The Ten Biggest Mistakes Letter Writers Make," which appears in *Sales Management* from April 17 through September 4, 1964. These articles cover questions of tone, organization, audience analysis, the writer's image, maintaining interest, bad manners to be avoided, and principles of direct mail selling. See the main References for specific references.

Other writers have also concentrated on specific aspects of sales letters. C. J. Schaefer in "Prospects Will Read You If Your..." (1958) lists ten qualities openings should possess that will encourage readers to finish reading sales letters.

The opening must present a clear benefit, raise interesting questions, consist of a short paragraph, be personal, get to the point quickly, and so forth. George B. Anderson in "Dear Mr. Pflug, Here's a Product" (1972) suggests that salespeople view letters as methods for opening, not closing, sales. Writers should, therefore, not try to cover all aspects of the subject or to sell their products too vigorously until they see the customer. Writing for real estate agents, Mark J. Cohen in "Don't Call Them, They'll Call You" (1978) explains his system for convincing an absentee landlord to sell property through a real estate agent. Such letters must be personalized and must create a favorable impression in order to elicit new information, verify old information, and make an appointment. Finally, Robert C. May in "How to Improve Your Sales Correspondence" (1965) discusses the special problems of responding to customer inquiries. He develops a four-step approach that consists of (1) getting to the point quickly, (2) answering all questions carefully, (3) presenting arguments and proofs to defend products, and (4) trying to close a deal if appropriate.

Three articles discuss systems for developing effective sales letter programs in businesses. John D. Yeck in "Reducing Cost of Sales Through Marketing Support Mail" (1977) argues that mail can replace, support, or improve a sales force. He discusses four functions letters can perform for the sales manager: they can (1) find new customers, (2) organize sales time by making appointments, (3) introduce new products, and (4) build good will. "How Every Salesman Can Send Selling Letters" (1965) describes Freemont Industry's "Silent Salesman Kit" that contains eight guide letters for common sales situations. When salespeople want to use a guide letter, they call into the main office where the letter is typed the same day and is readied for their signature and personalized note if one is needed. Finally, Ron Kolgraf in "Put It in Writing" (1980) describes a system that helps the salesperson, who often dislikes writing, construct effective letters.

One specialized kind of sales letter falls under the general category of direct mail advertising: sales letters that are sent directly to the consumer. Because of the glut of junk mail most Americans now receive, these letters must be carefully planned and written in order to be successful. Richard S. Hodgson's *The Dartnell Direct Mail and Mail Order Handbook* (1980) is the best single source of information on the subject. The book is particularly useful because Hodgson acts as an editor, bringing together extensive material from other experts on the subject. Chapters 24, 25, and 26 cover writing and formatting direct mail letters, and these discussions provide both philosophical background and practical advice. A dated but still useful book is John D. Yeck and John T. Maguire's *Planning and Creating Better Direct Mail* (1961), which discusses the advantages of direct mail as well as ways to create effective letters. William G. Werner's "Putting Personality in Print" (1959) discusses various ways to personalize these letters, while in "Some Psychological Aspects of Business Letter Writing" (1963), W. P. Boyd wisely calls for more research to determine the psychological elements of writing these sales letters. However, William L. Shanklin's "Receiver Perspectives on Direct Mail Advertising'' (1975) is one of the few empirical studies we found. The article concludes that reader response suggests that writers should avoid occupant-addressed mail, use the mass media to build product and company recognition before mailing letters, appeal to women since they receive most mail, conduct preliminary research to see if direct mail suits the needs of their companies, and target mail carefully to specific groups.

Articles such as Robert A. Bachle and Goodwin Alarik's "Results—Producing Direct Mail'' (1968) and James H. Koch's "Put Direct Mail on Your Sales Team'' (1973) discuss the power of direct mail in the banking business. Several articles discuss the importance of courses in direct mail in business schools. John D. Yeck in "The Importance of Direct Mail in Business School Education'' (1975) argues that schools should emphasize this letter since it has proven itself so effective, and John T. Maguire in a three-part series entitled "An Outline for a Course in Direct Mail Offered at the University of Illinois'' (1969, 1970, and 1971) justifies, outlines, and provides an extensive, though now dated, bibliography of sources for a course in the subject.

Some work has appeared on special kinds of letters, such as bank, purchasing, personnel, CPA, and insurance letters. Robert H. Morrison and Trudy Sundberg's *Bank Correspondence Handbook* (1964) discusses fundamentals of good writing, various kinds of bank letters with numerous examples of each, and legal aspects of bank correspondence. A useful book because of its bibliography is Clyde O. Draughon's *Practical Bank Letter Writing* (1971). David H. Tuttle has written on bank letters in "Written Communication'' (1967), in which he argues that letters are an important tool for bank workers, who too often are poor letter writers. He recommends that banks give their employees a letter writing course and subscribe to monthly bulletins on letter writing. In "Better Business Writing for Banks'' (1979), Robert S. Mason suggests that major organizational problems within banks lead to poor letter writing. Most banks have no company style that all employees agree upon, and employees pick up bad habits because they use poor models with outdated jargon. In addition, some banks encourage bad correspondence by insisting their employees write to the files, not to people, in order to keep records up to date. Letters, he argues, can and should function as important sales and good will vehicles for banks. J. Ronald Mikels in "Successful Bank Letters'' (1974) also stresses that bank letters should be carefully planned and written to avoid misunderstanding and to engender good will.

In a thorough article, "Share Owner Correspondence Can Establish Corporate Personality'' (1964), William Lee Phyfe discusses the role letters can play within the corporation. Correspondence with investors and stockholders falls into two general categories. The first includes records of shares and action needed to be taken regarding them. These are best handled, he suggests, by the corporation's Treasury Department, which keeps stock records. The second category includes all other matters such as welcome, follow-up, and appreciation letters as well as letters answering questions. All of these, which should be handled by a manager in charge of share owner relations, must be written tactfully in order to establish and maintain good will with investors and potential investors. Joel J. Shulman's *Treasurer's and Comptroller's Letter Book* (1974) discusses the many kinds of letters that the officers of corporations must be able to write. Shulman also analyzes various kinds of form letters useful to corporations.

Lynn Harrington has written two articles on purchasing letters. In "Better Purchasing Letters and How to Write Them" (1966), she stresses that purchasing agents must write strong letters in order (1) to make complex arrangements with sellers and (2) to represent their companies to other firms. To accomplish these goals, letters must be forceful, impressive, and absolutely clear. In Part II of the same article (1966), she discusses the many problems of grammar and usage that agents must avoid when writing.

In "Management Letters" (1967), Mitchell O. Humphrey writes a similar article for CPAs, emphasizing that CPAs should write management letters to their clients to keep them informed and to engender good will. Gordon Prager in "Dear Insured" (1980) argues that insurance agents and executives should write explanatory letters to new insurance policy holders to explain information they might not understand. This, too, generates good will. Mary K. Menger in "Unique Insurance Firm Demonstrates Effective Correspondence System" (1960) describes how the United Services Automobile Association designed a specialized system to train its correspondents to respond to the particular problems their military clients faced. In a highly specialized article, "Correspondence" (1976), Keith Le Rossignol outlines how commercial officers abroad should deal with the complexities of their correspondence. He makes suggestions for using diplomatic pouches, for systematically processing incoming mail, for keeping accurate files of outgoing mail, and for handling other specialized concerns. Another article on a highly specialized kind of letter is Stephen A. Kliment's "Writing for Marketing Impact" (1977), in which he explains how architects can write effective "letters of interest" to potential clients.

We found only two articles on writing personnel and reference letters. "How to Communicate with Employees Through Letters" (1971) describes a plan for increasing employee satisfaction by launching a company letter campaign. These letters should (1) emphasize employee benefits, (2) be easy to read, (3) be convincing and sincere, and (4) tell the employees what they need to know. Such letters can correct misinformation, quell rumors, and establish common ground between executives and workers. T. J. Halatin in "Writing Letters of Reference That Get Results" (1980) establishes useful guidelines for writing letters of recommendation for employees and colleagues. The author suggests that writers evaluate their commitment to the person; help find a stronger reference if they cannot support the person; review thoroughly all qualifications, accomplishments, and skills; and call up the company receiving the letter to learn what information to include and emphasize.

One of the few areas that has been extensively researched using controlled experiments is the cover letter and other letters associated with mailed questionnaires. Paul L. Erdo's *Professional Mail Surveys* (1970), which is based on experimental findings, covers the field of mail surveys in general. In Chapter 12, "The Accompanying Letter," he outlines the principles of writing cover letters that encourage responses. These include such elements as being brief, enclosing a stamped return envelope, and emphasizing reader benefit.

Arnold S. Linsky in "A Factoral Experiment in Inducing Responses to a Mail Questionnaire" (1965) tested four factors in cover letters that affected the rate of return of questionnaires. He found that only the personalization of the letter and the explanation of the importance of the respondent to the study increased the response rate, while the argument for the research's social utility and the appeal for help in conducting the experiment had no significance. In a similar study, described in "The Effects of Source and Appeal on Mail Survey Response Patterns" (1977), Michael J. Houston and John R. Nevin tested three kinds of appeals to questionnaire receivers to encourage response. The first is social utility, or the benefit the study will have for consumers in general. The second emphasizes the assistance the receiver will lend to the organization preparing the study. The third is egoistic appeal—the opportunity for respondents to make themselves heard. The authors also tested various combinations of these appeals. They found that different appeals worked best, depending on whether the sponsor of the study was a business or a university. The social utility appeal worked best for university-sponsored research, while the egoistic appeal worked best for commercial sponsors. Finally, in terms of speed and completeness of the response, appeals one and two seemed to work best for both sponsors. In "Questionnaire Response Rates" (1969), Dean J. Champion and Alan M. Sear found that egoistic appeals emphasizing what benefits the respondent would receive worked best for the lower classes, while altruistic appeals emphasizing the benefits of the study to the research firm worked best for the upper classes. Writers should, they conclude, vary their appeals according to the group addressed.

Other studies have tested more mechanical questions. Raymond Simon in "Responses to Personal and Form Letters in Mail Surveys" (1967) found that in some situations, such as when respondents wish to remain anonymous, form letters lead to higher response rates than do individualized letters. Neil M. Ford in "The Advance Letter in Mail Surveys" (1967) established that advance letters affect only the rate of questionnaire return, not other factors such as quickness or thoroughness of response. Waldeman M. Goulet in "Efficacy of a Third Request Letter in Mail Surveys of Professionals" (1977) demonstrated that when surveying business executives persistence pays off: the third request letter prodded 24 percent of the non-respondents to send in the completed questionnaire. James H. Meyers and Arne F. Haug in "How a Preliminary Letter Affects Mail Survey Return and Costs" (1969) found that a preliminary or preparatory letter increased returns about 28 percent. The additional mailing was so expensive, however, that it appears to be wiser just to send out questionnaires to a large enough sample to begin with. Michael A. McGinnis and Charles J. Hollon in "Mail Survey Response Rate and Bias" (1977) found no difference in response rate if the questionnaire was sent to the executives' home or office. Leslie Kanuk and Conrad Berenson in "Mail Surveys and Response Rates" (1975), after reviewing previous studies, argue that personalizing such correspondence by typing and signing individual letters does little good. Finally, Donald P. Robin and C. Glenn Walters in "The Effect on Return Rate of Messages Explaining Monetary Incentives" (1976) established that any kind of monetary incentive (enclosing 10 cents in this case) makes cover letters more effective.

One study of cover letters that has caused some controversy is John W. Anderson's "Determining the Effects of Order of Presentation in Special Request Letters" (1970). Anderson tested the Attention, Interest, Desire, Conviction, Action (AIDCA) method of organization in which the writer organizes a letter sequentially to attract attention, stimulate interest and desire, gain reader conviction, and galvanize readers to action. Anderson constructed a letter that would read coherently no matter how each of these parts was ordered and sent different versions to four groups of companies asking their presidents to fill out a questionnaire. He concluded that the traditional AIDCA organization pattern had no significant influence. G. H. Douglas, editor of the *Journal of Business Communication* at the time, published a critique of the study, arguing that it was trivial because teachers would still teach traditionally sound, orderly methods of organization even if studies suggested poorly written ones were as effective ("Editor's Comment [1970]). In a second article, "The Effect of Order of Information in a Questionnaire Cover Letter Situation" (1976), Anderson reports on a somewhat broader study that supports the results of his first one.

One point often made about business letters is that they should always establish and develop good will. In an excellent overview of the importance of letter writing in general, Walter Weir in "Is Business Correspondence a Bothersome Chore?" (1977) argues that letters are the most important single form of communication in business because they have the potential to establish and foster good will. As Luther A. Brock argues in *How to Build Goodwill Through Credit Correspondence* (1976), even in collection letters writers should foster good will. In two articles, "Write a Better Letter" (1978) and "Business Letters That Aren't All Business" (1971), Brock maintains that the human touch in any letter leads to good will. One of the simplest ways to generate good will, Malcolm S. Forbes comments in "No Answer Is No Answer" (1965), is to respond to all correspondence as soon as it arrives. As A. Donald Brice in "Write? Right!" (1960) and Richard R. Conarroe in "How Public Relations Helps Sales" (1973) point out, letters are one of the most effective public relations tools a company has.

Other articles offer practical suggestions for creating good will. Sidney C. Duerr in "How Best to Sell Yourself to the Boss?" (1961) suggests that credit departments write courtesy letters to paying customers during special occasions. Al W. Switzler in "Goodwill, Generosity, and Grammar" (1977) argues that all letters have two messages, the intended and the unintended. Sloppy, dirty, poorly written letters suggest an ungenerous spirit and undermine good will. C. W. Fishbaugh in "What Happened to Letter Writing?" (1973) encourages bankers to write good will letters regularly to customers, and George W. Leffler, writing to real estate agents in "Contact Through Correspondence" (1980), argues that good will letters are one of the best ways to maintain contact with customers.

Letters that affect readers negatively—such as collection, complaint, and bad news letters—have also received recent attention. Richard H. Morris's *Credit and Collection Letters* (1960), after reporting on a study of 500,000 weak collection letters, isolates three qualities effective ones should demonstrate: (1) a personal quality, (2) a strong writing style, and (3) a knowledge of human nature. Morris gives many examples of effective letters from actual company correspondence, and Chapter 27 answers the most common questions asked about these kinds of letters. In "Badly-Written Collection Letters Blamed on Aloof Top Management, Inadequate Training" (1961), Morris blames poor letters on managers who do not recognize the importance of these letters. In *How to Build Goodwill Through Credit Correspondence* (1976) and "Make Your Collection Letters Persuade—Not Plead!" (1968), Luther Brock outlines a series of appeals which writers can use to encourage customers to pay bills without antagonizing them. Writers can appeal to the customers' pride, sense of fairplay, need for the company's products and services, and desire to maintain favorable credit rating. Kenneth J. Forshee in "Every Letter a Sales Letter" (1960) argues that collection letters must be persuasive—they should convince, not force, the reader to pay the bill. These letters should be friendly and should make it easy for the reader to react. "Communicating with Past-Due Accounts" (1976) argues that getting money from past-due customers is a psychological process. Most dunning letters fall into an adult/child pattern when they should either be adult/adult or parent/child. In the first letter, the writer should assume the reader is an adult, but if no response results, the writer should resort to treating the reader as a child who wants to be told what to do in a gentle but firm manner. "Talking Convincingly to Customers By Personalizing Friendly Letters" (1961) argues that credit managers should communicate regularly in a friendly manner to all of their customers to educate them about credit policy, help them solve problems, and establish long-term friendships. Because of the problems of getting customers to respond to follow-up collection letters, Forest F. Bales in "New Twist in Collection Letters" (1963) developed the technique of enclosing a questionnaire in the letters. This greatly improved customer response—70 percent of the questionnaires were returned and 30 percent of these came with checks. John Sklar in "Make Your Follow-ups Work" (1968) explains a system for sending out and keeping track of followup letters, and "Mass Mailing in Minutes" (1975) reports that collection letters can be sent out through Western Union's Mailgram program by renting a TelePost consisting of a screen and a keyboard.

Businesses must be able to handle letters of complaint effectively, as Stanley J. Fenvessy argues in the impressive "Customer Mail" (1970). He outlines a system companies can use to handle and control these letters by (1) keeping track of when letters are received, (2) having staff members specialize in problems, (3) making the most effective letter writers the mail sorters so that important complaints receive attention first, (4) developing systems to help readers make decisions quickly, (5) creating form or guide letters for each major problem, (6) curtailing incoming letters by making sure that all company literature is in plain talk to avoid misunderstanding, and (7) following the maxim that the "customer is always right." In "Cereal Companies Get Letters That Go Snap, Crackle and Pop" (1972), Sandra Ekberg Jordan reports on an empirical study proving that large companies in the cereal industry take complaint letters seriously. She sent 90 complaint letters of various degrees of reasonableness and received 78 answers (86.7 percent). The more reasonable the complaint, she found, the longer the answer. She concludes that letter writing is a serious concern for these companies and that the responses were generally courteous and comprehensive. In another study, "The Complaint Letter" (1977), Peter Mears and Robert Cosenza analyzed the answers they received from 30 companies in the *Fortune* 500 to whom they had sent complaint letters. They isolated three important factors in successful answers: (1) empathy and general helpfulness; (2) "structurality," which includes addressing the specific problem, locating previous correspondence, and providing information to facilitate additional communication; and (3) diplomacy. Although this research suggests that large companies take letters of complaint seriously, "Put Your Complaint in Writing" (1965) argues that government agencies like the Federal Trade Commission can do little to help individual consumers who have been cheated. The article suggests that complaints always be written in letter form and sent first to retailers, and, if the problem is not resolved, to the manufacturing company.

Several researchers have explored the technique of writing letters denying a request. Luther A. Brock in "The 'No' Letter with the 'Yes' Sound" (1969) outlines a five-part structure for a letter of refusal: (1) start with a "buffer paragraph" that establishes common ground with the reader; (2) give logical reasons for the refusal; (3) mention the bad news of the rejection only once in the middle of the letter; (4) present another buffer, such as a counterproposal, to mitigate the effect of the bad news; and (5) and end either by suggesting that the reader take some action or by looking to some positive situation in the future. Vanessa Dean Arnold and Mossetta S. Soskis in " 'We Regret to Inform You' " (1977), Michael H. Murray in "Can You Say 'No' Without Twisting the Knife?" (1974), Ethel Kaplan in "Writing Effective Letters to Customers" (1966), and Bette Ann Stead in "Make a Good Impression When You Write" (1971) discuss similar methods of organizing these letters. Only Frederick W. Harbaugh in " 'No' Letters to Applicants" (1977) argues for starting with the bad news first in job rejection letters on the grounds that such directness is more honest and fair than avoiding the truth. In contrast to the bad news letter, the good news letter is easier to write. As Luther A. Brock in "Give Good News First!" (1969) and John A. Brown in "The Reader-Centered Letter" (1961) show, this letter should begin with what the reader considers good news and then give necessary background information.

Two articles address the question of how to write persuasive letters. John A. Brown's "Letters That Get Action" (1960) argues that the first 10 to 12 words of a persuasive letter are the most important because they must capture the reader's attention and present the most persuasive idea. In an excellent and innovative article, "Writing the Persuasive Business Letter" (1980), Daniel L. Plung develops the "motivated sequence," which is a method of organizing a letter based on John Dewey's problem-solving method. This sequence consists of five stages: (1) locating and defining a problem, (2) analyzing the problem, (3) establishing goals for the solution, (4) selecting the best solution from among those evaluated, and (5) putting the plan into action. Plung makes each of these steps into a rhetorical stage in the letter that leads the reader from recognizing a problem to accepting a solution to it to taking action to implement the solution. The method works well, Plung shows, when writing sales letters. Michael G. Moran in "Writing Business Correspondence Using the Persuasive Sequence" (1984) develops a similar approach.

With the increasing cost of sales and other letters because of rising postage, paper, and labor costs, many companies have turned to form and guide letters to save time and money. Several recent books have appeared that discuss various kinds of form letters. Martha W. Cresci's *Complete Book of Model Business Letters* (1976) discusses numerous kinds of common business letters, while Julien Elfenbein's *Handbook of Business Form Letters and Forms* (1972) emphasizes the 18 most typical kinds. A more specialized volume is Claire Neff Eddings's *Secretary's Complete Model Letter Handbook* (1965), which gives examples of typical letters secretaries might have to write and answer. Joseph L. Kish in "High Correspondence Costs?" (1966) describes a procedure for developing appropriate form letters: (1) classify all letters and memos that go out over a two-month period; (2) review all letters in each class for similarities and differences; and (3) determine which types can be made into form letters. Bess Ritter in "How to Reduce Bank Correspondence" (1973) suggests that companies start with a few form letters and gradually increase the number as the need arises. She also suggests that companies compile a "Form Letter Catalog" with all the standardized letters that all personnel can use. In "Improving Business Correspondence" (1966), Guy Fergason gives similar advice.

Not all experts believe that form letters are effective, however. David A. Kraft in "Sometimes a Form Letter Is Not the Right Answer" (1970) argues that form letters are often impersonal and that 20 percent of such correspondence he surveyed missed the mark and damaged customer relations. "The Art of Wooing Customers" (1967) argues that form letters lead to cold, impersonal correspondence and suggests that insurance agents take a course to learn how to personalize their letters.

One minor but significant element of business letters concerns their beginnings and endings. As "Business Letters Don't Have to Be Dreary" (1967) points out, these places tend to contain the most hackneyed phrases and expressions.

The salutation particularly tends to be dreary and repetitious. To remedy this, E. B. Weiss in "The Death of 'Dear Mr.'" (1965) attacks the conventional address by suggesting that writers substitute "Good Morning" for "Dear" or use a functional salutation with the person's name embedded in the opening line. "Most Business Letters Could Be Improved" (1973) suggests that letters begin with friendly openings such as "Good Morning, Mr. Jones!" and end with such injunctions as "I hope this is a great year for you!"

A related concern is sexist language. Luther A. Brock in "Liberate Your Sales Letters" (1974) argues that sales letters, often read by women executives, cannot continue using sexist openings. He suggests dropping "Dear Gentleman" or "Dear Sir" and replacing it with "Dear Person." In a more thorough treatment of the subject, J. H. Foegen in "What If the 'Gentlemen' Are Ladies?" (1979) makes a number of recommendations. If writers do not know the reader, they can use "Greetings" or drop the salutation altogether. If they know the person, they can use the name inside the letter with no initial salutation. Another suggestion is to use MM to refer to all people rather than Mr., Mrs., Miss, or Ms. Martha H. Rader suggests in "Rediscovering the Simplified Letter" (1976) that the problem can be solved by using World War II's simple letter form, one that does away entirely with salutations and complimentary closes. This letter form also saves time and money. In the only article of its kind, entitled "The Complimentary Close in Business Letters" (1981), Chester Wolford discusses the etymologies of the various letter closes. Partly tongue-in-cheek, he rejects "Yours," "Respectfully," "Cordially," and "Truly," deciding that "Sincerely" is the best compromise between logic and politeness.

The legal ramifications of business letters have also received some recent attention. Max Rose has written two articles on this question. In "How Not to Write a Libelous Letter" (1980), he argues that all writers should be aware of what a libelous letter is. For instance, to be libelous, a letter must be read by a third party outside the writer's company and must contain false and malicious information that injures the person or the person's memory. In "Is It 'Just Business Correspondence' or Is It a Contract?" (1981), Rose reminds us that letters can, under some circumstances, become legally binding contracts. Usually this occurs when a first letter is a proposal that the receiver accepts in a second, signed letter. In general, Rose warns, writers should check out questionable letters with an attorney before signing and sending them. In "Letters of Intent Can Turn into Contracts" (1976), Russell Decker reminds us that because courts have considerable latitude in determining the legality of letters of intent—even those lacking important terms of agreement—all letters should be written with care to avoid potential misunderstanding.

The final section of this part of our essay covers teaching business letters. A full discussion of all textbooks with sections on letters is beyond the scope of this work, but Beverly Stokes and Richard A. Hatch in "Primary Principles of Good Letter Writing Found in Business Communication Texts" (1975) summarize the major ideas discussed in the six most popular business communication texts. These include such principles as writing concisely, clearly, simply, vividly, positively, and coherently.

Several articles discuss pedagogical techniques for teaching the business letter. Enoch Haga's "1-2-3" (1977) argues that students should learn to write three-paragraph letters that state a problem or make a point, elaborate and provide details, and state what should be done. For high school courses, Mayly Chin Hagemann argues in "Taking the 'Wrench' Out of Letter Writing" (1980), teachers should design assignments that have students write to actual people and agencies in order to elicit replies. She discusses several appropriate assignments that have worked well for her. Richard D. Rowell in "Group Dynamics and Letter Writing" (1975) describes a peer evaluation system for letter writers. Thomas E. Walker, an English teacher, writes in "Can Words Cut Costs?" (1962) that businesses should help schools educate business writers by publicly proclaiming that they desire literate employees, by complaining to local schools if graduates cannot write well, and by sponsoring workshops for English teachers to develop effective business writing programs. Finally, in the only article reflecting the new process-oriented pedagogy, Allen Weiss in "Fear of the Blank Page. . . and How to Overcome It" (1978) describes his structured system for teaching blocked writers to work through the writing process.

Two textbooks on business letters stand out. Joel P. Bowman and Bernadine P. Branchaw's *Effective Business Correspondence* (1979) thoroughly covers most areas of business correspondence. Not only does it discuss all important kinds of letters, but it also gives excellent examples of each. Its Appendix A, which lists 50 realistic problems requiring letters, is a goldmine for classroom exercises and assignments. Another good book is James M. Reid, Jr., and Robert Wendlinger's *Effective Letters* (1978); this programmed text is particularly strong on matters of style—conciseness, emphasis, tone, and so on. Developed by the authors in collaboration with the New York Life Insurance Company, the book teaches practical skills needed on the job. Because users move at their own pace and evaluate their own work, it is an excellent approach for the working professional who wishes to develop sound letter writing skills.

Memoranda

Like the business letter, the memo has received little serious scholarly attention. It is usually dealt with briefly in textbook chapters on informal reports or in superficial "how-to" articles in business journals. These treatments are generally limited to a discussion of the memo's purpose (memos are written for brief in-house communication of business matters), style (they should be concise and to the point), and format ("TO," "FROM," and so forth, should be placed at the top of the page). However, there are a number of articles and textbook chapters that stand out, either because they treat an unusual aspect of memo writing or because they do an exceptionally good job of discussing the conventional concerns. It is these kinds of works that we will review.

One cluster of articles is primarily concerned with justifying the writing of memos. These pieces are apparently a response to the popular view that written communication in the business world is becoming obsolete. Robert L. Stearns, for example, in "Is the Much-maligned Memo Really As Bad As Some Say?" (1972), defends the memo against those who argue that a phone call or face-to-face talk is more personal. Among the advantages of memo communication are the following: the memo serves as a permanent record; it does not force the receiver to respond immediately; it allows both the writer and the reader to work out their thoughts; and it allows the writer to communicate information to many people at once. Sam B. Vitt ("In Praise of Memos" [1966]) also discusses the benefits of this form of communication, emphasizing that it forces the writer to think more clearly and state policy more clearly than does face-to-face or phone communication.

Others who make a good case for memo writing are Auren Uris (*Memos for Managers* [1975]), Max Rose ("A Memorandum about Memos" [1980]), and J. H. Menning, C. W. Wilkinson, and Peter B. Clarke ("Letters about Employment," [1978]). These and other articles include advice about which situations warrant memo writing and which do not. For example, Tom Adams, in "Developing a Meeting Memo" (1980), suggests that a memo be composed after every meeting to summarize it. He discusses thirteen essential elements of a good meeting memo and provides samples.

An excellent discussion of the situational considerations involved in memo writing is provided by Carla Butenhoff in "Bad Writing Can Be Good Business" (1977). A teacher of business writing, she believes that too much emphasis has been put on the style and mechanics of business correspondence and not enough on the political considerations. Students must understand these considerations, so as not to be naive about their memo writing when they enter the business world. Among the political realities she reveals are the following: the memo is almost never written for the person to whom it is addressed but for the person(s) receiving copies; how the memo is routed (whose names are listed at the top, who gets copies, whether the copies are "carbon" or "blind") is at least as important as what it says; equals almost never send each other memos (if you author a memo, then you are putting yourself up one or down one with respect to the receivers); and memos are often used to take credit or avoid blame.

Those who criticize memo writing usually concentrate on its abuses. Arthur G. Sharp, in "Breaking the Memo-Writing Habit" (1977), fears that management by memo is beginning to take over the business world. He warns that excessive written rather than oral communication has a negative impact on manager-employee relations. There have also been a number of tongue-in-cheek and parodic discussions of memo abuse. For example, the author of "How to Build Your Career by Memo Writing" (1970) suggests that many memos are self-serving rather than communicative: employees often write memos regarding some trivial issue simply to make themselves stand out and appear in-the-know. James Baar takes a similar approach in "The Art—and Craft—of the Memo" (1964), revealing that some employees use the memo to insult another employee without the awkwardness of a face-to-face encounter, and others use it to expose the receiver's ignorance to superiors. Finally, Eric Webster, in "Memo Mania" (1967), argues that many memos do not accomplish their avowed communicative purpose because they are written in an obscure, jargon-ridden style.

This problem of the pretentious, wordy style of much business writing has received most attention from writing experts. "How-to" articles always urge business people to write concisely and to limit their memos to one page. Harold Mayfield ("In Praise of the One-Page Memo" [1968]) claims that the chances of a one-page memo getting immediate attention are 90 percent, whereas those for a longer memo drop to 10 percent. Charles B. Cleveland agrees, pointing out in "Coming to Grips with Memo Mania" (1981) that many top executives, including President Reagan, will not read or will give low priority to memos of more than one page. He cites a management study that found that top executives spend an average of nine minutes on any one issue; therefore, if a memo cannot be read quickly, chances are that it will not be read at all.

Cleveland gives a number of detailed suggestions for writing clearly, avoiding jargon, and sticking to the point. A similar approach is taken by Somerby Dowst in "Informal Correspondence Gets Results" (1969). He advises an informal style in business correspondence in order to stem the tide of "bureaucratese," to save time, to get better responses, and to project a more human image of oneself. His specific suggestions for achieving such a style are to use active rather than passive voice, short, everyday words, short sentences and paragraphs, and occasional bits of humor.

One of the most detailed, helpful articles on how to write clearly is Marvin H. Swift's "Clear Writing Means Clear Thinking Means. . ." (1973). Swift does a close analysis of a sample executive memo, pointing out its wordiness (which diffuses the message), its tone (which is harsher than the writer would actually like to project), and its content (which muddles rather than clarifies the policies under discussion). He then presents a series of revisions, in which the deadwood is gradually eliminated, the tone made more human, and the message clarified.

Others who provide good advice on eliminating wordiness and jargon from memos are D. E. McCauley, Jr. ("Memo on Memos" [1963]) and Kenneth Roman and Joel Raphaelson (*Writing That Works* [1981]). The latter work devotes part of a chapter to memo writing, but the chapter on style is more helpful.

Closely related to the issue of style is the issue of audience analysis. Many articles point out that the style of a memo should be determined by the readers— their level of education, their relationship to the memo's writer, and so on. Cleveland, for example, in the article cited above, advises that memo writers consider first how close they are to the reader and how close the reader is to the project under discussion. In general, he says, memo style and tone should be "upgraded conversational"—tighter than conversation but not as rigid as formal writing.

Luther A. Brock suggests in "Do Your Memos Confuse or Communicate?" (1974) that the average length for memo sentences should be fifteen to twenty words if the audience is of average educational level (that is, high school graduates) and ten words if they are of lower than average. He points out that most people prefer short sentences and will not take the time to read long ones. Brock also urges the writer to be aware of the connotations of words and to project a pleasant, thoughtful image by making much use of the words "please" and "thank-you."

The importance of coming across as human, sincere, and considerate in business correspondence is emphasized by George T. Tade in "How to Write a Better Memo" (1971). He also provides examples of the errors and waste that can occur when memo writers do not properly consider the effects their words will have on readers. Luther A. Brock is concerned about the negative effects which sexist language can have on women readers. In "Liberate Your Sexist Memos!" (1979) he suggests ways memo writers can avoid using the masculine pronoun unnecessarily, and he discusses the possibility of new, neuter pronouns being introduced into business writing.

Another article concerned with audience awareness, Marilyn Jakes Church's "Writing Meaning into a Memo" (1981), suggests that in addition to gearing a memo's style and tone to a particular audience, the writer should also consider reader needs by making it immediately clear how the recipients are involved with the message and what actions are expected of them.

A final aspect of memo writing that is discussed in the advice articles is format. In "Memos That Get Things Moving" (1973), Harold K. Mintz gives detailed explanations of the different kinds of organization a memo can have, including cause-effect, general to specific, and question-answer. J. N. Menning, C. W. Wilkinson, and Peter B. Clarke, in "Letters About Employment" (1978), also give examples of various formats, as does Auren Uris in *Memos for Managers* (1975). Uris's examples are particularly helpful because they are taken from the files of actual executives, and he explains how these models can be used by others. Two final works containing good format suggestions are Marion W. Lamb and Eugene H. Hughes's *Business Letters, Memorandums, and Reports* (1967) and Pilson W. Kelly's "Do You Write Memos They Want to Read?" (1962).

Job Letters and Resumés

Because it is becoming increasingly common for top and middle-level business people to change jobs at least once during the course of their careers, many articles have been written in recent years giving job-search and resumé-writing advice to experienced white-collar workers. The following survey will cover the best and most representative of these works as well as those geared to first-time job-hunters. Few articles focus exclusively on resumé construction because most also include advice on how to write the accompanying cover letter (and some even discuss how to seek out job openings and how to behave in interviews). These articles generally point out that the cover letter should highlight the important parts of the resumé, explain any information in the resumé that could be construed negatively, and indicate what the job-seeker knows about and has to offer the company being applied to. There are, however, a few articles that offer more detailed treatment of cover letters, and these will be reviewed at the end of this survey.

Some of the best articles on the resumé focus on the pre-writing stage, explaining how to take an inventory of one's skills and strengths before constructing the resumé. This kind of article is particularly helpful for beginners and for people changing careers, who worry that they have no pertinent job experience to cite. The most comprehensive of these discussions is Richard N. Boles's "Only You Can Decide," a chapter in his book *What Color Is Your Parachute?* (1978). Michael Stimac's article, "Writing a Skills Resume" (1977), is also helpful. It advocates the use of a four-part procedure in composing a resumé, consisting of (1) logging one's achievements, (2) factoring these achievements for skills, abilities, and talents, (3) gleaning from the factored data generic skills and summarizing them, and (4) writing the resumé. June V. Wyant and Ruth Vise ("Resume Writing" [1979]) also provide step-by-step instructions for determining and organizing one's skills and significant experiences. Although this article is written to librarians seeking new jobs, its advice is more generally applicable.

Other articles that advocate this approach for executives and/or middle-level business people are "Could You Get Laid Off?" (1974), David Huggins's "The Resume Is the Foot in the Door" (1977), J. C. Perham's "What's Wrong with Executive Resumes?" (1975), Christine Egan's "Writing Resumes and Cover Letters" (1981), and Carl R. Boll's "The Do's and Don't's of Executive Resumes" (1970). Boll differs from the others, however, in that he suggests that after drawing up an inventory of accomplishments one should seek out interviews before composing the resumé. This way, the candidate can take advantage of the information gathered in the interview and shape each resumé to fit each job applied for. Harold B. Leeper, Jr. ("Can You Sell Yourself?" [1962]) points out that people who are excellent at selling products are often poor at selling themselves. He explains how candidates in the advertising field can assess their skills and market themselves.

One of the benefits of the inventory-taking method—in addition to the fact that it helps unearth material for one's resumé—is that it causes the candidate to take a more creative approach to resumé construction. Rather than regard the resumé as a rigid form with certain standard categories, arranged in a standard order, the candidate comes to see it as a flexible document to be shaped to one's own advantage. Although most business and technical writing textbooks continue to offer the traditional advice about placing personal information first and following it with an education category and a job experience category, a number of articles suggesting more innovative approaches have appeared in professional journals in recent years.

One such type of article argues that there is nothing sacrosanct about the reverse-chronology order traditionally used to list work experience. These articles point out that there are times when it might be to the candidate's advantage to use a functional arrangement instead, in which past jobs are grouped according to skills involved rather than according to chronology. Christine Egan, in the aforementioned article, does not favor one organization over the other, but rather says that the arrangement should depend upon one's strengths and weaknesses. For example, if one's job experience is narrow or sketchy, the functional approach might be better. Bridgford Hunt, in "The New You" (1981), advises the reverse-chronological order unless one's job history looks suspicious, in which case the functional approach is preferable.

Marshall Austin, in Chapter 9 of his book *How to Get a Better Job* (1976), argues that of the four typical resumé formats—chronological, functional, "original idea," and chronological-functional—the functional or chronological-functional is the best. Chronological resumés all look too much the same, and while the "original idea" approach stands out, it is often considered gimmicky and in poor taste. The functional approach, on the other hand, has the double advantage of making one's individuality come across and of specifying exactly what type of job one is seeking. In Chapter 10 Austin provides a step-by-step explanation of how to compose a functional resumé.

Burdette E. Bostwick, in the chapter on resumés in his book *Finding the Job You've Always Wanted* (1977), lists an even larger number of possible resumé formats: basic, chronological, chronological with summary, functional, functional-by-company, Harvard, creative, narrative, professional, and accomplishment. He gives samples and detailed explanations of when to use which type. With resumé style so crucial today—Bostwick estimates that resumé review screens out 90 percent of job applicants—it is important for candidates to choose the optimal format for their situations.

According to Patricia L. Rivers, in "Resumes" (1981), ten seconds is the maximum amount of time one can expect to be given one's resumé. Therefore, she suggests that key information should be made to stand out by being placed in the "hot zone"—the top half of the page. She advises against cluttering this space up with personal information.

Several other articles discuss ways to highlight one's strengths and minimize one's weaknesses. Gretchen Schoenfeld, in "Make Your Resume Sell" (1960), suggests that one should not elaborate upon responsibilities that anyone in the same position would have held but instead should play up unusual accomplishments. She also gives specific suggestions for ways to state these accomplishments without appearing boastful. Abbott P. Smith, in "How to Make Sure Your Next Resume Isn't an Obituary" (1977), explains how to examine all one's experience and turn it to one's advantage, using a functional approach. He also points out that most resumés erroneously focus on the past—what a candidate has done—rather than on what the candidate wants to do and can do for the company being applied to.

An exceptionally detailed discussion of how to highlight the positive is provided by Robert Half in "How to Write (or Read) a DP Resume" (1982). In addition to his advice on what to include and how to arrange the data, he lists a number of action verbs that can effectively state accomplishments and a number of appealing adjectives that can describe personal qualities. In another article, "How to Write (or Read) a Resume" (1981), Half discusses how to handle certain problem situations in a resumé, such as unfavorable personal data (age or marital status), not being a college graduate, a record with too many jobs, a one-company record, or a background exclusively government or military.

"Write a Resume That Gets the Job" (1975) gives pointers about how to phrase information effectively in the resumé. It also suggests, as do many of the other articles on creating a positive image, that the candidate not have the resumé professionally prepared. Employers usually can sense when this has been done, and it makes them suspect that the candidate lacks writing and organization skills.

How to make a resumé read like a success story is explained by Thomas Lynch in "Writing a Resume to Sell Yourself" (1976). He shows how the job experience section should be worded and organized so as to reveal greater responsibility and authority with each successive job. Edward J. Harrick and John M. Penrose in "Increase Interviews" (1975) explain how to turn not-so-good experiences to one's advantage by particular phrasing and emphasis. Finally, the author of "Resumes, like Sporty Cars, Should Be Compact and Well-designed" (1982) believes that nowadays computer training is a plus and should always be listed if possible.

With the same idea of highlighting the positive in mind, some of the articles surveyed give advice on whether and where to include certain personal information, such as age, race, marital status, and hobbies, and whether to include a photograph. Although inclusion of such personal data used to be routine, more and more it is being advised against because employers are leery of possible discrimination charges. An article that sets forth helpful guidelines on this matter, in line with federal affirmative action policies, is Stephen D. Lewis's "Are You Teaching a Practical, Up-to-Date Job Resume?" (1977).

While the authors of the best articles on resumé construction suggest using an imaginative rather than a formulaic approach, they generally frown upon overly creative or gimmicky formats. (The only field where such resumés seem to meet with approval is that of advertising. See, for example, Stephen Baker's "Do Resumes Have to Be Dull?" [1965] and David Liemer's "Pizza Resume Gets Young Adman First Job—Almost" [1979].) Contrary to popular opinion, a slick appearance—expensive or fancy paper and printing—does not create a good impression; often it seems to be a cover-up for inadequate credentials.

Among the articles that make this point are Tony Reynes's "You Sell Products" (1979), Bruce Jacobs's "Job-hunting on the Sly" (1981), Paul E. Sussman's "Executive Job Hunting" (1974), and "Make Your Availability Known When You Plan to Change Jobs" (1968).

Perhaps the most helpful articles are those that report the results of questionnaire surveys in which personnel or recruitment directors, who review hundreds of job applications each year, are asked to indicate what types of resumés and cover letters receive the best attention. Hubert S. Feild and William H. Holley ("Resume Preparation" [1976]) received questionnaire responses from 205 personnel directors of eight kinds of industries and tabulated the results so as to indicate preferred content, arrangement, format, and so forth. Deslie Beth Lawrence and Iris D. Rosendahl, in "Resume Vibes" (1979), describe a similar questionnaire survey distributed to college recruiters and personnel directors of 100 of the *Fortune* 500 firms. They report their respondents' remarks about various aspects of the resumé and cover letter, including physical appearance (for example, good quality paper and regular rather than fancy print create a favorable impression) and phrasing (for example, trite expressions are annoying). Other articles that report on similar surveys are Carmella E. Mansfield's "We Hear You Mr./Ms. Business" (1976), Harold D. Janes's "The Cover Letter and Resume" (1969), R. Neil Dortch's "What Businessmen Look for in the Resume" (1975), and "Writing Your First Resume" (1975).

An experiment by John M. Penrose, reported in "Does Order Make a Difference in Resumes?" (1973), sought to discover whether it is more effective to place the most impressive qualifications at the beginning or at the end of the resumé. Recruiters were asked to rank a number of resumés, some with the important information at the beginning, others with it at the end. The results suggested that order makes no difference: the entire content of the resumé and the preference of the particular recruiter appeared to be the most important determiners of a favorable response. These findings contradicted those of an earlier study by Roger Hayen and John H. Jackson, reported in "Behavioral Research and Computer Methods Applied to Managerial Resume Design" (1972), which indicated that the order of presentation of information on a resumé was more important than the information itself. These authors argue that for the most favorable response one should put the impressive information first, even if that means disregarding standard resumé format.

An article similar to the survey type is Stephen E. Fitzgerald's "Notes on the Resume" (1961). The author, a public relations specialist, says that of the 5,000 or so resumés he has read in his career, he can recall only half a dozen effective ones. He then goes on to list what is wrong with most resumés. These flaws include the following: candidates don't tell the prospective employers how they can help *them*; they usually don't indicate any knowledge about the employer's business, clients, or needs; the writing style is often frightful; and jobs are listed with no mention of why the candidate left each.

Another category of articles directs advice to employers and personnel directors on how to interpret and read between the lines of resumés. These articles are also helpful for the candidates themselves (and for instructors teaching resumé writing) because they indirectly provide advice on what to do and what not to do in a resumé. For example, "How to Read an Employee Application" (1966) reveals the bad impression made upon employers by vagueness about job history, poor penmanship, gaps in work or school experience, and the like. Equally helpful are Pearl Meyer's "How to Read a Resume" (1970) and Sylmar Van Nuys's "Resume Reading" (1970).

Many articles in this category expose the vast amount of resumé fraud that exists today. Ever since Janet Cooke won the Pulitzer Prize in 1979 and was subsequently discovered to have concocted a phony resumé, article after article on this problem has poured out. These articles list the various forms resumé-lying can take, from embellishment of a job title and exaggerations about responsibilities to false claims of holding an M.B.A. It is helpful for job candidates to know that employers are on to such fraud—indeed, they nowadays assume that most resumés are somewhat inflated—and to realize that using fancy terms like "conceived" or "implemented" to describe routine job activities fools no one and only gives the impression that the candidate is trying to hide inadequacies. Articles that discuss this issue are Walter Kiechel III's "Lies on the Resume" (1982), John Leo's "Embellishment Yes, Lying No" (1983), Kevin McManus's "They're Still Lying on Their Resumes" (1982), "Resume Fraud" (1981), Merle P. Martin's "The Instant Analyst-Resumes" (1981), Susan Margetts's "The 'Creative' Resume" (1972), "Faking It" (1981), and "Bogus Degrees" (1981).

A miscellaneous group of articles provides advice for job candidates in special situations. Sarah Augusta Taintor, Kate M. Monro, and Margaret D. Shertzer, in "Applying for a Job" (1969), explain how women going back to work after several years as housewives can explain the gap in their job history to their advantage. "Four Ways of Explaining a Physical Handicap in the Application Letter and Resume" (1975) does just what its title implies. Robert E. Andreyka, in "Job Resumes for Vocational Graduates" (1970), tells how to adapt the standard resumé to the needs of vocational school graduates. And Tim Whalen, in "Proposal Resumés" (1980), explains how a company can create a group resumé to submit as part of a proposal when it bids for a contract.

In addition to articles in professional journals, a number of books and workbooks on the market provide detailed guidelines for resumé construction. Most of these routinely point out the purposes of resumés; discuss the do's and don't's of style, content, and format; explain the various ways the data can be organized; discuss the elements of effective cover letters; and offer sample resumés and cover letters. Michael P. Jacquish, in *Personal Resume Preparation* (1968), covers the standard ground but also provides an interesting explanation of the historical development of the resumé and a discussion of professional resumé-preparing services. Jacob Israel Biegeleisen's book, *Job Resumes* (1969), is unusual in that it contains a list of approximately 200 job titles and provides sample resumés for each. Juvenal L. Angel takes a similar approach in *Why and How to Prepare an Effective Job Resume* (1961), giving detailed descriptions of various jobs and sample resumés for them.

Carolyn F. Nutter, in *The Resume Workbook* (1963), and Tom Jackson, in *The Perfect Resume* (1981), use workbook approaches. Both books, especially Jackson's, have excellent chapters on analyzing and blocking one's skills and interests and on targeting jobs that will match up with them. Both discuss the advantages and disadvantages of the various methods of organization—chronological, functional, creative, and so forth—and show how to construct each kind. In addition, Jackson has an excellent section on style, including a list of action verbs to help create a positive image.

Other helpful standard books on resumé construction are Theron Miller's *How to Write a Job-Getting Resume* (1967), Leonard Corwen's *Your Resume* (1976), Kenneth R. Adler's *Pathway to Your Future* (1971), Adele Lewis's *How to Write Better Resumes* (1976), and Maury Shyking's *Resumes for Job Hunters* (1976).

The remaining articles in this survey discuss the cover letter or when to use alternatives to the resumé. "Job Hunting" (1973) advises job candidates not to send a resumé because it could prejudice an employer against them; a personal letter conveys a truer picture of them and their qualifications. Mark Bernheim, in "The Written Job Search" (1982), and Francis W. Weeks, in "Data Sheets and Resumes" (1975), explain the difference between a data sheet (it merely lists) and a resumé (it focuses, emphasizes, and explains). Weeks suggests which is applicable for which kinds of job situations. A similar article, "Personal Business" (1966), explains the difference between a bio and a resumé: the bio is a briefer, less promotional version of the resumé. This article points out that generally the resumé is used by candidates on the way up, trying to sell themselves, while the bio is used by top executives seeking new positions (they write only a letter of application and then present the bio at the interview).

Menning, Wilkinson, and Clarke, in "Letters about Employment" (1978), suggest that, even if candidates are not going to include a resumé with a job letter, they should compile one in order to help them focus the letter. This discussion is part of an excellent chapter on writing the various types of letters related to the job search (prospecting letters, solicited job application letters, post-interview letters, letters turning down a job offer). The authors emphasize the similarities between job application letters and sales letters, giving detailed advice about how to stress one's central selling point, how to overcome deficiencies that may be implied in one's resumé, and how to talk the special language of the reader's business. The chapter includes several helpful examples of effective and ineffective job search-related letters and suggests how one can learn from the effective examples without slavishly imitating them.

In Marshall Austin's chapter on cover letters in *How to Get a Better Job* (1976), the author cautions candidates not to be oversolicitous and to avoid flattery and exaggerated expressions of gratitude. He goes on to list five essential ingredients of a letter of application and then develops detailed discussions of each: (1) begin with a brief observation regarding either the reader or the company he represents, (2) briefly describe the scope of your experience, (3) call attention to your resumé and cite one or two examples from it, (4) tell the prospective employer you want to work for him and specify the job title, and (5) ask for an appointment for an interview. Austin's chapter also contains examples of effective cover letters and a checklist.

Another superior discussion of job application letters is E. Michael Walsh's "Teaching the Letter of Application" (1977), with detailed pedagogical suggestions for technical/business writing instructors as well as regular composition teachers. The standard textbook treatment of the job application letter—to regard it as a fill-in-the-blanks exercise—ignores the reality that people often apply for jobs for which they are not apparently trained. Walsh, therefore, advocates an inventory-taking approach, in which candidates analyze both their own skills and the component parts of the desired job and then creatively match up the two. The article contains some excellent suggestions for exercises that will help students both to discover their own qualifications and to highlight them in the letter.

Other articles that give detailed advice about how to sell oneself in a job application letter are Natalie R. Seigle's "How to Have a Prospecting Letter of Application Read" (1975), "How to Write the Prospecting (or Unsolicited) Application" (1975), and "How to Start Your Letter" (1975). Marcia R. Fox, in "The Cover Letter" (1981), discusses the appropriate style and tone to use in cover letters and analyzes the effects various phrasings of the same information would have on the prospective employer/reader.

Leonardo Da Vinci's "A Classic Letter of Application" (reprinted in 1975), in which the famous artist-inventor appeals to the Duke of Milan by cogently delineating the ten ways he could benefit the Duke, remains an excellent model for contemporary job applicants. Finally, Dorothea Chandler explains in "Writing the Post-Interview Thank-You Letter" (1975) how a good followup letter can promote one's candidacy.

Conclusion

As this discussion of research on letters, memos, and resumés suggests, much research is needed on this neglected area of writing. The majority of extant articles assume that certain principles of sound writing are givens and not deserving of serious research. This attitude has encouraged the research to remain at the level of description and practical advice. Yet the area is filled with interesting questions about the history of business correspondence, about the effectiveness of some of our cherished beliefs about effective business writing, and about the rhetoric of business correspondence in the modern world. Perhaps this essay will stimulate further research.

References

Business Letters

Anderson, George B. "Dear Mr. Pflug, Here's a Product." *Sales Manag*, 30 Oct. 1972, pp. 51–52.

Anderson, John W. "Determining the Effects of Order of Presentation in Special Request Letters." *J Bus Comm*, 7 (1970), 31–40.

———. "The Effect of Order of Information in a Questionnaire Cover Letter Situation." *J Bus Comm*, 13 (1976), 11–15.

Arnold, Vanessa Dean, and Mosetta S. Soskis. " 'We Regret to Inform You'—News of Disappointment." *ABCA Bul*, 40 (June 1977), 37–38.

"The Art of Wooing Customers." *Best's Insur N*, 67 (1967), 85–86.

"As a Designer Sees a Letterhead." *Office*, 55 (June 1962), 87, 91.

Bachle, Robert A., and Goodwin Alarik. "Results—Producing Direct Mail." *Bankers Month*, 85 (Aug. 1968), 44–45.

Bales, Forest F. "New Twist in Collection Letters." *Cred Fin Manag*, 65 (May 1963), 14–15.

Bender, Donald H. "A Convergence of Data Processing and Word Processing." *Best's Rev (L/H Ed)*, 81 (Mar. 1981), 38, 42, 44, 46.

Bergeron, Lionel L. "Managing a Correspondence Center." *J Sys Manag*, 26 (Sept. 1975), 22–25.

Boettcher, Richard A. "Word Processing Works Well Here." *Office*, 80 (Sept. 1974), 80, 84, 86.

Bowman, Joel P., and Bernadine P. Branchaw. *Effective Business Correspondence*. New York: Harper, 1979.

Bowman, Mary Ann. "Books on Business Writing and Technical Writing in the University of Illinois Library." *J Bus Comm*, 12 (1975), 33–67.

———, and Joan D. Stamas. *Written Communication in Business: A Selective Bibliography, 1967–1977*. Champaign, Ill.: American Business Communication Association, 1980.

Body, W. P. "Some Psychological Aspects of Business Letter Writing." *J Bus Comm*, 1 (1963), 37–44.

Brice, A. Donald. "Write? Right!" *Pub Rel J*, 16 (1960), 15–16.

Broadbent, Christopher. "British Letterhead Awards." *Director*, 34 (July 1981), 8–9.

Brock, Luther A. "Business Letters That Aren't All Business." *Sup Manag*, 16 (Apr. 1971), 7–10.

———. "Give Good News First!" *Office*, 70 (Nov. 1969), 76.

———. *How to Build Goodwill Through Credit Correspondence*. New York: National Association of Credit Management, 1976.

———. *How to Communicate by Letter and Memo*. New York: McGraw-Hill, 1974.

———. "Liberate Your Sales Letters." *Sales Manag*, 11 Nov. 1974, pp. 46, 48.

———. "Make Your Collection Letters Persuade—Not Plead!" *Cred Fin Manag*, 70 (Mar. 1968), 30–31.

———. "The 'No' Letter with the 'Yes' Sound." *Office*, 69 (Mar. 1969), 61–62.

———. "Write a Better Letter: And See Good Will—and Business—Grow." *Fed Home Loan Bank Board J*, 11 (Nov. 1978), 37–38.

Bromage, Mary C. "The Management of Communications." *S.A.M. Adv Manag J*, 38 (Apr. 1973), 42–46.

Brown, Clement F. "How Not to Write a Business Letter." *Indus Week*, 7 Aug. 1972, p. 49.

———. "Ten Steps to Stuffy Business Letters." *Sup Manag*, 17 (Nov. 1972), 31–32.

Brown, John A. "Letters That Get Action." *Am Bus*, 30 (1960), 38–39.

———. "The Reader-Centered Letter." *Office Ex*, 36 (May 1961), 16.

"Business Letters Don't Have to Be Dreary." *Sup Manag*, 12 (Aug. 1967), 34–36.

Carter, David E., ed. *Letterheads/1: The International Annual of Letterhead Design.* New York: Art Direction Book Co., 1977.

Champion, Dean J., and Alan M. Sear. "Questionnaire Response Rates: A Methodological Analysis." *Soc Forces*, 47 (Mar. 1969), 335–39.

Cohen, Mark J. "Don't Call Them, They'll Call You." *Real Est Today*, 11 (1978), 20–23.

"Communicating with Past-Due Accounts." *Fueloil Oil Heat*, 35 (July 1976), 30–31.

Conarroe, Richard R. "How Public Relations Helps Sales." *Sales Manag*, 19 Mar. 1973, pp. 58, 60–63.

"Copying Letters Saves Firm $2,600." *Admin Manag*, 26 (May 1965), 68–70.

"Costly Words." *Dun's*, 110 (July 1977), 74.

Cresci, Martha W. *Complete Book of Model Business Letters.* West Nyack, N.Y.: Parker, 1976.

" 'Customized Communications' Can Help Improve Company Sales, Bryant Says." *Nat Underw Life (Insur Ed)*, 1 June 1974, p. 2.

"Cutting Your Mail Costs." *Admin Manag*, 26 (Jan. 1965), 40–41.

Decker, Russell. "Letters of Intent Can Turn into Contracts." *Purchasing*, 9 Nov. 1976, pp. 81, 83.

Douglas, G. H. "Editor's Comment." *J Bus Comm*, 7 (1970), 41–42.

Draughon, Clyde O. *Practical Bank Letter Writing: Written by a Banker for Bankers.* Boston: Bankers Publishing, 1971.

Duerr, Sidney E. "How Best to Sell Yourself to the Boss?" *Cred Fin Manag*, 63 (Sept. 1961), 40–41.

Dyer, Frederick C. "Managing Other People's Writing." *Manag Rev*, 51 (Feb. 1962), 62.

Eddings, Clair Neff. *Secretary's Complete Model Letter Handbook.* Englewood Cliffs, N.J.: Prentice-Hall, 1965.

"Electronic Mail for Business Communication." *Office*, 88 (July 1978), 103.

Elfenbein, Julien. *Handbook of Business Form Letters and Forms.* New York: Simon, Schuster, 1972.

Erdo, Paul L. *Professional Mail Surveys.* New York: McGraw Hill, 1970.

Fenvessy, Stanley J. "Customer Mail: How to Keep Friends." *Admin Manag*, 31 (July 1970), 44–46.

Fergason, Guy. "Improving Business Correspondence." *Best's Insur N (Life Ed)*, 67 (1966), 80, 82.

Fishbaugh, C. W. "What Happened to Letter Writing?" *Banking*, 65 (May 1973), 114–15.

Foegen, J. H. "What If the 'Gentlemen' Are Ladies?" *Human Res Manag*, 18 (Spring 1979), 72–74.

Forbes, Malcolm S. "No Answer Is No Answer." *Forbes*, 15 Nov. 1965, p. 12.

Ford, Neil M. "The Advance Letter in Mail Surveys." *J Mark Res*, 4 (May 1967), 202–204.

Forshee, Kenneth J. "Every Letter a Sales Letter." *Cred Fin Manag*, 62 (Feb. 1960), 18–19.

Frailey, L. E. *Handbook of Business Letters*. Rev. Ed. Englewood Cliffs, N.J.: Prentice-Hall, 1965.

"From Longhand to Dictation in One Easy System." *Banking*, 66 (Oct. 1974), 14, 32.

"The General Manager's Mail, 1879." *Bus Hist Rev*, 40 (1966), 369–71.

Gold, Lawrence. "Students Can Design and Print Their Own Stationery." *ABCA Bul*, 40 (Sept. 1977), 11–12.

Gottheimer, Debra. "Mail the Postman Doesn't Carry." *Admin Manag*, 38 (Mar. 1977), 36–38, 43–44, 46, 48, 50, 120.

Gould, John D., and Stephen J. Boies. "Writing, Dictating, and Speaking Letters." *Science*, 22 Sept. 1978, 1145. Also in *IEEE Trans Prof Comm*, PC–22 (Mar. 1979), 16–18.

Goulet, Waldeman M. "Efficacy of a Third Request Letter in Mail Surveys of Professionals." *J Mark Res*, 14 (Feb. 1977), 112–14.

Griesinger, Frank K. "Wiring the Written Word." *Admin Manag*, 35 (Sept. 1974), 24–34.

Haga, Enoch. "1–2–3: A New Way to Read and Write Letters." *J Bus Educ*, 52 (Feb. 1977), 229–30.

Hagemann, Mayly Chin. "Taking the 'Wrench' Out of Letter Writing." *Engl J*, 69 (Mar. 1980), 38–40.

Hairston, Clifford J., Jr. "How Often Do Executives Delegate Correspondence?" *Manag World*, 7 (1978), 12–14.

Halatin, T. J. "Writing Letters of Reference That Get Results." *Sup Manag*, 25 (Dec. 1980), 32–34.

Hanford, Robert B., Jr. "Bad Manners." *Sales Manag*, 7 Aug. 1964, pp. 41–46.

———. "Creating Candidates for the Wastebasket." *Sales Manag*, 3 July 1964, pp. 45–48.

———. "Failing to Capture Attention Early." *Sales Manag*, 19 June 1964, pp. 39–44.

———. "Failing to Organize Your Thoughts." *Sales Manag*, 1 May 1964, pp. 47–50.

———. "Failing to Understand the Other Man." *Sales Manag*, 15 May 1964, pp. 71–74.

———. "Neglecting Direct Mail Basics." *Sales Manag*, 21 Aug. 1964, pp. 43–48.

———. "Neglecting Your Image." *Sales Manag*, 5 June 1964, pp. 61–65.

———. "Sell Too Hard." *Sales Manag*, 17 July 1964, pp. 43–46.

———. "Sounding the Wrong Tone." *Sales Manag*, 17 Aug. 1964, pp. 34–36.

———. "Using the Wrong Direct Mail Format." *Sales Manag*, 4 Sept. 1964, pp. 49–54.

Harbaugh, Frederick W. " 'No' Letters to Applicants: Let's Tell It Straight." *ABCA Bul*, 40 (Sept. 1977), 28.

Hardy, Michael G. "Take A Letter, Plain and Simple." *Sales Mark Manag*, 8 June 1981, pp. 37–38.

Harrington, Lynn. "Better Purchasing Letters and How to Write Them." *Purchasing*, 25 Aug. 1966, pp. 86–90.

———. "Better Purchasing Letters and How to Write Them—Part II." *Purchasing*, 8 Sept. 1966, pp. 64–66.

Hodgson, Richard S. *The Dartnell Direct Mail and Mail Order Handbook*. 3rd ed. Chicago: Dartnell, 1980.

Houston, Michael J., and John R. Nevin. "The Effects of Source and Appeal on Mail Survey Response Patterns." *J Mark Res*, 14 (1977), 374–78.

"How Every Salesman Can Send Selling Letters." *Indus Mark*, 50 (Aug. 1965), 106–07.

"How to Communicate with Employees Through Letters." *Pers J*, 50 (1971), 878–79.

"How to Cut Letter Writing Costs." *Purchasing*, 5 Nov. 1962, p. 128.

Humphrey, Mitchell O. "Management Letters—Image Builders for the CPA." *J Account*, 123 (Jan. 1967), 27–32.

"Insurance Company's Letters Are Links with Customers." *Office*, 91 (Mar. 1980), 42–46, 50–55.

Janis, J. Harold. "Business Writing: In Defense of the Cliche." *Manag Rev*, 54 (Oct. 1965), 25–28.

Jordan, Sandra Ekberg. "Cereal Companies Get Letters That Go Snap, Crackle and Pop." *Pub Rel J*, 28 (May 1972), 19–21, 24.

Kanuk, Leslie, and Conrad Berenson. "Mail Surveys and Response Rates: A Literature Review." *J Mark Res*, 12 (Nov. 1975), 440–53.

Kaplan, Ethel. "Writing Effective Letters to Customers." *Manag Rev*, 55 (July 1966), 42–45.

"Keep Your Letters Interesting." *Sup Manag*, 16 (Feb. 1971), 27–29.

Kish, Joseph L. "High Correspondence Costs? Try Form Letters." *Sup Manag*, 11 (Sept. 1966), 41–42.

———. "We Improved Correspondence and Reduced Its Cost." *Office*, 56 (Nov. 1962), 101–15.

Kliment, Stephen A. "Writing for Marketing Impact: Letters, Brochures, Proposals." *Architec Rec*, 161 (June 1977), 71, 73.

Koch, Bryon J. "Producing Complete Letters from Name and Address File." *Comput Auto*, 20 (July 1971), 16–17.

Koch, James H. "Put Direct Mail on Your Sales Team." *Banking*, 65 (May 1973), 106.

Kolgraf, Ron. "Put It in Writing." *Indus Distrib*, 70 (Aug. 1980), 45.

Kraft, David A. "Sometimes a Form Letter Is Not the Right Answer." *Office*, 71 (Apr. 1970), 34–38.

"Large Businesses Dispatch Over 200 Letters a Day with New Electronic Mail System." *Admin Manag*, 35 (Aug. 1974), 81.

Leffler, George W. "Contact Through Correspondence." *Real Est Today*, 13 (Aug. 1980), 25–26.

Le Rossignol, Keith. "Correspondence: Handle It with Care." *Int Trade For*, 12 (July/Sept. 1976), 16–18, 26–29.

"Letters Are Better." *Forbes*, 68 (Feb. 1980), 65–66.

"Letters That Sell." *Roy Bank Can Month N*, 55 (May 1974), 1–4.

Lewis, Leslie Llewellyn. *The Dartnell Business-Letter Deskbook*. Chicago: Dartnell, 1969.

Linsky, Arnold S. "A Factoral Experiment in Inducing Responses to a Mail Questionnaire." *Soc Social Res*, 49 (1965), 183–89.

Lipman, Michael. "How to Sell with the Written Word." *Bus Manag*, 20 (Sept. 1961), 61–64.

"Longhand Correspondence Still Rates Consideration." *Admin Manag*, 27 (Jan. 1966), 48.

McGinnis, Michael A., and Charles J. Hollon. "Mail Survey Response Rate and Bias: The Effect of Home Versus Work Address." *J Mark Res*, 14 (1977), 383–84.

McKeon, William R. "Thin Paper for Thin Budgets." *Office*, 82 (Oct. 1975), 82.

Maguire, John T. "An Outline for a Course in Direct Mail Offered at the University of Illinois." *ABCA Bul*, 32 (1969), 22–30; 33 (1970), 27–40; and 34 (1971), 1–50.

"Making Business Letters Interesting." *Roy Bank Can Month N*, 51 (July 1970), 1–4.

"Management's Alternatives to the Mails." *Admin Manag*, 38 (Nov. 1977), 52.

Mason, Robert S. "Better Business Writing for Banks." *Banker's Mag*, 162 (Jan. 1979), 56–60.

"Mass Mailing in Minutes." *Cred Fin Manag*, 77 (May 1975), 30–31.

May, Robert C. "How to Improve Your Sales Correspondence." *Indus Manag*, 50 (Oct. 1965), 86–90.

Mayotte, Robert L. "Are You Getting Your Share of Letterhead Business?" *Inland Print/ Amer Lith*, 154 (Oct. 1964), 48–49.

———. "How You Can Help Your Customers Design Better Letterheads." *Inland Print/ Amer Lith*, 163 (July 1969), 28–29.

Mears, Peter, and Robert Cosenza. "The Complaint Letter: Forgotten Communication Medium." *Pub Rel J*, 33 (June 1977), 20.

Medlin, John. "Paper Your Correspondence." *Admin Manag*, 28 (June 1967), 70–77.

Menger, Mary K. "Unique Insurance Firm Demonstrates Effective Correspondence System." *Am Bus*, 30 (1960), 21–22.

Menning, J. H., et al. *Communicating Through Letters and Reports.* 6th ed. Homewood, Ill.: Irwin, 1976.

Meyers, James H., and Arne F. Haug. "How a Preliminary Letter Affects Mail Survey Return and Costs." *J Adver Res*, 9 (Sept. 1969), 32–33.

Mikels, J. Ronald. "Successful Bank Letters—A Matter of Planning." *Bur Clear House*, 58 (Apr. 1974), 26, 62–63.

Monaghan, Patrick. *Writing Letters That Sell: You, Your Ideas, Products and Services.* New York: Fairchild, 1968.

Moran, Michael G. "Writing Business Letters Using the Persuasive Sequence." *ABCA Bul*, 47 (June 1984), pp. 24–27.

Morris, Richard H. "Badly-Written Collection Letters Blamed on Aloof Top Management, Inadequate Training." *Cred Fin Manag*, 63 (Feb. 1961), 20–21.

———. *Credit and Collection Letters: New Techniques to Make Them Work.* Great Neck, N.Y.: Channel Press, 1960.

———. "Letters You'll Be Proud Of." *Sales Manag*, 7 Nov. 1958, pp. 54–57.

Morrison, Robert H., and Trudy Sundberg. *Bank Correspondence Handbook.* Boston: Banker Publishing, 1964.

"Most Business Letters Could Be Improved." *Office*, 77 (Apr. 1973), 42, 46.

Murray, Michael H. "Can You Say 'No' Without Twisting the Knife?" *Sup Manag*, 19 (Nov. 1974), 16–20.

———. "If You Have Any Questions, Please Don't Hesitate to Contact Us." *Best's Rev (L/H Ed)*, 75 (Feb. 1975), 74–76.

Nance, Harold W. "Is Word Processing a Substitute for a Poor Typist?" *Office*, 78 (Dec. 1973), 67, 117.

Naugheim, Ferd. *Letter Perfect: How to Write Business Letters That Work*. New York: Van Nostrand, Reinhold, 1982.

O'Brien, Richard J. "Uniform Letter Size: Is an Agreement Possible?" *Office*, 93 (Apr. 1981), 106.

O'Conner, D. M. "Improving Your Correspondence." *Office*, 68 (Sept. 1968), 41, 154–55.

Parr, William M. *Executive's Guide to Effective Letters and Reports*. West Nyack, N.Y.: Parker, 1976.

"Personalized Printing at 280 Lines Per Minute." *Admin Manag*, 33 (Sept. 1972), 72–74.

Phyfe, William Lee. "Share Owner Correspondence Can Establish Corporate Personality." *Pub Rel J*, 20 (Aug. 1964), 23–24.

Plung, Daniel L. "Writing the Persuasive Business Letter." *J Bus Comm*, 17 (Spring 1980), 45–49.

Pollock, Ted. "How Letters Can Multiply Your Sales Wallop." *Manag Methods*, 17 (Oct. 1959), 57–60.

Prager, Gordon. "Dear Insured." *Best's Rev (P/C Ed)*, 80 (Apr. 1980), 10, 86, 88–90.

"Producing an Effective Business Letter Manual." *Admin Manag*, 26 (Nov. 1965), 56.

"Put Your Complaint in Writing." *Consumer Bul*, 48 (Oct. 1965), 26–27.

Rader, Martha H. "Rediscovering the Simplified Letter." *ABCA Bul*, 39 (Sept. 1976), 27–28.

Reid, James M., Jr., and Robert Wendlinger. *Effective Letters: A Program for Self-Instruction*. 3rd ed. New York: McGraw-Hill, 1978.

Richardson, Malcolm. "The Earliest Business Letters in English: An Overview." *J Bus Comm*, 17 (Spring 1980), 19–31.

Ritter, Bess. "How to Reduce Bank Correspondence." *Bur Clear House*, 57 (Aug. 1973), 30.

Rivers, William E. "Lord Chesterfield on the Craft of Business Writing: The Relations of Reading and Writing." *J Bus Comm*, 17 (Fall 1979), 3–12.

Robin, Donald P., and C. Glenn Walters. "The Effect on Return Rate of Messages Explaining Monetary Incentives in Mail Questionnaire Studies." *J Bus Comm*, 13 (1976), 49–54.

Rose, Max. "How Not to Write a Libelous Letter." *Supervisor*, 42 (Jan. 1980), 6–7.

———. "Is It 'Just Business Correspondence' or Is It a Contract?" *Supervisor*, 43 (May 1981), 9–10.

Rosenblum, Sig. "Ten Secrets of Better Sales Letters." *Sales Mark Manag*, 16 May 1977, pp. 36–38.

Rowell, Richard D. "Group Dynamics and Letter Writing." *ABCA Bul*, 38 (Mar. 1975), 24–26.

"Santa Fe Puts Zip into Its Letter Writing System." *Railway Age*, 19 Aug. 1968, pp. 24–25, 28.

Schaefer, C. J. "Prospects Will Read You If Your. . . ." *Sales Manag*, 20 June 1958, p. 82.

"Selecting and Buying Executive Letterheads." *Admin Manag*, 26 (Aug. 1965), 36–40.

Shanklin, William L. "Receiver Prospectives on Direct Mail Advertising." *J Bus Comm*, 12 (1975), 24–31.

Shulman, Joel J. *Treasurer's and Controller's Letter Book*. Englewood Cliffs, N.J.: Prentice-Hall, 1974.

Simon, Raymond. "Responses to Personal and Form Letters in Mail Surveys." *J Adver Res*, 7 (Mar. 1967), 28–30.

Sklar, John. "Make Your Follow-ups Work." *Office*, 62 (May 1968), 64–65.

Smith, Sofrana L. "Balance Sheet for Letter Writing." *Office Ex*, 75 (1960), 26–28.

Stead, Bette Ann. "Make a Good Impression When You Write." *Sup Manag*, 16 (Oct. 1971), 15–18.

Stokes, Beverly, and Richard A. Hatch. "Primary Principles of Good Letter Writing Found in Business Communication Texts." *ABCA Bul*, 38 (Mar. 1975), 2–5.

Stone, Bob. "Here Are Some Ways You Can Write a Better Sales Letter." *Adver Age*, 31 Jan. 1972, pp. 55–56.

———. "Personalized Computer Letters Come of Age." *Adver Age*, 14 July 1969, pp. 54–56.

———. "20 Ways to Upgrade Sales Letters." *Adver Age*, 25 Mar. 1968, p. 172.

Swanson, Robert, and Ron Marthaller. "Efficiency in Policyholder Correspondence." *Best's Rev (L/H Ed)*, 79 (Mar. 1979), 78–79.

Switzler, Al W. "Goodwill, Generosity, and Grammar." *Pub Rel J*, 33 (Mar. 1977), 18–19.

"Talking Convincingly to Customers by Personalizing Friendly Letters." *Cred Fin Manag*, 63 (Sept. 1961), 40–41.

"Ten Ways to Speed Your Correspondence." *Admin Manag*, 28 (Feb. 1967), 32, 34, 36.

Tuttle, David H. "Written Communication." *Bankers Month*, 84 (July 1967), 42.

Viale, Patricia. "Standardizing and Simplifying Paperwork in Agency Correspondence." *Best's Rev (P/C Ed)*, 80 (July 1979), 93–94.

Walker, Thomas E. "Can Words Cut Costs?" *Dun's*, 79 (Jan. 1962), 67–68, 70.

Walsh, Ruth M. *Business Communication: A Selected Annotated Bibliography*. Urbana, Ill.: American Business Communication Association, 1973.

———, and Stanley J. Birkin. *Business Communication: An Annotated Bibliography*. Westport, Conn.: Greenwood, 1980.

Weart, J. P. "Consultant Personalizes Advice to Letterwriters." *Office*, 62 (Oct. 1965), 14–20.

Wecker, Jeffrey H. "Personalized Computer Letters: A Quality Touch." *Indus Mark*, 66 (Aug. 1981), 97.

Weir, Walter. "Is Business Correspondence a Bothersome Chore? Beware!" *Adver Age*, 12 Sept. 1977, pp. 64, 67.

Weisman, Herman M. *Technical Correspondence: A Handbook and Reference Source for the Technical Profession*. New York: Wiley, 1968.

Weiss, Allen. "Fear of the Blank Page . . . and How to Overcome It." *S.A.M. Adv Manag*, 43 (Autumn 1978), 22–29.

Weiss, E. B. "The Death of 'Dear Mr.' " *Adver Age*, 3 May 1965, pp. 84–85.

Wendlinger, Robert M. "How New York Life Writes Effective Letters." *Office*, 61 (Apr. 1965), 14–31, 217–18.

Werner, William G. "Putting Personality in Print." *Pub Rel J*, 15 (July 1959), 10–12.

White, William. "World's Shortest Letters." *J Bus Comm*, 9 (1972), 40.

Wolff, Luella M. "A Brief History of the Art of Dictamen: Medieval Origins of Business Letter Writing." *J Bus Comm*, 16 (Winter 1979), 3–11.

Wolford, Chester. "The Complimentary Close in Business Letters: Closing Some Closings." *Tech Writ Teach*, 8 (1981), 91–92.

"WP Center Produces 500 Letters Each Day." *Admin Manag*, 34 (Mar. 1973), 76.

Yeck, John D. "The Importance of Direct Mail in Business School Education." *J Bus Comm*, 12 (1975), 11–16.

————. "Reducing Cost of Sales Through Marketing Support Mail." *Indus Mark Manag*, 6 (1977), 95–97.

————, and John T. Maguire. *Planning and Creating Better Direct Mail*. New York: McGraw-Hill, 1961.

Tips on Writing Business Letters

"The Art of Wooing Customers by Mail." *Best's Insur N*, 67 (Apr. 1967), 86–87.

Born, Jess W. "Write It Right!" *Fueloil Oil Heat*, 21 (Nov. 1962), 61.

Brock, Luther A. "A Few Words About Using Fewer Words." *Trusts Est*, 113 (Nov. 1974), 722–23.

————. "Are Your Letters 'Dead'? Cut 'Em Down and Spice Them Up." *Manag World*, 7 (Aug. 1978), 12–14.

"A Direct Approach to Writing." *Admin Manag*, 28 (Jan. 1967), 35.

Dowst, Somerby. "Informal Correspondence Gets Results." *Purch Mag*, 9 Jan. 1969, pp. 117–18.

"Do You Want Your Letters to Be Read?" *Indus Week*, 9 Dec. 1974, pp. 47–48.

Emmett, James. "Improve Your Letterwriting." *Supervision*, 38 (1976), 16–17.

Estrada, Dan. "Does Your Writing Communicate?" *Indus Week*, 18 June 1973, pp. 49–50.

Gladwin, Ellis. "Write Fewer Words and Save More Money." *Office*, 64 (Oct. 1966), 94–103.

Hanft, P., and M. Roe. "How to Write Well in Business." *CA Mag*, 111 (May 1978), 72–74.

————. "How to Write Well in Business (2)." *CA Mag*, 111 (July 1978), 46–47.

Hayes, Joseph R., and Dugan Laird. "Letters That Get Results." *Pers J*, 43 (1964), 380–81, 388.

Hays, Robert. "An Open Letter...About Letters." *Super Manag*, 3 (July 1958), 37–40.

Ireland, Otto M. "Tailor Your Letter to the Reader." *Super Manag*, 6 (Apr. 1961), 29–33.

Johnson, Frank M. "Writing Letters to Busy People." *Super Manag*, 11 (Jan. 1966), 14–15.

Kimberly-Clark Corporation. "Tips on Writing Better Letters." *Super Manag*, 13 (May 1968), 16–20.

Koch, Robert G., and Eugene H. Fram. "Use This Checklist to Write Better Business Letters." *Am Bus*, 30 (1960), 11–12.

Lipman, Michael. "How to Sharpen Your Business Writing." *Bus Manag*, 20 (Aug. 1961), 34–35, 66.

McQueen, Roderick. "An Open Letter to Letterwriters." *Can Banker TCB Rev*, 86 (Apr. 1979), 40–42.

Mathies, Leslie H. "Let People Show in Your Writing." *Office*, 51 (May 1960), 12–13, 191.

————. "Why Johnny Don't Write So Good." *Office*, 72 (Sept. 1970), 70.

"Max-Imizing Your Letter Writing." *Sales Manag*, 15 June 1969, pp. 52-53.

May, Mair. "Better Business Letters? Here's How." *Super Manag*, 10 (Nov. 1965), 36–38.

Murray, Michael H. "Making a $4.17 Letter Worth It." *Banking*, 69 (May 1977), 124, 126, 128.

Ross, Maxwell C. "Formula for Easy Reading: Use Five-letter Words." *Adver Age*, 11 Nov. 1974, p. 50.

———. "Little Words Have Big Drawing Power in Direct Mail and Advertising." *Adver Age*, 8 July 1974, p. 40.

Ryan, Edward M. "Your Business Letters Have Become a First-class Expense." *Admin Manag*, 23 (1962), 56–57.

"Ten Ways to Speed Up Your Correspondence." *Admin Manag*, 28 (Feb. 1967), 32–36.

Whalen, John J. "Your Letters as Self-Portraits." *Office*, 53 (Apr. 1961), 84–85, 263.

Yeck, John D. "Hints on Letter Writing." *Sales Manag*, 5 Sept. 1958, p. 116.

Young, A. E. "Mean Business in Your Writing." *Admin Manag*, 40 (Apr. 1979), 62–64, 65.

Memoranda

Adams, Tom. "Developing a Meeting Memo." *Sup Manag*, 25 (July 1980), 39–42.

Baar, James. "The Art—and Craft—of the Memo." *Manag Rev*, 53 (May 1964), 31–33.

Bovee, Courtland L. *Techniques of Writing Business Letters, Memos, and Reports*. San Diego: Grossmont, 1974.

Brock, Luther A. "Do Your Memos Confuse or Communicate?" *Sup Manag*, 19 (Sept. 1974), 18–21.

———. "Liberate Your Sexist Memos!" *Manag World*, 8 (Apr. 1979), 12–14.

Brown, Leland. *Communicating Facts and Ideas in Business*. 2nd ed. Englewood Cliffs, N.J.: Prentice-Hall, 1970.

Butenhoff, Carla. "Bad Writing Can Be Good Business." *ABCA Bul*, 40 (June 1977), 12–13.

Church, Marilyn Jakes. "Writing Meaning into a Memo." *Supervision*, 43 (Dec. 1981), 3–4.

Cleveland, Charles B. "Coming to Grips with Memo Mania." *Indus Week*, 21 Sept. 1981, pp. 89–90.

Dowst, Somerby. "Informal Correspondence Gets Results." *Purchasing*, 9 Jan. 1969, pp. 117, 119.

"How to Build Your Career by Memo Writing." *Bus Manag*, 39 (Nov. 1970), 44.

Kelly, Pilson W. "Do You Write Memos They Want to Read?" *Sup Manag*, 7 (Oct. 1962), 8–12.

Lamb, Marion W., and Eugene H. Hughes. *Business Letters, Memorandums, and Reports: A Basic Text in Business Communications*. New York: Harper, 1967.

McCauley, D. E. Jr. "Memo on Memos: Write Less, Say More." *Sup Manag*, 8 (May 1963), 8–9.

Mayfield, Harold. "In Praise of the One-Page Memo." *Sup Manag*, 13 (Feb. 1968), 8–9.

Menning, J. H., C. W. Wilkinson, and Peter B. Clarke. "Writing Short Reports." In

Communicating Through Letters and Reports. 6th ed. Homewood, Ill.: Richard
    D. Irwin, 1976.
Mintz, Harold K. "Memos That Get Things Moving." *Sup Manag*, 18 (Aug. 1973), 2–
    9.
Roman, Kenneth, and Joel Raphaelson. *Writing That Works: How to Write Memos,
    Letters, Reports, Speeches, Resumes, and Other Papers That Say What You Mean
    and Get Things Done*. New York: Harper, 1981.
Rose, Max. "A Memorandum About Memos." *Supervision*, 42 (Mar. 1980), 6–8.
Sharp, Arthur G. "Breaking the Memo-Writing Habit." *SAM Adv Manag J*, 42, No. 3
    (1977), 48–51.
Stearns, Robert L. "Is the Much-maligned Memo Really As Bad As Some Say?" *Pub
    Rel J*, 28 (Feb. 1972), 44.
Strong, Earl Poe, and Robert H. Weaver. *Writing for Business and Industry: Reports,
    Letters, Minutes of Meetings, Memos, and Dictation*. Boston: Allyn, Bacon, 1962.
Swift, Marvin H. "Clear Writing Means Clear Thinking Means. . . ." *Harvard Bus Rev*,
    51 (Jan. 1973), 59–62.
Tade, George T. "How to Write a Better Memo." *Sup Manag*, 16 (May 1971), 12–15.
Uris, Auren. *Memos for Managers*. New York: Crowell, 1975.
Vitt, Sam B. "In Praise of Memos." *Nation's Bus*, 54 (Nov. 1966), 70.
Webster, Eric. "Memo Mania: Its Causes, Carriers and Cures." *Manag Rev*, 56 (Sept.
    1967), 32–36.
Weeks, Francis W., and Richard A. Hatch. *Business Writing Cases and Problems: Letters,
    Memorandums, and Reports*. Champaign, Ill.: Stipes Publishing, 1972.

Job Letters and Resumés

Adler, Kenneth R. *Pathway to Your Future: The Job Resumé and Letter of Application*.
    Cambridge, Mass.: Bellman, 1971.
Andreyka, Robert E. "Job Resumés for Vocational Graduates." *Am Vocat J*, 45 (Jan.
    1970), 34, 36.
Angel, Juvenal L. *Why and How to Prepare an Effective Job Resumé*. 3rd ed. New York:
    World Trade Academy Press, 1961.
Austin, Marshall. *How to Get a Better Job*. New York: Hawthorn, 1976.
Baker, Stephen. "Do Resumés Have to Be Dull?" *Adver Age*, 8 Mar. 1965, p. 117.
Bernheim, Mark. "The Written Job Search—Doubts and 'Leads.' " *Tech Writ Teach*,
    10 (1982), 3–7.
Biegeleisen, Jacob Israel. *Job Resumés: How to Write Them, How to Present Them*. New
    York: Grosset, Dunlap, 1969.
Blumenthal, Lassor A. *Successful Business Writing: How to Write Effective Letters,
    Proposals, Resumés, Speeches*. New York: Grosset, Dunlap, 1976.
"Bogus Degrees." *Forbes*, 25 May 1981, pp. 155–56.
Boles, Richard N. *What Color Is Your Parachute?* Berkeley, Calif.: Ten Speed, 1978.
Boll, Carl R. "The Do's and Don't's of Executive Resumés." *Dun's*, 95 (Feb. 1970),
    47–48.
Bostwick, Burdette E. *Finding the Job You've Always Wanted*. New York: Wiley, 1977.
———. *Resumé Writing: A Comprehensive How-to-do-it Guide*. New York: Wiley, 1976.
Bovee, Courtland L. *Better Business Writing for Bigger Profits*. New York: Exposition,
    1970.

Chandler, Dorothea. "Writing the Post-Interview Thank-You Letter." *ABCA Bul*, 38 (Dec. 1975), 11.

Corwen, Leonard. *Your Resumé: Key to a Better Job*. New York: Arco, 1976.

"Could You Get Laid Off? Then Be Prepared." *Indus Week*, 2 Dec. 1974, pp. 43–46.

Da Vinci, Leonardo. "A Classic Letter of Application." *ABCA Bul*, 35 (Dec. 1975), 17.

Dickhut, H. W., and J. Marvel Davis. *Professional Resumé/Job Search Guide*. 3rd ed. Chicago: Management Counselors, 1974.

Dortch, R. Neil. "What Businessmen Look for in the Resumé." *Pers J*, 54 (Oct. 1975), 516.

Egan, Christine. "Writing Resumés and Cover Letters." *IEEE Trans Prof Comm*, 24 (1981), 156–60.

"Faking It." *Manag Rev*, 70 (Sept. 1981), 6–7.

Feild, Hubert S., and William H. Holley. "Resumé Preparation: An Empirical Study of Personnel Managers' Perceptions." *Voc Guid Q*, 24 (Mar. 1976), 229–36.

Figgins, Ross F. *Techniques of Job Search*. San Francisco: Canfield, 1976.

Fitzgerald, Stephen E. "Notes on the Resumé." *Pub Rel J*, 17 (Feb. 1961), 24.

"Four Ways of Explaining a Physical Handicap in the Application Letter and Resumé." *ABCA Bul*, 38 (Dec. 1975), 20.

Fox, Marcia R. "The Cover Letter." *IEEE Trans Prof Comm*, 24 (1981), 163–65.

Gruber, Edward C. *Resumés That Get Jobs*. New York: Arco, 1976.

Half, Robert. "How to Write (or Read) a DP Resume." *Data Manag*, 20 (Feb. 1982), 34–37.

———. "How to Write (or Read) a Resumé." *Prac Account*, 14 (May 1981), 63–67.

Harrick, Edward J., and John M. Penrose. "Increase Interviews: Effective Use of the Resumé." *ABCA Bul*, 38 (Dec. 1975), 9–11.

Hayen, Roger, and John H. Jackson. "Behavioral Research and Computer Methods Applied to Managerial Resumé Design." *Pers J*, 51 (Oct. 1972), 728–32.

"How to Read an Employee Application." *Sup Manag*, 11 (May 1966), 44–45.

"How to Start Your Letter." *ABCA Bul*, 38 (Dec. 1975), 28.

"How to Write the Prospecting (or Unsolicited) Application." *ABCA Bul*, 38 (Dec. 1975), 27–28.

Huggins, David. "The Resumé Is the Foot in the Door." *Can Bus*, 50 (July 1977), 35–36, 38.

Hunt, Bridgford. "The New You—Researched, Resuméd, and Rarin' to Go." *IEEE Trans Prof Comm*, 24 (1981), 160–62.

Irish, Richard K. *Go Hire Yourself an Employer*. Garden City, N.Y.: Anchor Books, 1973.

Jackson, Tom. *The Perfect Resumé*. Garden City, N.Y.: Anchor Books, 1981.

Jacobs, Bruce. "Job-hunting on the Sly." *Indus Week*, 9 Mar. 1981, pp. 26–27.

Jacquish, Michael P. *Personal Resumé Preparation*. New York: Wiley, 1968.

Janes, Harold D. "The Cover Letter and Resumé." *Pers J*, 48 (Sept. 1969), 732–33.

"Job Hunting: Sell Yourself." *Sales Manag*, 11 June 1973, p. 12.

"Job Resumé: Write It Right." *Chang Times*, 18 (Sept. 1964), 18.

Kiechel, Walter, III. "Lies on the Resumé." *Fortune*, 23 Aug. 1982, pp. 221, 223–24.

Lathrop, Richard. *Who's Hiring Who*. Berkeley, Calif.: Ten Speed, 1977.

Lawrence, Deslie Beth, and Iris D. Rosendahl. "Resumé Vibes—Reading Between the Lines." *Pers*, 56 (Mar. 1979), 53–56.

Leeper, Harold B., Jr. "Can You Sell Yourself?" *Adver Age*, 3 Dec. 1962, pp. 81–82, 84, 86.

Leo, John. "Embellishment Yes, Lying No." *Time*, 9 May 1983, p. 82.

Lewis, Adele. *How to Write Better Resumés*. Woodbury, N.Y.: Barron's Educational Series, 1976.

Lewis, Stephen D. "Are You Teaching a Practical, Up-to-date Job Resumé?" *ABCA Bul*, 40 (Sept. 1977), 15–17.

Liemer, David. "Pizza Resume Gets Young Adman First Job—Almost." *Adver Age*, 1 Jan. 1979, p. 19.

Lynch, Thomas. "Writing a Resumé to Sell Yourself." *Int Manag*, 31 (June 1976), 41–43.

McManus, Kevin. "They're Still Lying on Their Resumés." *Forbes*, 4 Jan. 1982, pp. 288–89.

"Make Your Availability Known When You Plan to Change Jobs." *Admin Manag*, 29 (Feb. 1968), 76–77.

Mansfield, Carmella E. "We Hear You Mr./Ms. Business: The Resumé and Cover Letter." *ABCA Bul*, 39 (Sept. 1976), 20–22.

Margetts, Susan. "The 'Creative' Resumé." *Dun's*, 99 (Feb. 1972), 73–74.

Marshall, Austin. *How to Get a Better Job*. New York: Hawthorn, 1976.

Martin, Merle P. "The Instant Analyst-Resumés." *J Sys Manag*, 32 (June 1981), 6–11.

Menning, J. H., C. W. Wilkinson, and Peter B. Clarke. "Letters About Employment." In *The Practical Craft: Readings for Business and Technical Writers*. Ed. W. Keats Sparrow and Donald H. Cunningham. Boston: Houghton Mifflin, 1978.

Metzger, H. P. "How to Write an Effective Resumé." *Printers' Ink*, 31 Mar. 1961, p. 58.

Meyer, Pearl. "How to Read a Resumé." *Dun's*, 96 (Dec. 1970), 49–50, 52.

Miller, Theron. *How to Write a Job-Getting Resumé*. New York: Vantage, 1967.

Noer, David. *Jobkeeping, A Hireling's Survival Manual*. Radnor, Pa.: Chilton's Book, 1976.

Nutter, Carolyn F. *The Resumé Workbook*. Cranston, R.I.: Carroll, 1963.

Penrose, John M. "Does Order Make a Difference in Resumés?" *J Bus Comm*, 10, No. 3 (1973), 15–19.

Perham, J. C. "What's Wrong with Executive Resumés?" *Dun's*, 105 (May 1975), 50–52, 94, 96.

"Personal Business." *Bus Week*, 21 Sept. 1963, pp. 133–34.

"Personal Business." *Bus Week*, 15 Oct. 1966, pp. 173–74.

Read, Jean, ed. *Resumés That Get Jobs*. New York: Arco, 1977.

"Resumé Fraud." *Pers J*, 60 (Dec. 1981), 914.

"Resumés, Like Sporty Cars, Should Be Compact and Well-designed." *Iron Age*, 3 May 1982, p. 65.

Reynes, Tony. "You Sell Products—Now Learn to Sell Yourself Likewise." *Adver Age*, 1 Jan. 1979, pp. S6, S15–S16, S18.

Rivers, Patricia L. "Resumés: Up Close and Personal." *Sec Manag*, 25 (Apr. 1981), 81–82.

Schoenfeld, Gretchen. "Make Your Resumé Sell." *Office Ex*, 35 (Sept. 1960), 24–25.

Sears, Raymond W. "How to Improve Your Resumé." *Physics Today*, 29 (May 1976), 9.

Seigle, Natalie R. "How to Have a Prospecting Letter of Application Read." *ABCA Bul*, 35 (Dec. 1975), 15–16.

Shyking, Maury. *Resumés for Job Hunters*. 2nd ed. New York: Arco, 1976.

Smith, Abbott P. "How to Make Sure Your Next Resumé Isn't an Obituary." *Training*, 14 (May 1977), 63–64.

Stimac, Michael. "Writing a Skills Resumé—Translating Nonwork Experience into Highly Marketable Skills." *S.A.M. Adv Manag J*, 42 (Summer 1977), 52–64.

Sussman, Paul E. "Executive Job-Hunting: It's Still a Tough Market." *Fin Ex*, 42 (Feb. 1974), 20–24.

Taintor, Sarah Augusta, Kate M. Monro, and Margaret D. Shertzer. "Applying for a Job." In *The Secretary's Handbook: A Manual of Correct Usage*. 9th ed. New York: Macmillan, 1969, pp. 257–73.

"To Attract Good Men, Drop Resumés." *Iron Age*, 29 Aug. 1968, p. 23.

Van Nuys, Sylmar. "Resumé Reading." *Datamation*, 15 July 1970, pp. 60, 62, 64.

Vogel, Erwin. *How to Write Your Job-Getting Resumé and Covering Letter*. Brooklyn, N.Y.: Copy-Write Creations, 1971.

Walsh, E. Michael. "Teaching the Letter of Application." *CCC*, 28 (1977), 374–76.

Weeks, Francis W. "Data Sheets and Resumés." *ABCA Bul*, 38 (Dec. 1975), 13–14.

Whalen, Tim. "Proposal Resumés: A Study of Styles." *Tech Comm*, 27, No. 3 (1980), 26–29.

"Write a Resumé That Gets the Job." *Chang Times*, 29 (July 1975), 25–28.

"Writing Your First Resumé—Marketing Your Potential." *S.A.M. Adv Manag J*, 40 (Autumn 1975), 53–59.

Wyant, June V., and Ruth Vise. "Resumé Writing: Form and Function." *Sp Libr*, 70 (Aug. 1979), 328–32.

Part IV

Related Concerns and Specialized Forms of Technical Communication

Computing and the Future of Technical Communication

WILLIAM L. BENZON

A microcomputer purchased as recently as the summer of 1978 is now obsolete; one can now buy a computer with five to ten times as much computing capacity for approximately the same real cost. As you read this article, this new machine will be fading into the same obsolescence. The moral is simple: Computing technology is changing rapidly.

In this situation reviewing the current literature on the uses of computers in technical communication is pointless, for the equipment discussed in that literature will be obsolete by the time this review becomes available. Much of that literature has the form of "reports from the trenches" and, as such, is a valuable record of the uses technical communicators have found for computers and of the problems they have encountered in using computers. But that literature is not an adequate basis for conducting research into how computing technology can enhance and transform the conduct of technical communication. For that literature gives no sense of the broad capacities of computing technology or of the direction of future developments. Consequently, this chapter has little to say about that literature; it is readily available in standard journals, such as *Technical Communication, Journal of Technical Writing and Communication, IEEE Transactions on Professional Communication*, and proceedings of conferences, such as the International Technical Communication Conference, the AFIPS Conference on Office Automation, or the National Online Information Meeting.

Instead, this essay takes a broad look at computers and at technical communication to identify those areas where developments in computing are most likely to yield tools for technical communication. However, since computing is changing the ways in which we think about perceptual, cognitive, and linguistic processes, we also take a brief look at work in cognitive psychology, computational linguistics, and artificial intelligence which has promise of yielding insight into the processes of technical communication. This is particularly important, since today's abstract computational models of mental processes can become the practical tools of tomorrow. If we can use a computer to simulate, in a small way, what people do when they write, read, look at a picture, and so on, then we can develop that model into a tool that technical communicators, for example, can use in writing or in devising graphics. Thus, through the medium of the computer, current theoretical studies can point the way to the tools of tomorrow.

This article first provides a general discussion of computers and their social impact and then discusses three general task areas within technical communication:

> Linearization: In our minds, knowledge is intimately and complexly interlinked and cross-correlated. But we communicate, whether as the addressor or the addressee, one idea at a time, idea after idea. Linearization is the process of going back and forth between the simultaneous interconnectedness of thought and the linearity of communication.

> Adaptation: Different populations have different interests, needs, and levels of understanding. Adaptation is the process of tailoring communication to reflect these differences appropriately.

> Mode: We can communicate through writing and through visual images; and either can be done in printed copy or through on-line media. These are differences of mode.

Under each heading consideration is given to currently practical technology and research directions leading to the practical tools of tomorrow. As appropriate, suggestions will be made as to the likely directions for research and new computer-based tools which are likely to be developed.

As you read this article, you might imagine that you are that technical communicator of the future. And so you are reading it on a terminal: not a bulky TV-like device, but a relatively small terminal about the size of a book which includes both screen and keyboard and/or voice input. When you come across an item that seems interesting, you can read it immediately simply by calling it up on the screen. Or you can make a list of items and call them up when you have finished this article. You can also contact the authors of any of these articles or books and leave questions for them or direct their attention to material you think might interest them. You might also want to comment on the usefulness of various items mentioned here. You might even go so far as to call an on-line conference to discuss some area of particular interest. Finally, your terminal will be able to handle high-resolution color images. Hence, the version of this essay you will read in the future will have many graphs, diagrams, and pictures. This is very important, for one needs a highly developed visual imagination in order to understand computing and computers easily. Beyond this, some of these visual aids will be animated, for computing is a process, and time is intrinsic to it. Hence, moving pictures will provide a means for acquiring an intuitive understanding of very complex mathematical processes.

The World of Computing

This section briefly considers computing in general and then looks at some of the literature on the social and economic consequences of computing. From there, it moves to a general look at the automated office and computer networks, and concludes by considering artificial intelligence and cognitive science.

The state of the current computing art has been well reviewed in a special issue of *Science* (1982) devoted to computers and electronics and containing articles on software (that is, programs), hardware (that is, machines), graphics, scientific and commercial applications, communications, and information retrieval. The articles, some to be reviewed below, are relatively informal, and many of the illustrations are superb. The world of microelectronics (that is, the semiconductor "chips" in which the microminiaturized electronic circuits of computers are embedded) was covered in the September 1977 issue of *Scientific American*, which has been reissued as a book, *Microelectronics*.

The best general textbook is Michael Arbib's *Computers and the Cybernetic Society* (1977), which was written for relative novices in a way that invites serious attention from old hands. Arbib covers the basic principles of computing hardware, the electronic circuitry that actually performs the computation, and of software, the instructions that assemble the elementary operations of the hardware into complex programs of computational activity. The section on writing large programs is essential reading for anyone who wants to understand the role of documentation in software development and use. Large programs, often consisting of 100,000 or more lines of program code, must be written as a set of quasi-independent modules, each of which handles a part of the overall problem. Accurate documentation is absolutely essential to insuring that the modules interact properly. Hence, as F. H. Brooks, Jr., makes clear in his book on managing software development, *The Mythical Man-Month* (1975), good programming begins and ends in good documentation.

Arbib approaches the use of computers in simulating large and complex systems by discussing models for the interaction of predators and prey in an ecosystem and by discussing global economic models. This material, along with that on data banks and on planning systems, can be combined with the chapters on "Economic Rationality," "The Science of Design," and "Social Planning" from Herbert A. Simon's *The Sciences of the Artificial* (1981) to provide an overview of the basic concepts behind management information systems and decision support systems. Arbib also has useful treatments of artificial intelligence and of computer-aided instruction.

One should also consult the annual proceedings of the National Computer Conference (NCC). NCC is sponsored by American Federation of Information Processing Societies, Inc. (AFIPS), which is constituted by various professional associations involved in computing, and the NCC proceedings cover all phases of computing, from hardware to social consequences. Among the most central and general journals in computing are *Communications of the ACM* (ACM:

Association for Computing Machinery), *IEEE Computer* (IEEE: Institute of Electrical and Electronics Engineers), *Journal of the American Society for Information Science*, and *Computing Reviews*, which reviews recent books and articles in computing. *The Annual Review of Information Science and Technology* and *Advances in Computers* publish good review articles which, over about a three-year cycle, review the whole field. Most articles in the field are abstracted in *Computer and Control Abstracts* and in *Information Science Abstracts*. All work done under federal contracts which is not classified is available from the National Technical Information Service (NTIS), which lists reports, along with abstracts, in *Government Reports Announcements*. Much university work is available in technical reports before it appears in the archival literature; the most active computer science departments include those at Massachusetts Institute of Technology, Stanford, Carnegie-Mellon, Cornell, and the University of California at Berkeley.

One way to make a transition from considering the nature of computing technology to considering its social and economic consequences is to examine the two-volume report, Raymond T. Yeh and Paul B. Schneck's *Computer Science* (1982), which is the result of a study NASA commissioned to examine how computing can enhance NASA's operations. A series of appendices reviews broad areas of computing technology, while the body of the report culminates in a general plan for coordinating NASA's use of computing technology. This plan makes it quite clear that anything approaching full utilization of computing technology is, ipso facto, social engineering and, as such, must carefully consider the agency's goals, present organization, and personnel needs. With this in mind, the plan suggests that NASA could, in stages, evolve into a highly flexible, adaptive, and intelligent organization, one in which control and authority are decentralized and various groups can readily form to meet special needs, then dissolve when those needs have been met. Implementing this plan requires the judicious use of computer networks, decision support systems, and a wide variety of databases, especially those about the agency and its clients.

One of the earliest and most forceful essays on the general role of information in society is Norbert Wiener's "Information, Language, and Society" (1961), which was originally published in 1948. The point is a simple one: Social organization and processes are mediated by information flow; to control and regulate that organization and its processes we need only control the information flow. Decisions are based on information and themselves constitute a higher form of information. If we can influence the information on which any decision is to be based, then we can influence the decision. Wiener also states a theme that has loomed larger and larger in the social sciences. The social scientist is not external to the system he is studying; he is, to some irreducible extent, a part of that system. Thus, the very act of conducting that study will, in some way—perhaps small and certainly unpredictable—change the system he is studying. This apparently abstract question will become increasingly concrete as we become more and more interlinked through computer networks. For the administrative mechanisms that regulate the computer networks will, in effect, be studying the social organization of the network users. The administrative decisions made will have direct and immediate impact on the organization of interaction among users of the network.

Robert Theobald's essay, "Cybernetics and the Problems of Social Reorganization" (1967), remains one of the most perceptive treatments of the general impact of computing technology. He argues that through computers "we possess the technological potential to call forth enough goods and services to meet our needs" (p. 45). Achieving this, however, requires basic changes in our institutions, and in making such changes we will have to be particularly careful to preserve and even to enhance the rights of individuals. Finally, and here Theobald echoes Weiner's point about self-reflexiveness, we can use the computer to anticipate and to plan for the changes which the computer will itself bring about.

The most comprehensive book-length treatment of these issues is Abbe Mowshowitz's *The Conquest of Will* (1976), with treatments of computers in education, health care, business, and politics. In exploring these issues, Mowshowitz is particularly concerned with the distribution of power and with individual responsibility. The book begins with a chapter on the role of technology in Western culture, followed by one on the history of computing machines from the mechanical devices of the Renaissance through the current electronic computer. The book closes with a section on the computer as it functions as a mirror and metaphor for our understanding of ourselves, with the final chapter devoted to images of the computer in literature. Mowshowitz thus provides a very full image of computing and its implications, an image that can usefully be supplemented by the essays in Michael L. Dertouzos and Joel Moses, *The Computer Age* (1979). Finally, one should also examine Adam Osborne's *Running Wild* (1979) and Ted Nelson's *Computer Lib/Dream Machines* (1974). Osborne is himself one of the "wonderkids" of the current microcomputer revolution (Bro Uttal, "A Computer Gadfly's Triumph," [1982]), and he predicts that by 1990 90 percent of the computers in use will be powerful microcomputers, and only 10 percent will be the large mainframe computers that are the centerpieces of the product lines of corporations such as IBM, Control Data Corporation, Burroughs, and Digital Electronics Corporation. Ted Nelson is something of a guru in an anticorporate computer underground, and his book projects an outrageously imaginative understanding of how computers work and how they can be made to work for people, not against or over people.

Focusing specifically on the economic implications of computing, A. B. Oettinger's article, "Information Resources" (1980) reviews a variety of literature, including Marc U. Porat's well-known study *The Information Economy* (1977), which shows that almost half of the U.S. labor force is employed in the information sector. Oettinger suggests that the information sector of the economy is currently the least productive sector and "hence the ripest for displacement by more capital-intensive information resources" (p. 197) based on computing and computing technology.

In "The Distribution of Work and Income" (1982) Wassily W. Leontief reports the results of a study of the short-term (to 1990) implications of computing technology on the Austrian economy. (Austria is the only nation that has so far produced such a study.) The result is clear; if the work week is not shortened, then Austria will experience its highest unemployment since the 1930s. Finally, those who still insist on believing that the number of jobs created by high-technology industries will make up for the number of jobs lost through automation should read James E. Long and Timothy J. Healy, "Advanced Automation for Space Missions" (1980) which argues that it would take only about 20 years to develop computers and robots so sophisticated that they could be landed on the moon and then proceed to establish a manufacturing operation capable of producing robots capable of setting up a manufacturing operation capable of producing and so on. If a robot is capable of manufacturing a robot, then there is no reason whatever to believe that the long-term outcome of high technology will be more jobs. Unfortunately, no one is thinking seriously about these issues.

It is not immediately obvious, however, that computers of the requisite sophistication can be produced, that is, within the provenance of artificial intelligence, computational linguistics, and cognitive science. Whether or not the self-replicating robot is possible, these disciplines are important to technical communication because they have recently produced many sophisticated theories about higher mental processes. If technical communicators want to achieve a deeper understanding of how we read and write, how we perceive and think about drawings and diagrams, and how we understand abstract concepts, then this material must be confronted.

Douglas R. Hofstader's *Godel, Escher, Bach* (1979) is an entertaining way in, while Herbert A. Simon's *The Sciences of the Artificial* (1981) remains a classic statement of basic principles of cognition, including the value of modular, hierarchic organization, and the need for perspicuous grouping and organization of material. Patrick H. Winston's *Artificial Intelligence* (1977) is a good introductory textbook, but it does require a serious confrontation with technical detail. A great deal of the work in cognitive psychology and linguistics has been brought together in *Language and Perception* by George A. Miller and Philip N. Johnson-Laird (1976). Important review articles include "Computational Linguistics and the Humanist" (William L. Benzon and David G. Hays [1976]), "Information Processing Models of Cognition" (Herbert A. Simon [1981]), and "The Organization and Use of Information" (Donald E. Walker [1981]). The central journals are *Artificial Intelligence, International Journal of Man-Machine Studies, Cognition, Cognitive Psychology, Cognitive Science, IEEE Transactions on Pattern Analysis and Machine Intelligence, IEEE Transactions on Acoustics, Speech, and Signal Processing, SIGART Newsletter* (SIGART: Special Interest Group in Artificial Intelligence), *American Journal of Computational Linguistics* (which publishes a large number of abstracts of articles and technical reports), and, in a more interdisciplinary context, *Behavioral and Brain Sciences* and *Cognition and Brain Theory*.

Work in this area is exceedingly controversial. Some of the controversy is concerned only with whether or not artificial intelligence and cognitive science can live up to their strongest claims, to provide fundamental insight into the nature of perception, reasoning, speaking, thinking, and reading. These questions have been covered in a series of articles that have appeared in *Behavioral and Brain Sciences*, beginning with Zenon Pylyshyn's "Computational Models and Empirical Constraints" (1978), John Haugeland's "The Nature and Plausibility of Cognitivism" (1978), and continuing with "On the Demystification of Mental Imagery" (Stephen M. Kosslyn, et al. [1979]), Noam Chomsky's "Rules and Representations" (1980), Zenon Pylyshyn's "Computation and Cognition" (1980), and John R. Searle's "Minds, Brains, and Programs" (1980). The central issues are: (1) Is the computational approach inherently plausible or is it intrinsically flawed (Searle and Haugeland); (2) what is the link between these complex models and empirical evidence (Haugeland and Pylyshyn); and (3) are mental processes essentially analogue or Gestalt, or are they digital, propositional, logical (Haugeland, Chomsky, Kosslyn, and Pylyshyn)? There is not, as yet, any consensus on these matters.

Beyond the purely conceptual controversy, there is considerable controversy about the ethical implications of this work. Mowshowitz (1976) discusses these issues, as does Hofstader (1979), albeit in a rather quixotic way. Perhaps the central statement is Joseph Weizenbaum's *Computer Power and Human Reason* (1976), in which Weizenbaum argues that we are perilously close to turning over major responsibility to computers and thereby evading responsibility for important decisions. In a perceptive review of Weizenbaum, David G. Hays (*Computers and the Humanities* [in press]) argues that, while the issues Weizenbaum raises are important and deserve our deepest thought, Weizenbaum is caught in the inadequacies of the views he is criticizing. Although he does not realize it, Weizenbaum has no substantial view of human nature other than the computational view he criticizes. Thus, Weizenbaum's critique is inadequate because it fails to call on our best knowledge of human actions and behavior. Hays would prefer that we have greater respect for the current depth of our ignorance and, in particular, that we recognize the intellectual weakness of artificial intelligence without rushing to hasty judgment about the ultimate intellectual and moral value of computation as a way of modeling human mental processes.

These issues are particularly important for technical communication, for the profession of technical communication has a central role to play in the development of computing. On the one hand, we write much of the documentation that interprets computer technology to lay users. On the other hand, precisely because technical communication is so important to the industrial and business worlds, we will make many of the practical applications of advanced computing technology, based on work in cognitive science and artificial intelligence. In adapting this technology, we must be sensitive to the ethical issues as well as to the basic pragmatic and conceptual issues.

Linearization

Linearization concerns the structure of attention when we are picking up information, percepts, and concepts. It is thus primarily a phenomenon of listening, reading, and looking. Of course, writing, speaking, and drawing must also involve linearization; for we can utter or write only one word at a time, and we can draw only one line at a time. But the linearity of production is ultimately regulated by the linearity of comprehension. We utter what makes sense when we listen to ourselves talk; if it doesn't make sense, then we backtrack and make corrections. Writing and drawing are similar; the production process is regulated to meet the standards of the comprehension process.

Thus, linearization concerns how we attend to written, spoken, and graphic material in our attempts to comprehend it and also how we produce such material so that it is comprehensible. Linearization is obviously related to both adaptation and to mode. Different types of audiences will have attention structures that differ according to their interests and cognitive capacities. Mode is also important. A given body of material will be organized one way for effective oral presentation, while a different order will be appropriate in written presentation.

Modal difference becomes particularly important when we consider the possibilities of computerized documents. Hardcopy documents at least present the illusion of linearity, for such documents generally have their pages numbered consecutively. It may never be the case that anyone reads those pages in order; many people skip around in documents, looking only at what is most immediately relevant. Hence, the order in which people assimilate the written text is not the same linearization imposed on it by the author. In the case of computerized documents, even the convention of linear order is unnecessary. Such documents can be stored in databases where the notion of numerically ordered pages is meaningless. Instead, various fragments of a document can be linked to other fragments according to conceptual association.

Thus, we enter the world which Ted Nelson has envisioned in *Literary Machines* (1981). In this world, new documents are very likely to take the form of relatively small modules of text which serve primarily to create links between already existing text modules. After all, much of the content of research articles, and certainly the content of review articles, is simply a summary of material in other articles. In an electronic environment, all articles would be accessible from any given terminal; thus, it might be more convenient simply to cite these other articles and, rather than review them, provide only that new text which is needed to present new information and make new connections between items already in the system. In order for such a system to work smoothly, it will be necessary for people to learn to structure their material into relatively small (250 to 1,000 words) quasi-independent text modules—a practice good technical writers are already adept at. It would also be wise to summarize the main point of each module in a single line at the beginning of the module. In such an informatic environment, readers would browse around quite freely, starting with the text module that is most relevant to their current needs and capacities, and then moving to other modules as they please. The linear order in which material is attended to would thus be largely under the control of the reader, where it should be, rather than being subject to the arbitrary demands of sequential hardcopy organization.

That, however, is still in the future. For the present, the most obvious computer tools are word processing tools. These tools help the writer with his or her linearizing, composing. A wide variety of office technology is ably reviewed in David Barcomb's book *Office Automation* (1981). Some of the best articles are David Becker, "Automated Language Processing" (1981), Vincent E. Giulano, "The Mechanization of Office Work" (1982), R. J. Spinrad, "Office Automation" (1982), and James A. Levin, "Interpersonalized Media" (1980). An account of some of the programming techniques used in text and word processing can be found in A. B. Tucker's book, *Text Processing* (1979). But the most important technical treatment is Donald E. Knuth's *TEX and METAFONT* (1979), which is a description of programs Knuth developed for page layout of technical material, with particular attention given to dealing with equations and formulas, and for the development of a wide variety of typefonts. In working on the latter programs, Knuth had to develop a mathematical theory of the geometry of typefaces. The theory is an important one and, while full comprehension requires substantial mathematics, the basic ideas can be grasped by reading through the text and looking at the examples.

Beyond word processing, a variety of tools are being developed to aid writers. See Wayne Holder, "Software Tools for Writers" (1982), or Linda Cherry, "Computer Aids for Writers" (1981), Mark S. Fox, Donald J. Bebel, and Alice C. Parker, "The Automated Dictionary" (1980), Ira Goldstein, "Writing with a Computer" (1981), William E. Linn, Jr., and Walter W. Reitman, 'Autonote2" (1975), and Lance A. Miller, George E. Heidorn, and Karen Jensen, "Text-Critiquing with the EPISTLE System" (1981). These systems do a variety of things, from checking spelling, assessing readability according to one of the standard formulas, through checking grammar and stylistic attributes. The last-named capabilities are as of this writing experimental or, at best, in the early stages of prototype development. These systems employ theoretical models developed in computational linguistics, artificial intelligence, and cognitive science and, as such, represent one avenue through which theoretical work in cognition and linguistics is made into practical tools that can be used by technical communicators. But if these tools are to be of maximum service, then technical communicators must become involved in developing the theories on which they are based.

The best way to move from the practical to the theoretical is machine translation, which is the use of computers to translate documents from one language into another. With the development of multinational corporations, the problem has become urgent, though most of the past research was sponsored by the Defense Department, which needs machine translation as an adjunct to its intelligence operations. Martin Kay's "Automatic Translation of Natural Languages" (1973) gives a brief history and evaluation of the work in the area. He states that high-quality translation is not yet within our grasp but that we have made much theoretical progress. The evaluation is still valid; see also David G. Hays and J. Mathias's "FBIS Seminar on Machine Translation" (1976), and Wayne Zachary's bibliography, "Machine Aids to Translation" (1978). In the early days machine translation was little more than dictionary lookup systems: take a word in the source language, look it up in the dictionary, and then find the equivalent word in the target language. Such systems failed, and so attempts were made to employ syntactic information as well. This method worked better but was still inadequate. It is now quite obvious that high-quality machine translation has to be semantically based; the computer translating system has to implement a theory of meaning.

Thus, while the work on machine translation had a practical motivation, the most significant result has been a variety of theoretical models of language processes, models from which a new discipline of technical communication can be created.

A great deal of work has been done in these general areas. Good reviews include William L. Benzon and David G. Hays, "Computational Linguistics and the Humanist" (1976), David Becker, "Automated Language Processing" (1981), Herbert A. Simon, "Information Processing Models of Cognition" (1981), and Donald E. Walker, "The Organization and Use of Information" (1981), while Harry Tennant's *Natural Language Processing* (1981) is a good textbook. In the early 1970s, the Defense Department sponsored a major research project aimed at producing computer systems that could accept natural language voice input and respond appropriately (that is, if a question was asked, then the computer would answer it). The results of this work have been reviewed in Stanley R. Petrick's "Report of the ACL 1977 Annual Meeting Panel on Speech Understanding and Computational Linguistics" (1977), while Donald E. Walker's *Understanding Spoken Language* (1978) provides a detailed account of the systems developed by SRI International, which produced the soundest theoretical work in this project. Other major theoretical approaches include the conceptual dependency theory of R. C. Schank and R. P. Abelson, *Scripts, Plans, Goals, and Understanding* (1977), the network model of Donald A. Norman and David E. Rumelhart, *Explorations in Cognition* (1975), which draws heavily on psychological experimentation, Naomi Sager, *Natural Language Information Processing* (1981), which includes applications to medical recordkeeping, and George A. Miller and Philip N. Johnson-Laird, *Language and Perception* (1976), which attempts to synthesize a massive amount of perceptual and cognitive theorizing and experimentation into a formal account of language and meaning.

One particularly important area of language processing research concerns parsing, which is the process through which a linear sequence of linguistic units, whether uttered aloud or written, is related to an essentially relational, multidimensional, and non-linear semantic base. Ralph Grishman has reviewed much of the literature on parsing in his "A Survey of Syntactic Analysis Procedures for Natural Languages" (1976), which includes a five-page bibliography. The topic is complex and important because language is infinitely variable; Noam Chomsky's fame comes from his early arguments, which became widely known through his *Syntactic Structures* (1957), establishing that language structure is infinite in a precise, mathematically intelligible way. From this infinite variability, it follows that there are many ways to parse a given sentence, many ways to relate its surface structure to the underlying deep structure from which it was generated and through which it is related to semantics, cognition, and perception. The trick of successful parsing is to identify the one structure that is relevant to the sentence at hand. It is not yet a trick that can be performed with routine success.

Parsing is concerned primarily with sentences. For a review of work on mechanisms for understanding connected discourse, Robert Young's "Text Understanding" (1977) is useful. Walter Kintsch, in *The Representation of Meaning in Memory* (1974), reports his extensive experimentation in text understanding and concludes that we remember text meanings in a non-linguistic form. We do not remember sentences or clauses; we remember the underlying propositions from which they are derived.

While most of the work in cognitive science and computational linguistics has been devoted to language comprehension, there has been some done on production, for example, the work that William C. Mann and James A. Moore have done on the "Computer Generation of Multiparagraph English Text" (1981). This general conceptual approach informs the most interesting current work in composing theory, such as the work of Bertram Bruce, Allan Collins, Ann D. Rubin, and Dedre Genter on "A Cognitive Science Approach to Writing" (1981) and Linda S. Flower and John R. Hayes on "Problem Solving and the Cognitive Process of Writing" (1981).

Finally, we need briefly to mention work embodying a cybernetic approach to psychology. The basic concepts come from Norbert Wiener in *Cybernetics* (1961), and they have been ably elaborated by William T. Powers in his *Behavior* (1973). Powers argues that perception and cognition are organized into distinct orders, in which higher level orders obtain their input from lower level orders and in turn regulate those lower level orders. The lowest perceptual level involves intensities, the immediate sensations present in sensory organs, the eyes, ears, nose, skin, joint and tendon sensors, and so on. Intensities are in turn organized into sensations, such as sweet, bitter, cold, dry, heavy, red, and rapid. At the next level of regulation, sensations are compounded into configurations, such as dog, square, standing, sitting, and the taste of an apple or steak. Configurations are organized into transitions, and transitions then constitute sequences, such as run, walk, fly, and a bird's song. Powers discusses several levels that are even higher, including relationships, programs, principles, and systems concepts, but the general idea should now be clear enough. Powers has gone beyond vague ideas of hierarchical systems organization to a specific proposal about the structure of our perceptual and cognitive systems. At each level in Powers's hierarchy, a distinctly different level of phenomenon is regulated.

David G. Hays has taken the general approach of cognitive science and computational linguistics and has combined it with Powers's model in his account of *Cognitive Structures* (1981). William L. Benzon and David G. Hays have taken that model and provided it with a neurological foundation in their essay, "Principles and Development of Natural Intelligence" (submitted for publication). The result of this theoretical synthesis is a cybernetic model for language in which structure and processes are inextricably interwoven. Nouns represent schemas of configuration order (in Powers's model discussed in the previous paragraph), while verbs represent schemas of the sequence and program orders; adjectives and adverbs represent sensation schemas. Thus, the basic parts of speech can be derived from the hierarchical structure of cognitive and perceptual processes. A similar justification can be provided for the division of language processes into phonological processes (having to do with the sound structure of syllables), morphological processes (the combination of syllables into words), syntactic processes (the combination of words into sentences), and pragmatics (the relation of language to its communicative context). While the most recent version of Hays's model has not been embodied in a computer simulation, Brian Phillips did program an earlier version of the theory and used it to study discourse structure in "A Model for Knowledge and Its Application to Discourse Analysis" (1978).

We can now look back over this brief review of linearization and computing. The current technology offers word and text processing to eliminate much of the slop, clutter, and wasted time involved in document preparation, leaving more time for the communicator to attend to style, content, and graphic form. Experimental work in the cognitive sciences—linguistics, cognitive psychology, computational linguistics, and artificial intelligence—is providing a rich assortment of models and theories about language processes; some of this work is already being incorporated into tools that help writers with grammar and style. It is clear that technical communicators will have to become familiar with these models and theories if they are to develop a deeper understanding of language processes and if they are to further develop computer tools to help them in their work.

Adaptation

People's needs for knowledge and information differ along three dimensions: (1) interest, (2) specific background knowledge, and (3) general capacity for abstract thought. While we may have no specific theories about the first dimension, it is much discussed and well understood; for example, managers, engineers, and market analysts have different interests and responsibilities for a product, and their need for information differs accordingly.

The need to adapt to different levels of abstraction and to differences in background knowledge is also discussed, but it is not well differentiated. Neither a plumber nor a Ph.D. paleontologist is likely to have any specific knowledge that is relevant to understanding the techniques of designing and fabricating large-scale integrated (VLSI) semiconductor chips. But the plumber is unlikely to be able to follow reasoning at as high a level of abstraction as the paleontologist can. Documents on VLSI design and fabrication aimed at these two groups of people should keep this point in mind. This difference in level of abstraction is, in effect, the primary difference between *Scientific American* and *Science Digest*. Both are likely to have articles on VLSI techniques, and neither is likely to assume specific background knowledge. But the articles will be aimed at different levels of abstraction.

On the other hand, the Ph.D. paleontologist is likely to be operating at the same level of abstraction as a Ph.D. chemist, but they are applying that relatively high level of abstract thought to different intellectual domains, different conceptual backgrounds. Similarly, the plumber and the carpenter operate at the same level of abstraction, but in different conceptual domains.

Thus, the likely background knowledge of an audience is one aspect of the communication situation while the level of abstract conceptualization of typical members of the audience is clearly a different aspect of the communication situation. The technical communicator must deal with both of these factors as well as the different interests people have as a function of the different roles they play with respect to the technical material discussed in the document.

Let us begin our discussion with the work of Yuzo Yamamoto, Richard V. Morris, Christopher Hartsough, and E. David Callender, "The Role of Requirements Analysis in the System Life Cycle" (1982). They are concerned with the problem and role of documentation in developing large and complex information systems. They argue that in designing and implementing such systems, six different points of view must be accommodated: (1) User Needs, (2) User Design, (3) User Operations, (4) Implementation Design, (5) Implementation Training, and (6) Implementation Testing. The User Needs viewpoint can be captured in scenarios depicting how various users of the system—whether it be a word processing system, a database system, or a graphics system—would interact with it. The factors common to all these scenarios are expressed in the User Design viewpoint, from which the basic systems requirements are extracted. The User Operations viewpoint takes the system, as it is constructed, and applies it to the users' problems; experience gained from this viewpoint can then be used to modify the developing system.

The Implementation Design viewpoint is concerned with matching the general design of the system to the requirements of the User Design viewpoint. Details of the system are fine tuned from the Implementation Training viewpoint; in training prospective users to use the developing system, the implementers learn how to adapt the system of human capacities. Finally, the Implementation Testing viewpoint is concerned with integrating the various parts of the system into a coherent whole and testing their interaction.

Yamamoto and colleagues find it necessary to specify these different points of view because different kinds of information are relevant to different tasks, and those differing kinds of information often require different types of conceptual realization. Thus, user needs are best expressed in the concepts users employ in conducting their business—for example, market analysis, inventory control, long-range facilities planning—while the implementation design must be expressed in the concepts of hardware and software systems organization—for example, megabytes, RAM, hard disk, relational database, FIFO stack. Only by keeping these differences clear and distinct is it possible to step to the side, as it were, and look across the full set of viewpoints to coordinate the development of the system.

This concept of system viewpoints has been developed in conjunction with work on "Document Production from a Formal Database" by Christopher Hartsough, Yuzo Yamamoto, and E. David Callender (1982). The design of large information systems is so complicated that various computer tools are used in the design process, with the design being stored in a database. The different viewpoints then become part of the system for retrieving information from the database; the nature of the information retrieved in response to a specific question will depend on the viewpoint from which the query was made. Other work on computer tools for document development includes Roy E. Anderson's "Modular Documentation" (1981), which takes the position that "documents are written, not for the purpose of providing 'documentation'. . . but for the purpose of providing a system design to guide the system's 'construction' " (p. 401), (a position consistent with that of Yamamoto and colleagues [1982]); and Edgar H. Sibley, P. Gerard Scallan, and Eric K. Clemons, "The Software Configuration Management Database" (1981), which discusses a database system that supports Software Configuration Management, a set of techniques used by suppliers of large data processing systems to the U.S. government to ensure the coherence and integrity of a system as it is developed and goes through the inevitable changes, both major and minor, which are necessary.

The discussion so far has concerned information concepts and computing tools for documenting computer systems, but they may also apply to documenting any system or product. Computer-aided design (CAD) and computer-aided manufacturing (CAM) concern the use of computer tools in product design and manufacturing across the full range of industrial products; see Thomas G. Gunn, "The Mechanization of Design and Manufacturing" (1982), and C. A. Hudson, "Computers in Manufacturing" (1982). CAD/CAM tools are used in designing everything from simple mechanical parts, such as a ball bearing assembly, to complex integrated circuit chips. The ultimate application of CAD/CAM techniques is the automatic factory, in which a designer creates a product using a CAD system, which is directly linked to a CAM system so that, once the design is complete, the product can be manufactured automatically. In this world, all the documentation will be created in and continue to reside in a computer-realized information system. No doubt hardcopy will be needed, but that copy will be generated from the material stored in an information system. Therefore, the techniques that are being developed to manage documentation for computing systems will be applicable to all documentation in the factory of the future.

With the prospect of all documentation being created and maintained in information systems, Gerard Salton's works, *Dynamic Information and Library Processing* (1975) and 'SMART'' (1979), become critically important. Salton has been interested in techniques for indexing free text material stored in databases and so has developed the SMART (System for the Mechanical Analysis and Retrieval of Text) system. The object of text retrieval is to provide users with a set of texts containing information relevant to their interests. The most obvious example is bibliographic retrieval, where the user wants a list of citations to articles, reports, books, and monographs on a given topic. The database will contain a list of items along with abstracts of each. Although Salton's methods have not been tried on full-scale bibliographic systems, they have been tested on small samples, and here they perform better than conventional bibliographic systems. They retrieve a higher percentage of the items in the system which are relevant to the user's query and a relatively smaller percentage of useless items.

Other advantages of Salton's system are that (1) it accepts queries in ordinary English; (2) it will modify its retrieval strategy in response to user feedback about how useful the retrieved items are; and (3) its internal structure is dynamic so that over a long period of time it will adapt itself to the changing interests and needs of its users. The overall effect of Salton's methodology is to create a system that orders its documents according to their relevance to a particular user's point of view. Knowledge is complexly interlinked; everything is related to everything else, but some linkages are relatively close (for example, composing theory and rhetoric) while others are relatively distant (for example, composing theory and quantum mechanics, which might be linked through the theme of indeterminacy as it applies to our knowledge of ourselves, of composing theory, and of the physical universe, quantum mechanics). What a user wants from a bibliographic retrieval system is that it orders its citations according to the point of view implicit in the user's query; the items most relevant are at the top of the order while the items least relevant are at the bottom of the order. And that is what Salton's system does.

Thus, if Salton's SMART system is used to index, for example, business correspondence, proposals, and user's manuals, it will automatically adapt to the various points of view present among its various users. It will, therefore, be a crucial tool which the technical communicator of the future can use to adapt documentation to various user points of view. By writing documents in relatively small modules, the communicator can allow SMART to index the modules in a way that will link them together into larger information clusters according to the interests and needs of the user.

The computer tools discussed so far assume users who are only interested in material they can immediately understand. A rather different set of tools, those of computer-aided instruction (CAI), could be used actively to train users for some system or device. The work in CAI has been ably reviewed by Patrick Suppes, one of the pioneers in the field, in "Current Trends in Computer-Assisted Instruction" (1979). The general idea is to prepare a set of lessons in much the same way in which programmed learning modules or texts are prepared. Each lesson teaches one concept or fact, and after a set of lessons students are tested. If they answer the questions satisfactorily, then new material is made available; otherwise, old material will be repeated.

In *Mindstorms* (1980), Seymour Papert argues that most CAI proceeds from mistaken assumptions. Although it does provide some flexibility, it assumes a passive learner. Papert advocates the use of techniques from artificial intelligence to create a much more active style of CAI in which the student becomes an active learner, creating relatively small and simple programs that embody or illustrate various concepts. Papert is particularly interested in teaching mathematical concepts and reports work done in his laboratory which demonstrates that by using his methods of CAI, students who show no interest in or aptitude for mathematics can become surprisingly proficient in a relatively short time. Since a knowledge of mathematics is essential to understanding advanced technology in all areas, Papert's work deserves close consideration from technical communicators, for training modules patterned after Papert's work might well become parts of on-line documentation packages for all technical domains.

Going beyond the use of artificial intelligence techniques to construct CAI programs, one can use these techniques to model the learning process, as John Seely Brown, Allan Collins, and Gregory Harris have done in "Artificial Intelligence and Learning Strategies" (1978). They found that the same general processes used in understanding stories are also used in understanding elementary mathematics and electronic circuit design. In all three cases, there is a surface structure that is readily available and a deep structure that must be actively learned.

Finally, let us consider some recent theoretical work that has been done on levels of abstraction. A basic theory has been set forth by David G. Hays in *Cognitive Structures* (1981), and a simplified exposition can be found in "Lust in Action" by William L. Benzon (1981), in which the theory is applied to one of Shakespeare's sonnets. Other expositions of the theory include William L. Benzon, "Cognitive Networks and Literary Semantics" (1976), David G. Hays, "Machine Translation and Abstract Terminology" (1977), David G. Hays and William L. Benzon, "Metagram Software" (1981), and Brian Phillips, "A Model for Knowledge and Its Application to Discourse Analysis" (1978). Benzon and Hays have sketched out the neural basis of abstraction in "Principles and Development of Natural Intelligence" (submitted for publication).

The basic idea is simple. Abstract concepts are defined by the stories that exemplify them. Thus, the abstract concept of "charity" can be defined by the general story, "when someone does something nice for someone without thought of reward." Any particular story in which specific actors do specific deeds in a way that satisfies the general pattern is an instance of charity. Charity is not any one of those deeds or thoughts or actors; rather, it resides in the pattern linking the actors to one another and to their thoughts and deeds.

Abstract definition, in Hays's sense, is recursive. Terms that have been abstractly defined can appear in the stories that provide the conceptual base for higher order abstractions. Thus, in the definition of "charity," both "nice" and "reward" are abstract concepts. One can easily enough make lists of deeds that are nice and things that are rewards; but "niceness" and "rewardhood" don't appear in those lists—they are abstract properties—and the lists of deeds and things exhibiting those properties are specific to individuals. What is nice or rewarding for Dick may not be so for Jane. Thus, "niceness" and "rewardhood" exist only in the relationship between deeds, things, and the needs and desires of individuals. If "nice" and "reward" were first order abstractions, then "charity" would be a second order abstraction; an abstract concept defined over stories containing "charity" would then be a third order abstraction.

The technique of abstract definition is thus a method by which an information processing system, in this case, the human mind, can continually build new conceptual structures by noticing patterns in the way it interacts with the world (that is, in the stories in which it participates). It is thus akin to the concept of reflexive abstraction which Jean Piaget has elaborated in his *Genetic Epistemology* (1970) and *Understanding Causality* (1974). Piaget believes that intelligence develops by creating newer high-level structures to reorganize and regulate older structures; abstract definition is one way of doing this. Because abstract definition is recursive and can thus build on itself indefinitely, it provides a mechanism for explaining conceptual growth beyond adolescence, which is the last developmental period Piaget's theory accounts for. Thus, abstract definition might be the mechanism underlying the post-adolescent growth in moral development which Lawrence Kolhberg explores in *Essays on Moral Development* (1981) or the various forms of post-adolescent conceptual development probed in Deanna Kuhn's collection of pieces on *Intellectual Development Beyond Childhood* (1979).

Thomas Kuhn's account, *The Structure of Scientific Revolutions* (1962), also has affinities with the mechanism of abstract definition. Kuhn sees science progressing through abrupt and discontinuous stages in which scientific concepts are defined over particular examples (paradigms) of observation and experiment. These paradigmatic examples correspond to the stories that are the basis of abstract definition, while the scientific concepts are the abstractly defined terms.

Finally, both A. R. Luria and Eric A. Havelock have argued that learning to write plays has an essential role in developing abstractive capacity. Luria's argument, presented in *Cognitive Development* (1976), is based on observations he made of Uzbekistani peasants before and after they had learned to write. Eric Havelock's argument is based on his examination of classical Greek texts and is presented in *The Literate Revolution in Greece and Its Cultural Consequences* (1982). This work concludes with a superb essay, "Aftermath of the Alphabet" (pp. 314–50), in which Havelock suggests that the next major intellectual revolution after the invention of writing was spurred by the introduction of the Hindu-Arabic system of positional notation for numbers (that is, the use of zero and the decimal point) into Europe in the twelfth century. Luria and Havelock suggest that the structure of our communication systems, the tools we have for notating our concepts and calculations, plays an essential role in the way we formulate those concepts and influences the level of abstraction we can develop. This suggests that the ultimate fruit of computing will be conceptual structures of even higher levels of abstraction, for computing provides a new means of structuring, storing, and transmitting information which is as revolutionary in its potential as writing and positional notation have proven to be. By taking the initiative in adapting computing technology to the task of communicating technical information, technical communicators can play a central role in this intellectual revolution.

Hays's work on a computational approach to abstraction, in conjunction with appropriate work in psychology and the history of science, suggests the possibility of computer programs that take material at one level of abstraction and recast it at a lower level of abstraction. That suggestion, however, is not yet explicit enough to be the basis of a research and development program. But the theory could be used to classify concepts according to their levels of abstraction, which is roughly in accord with the broad historical order in which the concepts have evolved; see Hays and Benzon, "Metagram Software" (1981) (pp. 15–16, 42–45, 56–57). This classification could then be incorporated into text production systems to be part of the technical writer's tool kit for adapting material to the level of abstraction typical of the audience for a given document. Metaphors and analogies could also be classified according to the level of abstract conceptualization they embody. This classification, in conjunction with the classification of concepts, could then be used to select metaphors and analogies appropriate for explaining highly abstract concepts to audiences operating on a lower level of abstraction. If this material were created and maintained in an on-line system, it would be easy to add new analogies and concepts to the system. Thus, the technical communication community would be provided with a library of devices for adapting texts to different levels of abstraction. Since this work does not require the computer simulation of intellectual processes, it could be done now. In conjunction with current word and text processing technology and the emerging systems for checking style and grammar, this library would enable technical communicators to increase their productivity and the quality and challenge of their work.

Mode

The critical modal distinctions are between hardcopy and on-line presentation and between verbal and visual presentation. This section concentrates first on the contribution that computing can make to visual communication, then moves on to a discussion of the potentials of on-line documentation, and concludes with a discussion of Hays's concept of the automatic library.

Turner Whitted's "Some Recent Advances in Computer Graphics" (1982) is a good introduction to the state of the art capabilities. It includes a feast of gorgeous color pictures, one of which is a page from a repair manual that is implemented on a computer, as opposed to hardcopy (p. 774). The basic text in computer graphics is W. M. Newman and R. F. Sproull, *Principles of Interactive Computer Graphics* (1979). Currently, the most extensive use of computer graphics is in computer-aided design (CAD), which is reviewed in C. A. Hudson, "Computers in Manufacturing" (1982), and Thomas G. Gunn, "The Mechanization of Design and Manufacturing" (1982). CAD packages allow designers to work directly on a graphics screen. Once the basic design for an object (for example, an airplane fusilage, a gear assembly, an engine block) has been entered into the computer, variations can be made quickly and easily. It is even possible to simulate how various designs will work in actual use. Thus, the process of design and testing is made considerably easier and cheaper.

Much of the most imaginative work in graphics has been done by people at Xerox's Palo Alto Research Center. Some of this work has been reviewed by Alan Kay in "Microelectronics and the Personal Computer" (1977); Kay is particularly interested in educational applications. The August 1981 issue of *Byte* contains thirteen articles on Smalltalk, the language which the Xerox group has developed to implement its concepts. Much of the material in these articles is relatively non-technical, and one can get a good feel for the possibilities of computer graphics simply by looking at the illustrations.

The Smalltalk language allows one to mix text and high resolution graphics in a single frame, and the text can be in several different fonts. Furthermore, a single frame can accommodate several different "windows" simultaneously, where each different window is dealing with a different task. One window, for example, might be the system command window; this contains a record of the last few commands that have been entered into the system. Another window might contain a fragment of a program that the user is working on, while a third window contains documentation for that program fragment. A fourth window could contain a visual image—for example, a box within a box within a box, a tree structure, a spiral—which is the graphic analogue to the logical structure of the program fragment. Meanwhile, a fifth window appears with a schedule of today's appointments. The essential point is that in Smalltalk it is possible, even easy, to intermix text and graphics and to present fragments from several texts simultaneously. Some of the concepts worked out in Smalltalk have been incorporated into Xerox's Star Information System, which is described in David C. Smith and colleagues, "Designing the Star User Interface" (1982). With such a tool it becomes easy for technical communicators to do much of their own composition and layout, for the text is right there on the screen, in several different fonts, and graphics can be created at the same time. When the system is linked to a high resolution laser printer, then the image on the screen is the image that will be printed out. And that printed image will be the camera-ready copy so beloved by editors and printers.

With such tools now available, there is a clear need for good theories about the nature of visual perception and, in particular, about the relationship between visual perception and thinking and verbal thinking. Ulric Neisser's *Cognition and Reality* (1976) is a fine and readable introduction to contemporary cognitive psychology, and R. L. Gregory's classic *Eye and Brain* (1966) is still rewarding. James J. Gibson's *An Ecological Approach to Visual Perception* (1979) is perhaps the most challenging theoretical statement since it argues directly against much current work in cognitive psychology. The cognitive psychologists argue that the visual world is created in the mind through elaborate propositional constructs, while Gibson argues that, on the contrary, the structure of the visual world is directly available, if not exactly to the mind, then to the eye.

To assert that visual perception is direct and Gestalt-like is to assert that we perceive and identify whole objects without having to analyze them into parts. We see the tree without having to analyze it into trunk, leaves, and branches. This is Gibson's position, and Stephen M. Kosslyn and colleagues take a similar position in "On the Demystification of Mental Imagery" (1979).

To assert that visual perception involves propositional construction is to assert that we do analyze visual objects into parts and then make identifications by noting the structure of parts. Zenon Pylyshyn's "Computation and Cognition" (1980) and S. Ullman's "Against Direct Perception" (1980) argue this position, while Patrick H. Winston's book, *The Psychology of Computer Vision* (1975), explains programs that implement such a model.

William L. Benzon, in "System and Observer in Semiotic Modeling" (1982) and Benzon and Hays, in "Principles and Development of Natural Intelligence" (submitted for publication), suggest that the controversy is fundamentally mistaken and that visual thinking involves both modes, direct Gestalt-like perception, and computationally mediated propositional construction. Gestalt processes are regarded as fundamental, while propositional constructions are derived from the basic Gestalts. The basic clue to the nature of these constructions is in the paths which the eyes scan across images, discussed in D. Noton and L. Stark, "Eye Movements and Visual Perception" (1971). These scan paths connect a succession of fixation points; at some of these fixation points the eye looks at large portions of the scene or at whole objects, while at other fixation points the eye is focused on local details, an eye, a nose, a button, a leaf. Each individual image is a Gestalt, but the program that directs the eye from image to image and thereby fixes the relationships of the images to one another is a propositional construction.

If we wish a deeper insight into the ways we comprehend complex visual objects, it is necessary to go beyond even the most computationally sophisticated perceptual and cognitive psychology. Ernst H. Gombrich's *Art and Illusion* (1961) is the finest work that has been done on visual thinking. Gombrich is an art historian, and *Art and Illusion* is his study of the various conventions that were developed in Western art to give the visual illusion of realistic representation. The task for technical communicators is to take Gombrich's insights, translate them into an account of the interaction between propositional and Gestalt processes in complex visual thinking, and then use that account to analyze the ways in which we see circuit diagrams and flowcharts, line drawing, and photographs. As this analysis progresses, it can be linked up to work on the structure of technical prose, and through that we can work on the relationship between prose structure and image structure. The theories and models that result from that work can feed right back into that work in computer-aided instruction which emphasizes graphical presentation, as Seymour Papert discusses in *Mindstorms* (1980) and Michael J. Wozny discusses in "Key Issues in Instructional Computer Graphics" (1981).

This work will automatically lead us to a consideration of the brain, for it is now well known that the left cerebral hemisphere is primarily verbal while the right hemisphere is primarily visual. For a review see J. L. Bradshaw and N. C. Nettleton, "The Nature of Hemispheric Specialization in Man" (1981), and Roger Sperry, "Some Effects of Disconnecting the Cerebral Hemispheres" (1982). There is, of course, much more to the neurosciences than work on hemispheric specialization, but that is the topic most immediately germane to technical communication. If we are to insure the convenience of our new tools, however, we will ultimately have to delve more deeply into the neurosciences. Only through a study of the brain can we learn just how to engineer computer systems and on-line documentation to suit human capacities.

A great deal has been said here about the on-line environment; it only remains to pick up a few loose ends. There is an extensive literature on computer networks, computers in various locations—different rooms of the same building, different buildings in the same city, different cities, states, nations—linked together. This work has been reviewed in A. Newell and R. F. Sproull's "Computer Networks" (1982), and Joshua Lederberg's "Digital Communications and the Conduct of Science" (1978). The most extensive book-length treatment is Starr Roxanne Hiltz and Murray Turoff's *The Network Nation* (1978) which is, unfortunately, a bit simpleminded. F. W. Lancaster puts this work in context with work on library information systems in his *Toward Paperless Information Systems* (1978). The chief effect of networks is to dissolve the barriers of time and geography. Any document, program, or database that is in the network is available to all computers hooked in to the network, no matter where they are. If you wish to send a message to other people, you don't have to worry about whether or not they are in the office (that is, at their terminal); you can send the message and expect them to get it as soon as they check in. If your addressee is on the system when you send the message, it is a simple matter to have a conversation. A complete record of the transaction can be kept in the computer. Nor does it make any difference whose computer keeps the record since both of you have access to it through the network.

Finally, we should look at the automatic encyclopedia, a concept elaborated by David G. Hays in "Information Handling" (1974). This concept presupposes an understanding of human cognition and an implementation of that understanding in computer programs which exceeds our present knowledge—though glimpses can be seen in Bruce G. Buchanan's "Research On Expert Systems" (1981) and Wendy G. Lehnert's *The Process of Question Answering* (1978). The automatic encyclopedia is simply a vast information system that answers people's questions in standard ways. It would not have the capacity to generate new knowledge, but it would be a repository of that which has been verified by the intellectual community. Hays asks us to imagine "the whole scientific community may be in constant touch with a single network of knowledge; the experimental data going directly from measuring probe to computer, the theoretical calculations never stopping, the thinkers surrounding the system and watching it at work" (p. 2735). Through the contributions of technical communicators, people with different backgrounds and interests, and thinking at different levels of abstraction, could make queries of the system and expect answers in a form suited to their needs.

The automatic encyclopedia would be the central repository of human knowledge. As we make new observations, ponder new theories, and create new interpretations, we will modify the contents of the encyclopedia. The encyclopedia will constantly review its contents for cross-correlations and inconsistencies, and, by using techniques such as Eugene Garfield has explored in *Citation Indexing* (1979), it might occasionally suggest new avenues of inquiry and emerging disciplinary specializations to its users, that is, to us.

This is, admittedly, a fantasy, but unless one believes that our capacity to understand thought and perception is intrinsically limited, one should not dismiss this fantasy too easily. It may someday become an actuality, an actuality in which technical communication has played a crucial role.

Conclusion

Situated as it is between commerce, government, and academe, using the knowledge, insights, and methods of the humanities and the social and behavioral sciences to interpret science and technology to many sectors of the population, technical communication can play a major role in the wise and human use of computing technology. As writers of the documentation which makes that technology intelligible to computer-naive users, we are the pivotal influence in the development of various computing products. As users of computing technology, we translate abstract theoretical knowledge about human cognitive capacities into practical tools through which those cognitive capacities can be extended. The tools we develop to help us in our work can be used by many groups of professionals. Because our work is so important to the emerging high-technological industrial world, we will obtain the resources to develop these tools before many other professional groups have them. Thus, we have a critical role to play in bringing other professionals into the information age.

References

Anderson, Roy E. "Modular Documentation: A Software Development Tool." *AFIPS Conference Proceedings*. Vol. 50. 1981 National Computer Conference. May 1981. Montvale, N.J.: AFIPS Press, 1981, pp. 401–405.

Arbib, Michael. *Computers and the Cybernetic Society*. New York: Academic, 1977.

———, and David Caplan. "Neurolinguistics Must be Computational." *Behav Brain Sci*, 2 (1979), 449–83.

Bacon, G. "Software." *Science*, 215 (1982), 775–79.

Barcomb, David. *Office Automation: A Survey of Tools and Technology*. Bedford, Mass.: Digital, 1981.

Becker, David. "Automated Language Processing." In *Annual Review of Information Science and Technology*. Vol. 16. Ed. Martha E. Williams. White Plains, N.Y.: Knowledge Industry Publications, 1981, pp. 113–38.

Benzon, William L. "Cognitive Networks and Literary Semantics." *MLN*, 91 (1976), 952–82.

———. "The Computer and Technical Communication." *J Tech Writ Comm*, 11 (1981), 103–14.

———. "Lust in Action: An Abstraction." *Lang Style*, 14 (1981), 251–70.

———. "System and Observer in Semiotic Modeling: An Essay on Semiotic Realism." In *Semiotics 1980*. Ed. Michael Herzfeld and Margot Lenhart. New York: Plenum, 1982, pp. 27–36.

———, and David G. Hays. "Computational Linguistics and the Humanist." *Comput Hum*, 10 (1976), 265–74.

———, and David G. Hays. "Principles and Development of Natural Intelligence." Unpublished manuscript.

Blasgen, M. W. "Database Systems." *Science*, 215 (1982), 869–72.

Bradshaw, J. L., and N. C. Nettleton. "The Nature of Hemispheric Specialization in Man." *The Behav Brain Sci*, 4 (1981), 51–91.

Brooks, F. P. *The Mythical Man-Month: Essays on Software Engineering*. Reading, Mass.: Addison-Wesley, 1975.

Brown, John Seely, Allan Collins, and Gregory Harris. "Artificial Intelligence and Learning Strategies." In *Learning Strategies*. Ed. H. F. O'Neil. New York: Academic, 1978, pp. 107–39.

Bruce, Bertram, Allan Collins, Ann D. Rubin, and Dedre Gentner. "A Cognitive Science Approach to Writing." In *Process, Development and Communication*. Ed. C. H. Frederiksen and J. D. Dominic. Hillsdale, N.J.: Erlbaum, 1981.

Buchanan, Bruce G. "Research on Expert Systems." Stanford University, Heuristic Programming Project, Report No. HPP–81–1. Feb. 1981.

Cherry, Lorinda. "Computer Aids for Writers." *Sigplan Notices*, 16 (1981), 61–67.

Chomsky, Noam. "Rules and Representations." *Behav Brain Sci*, 3 (1980), 1–61.

———. *Syntactic Structures*. The Hague: Mouton, 1957.

Date, C. J. *An Introduction to Database Systems*. 2nd ed. Reading, Mass.: Addison-Wesley, 1977.

Davis, Ruth M. "Computers and Electronics for Individual Services." *Science*, 215 (1982), 852–56.

de Beaugrande, Robert. "Theoretical Foundations of the Automatic Production and Processing of Technical Reports." *J Tech Writ Comm*, 9 (1979), 239–69.

Dertouzos, Michael L., and Joel Moses, eds. *The Computer Age: A Twenty-Year View*. Cambridge, Mass.: MIT Press, 1979.

Dordick, Herbert S., Helen G. Bradley, and Burt Nanus. *The Emerging Network Marketplace*. Norwood, N.J.: Ablex, 1981.

Doszkos, T. E., B. A. Rapp, and H. M. Schoolman. "Automated Information Retrieval in Science and Technology." *Science*, 208 (1980), 25–30.

Ernst, Martin L. "The Mechanization of Commerce." *Sci Am*, 247, No. 3 (1982), 132–45.

Flower, Linda S., and John R. Hayes. "Problem Solving and the Cognitive Process of Writing." In *Writing: Process, Development, and Communication*. Vol. 2 of *Writing: The Nature, Development, and Teaching of Written Communication*. Ed. C. H. Frederiksen and J. F. Dominic. Hillsdale, N.J.: Erlbaum, 1981, pp. 39–58.

Fox, Mark S., Donald J. Bebel, and Alice C. Parker. "The Automated Dictionary." *Computer*, 13, No. 7 (1980), 35–48.

Garfield, Eugene. *Citation Indexing—Its Theory and Application in Science, Technology, and Humanities*. New York: Wiley, 1979.

Gibson, James J. *An Ecological Approach to Visual Perception*. Boston: Houghton Mifflin, 1979.

Giuliano, Vincent E. "The Mechanization of Office Work." *Sci Am*, 247, No. 3 (1982), 148–64.

Goldstein, Ira. "Writing with a Computer." *Proceedings of the 3rd Annual Conference of the Cognitive Science Society*, Aug. 1981, pp. 145–48.

Gombrich, Ernst H. *Art and Illusion*. 2nd ed. Princeton, N.J.: Princeton University Press, 1961.

Gregory, R. L. *Eye and Brain*. New York: McGraw-Hill, 1966.

Grishman, Ralph. "A Survey of Syntactic Analysis Procedures for Natural Languages." *Am J Comput Linguist*, Microfiche 47, 1976.

Gunn, Thomas G. "The Mechanization of Design and Manufacturing." *Sci Am*, 247, No. 3 (1982), 114–30.

Haas, W. J. "Computing in Documentation and Scholarly Research." *Science*, 215 (1982), 857–61.

Hartsough, Christopher, Yuzo Yamamoto, and E. David Callender. "Documentation Production from a Formal Database." *ACM SIGDOC, SIGOA International Conference on Systems Documentation*, 22–23 Jan. 1982.

Haugeland, John. "The Nature and Plausibility of Cognitivism." *Behav Brain Sci*, 1 (1978), 215–60.

Havelock, Eric A. *The Literate Revolution in Greece and Its Cultural Consequences*. Princeton, N.J.: Princeton University Press, 1982.

Hawkins, Donald T. "Online Information Retrieval Systems." In *Annual Review of Information Science and Technology*. Vol. 16. Ed. Martha Williams. White Plains, N.Y.: Knowledge Industry Publications, 1981, pp. 171–208.

Hays, David G. *Cognitive Structures*. New Haven, Conn.: HRAF Press, 1981.

———. "Information Handling." *Current Trends in Linguistics*. Vol. 12. Ed. T. A. Sebeok. The Hague: Mouton, 1974, pp. 2719–40.

———. "Machine Translation and Abstract Terminology." In *Studies in Descriptive and Historical Linguistics: Festschrift for Winfred P. Lehmann*. Ed. Paul J. Hopper. Amsterdam: John Benjamins B.V., 1977, pp. 95–108.

———. Review of *Computer Power and Human Reason*, by Joseph Weizenbaum. *Computers and the Humanities*, in press.

————, and William L. Benzon. *Metagram Software—A New Perspective on the Art of Computation*. Rome Air Development Center, Griffiss Air Force Base, New York. Final Technical Report RADC–TR–81–118, Oct. 1981.

————, and J. Mathias, eds. "FBIS Seminar on Machine Translation." *Am J Comput Linguist*, Microfiche 46, 1976.

Hiltz, Starr Roxanne, and Murray Turoff. *The Network Nation: Human Communication via Computer*. Reading, Mass.: Addison-Wesley, 1978.

Hofstader, Douglas R. *Godel, Escher, Bach: An Eternal Golden Braid*. New York: Basic, 1979.

Holder, Wayne. "Software Tools for Writers." *Byte*, July 1982, pp. 138–63.

Hudson, C. A. "Computers in Manufacturing." *Science*, 215 (1982), 818–25.

Kay, Alan. "Microelectronics and the Personal Computer." In *Microelectronics*. San Francisco: Freeman, 1977, pp. 124–35.

Kay, Martin. "Automatic Translation of Natural Languages." *Daedalus*, 102, No. 3 (1973), 217–30.

Kintsch, Walter. *The Representation of Meaning in Memory*. Hillsdale, N.J.: Erlbaum, 1974.

Kling, Rob, and Walt Scacchi. "Computing as Social Action: The Social Dynamics of Computing in Complex Organizations." In *Advances in Computers*, Vol. 19. Ed. Marshall C. Yovits. New York: Academic, 1980, pp. 250–327.

Knuth, Donald E. *TEX and METAFONT: New Directions in Typesetting*. Bedford, Mass.: Digital, 1979.

Kohlberg, Lawrence. *Essays on Moral Development, Volume 1. The Philosophy of Moral Development: Moral Stages and the Idea of Justice*. New York: Harper, 1981.

Kosslyn, Stephen M., Steven Pinker, George E. Smith, and Steven P. Shwartz. "On the Demystification of Mental Imagery." *Behav Brain Sci*, 2 (1979), 535–81.

Krauthamer, Helene. "The Prediction of Passive Occurrence." *Linguistics*, 19 (1981), 307–24.

Kuhn, Deanna, ed. *Intellectual Development Beyond Childhood. New Directions for Child Development*, No. 5. San Francisco: Jossey-Bass, 1979.

Kuhn, Thomas. *The Structure of Scientific Revolutions*. Chicago: University of Chicago Press, 1962.

Lancaster, F. W. *Toward Paperless Information Systems*. New York: Academic, 1978.

Lederberg, Joshua. "Digital Communications and the Conduct of Science: The New Literacy." *IEEE Proc*, 66 (1978), 1314–19.

Lehnert, Wendy G. *The Process of Question Answering—A Computer Simulation of Cognition*. Hillsdale, N.J.: Erlbaum, 1978.

Leontief, Wassily W. "The Distribution of Work and Income." *Sci Am*, 247, No. 3 (1982), 188–204.

Levin, James A. "Interpersonalized Media: What's News?" *Byte*, June 1980, pp. 214–28.

Linn, William E., Jr., and Walter Reitman. "Autonote2: Network-Mediated Natural Language Communication in a Personal Information Retrieval System." *Am J Comput Linguist*, Microfiche 23, 1975.

Linvill, J. G. "University Role in the Computer Age." *Science*, 215 (1982), 802–806.

Long, James E., and Timothy J. Healy. "Advanced Automation for Space Missions." University of Santa Clara, 15 Sept. 1980.

Luria, A. R. *Cognitive Development: Its Cultural and Social Foundations*. Cambridge, Mass.: Harvard University Press, 1976.

Mann, William C., and James A. Moore. "Computer Generation of Multiparagraph English Text." *Am J Comput Linguist*, 7 (1981), 17–30.

Masterman, Margaret. "The Nature of a Paradigm." *In Criticism and the Growth of Knowledge*. Ed. Imre Lakatos and Alan Musgrave. Cambridge: Cambridge University Press, 1970, pp. 59–89.

Miller, George A., and Philip N. Johnson-Laird. *Language and Perception*. Cambridge, Mass.: Harvard University Press, 1976.

Miller, Lance A., George E. Heidorn, and Karen Jensen. "Text-Critiquing with the EPISTLE System: An Author's Aid to Better Syntax." *AFIPS Conference Proceedings*. Vol. 50. 1981 National Computer Conference, May 1981. Montvale, N.J.: AFIPS Press, 1981, pp. 649–55.

Mowshowitz, Abbe. *The Conquest of Will: Information Processing in Human Affairs*. Reading, Mass.: Addison-Wesley, 1976.

Nagao, Makoto, and Jun-Ichi Tsujii. "Analysis of Japanese Sentences by Using Semantic and Contextual Information." *Am J Comput Linguist*, Microfiche 41, 1976.

Needham, Joseph. *Science in Traditional China*. Cambridge, Mass.: Harvard University Press, 1981.

Neisser, Ulric. *Cognition and Reality*. San Francisco: Freeman, 1976.

Nelson, Ted. *Computer Lib/Dream Machines*. Schooleys Mountain, N.J.: Ted Nelson, 1974.

———. *Literary Machines*, Swarthmore, Pa.: Ted Nelson, 1981.

Newell, A., and R. F. Sproull. "Computer Networks: Prospects for Scientists." *Science*, 215 (1982), 843–52.

Newman, W. M., and R. F. Sproull. *Principles of Interactive Computer Graphics*. New York: McGraw-Hill, 1979.

Norman, Donald A., and David E. Rumelhart. *Explorations in Cognition*. San Francisco: Freeman, 1975.

Noton, D., and L. Stark. "Eye Movements and Visual Perception." *Sci Am*, 224, No. 6 (1971), 34–43.

Novak, Gordon S. Jr. "Computer Understanding of Physics Problems Stated in Natural Language." *Am J Comput Linguist*, Microfiche 53, 1976.

Oettinger, A. G. "Information Resources: Knowledge and Power in the 21st Century." *Science*, 209 (1980), 191–98.

Osborne, Adam. *Running Wild: The Next Industrial Revolution*. Berkeley: Osborne/McGraw-Hill, 1979.

Papert, Seymour. *Mindstorms*. New York: Basic, 1980.

Petrick, Stanley R. "Report of the ACL 1977 Annual Meeting Panel on Speech Understanding and Computational Linguistics: A Critical Examination of the ARPA Project." *Am J Comput Linguist*, Microfiche 64 (1977), frames 2–15.

Phillips, Brian. "A Model for Knowledge and Its Application to Discourse Analysis." *Am J Comput Linguist*, Microfiche 82 (1978).

Piaget, Jean. *Genetic Epistemology*. New York: Columbia University Press, 1970.

———. *Understanding Causality*. New York: Norton, 1974.

Porat, Marc U. *The Information Economy: Definition and Measurement*. Washington, D.C.: U.S. Department of Commerce, Office of Telecommunications, May 1977.

Powers, William T. *Behavior: The Control of Perception*. Chicago: Aldine, 1973.

Pylyshyn, Zenon. "Computational Models and Empirical Constraints." *Behav Brain Sci*, 1 (1978), 93–127.

———. "Computation and Cognition: Issues in the Foundation of Cognitive Science." *Behav Brain Sci*, 3 (1980), 111–69.

Rosenfeld, Azriel. "Image Processing and Recognition." In *Advances in Computers*. Vol. 18. Ed. Marshall C. Yovits. New York: Academic, 1979, pp. 1–58.

Sager, Naomi. *Natural Language Information Processing: A Computer Grammar of English and Its Applications*. Reading, Mass.: Addison-Wesley, 1981.

Salton, Gerard. *Dynamic Information and Library Processing*. Englewood Cliffs, N.J.: Prentice-Hall, 1975.

———. "SMART." *Encyclopedia of Computer Science and Technology*. 1979.

Schank, R. C., and R. P. Abelson. *Scripts, Plans, Goals, and Understanding*. Hillsdale, N.J.: Erlbaum, 1977.

Scott, A. Carlisle, William J. Clancey, Randall Davis, and Edward H. Shortliffe. "Explanation Capabilities of Production-Based Consultation Systems." *Am J Comput Linguist*, Microfiche 62, 1977.

Scott, Joan Wallach. "The Mechanization of Women's Work." *Sci Am*, 247, No. 3 (1982), 166–87.

Searle, John R. "Minds, Brains, and Programs." *Behav Brain Sci*, 3 (1980), 417–57.

Sgall, Petr, and Eva Hajicova. "A Linguistic Approach to Information Retrieval—I." *Inform Stor Retrieval*, 10 (1974), 411–17.

Sibley, Edgar H., P. Gerard Scallan, and Eric K. Clemons. "The Software Configuration Management Database." *AFIPS Conference Proceedings*. Vol. 50. 1981 National Computer Conference, May 1981. Montvale, N.J.: AFIPS Press, 1981, pp. 249–55.

Simon, Herbert A. "The Behavioral and Social Sciences." *Science*, 209 (1980), 72–78.

———. "Information Processing Models of Cognition." *J Am Soc Inf Sci*, 32 (1981), 364–77.

———. *The Sciences of the Artificial*. 2nd ed. Cambridge, Mass.: MIT Press, 1981.

Smith, David C., Charles Irby, Ralph Kimball, Bill Verplank, and Eric Harslem. "Designing the Star User Interface." *Byte*, Apr. 1982, pp. 242–83.

Smith, Linda C. "Artificial Intelligence Applications in Information Systems." In *Annual Review of Information Science and Technology*. Ed. Martha E. Williams. White Plains, N.Y.: Knowledge Industry Publications, 1980, pp. 67–105.

Sparck Jones, Karen, and Martin Kay. *Linguistics and Information Science*. New York: Academic, 1973.

Sperry, Roger. "Some Effects of Disconnecting the Cerebral Hemispheres." *Science*, 217 (1982), 1223–26.

Spinrad, R. J. "Office Automation." *Science*, 215 (1982), 808–13.

Suppes, Patrick. "Current Trends in Computer-Assisted Instruction." In *Advances in Computers*, Vol. 18. Ed. Marshall C. Yovits. New York: Academic, 1979, pp. 173–229.

Tennant, Harry. *Natural Language Processing*. Princeton, N.J.: Petrocelli Books, 1981.

Terrant, Sheldon W. "Computers in Publishing." In *Annual Review of Information Science and Technology*. Ed. Martha E. Williams. White Plains, N.Y.: Knowledge Industry Publications, 1980, pp. 191–219.

Theobald, Robert. "Cybernetics and the Problems of Social Reorganization." In *The*

Social Impact of Cybernetics. Ed. Charles R. Dechert. New York: Clarion, 1967, pp. 39–70.

Thorndyke, P. M. "Cognitive Structures in Comprehension and Memory of Narrative Discourse." *Cog Psychol*, 9 (1977), 77–110.

Tucker, A. B. *Text Processing: Algorithms, Languages and Applications*. San Francisco: Academic, 1979.

Ullman, S. "Against Direct Perception." *Behav Brain Sci*, (1980), 373–415.

Uttal, Bro. "A Computer Gadfly's Triumph." *Fortune*, 8 Mar. 1982, pp. 74–76.

Walker, Donald E. "The Organization and Use of Information: Contributions of Information Science, Computational Linguistics, and Artificial Intelligence." *J Am Soc Inf Sci*, 32 (1981), 347–63.

————, ed. *Understanding Spoken Language*. New York: Elsevier North-Holland, 1978.

Weber, David J., and William C. Mann. "Prospects for Computer-Assisted Dialect Adaptation." *Am J Comput Linguist*, 7 (1981), 165–77.

Weizenbaum, Joseph. *Computer Power and Human Reason: From Judgement to Calculation*. San Francisco: Freeman, 1976.

Whitted, Turner. "Some Recent Advances in Computer Graphics." *Science*, 215 (1982), 767–74.

Wiener, Norbert. "Information, Language, and Society." In *Cybernetics: Or Control and Communication in the Animal and the Machine*. Cambridge, Mass.: MIT Press, 1961, pp. 155–65.

Winston, Patrick H., ed. *Artificial Intelligence*. Reading, Mass.: Addison-Wesley, 1977.

————. *The Psychology of Computer Vision*. New York: McGraw-Hill, 1975.

Wiora, Walter. *The Four Ages of Music*. New York: Norton, 1965.

Wozny, Michael J. "Key Issues in Instructional Computer Graphics." *Comput Educ*, 5 (1981), 183–92.

Yamamoto, Yuzo, Richard V. Morris, Christopher Hartsough, and E. David Callender. "The Role of Requirements Analysis in the System Life Cycle." *AFIPS Conference Proceedings*. Vol. 51. 1982 National Computer Conference. Montvale, N.J.: AFIPS Press, 1982, pp. 381–87.

Yeh, Raymond T., and Paul B. Schneck, Co-Directors. *Computer Science: Key to a Space Program Renaissance*. 2 vols. Technical Report 1168. College Park, Md.: University of Maryland, 1982.

Young, Robert. "Text Understanding: A Survey." *Am J Comput Linguist*, Microfiche 70 (1977).

Zachary, Wayne. "Machine Aids to Translation: A Concise State of the Art Bibliography." *Am J Comput Linguist*, Microfiche 77 (1978), frames 34–39.

Oral Presentation and Presence in Business and Industry

BERTIE E. FEARING

The spoken word is power in business and industry, and it is money. According to Harold P. Zelko and Frank E.X. Dance in *Business and Professional Speech Communication* (1978), the bottom line in business and industry is making money, selling more products, or offering better services than the competitor. "Internally this means greater efficiency of operation; and externally it means a better public image" (pp. 22–23), and oral communication plays an integral part in both.

Speechmaking by corporate executives is "one of the biggest booms in the nation" (p. 84), to quote *Time* magazine, "Boom in Speechmaking" (1960). Not only are corporations spending huge sums of money on speech courses for executives, but they are also training employees of lesser rank to make public relations speeches. James N. Holm in *Productive Speaking for Business and the Professions* (1967) reports, for example, that in one year Ohio Bell employees gave 3,744 presentations to audiences, totaling 214,000 listeners; and within five years, the speaking staff at Smith, Kline, French grew from 12 to 400 individuals, who delivered presentations to more than 5 million people.

Yet most presentational communication in business and industry takes place within the corporation, especially in the meeting room, where up-and-coming managers present their proposals, where technical experts from research and development explain their latest findings, and where executives listen and make their decisions. In *Effective Technical Presentations* (1968), James E. Connolly states that one of industry's major goals is to convert research into marketable products and services, and that the success or failure of this conversion hinges on two factors: (1) the practical feasibility of the product, and (2) the technical expert's ability to explain the technology clearly and effectively to a heterogeneous in-house audience of decision-makers. If the presentation fails, the product or the service or the proposal is likely not to be born.

Almost every technical writing textbook has a chapter on the oral presentation, but there are several sources devoted almost exclusively to the topic. In addition to the three books mentioned above, the following texts are especially helpful: Edward A. Rogge and James C. Ching's *Advanced Public Speaking* (1966), William S. Howell and Ernest G. Bormann's *Presentational Speaking for Business and the Professions* (1971), George R. Rodman's *Speaking Out* (1978), Morris R. Bogard's *The Manager's Style Book* (1979), and Paul R. Timm's *Functional Business Presentations* (1981). The Institute of Electrical and Electronics Engineers also has two publications of value to the industrial speaker: Robert M. Woelfe's *A Guide to Better Technical Presentations* (1975), and a special issue of the *IEEE Transactions on Professional Communication* on "Public Speaking for Engineers and Scientists" (1980). Finally, two bibliographies on the topic are Arthur E. Workun's "Speech for the Technician" (1974) and Bertie E. Fearing and Thomas M. Sawyer's "Speech for Technical Communicators" (1980).

Oral presentation is a communication form that has been studied and practiced for thousands of years, and because one can most assuredly learn from the past, this chapter introduces in the first section, Traditional Studies in Rhetoric, a brief overview of the history of oratory and speech criticism. The second part, Quantitative Studies in Rhetoric, traces the history and contributions of empirical research in speech criticism. The longest section, Applied Rhetorical Theory, presents audience analysis, message analysis, and delivery analysis from the perspective of how best to persuade the listener.

The citations in these sections are from speech historians, theorists, practitioners, and empirical researchers. Because speech is a social activity, the research is multidisciplinary, involving many fields: psychology, sociology, linguistics, and political science, to name a few.

Traditional Studies In Rhetoric

The term "rhetoric" is a Lewis Carroll-Humpty Dumpty word, requiring careful definition, lest it mean anything Humpty Dumpty wants it to mean. Is rhetoric written discourse? or is it oral discourse? or is it both? According to Donald C. Bryant in "Rhetoric" (1953), rhetoric refers to oral discourse, but so does oratory. He explains that in ancient Greece and Rome, oratory was an integral part of rhetoric (that is, the preparation and delivery of a speech). To clarify this confusion of terms, Bryant explains that "essentially rhetorical performances," whether already delivered or to be delivered, were often written down and circulated to be read as well as heard (p. 410). Traditionally, however, rhetoric has referred to the theory, and oratory to the practice. The history of both is an attempt to establish the relationship between the two. Richard Young has written an excellent bibliographical essay on the history of rhetoric as it pertains to "Invention" (1976), and although some of his recommended readings are duplicated here, this section of the chapter focuses on the history of rhetoric as it pertains to oratory and to speech criticism.

Lester Thonssen, A. Craig Baird, and Waldo W Braden's *Speech Criticism* (1970), a classic work on the theory and critical standards in public speaking, is valuable not only for its excellent history of rhetoric and oratory—from the ancients to the moderns—but also for its extensive bibliography. Short historical surveys include O. Thomas Sloane and Chaim Perelman's "Rhetoric" (1979), Gerilyn Tandberg's "History of Oratory" (1974), Douglas Ehninger's "History of Rhetoric and Public Address" (1965), Herbert A. Whicheln's "The Literary Criticism of Oratory" (1962), and Edward P.J. Corbett's "A Survey of Rhetoric" (1971). Corbett's book has a thorough bibliography on classical rhetoric.

For short histories of rhetoric and speech, plus their development in American education, the following two articles are useful: Hugh F. Seabury's "Speech" (1969) and Robert M. Gorrell's "Teaching of Rhetoric" (1971). Karl R. Wallace provides a more detailed survey in the *History of Speech Education in America* (1954). Carroll C. Arnold's "Some Preliminaries to English-Speech Collaboration in the Study of Rhetoric" (1967) is especially helpful in delineating the similar and dissimilar interests between the theorists of literature and the theorists of oratory. Arnold also makes useful distinctions among "Oral Rhetoric, Rhetoric, and Literature" (1968).

For more specialized studies of rhetoric in the various historical periods in Europe, see Young (1976), especially pp. 4–5. For specialized studies on oratory in the United States, there are Marie K. Hochmuth's *A History and Criticism of American Public Address*, III (1955), William Norwood Brigance's *A History and Criticism of American Public Address*, 2 vols. (1960), and the more recent Robert T. Oliver's *History of Public Speaking in America* (1978).

A cross-section of views on rhetorical theory and criticism can be found in anthologies of scholarly essays. Three excellent anthologies are Joseph Schwartz and John A. Rycenga's *The Providence of Rhetoric* (1965), Thomas R. Nilsen's *Essays on Rhetorical Criticism* (1968), and Richard L. Johannesen's *Contemporary Theories of Rhetoric* (1971). Raymond F. Howes's *Historical Studies of Rhetoric and Rhetoricians* (1961), Martin Steinmann, Jr.'s *New Rhetorics* (1967), Lloyd F. Bitzer and Edwin Black's *The Prospect of Rhetoric* (1971), Douglas Ehninger's *Contemporary Rhetoric* (1972), and Eugene E. White's *Rhetoric in Transition* (1980) also focus on the nature, use, and future of rhetoric from the different contributors' points of view.

Quantitative Studies in Rhetoric

"Dissatisfaction with the status of rhetorical theory is at least as old as Plato and Aristotle, both of whom objected vigorously to the practices and the writings of their predecessors and contemporaries" (p. 3), writes Wayne N. Thompson in his historical survey, *Quantitative Research in Public Address and Communication* (1967). Yet it was only about 70 years ago that anyone called for quantitative and experimental research in speech communication. Charles Henry Woolbert in "Suggestions as to the Methods in Research" (1916) asserted, "I stand for the facts; the facts of how speaking is done; of what its various effects are under specified conditions; how these facts can be made into laws and principles; and how other people can best be taught to apply them'' (p. 26). Before scientific or behavioral methods were applied to oratory, scholars contemplated or spun new theories from the classical principles of rhetoric. With the application of scientific methods to communication, these classical precepts were to become hypotheses for experimental testing.

It is only fitting that the first experimental study on speech was also published by Charles Henry Woolbert; entitled ''Effects of Various Modes of Public Reading,'' it appeared in 1920. Like Woolbert's initial study, most of the early experimental research in speech involved some physical aspect of delivery such as vocal rate or pitch; but some early probes also studied various linguistic and rhetorical concerns. Raymond H. Barnard, for example, studied the classification of sentences, sentence- and word-length, and personal pronouns in ''An Objective Study of the Speeches of Wendell Phillips'' (1932), Gilbert S. Macvaugh studied the types of introductions and conclusions in his ''Structural Analysis of the Sermons of Dr. Harry Emerson Fosdick'' (1932), and Gladys L. Borchers studied the differences between oral and written styles in ''An Approach to the Problem of Oral Style'' (1936). For summaries about research in the 1920s and 1930s, see Henry L. Ewbank's ''Four Approaches to the Study of Speech Style'' (1931) and ''The Statistical Analysis of Speech Style'' (1932).

In the 1930s, a conflict arose between the traditional scholars and the experimental researchers. William Norwood Brigance in ''Whither Research?'' (1933) objected to the ''attempt to overscientize our studies in rhetoric and oratory'' (p. 561). Yet experimentalists continued to lay the groundwork in quantitative research and to strengthen research methodologies. Studies became stronger and topics freer ranging. For example, Franklin H. Knower conducted ''Experimental Studies of Change in Attitudes'' (1935), and Howard Gilkinson reported on ''Experimental and Statistical Research in General Speech'' (1944).

In his survey of behavioral research from 1933 to 1963, Wilber L. Schramm in *The Science of Communication* (1963) cites four men as the ''founding fathers'' of behavioral research in the United States. Not one was in the field of rhetoric or oratory. Paul Lazarfeld, a sociologist interested in mass media, specialized in survey research. Lazarfeld thought it much more practical and significant to study the audience's reaction to media than to study the medium itself. A Gestalt psychologist, Kurt Lewin was an expert in experimental communication research. Harold Lasswell, a political scientist, pioneered in the study of propaganda research. In his study of political speeches, Lasswell contributed to the development of scientific content analysis. The fourth, and perhaps most influential, was experimental psychologist Carl Hovland, whose interest was the impact of communication on attitude change. In his research studies, Hovland isolates a single variable, controls the other variables, and tests hypothesis after hypothesis, building a systematic theory of modern rhetoric.

Based on the work of these four founding fathers, behavioral research grew and flourished in the 1950s and 1960s under the direction of their students and followers: Theodore Clevenger, Jr., Kenneth Anderson, and Gary Cronkhite, to name just a few. Many of their articles and books reported research; many also attempted to educate their readers about experimental research methods. See, for example, Theodore Clevenger, Jr.'s "Toward an Understanding of Experimental Rhetoric" (1964), Jack Matthews's "A Behavioral Science Approach to the Study of Rhetoric" (1964), and Samuel L. Becker's "Methodological Analysis in Communication Research (1965).

Samuel L. Becker in his assessment of "Rhetorical Scholarship in the Seventies" (1974) characterizes the state of scholarship as "chaotic" and in a turmoil wherein humanism and behavioralism go round and round. Both Robert J. Kibler and Larry L. Barker's anthology, *Conceptual Frontiers in Speech-Communication* (1969), and Bitzer and Black's anthology (1971) reflect the uncertainty, the questioning, the reexamination characteristic of rhetorical studies in the 1970s.

Walter R. Fisher attempts to bring the two schools of scholarship together in his anthology, *A Tradition in Transition* (1974). The first half of the book consists of "Studies in the Continuing Tradition"; the second half, on "Studies in Transition," reflects a broadening scope of rhetoric and the merging of the humanistic and behavioral approaches. Ehninger (1972) reporting on the scholarship of contemporary rhetoric agrees with Fisher. Ehninger sees the following essays as indications that both camps are trying to come together, to be mutually reinforcing: Wayne N. Thompson's "A Conservative View of a Progressive Rhetoric" (1963), John Waite Bowers's "The Pre-Scientific Function of Rhetorical Criticism" (1968), and Theodore Clevenger, Jr.'s "The Interaction of Descriptive and Experimental Research in the Development of Rhetorical Theory" (1972).

Several modern college textbooks integrate modern theory and behavioral research with the traditional teachings of the past. Foremost among these is James C. McCroskey's *An Introduction to Rhetorical Communication* (1982), now in its fourth edition. Gary Cronkhite nicely blends communication theory and research into his text, *Public Speaking and Critical Listening* (1978). James R. Andrews's *Essentials of Public Communication* (1979) gives excellent coverage on the basics of presentation: the speaker, the message, the audience—all based on research reported in his extensive bibliographies at the end of each chapter. A well-written and well-documented text with a wider scope—emphasizing transactional communication in private, public, organizational, and mass media situations—is Stewart L. Tubbs and Sylvia Moss's *Human Communication* (1980).

For those interested in the methods of behavioral research, Philip Emmert and William D. Brooks's *Methods of Research in Communication* (1970) is designed to help readers conduct their own experimental studies. Larry L. Barker and Robert J. Kibler in *Speech Communication Behavior* (1971) introduce psycholinguistic, human processing, and psychophysiological research; and Raymond

G. Smith in *The Message Measurement Inventory* (1978) introduces an instrument that judges the effectiveness of a speaker. It measures sixty facets of speech delivery (for example, nuances of intonation, message organization, speaker credibility).

For those not inclined to conduct their own research, but who want to know about recent research findings in persuasive communication, five books are indispensable: Daryl J. Bem's *Beliefs, Attitudes, and Human Affairs* (1970); Carl I. Hovland, Irving L. Janis, and Harold H. Kelley's *Communication and Persuasion* (1974), Winston L. Brembeck and William S. Howell's *Persuasion* (1976), Philip G. Zimbardo, Ebbe B, Ebbesen, and Christina Maslach's *Influencing Attitudes and Changing Behavior* (1977), and Erwin P. Bettinghaus's *Persuasive Communication* (1980). Annual bibliographies on research are available in the *Quarterly Journal of Speech* from 1947 to 1950 and in *Speech Monographs* from 1951 to 1974, renamed *Communication Monographs* in 1975. James W. Cleary and Frederick W. Haberman's *Rhetoric and Public Address* (1974) is useful, as is the bibliography in Thonssen, Baird, and Braden (1970).

A definite proponent of behavioral research, Ehninger (1972) states that "the character of rhetorical theory has begun to be significantly modified by the scientific-empirical point of view" (p. 7), forcing scholars to reexamine the definition and scope of rhetoric as well as its purposes and methods. Ehninger states emphatically that "the formulation of new and provocative hypotheses concerning message organization, sources of speaker/writer credibility, and the potency of emotional appeals, are exerting a major influence on the present state and future course of rhetoric as a discipline" (p. 8).

Applied Rhetorical Theory

As Howell and Bormann (1971) point out, the in-house corporate presenter is typically a change agent, a speaker who presents a budget, a proposal, or a new technological finding to executives who have the power to accept or reject those findings. "Typically, the entire proposal is accepted or rejected in the session initiated by the presentation" (p. 10). Therefore, to be successful, the presenter must ask, *What aspects of the communication situation under my control will most likely cause the audience to accept my proposal?* More specific questions concerning the preparation and delivery of the presentation include, *What are the interests and needs of my audience? How much content should I include? How should I organize the content? Which verbal embellishments are appropriate? What visual aids should I plan? What are the most successful methods of delivery?*

This section of the chapter encompasses not only the theoretical but also the empirical approach to three aspects of presentational communication: audience analysis, message analysis, and delivery analysis. Two caveats are in order here: These three aspects are not mutually exclusive; and the research is ongoing, incomplete, and sometimes conflicting. However, only reputable, representative studies and, whenever possible, summaries of research are cited.

Audience Analysis

Of all the variables affecting the persuasiveness of a presentation, the credibility of the speaker may be the most important in achieving change. Aristotle, of course, said it first, but modern research in communication supports his statement that "character" may be "the most potent of all the means to persuasion" (p. 9), in *The Rhetoric of Aristotle*, edited by Lane Cooper (1932). Credibility, as defined by McCrosky (1982), is the attitude that the audience holds toward the speaker, especially as regards the speaker's expertise or knowledge, prestige or status, trustworthiness or integrity, and dynamism or confidence.

Tubbs and Moss (1980) discuss two aspects of credibility: intrinsic and extrinsic. Intrinsic credibility is the impression the speaker creates while speaking; extrinsic credibility is the reputation the speaker has before speaking. Extrinsic credibility is especially crucial in the corporate setting. Howell and Borman (1971) point out that there are two additional facets of credibility in the corporate organization: (1) the official position of the speaker in the *formal* organizational structure and (2) the personal reputation of the speaker in the *informal* organizational structure. In the organization, staff members get to know one another, making friends or enemies, forming judgments about the responsible versus the irresponsible worker, sizing up the intellectually talented versus the intellectually weak employee. These informal opinions are as influential as the more formal status of the speaker. On the opposite side of the lectern, "the presentation will have the greatest impact if its preparation, content, and delivery recognize the formal status, authority, and responsibility of the listeners." In other words, the effective corporate speaker never underestimates "the importance of according each member of the audience the status... provided by his position in the formal organization" (p. 30). Thus, audience analysis is a key consideration in preparing the persuasive message.

One of the most helpful guides to audience analysis appears in *The Psychology of the Audience* (1935), in which H. L. Hollingworth designates five types of audiences according to their orientation to the topic and suggests how the speaker can meet the rhetorical needs of each audience. Theodore Clevenger, Jr., in *Audience Analysis* (1966), expands Hollingworth's approach to include not only rhetorical analysis but also demographic analysis. In his *The Psychology of the Speaker's Audience* (1970), Paul D. Holtzman identifies four main groups of audience factors: speaker image, listener motivation, environment, and group membership. Rodman (1978) also agrees on four message strategies: audience interest, explanation, persuasion, and humor. According to Rodman, speakers must gain audience attention before they can explain, and they must explain before they can persuade. In *The Speech Communication Process* (1971) both Theodore Clevenger, Jr., and Jack Matthews concur that speakers "cannot hope to inform, persuade, or move to action without first capturing and holding attention'' (p. 3).

In their summary of research on *Speech Communication* (1968), Howard Martin and Kenneth E. Anderson report that studies on the human attention span began early in the century. These findings, as summarized by William James in *Talks to Teachers on Psychology* (1958), indicate that the longest a human being can attend to a simple stimulus before attention begins to wander is only a few seconds. Gary Cronkhite in *Communication and Awareness* (1976) thinks that the introduction is the first and best place to capture the audience's attention, ''but you do not 'capture' it in the sense that it can be securely caged and then left alone. Instead, you will have to use devices to gain attention at the outset of the message, and devices to maintain it throughout'' (p. 333). Devices to gain and hold attention, frequently cited by authorities, are organization of content; specificity; variety; emphasis; explanation by example, illustration, analogy, and anecdote; and non-verbal elements such as gestures, eye contact, and voice quality. However, of all the attention devices, the appeal to audience needs and interests is perhaps the most important. Brembeck and Howell (1976) believe that audience interest is the direct result of relating to audience needs, that a message which exploits the audience's needs is more effective than one that does not, and that a message which promises to lead to the attainment of one or more of the audience's goals is more likely to be accepted by that audience. For reviews of the relevant research on audience needs, see Dorwin Cartwright and Alvin Zander, *Group Dynamics* (1968) and Bem (1970).

Message Analysis

In his award-winning article ''Preparing and Delivering an Oral Presentation'' (1979), Thomas M. Sawyer advises technical communicators to make their oral presentations short, to make the organization obvious, and to make the ideas simple and vivid. Sawyer's advice is sound according to Clevenger and Matthews (1971), who concur that ''the most widely accepted theory of speech organization'' is still that ''a well built speech can be represented as a hierarchically arranged network of ideas.'' Main points are divided into sub-points, which are divided into supporting materials such as examples, illustrations, comparisons, and contrasts that ''enliven, clarify, or prove points'' (p. 98). This classical rhetorical precept is now partially, if not totally, supported by research.

Over 30 years of research in human information processing has indicated that an audience will better understand the content of a presentation if it is built around a limited number of points. See, for example, Charles Petrie's ''Informative Speaking'' (1963) and George A. Miller's *The Psychology of Communication* (1975).

Having selected a limited number of main points to include in a presentation, the speaker is then advised to organize those points. A great deal of research on message analysis has, in fact, focused on the overall organization of the message.

The focal question has not always been *How should the message be organized?* but *Is organization important, either in increasing comprehension or in achieving attitude change?*

According to R. Wayne Pace, Robert R. Boren, and Brent D. Peterson in *Communication Behavior and Experiments* (1975), the majority of research on careful organization of oral presentation does not support the claim that there is a correlation between speech organization and audience comprehension. However, early studies by Raymond H. Wheeler and Francis T. Perkins in *Principles of Mental Development* (1932) report that the more orderly the message, the more quickly learning occurs; and the more lengthy the content, the more important the organization. Wheeler and Perkins also conclude that comprehension is best achieved when the organization of the message is explicitly stated at the outset and that the listeners will become confused if they expect but do not receive a well-organized talk. Several other studies too numerous to mention here support Wheeler and Perkins's findings. See, for example, Donald L. Thistlewaite, Henry DeHann, and Joseph Kamenentsky's "The Effect of 'Directive' and 'Non-Directive' Communication Procedures on Attitudes" (1955) and Ernest Thompson's "An Experimental Investigation of the Relative Effectiveness of Organizational Structure in Oral Communication" (1960). One later study, in fact, demonstrates that changing the sequences of sentences within a paragraph adversely affects comprehension. See Donald K. Darnell, "The Relation Between Sentence Order and Comprehension" (1963).

Most studies on the organization of the persuasive message favor the organized over the disorganized presentation. Raymond G. Smith's "An Experimental Study of the Effects of Speech Organization upon the Attitudes of College Students" (1951) indicates that an extremely disorganized message hampers persuasion. Harry Sharp, Jr., and Thomas McClung in "Effects of Organization on the Speaker's Ethos" (1966) agree that disorganization can lower the audience's opinion of the speaker, and James C. McCroskey and R. Samuel Mehrley in "The Effects of Disorganization and Nonfluency on Attitude Change and Source Credibility" (1969) report that an organized message presented in a fluent manner is more persuasive than a disorganized message presented in a fluent manner. It appears that audiences expect presentations to be organized and that audiences are distracted by a poorly organized message, losing interest in the topic and respect for the speaker.

A second facet of organization involves choosing organizational patterns. Chronology, division classification, spatial sequence, inquiry, comparison, and contrast, and elimination are familiar rhetorical modes found in freshman and advanced composition textbooks alike. One not-so-familiar organizational pattern is Monroe's Motivational Sequence, described in Alan H. Monroe and Douglas Ehninger's *Principles and Types of Speech Communication* (1975). There are five steps: the attention step, the need step, the satisfaction step, the visualization step, and the action step. At least two studies indicate the persuasive effect of the speaker's specific recommendation for action. See Howard Leventhall, Robert

Singer, and Susan Jones's "Effects of Fear and Specificity of Recommendations upon Attitudes and Behavior" (1965) and P. R. Biddle's "An Experimental Study of Ethos and Appeal for Overt Behavior in Persuasion" (1966).

Another topic of interest to speech researchers is where to place the most important points of presentation: in the first, middle, or last position? Percy Tannenbaum reports in "Effect of Serial Position on Recall of Radio and News Stories" (1954) that audience comprehension, retention, and recall are better when material is placed either first or last rather than in the middle of a message. Gary Cronkhite agrees in *Persuasion* (1969), that audiences tend to listen more carefully at the beginnings and endings of presentations. Marvin Karlins and Herbert I. Abelson in *Persuasion* (1970) concur that whatever is presented first and last is remembered longer than whatever is presented in the middle, and Ernest Thompson in "Some Effects of Message Structure on Listeners' Comprehension" (1967) reports that points made first have the strongest impact, while points made last are remembered longest.

In their research summary on climactic versus anti-climactic ordering of materials, Hovland, Janis, and Kelley (1974) advise using climactic order if the audience is interested in the topic or proposition but using anti-climactic order if the audience is not interested. If the audience is hostile to the speaker's stance, the speaker should present acceptable ideas first before introducing new ideas. Substantial evidence suggests too that it may not be wise to announce the intention to persuade. Representative studies on this topic include Jane Allyn and Leon Festinger's "The Effectiveness of Unanticipated Persuasive Communications" (1961) and Charles A. Kiesler and Sara B. Kiesler's "Role of Forewarning in Persuasive Communication" (1971).

Before persuasion can be effected, however, belief must be established. In choosing materials to support generalizations and enhance belief, Connolly (1968) advises speakers to ask themselves one question: *Will the material they intend on using increase the probability of belief and, thus, make the persuasive goal more attainable?* Some evidence exists to support Otis M. Walter and Robert L. Scott's statement in *Thinking and Speaking* (1973) that the presentation that uses explanatory devices will be clearer than one that does not. In their summary of research, Clevenger and Matthews (1971) say that using evidence to support assertions, along with interesting content and emotional appeals, appears to effect change in the persuasive presentation. James C. McCroskey's "A Summary of Experimental Research on the Effects of Evidence in Persuasive Communication" (1969) finds that evidence increases the amount of attitude change *if* the evidence is new to the audience. Furthermore, the use of examples and illustrations that appeal to the audience increases motivation to listen and to comprehend. Finally, T. B. Hart in "The Effects of Evidence in Persuasive Communication" (1976) reports that citing expert testimony has a positive effect especially if the speaker has low credibility and the audience is initially opposed to the speaker's stance.

Research has also been conducted on rhetorical devices such as repetition and restatement. As early as 1945, Ray Ehrensberger in "An Experimental Study of the Relative Effects of Certain Forms of Emphasis in Public Speaking" found that these devices have a positive effect. Research by Thistlewaite, DeHaan, and Kamenentsky (1955) suggests that a presentation is better comprehended and accepted when transitions are employed.

The level of vocabulary used by the speaker has been studied in two ways: (1) as vocabulary correlates with audience perception and comprehension and (2) as vocabulary correlates with audience expectations of the speaker. William N. Dember in *The Psychology of Perception* (1960) summarizes experiments in perception which suggest that matching vocabulary to the audience's level increases perception, thus, comprehension and motivation. On the other hand, several studies indicate that the vocabulary level should not match the audience's level but the audience's expectations of the speaker's level. See, for example, William D. Brooks and Philip Emmert, "The Effect of Language Usage Congruency upon Source Credibility, Attitude Change, and Retention" (1967) and Paula J. Adrian, "A Study of the Relationship Between Language Usage and Congruency and Perceived Ethos" (1967).

Some research has also been conducted on the use of verbal embellishments such as metaphor and analogy. W. J. Jordan and M. L. McLaughlin in "Figurative Language as an Independent Variable in Communication Research" (1976) have found that listeners can distinguish between literal and figurative language. James C. McCroskey and W. H. Coombs in "The Effects of the Use of Analogy on Attitude Change and Source Credibility" (1969), have documented that analogy is an effective explanatory device.

Since a corporate presentation is generally a persuasive one, there is a place for emotional appeal if it is done with propriety. Research shows that emotional appeals, both rewards and threats, bring about greater attitude change than appeals to the intellect alone. For reviews of the relevant research on emotional appeals in persuasion, see C. A. Insko, *Theories of Attitude Change* (1967).

On the other end of the spectrum is humor. Research into this area is sparse, but there is some indication that humor appropriately applied makes a dull message more interesting and thus more effective. Dorothy Markiewicz has studied the positive "Effects of Humor on Persuasion" (1974), as has Charles R. Gruner in "The Effects of Humor on Dull and Interesting Informative Speeches" (1970). Gruner reports that an audience tends to like speakers more when they use humor.

For a comprehensive treatment of content analysis, consult George Gerbner and colleagues, *The Analysis of Communication Content* (1969). Erwin P. Bettinghaus in *Message Preparation* (1972) thoroughly covers the relationship between arrangement of content and shaping of belief.

Careful selection of content, organization of that content, choice of diction, verbal embellishments, and use of emotional appeals and humor are not enough, however, to ensure that the message will be understood or appreciated by the audience. Research in business, industry, education, and the military indicates that oral presentations are better comprehended and received when the speaker uses visual aids. See, for example, Franklin H. Knower, David Phillips, and Fern Keoppel's "Studies in Listening to Informative Speaking" (1945), Kenneth Kurtz and Carl I. Hovland's "The Effect of Verbalization During the Observation of Stimulus Objects upon Accuracy of Recognition and Recall" (1953), William H. Allen's "Research in Film Use" (1957), John Holway Ulrich's "An Experimental Study of the Acquisition of Information" (1957), and W. J. Seiler's "The Effects of Visual Material on Attitudes, Credibility, and Retention" (1971).

Two theories are supported by this research. The first proposes that human beings can absorb more information visually than aurally and that presentations accompanied by visuals increase recall. William A. Linkgugel and David N. Berg in *A Time to Speak* (1970) found in repeated experiments that visuals increase listener recall from 15 to 55 percent: immediate recall is 85 percent with a visual presentation versus 75 percent without visuals, and later recall is 65 percent with visuals versus 10 percent without visuals. The second theory deals with audience involvement. According to Edgar Dale in *Audiovisual Methods in Teaching* (1969), there are three levels of learning experiences: (1) participation in the activity, (2) observation of the activity, and (3) perception of verbal symbols. Visuals increase the audience's involvement to the level of observation, thus supplementing the speaker's main reliance upon words.

Although several textbooks have excellent chapters on visuals, there are hundreds of books, monographs, and articles on graphics and audiovisuals. Two helpful annotated bibliographies on these sources are Dixie E. Hickman's "Self-Education in Graphics for Teachers of Technical Writing" (1981) and Kaye E. White's "Back to Hieroglyphics" (1981).

Three sourcebooks for using visuals in an oral presentation are the U.S. Civil Service Commission's *Visual Materials* (1971), Edward O. Minor's *Handbook for Preparing Visual Instructional Materials* (1979), and Eastman Kodak's *Speechmaking...More Than Words Alone* (1979). A specialized book by J. H. Benson and A. G. Carey on *The Elements of Lettering* (1962) is also available.

A handful of articles on preparing or handling visuals for the oral presentation are James M. Lufkin's "The Slide Talk" (1968), C. R. Gould's "⊕*@£‡]#!!! The Overhead Projector" (1972) and "Visual Aids" (1973), Charles R. Stratton and Edward J. Breidenbach's "Inexpensive Visuals for Oral Presentation" (1976), and Glenn Kerfoot's "Let the Audience *See* Your Presentation" (1980).

Eastman Kodak has two excellent monographs: *Graphic Design* (1979) and *Planning and Producing Slide Programs* (1975). Two other helpful works on slides are Jeff Wein's *The Big Picture* (1977), and Don Pratt and Lev Ropes's *35-mm Slides* (1978).

Many sources address the use of audiovisual materials. See, for example, Walter A. Wittich and Charles F. Schuller's *Audiovisual Materials* (1967), James S. Kinder's *Using Instructional Media* (1973), James I. Meyer's "The Effective Use of Audiovisual Aids in Presenting Technical Information Orally" (1977), and Jerrold E. Kemp's *Planning and Producing Audiovisual Materials* (1980).

For a special issue on "Audiovisual Communication," see *IEEE Transactions on Professional Communication* (1978).

Advanced technology has brought about the multimedia presentation. Several articles address this topic in journals: Anthony C.L. Bishop's "The Multimedia Presentation of Technical Information" (1970), J. S. Russell's "Multimedia Communication" (1974), and Bernard M. Fradkin's "Effectiveness of Multi-Image Presentations" (1975). For a good discussion of presenting information via the various media (for example, video tape, sound-on-slide, film, tape recordings), see Joseph T. Klapper's *The Effects of Mass Communication* (1960). Klapper warns, however, that overemphasizing audiovisuals can reduce audience involvement; therefore, he recommends using visuals since the oral presentation already relies heavily on the audience's sense of hearing.

Delivery Analysis

Having analyzed the audience and prepared the message, the corporate speaker is ready to deliver the presentation. If speakers are recognized experts who are also considered trustworthy and who are dynamic in the presentation, they are likely to be successful. See, for example, Elliott R. Siegal, Gerald R. Miller, and C. Edward Wotring, "Source Credibility and Credibility Proneness" (1969). If speakers lack credibility or are perceived as untrustworthy, Carl I. Hovland and Walter Weiss in "The Influence of Source Credibility on Communication Effectiveness" (1951) have found that the audience may discount them and reject their messages. In Franklyn S. Haiman's "An Experimental Study of the Effect of Ethos in Public Speaking" (1949), the audience responded favorably to the issue of public health insurance when the speech was attributed to Thomas G. Parran, Surgeon-General of the United States, but reacted unfavorably when the same speech was attributed to Eugene Dennis, Secretary of the Communist party of the United States. In another study of audience reaction to the prior reputation of the speaker, William E. Arnold and James C. McCroskey, in "Experimental Studies of Perception Distortion and the Extensional Device of Dating" (1967), prepared a moderate position paper that contained both positive and negative statements about busing schoolchildren. When the paper was attributed to Martin Luther King, Jr., the audience perceived the message as pro busing; when the paper was attributed to George Wallace, the audience's perception was the opposite.

When a speaker's credibility is low or suspect, all is not lost. Speakers can increase their credibility through effective message preparation and through the dynamic, effective delivery of that message. Body movement, eye contact, vocal carriage, and dress—all can enhance credibility.

Robert D. Brooks and Thomas M. Scheidel in "Speech as a Process' (1968) have documented that a speaker can establish credibility early in a presentation. *Walk briskly to the platform, address the audience physically, and pause for a moment to gain the audience's attention* is advice found in most freshman speech textbooks. Yet according to a survey by R. H. Bruskin Associates reported in "Fears" (1973), public speaking is one of the most common fears: 40.6 percent of the population reported a fear of public speaking. For "Apprehension About Speaking in the Organizational Setting" (1979), see Donald Kloph and Ronald Cambra. In *The Quiet Ones* (1980), James C. McCroskey and Virginia Richmond document what causes communication shyness, how to detect it, and what to do about it. Studies, summarized by James C. McCroskey and Lawrence Wheeless in *Introduction to Human Communication* (1976) and again by McCroskey (1982), give reassuring evidence that stage fright is only natural. Reassuring evidence also comes from William James in *Psychology* (1907) that positive body language (for example, walking assertively to the platform) reinforces confidence. W. M. Parish in "Implications of Gestalt Psychology" (1928) supports James's contention that emotional well-being, such as confidence, is an outgrowth of physical action, not the cause of it. See Theodore Clevenger, Jr., for "A Synthesis of Experimental Research in Stage Fright" (1959) and James C. McCroskey for "Oral Communication Apprehension" (1977).

Eye contact is a second aspect of body language important in delivery. Audiences prefer direct eye contact, according to Martin Cobin in "Response to Eye Contact" (1962). P. C. Ellsworth and J. M. Carlsmith in "Effects of Eye Contact and Verbal Content in Affective Response to a Dyadic Interaction" (1968) have found that eye contact increases audience interest and makes the speaker more attractive. H. J. Leavitt and R.A.H. Mueller in "Some Effects of Feedback on Communication" (1951) assert that eye contact increases the audience's understanding and satisfaction with the speaker because the speaker can respond to audience feedback. Eye contact is also important in regard to the speaker's proximity to the audience: Lawrence Rosenfeld and Jean M. Civikly summarize the research on the "audience action zone" in *With Words Unspoken* (1976), concluding that the most interested members of the audience usually sit closest to the speaker while those less interested sit farther back.

Non-verbal communication speaks louder that words, some say. In fact, some researchers believe that over 90 percent of a person's attitude is transmitted through non-verbal signals. See, for example, Albert Mehrabian and Morton Wiener's "Decoding of Inconsistent Communication" (1967) and Albert Mehrabian and S. R. Ferris's "Inference of Attitudes from Nonverbal Communication in Two Channels" (1967). For a thorough treatment of non-verbal communication, see Haig A. Bosmajian, *The Rhetoric of Nonverbal Communication* (1971).

Audiences also develop impressions on the basis of the speaker's non-verbal auditory cues such as vocal rate and pitch. In an early study, William Norwood Brigance determined the rate of delivery of winners in intercollegiate oratorical contests. In "How Fast Do We Talk?" (1926), Brigance reported that the winners spoke at approximately 120 words per minute. Additional research, summarized by Wayne N. Thompson in *Quantitative Research in Public Address and Communication* (1967), indicates that message reception is best when the presenter speaks between 125 and 190 words per minute. Along with pace, pitch is a decisive variable. Several studies, including David W. Addington's "The Relationship of Selected Vocal Characteristics to Personality Perception" (1968) and his "The Effect of Vocal Variations on Ratings of Source Credibility" (1971), indicate that as pitch diminishes toward monotone, listeners judge the speaker as less and less credible. Exaggerated pitch changes are even more detrimental to the speaker's credibility than monotone or soporific tones, according to Barbara J. Eakins's "The Relationship of Intonation to Attitude Change, Retention, and Attitude Toward Source" (1969). As one would suspect, a pleasant, resonant voice is preferable to a shrill, harsh voice. Ned Bowler reports on this finding in "A Fundamental Frequency Analysis of Harsh Vocal Quality" (1964). For additional research on non-verbal auditory cues, see Joel R. Davitz and Linda Davitz, "The Communication of Feelings by Content-Free Speech" (1959) and L. Stanley Harms, "Listener Judgments of Status Cues in Speech" (1961).

The speaker's credibility can be damaged by vocalized nonfluencies as well. There are three types of vocalized nonfluencies: vocalized pauses such as "er," "um," "ah"; parenthetical expressions such as "you know," "like," "OK?"; and unnecessary repetitions of words. Kenneth K. Sereno and Gary J. Hawkins in "The Effects of Variations in Speaker's Nonfluency" (1967) found that whereas such nonfluencies do not impair the persuasive effect, they do lower the audience's estimate of the speaker. J. J. Bradac, C. W. Konsky, and R. A. Davies in "Two Studies of the Effects of Linguistic Diversity" (1976) and J. J. Bradac and colleagues in "The Effects of Perceived Status and Linguistic Diversity" (1976) say that parenthetical expressions suggest high speaker anxiety and low competence. Gerald R. Miller and Murray A. Hewgill in "The Effect of Variations in Nonfluency" (1964) have discovered that as the number of nonfluencies increases, speaker credibility decreases. The effect is even more pronounced when the nonfluencies are repetitions. Although nonfluencies may not detract from the persuasiveness of the message, as Sereno and Hawkins (1967) found, at least one reputable study disagrees: McCroskey and Mehrley (1969) have found that fluency not only increases credibility but also increases the persuasive effect.

How do dialects affect credibility? Most research, such as that conducted by Howard Giles and Peter F. Powesland in *Speech Style and Social Evaluation* (1975), indicates that regional dialects and poor usage can create a negative impression. A person's speech and dress are considered indices to one's social class, and both are directly related to judgments of competence, according to Fred L. Strodbeck, Rita M. James, and Charles Hawkins in "Social Status in Jury Deliberations" (1958).

Researchers have also long been interested in such variables as the height, sex, dress, and general attractiveness of the speaker and the relationship between these variables and speaker credibility. The findings suggest that whereas tall people are not automatically perceived as more authoritative than short people (see Eldon E. Baker and W. Charles Redding, "The Effects of Perceived Tallness in Persuasive Speaking" [1962]), men are generally perceived as more authoritative and thus more credible than women (see James Whittaker, "Sex Differences and Susceptibility to Interpersonal Persuasion" [1965]). In a classic study, "Male Chauvinism and Source Competence" (1973) conducted by Gerald R. Miller and Michael McReynolds, two audiences were read a message favoring an expanded armed ballistic missile system. The author of the message was identified as a Ph.D. in nuclear physics who was also a director of a radiology laboratory and a scientific advisor to the National Security Council. For one group, the author was further identified as Dr. Robert Stapleton; for the other, Dr. Gretchen Stapleton. Female subjects rated Dr. Robert Stapleton slightly higher than did the males, and female subjects rated Dr. Robert Stapleton significantly higher than they did Dr. Gretchen Stapleton. Most research studies seem to substantiate that male speakers are more credible and more persuasive than female speakers; yet these findings may be a part of our culture that is now changing. Lawrence Rosenfeld and Vickie Christie in "Sex and Persuasibility Revisited" (1974) insist that it is ludicrous to conclude that one sex is more persuasive than the other.

Tall or short, male or female, a person who wears glasses does not tend to project an image of intelligence and competence, according to a study by George Russell Thornton, "The Effects of Wearing Glasses" (1944). Dress matters, too. Not only do clothes reveal one's self-image, personality, and social status, but they also help others to identify with the speaker. In a study focused on dress, Haiman (1949) made the same presentation to two different audiences. Before one audience, he appeared neatly dressed and cleanly shaven; before the other, unkempt and unshaven. He favorably impressed the first group, not the second. Haiman concluded that a speaker can woo audiences by sharing in its values and meeting its expectations. Later research by Michael Burgoon in *Approaching Speech Communication* (1974) shows that audiences respond favorably to speakers who are similar to them, yet prefer that the similarity be on the conservative rather than the liberal side. For example, in 1972 when long hair on men was still a relatively new fashion or fad, even long-haired listeners perceived long-haired speakers as less credible than short-haired speakers (Rosenfeld and Civikly [1976]).

An experiment with rather surprising results is Timothy C. Brock's "Communicator Recipient Similarity and Decision Change" (1965). Brock wanted to see if a persuader identified as similar to the audience could be more persuasive than a persuader identified as an expert. The results favored the similar, not the expert, persuader. William J. McGuire in "The Nature of Attitude Change" (1969) thinks that similarity and liking are the major characteristics contributing to attractiveness of the speaker. Judson Mills and Elliot Aronson in "Opinion Change as a Function of a Communicator's Attractiveness and Desired Influence" (1965) found that an attractive speaker's open admission to persuade was the single most effective device. In a follow-up study, Judson Mills in "Opinion

Change as a Function of the Communicator's Desire to Influence'' (1966) found that the same admission by an unattractive speaker resulted in decreased effectiveness. In short, according to Paul H. Wright's "Attitude Change under Direct and Indirect Interpersonal Influence" (1966), efforts to persuade may be ineffective unless the audience likes the speaker. It seems that a speaker who is similar to and is liked by the audience has a better chance to persuade.

The importance of personal ethos is vividly illustrated by Ann Nietzke's study "The Seductive Doctor Fox" (1974): an actor was hired to deliver a lecture to a group of trained psychologists. The lecture was complete gobbledygook, absolutely meaningless in content, but well delivered. The psychologists found the speaker highly credible and were impressed with his knowledge. Two summaries of research—Erwin P. Bettinghaus's "The Operation of Congruity in an Oral Communication Situation" (1961) and Kenneth Anderson and Theodore Clevenger, Jr.'s "A Summary of Experimental Research in *Ethos*" (1963)—conclude that without doubt effective delivery contributes to the credibility of the speaker and to the persuasiveness of the message. Thompson in *Quantitative Research* (1967) writes, "Such unanimity is unusual in the behavioral sciences, where the complexity of variables and the test situations make nonsignificant and conflicting findings common" (p. 84).

Conclusion

Although empirical research in speech communication may not have revolutionized traditional rhetorical theory, the corporate speaker may take confidence in the fact that most of the traditional rhetorical precepts have been at least partially substantiated by quantitative research. The two approaches do, indeed, complement one another.

References

Addington, David W. "The Effect of Vocal Variations on Ratings of Source Credibility."*Speech Mon*, 38 (1971), 242–47.
———. "The Relationship of Selected Vocal Characteristics to Personality Perception." *Speech Mon*, 35 (1968), 492–503.
Adrian, Paula J. "A Study of the Relationship Between Language Usage and Congruency and Perceived Ethos." Thesis University of Kansas, 1967.
Allen, William H. "Research in Film Use; Student Participation." *AV Comm Rev*, 5 (1957), 423–50.
Allyn, Jane, and Leon Festinger. "The Effectiveness of Unanticipated Persuasive Communications." *J Abnorm Soc Psychol*, 62 (1961), 35–40.
Anderson, Kenneth, and Theodore Clevenger, Jr. "A Summary of Experimental Research in *Ethos*." *Speech Mon*, 30 (1963), 59–78.
Andrews, James R. *Essentials of Public Communication*. New York: Wiley, 1979.
Arnold, Carroll C. "Oral Rhetoric, Rhetoric, and Literature." *Phil Rhet*, 1 (1968), 191–210.

————. "Some Preliminaries to English-Speech Collaboration in the Study of Rhetoric." In *Rhetoric: Theories for Application*. Ed. Robert M. Gorrell. Champaign, Ill.: National Council of Teachers of English (NCTE), 1967, pp. 30–36.

Arnold, William E., and James C. McCroskey. "Experimental Studies of Perception Distortion and Extensional Device of Dating." Speech Communication Association Convention, Los Angeles, 1967.

"Audiovisual Communication" Special Issue. *IEEE Trans Prof Comm*, PC–21, No. 3 (1978).

Baker, Eldon E., and W. Charles Redding. "The Effects of Perceived Tallness in Persuasive Speaking." *J Comm*, 12 (1962), 51–53.

Barker, Larry L., and Robert J. Kibler, eds. *Speech Communication Behavior: Perspectives and Principles*. Englewood Cliffs, N.J.: Prentice-Hall, 1971.

Barnard, Raymond H. "An Objective Study of the Speeches of Wendell Phillips." *Q J Speech*, 18 (1932), 571–84.

Becker, Samuel L. "Methodological Analysis in Communication Research." *Q J Speech*, 51 (1965), 382–91.

————. "Rhetorical Scholarship in the Seventies." In *A Tradition in Transition*. Ed. Walter R. Fisher. East Lansing, Mich.: Michigan State University Press, 1974, pp. 3–15.

Bem, Daryl J. *Beliefs, Attitudes, and Human Affairs*. Belmont, Calif.: Brooks/Cole, 1970.

Benson, J. H., and A. G. Carey. *The Elements of Lettering*. 2nd ed. New York: McGraw-Hill, 1962.

Bettinghaus, Erwin P. *Message Preparation: The Nature of Proof*. 2nd ed. Indianapolis: Bobbs-Merrill, 1972.

————. "The Operation of Congruity in an Oral Communication Situation." *Speech Mon*, 28 (1961), 131–42.

————. *Persuasive Communication*. 3rd ed. New York: Holt, 1980.

Biddle, P. R. "An Experimental Study of Ethos and Appeal for Overt Behavior in Persuasion." Diss. University of Illinois, 1966.

Bishop, Anthony C.L. "The Multimedia Presentation of Technical Information." *IEEE Trans Prof Comm*, EWS–13, No. 1 (1970), 24–27.

Bitzer, Lloyd F., and Edwin Black, eds. *The Prospect of Rhetoric*. Englewood Cliffs, N.J.: Prentice-Hall, 1971.

Bogard, Morris R. *The Manager's Style Book: Communication Skills to Improve Your Performance*. Englewood Cliffs, N.J.: Prentice-Hall, 1979.

"Boom in Speechmaking." *Time*, 8 Feb. 1960, p. 84.

Borchers, Gladys L. "An Approach to the Problem of Oral Style." *Q J Speech*, 22 (1936), 114–17.

Bosmajian, Haig A. *The Rhetoric of Nonverbal Communication: Readings*. Glenview, Ill.: Scott Foresman, 1971.

Bowers, John Waite. "The Pre-Scientific Function of Rhetorical Criticism." In *Contemporary Rhetoric: A Reader's Coursebook*. Ed. Douglas Ehninger. Glenview, Ill.: Scott Foresman, 1972, pp. 163–73.

Bowler, Ned. "A Fundamental Frequency Analysis of Harsh Vocal Quality." *Speech Mon*, 31 (1964), 128–34.

Bradac, J. J., et al. "The Effects of Perceived Status and Linguistic Diversity upon

Judgments of Speaker Attributes and Message Effectiveness.'' *J Psychol*, 93 (1976), 213–20.

————, C. W. Konsky, and R. A. Davies. "Two Studies of the Effects of Linguistic Diversity upon Judgments of Communicator Attributes and Message Effectiveness." *Comm Mon*, 43 (1976), 70–79.

Brembeck, Winston L., and William S. Howell. *Persuasion: A Means of Social Influence*. 2nd ed. Englewood Cliffs, N.J.: Prentice-Hall, 1976.

Brigance, William Norwood. *A History and Criticism of American Public Address*. 2 vols. New York: Russell, 1960.

————. "How Fast Do We Talk?" *Q J Speech*, 12 (1926), 337–42.

————. "Whither Research?" *Q J Speech*, 19 (1933), 552–61.

Brock, Timothy C. "Communicator Recipient Similarity and Decision Change." *J Pers Soc Psychol*, 1 (1965), 650–54.

Brooks, Robert D., and Thomas M. Scheidel. "Speech as a Process: A Case Study." *Speech Mon*, 35 (1968), 1–7.

Brooks, William D., and Philip Emmert. "The Effect of Language Usage Congruency upon Source Credibility, Attitude Change, and Retention." SAA Convention, Los Angeles. 28 Dec. 1967.

R. H. Bruskin Associates. "Fears." *Spectra*, 9 (Dec. 1973), 4.

Bryant, Donald C. "Rhetoric: Its Functions and Its Scope." *Q J Speech*, 39 (1953), 401–24. Rpt. in *A Tradition in Transition*. Ed. Walter R. Fisher. East Lansing, Mich.: Michigan State University Press, 1974, pp. 195–230.

Burgoon, Michael. *Approaching Speech Communication*. New York: Holt, 1974.

Cartwright, Dorwin, and Alvin Zander. *Group Dynamics*. 3rd ed. New York: Harper, 1968.

Cleary, James W., and Frederick W. Haberman. *Rhetoric and Public Address: A Bibliography, 1947–1961*. Madison, Wis.: University of Wisconsin Press, 1974.

Clevenger, Theodore, Jr. *Audience Analysis*. Indianapolis: Bobbs-Merrill, 1966.

————. "The Interaction of Descriptive and Experimental Research in the Development of Rhetorical Theory." In *Contemporary Rhetoric: A Reader's Coursebook*. Ed. Douglas Ehninger. Glenview, Ill.: Scott Foresman, 1972, pp. 174–80.

————. "A Synthesis of Experimental Research in Stage Fright." *Q J Speech*, 45 (1959), 134–45.

————. "Toward an Understanding of Experimental Rhetoric." *Penn Speech A*, 21 (1964), 23–27.

————, and Jack Matthews. *The Speech Communication Process*. Glenview, Ill.: Scott, Foresman, 1971.

Cobin, Martin. "Response to Eye Contact." *Q J Speech*, 48 (1962), 415–18.

Connolly, James E. *Effective Technical Presentations*. St. Paul, Minn.: 3M Business Press, 1968.

Cooper, Lane, ed. *The Rhetoric of Aristotle*. New York: Appleton-Century-Crofts, 1932.

Corbett, Edward P.J. "A Survey of Rhetoric." In *Classical Rhetoric for the Modern Student*. 2nd ed. New York: Oxford University Press, 1971, pp. 594–641.

Cronkhite, Gary. *Communication and Awareness*. Menlo Park, Calif.: Cummings, 1976.

————. *Persuasion: Speech and Behavioral Change*. Indianapolis: Bobbs-Merrill, 1969.

————. *Public Speaking and Critical Listening*. Menlo, Park, Calif.: Benjamin/Cummings, 1978.

Dale, Edgar. *Audiovisual Methods in Teaching*. 3rd ed. New York: Holt, 1969.

Darnell, Donald K. "The Relation Between Sentence Order and Comprehension." *Speech Mon*, 30 (1963), 97–100.

Davitz, Joel R., and Linda Davitz. "The Communication of Feelings by Content-Free Speech." *J Comm*, 9 (1959), 6–13.

Dember, William N. *The Psychology of Perception*. New York: Holt, 1960.

Eakins, Barbara J. "The Relationship of Intonation to Attitude Change, Retention, and Attitude Toward Source." Speech Association of America Convention, New York, Dec. 1969.

Ehninger, Douglas, ed. *Contemporary Rhetoric: A Reader's Coursebook*. Glenview, Ill.: Scott, Foresman, 1972.

———. "History of Rhetoric and Public Address." In *Introduction to the Field of Speech*. Ed. Ronald Reid. Chicago: Scott, Foresman, 1965, pp. 163–83.

Ehrensberger, Ray. "An Experimental Study of the Relative Effects of Certain Forms of Emphasis in Public Speaking." *Speech Mon*, 12 (1945), 94–111.

Ellsworth, P. C., and J. M. Carlsmith. "Effects of Eye Contact and Verbal Content in Affective Response to a Dyadic Interaction." *J Pers Soc Psychol*, 10 (1968), 15–20.

Emmert, Philip, and William D. Brooks. *Methods of Research in Communication*. New York: Houghton Mifflin, 1970.

Ewbank, Henry L. "Four Approaches to the Study of Speech Style." *Q J Speech*, 17 (1931), 458–65.

———. "The Statistical Analysis of Speech Style." *Q J Speech*, 18 (1932), 117.

Fearing, Bertie E., and Thomas M. Sawyer. "Speech for Technical Communicators: A Bibliography." *IEEE Trans Prof Comm*, PC–23, No. 1 (1980), 53–60.

Fisher, Walter R., ed. *A Tradition in Transition*. East Lansing: Michigan State University Press, 1974.

Fradkin, Bernard M. "Effectiveness of Multi-Image Presentations." *J Educ Tech*, 5 (1975), 53–68.

Gerbner, George, et. al. *The Analysis of Communication Content*. New York: Wiley, 1969.

Giles, Howard, and Peter F. Powesland. *Speech Style and Social Evaluation*. London: Academic, 1975.

Gilkinson, Howard. "Experimental and Statistical Research in General Speech: Effects of Training and Correlates of Speech Skill." *Q J Speech*, 30 (1944), 95–101.

Gorrell, Robert M. "Teaching of Rhetoric." *Encyclopedia of Education*. 1971 ed.

Gould, C. R. "⊕*@£‡#!!! The Overhead Projector." *IEEE Trans Prof Comm*, PC–15, No. 1 (1972), 2–6.

———. "Visual Aids—How to Make Them Positively Legible." *IEEE Trans Prof Comm*, PC–16, No. 2 (1973), 35–40.

Graphic Design. Rochester, N.Y.: Eastman Kodak, 1979.

Gruner, Charles R. "The Effects of Humor on Dull and Interesting Informative Speeches." *C S Speech J*, 21 (1970), 160–66.

Haiman, Franklyn S. "An Experimental Study of the Effects of Ethos in Public Speaking." *Speech Mon*, 16 (1949), 190–202.

Harms, L. Stanley. "Listener Judgments of Status Cues in Speech." *Q J Speech*, 47 (1961), 164–70.

Hart, T. B. "The Effects of Evidence in Persuasive Communication." *C S Speech J*, 27 (1976), 42–46.

Hickman, Dixie E. "Self-Education in Graphics for Teachers of Technical Writing." *Proceedings of the 1981 CCC Sessions on Technical Communication*. Washington, D.C.: NASA, 1981, pp. 107–13.

Hochmuth, Marie K., ed. *A History and Criticism of American Public Address*. Vol. III. New York: Russell, 1955.

Hollingworth, H. L. *The Psychology of the Audience*. New York: American Book Co., 1935.

Holm, James N. *Productive Speaking for Business and the Professions*. Boston: Allyn, Bacon, 1967.

Holtzman, Paul D. *The Psychology of the Speaker's Audiences*. Glenview, Ill.: Scott, Foresman, 1970.

Hovland, Carl I., Irving L. Janis, and Harold H. Kelley. *Communication and Persuasion: Psychological Studies of Opinion Change*. 2nd ed. New Haven: Yale University Press, 1974.

———, and Walter Weiss. "The Influence of Source Credibility on Communication Effectiveness." *POQ*, 15 (1951), 635–50.

Howell, William S., and Ernest G. Bormann. *Presentational Speaking for Business and the Professions*. New York: Harper, 1971.

Howes, Raymond F., ed. *Historical Studies of Rhetoric and Rhetoricians*. Ithaca, N.Y.: Cornell University Press, 1961.

Insko, C. A. *Theories of Attitude Change*. New York: Appleton-Century-Crofts, 1967.

James, Williams. *Psychology: Briefer Course*. New York: Henry Holt, 1907.

———. *Talks to Teachers on Psychology*. New York: Norton, 1958.

Johannesen, Richard L., ed. *Contemporary Theories of Rhetoric: Selected Readings*. New York: Harper, 1971.

Jordan, W. J., and M. L. McLaughlin. "Figurative Language as an Independent Variable in Communication Research." *Comm Q*, 24 (1976), 31–37.

Karlins, Marvin, and Herbert I. Abelson. *Persuasion: How Opinions and Attitudes Are Changed*. 2nd ed. New York: Springer, 1970.

Kemp, Jerrold E. *Planning and Producing Audiovisual Materials*. 4th ed. New York: Harper, 1980.

Kerfoot, Glenn. "Let the Audience *See* Your Presentation." *IEEE Trans Prof Comm*, PC–23, No. 1 (1980), 50–52.

Kibler, Robert J., and Larry L. Barker, eds. *Conceptual Frontiers in Speech-Communication*. New York: Speech Association of America, 1969.

Kiesler, Charles A., and Sara B. Kiesler. "Role of Forewarning in Persuasive Communication." *J Abnorm Soc Psychol*, 18 (1971), 210–21.

Kinder, James S. *Using Instructional Media*. New York: Nostrand, 1973.

Klapper, Joseph T. *The Effects of Mass Communication*. New York: Free Press, 1960.

Kloph, Donald, and Ronald Cambra. "Apprehension About Speaking in the Organizational Setting." *Psychol Rep*, 45 (1979), 58.

Knower, Franklin H. "Experimental Studies of Change in Attitudes. I. A Study of the Effect of Oral Argument in Change in Attitudes." *J Soc Psychol*, 6 (1935), 315–47.

———, David Phillips, and Fern Keoppel. "Studies in Listening to Informative Speaking." *J Abnorm Soc Psychol*, 40 (1945), 82–88.

Kurtz, Kenneth, and Carl I. Hovland. "The Effect of Verbalization During the Observation of Stimulus Objects upon Accuracy of Recognition and Recall." *J Exp Psychol*, 45 (1953), 157–64.

Leavitt, H. J., and R.A.H. Mueller. "Some Effects of Feedback on Communication." *Human Relat*, 4 (1951), 401–10.

Leventhall, Howard, Robert Singer, and Susan Jones. "Effects of Fear and Specificity of Recommendations upon Attitudes and Behavior." *J Pers Soc Psychol*, 2 (1965), 20–29.

Linkgugel, William A., and David N. Berg. *A Time to Speak*. Belmont, Calif.: Wadsworth, 1970.

Lufkin, James M. "The Slide Talk: A Tutorial Drama in One Act." *IEEE Trans Eng Writ Speech*, EWS–11, No. 2 (1968), 7–14.

McCroskey, James C. *An Introduction to Rhetorical Communication*. 4th ed. Englewood Cliffs, N.J.: Prentice-Hall, 1982.

———. "Oral Communication Apprehension: A Summary of Recent Theory and Research." *HCR*, 4 (1977), 78–86.

———. "A Summary of Experimental Research on the Effects of Evidence in Persuasive Communication." *Q J Speech*, 55 (1969), 169–76.

———, and W. H. Coombs. "The Effects of the Use of Analogy on Attitude Change and Source Credibility." *J Comm*, 19 (1969), 333–39.

———, and R. Samuel Mehrley. "The Effects of Disorganization and Nonfluency on Attitude Change and Source Credibility." *Speech Mon*, 36 (1969), 13–21.

———, and Virginia Richmond. *The Quiet Ones: Communication Apprehension and Shyness*. Dubuque: Gorsuch Scarisbrick, 1980.

———, and Lawrence Wheeless. *Introduction to Human Communication*. Boston: Allyn, Bacon, 1976.

McGuire, William J. "The Nature of Attitude Change." In Vol. III, *The Individual in a Social Content*, of *The Handbook of Social Psychology*. 2nd ed. Ed. Gardner Lindzey and Elliot Aronson. Reading, Mass.: Addison-Wesley, 1969, pp. 136–314.

Macvaugh, Gilbert S. "Structural Analysis of the Sermons of Dr. Harry Emerson Fosdick." *Q J Speech*, 18 (1932), 531–46.

Markiewicz, Dorothy. "Effects of Humor on Persuasion." *Sociometry*, 37 (1974), 407–22.

Martin, Howard, and Kenneth E. Anderson. *Speech Communication: Analysis and Readings*. Boston: Allyn, Bacon, 1968.

Matthews, Jack. "A Behavioral Science Approach to the Study of Rhetoric." *Penn Speech A*, 21 (1964), 55–60.

Mehrabian, Albert, and S. R. Ferris. "Inference of Attitudes from Nonverbal Communication in Two Channels." *J Consult Psychol*, 31 (1967), 248–52.

———, and Morton Wiener." Decoding of Inconsistent Communication." *J Pers Soc Psychol*, 6 (1967), 109–14.

Meyer, James I. "The Effective Use of Audiovisual Aids in Presenting Technical Information Orally." *J Tech Writ Comm*, 7 (1977), 45–49.

Miller, George A. *The Psychology of Communication*. New York: Basic, 1975.

Miller, Gerald R., and Murray A. Hewgill. "The Effect of Variations in Nonfluency on Audience Ratings of Source Credibility." *Q J Speech*, 50 (1964), 36–44.

———, and Michael McReynolds. "Male Chauvinism and Source Competence: A Research Note." *Speech Mon*, 40 (1973), 154–55.

Mills, Judson. "Opinion Change as a Function of the Communicator's Desire to Influence and Liking for the Audience." *J Exp Soc Psychol*, 2 (1966), 152–59.

————, and Elliot Aronson. "Opinion Change as a Function of a Communicator's Attractiveness and Desired Influence." *J Pers Soc Psychol*, 1 (1965), 173–77.

Minor, Edward O. *Handbook for Preparing Visual Instructional Materials*. New York: McGraw-Hill, 1979.

Monroe, Alan H., and Douglas Ehninger. *Principles and Types of Speech Communication*. 7th ed. Glenview, Ill.: Scott, Foresman, 1975.

Nietzke, Ann. "The Seductive Doctor Fox." *Human Behav*, 3, No. 10 (1974), 42–44.

Nilsen, Thomas R., ed. *Essays on Rhetorical Criticism*. New York: Random House, 1968.

Oliver, Robert T. *History of Public Speaking in America*. Westport, Conn.: Greenwood, 1978.

Pace, R. Wayne, R. Boren, and Brent D. Peterson. *Communication Behavior and Experiments: A Scientific Approach*. Belmont, Calif.: Wadsworth, 1975.

Parish, W. M. "Implications of Gestalt Psychology." *Q J Speech*, 14 (1928), 8–30.

Petrie, Charles. "Informative Speaking: A Bibliography of Related Research." *Speech Mon*, 30 (1963), 79–91.

Planning and Producing Slide Programs. Rochester, N.Y.: Eastman Kodak, 1975.

Pratt, Don, and Lev Ropes. *35-mm Slides: A Manual for Technical Presentations*. Tulsa: American Association of Petroleum Geologists, 1978.

"Public Speaking for Engineers and Scientists" Special Issue. *IEEE Trans Prof Comm*, PC–23, No. 1 (1980).

Rodman, George R. *Speaking Out: Message Preparation for Professionals*. New York: Holt, 1978.

Rogge, Edward A., and James C. Ching. *Advanced Public Speaking*. New York: Holt, 1966.

Rosenfeld, Lawrence, and Vickie Christie. "Sex and Persuasibility Revisited." *W J Speech Comm*, 38 (1974), 244–53.

————, and Jean M. Civikly. *With Words Unspoken*. New York: Holt, 1976.

Russell, J. S. "Multimedia Communication—It's Affordable." *Proceedings of the Society for Technical Communication 21st ITCC*, 15–18 May 1974, pp. 193–98.

Sawyer, Thomas M. "Preparing and Delivering an Oral Presentation." *Tech Comm*, 26, No. 1 (1979), 4–7.

Schramm, Wilber L., ed. *The Science of Communication: New Directions and New Findings in Communication Research*. New York: Basic, 1963.

Schwartz, Joseph, and John A. Rycenga, eds. *The Providence of Rhetoric*. New York: Ronald, 1965.

Seabury, Hugh F. "Speech". *Encyclopedia of Educational Research*. 1969 ed.

Seiler, W. J. "The Effects of Visual Material on Attitudes, Credibility, and Retention." *Speech Mon*, 38 (1971), 331–34.

Sereno, Kenneth K., and Gary J. Hawkins. "The Effects of Variations in Speaker's Nonfluency upon Audience Ratings of Attitude Toward the Speech Topics in Speaker's Credibility." *Speech Mon*, 34 (1967), 58–64.

Sharp, Harry, Jr., and Thomas McClung. "Effects of Organization on the Speaker's Ethos." *Speech Mon*, 33 (1966), 182–83.

Siegal, Elliott R., Gerald R. Miller, and C. Edward Wotring. "Source Credibility and Credibility Proneness: A New Relationship." *Speech Mon*, 36 (1969), 118–25.

Sloane, O. Thomas, and Chaim Perelman. "Rhetoric." *The New Encyclopedia Britannica: Macropaedia*. 1979 ed.

Smith, Raymond G. "An Experimental Study of the Effects of Speech Organization upon the Attitudes of College Students." *Speech Mon*, 18 (1951), 292–301.

————. *The Message Measurement Inventory: A Profile for Communication Analysis*. Bloomington: Indiana University Press, 1978.

Speechmaking...More than Words Alone. Rochester, N.Y.: Eastman Kodak, 1979.

Steinmann, Martin, Jr., ed. *New Rhetorics*. New York: Scribner's, 1967.

Stratton, Charles R., and Edward J. Breidenbach. "Inexpensive Visuals for Oral Presentation." *Tech Comm*, 23, No. 2 (1976), 2–5.

Strodbeck, Fred L., Rita M. James, and Charles Hawkins. "Social Status in Jury Deliberations." In *Readings in Social Psychology*. Ed. E. E. Maccoby, T. H. Newcomb, and E. L. Hartley. New York: Holt, 1958, pp. 379–88.

Tandberg, Gerilyn. "History of Oratory." In *Research Guide in Speech*. Morristown, N.J.: General Learning Press, 1974, pp. 179–205.

Tannenbaum, Percy. "Effect of Serial Position on Recall of Radio and News Stories." *Journ Q*, 31 (1954), 319–23.

Thistlewaite, Donald L., Henry DeHann, and Joseph Kamenentsky. "The Effect of 'Directive' and 'Non-Directive' Communication Procedures on Attitudes." *J Abnorm Soc Psychol*, 51 (1955), 107–18.

Thompson, Ernest. "An Experimental Investigation of the Relative Effectiveness of Organizational Structure in Oral Communication." *S Speech J*, 26 (1960), 59–69.

————. "Some Effects of Message Structure on Listeners' Comprehension." *Speech Mon*, 34 (1967), 51–57.

Thompson, Wayne N. "A Conservative View of a Progressive Rhetoric." *Q J Speech*, 49 (1963), 1–7.

————. *Quantitative Research in Public Address and Communication*. New York: Random House, 1967.

Thonssen, Lester, A. Craig Baird, and Waldo W. Braden, eds. *Speech Criticism*. 2nd ed. New York: Ronald, 1970.

Thornton, George Russell. "The Effects of Wearing Glasses upon Judgments of Personality Traits of Persons Seen Briefly." *J Appl Psychol*, 28 (1944), 203–07.

Timm, Paul R. *Functional Business Presentations: Getting Across*. Englewood Cliffs, N.J.: Prentice-Hall, 1981.

Tubbs, Stewart L., and Sylvia Moss. *Human Communication*. 3rd ed. New York: Random House, 1980.

Ulrich, John Holway. "An Experimental Study of the Acquisition of Information from Three Types of Recorded Television Presentations." *Speech Mon*, 24 (1957), 39–45.

Visual Materials: Guidelines for Selection and Use in Training Situations. U.S. Civil Service Commission. Washington, D.C.: U. S. GPO, 1971.

Wallace, Karl R., ed. *History of Speech Education in America*. New York: Appleton-Century-Crofts, 1954.

Walter, Otis M., and Robert L. Scott. *Thinking and Speaking: A Guide to Intelligent Oral Communication*. 3rd ed. New York: Macmillan, 1973.

Wein, Jeff. *The Big Picture: Photography and Slides in the Classroom*. Waitsfield, Vt.: Vermont Crossroads Press, 1977.

Wheeler, Raymond H., and Francis T. Perkins. *Principles of Mental Development*. New York: Crowell, 1932.

Whichelns, Herbert A. "The Literary Criticism of Oratory." In *Studies in Rhetoric and Public Address in Honor of James Albert Winans*. New York: Russell, 1962, pp. 181–216.

White, Eugene E., ed. *Rhetoric in Transition: Studies in the Nature and Use of Rhetoric*. University Park, Pa.: Pennsylvania State University Press, 1980.

White, Kaye E. "Back to Hieroglyphics: A Rhetoric of Graphic Communication." Thesis East Carolina University, 1981.

Whittaker, James. "Sex Differences and Susceptibility to Interpersonal Persuasion." *J Soc Psychol*, 66 (1965), 91–94.

Wittich, Walter A., and Charles F. Schuller. *Audiovisual Materials: Their Nature and Use*. New York: Harper, 1967.

Woelfe, Robert M., ed. *A Guide to Better Technical Presentations*. New York: Institute of Electrical and Electronics Engineers Press, 1975.

Woolbert, Charles Henry. "Effects of Various Modes of Public Reading." *J Appl Psychol*, 4 (1920), 162–85.

———. "Suggestions as to the Methods in Research." *Q J Speech Educ*, 3 (1916), 12–26.

Workun, Arthur E. "Speech for the Technician: A Bibliography." *J Tech Writ Comm*, 4 (1974), 331–39.

Wright, Paul H. "Attitude Change Under Direct and Indirect Interpersonal Influence." *Human Relat*, 19 (1966), 199–211.

Young, Richard. "Invention: A Typographical Survey." In *Teaching Composition: 10 Bibliographical Essays*. Ed. Gary Tate. Fort Worth: Texas Christian University Press, 1976, pp. 1–43.

Zelko, Harold P., and Frank E.X. Dance. *Business and Professional Speech Communication*. 2nd ed. New York: Holt, 1978.

Zimbardo, Philip G., Ebbe B. Ebbesen, and Christina Maslach. *Influencing Attitudes and Changing Behavior*. 2nd ed. Reading, Mass.: Addison-Wesley, 1977.

Resources for Teaching Legal Writing

RUSSELL RUTTER

Legal writing has been a target of ridicule by people who believe that it is often needlessly complex and obscure to the point of perversity. A story is told and re-told in the literature on this subject of an English chancellor who in 1596 ordered a hole cut in a 120-page document so that the draftsman's head could be stuck through it. This unfortunate wretch was then paraded around Westminster Hall much to the onlookers' glee. Over 40 years ago William L. Prosser, in "English as She Is Wrote" (1939), asserted that the average lawyer in the course of a lifetime writes more than a novelist does, and yet his law students experienced "utter consternation at the prospect of a little original writing" (p. 48). Twenty-five years later Hans J. Gottlieb, one of the first writing specialists to teach composition in a law school, lamented in "Teaching English in a Law School" (1963) that papers produced by law students were so ill-written that they could not conceivably have earned passing grades in the very colleges from which the writers had graduated. Although the complaint has been voiced repeatedly by both law professionals and the public, no systematic study of the techniques used to teach writing in American law schools was available until 1973, when Marjorie Dick Rombauer, dean of the University of Washington School of Law, published "First-Year Legal Research and Writing" (1973). The information in Rombauer's study was developed from responses to questionnaires sent to all persons listed in the 1968–70 *Directory of Law School Teachers* as teaching a "Legal Research and Writing" course. The tabulated responses led Dean Rombauer to several conclusions especially important to the teacher of legal writing. For example, law students, though they consider the legal writing courses "relevant," say (and their professors agree) that these courses carry too little credit for the quantity of work they require. In addition, the single most frequently listed objective of such courses is not legal writing but mastery of legal research methods and legal bibliography. Furthermore, fewer than half the teachers of legal writing courses require systematic revision of papers written. In other words, legal writing is often conflated with other activities and in some cases is virtually crowded out. In "Teaching Legal Writing in the Law Schools" (1979) Reed Dickerson, writing from long experience as a leading authority on legal drafting, supports the findings of Dean Rombauer. He castigates law professors for "trivializing" legal writing, making it seem merely a matter of teaching surface correctness, and thereby ignoring the fact that "expository writing... is a basic discipline, perhaps the most basic of all disciplines" (p. 85). At the source of the problem, of which Rombauer's findings are but signs, is the long-standing conviction among law professors that writing, alleged to be merely a skill, is far less intellectually respectable and challenging than content disciplines such as torts or contract law. It does not necessarily follow that someone who took a course called "Legal Writing" in fact learned legal writing.

Resource materials on good legal writing, as opposed to materials that purport to discuss legal writing but instead treat legal research and bibliography, have been developed only in the last fifteen years. Even Dean Rombauer's widely accepted *Legal Problem Solving* (1978), which seems at first glance to offer a problem-solving approach to legal writing, is a highly research-oriented text somewhat in the category of Morris Cohen's standard introduction to legal studies, *How to Find The Law* (1976) (only recent editions of which even discuss writing at all).

The newcomer to legal writing studies will notice that, while few long works have been published on the subject, many articles are available, and that these articles duplicate one another in ways not usually found in other areas. A word about this is in order. The main organizational unit for law professionals is the state bar association. Virtually every state has its own law reviews and law journals, which are aimed at state-wide audiences. This is because laws differ from state to state, and a person licensed to practice law in one state is not necessarily prepared to do so in another. However well this organizational method serves the interests of substantive law and legal interpretation, which differ from state to state, it does not serve well the interests of good legal writing, which, of course, is the same everywhere. While it is fortunate that articles have been written for each state on, say, vehicular homicide, it is frustrating to find several articles saying almost the same thing about topics like the use of the hybrid "and/or" or about the problems created by needless legal jargon. When such duplication occurs, this essay discusses the best article and perhaps mentions one or two others, either in the text or in the references.

Two major bibliographies may be consulted for references to works on legal writing and related issues: the *Index to Legal Periodicals* (1925–) and the American Association of Law Libraries' *Current Publications in Legal and Related Fields* (1953–). The *Index to Legal Periodicals* is very complete: it monitors hundreds of legal publications, and each year lists thousands of entries on all aspects of law, not just legal writing. It is updated several times a year with supplements that are now collected annually and in the past have been collected every two or three years. *Current Publications in Legal and Related Fields* covers the one area excluded in the *Current Index*, book-length studies and monographs. Both of these bibliographies monitor legal writing in its largest sense, that is, writing done not only by lawyers but also by judges, probation officers, police officers, and various court services personnel. The writing specialist seeking information about more specialized legal writing may consult, for business law, the bibliographies published annually by *The Business Lawyer* and, for other fields, those listed in Morris Cohen's *How to Find the Law*. These more limited bibliographies are consulted merely for convenience, however. Because only rarely do they contain entries not also listed in either the *Index* or the *Current Publications*, it is normally sufficient to consult only these two major bibliographies.

The discussion is divided into three sections:

1. Legal training and legal forms.

2. Legal style and the plain language laws.

3. Resources for teaching legal writing.

These sections are meant to reflect the three most significant formative influences on legal writing studies: law school curricula; the discontent with legal style that has prompted attempts to clarify it; and the development of college, university, and in-service writing courses for law students and law professionals. Because legal writing is an emerging discipline without a long history of quality resource materials, a topical rather than chronological organization has been developed within these sections to indicate the areas in which significant studies are being published.

Legal Training and Legal Forms

Anyone who studies the literature on law school curricula soon understands that they generally do not give legal writing and communication skills high priority. David M. Hunsaker in "Law, Humanism and Communication" (1980), an essential item of background reading for the teacher of legal writing, explains why this is so. Drawing upon his experience as a judge in the Interscholastic Mock Law Office competition of the University of San Diego, Hunsaker notes that only 35 percent of the points that a student participant can earn are given to interpersonal skills—and only 5 percent to writing results and preparatory memoranda. These statistics are all the more convincing when it is observed that 3 percent of the points are awarded for effective use of the dictaphone. Obviously, Hunsaker concludes, communicative skills will continue to be slighted as long as almost two-thirds of the credit given in Mock Law Office competition (which like Moot Court is a law school training ground for law practice itself) goes only to accuracy of fact and clarity of logic.

Alan Crouch makes this point in a different way in "Barriers to Understanding in the Legal Situation" (1979), which emphasizes that any working definition that identifies lawyers merely as finders of facts and arguers before the court is too limited to be useful. Because such weight is given to cognitive skills, "the whole caring and attending approach, which is the fore-runner of adequate communication" (p. 505), is largely neglected. Hunsaker, in observing Mock Law Office Competition, was "struck by the lack of sensitivity" on the part of most law students "to the anxieties and emotional concerns" of the persons relating their problems. Both Crouch and Hunsaker perceive a clear relationship between lawyers' communicative skills and their ability to understand the needs and fears of their clients as well as the facts of their cases. The teacher of legal writing soon discovers that many practicing lawyers have received—and will say that they have received—too little training in communicative skills. Many practicing lawyers have never thought of language as "a symbolic means of inducing cooperation in beings that by nature respond to symbols" (Kenneth Burke, *A Rhetoric of Motives* [1950], p. 43), largely because law schools often do not consider use of legal language a discipline in its own right.

The context in which legal writing is taught in law school is described by Wesley Gilmer, Jr., in "Teaching Legal Research" (1973). Citing the common (and valid) idea that writing is perfected in the doing, Gilmer writes that law students should begin with case studies that present legal problems and provide detailed precedent cases that can be used in formulating solutions. The course that ostensibly emphasizes writing soon becomes a course in legal research. Gilmer, typical in his assertion that writing is perfected in the doing, is also typical in his heavy emphasis on case studies and the use of precedent cases as well as on teaching methods for citing the law and using resources such as the *Uniform System of Citation*. Ideally, "one written paper in every course, certainly after the first year, and perhaps even in the first year, should be the goal," but "realistically," he concludes (and in this he speaks for other law professors), such a goal requires too much faculty effort to be attainable. Many law professors, like Gilmer, assert the need for more training in composition but then quickly equate legal writing with legal research and finally subordinate legal writing altogether.

Specialists who have written about subjects that seem closely related to writing in fact spend little time discussing writing. For example, Stephen Jay Schwartz ("Effective Brief-writing for the Michigan Board of Appeals" [1979]) asserts unequivocally, "an attorney who fumbles through an appellate brief reduces the chances of success on appeal. Similarly, one with solid brief-writing skills will have a better chance of winning an appeal" (p. 240). But the article, certainly useful to the writing consultant, emphasizes the technique of selecting issues and the workings of the appellate court as heavily as it emphasizes writing skills. One learns more about appellate court procedure than about how to write briefs.

Richard Wincor carries this process further in *Contracts in Plain Language*

(1976). The book begins with an eloquent description of "the Position-taking Style" that Wincor deems essential to all good contracts:

The Position-taking Style is above all unspontaneous and controlled. It is also courteous, precise, and evasive by turns, wary of commitments but quick in their recognition. It may be thought of as simplified legalese of a low dialect of diplomacy. Its trademark is caution, its *raison d'etre* the potency of words, its usefulness incalculable. The Position-taking Style makes communication into a game of chess (p.xiii).

Furthermore, Wincor insists that "the best way to know English is to read its classics. Contract language comes later. Shakespeare and Milton are better training, and a passage from Jane Austen is worth twenty 'whereas' clauses" (p. 27). With this impressive beginning, the reader might expect a book that explains how to acquire the skill needed to use this valuable style. But *Contracts* does not provide this explanation. After a brief section on legal terms and phrases, Wincor turns to the real topic of his book, contract analysis. He provides a splendid analysis of a set of contract proposals (pp. 45–58) and includes a section that reproduces parallel English, German, and French versions of a single contract (pp. 99–135). Writing consultants working in the area of contract drafting and contract law will find this book a mine of useful examples, sample contracts, and bits of negotiating advice. But they won't find out how to acquire the position-taking style. An experienced contract lawyer or negotiator might, by studying the book's sample contracts and poring over Wincor's commentary, glean some tips on how to achieve a good position-taking style. But the book, after an elaborate bow toward writing, develops into a negotiator's text—and a fine one—not a writing text.

Similarly limited are works like John A. Yogis and Innis M. Christie's *Legal Writing and Research Manual* (1974) designed "primarily for use by first year law students as an aid in legal writing and research" (p. 1). It should be noted that "legal writing and research" are once again equated. Moreover, more space is given to proper citation and footnote form than to legal writing itself. Finally, the largest section—two-thirds of the book—is devoted to a descriptive survey of legal materials available to the researcher. It is small wonder that the first-year law students to whom the *Manual* is directed develop the idea that writing is of minimal importance compared with research methods and analytic skill.

The teacher of legal writing should not think, after reading these pages, that the materials discussed are useless or of poor quality. To the contrary, they are selected for discussion here because they are the best works of their type. The point is that many resources that purport to discuss legal writing in fact discuss legal research, legal bibliography, legal argumentation, legal citation, or legal procedure. These resources are essential reading for anyone who wishes to know the contexts in which law is taught and practiced and the forms that the law requires. They also reveal—by their bulk if in no other way—that legal writing is inadequately defined and thus often poorly taught. The chief contribution that legal writing teachers can make is to identify legal writing as a discipline in its own right and to apply to this discipline the teaching methods developed over the years by composition specialists.

Legal Style and the Plain Language Laws

The subject of legal style has received extensive attention, much of it from practicing attorneys and some from writing specialists, including law professors who have made this one of their areas of professional interest. More recently, debate has centered on the plain language laws enacted by several states and pending in many more. These laws, tied to readability formulas, have been created out of the widespread conviction that legal documents, especially in consumer-oriented areas (for example, credit forms, automobile insurance forms, Social Security guidelines), should be required to be written in "plain English.".

The best brief, general overview of legal style may be found in George D. Gibson's early "Elements of Legal Style" (1967) and his more recent "Effective Legal Writing and Speaking" (1980). In the latter, Gibson criticizes legal writing as "poor, wordy, vague, uncertain" (p. 1) and advocates restraint in the use of language, insisting that "if unnecessary words are eliminated, ideas will prevail" (p. 3). Brevity, "is not only the soul of wit, it is also the source of power." Besides, most people would rather do or think about something else than listen. "Elements of Legal Style" is cast in the form of instructions based on the premise that the reader "is not going to make more of an effort for you than he has to" (p. 547). The article discusses the styles proper to memoranda, letters, contracts, briefs, and arguments—the forms most often employed by the law practitioner.

The best and most complete book-length treatment of the subject is Henry Weihofen's *Legal Writing Style*, first published in 1960 and now available in a new edition (1980). Incisive phrasing and perceptive comment make the book memorable to quote and enjoyable to read as well as useful to assign. Here are some samples of Weihofen's well-written advice:

If the judge reading your brief is impressed merely with how well you write, you have defeated yourself. You want to make him feel that your client has a good case, not merely that he has a good lawyer (p. 5). If a person for whom you are writing cannot understand you, you have not written clearly. The fact that your words would be clear to someone else is irrelevant (p. 66). Just as water cannot rise above its source, so you cannot write more clearly than you think (p. 135). If a cliche is a has been, a platitude never was (p. 120).

Weihofen liberally cites pertinent legal opinions that illustrate good style, and he quotes freely from the works of prose stylists and from books on style by authorities such as Theodore Bernstein and William Strunk and E. B. White.

His book, intended for law students, contains two types of material: information on how to write and revise (Chapters 1–7, 13) and information on how to write specialized legal documents (Chapters 8–12). The material in the second category presupposes legal training or the opportunity to work closely with a law professional; the material in the first category does not.

Since *Legal Writing Style* contains almost no exercises for the student, the instructor must develop such material or else use the book in tandem with a book that contains them, such as John O. White and Norman Brand's *Legal Writing: The Strategy of Persuasion* (discussed below). This aside, the book is an excellent resource for students and for teachers new to legal writing. For a course that addresses law students only, it is indispensable—by far the best book of its kind available.

The best brief books on legal style are Richard C. Wydick's *Plain English for Lawyers* (1979) and Elliott Biskind's *Simplify Legal Writing* (1975). Wydick's *Plain English for Lawyers*, unlike Weihofer's books, contains numerous exercises on editing, subordination, elimination of redundancies, breaking up passages of clumsy jargon, and a host of other topics. A separate chapter presents suggested responses to these exercises and more supplementary exercises.

An appended "Index and Lawyer's Word Guide" is a classification of legal terms and legal-sounding phrases equaled only by the one in David Mellinkoff's *Legal Writing* (1982). Entries like "*Hereinbefore*, a lawyerism" or "*At that point in time*, useless compound construction" or "*It is interesting to point out that*, a throat clearing phrase" help the student or practicing lawyer who possesses the requisite persistence to identify the causes of wordiness and achieve a leaner style. This is Wydick's chief aim: he observes that the development of word processors and electronic research systems, a blessing in many areas, can also be a curse because they increase the power to multiply jargon-laden formulaic redundancies. The professional, he urges, should "keep a card file of slain redundancies" because "such trophies distinguish a lawyer from a scrivener" (p. 20). Wydick's book, in addition to treating briefly issues that Weihofen's treats exhaustively, focuses more on writing and editing as processes, whereas Weihofen emphasizes the products of good writing and editing—clear, graceful statements of even complex thoughts.

Elliot Biskind's *Simplify Legal Writing* (1975), based on his long-standing column in *The New York Law Review*, is, like Wydick's *Plain English*, much respected by lawyers, but the writing teacher must use it with care. A skilled writer will readily see that Biskind's numerous revisions of flawed originals are improvements of those originals, but most students will need to be told how the improvement is achieved. Biskind appears to rely heavily on the assumption that to see a poor original and a better revision side by side is to understand why this revision is better and to be able to produce similar revisions. Although certain sections of the book are more self-contained, the book sorely needs commentary, and it would benefit from clearer organization. Chapters on drafting of contracts and wills and extensive sections drawn from briefs, contracts, and court opinions show that the book is intended for practicing lawyers. Because the book is not a classroom text at all, it is most useful as a reference work for the office or in the in-service setting with groups of law professionals.

Since the coming of plain language legislation, the best overview of which is James T. Plack's "The Plain Language Movements" (1980), readability formulas have gained new currency despite the skepticism with which writing specialists view them. The best study of readability formulas in legal writing is Janice C. Redish's "Readability" (1979), which defines the concept of readability and describes the origin of readability formulas in the textbook publishing field of the 1920s. Redish discusses in particular detail Flesch's Reading Ease Scale, Gunning's Fog Index, and the Dale-Chall readability formula, stressing that all formulas are limited because they have been tested only against one another and because they are based ultimately upon data originally developed for children. This justifiable skepticism is tempered by the pragmatic observation that one positive reason for using formulas is that they afford a ready means of quantifying and thus talking about the features of legal discourse.

Redish also discusses what readability formulas cannot do (for example, serve as a guide for re-writing or evaluate logical sequence or the lack of it). She provides examples of sentences—one clear and the other so convoluted as to be nonsensical—that, nonetheless, measure the same on the Flesch and Gunning scales. Supplementing this discussion of readability formulas and what they can and cannot accomplish is a bibliography of pertinent literature published since Rudolf Flesch's *The Art of Readable Writing* (1949).

Numerous article-length discussions have been published on the plain language movement itself. Many of them have appeared in law reviews and were thus intended for a state-wide readership. As a result, they overlap one another considerably. Several essays on the plain language laws enacted in several states and pending in many more are more generally relevant, however, because they have been published in journals aimed at wider audiences.

In addition to Plack's study just mentioned is John Willis's "Making Legal Documents Readable" (1978), which studies the American movement from the perspective of an outsider. Willis is an Australian law professional disturbed that Australian law on "matters of vital concern" such as social security, marriage and divorce, and taxation, is often too difficult for the ordinary person to understand. Because it discusses and reproduces fully documents such as the Massachusetts automobile insurance forms as they were before plain language laws were enacted and in their revised form, Willis's essay is especially useful in its discussion of the role of formatting, typesetting, and leading in clarifying the law. Valuable for its detachment and thoroughness is Irving Kellogg's "How to: A Plan for Drafting in Plain English" (1981). Like Willis, Kellogg supplies before and after versions of a document that has been re-drafted to improve its readability. Kellogg supports plain language legislation because, he says, a document that a client cannot understand cannot be said to carry out the client's intentions. Kellogg also provides a working bibliography that is useful for anyone interested in drafting consumer credit forms or other types of documents that must be readable to a wide public. Generally, articles that discuss plain language laws provide neither the visuals nor the bibliography provided by Willis and Kellogg, and it is therefore best to consult these two before proceeding to read the rest.

Robert C. Dick's "Plain English in Legal Drafting" (1978) and William C. Prather's "In Defense of the People's Use of Three Syllable Words" (1978) best represent the reasoning of law professionals who oppose plain language legislation. Dick, a Canadian law professional of national standing, worries that, while large corporations like Citibank have adopted simplified legal forms without encountering a rash of litigation caused by the presence of real or imagined loopholes in their contracts, plain English style is "a significant, untested departure from traditional legal draftsmanship" (p. 513). It may, he believes, lead to writing to satisfy readability formulas rather than to the necessary "good substantive analysis" of the problems that any legal drafting presents. Writing plainly is an undoubted good, Dick concludes, but legislating plain style is unfortunate because it forces draftsmen into a mold while not requiring them to address the basic sources of unclear writing: poor analysis of audience and poor conceptualization of issues. Prather defends legal language as it is on the grounds that it is precise (but see Mellinkoff, *Language of the Law* [1963], pp. 291–398, for evidence to the contrary). He suggests that "language simplifiers" are mainly do-gooders seeking re-election or anti-intellectuals who want to banish the French and Latin heritage of the English language. "All English," Prather concludes, "is everyday English" (p. 399).

To the writing specialist it may seem unclear why some law professionals oppose plain language legislation. Prather's reasoning may appear specious. The important thing, however, is that for reasons that are surprisingly compelling, plain language legislation is not universally welcomed even by specialists who admit that the average consumer contract is difficult to interpret. It is important for the writing specialist, who is probably inclined to consider all such legislation good, to understand the formidable objections made against it by the kind of people they may teach.

Ever since the publication of Margaret N. Bryant's *English in the Law Courts* (1930), articles in staggering numbers have been appearing on the various details of style. Bryant's book, in bulk daunting to read yet fascinating to dip into, describes with copious illustration from court proceedings the ways in which "little words" like prepositions have determined the fates of towns, cities, corporations, and individuals engaged in litigation. The best recent discussion of poor writing in legal documents is Kermit L. Dunahoo's "Avoiding Inadvertent Syntactic Ambiguity" (1970). Referring to "three major curable diseases [that] infect language: ambiguity, vagueness, and generality" (p. 139), Dunahoo focuses, with copious examples, on the way in which misused form words, especially conjunctions, can render unclear the meaning of any statement. Her discussion of the legal nemesis, "and/or," should be supplemented by Dwight

G. McCarty's "That Hybrid 'and/or'" (1960) which traces the term from its origins in British maritime law (earliest occurrence: 1855) to the present. This standard article on a syntactic matter that has become a *cause célèbre* for those engaged in legal drafting cites the overwhelmingly negative judicial comments about the use of "and/or" from the turn of the century to the present. In the process it furnishes all the ammunition a legal writing instructor could ever wish for to persuade students who use the term thoughtlessly to avoid using it at all.

Finally, two studies especially useful to the writing teacher that treat legal sentence structure are Gertrude H. Block's "Improving Legal Writing" (1978) and James C. Raymond's "Legal Writing" (1978). Block emphasizes with telling effectiveness a point obvious to most writing specialists but new to most law professionals, that lawyers write legalese because they read so much of it. The essay is a good one with which to begin a legal writing course. Raymond's essay, which focuses on the misuse of periodic sentences, emphasizes that delaying closure for no good reason often produces the very legalese so often decried. Like Reed Dickerson (*Legal Drafting* [1978]), he recommends verbalizing a draft to make the initial writing of it easier, and, like Dwight W. Stevenson ("Writing Effective Opinions" [1975]), he observes that law professionals, because they are not audience-oriented, tend to list facts without indicating which are most vital. The instructor who wishes to use articles on style in a legal writing course will find those by Block and Raymond the best currently available—incisive, readable, and clear even to the beginning law student.

Resources for Teaching Legal Writing

The teacher of legal writing can draw upon four basic types of resources for classroom teaching: overviews of legal writing, studies of specialized writing forms or separate law-related professions, full-length writing textbooks, and descriptions of legal writing programs now in place.

Mary Ellen Gale, in "Legal Writing" (1980), provides an overview of legal writing in relation to other law-related activities. Legal writing courses, she remarks, have been "stigmatized as beaching places for scholars *manques* whose inability to think deeply about anything that matters has relegated them to the shallow waters of training students for the supposed least of the practitioner's arts: the ability to say clearly what he means" (p. 342). What is needed is a new definition of "legal writing," one that transcends the view that it is a subject which, lacking content, consists of drills on spelling and punctuation. Gale's extensive description of the categories of legal writing forms a kind of generalized syllabus for a legal writing course. She is one of a growing number of commentators who insist that analysis, so heavily emphasized in legal curricula, is only one of a substantial number of skills needed by the practicing lawyer.

College Composition and Communication has published a series of articles that treat in a specific manner various aspects of legal writing. Dwight W. Stevenson's "Rhetoric and Law" (1978) complements Gale's general paradigm for legal writing by describing in non-specialist's language the six communication skills that law professionals need most: the abilities to state what the law is, identify legal issues, state the facts of a case, construct arguments that show how those facts are related to principles of law, explain the law to non-specialists, and use effective oral communication and written memoranda. A given case presents a large number of potentially pertinent facts, and hundreds of laws and opinions are already on the books. In order to communicate effectively, law professionals must learn how to select from a mass of available materials the details necessary in a given communication situation. The writing specialist, by teaching the principles of classical rhetoric, can help the law professional acquire this skill in selection of information, Stevenson insists, because "virtually no one in law school today is trained in report writing, business communication, or interpersonal communication" (p. 34).

John O. White and Norman Brand build on Stevenson's useful discussion of the types of writing law professionals do in their "Composition for the Pre-Professional" (1976). This work contains the best brief description available for a university writing course designed to teach students to do the kinds of writing Stevenson describes. They speak reassuringly to new teachers (legal writing "is not so different from any other kind of writing as to confound the potential instructor") and authoritatively about the assumptions that any instructor should make. They assert unequivocally that (1) clear expression is the focus of the course, (2) success in law school depends heavily on writing ability, (3) much legal writing is the application of rules of law to particular situations so that logical conclusions result, (4) law students write mostly memoranda and briefs (these are well defined), and (5) most pre-law students need specific training in the writing of law examination answers.

The writing instructor, White and Brand urge, will find clear understanding of rhetoric more useful than extensive knowledge of law. The authors present sample case studies, some hypothetical and some drawn from law examinations, and they frankly recommend that writing instructors turn to law faculty for materials they can use to construct more case studies.

White and Brand's article, with its blend of assurance, advice about the law, and sample assignments, is especially helpful to the teacher assigned a legal writing course for the first time. Its blend of theory and practice, together with its deftly sketched description of the world pre-law students are about to enter, makes it essential reading for the beginning teacher and good reading for any teacher of legal writing.

Persons seeking information about writing courses for other law-related professions may consult Terence Collins's "Further Notes on Legal Writing" (1980) and Russell Rutter's "Teaching Writing to Probation Officers" (1982). By applying White and Brand's methodology and supplying new case study materials, Collins offers ready-to-use materials and resources for writing courses aimed at paralegal students and paralegal professionals already on the job. Rutter's study, while it describes the kinds of writing probation officers do, is mainly a discussion of the resources available for teaching this kind of writing. Accordingly, it discusses some of the problems encountered in the in-service context and provides bibliographic references to various articles, books, and government publications devoted to writing tasks typically performed by probation and court services personnel.

Dwight W. Stevenson's "Writing Effective Opinions" (1975) treats a specific branch of legal writing (judicial opinion-writing), but, like the articles just discussed, is more accurately seen as a methodology for applying the principles of classical rhetoric to legal writing. Drawing on his work as a writing consultant to the American Academy of Judicial Education, Stevenson observes that most judicial opinions are too long and too filled with notes and legal jargon—and that many judges, though they recognize this problem, do not know how to eliminate it. The problem arises because judges fail to define fully their purpose in writing or the audiences they address. As a result, their opinions, instead of being decision-oriented and tailored to an audience, duplicate their own decision-making process.

Stevenson introduces the pattern of organization developed by the ancient Greeks for persuasive discourse held in the public forum: *exordium*, *narratio*, *divisio*, *confirmatio*, *confutatio*, and *peroratio*. He shows how this pattern can be imposed on a judicial opinion, so that instead of offering a "detailed start-to-finish history of the case," that opinion presents foremost the judge's decision (which interests litigants, attorneys, news media, and the community) and only secondarily and in abbreviated form, if at all, describes the decision-making process (usually of interest only to legal scholars).

Much legal writing involves the generation of specialized agreements which, duly signed and witnessed, become legally binding and, inexpertly written, become sources of litigation or simple bafflement. Because this form of writing, called drafting, demands extreme precision in the use of language, it receives much of the attention given to legal writing. The essential work on this subject is Reed Dickerson's exhaustive and highly specialized *Fundamentals of Legal Drafting* (1965). Those seeking a shorter, less specialized treatment of the subject, particularly of the writing processes used, should consult Reed Dickerson's "Legal Drafting" (1978) and Janice C. Redish's "How to Draft More Understandable Legal Documents" (1979).

Dickerson develops a useful comparison between legal drafting and scientific investigation. The draftsman should begin writing, before research is completed, whenever the information obtained from research becomes unwieldy or difficult to keep in mind, and then renew the research process after a rough draft has been written, just as the scientist "switches from hypothesis to verification to modified hypothesis" (p. 376). It is this constant movement from research to drafting to questioning the draft to renewing the research process that prompts what Dickerson calls talk-back. Dickerson insists on the use of a "severely hierarchic arrangement" or outline, which is not final but rather a means of displaying ideas for the time being so that their relationship can be visualized and the validity of that relationship questioned and tested.

Redish's "How to Draft" (1979) focuses on specific steps that can be taken to improve a drafted document. This work complements nicely Dickerson's more theoretical article (and, of course, his text) on drafting methodology in general. Redish bases her article on seven assertions about legal drafting (for example, much legal writing is unintelligible even to lawyers, or legal language can be made clear without loss of necessary precision). Redish's assertions are in themselves useful to the writing specialist because they constitute an expert's testimony about the language of drafting and obviate the need of any such testimony on the part of the writing teacher, who in most cases is not a law professional.

Redish defines drafting as "a *process* that starts with figuring out *what* you need to say, *why* you are writing it, *whom* you are writing for" (p. 128). The talk-back process recommended by Dickerson is intended to answer just the kinds of questions Redish poses in her definition. Her own study emphasizes stylistic devices and formatting. She cites ten qualities for better drafting (for example, cross out unnecessary words or break up long sentences), fully illustrating each with "before and after examples" that in themselves are useful to the instructor. Another nice touch is her illustration of poor formatting: she includes an eye-splitting section of 4-point type from a bond, and she (like Willis, above) reproduces an automobile insurance policy form used at one time by the state of Massachusetts, comparing it to the present, attractively laid out, clearly written form.

George D. Gopen describes in "A Composition Course for Pre-Law Students" (1978) an approach to course planning that complements that of White and Brand. Gopen relies less on presentation of case studies, however, and more on what one might term working principles for a pre-law writing course. Although writing is so important that law schools might properly make composition courses that emphasize logic and rhetoric prerequisites to admission, the fact is that most undergraduates believe that courses in legal history or political science will help them more. Gopen thus believes that the major goal of a writing course for pre-law students is to banish their general tendency to belittle the power of words and teach them the subtlety of language and the complexity of supposedly simple issues.

Gopen both defines course goals (for example, ability to articulate the steps in a logical argument or appreciation for "the shaping powers of words") and offers a set of assignments that focus on definition, translation, consistency, complexity and rule-making, arguing both sides of a case. Gopen's article is stimulating in its assertion that the student must be taught to appreciate the enormous power of words and the care needed to use them properly. His observations are often trenchant and witty (for example, "pre-law" is more a state of mind than a curriculum). For these very reasons, however, his article is suited more to the experienced teacher of professional writing than to the beginner.

The advice it offers and the resources it contains are more easily worked by experienced teachers into existing courses than used by new teachers as a recipe for getting started.

Gopen is also the author of the most comprehensive textbook in the field, *Writing from a Legal Perspective* (1981). The book emphasizes a limited number of concepts extremely well. Some of them are identified in the article discussed above. Unlike several other texts, it contains *both* copious examples *and* guided exercises for the student. Without presupposing that the instructor is a lawyer (Gopen himself holds doctorates in English and law), it offers an excellent blend of precepts, examples, and other exercises.

Gopen's text contains chapters on the history of legal language (brief but excellent), weak verbs and how to eliminate them, words and contexts, legal definition, briefs and memoranda, working with facts and inferences, translating the law for non-specialists, and persuasion. Several special facets of the book merit more extensive description. Gopen offers a complete system for determining how much of one's intended meaning reaches the page. This system, idiosyncratic and frankly a device, forces students to consider how language works and how meaning develops from it, and it is the best model of its type available. Also superior is the sequence of models and exercises intended to sharpen the student's power of definition. Gopen further includes extensive transcripts of interviews and courtroom dialogue from which the student is asked to extract items of fact and items of inference. Gopen's obvious interest in the way meaning occurs—in semantics— is nowhere more evident than in the extensive treatment of the way fact and inference tend to become confused with each other in the mind of the law student. No student who reads Gopen's discussion and is led through the fine exercises he provides can leave a legal writing class complacent about "mere" words. When legal language is the topic of consideration, it is readily observable that some books focus more on "legal" than on "language," and vice versa. Of all the teaching texts available, Gopen's book emphasizes most heavily the language component. This emphasis makes it at once accessible to the writing teacher who is not a law professional and valuable, perhaps more than any other text, to students who will one day practice law: as Gopen says in "A Composition Course" (above), "Without the control of words, the lawyer can neither control nor articulate his thoughts" (p. 223).

Norman Brand and John O. White's *Legal Writing* (1976), like Gopen's text, emphasizes that "the goal of a legal-writing class is simply clarity of expression" (p.ix). The book contains chapters on the principles of persuasion, strategies for legal persuasion, techniques of legal writing, mechanics, style, and logic and argumentation. More than Gopen's book, Brand and White's book is a standard composition text that uses legal materials. Like most standard composition texts it gives more peripheral attention to subjects like semantics, the nature of evidence, and the development of the English language (and, within it, legal language).

The book has several major strengths. It contains, for one thing, case studies on such legal matters as criminal trespass, traffic accident liability, and division of assets and liabilities after divorce. These case studies, found in the body of the text, are supplemented by a 40-page appendix that contains three more case studies, sample responses, and analyses of these sample responses. Throughout the book, in addition to case studies, are extended examples and numerous writing assignments. Because up to half of any given chapter is comprised of assignments, sample briefs, case studies requiring student responses, and miscellaneous other materials, the book is almost a combination writing text and reader—again like several standard composition texts now being marketed.

Much of the advice given on style, mechanics, logic, and persuasion is standard. This is not a bad thing, but readers of the book will notice, many with approval, that in its approach to these matters it resembles books like James M. McCrimmon's *Writing with a Purpose* (1980), a text usually used in freshman composition. The books by Gopen, Weihofen, and Mellinkoff—to name just a few—are more detailed, more advanced, and more interestingly written. Moreover, they treat the topics (like semantics) remarked on only tangentially by Brand and White. Both Gopen and Mellinkoff are clearly more intent on discussing the ways language can be used to create or obscure meaning, and they are thus more theoretical. (One is tempted to say more daring and innovative and less conservative and less intent on teaching legal correctness.) This may mean that Brand and White's text is better for less advanced students or that it will appeal to teachers unconvinced that teaching students how language creates meaning bears a necessary relationship to teaching them to produce finished briefs and arguments.

David Mellinkoff's *The Language of the Law* (1963), published 20 years ago, is the most frequently cited book on the origin, growth, nature, and limitations of legal language. Although it is an indispensable book for the teacher of legal writing, it is not a legal writing text. After a long hiatus, however, Mellinkoff has translated the scholarship of *The Language of the Law* into a writing book, *Legal Writing* (1982). The plan of this extraordinary book calls for comment. Seven chapters that constitute the first of its two parts have titles that are one-word rules: peculiar, precise, English, clear, law, plan, cut! For example, Chapter 1 is called "Rule 1. Peculiar." This is expanded into an epigraph: "The language of the law is more peculiar than precise. Don't confuse peculiarity with precision." The epigraph is expanded to a sentence: "Precision is sometimes peculiarly expressed, but don't be taken in by the peculiar expression of nonsense." At this point sub-division 1.1 ("Point 1. Precision rare") occurs. These points are divided and re-divided so that 1.1.a.1, "Ordinary Old and Middle English Words," is a sub-division of 1.1.a, "Junk critiques of legal vocabulary." This plan, while obviously cumbersome to explain, is remarkably easy to follow and makes the book a delight to consult, a manual full of information on language and composition and written with a clarity and verve rarely encountered in manuals. Moreover, the typesetting, which, as with any manual, could have obscured the work's plan, is intelligently varied, and the sections are liberally cross-referenced. An excellent format combined with plentiful examples and lucid, witty writing yields a valuable book.

Following the seven chapters that constitute the first part of the book is "Part 2. Blunders and Cures," which Mellinkoff calls "a series of practical demonstrations of how to go about analyzing and rewriting your own or someone else's legal writing" (p. 145). This section emphasizes the analysis of writing, which Mellinkoff sees as a process of creating a rationale for revising rather than revising to imitate slavishly a model. One of the most attractive features of the book is that it insists on explaining why a given revision is superior to its original when other books rely more on presenting models to be emulated, and then compel the student to execute a revision using the models provided.

The numerous appendices list Old English and Middle English words, abused formalisms, law Latin and law French terms, legal argot, legal terms of art and their definitions, and the texts (with commentary) of plain language laws.

Mellinkoff's *Legal Writing* is a good textbook; it is far less stodgy than the average. It is arranged like a manual, but its pungent rhetoric, which mixes the formal and the colloquial, makes it more hard-hitting, less bland, than any manual could be. Some samples from it may suggest the flavor of the book:

> The essence of the shell game is that the pea, obviously under this shell, isn't. It is played out on a dozen fronts in legal writing (p. 112).
>
> Most legal writing isn't written for anybody or all. Most legal writing is written to get it written. There. I've done it (p. 65).
>
> Do not use one word to convey more than one of your meanings (A = gawk; and A = squawk). And do not use more than one word to convey your same meaning (A = gawk; and B = gawk). Context affects these efforts, but you can affect context (p. 20).
>
> For centuries there was little or no guidance to a modern English grammar. The lawyers got along without it, and many of them have been getting along without it ever since (p. 45).

Mellinkoff does not define an audience for the book. Its repeated reference to arguing cases, writing memoranda, and drafting contracts may suggest that it addresses law students or lawyers. But the appendices, the definitions of elementary legal terms, and the occasional descriptions of what law school is like make it clear that the book is meant not just for law professionals but for anyone interested in the language of the law. The book is easy to read or dip into for reference. It presents clearly a large body of information, demonstrating the truth of its thesis, that legal writing, if it is good, is clear writing. Mellinkoff, perhaps acting on the legal commonplace that a good lawyer is a good wordsmith, combines concern with the correct style and insistence on treating the philosophic question of how language conveys meaning. The product is the best legal writing reference manual now available. What is true of other innovative and daring books is true of this one: it appeals at once to the lover of language, but many instructors, knowing that not all students *are* lovers of language, may at least consider using a "safer" text like Gopen's or Brand and White's. Still, no student should leave a legal writing course without some acquaintance with this stimulating book.

A final resource for the legal writing teacher is the corpus of published studies on legal writing programs in various law schools. The quarterly *Journal of Legal Education* includes such studies regularly. Two informative studies are Margit Livingston's "Legal Writing and Research at DePaul" (1980) and Lynn B. Squires's "A Writing Specialist in the Legal Research and Writing Curriculum" (1980). Squires holds a doctorate in English and has academic rank in the University of Washington School of Law. Her thesis that "a writing specialist without formal legal training is potentially more useful to a law school than one with it" (p. 419) is demonstrated by her account of the ways in which she has been able to assist law students admitted to the Basic Legal Skills program, designed for promising students with deficiencies in writing. In addition to providing information on use of conference and tutorial methods of teaching legal writing, Squires also supplies a bibliography of law books and articles that she found helpful in adapting her skills in composition pedagogy to the law school setting.

Resources for teaching legal writing are plentiful, but a survey of the available material indicates at once how slowly recent research in composition has been adapted to create better ways of teaching law professionals to write clearly. Promising developments, such as the Symposium on Teaching Legal Writing (see *Albany L Rev*, 44 [1980]), suggest that some are starting to use this research, but articles like Stevenson's and books like Mellinkoff's are still too rare. A need exists for systematic study of legal discourse, study oriented not toward substantive law on one hand or emulation of models on the other. The results of that study need to be translated into writing courses, in school or in service, that are not also freighted with legal research, legal bibliography, legal citation, and legal format.

References

American Association of Law Libraries. *Current Publications in Legal and Related Fields*. 30 vols. Littleton, Colo.: Rothman, 1953–.

Bernstein, Theodore M. *The Careful Writer: A Modern Guide to English Usage*. New York: Atheneum, 1965.

Biskind, Elliot L. *Legal Writing Simplified* . New York: Boardman, 1971.

————. *Simplify Legal Writing*. New York: Arco, 1975.

Block, Gertrude H. "Improving Legal Writing." *Fla B J*, 52 (1978), 778–82.

Brand, Norman. "Legal Writing, Reasoning, and Research: An Introduction." *Albany L Rev*, 44 (1980), 292–97.

————, and John O. White. *Legal Writing: The Strategy of Persuasion*. New York: St. Martin's, 1976.

Bridge, William J. "Legal Writing After the First Year of Law School." *Ohio North L Rev*, 5 (1978), 411–31.

Bryant, Margaret N. *English in the Law Courts, the Part that Articles, Prepositions, and Conjunctions Play in Legal Decisions*. 1930; rpt. New York: Ungar, 1962.

Burke, Kenneth. *A Rhetoric of Motives*. New York: Prentice-Hall, 1950.

Cohen, Morris, gen. ed. *How to Find the Law*. 7th ed. St. Paul, Minn.: West, 1976.

Collins, Terence. "Further Notes on Legal Writing: Designing the Course for Legal Paraprofessionals." *CCC*, 31 (1980), 58–62.

Crouch, Alan. "Barriers to Understanding in the Legal Situation." *L Inst J*, 53 (1979), 505–508.

Dick, Robert C. "Plain English in Legal Drafting." *Alberta L Rev*, 18 (1980), 509–14.

Dickerson, Reed. *Fundamentals of Legal Drafting*. St. Paul, Minn.: West, 1965.

————. "Legal Drafting: Writing as Thinking, or, Talk-Back from your Draft and How to Exploit It." *J Legal Educ*, 29 (1978), 373–79.

————. "Teaching Legal Writing in the Law Schools (with a Special Nod to Legal Drafting)." *Idaho L Rev*, 16 (1979) 85–91.

Driedger, E. A. "Are Statutes Written for Men Only?" *McGill L J*, 22 (1976), 666–72.

Dunahoo, Kermit L. "Avoiding Inadvertent Syntactic Ambiguity." *Drake L Rev*, 20 (1970), 137–58.

Flesch, Rudolf. *The Art of Readable Writing*. New York: Harper, 1949.

————. *How to Write Plain English: A Book for Lawyers and Consumers*. New York: Harper, 1979.

Gale, Mary Ellen. "Legal Writing: The Impossible Take a Little Longer." *Albany L Rev*, 44 (1980), 298–343.

Gibson, George D. "Effective Legal Writing and Speaking." *Bus Law*, 36 (1980), 1–9.

————. "Elements of Legal Style." *Bus Law*, 22 (1967), 547–55.

Gilmer, Wesley, Jr. "Teaching Legal Research and Legal Writing in American Law Schools." *J Legal Educ*, 25 (1973), 571–81.

Gopen, George D. "A Composition Course for Pre-Law Students." *J Legal Educ*, 29 (1978), 222–31.

————. *Writing from a Legal Perspective* . St. Paul, Minn.: West, 1981.

Gottlieb, Hans J. "Teaching English in a Law School." *ABA J*, 49 (1963), 666–69.

Gross, Peter W. "California Western Law School's First-Year Course in Legal Skills." *Albany L Rev*, 44 (1980), 369–91.

————. "On Law School Training in Analytic Skill." *J Legal Educ*, 25 (1973), 261–311.

Hunsaker, David M. "Law, Humanism and Communication: Suggestions for Limited Curricular Reform." *J Legal Educ*, 30 (1980), 417–36.

Index to Legal Periodicals. 21 vols. New York: Wilson, 1925–.

Kellogg, Irving. "How to: A Plan for Drafting in Plain English." *Calif S B J*, 56 (1981), 154–59.

Livingston, Margit. "Legal Writing and Research at De Paul University: A Program in Transition." *Albany L Rev*, 44 (1980), 344–68.

McCarty, Dwight G. "That Hybrid 'and/or.' " *Mich S B J*, 39 (1960), 9–17.

McCrimmon, James M. *Writing With a Purpose*. 7th ed. Boston: Houghton Mifflin, 1980.

Mellinkoff, David. *The Language of the Law*. Boston: Little, Brown, 1963.

————. *Legal Writing: Sense and Nonsense*. New York: Scribner's, 1982.

Nafziger, James A.R. "Teaching Legal Writing in the United States." *Mon L Rev*, 7 (1980), 67–76.

Plack, James T. "The Plain Language Movement: An Overview with Recent Developments." *Mo B J*, 36 (1980), 40–47.

Prather, William C. "In Defense of the People's Use of Three Syllable Words." *Ala Law*, 39 (1978), 394–400.

Prosser, William L. "English as She Is Wrote." *Engl J*, 28 (1939), 38–45.

Raymond, James C. "Legal Writing: An Obstruction to Justice." *Ala L Rev*, 30 (1978), 1–17.

Redish, Janice C. "How to Draft More Understandable Legal Documents." *Drafting Documents in Plain English*. New York: Practising Law Institute, 1979, pp. 121–56.

————. "Readability." *Drafting Documents in Plain English*. New York: Practising Law Institute, 1979, pp. 157–74.

Ritchie, Marguerite E. "Alice Through the Statutes." *McGill L J*, 21 (1975), 685–707.

————. "The Language of Oppression—Alice Talks Back." *McGill L J*, 23 (1977), 535–44.

Rombauer, Marjorie Dick. "First-Year Legal Research and Writing: Then and Now." *J Legal Educ*, 25 (1973), 538–52.

————. *Legal Problem Solving*. 3rd ed. St. Paul, Minn.: West, 1978.

Rutter, Russell. "Teaching Writing to Probation Officers: Methods, Problems, and Resources." *CCC*, 33 (1982), 288–95.

Schlesinger, Edward S. "English As a Second Language for Lawyers." *1978 Institute on Estate Planning*. N.p., n.d. Chapter 7. Para. 700–16.

Schwartz, Stephen Jay. "Effective Briefwriting for the Michigan Court of Appeals." *Mich B J*, 58 (1979), 240–44.

Squires, Lynn B. "A Writing Specialist in the Legal Research and Writing Curriculum." *Albany L Rev*, 44 (1980), 412–20.

Statsky, William P., and R. John Wernet, Jr. *Case Analysis and Fundamentals of Legal Writing*. St. Paul, Minn.: West, 1977.

Stevenson, Dwight W. "Rhetoric and Law: Designing a Program in Communication for Law Students." *CCC*, 29 (1978), 30–35.

————. "Writing Effective Opinions." *Judicature*, 59, No. 3 (Oct. 1975), 134–39.

Strunk, William, Jr. *The Elements of Style*. Rev. E. B. White. 3rd ed. New York: Macmillan, 1979.

Thurman, Ruth Fleet. "Blueprint for a Legal Research and Writing Course." *J Legal Educ*, 31 (1981), 134–39.

Weihofen, Henry. *Legal Writing Style*. 2nd ed. St. Paul, Minn.: West, 1980.

White, John O., and Norman Brand. "Composition for the Pre-Professional: Focus on Legal Writing." *CCC*, 27 (1976), 41–46.

————. *Legal Writing: The Strategy of Persuasion*. New York: St. Martins, 1976.

Willis, John. "Making Legal Documents Readable: Some American Initiatives." *L Inst J*, 52 (1978), 513–22.

Wincor, Richard. *Contracts in Plain English*. New York: McGraw-Hill, 1976.

Word, Thomas S., Jr. "A Brief for Plain English Wills and Trusts." *U Richmond L Rev*, 14 (1980), 471–81.

Wydick, Richard C. *Plain English for Lawyers*. Durham, N.C.: Carolina Academic Press, 1979.

Yogis, John A., and Innis M. Christie. *Legal Writing and Research Manual*. 2nd ed. Toronto: Butterworths, 1974.

Writing for the Government

ROBERT SCOTT KELLNER

There are two ways a person can become involved in writing for the government: as someone working for the government who writes for both other government workers and the general public; or as a business person or individual writing to obtain something from the government. In both cases, numerous books, pamphlets, and articles describe—and in many instances prescribe—the proper and approved methods of writing.

Most people who write for the government are not government specialists. Defining these writers in terms of job function, as we can do of medical and legal writers, for example, is not possible. Writing for the government touches upon almost every field. This is true not only for business people trying to obtain government contracts or grants, but also for government-employed writers. The civil service now lists twenty-one mid-level occupational codes for technical writers, covering such diverse fields as agriculture, the fine arts, and military history. Robert Scott Kellner's article "Preparing Technical Writing Students to Write for the Government" (1980) points out that one out of every eight technical writers finds work in the civil service. As we might expect, many of the government agencies employing these writers produce their own standards and style of manuals to achieve correctness and a degree of uniformity in their written communication. The waste and duplication that we associate with our government bureaucracies are never more evident than in this instance.

We do not yet have a comprehensive bibliography of the countless guidelines for writing for the government. Bibliographers have been more interested in the finished product of government writers. An early attempt to list government publications is Benjamin Poore's *A Descriptive Catalog of the General Publications of the United States, September 5, 1774-March 4, 1881* (1885) which runs over 1,300 pages. William Buchanan and Edna Kanely's voluminous *Cumulative Subject Index to the Monthly Catalog of U.S. Government Publications, 1900-1971* (1973), an alphabetical listing of more than one million publications, and John L. Andriot's *Guide to U.S. Government Serials and Periodicals* (1962–), take up where Poore leaves off. There are also Ellen Jackson's *Subject Guide to Major United States Government Publications* (1968) and Linda C. Pohle's *A Guide to Popular Government Publications* (1972). Pohle's table of contents, in which almost 100 topics are listed, reveals the government writers' far-ranging interests.

According to the *Monthly Catalog of United States Government Publications*, published by the Superintendent of Documents since 1895, thousands of pamphlets are currently available to the general public, many of them free of charge. The *Monthly Catalog* is supplemented by a bi-weekly annotated list of selected government publications. The distribution center in Pueblo, Colorado, known to many through its television commercials, responds to as many as 25,000 requests for publications weekly. This impressive figure is relatively small when we consider the yearly production of the Government Printing Office (GPO). The 6,200 employees of the GPO, the world's largest printing plant, produce as many as 75 million copies of printed matter in a single year. Robert E. King, Jr., documents the history of the GPO in *The Government Printing Office* (1970). The GPO itself produced a similar book, *100 GPO Years, 1861–1961* (1961).

An indispensable aid in finding one's way through literally the mountains of government publications is Joe Morehead's *Introduction to United States Public Documents* (1978). Intended for librarians, it presents one of the clearest pictures possible of the GPO and of government writing. A useful supplemental text is Laurence F. Schmeckebier and Roy B. Eastin's *Government Publications and Their Use* (1970).

On the state and local levels, the Library of Congress produces a *Monthly Checklist of State Publications* (1910–), which is the best and easiest reference for the major publications of the 50 states. Also helpful in this category is *The Dynamics of Information Flow* (1968).

This article focuses on those publications that describe the requirements for writing for the government. Many of these publications appear for the first time in such a bibliography. A general ordering of the material produces two major categories: Style Guides, which includes publications about format techniques; and Specifications and Standards. Because most of the material cited is not readily obtainable in either bookstores or libraries, a concluding section, Obtaining Government Publications, is included in this essay.

Style Guides

If any one book can take credit as a major unifying force for the staggering output of the government agencies, it is the *U.S. Government Printing Office Style Manual* (1973). This manual was reprinted in 1979 and is currently undergoing another printing. The long-awaited revision of this book is scheduled for late 1983 or early 1984. The 190-page supplement to the *Style Manual, Word Division* (1976), is in its seventh edition.

Issued by the Public Printer under the authority of an act of Congress, the GPO *Style Manual* standardizes the form and style of government printing. While the manual contains elements helpful to authors and editors, it is primarily a printer's stylebook. Contrary to our expectations of a style manual, this one does not have many explanations of grammatical rules. There are helpful sections on capitalization, spelling, punctuation, and compounding, but they are limited in scope. Over half of the book is devoted to formats for the *Congressional Record* and Senate and House journals, and tabular and leader work. In addition, there is a lengthy, 100-page section on foreign languages: eighteen allied countries as well as the Slavic languages and their alphabets. For detailed information on grammatical usage and general formats, the *Style Manual* directs its readers to the *Macmillan Handbook of English* and the University of Chicago's *A Manual of Style*.

Throughout the federal government, the individual agencies have used the GPO *Style Manual* as a precedent for creating their own. The proliferation of style guides and handbooks about writing techniques reflects more than just a lack of communication between government agencies. As Joe Morehead states in his *Introduction to United States Public Documents* (1978), "Governments must be seen to exist. They publish numerous records of their activities as a way of establishing and validating their existence" (p. xxiii). Under this premise, it would be institutional suicide for one agency to use another's style guide. So we discover the National Archives and Records Services of the General Services Administration (GSA) distributing to their employees *Plain Letters* and *Form Letters* (1979), while the U.S. Civil Service Commission distributes *Letterwriting for Secretaries* (1973), *How to Write Position Descriptions* (1975), and *Writing Effective Letters* (1977). This last-named work is perhaps the most refreshing of their style manuals. In the section labeled "Write for Your Reader," we find this quote by Sir Ernest Gowers:

Get into his skin and adapt the atmosphere of your letter to suit that of his. If he is troubled, be sympathetic. If he is rude, be specially courteous. If he is muddle-headed, be specially lucid. If he is pig-headed, be patient. If he is helpful, be appreciative. If he convicts you of a mistake, acknowledge it freely and even with gratitude. But never let a flavour of the patronising creep in. (p. 9)

This sound advice, if followed, would soon endear our government bureaucrats to us.

Although the GPO *Style Manual* should suffice as a primary source for all government agencies, it cannot address all specific cases. Therefore, some of the individual agencies (there are more than 500 in the federal government) are justified in preparing style guides for their own needs. One of the most notable is the *Handbook for Preparing Office of Research and Development Reports* (1976) which is compiled by the Technical Information Staff of the Office of Research and Development in Cincinnati, Ohio. Besides the typical information presented in such manuals, this one offers advice on copyright laws, metric units of measure, proper use of fold-ins and dividers, and the preparation of forms pertaining to the Environmental Protection Agency. To avoid any misinterpretation, two-thirds of the pages in the *Handbook* have illustrations that clarify the text.

The General Accounting Office (GAO) has style guides for its many writers. The GAO was established in 1921 to oversee the expenditures of Congress and the executive branch. It produces hundreds of reports each year. (The Government Printing Office produces a monthly list of GAO reports.) To ensure uniformity of format and style, the GAO publishes the quarterly *GAO Review*. Two typical articles are Lowell Mininger's "A Commonsense Approach to Writing Reports" (1978) and David M. Rosen's "Communicating Effectively Through GAO Reports" (1978). More recently, H. Rosalind Cowie in "Training at GAO" (1981) discusses the GAO's writing program: "The Writing Program creatively adapts current college techniques for teaching writing to GAO's unique requirements for report writing. The program has given the agency a common language for discussing writing problems and has helped to standardize report writing practices" (p. 28). Typical of the government's predilection for acronyms, the General Accounting Office has adopted POWER as its slogan: Producing Organized Writing and Effective Reviewing.

The General Accounting Office is also responsible for Floyd L. Bergman's *From Audit to Editing* (1976), a handbook designed to combat the rise of gobbledygook in government reports. This book was originally conceived to assist GAO auditors in report writing, but it is useful for anyone in government or private industry who needs to improve memo and report writing.

The Superintendent of Documents at the Government Printing Office is quite receptive to manuscripts dealing with writing problems and techniques. The GPO's publications range from the general to the specific, from short pamphlets to full-length studies. For example, *Clarity in Technical Reporting* (1977) is 25 pages long, while the more specific *Effective Revenue Writing* (1976) has 268 pages. The first volume of this two-volume series is a basic course designed to give a practical review of writing principles. The companion volume, Number 2 (1978), is a 198-page advanced course to help experienced writers and reviewers diagnose and cure writing problems.

Other Government Printing Office publications include *Getting Your Ideas Across Through Writing* (1973), *Writing Words That Work* (1978), *Levels of Edit* (1980), and *Gobbledygook Has Gotta Go* (1978). Interest in omitting gobbledygook extends beyond the doors of the GPO. H. Lee Shimberg carries the baton for clear language in his article "Clarifying Federal Regulations by Using Plain English" (1980).

Until their most recent reprinting, the Government Printing Office provided information about employment in the field of writing. *Communications Related Occupations* (1978) gave the employment outlook for advertising workers, interpreters, newspaper reporters, public relations workers, technical writers, and occupations in radio and television broadcasting. *Printing and Publishing Occupations* (1978) also covered the field of technical writing as well as employment opportunities for printers. *Exploring Writing Careers* (1976), still in print but sorely in need of revision, is a student guidebook that provides information about qualifications, duties, and responsibilities, and also gives direct advice from working professionals.

The military services are vitally interested in clarity and uniformity in written communication. If quantity of material were considered as a criterion, the U.S. Air Force could probably claim the greatest interest in clear communication. A sampling of their more important publications includes *United States Air Force Effective Writing Course* (1980), which contains the written exercises for an Air Force course in plain language, *Writing Improvement* (1978), *Glossary of Standardized Terms* (1961), and *Preparing Correspondence* (1981). The Air University at Maxwell Air Force Base in Alabama publishes several manuals for its writing courses. The best known is Lt. Col. H. A. Staley's *Tongue and Quill* (1977). The Air University also publishes *Effective Writing* (1974), which is Volume IV in its *Communication Techniques* series. Other Air Force units separately produce their own style guides, such as *Report Writing Guide* (1958) published by the U.S. Air Force Engineering Development Center at Tullahoma, Tennessee.

The U.S. Navy is equally concerned about good writing but more centralized in its dissemination of information. It relies primarily on the hefty *Navy Comptroller Manual*, Vols. 1–7 (1975), and the *Correspondence Manual* (1972). The *Correspondence Manual* has detailed the proper procedures for preparing correspondence in the U.S. Navy for decades. Despite its singular focus on Navy examples, this manual is so complete and detailed that it could serve as a general guide for all the armed forces. Its sections on letter writing are particularly valuable.

The Department of the Army has its own manual, *Office Management Preparing Correspondence* (1972). There is also Richard P. Kern and colleagues' *Guidebook for the Development of Army Training Literature* (1976). The Marine Corps, as a branch of the Navy, relies on naval publications.

The above publications represent the "how-to" end of military writing. The actual writing for the armed forces goes far beyond these few texts. Richard M. Davis in "Technical Writing in Industry and Government" (1977) points out that writing for the government involves enormous resources in terms of words, time, and money. Using the F-15 fighter aircraft as an example, Davis informs us that the government's Request For a Proposal contained 10,000 pages, and that the proposals received from industry in response to the RFP averaged 40,000 pages. Davis quotes William G. Muller's "Useability Research in the Navy" from *Reading and Readability Research in the Armed Forces* (1976) to inform us that the Naval Air Systems Command supplies technical manuals for over 100 airplane models. The Naval Air Systems Command has an active inventory of 25,000 manuals with a total page count of approximately 3 million.

Since a separate and comprehensive bibliography of proposal writing appears elsewhere in this text, it will not be duplicated here. One of the leading authorities on proposal writing for government grants and contracts is Herman Holtz who, with Terry Schmidt, recently wrote *The Winning Proposal* (1981). Holtz also authored *Government Contracts* (1979). Other writers who focus on obtaining government grants are William Hill, *A Comprehensive Guide to Successful Grantsmanship* (1971), and Donald Orlich and Patricia Orlich, *The Art of Writing Successful R&D Proposals* (1978). An important article is Robert D. Dycus's "The Effect of Proposal Appearance on the Technical Evaluation Scoring of Government Proposals" (1977). This article helps to dispel the notion that the most elaborate proposals exert the greatest influence. Although evaluators are initially impressed by the appearance of proposals, their ultimate judgments, according to Dycus's study, are based solely on the content. The Society for Technical Communication has compiled 16 essays, previously published by the Society, that discuss procedures and guidelines for proposals. This book is entitled *Proposals and Their Preparation* (1975).

Up to this point we have considered mainly those publications written by government employees or produced by government presses. Advice on style and formats is abundant as well from non-government employees who seek to enlighten the business community about acceptable and successful approaches in writing for the government. Two general texts are Michael L. Murdock's *Effective Writing for Business and Government* (1978) and Judson Monroe's *Effective Research and Report Writing in Government* (1980). Monroe's book is by far more original, moving beyond the content of the typical style guide. For example, we find in Monroe a chapter on "Politics and Government Reports," and another entitled "Staffing and Quality Control in Research." Less commendatory is Monroe's choice of examples in some of his chapters. Like too many writers, Monroe does not always match his examples to the purpose of the text. For example, in Chapter Five, "Analyzing the Audience for the Report," instead of using a government report as an example, Monroe uses a narrative about someone buying blue jeans in a downtown department store and reporting on the purchase to a friend. Murdock is more careful to relate his examples to situations in business and government.

An older but still useful text is edited by B. H. Weil, *The Technical Report* (1954). Most pertinent in this book are Chapters Two and Thirteen, "The Technical Report in Government," by Lawson M. McKenzie, and "Security and Other Aspects of the Distribution of Governmental Technical Reports," by R. S. Bray.

Another helpful book is *Handbook of Technical Writing Practices*, Volumes 1 and 2 (1971), edited by Stello Jordan with Joseph Kleinman and H. Lee Shimberg. Volume 1 covers the production of various documents and publications, such as instruction handbooks, parts catalogs, reports, and proposals. Volume 2 is concerned with the activities and services that support the technical writing function, such as illustrating, editing, and data processing. It also contains chapters on the management of technical writing departments and on the production of guides and references used in technical communication: style manuals, data sources and uses, and so on. One other useful text is David Ewing's *Writing for Results in Business, Government, and the Professions* (1974).

Specifications and Standards

Specifications and standards are produced by individual businesses, professional associations, and government agencies. Their purpose is to establish and maintain engineering and technical standards. The federal government produces two types of specifications and standards: federal and military. Because the military standards are by far the most critical, many agencies outside of the Department of Defense require their suppliers to follow the military standards. Charles W. Strong and Donald Eidson in *A Technical Writer's Handbook* (1971) devote an entire chapter to formats for government publications. They go into particular detail about the preparation of military and commercial specifications and the format and style for technical manuals. The most authoritative source, however, for preparing standards and specifications is the Department of Defense. Their military standard MIL-STD-490 (1968) is a 76-page document that sets forth in detail the requirements for preparing specifications for the government. Military standard MIL-STD-962 (1975) is an outline of forms and instructions for the preparation of military standards and military handbooks.

There are well over 50,000 government specifications and standards. Those important to technical writers are listed in *List of Specifications and Standards Pertaining to Technical Publications* (1976). The *List* was compiled by the Manual Specification Review Committee of the Society for Technical Communication under the chairmanship of Joseph M. Kleinman and includes standards important to industry as well as government. The list is updated in the Society's journal, *Technical Communication*, under the department "Status of Technical Manual Specifications and Standards," edited by Joseph M. Kleinman.

Anyone involved in writing for the government should be familiar with at least military specification MIL-M-38784A (1978) and military standard MIL-STD-847A (1974). Each of these has been updated by amendments that are provided with the original documents. The specification MIL-M-38784A gives the general style and format requirements for technical manuals. It is a comprehensive specification that covers all the aspects of manual preparation, both format and text. A company selling equipment to the armed forces or to other government agencies that use Department of Defense standards should prepare technical manuals as prescribed by MIL-M-38784A. Some government agencies, even within the Department of Defense, have as their main criterion for accepting technical manuals the accessibility of the information: the organization of content and the clarity of writing. These agencies will accept manuals that deviate from MIL-M-38784A. But other agencies insist on exactness as outlined in the government specification.

Besides MIL-M-38784A, there are other specifications for the production of technical manuals. Military specification MIL-M-7298B (1969) gives the minimum requirements for acceptable commercial manuals. An important section to note is 3.1, which states that acceptance of a manual will not be based on content alone but also on the convenience of using the manual. In this regard, such things as type size and page size are important. This specification goes into detail about such requirements.

The various service branches within the Department of Defense want manuals produced according to their specific needs. For example, the Bureau of Naval Weapons in the Department of the Navy refers to military specification MIL-M-81273A (1966), which covers the preparation of manuals for ordnance and support equipment (except in the case of avionics manuals). Where there is any question about proper procedure for any of the services, the military handbook MIL-HDBK-63038-1(TM) (1977) is designed to supplement the various and sometimes conflicting specifications.

A fascinating, although outdated, account of the production of technical manuals for the military is found in the *Proceeding of the 1959 Institute in Technical and Industrial Communications* (1960), edited by Herman M. Weisman and Roy C. Nelson. In his paper "Government Technical Manuals," Colonel William E. Frame relates how the U.S. Army works with industry to produce comprehensive and readable manuals. According to Frame, 20 years ago the Department of Defense allocated approximately $500 million of its annual budget to publication production. Frame's description of the preparation of technical manuals in the late 1950s shows that a shift in emphasis has taken place over the years. A major consideration in the preparation of technical manuals today is the readability level of the document, a subject only briefly mentioned in Frame's article. The decline in literacy in America has perhaps affected the military services more than it has any other segment of our nation. A study by the General Accounting Office, "A Need to Address Illiteracy Problems in the Military Services" (1977, shows that the average reading ability of enlisted men is below the ninth grade level. In the case of certain selected groups, the reading level is closer to the sixth grade. When we consider the high technology involved in weaponry in today's army, these low figures are disturbing.

To deal with this problem, Amendment 5 to military specification MIL-M-38784A imposes new readability requirements for military technical manuals. A variation of the Flesch formula is prescribed. J. Douglas Kniffin explains the new requirements in "The New Readability Requirements for Military Technical Manuals" (1979).

For the preparation of reports, military standard MIL-STD-847A is indispensable. This standard gives the format requirements for scientific and technical reports prepared by or for the Department of Defense. This standard sets forth in detail information that must be on the front cover as well as in other sections of the report; it explains footnoting techniques; it gives the requirements for the reference section: when to use glossaries, lists of abbreviations, or indexes; and it provides a great deal of other necessary information about form and style. Some other military standards for the preparation of reports include MIL-STD-1602(AS) (1973), which gives the requirements for progress reports for research and development equipment, and *AFWL Standards for Scientific and Technical Reports* (1979). The AFWL standard implements MIL-STD-847A and presents the standards for preparing, editing, reproducing, and distributing technical reports for the Air Force Weapons Laboratory.

Agencies outside the Defense Department prepare their own standards when necessary. For example, the Department of Transportation relies on its standard DOT-TST-72-1, *Format and Distribution Requirements for DOT Scientific and Technical Reports* (1972), and on a supplementing booklet, *Repro Copy Requirements for Technical Reports* (1973). An overall guideline for these non-military agencies is a report prepared by the Committee on Scientific and Technical Information of the Federal Council for Science and Technology, *Guidelines to Format Standards for Scientific and Technical Reports Prepared by or for the Federal Government* (1968). This COSATI report is meant to standardize report writing procedures among the government agencies. On an even broader scale we find the *Requirements for Recurring Reports to the Congress* (1980). This directory, issued by the Comptroller General, identifies congressional information needs and monitors the various reporting requirements of the Congress.

To ensure ready access to all the reports written by and for the government, the Department of Commerce established the National Technical Information Service (NTIS) in 1970 as a clearinghouse of scientific and technical literature. Designed to collect and distribute information on a self-supporting basis, NTIS gathers information from foreign, federal, state, and local governmental bodies and their contractors in the private sector at the rate of more than 70,000 items annually. As the most important central source for these documents, NTIS responds to over 20,000 document requests daily, which makes it one of the world's largest processors of technical information. In all, the NTIS program gives researchers access to 700,000 reports on completed U.S. government research.

Obtaining Government Publications

There are over 21,000 different publications, periodicals, and subscription services for sale by the Superintendent of Documents, U.S. Government Printing Office, Washington, D.C. 20402. Approximately 3,000 new titles enter the GPO sales inventory each year, and a similar number become outdated or superseded by revised editions. Instead of publishing a single catalog listing all of the titles sold, the GPO has available 250 subject bibliographies which list publications on a single subject or field of interest. Technical writers may send for the Subject Bibliography Index to identify the particular subject bibliography that contains titles relating to their needs. For example, Subject Bibliography SB-087, November 16, 1981, entitled *Stenography, Typing and Writing*, lists 26 publications relating to writing.

It is equally easy to obtain government specifications and standards. The Naval Publications and Forms Center, 5801 Tabor Avenue, Philadelphia, Pennsylvania 19120, is the central stock point for all government specifications and standards. They will send upon request an order form, DD Form 1425, Specifications and Standards Requisition Form. Five items may be ordered on each form, with up to ten copies of each item. There is no charge for specifications and standards. The Naval Publications and Forms Center also offers a subscription service for each of the Federal Supply Classifications (numbers assigned to different industries). The subscription service automatically provides the subscriber with updated and new specifications and standards. Technical writers interested in maintaining a library of pertinent technical publications for their industry will want to subscribe to this service.

No bibliography about writing for the government would be complete without reference to Elliott R. Morss and Robert F. Rich's *Government Information Management* (1980). The authors refer to the work done by the Commission on Federal Paperwork, which spent $9 million between 1974 and 1977 studying government writing, yet failed to provide a satisfactory solution for the enormous information-reporting burden within the public sector. Morss and Rich identify what they believe are the primary causes for the excessive amount of paperwork generated by the government, and provide direction for future government information management efforts. In short, they blame an absence of national priorities, bureaucratic and political dynamics, and citizen distrust as causes of paperwork overkill. Although these authors make no claim to cure the paperwork problem, they do offer suggestions to streamline government operations to make them more efficient and more useful. Their suggestions are to establish criteria for value judgments, set priorities, do a comparative agency analysis, and customize and update the automated management information system for the individual agencies. It is quite likely that the last suggestion will have the most impact. As the government (as well as libraries) makes progress in automating its documents, duplication of material will become more apparent and, one hopes, eradicated.

References

AFWL Standards for Scientific and Technical Reports. Washington, D.C.: Air Force Weapons Laboratory, 1979.

Andriot, John L. *Guide to U.S. Government Serials and Periodicals*. 3 vols. McLean, Va.: Documents Index, 1962–.

Bergman, Floyd L. *From Audit to Editing*. Washington, D.C.: U.S. GPO, 1976.

Buchanan, William, and Edna Kanely. *Cumulative Subject Index to the Monthly Catalog of U.S. Government Publications, 1900–1971*. Washington, D.C.: Carrollton, 1973.

Clarity in Technical Reporting. Washington, D.C.: U.S GPO, 1977.

Communications Related Occupations. Washington, D.C.: U.S. GPO, 1978.

Correspondence Manual. Washington, D.C.: Naval Records Management Division, 1972.

Cowie, H. Rosalind. "Training at GAO: A Systematic Approach." *GAO Rev*, 16, No. 4, (1981), 28–30.

Davis, Richard M. "Technical Writing in Industry and Government." *J Tech Writ Comm*, 7 (1977), 235–42.

Dycus, Robert D. "The Effect of Proposal Appearance on the Technical Evaluation Scoring of Government Proposals." *J Tech Writ Comm*, 7 (1977) 285–93.

The Dynamics of Information Flow: Recommendations to Improve the Flow of Information Within and Among Federal, State, and Local Government. Washington, D.C.: U.S. GPO, 1968.

Effective Revenue Writing. 2 vols. Washington, D.C.: U.S. GPO, 1976, 1978.

Effective Writing. Air University's *Communication Techniques* Series, Vol. 4. Alabama: Maxwell Air Force Base, 1974.

Ewing, David. *Writing for Results in Business, Government, and the Professions*. New York: Wiley, 1974.

Exploring Writing Careers. Washington, D.C.: U.S. GPO, 1976.

Format and Distribution Requirements for DOT Scientific and Technical Reports. DOT–TST–72–1. Washington, D.C.: U.S. Department of Transportation, 1972.

Format Requirements for Scientific and Technical Reports Prepared by or for the Department of Defense. MIL–STD–847A. Washington, D.C.: U.S. Department of Defense, 1978.

Form Letters. By the General Services Administration. Washington, D.C.: U.S. GPO, 1979.

Frame, Colonel William E. "Government Technical Manuals." *Proceedings of the 1959 Institute in Technical and Industrial Communications*. Ed. Herman M. Weisman and Roy C. Nelson. Fort Collins, Colo.: Colorado State University, 1960.

Getting Your Ideas Across Through Writing. Washington, D.C.: U.S. GPO, 1973.

Glossary of Standardized Terms. Washington, D.C.: U.S. GPO, 1961.

Gobbledygook Has Gotta Go. Washington, D.C.: U.S. GPO, 1978.

Guidelines to Format Standards for Scientific and Technical Reports Prepared by or for the Federal Government. By the Committee on Scientific and Technical Information of the Federal Council for Science and Technology. Washington, D.C.: U.S. Department of Commerce, 1968.

Handbook for Preparing Office of Research and Development Reports. Washington, D.C.: Environmental Protection Agency, 1976.

Hill, William. *A Comprehensive Guide to Successful Grantsmanship*. Littleton, Colo.: Grand Development Institute, 1971.

Holtz, Herman. *Government Contracts: Proposalsmanship and Winning Strategies*. New York: Plenum, 1979.

———, and Terry Schmidt. *The Winning Proposal: How to Write It*. New York: McGraw-Hill, 1981.

How to Write Position Descriptions. By the U.S. Civil Service Commission. Washington, D.C.: U.S. GPO, 1975.

Jackson, Ellen. *Subject Guide to Major United States Government Publications*. Chicago: American Library Association, 1968.

Jordan, Stello, ed. *Handbook of Technical Writing Practices*. 2 vols. New York: Wiley, 1971.

Kellner, Robert Scott. "Preparing Technical Writing Students to Write for the Government." *J Tech Writ Comm*, 3 (1980), 177–82.

Kern, Richard P., et al. *Guidebook for the Development of Army Training Literature*. Alexandria, Va.: Human Resources Research, 1976.

King, Robert E., Jr. *The Government Printing Office*. New York: Praeger, 1970.

Kleinman, Joseph M. "Status of Technical Manual Specifications and Standards." *Tech Comm*. Continuing department in journal.

Kniffin, J. Douglas. "The New Readability Requirements for Military Technical Manuals." *Tech Comm*, 26, No. 3 (1979), 16–19.

Letterwriting for Secretaries. By the U.S. Civil Service Commission. Washington, D.C.: U.S. GPO, 1973.

Levels of Edit. Jet Propulsion Laboratory. Washington, D.C.: U.S. GPO, 1980.

List of Specifications and Standards Pertaining to Technical Publications. By the Manual Specification Review Committee. Washington, D.C.: Society for Technical Communication, 1976.

Manuals, Technical: Commercial Equipment. MIL–M–7298B. Washington, D.C.: U.S. Department of Defense, 1969.

Manuals, Technical, General Specifications for. MIL–M–81273A(WP). Washington, D.C.: U.S. Department of the Navy, 1966.

Manuals, Technical: General Style and Format Requirements. MIL–M–38784A. Washington, D.C.: U.S. Department of Defense, 1978.

Mininger, Lowell. "A Commonsense Approach to Writing Reports." *GAO Rev*, 13, No. 2 (1978), 40–47.

Monroe, Judson. *Effective Research and Report Writing in Government*. New York: McGraw-Hill, 1980.

Monthly Catalog of United States Government Publications. Washington, D.C.: U.S. GPO, 1895–.

Monthly Checklist of State Publications. Library of Congress. Washington, D.C.: U.S. GPO, 1910–.

Morehead, Joe. *Introduction to United States Public Documents*. Littleton, Colo.: Libraries Unltd., 1978.

Morss, Elliott R., and Robert F. Rich. *Government Information Management: A Counter-Report of the Commission on Federal Paperwork*. Boulder, Colo.: Westview, 1980.

Muller, William G. "Useability Research in the Navy." *Reading and Readability Research in the Armed Forces*. Ed. T. G. Sticht and D. Welty Zapf. Alexandria, Va.: Human Resources Research, 1976, pp. 249–250.

Murdock, Michael L. *Effective Writing for Business and Government*, 2nd ed. Washington, D.C.: Transemantics, 1978.

Navy Comptroller Manual. 7 vols. Washington, D.C.: Dept. of the Navy, 1975.

"A Need to Address Illiteracy Problems in the Military Services." Report No. FPCD–77–13, Washington, D.C.: U.S. General Accounting Office, 31 Mar. 1977.

Office Management Preparing Correspondence. Washington, D.C.: U.S. Department of the Army, 1972.

O'Hayre, John. *Gobbledygook Has Gotta Go*. Washington, D.C.: U.S. GPO, 1978.

100 GPO Years, 1861–1961: A History of United States Public Printing. Washington, D.C.: U.S. GPO, 1961.

Orlich, Donald, and Patricia Orlich. *The Art of Writing Successful R&D Proposals*. Pleasantville, N.Y.: Docent, 1978.

Outline of Forms and Instructions for the Preparation of Military Standards and Military

Handbooks. MIL–STD–962. Washington, D.C.: U.S. Department of Defense, 1972.

Plain Letters. General Services Administration. Washington, D.C.: U.S. GPO, 1979.

Pohle, Linda C. *A Guide to Popular Government Publications*. Littleton, Colo.: Libraries Unltd., 1972.

Poore, Benjamin. *A Descriptive Catalog of the General Publications of the United States, September 5, 1774-March 4, 1881*. Washington, D.C.: U.S. GPO, 1885.

Preparing Correspondence. U.S. Air Force. Washington, D.C.: U.S. GPO, 1981.

Printing and Publishing Occupations. Washington, D.C.: U.S. GOP, 1978.

Progress Reports for Research and Development Equipment. MIL–STD–1602(AS). Washington, D.C.: U.S. Department of Defense, 1973.

Proposals and Their Preparation. Society for Technical Communication Anthology, Series 1. Washington, D.C.: Society for Technical Communication, 1975.

Report Writing Guide. Tullahoma, Tenn.: U.S. Air Force Engineering Development Center, 1958.

Repro Copy Requirements for Technical Reports. Washington, D.C.: Federal Highway Administration, 1973.

Requirements for Recurring Reports to the Congress. Washington, D.C.: U.S. GPO, 1980.

Rosen, David M. "Communicating Effectively Through GAO Reports." *GAO Rev*, 13, No. 1 (1978), 18–21.

Schmeckebier, Laurence F., and Roy B. Eastin. *Government Publications and Their Use*. Washington, D.C.: Brookings Institute, 1970.

Shimberg, H. Lee. "Clarifying Federal Regulations by Using Plain English." *Tech Comm*, 27 No. 2 (1980), 6–10.

Specification Practices. MIL–STD–490. Washington, D.C.: U.S. Department of Defense, 1968.

Staley, Lt. Col. H. A. *Tongue and Quill: Communicating to Manage in Tomorrow's Air Force*. Alabama: Maxwell Air Force Base, 1977.

Strong, Charles W., and Donald Eidson. *A Technical Writer's Handbook*. New York: Holt, Rinehart, Winston, 1971.

Technical Manual Writing Handbook. MIL–HDBK–63038–1(TM). Washington, D.C.: U.S. Department of Defense, 1977.

U.S. Air Force Effective Writing Course. Washington, D.C.: U.S. GPO, 1980.

U.S. Government Printing Office Style Manual. Washington, D.C.: U.S. GPO, 1973, reprinted 1979.

Weil, B. H., ed. *The Technical Report: Its Preparation, Processing, and Use in Industry and Government*. New York: Reinhold, 1954.

Word Division. 7th ed. Washington, D.C.: U.S. GPO, 1976.

Writing Effective Letters. By the U.S. Civil Service Commission. Washington, D.C.: U.S. GPO, 1977.

Writing Improvement: Guide for Air Force Writing. Washington, D.C.: U.S. GPO, 1798.

Writing Words That Work. Washington, D.C.: U.S. GPO, 1978.

Appendices

Guide to Textbooks in Technical Communication

SUSAN HILLIGOSS

The growth of technical communication as an academic subject is reflected in the growing number of textbooks on the market. Choosing among them is difficult, not only because many cover essentially the same material, but also because many who now teach and select materials for technical communication courses are not experts in the field. This guide reviews a number of texts currently available.

The textbooks selected represent a range of approaches to overall course structure and teaching methodology. Nonetheless, introductory and comprehensive texts outnumber advanced and specialized ones; texts that stress both academic and professional forms of writing outnumber those that focus strictly on the professional. These biases reflect the hybrid nature of many technical communication courses. With the exception of engineering, textbooks that treat only one specialized subject have been omitted.

The following review describes examples of three types of books that instructors or text selection committees might consider adopting: (1) comprehensive texts in technical communication, (2) specialized texts such as reference guides and anthologies, and (3) general composition texts. The titles are representative of important, popular, and new texts available as of the 1982–1983 midyear supplement to *Books in Print*. For additional reviews, see issues of *The Journal of Technical Writing and Communication* and *The Technical Writing Teacher*.

The terms that designate appropriate audiences for a text overlap. "Introductory" means suited for students with relatively little adult writing experience, few college courses in a single field, and little or no work experience; that is, a text for freshman or sophomore courses in two- or four-year programs. "Intermediate" means suited for students with some knowledge of writing and elementary knowledge of their chosen field; that is, for post-freshman courses in technical communication. "Advanced" means suited for students who have not only some knowledge of writing, either from English courses or from on-the-job experience, but also some significant academic or professional preparation in their fields, for example, juniors, seniors, graduate students, professionals, and advanced technicians. These designations are suggestions only. Some basic texts, for example, have a no-nonsense tone and a selection of models and assignments that appeal to a wide audience.

Comprehensive Texts

Comprehensive texts, as the name suggests, aim at completeness. They often incorporate features of freshman composition texts and thus are intended for a wide range of readers. However, a comprehensive book many not be the best choice; consistency of approach or thorough coverage of particular problems or formats may be more important than completeness. The handbooks of these texts, for example, are often highly selective to make room for other material. Students with limited writing skills and those for whom English is not the first language may need another handbook.

Unless otherwise noted, each comprehensive text covers the importance of writing on the job, technical style, modes of exposition, the description of mechanisms and processes, graphics, information resources such as the library, oral reports, long written reports, and correspondence, including letters of application and resumés. Each also devotes 25 to 100 pages to topics in grammar, punctuation, mechanics, and usage, sometimes contained in a handbook or appendix, sometimes in separate chapters or sections. Each text has assignments and numerous models.

But that is the least common denominator. The texts described below vary in intended audience, overall approach, emphasis given particular topics, and special formats. The commentary tries to make some of those distinctions clear, beginning with the difficult problem of the audience addressed by the text and that addressed by the students as they write.

Comprehensive texts assume different student readerships. Two main audiences are technical majors, usually engineers, and freshmen or sophomores who are as yet unspecialized. Texts have often addressed the first audience. A classic example aimed squarely at advanced undergraduates and professionals in engineering and science is *Technical Reporting* (1972) by Joseph N. Ulman, Jr., and Jay R. Gould. The text assumes that the reader is a novice writer but a technical expert: the detailed models are written by professionals in government and industry for technicians, other experts, and managers in technical fields. The accompanying discussion is concise and organized by numbered headings. Special forms include both professional and academic writing, such as technical articles, proposals, laboratory reports, and theses. Somewhat dated in its models, format, and assumptions, it devotes one-third of its text to basic principles, one-third to writing style and visual presentation of information, and one-third to specimens of writing.

In contrast, *Technical Writing* by Gordon H. Mills and John A. Walter combines many features of technical communication and traditional composition texts. For example, Chapter 2 illustrates conciseness: it is a one-page list of the five basic principles of good technical writing. In turn, many of the student models illustrating expository modes are typical of freshman or advanced expository writing texts, making it appropriate for introductory and intermediate courses. Other models include excerpts from magazine feature articles and advertisements for technical equipment, as well as substantial specimens from trade journals and internal reports in business and industry. Outlines, abstracts, transitions, and introductions receive major coverage. Appendices include an extensive bibliography on technical writing.

Kenneth W. Houp and Thomas E. Pearsall bridge these two readerships in *Reporting Technical Information* (1980), an intermediate or advanced text. Aimed at future technical writers as well as the writing engineer or scientist, the text focuses on audience analysis, based on Pearsall's research on the information needs of different technical readers. It balances a professional's attitude toward research with a direct, open tone toward the student who may not yet have specialized knowledge of a scientific or technical field. Library research is introduced early, and many of the assignments are keyed to the student's major project. The research emphasis shows in the authors' own citation of papers in technical communication and in the 15-page annotated guide to technical references. However, the tone of the explanations and many of the models and assignments are geared to non-specialists—for example, investigating a local shade-tree planting program. Non-academic applications include proposals, progress reports, physical research (observation and experimentation) reports, feasibility reports, and group conferences. There are professional and some student models from many fields. Like many of the texts reviewed here, the layout makes liberal use of white space, headings and color.

One of the problems in realistically presenting audience to students is "Who will the students write for?" Steven E. Pauley's *Technical Report Writing Today* (1979) solves the problem by assuming that students will naturally address their writing to "an uninformed reader—the instructor" (p. xi). (For another view, see the discussion by Ingrid Brunner, and colleagues, *The Technician as Writer* [1980]). This text gives students' writing throughout, mostly from freshmen and sophomores. Explanations of writing principles are brief but to the point. Pauley also takes the rhetorician's stand that writing aids thinking, so that technical writing courses help students understand their disciplines. Special attention is given to statistical interpretation, recommendation reports, laboratory reports, proposals, feasibility reports, progress reports, and operation manuals. The text is suitable for technical and science majors in introductory or intermediate courses.

Audience is also central to John M. Lannon's introductory and intermediate text, *Technical Writing* (1982). However, Lannon expects students to search out readers beyond the instructor. Models throughout the book are introduced by giving the situation, the writer (for example, work-study student, nurse practitioner, builder), and the intended audience (chief librarian, students, professional engineer). The text has student and professional models from many fields, notably health care, giving it broad application. Each chapter is organized with the writing process in mind. Research is treated as a strategy of writing rather than as an end in itself; academic research reports are distinguished from professional analytical reports. Numerous topics for long reports are given. The handbook covers basic definitions of grammatical terms. Besides the analytical report, there is special attention to proposals and informal reports.

The Technician as Writer (1980), by Ingrid Brunner, J. C. Mathes, and Dwight W. Stevenson, takes a thoroughly professional view of the writer's audience. Technicians write in organizations, and they must be accustomed to addressing several audiences with different training and expectations all in the same document. Thus, the authors stress the rhetorical analysis of audience and a two-part structure for reports that can be used by multiple audiences. A shorter adaptation of *Designing Technical Reports* (see below) for technical or professional students in many disciplines, *The Technician as Writer* keeps the pioneering ideas of Mathes and Stevenson concerning the writer's role, but uses everyday situations in school and on the job to explain communication in organizations. The student and professional models come from many fields, such as health care, law enforcement, and engineering. Rather than explaining different formats of reports, the authors give methods of analysis and planning that apply to many types of technical writing. Oral reports and grammar exercises are included, but there is no section on library research or resumés. This text is suitable for many introductory or intermediate courses, especially those for vocational or technical majors.

Another rhetorical text that considers the problem of multiple audiences is Deborah

C. Andrews and Margaret D. Blickle's *Technical Writing* (1982). To stress that writing is done in specific contexts, the authors classify what readers read on the job and trace the network of readers a document may have. The chapter on library resources shows how to evaluate information. Applications include abstracts, proposals, progress reports, final reports, popular scientific articles, and literature reviews. The chapter on oral reports includes a list of goals for well-run meetings. This introductory and intermediate text gives student and professional models from many fields.

Hypothetical cases provide yet a different solution to the problem of audience. One text that uses the casebook approach is Ron S. Blicq's *Technically-Write!* (1981). Two "technically oriented" companies, one in the United States and one in Canada, are introduced to provide examples and situations for many of the writing assignments. The reader is drawn into the various situations through dialogue as well as explanation. Blicq divides many report formats into those "describing facts and events," such as progress reports, and those "describing ideas and concepts," such as feasibility studies and proposals, a division corresponding roughly to the distinction between the technician's and the professional's responsibility. There is no coverage of library research. The models, divided between technical, managerial, and employee matters, are mainly by professionals but are addressed to a variety of audiences, specialized and lay. The text is appropriate for introductory and intermediate courses, especially for technical and business majors.

Thomas E. Pearsall and Donald H. Cunningham are also concerned with the relation of student writers to their readers in *How to Write for the World of Work* (1982). But they deliberately do not give cases or traditional exercises; instead they give numerous "Suggestions for Applying Your Knowledge" addressed to both student and instructor. The same attention to audience that informs Houp and Pearsall's more advanced textbook is evident in *World of Work*: students are addressed without jargon and are shown ways to treat their readers likewise. As its title suggests, this text may be used for business as well as technical communication courses at the introductory or intermediate level. The authors have divided the book into two main parts, correspondence and reports. The types of reports include academic and professional writing: annotated bibliographies and literature reviews; periodic, accident, and trip reports; analytical reports; and proposals. Discussion of graphics is integrated into the discussion of writing, and the text is amply illustrated. The models are mainly professional, many intended for non-expert audiences.

Because people on the job often learn new writing skills by examining and imitating others' work, examples are the heart of *Technical Writing* by Bonnie Carter Brinegar and Craig Barnwell Skates (1983). The models, all by professionals, are presented in facsimile, with brief but frequent annotation by the authors. (Color and white space distinguish model from comment.) The text introduces basic ideas and provides transition between examples. There is considerable attention to situation and audience. Types of academic and professional writing covered include progress reports, abstracts, literature reviews, field and laboratory reports, surveys, recommendation reports, feasibility studies, critiques, proposals, and persuasive essays. The models are intended for audiences from lay to expert, in fields as diverse as health care, education, forestry, anthropology, and the military. There is no section on oral reports. This text is suited for intermediate and advanced majors in many fields.

Recent models showing current practice in government and industry may also be found in *Modern Technical Writing* by Theodore A. Sherman and Simon S. Johnson (1983). Like those in Brinegar and Skates, the models are professional, reproduced in facsimile. Many are intended for technical or expert readers, making this text especially appropriate for advanced students. The authors give extended exposition of traditional subjects in technical prose. The reports section consists of four chapters introducing aspects of reports, followed by specific formats. Formats covered include proposals, feasibility reports, laboratory reports, and environmental impact statements.

While many texts in technical communication give space to the writing process, some make it a major organizing principle. Lannon (cited above) presents one approach, including a flexible but consistent treatment of process in each chapter. Another, more prescriptive, approach for vocational students is exemplified in two texts by Nell Ann Pickett and Ann A. Laster: *Technical English* (1980) and *Occupational English* (1981). Both use plan sheets to help students think about writing. The worksheets are part of a step-by-step procedure for approaching specific writing tasks: objectives are set for each chapter, concepts are introduced, the intended readers discussed, and principles and procedure given. These texts are distinctive for their integration of speaking—orally giving instructions, for example—into the process of writing. The handbook includes exercises. Intended for introductory composition courses in two- and four-year programs, the texts emphasize instructions, summaries (including executive summaries), letters, and research reports. *Technical English* contains twelve readings, ranging from a cartoon to material on clear writing to selections by W. H. Auden and Robert Pirsig. *Occupational English* omits these and parts of the handbook; it also contains somewhat different assignments and models.

Another introductory or intermediate text that concentrates on the preliminaries of writing is David E. Fear's *Technical Communication* (1981). The first part, ''Basics,'' contains chapters on purpose, planning, writing, and revising, as well as modes of exposition and instructions. Fear stresses planning worksheets and gives several examples of their use. Included are many types of academic and professional writing: research papers, proposals, job descriptions, specifications, articles, and the design of forms. The handbook discusses basic grammar and common errors. One chapter is devoted to informal oral communication, such as listening and telephoning skills; another covers the ''job package.'' Models come from professionals and students in many fields.

Concerned solely with professional writing, *Technical Writing*, by James Miles, Donald Bush, and Allin Kaplan (1982), includes numerous models with a discussion of audience, purpose, the process of writing, and editing. Techniques of writing are shown through cases and situations. The applications covered are instructional manuals, technical proposals, progress reports, and feasibility studies. Because of its focus, the book includes no discussion of research papers or oral reports. This text is appropriate for intermediate and advanced students.

Specialized Texts

Three types of specialized texts in technical communication may be considered for course adoption or for the bookshelf: (1) texts for a special field that present original research and methods, (2) references and books on one aspect of communication, and (3) anthologies.

In the first group are two texts for engineers. J. C. Mathes and Dwight W. Stevenson, in an influential text, *Designing Technical Reports* (1976), analyze the rhetorical situation a professional engineer faces. Rather than describe separate formats, Mathes and Stevenson argue for and illustrate a handful of methods for writing, or designing, many documents, from one-page memos to lengthy studies and manuals. Working from the principles that "All audiences are particular audiences" and that audiences in organizations are multiple and complex, they develop the "egocentric organization chart" to aid writers in defining the readers of their work (p. 46). From the idea that a report addresses an organizational problem, they develop a three-part purpose statement that can help the writer as well as the reader to understand what is at issue. The section on "Designing the Report" proposes a two-part structure for reports, one for decision-makers and one for technical readers. The section on editing gives a method of revising paragraphs for coherence; sentence patterns are analyzed by the expectations they set up in readers. There are numerous examples, negative as well as positive. The text is suited for advanced students and professionals in engineering and technical writing. A shorter version for students in many fields, *The Technician as Writer*, is reviewed above.

James W. Souther and Myron L. White's text, *Technical Report Writing* (1977), also compares the process of writing with the engineering design process. Two introductory chapters define scientific and technical writing and outline the design approach to writing, a step-by-step method amplified in the next four chapters. Purpose, audience, organization for a managerial readership, and tone are discussed in detail, based on Souther's studies of the informational needs of managers at Westinghouse. Included is the classic organizational catechism, "What Managers Want to Know." The authors criticize overly standardized reports and advocate formats determined by purpose, use, and audience. Examples in this brief book are taken from professional reports, and the exercises assume that readers will be engaged in substantial projects. The text is appropriate for advanced students and professionals, particularly in engineering.

Three special-purpose books can be assigned as useful references, especially in intermediate or advanced classes. The first, *Handbook of Technical Writing*, by Charles T. Brusaw, Gerald J. Alred, and Walter E. Oliu (1982), is an encyclopedic dictionary of terms. As a composition handbook it covers grammar, punctuation, and usage. As a rhetoric it explains such topics as methods of development, modes of exposition, and analogy. As a technical writing guide it discusses and gives examples of many types of reports, illustrations, and layout. A full index and ample cross-referencing increase its usefulness.   The second book, *Technical Communication* by Thomas L. Warren (1978), is a review of the principles of technical writing and speaking in outline form. The truncated form of the explanations makes this book useful as a quick reference rather than as an introduction to concepts. There are few extended examples. Covering the same material as a comprehensive text, the outline gives considerable attention to pre-writing, audience, purpose, and revising. The book also contains six short essays on technical writing, ranging from the humorous to the classic "What to Report."

Texts that concern one aspect of writing or speaking can add an important dimension to a course. The third special-purpose book, *Revising Business Prose* (1981) by Richard A. Lanham, takes aim at a perennial problem, the excesses of bureaucratic style. Like *Revising Prose* (1979), Lanham's earlier work for advanced composition courses, this book presents the "Paramedic Method," a "first-aid kit" for sentences (p. viii). The examples, which give new meaning to the word "negative," are from actual documents. Lanham covers not just conciseness but also prose rhythm and the way revising can change meaning.

Anthologies can provide a common source of material in a class where most students are pursuing their own interests. The collections of readings currently available tend toward reflective essays about scientific and technical writing rather than models of that writing. One exception is Mary M. Lay's *Strategies for Technical Writing* (1982), which combines discussion of major principles of writing with numerous excerpts from technical documents as well as popular scientific writing. Courses with an emphasis on science might profit from *Writing About Science* edited by Mary Elizabeth Bowen and Joseph A. Mazzeo (1979) or *The Example of Science* edited by Robert E. Lynch and Thomas B. Swanzey (1981). Both include many readings aimed at educated lay audiences. *The Practical Craft*, edited by W. Keats Sparrow and Donald H. Cunningham (1978), contains advice on writing and articles on technical writing research. Kevin J. Harty emphasizes business writing, letters, and resumés as well as reports in his reader, *Strategies for Business and Technical Writing* (1980). Courses that attract many majors may need a broader selection, such as that in *Writing and Reading Across the Curriculum*, by Laurence Behrens and Leonard J. Rosen (1982), which has sections on computing, personality, and nuclear war and instructs students in summaries, syntheses, and critiques.

General Composition Texts

Finally, two recent textbooks for general composition deserve mention here. Both are adaptable to courses that combine the writing of professional reports and articles with typical college assignments. The first, *Writing in the Arts and Sciences* (1981) by Elaine P. Maimon and her colleagues at Beaver College, focuses on "academic writing, reading, and studying" and "the communication of reasoned belief." The book is divided into two sections. The first presents the process of composing and revising; the uses of journals in academic writing; and techniques for notetaking, writing essay examinations, and using the library. The second section applies the ideas of the first to typical writing assignments in the humanities, social sciences, and natural sciences. In the last two groups are term papers, case studies, laboratory reports, and "apprentice" professional papers such as review papers. Each chapter discusses "getting started," drafting, and revising a major form of academic writing. The APA and MLA styles of documentation are compared. The appendix presents four student papers in history, sociology, psychology, and biology. The text is designed for composition courses and writing-across-the-curriculum programs, but is also suitable for other courses that combine "functional" and "thinking" writing, such as introductory technical communication.

The second text in this category, Linda Flower's *Problem-Solving Strategies for Writing* (1981), addresses both professional and academic writing as "real-world" writing. In this respect Flower treats student writers no differently from writers on the job. The book gives strategies and alternatives rather than prescriptions—for composing, for adapting a piece of writing to the reader's needs, and for evaluating and editing one's own work. There is considerable explanation of how and why people write as they do, based on Flower's and others' research in cognitive psychology. The first three chapters present problem-solving, issue trees, and "weak" and "powerful" strategies for writing. The remaining nine chapters amplify the major tasks all writers must handle: planning, generating ideas, organizing, and writing for a reader. Some models are followed over more than one chapter through planning, drafting, and revision. Models include an internship application, a team consulting report, a research paper, and a proposal. Two chapters on editing discuss economy, forcefulness, subordination, and paragraph logic. The text is suitable for beginning and advanced students in many disciplines.

Conclusion

Instruction and research in technical and professional communication are expanding. New student audiences and new research findings have influenced the design of recent textbooks, including some in this review. If that growth continues, textbooks in technical communication will increase in variety as well as number.

References

Andrews, Deborah C., and Margaret D. Blickle. *Technical Writing: Principles and Forms*. 2nd ed. New York: Macmillan, 1982.

Behrens, Laurence, and Leonard J. Rosen. *Writing and Reading Across the Curriculum*. Boston: Little, Brown, 1982.

Blicq, Ron S. *Technically-Write! Communicating in a Technological Era*. 2nd ed. Englewood Cliffs, N.J.: Prentice-Hall, 1981.

Bowen, Mary Elizabeth, and Joseph A. Mazzeo, eds. *Writing About Science*. New York: Oxford, 1979.

Brinegar, Bonnie Carter, and Craig Barnwell Skates. *Technical Writing: A Guide with Models*. Glenview, Ill.: Scott, Foresman, 1983.

Brunner, Ingrid, J. C. Mathes, and Dwight W. Stevenson. *The Technician as Writer: Preparing Technical Reports*. Indianapolis: Bobbs-Merrill, 1980.

Brusaw, Charles T., Gerald J. Alred, and Walter E. Oliu. *Handbook of Technical Writing*. 2nd ed. New York: St. Martin's, 1982.

Fear, David E. *Technical Communication*. 2nd ed. Glenview, Ill.: Scott, Foresman, 1981.

Flower, Linda. *Problem-Solving Strategies for Writing*. New York: Harcourt, 1981.

Harty, Kevin J., ed. *Strategies for Business and Technical Writing*. New York: Harcourt, 1980.

Houp, Kenneth W., and Thomas E. Pearsall. *Reporting Technical Information*. 4th ed. New York: Macmillan, 1980.

Lanham, Richard A. *Revising Business Prose*. New York: Scribner's, 1981.

Lannon, John M. *Technical Writing*. 2nd ed. Boston: Little, Brown, 1982.

Laster, Ann A., and Nell Ann Pickett. *Occupational English*. 3rd ed. New York: Harper, 1981.

Lay, Mary M. *Strategies for Technical Writing: A Rhetoric with Readings*. New York: Holt, 1982.

Lynch, Robert E., and Thomas B. Swanzey, eds. *The Example of Science: An Anthology for College Composition*. Englewood Cliffs, N.J.: Prentice-Hall, 1981.

Maimon, Elaine P., et al. *Writing in the Arts and Sciences*. Cambridge, Mass.: Winthrop, 1981.

Mathes, J. C., and Dwight W. Stevenson. *Designing Technical Reports: Writing for Audiences in Organizations*. Indianapolis: Bobbs-Merrill, 1976.

Miles, James, Donald Bush, and Allin Kaplan. *Technical Writing: Principles and Practice*. Chicago: SRA, 1982.

Mills, Gordon H., and John A. Walter. *Technical Writing*. 4th ed. New York: Holt, 1978.

Pauley, Steven E. *Technical Report Writing Today*. 2nd ed. Boston: Houghton Mifflin, 1979.

Pearsall, Thomas E., and Donald H. Cunningham. *How to Write for the World of Work.* 2nd ed. New York: Holt, 1982.

Pickett, Nell Ann, and Ann A. Laster. *Technical English: Writing, Reading, Speaking.* 3rd ed. New York: Harper, 1980.

Sherman, Theodore A., and Simon S. Johnson. *Modern Technical Writing.* 4th ed. Englewood Cliffs, N.J.: Prentice-Hall, 1983.

Souther, James W., and Myron L.White. *Technical Report Writing.* 2nd ed. New York: Wiley, 1977.

Sparrow, W. Keats, and Donald H. Cunningham, eds. *The Practical Craft: Readings for Business and Technical Writers.* Boston: Houghton Mifflin, 1978.

Ulman, Joseph N., Jr., and Jay R. Gould. *Technical Reporting.* 3rd ed. New York: Holt, 1972.

Warren, Thomas L. *Technical Communication: An Outline.* Totowa, N.J.: Littlefield, 1978.

A Selection of Style Manuals

CAROLINE R. GOFORTH

One of the writer's most perplexing tasks is to make a piece of writing look and sound the way a particular audience expects it to. The appearance and the sound of writing are its style. Although all the elements of writing work together to create an organic whole, style can be examined as a distinct component consisting of two complementary aspects, editorial style and prose style.

Editorial style comprises grammatical usage, punctuation, capitalization, spelling, use of abbreviations, treatment of numbers, documentation, and bibliography, as well as the format—mechanical and organizational—required in a particular writing task. Prose style is shaped by diction, sentence structure, paragraphing, approach to audience, approach to subject, and level of grammatical usage. The interaction of these elements determines the voice preferred in a particular type of writing, as well as the writer's individual voice.

If the rules of style—editorial and prose—were clear-cut and unchanging from one type of writing to another, the writer's job would be easier; but written language would suffer from restricted flexibility and precision. For instance, comparable information on genetic engineering requires different handling for geneticists and for laymen if it is to be viewed as credible by the first group and as comprehensible by the second.

Guides to style abound. In fact, their number and variety may bewilder a novice, and even veteran writers may benefit from a survey of representative style manuals. The first problem in making such a survey is establishing its boundaries. At one end of their spectrum, style manuals shade into dictionaries and grammar handbooks; at the other, into rhetoric texts and "how-to" books on creative writing. Although some style manuals deal exclusively with editorial or prose style, many include a combination, varying in their breadth and depth of treatment and in their length from style sheets with fewer than 50 pages to exhaustive guides with over 500.

The first step in choosing a style manual for a particular writing project is to find out if the publication for which it is intended has its own guidelines—that is, its own house style. If it does not or if the piece of writing may have to be submitted to several publishers before it is accepted, choice of the style manual depends on the writer's expertise, the nature of the writing task, and the audience and type of publication for which it is intended. These criteria serve as a basis for selecting and presenting sources in this essay, which includes readily available style manuals, those recognized as authoritative in their fields, and recent publications. Excluded are style manuals used only within a narrow range, such as those produced by industrial corporations, or those published more than 25 years ago unless they have been reprinted, unless their coverage has not been duplicated, or unless their frequent appearance in the bibliographies of other style manuals indicates that they have become classics.

The most comprehensive listing of style manuals to date appears in Gerald J. Alred, Diana C. Reep, and Mohan R. Limaye's *Business and Technical Writing* (1981). Presented in a section separate from the main bibliography, the list of style manuals is unannotated and organized under such headings as "Industry and Society Style Guides," "Government and Military Style Guides," "Publishing," and "Style, Language, and Readability."

The style manuals selected for this essay are divided into three categories: those useful in a wide variety of subject areas and types of writing; those useful in most technical writing; and those prepared for specific academic fields, specific kinds of writing, and specific publications.

General Style Manuals

Most writers face their first stylistically demanding writing task in an academic report, usually a research paper. Long recognized as an authority in this area, Kate L. Turabian's *A Manual for Writers of Term Papers, Theses, and Dissertations* (1973) provides detailed coverage of the research report format, including extensive sections on reference footnotes and bibliography that contain numerous examples of citations for different types of sources—print, non-print, and legal and government documents. Turabian also discusses two citation systems often used in scientific papers—the reference list with internal documentation by author's last name and publication date; and the numbered reference list with internal documentation by corresponding numbers. A similar guide widely used in the liberal arts is Joseph Gibaldi and Walter S. Achtert's *MLA Handbook for Writers of Research Papers, Theses, and Dissertations* (1977), published by the Modern Language Association of America. Like Turabian's *Manual*, the *MLA Handbook* offers detailed information on the elements and format of research papers, including documentation and bibliography. Both also include sections on punctuation, capitalization, spelling, and treatment of quoted materials, numbers, and abbreviations—all stylistic concerns which are called "mechanical rules" in the remainder of this essay. Neither book deals with prose style.

Martha L. Manheimer approaches citation form from the librarian's standpoint in her *Style Manual* (1973). She calls her system "a compromise between traditional bibliographic form and the form used by the Library of Congress and other major libraries in their catalogs" (p. 45). This book covers citations for government documents, archival sources, computer programs and data banks, but lists few examples of non-print sources.

Especially helpful to foreign language students is Edward D. Seeber's *A Style Manual for Students* (1967), which contains extensive information on handling titles, words, and expressions in French, Italian, Spanish, German, Russian, Latin, and Greek. Both Seeber's manual and the *MLA Handbook* are based on the *MLA Style Sheet*—the *MLA Handbook* on the current *MLA Style Sheet* (1970) and Seeber's book on the 1951 edition. The *MLA Style Sheet*, a guide to the mechanics of scholarly writing, is accepted as a standard by numerous publications in the liberal arts. Because it is intended for professional scholarly writers, as opposed to student writers, it is less detailed in its coverage and more oriented toward publication than is the *MLA Handbook*. Seeber is also the author of a similar reference for publishing scholars, *A Style Manual for Authors* (1967).

A Handbook for Scholars (1978) by Mary-Claire van Leunen, though useful for both students and scholarly writers, advocates a style of embedded citations with a numbered reference list, which is not as widely accepted in the liberal arts as the MLA style. In van Leunen's system, bracketed numbers in the text correspond with numbers on the reference list, which is arranged in alphabetical order, in chronological order, or in order of mention in the text. Van Leunen uses an audience approach to writing references, basing form on the reader's needs in locating a particular source. She illustrates a variety of source types, including microfilm and microfiche, architecture, art works, computer programs, movies, music, radio and television programs, and unpublished interviews and studies. A chapter entitled ''Scholarly Peculiarities'' focuses on points of prose style that are particularly important to academic writers. Finally, an appendix deals with format and content of vitae.

Herbert H. Hoffman presents still another bibliographic style in *Bibliography Without Footnotes* (1978). Hoffman's internal documentation system is based on a numbered, title-first bibliography. Corresponding numbers, together with page numbers from sources, appear in parentheses in the text. This style, like Van Leunen's, is an alternative one and is not generally accepted as a standard.

Peyton Hurt's *Bibliography and Footnotes* (1968) generally follows MLA style, though there are differences in the two systems. Hurt also discusses reference citation styles used in scientific and technical publications, including illustrations from several representative journals. The advantage of Hurt's book is the examples cover a broad range of source types—U.S. government documents, as well as U.S. state, British and other foreign documents, and publications of international organizations, particularly those of the United Nations. These examples can be easily adapted to MLA style or to any of several scientific and technical styles.

A third book focusing on bibliographic form is *A Style Manual for Citing Microform and Nonprint Media* (1978) by Eugene B. Fleischer. This work presents general guidelines for constructing references and specific instructions and examples, including sample references for charts, dioramas, filmstrips, flash cards, games, globes, kits, maps, microforms, microscope slides, models, pictures, realia, and sound and video recordings.

The Writer's Manual (1979) by Roy E. Porter and others includes chapters on term papers, theses, dissertations, academic writing, creative writing, grammatical usage, and prose style.

Margaret Nicholson's *A Practical Style Guide for Authors and Editors* (1967) is a general introduction to book publishing. Nicholson touches on the author's and the editor's roles in producing a book, on the parts of a book and their sequence, on quotations, on handling references, on indexing, on proofreading, and on mechanical rules. Although the book is of equal value to non-fiction writers in all fields, treatment is basic and cursory. More comprehensive and more detailed is *Words into Type* (1974) by Marjorie E. Skillin, Robert M. Gay, and others. This book covers the whole writing-publishing process from preparation of the manuscript to production of the printed page. Extensive sections explore mechanical rules, grammar and syntax, and prose style. Another work that addresses the concerns of both book writers and printers is F. Howard Collins's *Authors and Printers Dictionary* (1973), which includes mechanical rules, difficult spellings, usage problems, and technical terms used in printing. All entries follow British usage.

In addition to general style manuals, many publishers—publishing companies, university presses, periodicals, national and international organizations, even corporations—produce their own style guides. An example is *The Chicago Manual of Style* (1982), published by the University of Chicago Press. The three divisions of this book—"Bookmaking," "Style," and "Production and Printing"—explore manuscript preparation, editorial style, and the printing process. The section on style includes guidelines for putting foreign languages into type—languages using the Latin alphabet, transliterated and Romanized languages, and Classical Greek, Old English, and Middle English. Also covered in detail are treatment of illustrations, captions, and legends; preparation of tables; and treatment of mathematical material. The chapter on documentation discusses four citation systems: author-date, endnotes, footnotes, and unnumbered notes; two styles for listing sources: reference list and bibliography; and two systems of bibliographic form, one of which is favored in literature, history, and the arts, and the other in the natural and social sciences. A chapter on indexing presents the principles of indexing with examples, principles of alphabetizing, typographical considerations, and examples of different index styles. Because of its comprehensiveness and its quality, *The Chicago Manual of Style*, now in its thirteenth edition, has become a standard reference work used by style manual writers as well as by numerous publications.

Another frequently used guide is the *U.S. Government Printing Office Style Manual* (1973). Although produced for printers of Government Printing Office materials, this style manual is useful to writers in all fields because it pulls together diverse information on editorial style. Examples are listings of mechanical rules; of problem spellings; of abbreviations for geographical locations and units of measure, as well as standard word abbreviations; of mathematical and scientific signs and symbols; of geologic terms, physiographic terms, plant and insect names; and of information on foreign countries.

Focused more on prose style than on editorial instructions, *A Guide to Writing for the United Nations* (1966) is audience oriented, emphasizing the clarity, consistency, and conciseness of style necessary in reports written for readers who speak a variety of languages. To illustrate their points, the editors include excerpts from unsatisfactory reports along with re-writes, as well as models of good reports.

Representative of style manuals produced by book publishers for writers and editors is *The McGraw-Hill Style Manual* (1983), edited by Marie Longyear. Its sections on mechanical rules, documentation, and table format make it a useful reference for writers of general non-fiction, educational texts from high school through postgraduate levels, and professional texts and reference books in most fields. Of particular interest to technical writers are sections on technical notation in mathematics, electronics, computer science, chemistry, and life sciences. A similar work, but less detailed, is *The Author-Publisher Handbook* (1980), edited by David T. Hunn for Aztex. Brooke Crutchley's *Preparation of Manuscripts and Correction of Proofs* (1970), prepared for the Cambridge University Press, is based on British printing conventions and usage.

Like academic publications and book publishers, newspapers establish house styles to insure consistency. Many use one of the two news service style books—*The UPI Stylebook* (1981), edited by Bobby R. Miller and published by United Press International, and *The Associated Press Stylebook and Libel Manual* (1977), edited by Howard Angione. Both list entries in alphabetical order, which include items related to spelling, capitalization, abbreviations, punctuation, and usage. Some large newspapers produce their own style guides like *The New York Times Manual of Style and Usage* (1976), revised and edited by Lewis Jordan.

Except for Porter's *The Writer's Manual*, the books discussed so far are primarily editorial style guides. *The Elements of Style* (1979) by William Strunk, Jr., and E. B. White focuses instead on prose style. This book's chief advantages are its compactness and directness. Strunk wrote the first edition over 60 years ago for his composition class, telescoping mechanical rules and grammatical usage into seven "Elementary Rules of Usage," a short section entitled "A Few Matters of Form," and a mini-dictionary of usage (less than 30 pages). He covered prose style in eleven "Elementary Principles of Composition." White in his revision added four rules of usage and a chapter entitled "An Approach to Style," which deals primarily with audience and voice. Reading *The Elements of Style* in one sitting is no strain; and, because of its size and arrangement, using it as a reference is quick and convenient.

Almost as ubiquitous as Strunk and White's classic in the reference lists of style manuals is *The Complete Plain Words* (1973), written by Sir Ernest Gowers and revised by Sir Bruce Fraser. Prepared for British bureaucrats, this guide concentrates on practical prose, advocating attention to audience, precision in diction, conciseness, and avoidance of jargon. Fraser illustrates these principles by analyzing eight writing samples.

Effective usage—an inextricable blend of grammatical rules, denotative and connotative definitions, prose style principles, and the personal preferences of scholars and authors—creates difficulties for all writers and raises constant controversy, which has bred a bevy of dictionaries of style and usage. One of the most recent and ambitious is Roy H. Copperud's *American Usage and Style* (1980). Arranged alphabetically like most usage dictionaries, the book consists of entries that attack problems long recognized as difficult or arguable points of style. The difference is that Copperud sets out to establish a consensus on each item he examines. First, this volume consolidates two earlier works by Copperud—*A Dictionary of Usage and Style* (1964) and *American Usage* (1970). Second, it represents a comparison of eight other authorities on usage. Controversial entries contain a discussion of dissenting opinions. The sources Copperud compares are *A Dictionary of Modern English Usage* (1965), written by Henry W. Fowler and revised by Sir Ernest Gowers; *The ABC Style* (1964) by Rudolph Flesch; *Modern American Usage* (1966) by Wilson Follett; *Encyclopedic Dictionary of English Usage* (1974) by Nathan H. Mager and Sylvia K. Mager; *Current American Usage* (1962), edited by Margaret M. Bryant; *Harper Dictionary of Contemporary Usage* (1975) by William and Mary Morris; *A Dictionary of Contemporary American Usage* (1957) by Bergen Evans and Cornelia Evans; and *The Careful Writer* (1965) by Theodore M. Bernstein.

Fowler's book, first published in 1926, is the classic dictionary of usage in the English language, on which succeeding usage authorities have based their work. While language scholars do not agree with Fowler on every point, they do use his dictionary as a reference point. *A Dictionary of American-English Usage* (1957) by Margaret Nicholson is an adaptation of Fowler's *Dictionary* for an American audience.

The *Harper Dictionary of Contemporary Usage* shares Copperud's democratic approach, with comments from 136 panelists, writers and scholars, sprinkled throughout its entries. *A Dictionary of Contemporary American Usage* deserves notice because it includes within its dictionary framework a full discussion of grammar, which the reader uses by starting at *parts of speech* and following cross-references.

Theodore M. Bernstein has written two other books similar to *The Careful Reader* (cited above)—*Miss Thistlebottom's Hobgoblins* (1971) and *Dos, Don'ts, and Maybes of English Usage* (1977). Because the first book deals with outmoded rules of usage, it can help relax a stilted style. The second book is based on Bernstein's syndicated *New York Times* column, "Bernstein on Words." Because most of its entries come from readers' questions, they are practical problems which writers in all fields are likely to confront.

Technical Style Manuals

This second category of style manuals is composed of books on technical writing style that are still general in the sense that they pertain to several or even to all technical writing fields. One of the most elementary guides is *Scientific Writing for Graduate Students* (1968), edited by F. Peter Woodford and produced by the Council of Biology Editors. Written for teachers of scientific writing, the first section of this book is organized around a course of twelve one-hour sessions that lead students step-by-step through the writing process. Other chapters include information on writing theses and research project proposals. Another basic style guide is *How to Write Scientific and Technical Papers* (1958) by Sam Farlow Trelease. Although this reference is an early one, it retains a place on the reference lists of many other, more recent style manuals.

One of the most comprehensive technical writing manuals is *Handbook of Technical Writing* (1982) by Charles T. Brusaw, Gerald J. Alred, and Walter E. Oliu. Alphabetical entries include detailed information on format for a variety of technical writing forms, on prose style, on grammar, and on handling references, indexes, tables, and illustrations.

Carolyn J. Mullins covers editorial and prose style in *The Complete Writing Guide* (1980); she presents material in a clearly marked, step-by-step writing process, with information arranged sequentially as the writer will use it. Mullins includes an unannotated bibliography of major style manuals in a variety of fields, as well as sample pages from a book manuscript for use as a style sheet. An unusual section explains the preparation and use of boiler plates—paragraphs, sections, chapters, and appendices that can be standardized and lifted from one manuscript for use in another with little or no alteration.

Robley Winfrey's *Technical and Business Report Writing* (1962) is outstanding in its treatment of different types of writing, including sections on formal reports, student laboratory reports, magazine feature articles, and papers for technical societies.

The strength of *How to Write and Publish a Scientific Paper* (1979) by Robert A. Day lies in its practical coverage of the format and content of each element in a scientific paper. Day includes special sections on preparing review papers, conference reports, and theses. His appendices contain lists of accepted abbreviations and symbols for scientific terms, prefixes and abbreviations of International System of Metrication (SI) units, words presenting problems in spelling or style, and frequently used jargon compared with preferred usage.

Publications of certain national and international organizations may also prove useful to writers in a variety of technical fields. The *American National Standard Guidelines for Format and Production of Scientific and Technical Reports* (1974) provides style guidance for research reports in science and engineering that are reproduced and distributed in the technical community but not published in journals or books. *General Notes on the Preparation of Scientific Papers* (1974), published by the Royal Society, sets style standards for scientific journal articles published in England. Maeve O'Connor and F. Peter Woodford attempt in *Writing Scientific Papers in English* (1975) to establish international style guidelines "for scientists of any nationality who want to submit papers to journals published in English" (p. 1). Grammatical usage and prose style points covered in this work therefore reflect the problems of writers whose native language is not English.

Edmond H. Weiss in *The Writing System for Engineers and Scientists* (1982) approaches editorial and prose style from a unique angle, setting up a writing project like any other technical problem and offering a system of strategies for handling reports, proposals, professional papers, articles, manuals, memorandums, and letters. He divides editing into five ascending levels of prose style quality: mechanical correctness, appropriateness of language, clarity, accessibility (the style level at which a reader is required to make a minimal effort to understand), and urgency (a lively, fluent style). Using copious examples, Weiss discusses prose style in two comprehensive sections: one on words and phrases, and one on sentences and paragraphs.

Another detailed work on technical prose style is *The Language of Science* (1961) by William Gilman. Although it contains plenty of specific rules and examples, this book also offers a survey of good scientific style for the writer who prefers to read it through in addition to using it as a reference. A similar work is *Scientists Must Write* (1978) by Robert Barrass. This book is a general overview of style in scientific writing, ranging from personal records to correspondence and internal reports to formal reporting and publication of research.

Technical professionals interested in writing for magazines read by the general public will find a comprehensive guide in *Writing for Technical and Business Magazines* (1969) by Robert H. Dodds. Emphasis in prose style is on writing for an audience. Dodds also covers editorial style in his section on format of magazine articles and in reprinted sections of mechanical rules from the 1967 edition of the *U.S. Government Printing Office Style Manual*.

Technical Editing (1975), edited by Benjamin H. Weill, is slanted for editors of technical books and journals, as well as for writers who work with project scientists and engineers. Another guide for technical writing professionals is Rufus P. Turner's *Technical Writer's and Editor's Stylebook* (1964). Packed with rules, examples, and lists of various types of usage items, this reference concentrates on editorial style.

The last three sources in this category are limited to specific areas of style. J. Christopher Rigg's *A Bibliography of Recommendations (ISO, BS, NEN, and ANSI) for the Preparation of Scientific Publications* (1972) concerns only systems of national and international standards for putting scientific material into publishable form. Divided into four sections, the bibliography lists publications of the International Organization for Standardization (ISO), of the British Standards Institute (BS), of the Netherlands Standardization Institute (NEN), and of the American National Standards Institute (ANSI). Many entries are annotated. Although the *Bibliography of Recommendations* is over ten years old, it can be used to locate the current publications listed or those available in new editions. *The Technical Speller* (1964), edited by Gessner G. Hawley and Alice W. Hawley, is a 130-page alphabetical list of words often used in technical writing. Finally, Nelson James Dunford's *A Handbook for Technical Typists* (1964) gives instructions for typing technical manuscripts.

Style Manuals Prepared for Specific Publications

To supplement general style guides, academic societies, individual publications, and experienced scholars have produced specialized manuals. In *Writing for Technical and Professional Journals* (1968), John H. Mitchell lists style manuals preferred by publications in biological sciences, agricultural sciences, medicine, mathematics, engineering, humanities, business, psychology, sociology, political science, government, history, law, fine arts, and education. However, currency is an important consideration in using this material. Although over half the book is a section in which excerpts from 16 style manuals are reprinted, about half of these publications have been revised since 1968. For example, the *MLA Style Sheet* was revised in 1970; moreover, since the more detailed *MLA Handbook* was published in 1977, some publishers prefer the newer version to its predecessor. Mitchell also suggests using the *NEA Style Manual for Writers and Editors* (1966) in writing for education journals, but that reference is out of print and is no longer available from the National Education Association's Publication Department.

The most widely preferred style guide in the biological sciences is the *Council of Biology Editors Style Manual* (1978). This reference covers both editorial and prose style, as well as special style conventions in plant sciences, microbiology, animal sciences, chemistry, and biochemistry. With its comprehensive annotated bibliography and reference lists for each chapter, the *CBE Style Manual* is particularly rich in sources. Examples of specialized guides in this field are the *Journal of Physiology* "Notice to Contributors" (1983) and "BIOSIS Guide to Abstracts" (1978), prepared by the BioSciences Information Service. Suggestions in "BIOSIS" include the elements of a biological abstract, its format, and instructions on handling names of chemicals and drugs, geographic locations, and scientific names of organisms as well as a list of abbreviations and symbols used in abstracts.

Agricultural scientists will find answers to their questions on style in the *Handbook and Style Manual for ASA, CSSA, and SSSA Publications* (1977), published by the American Society of Agronomy, the Crop Science Society of America, and the Soil Science Society of America. In addition to its material on editorial style, this reference includes submission requirements for the five journals published by member societies; for *Crops and Soils Magazine*, a semitechnical, popular-style magazine; and for monographs, books, and special publications. The authors also list sources for nomenclature used in fields related to agronomy and crop science, and provide instructions on writing abstracts of articles, selecting index words, and preparing reference citations.

Guides to medical writing abound. The authoritative style guide for journal articles in this field is the American Medical Association's *Manual for Authors and Editors* (1981) by William R. Barclay, M. Therese Southgate, and Robert W. Mayo. In addition to general information on editorial style, this book contains sections on notation of SI units, standard abbreviations of general and technical terms, format for mathematical material, and medical nomenclature.

Edward J. Huth's *How to Write and Publish Papers in the Medical Sciences* (1982) provides detailed information on editorial and prose style in medical research papers, case reports, reviews, case-series analyses, editorials, book reviews, and letters to the editor. Huth's bibliography and references combine to offer a comprehensive survey of writing resources in his field. *Writing Medical Papers* (1973) by James Calnan and Andras Barabas focuses on prose style and on the format and content of numerous types of medical writing, including examination papers, job applications, applications for research funds, research reports, conference reports, theses, and monographs. In *Medical Writing* (1972), Morris Fishbein tackles both editorial and prose style in the medical context.

Two books on prose style, both intended to be read as texts and not handbooks, are *Why Not Say It Clearly* (1978) by Lester S. King and *Dx + Rx* (1977) by John H. Dirckx. King's purpose is to enable his reader to discriminate between good and bad writing, to see style principles that make the difference, and to implement those principles. An outstanding feature is his chapter on translation and style. Dirckx stresses language—

grammar and syntax, grammatical usage, diction, sentence structure, and paragraph structure.

Nurses, too, have produced their share of writing guides. Andrea B. O'Connor presents a general overview of the writing process within the context of nursing in *Writing for Nursing Publications* (1976). *The Nurse's Guide to Writing for Publication* (1981) by Susan Kooperstein Mirin addresses the task of writing articles for journals. Philip C. Kolin and Janeen L. Kolin, in *Professional Writing for Nurses in Education, Practice and Research* (1980), write for an audience of nurses, graduate students, teachers, and administrators. Their scope is wide, with sections on mechanical rules, prose style, standard abbreviations used in health care, reports, client case documentation, student writing, professional correspondence, journal articles, and book writing.

In the United States the style of chemical publications is dominated by the *Handbook for Authors of Papers in American Chemical Society Publications* (1978). This reference describes the different types of contributions that appear in American Chemical Society publications and includes sections on mechanical rules; treatment of mathematical expressions; abbreviations and symbols for physical and chemical quantity units, chemical elements, chemical and biochemical compounds, and SI units; references for chemical nomenclature; instructions for presenting experimental details, tables, and illustrations; microform and non-print supplements; documentation; and useful references. A similar source, *Handbook for Chemical Society Authors* (1961) gives directions for format, preparation, and submission of papers to chemical journals in England. *Style Guide for Chemists* (1960) by Louis F. Fieser and Mary Fieser presents material on prose style, grammar and syntax, usage, and mechanical rules in a chemical context. *Writing Guide for Chemists* (1961) by Walter J. Gensler and Kinereth D. Gensler focuses on developing an effective technical writing style and on describing the content and format of a paper on chemistry by taking the reader through the writing process.

Physicists will find writing style suggestions in the *Style Manual* (1978) published by the American Institute of Physics and edited by David Hathwell and A.W. Kenneth Metzner. Included in this guide are a list of physics journals with statements of editorial policy; manuscript preparation instructions; mechanical rules; instructions for handling mathematical material; instructions on preparing figures; lists of spellings for frequently used words, units of measure, standard abbreviations, and journal title abbreviations; the Physics and Astronomy Classification Scheme; and a bibliography of useful references.

Most earth science journals follow *Suggestions to Authors of the Reports of the United States Geological Survey* (1978) by Elna E. Bishop and others. Focusing on editorial style, the authors give directions on format and content of different types of reports published by the Geological Survey and on manuscript preparation. Special sections present information on stratigraphic nomenclature and description, geographic names, petrologic terminology, chemical terminology, mineralogic terminology and descriptions, paleontologic matter, and the metric system. Other sections discuss use of the computer in preparing geologic reports and review English grammar, syntax, and mechanical rules. A more general guide is *Geowriting* (1979), edited by Wendell Cochran, Peter Fenner, and Mary Hill.

The American Mathematical Society has set stylistic standards for mathematical writing in *A Manual for Authors of Mathematical Papers* (1973). In addition to material on format and content of papers, this manual includes alternative systems of mathematical notation; criteria for selecting a notation system; instructions for presenting formulas and displays; instructions for preparing diagrams, illustrations, matrices, and tables; directions on selection and format of key words and phrases; instructions on abstract preparation; and documentation. Also published by the American Mathematical Society is Ellen Swanson's *Mathematics into Type* (1979), which emphasizes preparation of copy for the compositor by the copy editor.

Writers in all engineering fields can use Herbert B. Michaelson's *How to Write and Publish Engineering Papers and Reports* (1982) as a reference in preparing internal reports, journal papers, conference papers, trade magazine articles, and theses. Emphasizing the writer as a strategist who makes decisions based on the needs of his audience, Michaelson presents sections on prose style, abstracts, references, illustrations, and tables.

The thirty journals published by the American Institute of Electrical and Electronics Engineers follow guidelines set in three *IEEE Spectrum* articles—"Information for IEEE Authors" (1965), "A Supplement to 'Information for IEEE Authors' " (1966), and "IEEE Recommended Practice for Units in Published Scientific and Technical Work" (1966). The original guide gives information on content and format of articles, symbols and abbreviations, mathematical notation, references, illustrations, and captions. The supplement provides new instructions for preparation of titles, abstracts, and references to facilitate indexing by computer-based techniques. The third article makes recommendations on when to use metric units and when to use other systems of units and on usage in cases where a unit has more than one name. Also included are a translation of the International System of Units resolution, definitions of fundamental SI units, rules for conversion and rounding of units, and a list of equivalences for converting British-American units to SI units.

John Markus and Joan L. Fife in the *Electronics Style Manual* (1978) present the usage rules Markus followed in the fourth edition of his *Electronics Dictionary* (1978). The *Style Manual* includes rules for spelling words, rules for presenting numbers, and tables of standard abbreviations and spellings frequently used in writing about electronics.

In *Bibliographic References* (1968) Dorothy L. Anderson covers reference lists, bibliographies, footnotes, internal documentation, and quotations for engineers. Her citation forms are based on recommendations made by the Committee of Engineering Society Editors of the Engineering Joint Council at a 1966 meeting.

Many style guides exist for the social sciences. Marigold Linton suggests editorial style standards for these scientists in *A Simplified Style Manual* (1972). She devotes one section of the book to succinct discussion of mechanical rules, grammatical usage, and prose style. Basing her recommendations on the 1967 edition of the *Publication Manual of the American Psychological Association* (no longer current), she discusses content and form of articles. An especially helpful feature is the facsimile of a complete typewritten manuscript and of the same article as it would appear in the *Journal of Experimental Psychology*.

More wide-ranging is *A Guide to Writing and Publishing in the Social and Behavioral Sciences* (1977) by Carolyn J. Mullins. This work deals with writing not only research articles but also notes, short reports, comments, responses to comments, review articles, book reviews, books, monographs, textbooks, and edited collections. A key section discusses the seven basic documentation styles commonly used by journals in the social and behavioral sciences. Mullins also explains how to prepare a prospectus and includes a sample prospectus for a monograph. John S. Harris and Reed H. Blake in *Technical Writing for Social Scientists* (1976) apply technical writing methods to the social sciences, stressing scientific research procedures and clarity and precision in style.

The *Publication Manual of the American Psychological Association* (1974), accepted by numerous journals in its field, gives detailed information on format and content of experimental reports, deals with scientific prose style, and includes a list of APA journals with policy statements and a list of non-APA journals that use this manual.

In *Report Writing in Psychology and Psychiatry* (1961), Jack T. Huber concentrates on content and format of reports. He discusses the basic structure of reports, formulation of cases, and elements of psychological reports, reports on intelligence, therapy progress notes, psychiatric case studies, vocational reports, and reports for neurologists. Huber suggests that personnel workers, speech therapists, and reading specialists may find adaptations of his report guidelines useful.

Although law journals vary in style, legal writers can find useful recommendations in *A Uniform System of Citation* (1981). Published by the Harvard Law Review Association, this reference contains general rules for constructing citations; specific forms for cases, constitutions, statutes, legislative materials, administrative and executive materials, international materials, and services; and tables of federal, state and foreign government sources.

Robert W. Durrenberger in *Geographical Research and Writing* (1971) offers advice to beginning writers in geography, discussing both research techniques and paper preparation. The "Editorial Policy Statement" and "Style Sheet" of the *Association of American Geographers Annals* (1970) are reprinted in Durrenberger's book. These guides give specific instructions on preparing each element of an article.

The Preparation of Archaeological Reports (1974) by Leslie Grinsell, Philip Rahtz, and David Price Williams provides a basis for preparing excavation and non-excavation reports. It includes a section on preparing distribution maps, as well as directions on documentation and indexing.

Although the *MLA Handbook* gives information useful to contributors to some education journals, other guides address specific types of educational reports and materials. *A Guide for the Development of Proposals, Progress, and Final Reports* (1975) was prepared by the Kentucky Department of Education to assist vocational educators in applying for new program funds. Although the authors stress that program planners outside Kentucky should find out the specific requirements of their agencies, this guide may help administrators in other districts standardize application procedures. It may also provide a model for educators in districts with no standardized procedures. A similar publication is *Preparing Evaluation Reports* (1970) by David G. Hawkridge, Peggie L. Campeau, and Penelope K. Trickett. Written for educators reporting results of experimental programs to local, state, and federal administrators, this guide tells how to present and analyze data and includes a sample evaluation report. The authors also give instructions for preparing abstracts for the Educational Resources Information Center (ERIC). Although Lynn A. Emerson wrote *How to Prepare Training Manuals* in 1952, it remains a usable source because of its thorough coverage of writing instructional materials based on educational principles. Emerson includes a variety of samples illustrating prose style and typographical format.

More specialized than Emerson's work is *How to Write Computer Manuals for Users* (1982) by Susan J. Grimm. Written to illustrate the style it inculcates, the book is chronologically arranged with detailed steps explained in an active, clear, conversational prose style. Grimm covers format alternatives, mechanical rules, and treatment of examples and illustrations.

The kinds of writing required in business and in the study of business are given full treatment in *The Business Writer's Handbook* (1982) by Charles T. Brusaw, Gerald J. Alred, and Walter E. Oliu. Among the alphabetical entries are sections (including samples) on abstracts, journal articles, briefs, correspondence, essay examination answers, forms, instructions, job descriptions, memorandums, minutes of meetings, news releases, policies and procedures, proposals, questionnaires, reports, and resumés. Other entries focus on prose style, editorial style, and grammar rules.

Conclusion

This list of style manuals is by no means complete. There are other, equally valuable sources. None of these guides is sufficient for every writing task; none is the *right* one. The choice of a style manual or a combination of style manuals—like style itself—hinges on appropriateness to the writing assignment, the audience, and often the writer's own preferences.

References

Alred, Gerald J., Diana C. Reep, and Mohan R. Limaye. *Business and Technical Writing: An Annotated Bibliography of Books, 1880–1980*. Metuchen, N.J.: Scarecrow, 1981.

American National Standard Guidelines for Format and Production of Scientific and Technical Reports. New York: American National Standards Institute, 1974.

Anderson, Dorothy L. *Bibliographic References: A Manual for Engineering Reporters*. University Park: Pennsylvania State University, 1968.

Angione, Howard, ed. *The Associated Press Stylebook and Libel Manual*. New York: Associated Press, 1977.

Barclay, William R., M. Therese Southgate, and Robert W. Mayo. *Manual for Authors and Editors: Editorial Style and Manuscript Preparation*. 7th ed. American Medical Association. Los Altos, Calif.: Lange, 1981.

Barrass, Robert. *Scientists Must Write: A Guide to Better Writing for Scientists, Engineers and Students*. New York: Wiley, 1978.

Bernstein, Theodore M. *The Careful Writer: A Modern Guide to English Usage*. New York: Atheneum, 1965.

———. *Dos, Don'ts, and Maybes of English Usage*. New York: Times Books, 1977.

———. *Miss Thistlebottom's Hobgoblins: The Careful Writer's Guide to the Taboos, Bugbears and Outmoded Rules of English Usage*. New York: Farrar, Straus, Giroux, 1971.

BioSciences Information Service. "BIOSIS Guide to Abstracts." *Biol Abstr*, 65 (Jan. 1978), xxiii–xxvi.

Bishop, Elna E., et al. *Suggestions to Authors of the Reports of the United States Geological Survey*. 6th ed. Washington, D.C.: U.S. GPO, 1978.

Brusaw, Charles T., Gerald J. Alred, and Walter E. Oliu, *The Business Writer's Handbook*. 2nd ed. New York: St. Martin's, 1982.

———. *Handbook of Technical Writing*. 2nd ed. New York: St. Martin's, 1982.

Bryant, Margaret M., ed. *Current American Usage*. New York: Funk, Wagnalls, 1962.

Calnan, James, and Andras Barabas. *Writing Medical Papers: A Practical Guide*. London: Heinemann, 1973.

The Chicago Manual of Style, Thirteenth Edition, Revised and Expanded, for Authors, Editors, and Copywriters. Chicago: University of Chicago Press, 1982.

Cochran, Wendell, Peter Fenner, and Mary Hill, eds. *Geowriting: A Guide to Writing, Editing, and Printing in Earth Science*. 3rd ed. Falls Church, Va.: American Geological Institute, 1979.

Collins, F. Howard. *Authors and Printers Dictionary*. 11th ed. Revised by Stanley Beale. Oxford: Oxford University Press, 1973.

Copperud, Roy H. *American Usage and Style: The Consensus*. New York: Van Nostrand Reinhold, 1980.

———. *American Usage: The Consensus*. New York: Van Nostrand Reinhold, 1970.

———. *A Dictionary of Usage and Style*. New York: Hawthorn-Dutton, 1964.

Council of Biology Editors Style Manual: A Guide for Authors, Editors, and Publishers in the Biological Sciences. 4th ed. Arlington, Va.: Council of Biology Editors, 1978.

Crutchley, Brooke. *Preparation of Manuscripts and Correction of Proofs*. 6th ed. Cambridge Authors' and Printers' Guides, No. 2. Cambridge: Cambridge University Press, 1970.

Day, Robert A. *How to Write and Publish a Scientific Paper*. Philadelphia: ISI Press, 1979.

Dirckx, John H. *Dx + Rx: A Physician's Guide to Medical Writing*. Boston: Hall, 1977.

Dodds, Robert H. *Writing for Technical and Business Magazines*. New York: Wiley, 1969.

Dunford, Nelson James. *A Handbook for Technical Typists*. New York: Gordon, Breach, 1964.

Durrenberger, Robert W. *Geographical Research and Writing*. New York: Crowell, 1971.

"Editorial Policy Statement" and "Style Sheet." *Assn Am Geog Ann*, 60 (1970), 194–207.

Emerson, Lynn A. *How to Prepare Training Manuals: A Guide in the Preparation of Written Instructional Materials*. Albany, N.Y.: University of the State of New York, State Education Department, Bureau of Vocational Curriculum Development and Industrial Teacher Training, 1952.

Evans, Bergen, and Cornelia Evans. *A Dictionary of Contemporary American Usage*. New York: Random House, 1957.

Fieser, Louis F., and Mary Fieser. *Style Guide for Chemists*. New York: Reinhold, 1960.

Fishbein, Morris. *Medical Writing: The Technic and the Art*. 4th ed. Springfield, Ill.: Thomas, 1972.

Fleischer, Eugene B. *A Style Manual for Citing Microform and Nonprint Media*. Chicago: American Library Association, 1978.

Flesch, Rudolph. *The ABC of Style*. New York: Harper, 1964.

Follett, Wilson. *Modern American Usage: A Guide*. Ed. Jacques Barzun. New York: Hill, Wang, 1966.

Fowler, Henry W. *A Dictionary of Modern English Usage*. 2nd ed. Rev. by Sir Ernest Gowers. Oxford: Oxford University Press, 1965.

General Notes on the Preparation of Scientific Papers. 3rd ed. London: Royal Society, 1974.

Gensler, Walter J., and Kinereth D. Gensler. *Writing Guide for Chemists*. New York: McGraw-Hill, 1961.

Gibaldi, Joseph, and Walter S. Achtert. *MLA Handbook for Writers of Research Papers, Theses, and Dissertations*. New York: Modern Language Association (MLA), 1977.

Gilman, William. *The Langucge of Science: A Guide to Effective Writing*. New York: Harcourt, Brace, World, 1961.

Gowers, Sir Ernest. *The Complete Plain Words*. 2nd ed. Rev. by Sir Bruce Fraser. Baltimore: Penguin, 1973.

Grimm, Susan J. *How to Write Computer Manuals for Users*. Belmont, Calif.: Lifetime Learning-Wadsworth, 1982.

Grinsell, Leslie, Philip Rahtz, and David Price Williams. *The Preparation of Archaeological Reports*. 2nd ed. New York: St. Martin's, 1974.

A Guide for the Development of Proposals, Progress, and Final Reports. Kentucky Research in Vocational Education Series, No. 1. Frankfort, Ky.: Bureau of Vocational Education, Kentucky Department of Education, 1975.

A Guide to Writing for the United Nations. New York: United Nations Publication, 1966.

Handbook and Style Manual for ASA, CSSA, and SSSA Publications. Madison, Wis.: American Society of Agronomy, Crop Science Society of America, Soil Science Society of America, 1977.

Handbook for Authors of Papers in American Chemical Society Publications. Washington, D.C.: American Chemical Society, 1978.

Handbook for Chemical Society Authors. 2nd ed. Special Publication No. 14. London: Chemical Society, 1961.

Harris, John S., and Reed H. Blake. *Technical Writing for Social Scientists*. Chicago: Nelson-Hall, 1976.

Hathwell, David, and A.W. Kenneth Metzner, eds. *Style Manual for Guidance in the Preparation of Papers for Journals Published by the American Institute of Physics and Its Member Societies*. 3rd ed. New York: American Institute of Physics, 1978.

Hawkridge, David G., Peggie L. Campeau, and Penelope K. Trickett. *Preparing Evaluation Reports: A Guide for Authors*. AIR Monograph No. 6. Pittsburgh: American Institutes for Research, 1970.

Hawley, Gessner G., and Alice W. Hawley, eds. *The Technical Speller*. New York: Reinhold, 1964.

Hoffman, Herbert H. *Bibliography Without Footnotes*. 2nd ed. Newport Beach, Calif.: Headway, 1978.

Huber, Jack T. *Report Writing in Psychology and Psychiatry*. New York: Harper, 1961.

Hunn, David T., ed. *The Author-Publisher Handbook*. Tuscon, Ariz.: Aztex, 1980.

Hurt, Peyton. *Bibliography and Footnotes: A Style Manual for Students and Writers*. 3rd ed. Rev. by Mary L. Hurt Richmond. Berkeley: University of California Press, 1968.

Huth, Edward J. *How to Write and Publish Papers in the Medical Sciences*. Professional Writing Series. Philadelphia: ISI Press, 1982.

IEEE Standards Coordinating Committee 14 (Quantities and Units). "IEEE Recommended Practice for Units in Published Scientific and Technical Work." *IEEE Spectrum*, 3 (Mar. 1966), 169–73.

"Information for IEEE Authors." *IEEE Spectrum*, 2 (Aug. 1965), 111–15.

Jordan, Lewis, ed. *The New York Times Manual of Style and Usage: A Desk Book of Guidelines for Writers and Editors*. Rev. ed. New York: Times Books, 1976.

King, Lester S. *Why Not Say It Clearly: A Guide to Scientific Writing*. Boston: Little, Brown, 1978.

Kolin, Philip C., and Janeen L. Kolin. *Professional Writing for Nurses in Education, Practice and Research*. St. Louis: Mosby, 1980.

Linton, Marigold. *A Simplified Style Manual: For the Preparation of Journal Articles in Psychology, Social Sciences, Education, and Literature*. New York: Appleton-Century-Crofts-Meredith Corp., 1972.

Longyear, Marie, ed. *The McGraw-Hill Style Manual: A Concise Guide for Writers and Editors*. New York: McGraw-Hill, 1983.

"LSA Style Sheet for Publications of the Linguistic Society of America." *LSA Bul*, No. 71 (1976), 43–45.

Mager, Nathan H., and Sylvia K. Mager. *Encyclopedic Dictionary of English Usage*. Englewood Cliffs, N.J.: Prentice-Hall, 1974.

Maney, A.S., and R. L. Smallwood, eds. *MHRA Style Book: Notes for Authors and Editors*. Leeds, England: Modern Humanities Research Association, 1971.

Manheimer, Martha L. *Style Manual: A Guide for the Preparation of Reports and Dissertations*. New York: Marcel Dekker, 1973.

A Manual for Authors of Mathematical Papers. 5th ed. Providence, R.I.: American Mathematical Society, 1973.

Markus, John. *Electronics Dictionary*. 4th ed. New York: McGraw-Hill, 1978.

———, and Joan L. Fife. *Electronics Style Manual: A Concise Presentation of the Style Rules Followed in the Fourth Edition of the Electronics Dictionary*. New York: McGraw-Hill, 1978.

Michaelson, Herbert B. *How to Write and Publish Engineering Papers and Reports*. Philadelphia: ISI Press, 1982.

Miller, Bobby R., ed. *The UPI Stylebook: A Handbook for Writers and Editors*. Rev. ed. New York: United Press International, 1981.

Mirin, Susan Kooperstein. *The Nurse's Guide to Writing for Publication*. Wakefield, Mass.: Nursing Resources-Concept Development, 1981.

Mitchell, John H. *Writing for Technical and Professional Journals*. Wiley Series on Human Communications. New York: Wiley, 1968.

The MLA Style Sheet. 2nd ed. New York: MLA, 1970.

Morris, William, and Mary Morris. *Harper Dictionary of Contemporary Usage*. New York: Harper, 1975.

Mullins, Carolyn J. *The Complete Writing Guide to Preparing Reports, Proposals, Memos, Etc*. Englewood Cliffs, N.J.: Prentice-Hall, 1980.

———. *A Guide to Writing and Publishing in the Social and Behavioral Sciences*. New York: Wiley, 1977.

Nicholson, Margaret. *A Dictionary of American-English Usage, Based on Fowler's Modern English Usage*. New York: Oxford University Press, 1957.

———. *A Practical Style Guide for Authors and Editors*. New York: Holt, Rinehart, Winston, 1967.

"Notice to Contributors." *J Physiol*, 339 (June 1983), iii–viii.

O'Connor, Andrea B. *Writing for Nursing Publications*. Thorofare, N.J.: Slack, 1976.

O'Connor, Maeve, and F. Peter Woodford. *Writing Scientific Papers in English: An ELSE-Ciba Foundation Guide for Authors*. Amsterdam: Elsevier/Excerpta Medica/North-Holland, 1975.

Porter, Roy E., et al. *The Writer's Manual*. 2nd ed. Palm Springs, Calif.: Education and Training Consultants, 1979.

Power, Jane, et al., eds., *NEA Style Manual for Writers and Editors*. Washington, D.C.: National Education Association, 1966.

Publication Manual of the American Psychological Association. 2nd ed. Washington, D.C.: American Psychological Association, 1974.

Rigg, J. Christopher. *A Bibliography of Recommendations (ISO, BS, NEN, and ANSI) for the Preparation of Scientific Publications.* Wageningen, the Netherlands: Centre for Agricultural Publishing and Documentation (Pudoc), 1972.

Seeber, Edward D. *A Style Manual for Authors.* Bloomington: Indiana University Press, 1967.

————. *A Style Manual for Students for the Preparation of Term Papers, Essays, and Theses.* 2nd ed. Bloomington: Indiana University Press, 1967.

Skillin, Marjorie E., Robert M. Gay, et al. *Words into Type.* 3rd ed. Englewood Cliffs, N.J.: Prentice-Hall, 1974.

Strunk, William, Jr., and E. B. White. *The Elements of Style.* 3rd ed. New York: Macmillan, 1979.

"A Supplement to 'Information for IEEE Authors,' " *IEEE Spectrum,* 3 (May 1966), 91.

Swanson, Ellen. *Mathematics into Type: Copy Editing and Proofreading of Mathematics for Editorial Assistants and Authors.* 2nd ed. Providence, R.I.: American Mathematical Society, 1979.

Trelease, Sam Farlow. *How to Write Scientific and Technical Papers.* Baltimore: Williams, Wilkins, 1958.

Turabian, Kate L. *A Manual for Writers of Term Papers, Theses, and Dissertations.* 4th ed. Chicago: University of Chicago Press, 1973.

Turner, Rufus P. *Technical Writer's and Editor's Stylebook.* Indianapolis: Sams; New York: Bobbs-Merrill, 1964.

A Uniform System of Citation. 13th ed. Cambridge, Mass.: Harvard Law Review Association, 1981.

U.S. Government Printing Office Style Manual. Rev. ed. Washington, D.C.: U.S. GPO, 1973.

Van Leunen, Mary-Claire. *A Handbook for Scholars.* New York: Knopf, 1978.

Weill, Benjamin H., ed. *Technical Editing.* 1958; rpt. Westport, Conn.: Greenwood, 1975.

Weiss, Edmond H. *The Writing System for Engineers and Scientists.* Englewood Cliffs, N.J.: Prentice-Hall, 1982.

Wiles, Roy McKeen. *Scholarly Reporting in the Humanities.* 4th ed. Toronto: University of Toronto Press-Humanities Research Council of Canada, 1968.

Winfrey, Robley. *Technical and Business Report Preparation.* 3rd ed. Ames, Iowa: Iowa State University Press, 1962.

Woodford, F. Peter, ed. *Scientific Writing for Graduate Students.* New York: Rockefeller University Press, 1968.

The Technical Writing Profession

JULIE LEPICK KLING

This essay identifies and briefly reviews the more important and accessible literature on technical writing as a profession. The literature reviewed falls under three general rubrics:

Professional definition and identity
Professional status
Career guidance and preparation

This review, with few exceptions, concentrates on the literature published in the last 15 years, and does not consider relevant material in textbooks or the general areas of legal writing or writing for the government. Moreover, material on freelancing, consulting, and technical illustration has consciously been excluded. Therefore, the term "technical communication" is used interchangeably with "technical writing" and, frequently, with "technical editing."

Professional Definition and Identity

The origins of technical writing conceived as a special subject of study in college curricula can be traced back to the latter part of the nineteenth century in American education, as Robert J. Connors has shown in his well-documented study, "The Rise of Technical Writing Instruction in America" (1982).Technical writing as a separate and identifiable profession is a much more recent phenomenon, stemming from the dramatic technical achievements of World War II and the consequent explosion of technical and scientific information.

Today, technical writing is a recognized, if young, profession. As a profession, it is still in its formative stage. This is perhaps best reflected in the fact that technical writers are designated by a multitude of differing job titles: technical editor, documentation specialist, publications engineer, and so on.

While technical writers may be known by a variety of names, the functions they perform can be defined. The two-volume *Handbook of Technical Writing Practices* edited by Stello Jordan (1971), an indispensable reference work for both novice and experienced technical writers, offers a comprehensive collection of articles on all aspects of the technical writing profession. The *Handbook* is divided into four parts. Part One (Volume One) reviews the various kinds of documents produced by the technical writer: instruction manuals, parts catalogs, reports, proposals, even films. Parts Two, Three, and Four (Volume Two) respectively address the supporting services for technical writing (illustration and layout, data processing, composition and reproduction techniques, editing); the management of technical writing and its place in the overall organizational structure; and guides, style manuals, specifications, and other references for the technical writing professional.

Two articles in the *Handbook* specifically relate to the problem of professional identity and definition: Carl F. Whitesell, Jr.'s "Role and Scope of Technical Writing Activities" and Walter A. Skowron's discussion of "Job Classifications" (1971).

Whitesell's article describes the publication products and services that are within the range of a technical writer or technical writing group. Among products, he includes manuals, parts catalogs, provisioning documentation, reports, proposals, professional papers, journals and trade publications, displays, brochures, in-house publications, product support literature, and specifications. Among the services included in the technical writing function, Whitesell lists data management, editing, illustrating, titling of graphics, document production in all its media, and document storage, retrieval, and distribution. The author uses graphics to enhance the reader's understanding of the technical writing activity in the larger context of its parent organization. He concludes that the scope of technical writing is broadening and will increasingly come to include information management and related functions as technical advances are made in the fields of electronics, communications, and publishing.

The intrepid reader who is willing to wade through a good deal of turgid prose will find in Walter A. Skowron's article a comprehensive and informative listing of the various job titles by which technical communicators are classified, together with a description of the responsibilities and functions associated with each job category. As might be expected, many job classifications contain overlapping functions—the distinction between technical writer/technical editor is a case in point. Skowron, however, argues for the efficacy of clear and distinct job descriptions, and he provides one of the best available descriptions of what technical communicators at all levels of civilian and military organizations and under a variety of job titles actually do for a living. He also briefly summarizes a by-now-dated salary survey (for 1967); he concludes that computerization and automation of the publications industry will lead to a reduction in the demand for narrowly specialized writers and to a consequent increased need for broadly experienced publications personnel.

Of related interest is Carlin T. Kindilien's book, *Technical Writing and Communications* (1963). Kindilien's purpose is to provide company managers with a knowledge of technical writing practices that will enable them to develop and integrate technical communications into the larger organization. His information is based on that supplied by over 500 technical communications managers; it is eminently practical and covers such topics as staffing and organization of a technical writing group, workloads, training policies, wage scales, work methods, and costing procedures. Graphics and case studies increase the effectiveness of this work which, though dated, still presents a realistic portrait of the technical writing profession.

In his thoughtful and suggestive paper, *For the Technical Communicator* (1974), Eugene A. Cogan contrasts the incomplete state of development of the technical writing profession with the more mature legal and medical professions, and with other professions born out of World War II: operations research and systems analysis, computer technology, management sciences, and information retrieval. The technical writing profession is defined, like any other professional group, in terms of three criteria: services provided, characteristics of individuals in the profession, and overall group characteristics. Cogan offers prescriptions and proscriptions for achieving increased professional definition. He concludes that, while technical writing is still a nascent profession, it will become increasingly more defined and specialized; he also urges the development of a code of ethics for the technical communicator. Cogan's predictions have been validated by the recent concern among technical communicators with establishing professional certification and with problems in professional conduct.

One paper on the professional definition and identity of the technical writer which deserves much wider recognition than it has received is J. W. Dillingham's *"Technical Writing vs. Technical Writing"* (1981). Dillingham distinguishes between the technical writer, technical author, and editor. He argues that the designation "technical writer" is an occupational, not a professional, category, associated with lower salaries and status—a problem which, he suggests, can be circumvented by job titles, such as "engineering writer" or "technical publications specialist." According to Dillingham, industry needs technical authors and editors. He outlines the problems in preparing students for these positions and gives a real-world example of the technical writer's job as measured by the effort and number of drafts required to complete a manual written to Army specifications.

In two related articles in *Computerworld*, Lois Paul (1982) notes that the intended audience for many technical documents has shifted from technical personnel to end-users of many products. Paul points out that this shift has carried with it a change in the professional image of the technical writer. Technical writing is no longer a "twilight zone" of dissatisfied engineers, but a definite career path supported by graduate and undergraduate degree specializations. Today's technical writers may prefer to be called "documentation analysts" and are full-fledged communications specialists.

As much of the literature cited thus far makes clear, the distinction between technical writer and technical editor is not hard and fast. From the point of view of function, it is generally agreed that editing involves correcting mistakes of grammar and punctuation; improving sentence structure, paragraph cohesion, and overall organization; insuring that the style of a document is consistent with its audience, purpose, and the issuing organization's standards; and improving the readability of a piece of writing. In other words, an editor revises a text; a writer provides fodder for revision.

All technical writing, however, necessarily includes some editorial function. Nor is the distinction between technical writer and editor made clearer if approached in terms of job titles. In smaller organizations, the technical editor (or writer) may wear both hats simultaneously; in larger organizations, the job category "technical editor" usually refers to supervisory personnel who oversee technical writers and other workers involved in the production of a given document. The technical editor in such an organization usually answers to the production manager, who is in charge of all publications production.

The fact of the matter is that all technical writers will function as editors, and that many practicing professionals will agree that their profession or job classification is that of a technical editor. A considerable body of literature supports this claim.

Most discussions of technical editing assume that the editor possesses first-rate language skills. There is general agreement that equally important to an editor's success is the possession of the right psychological equipment: the successful editor must be able to work well with others. This qualification reflects the fact that a technical editor usually must supervise as well as work with others.

The individual who wishes to obtain an idea of the range of activities subsumed under the title "technical editor" should consult *Technical Editing* (1975). Edited by B. H. Weil, *Technical Editing* serves as a comprehensive review of the field and includes essays describing the editing of internal documents, journals, books, manuals, graphic aids, and translations. Originally published in the 1950s as an outgrowth of the "Symposium on Technical Editing" held in New York at the 1957 meeting of the Division of Chemical Literature of the American Chemical Society, the essays collected in this volume remain timely today for readers ranging from the student of technical editing to the experienced professional. In the initial essay, editor Weil outlines the "Psychological, Educational, and Professional Aspects" of technical editing. He emphasizes that good technical editors must become "student[s] of applied psychology" (p. 2) if they are to develop fruitful working relations with writers, management, illustrators, and printers. Weil briefly covers the educational requirements of the technical editor; he notes that employers tend to prefer the technically trained engineer or scientist, since technical editing "often calls for a form of technical collaboration rather than grammatical correction" (p. 14). Similar to Weil's *Technical Editing* in aim, although more limited in scope, is Lola M. Zook's *Technical Editing* (1975), a collection of 18 essays on the qualifications and responsibilities of the technical editor.

Zook (1981) has also authored a lively and straightforward description of the technical editor's lot in her article, "Editing and the Editor," printed in a special issue of *Technical Communication* (1981) devoted to technical editing. On the basis of her own experience as an editor, Zook lists the tangible knowledge, skills, and abilities required of a technical editor. She then suggests that these qualities must be supplemented by "certain intangibles," including a sense of order, logic, and appreciation for language, and an "instinct for what matters" (p. 8). She also gives practical advice to editors in negotiating the sometimes stormy tides that rise between editors, writers, and other co-workers.

An interesting portrait of the technical editor can be found in the *Guide for Beginning Technical Editors* (1979) developed by Wallace Clements and Robert G. Waite for the Lawrence Livermore Laboratories. An earlier draft was published in the Proceedings of the 26th International Technical Communication Conference. Developed to instruct new technical editors in editorial procedures, the guide offers an overview of the progress of a manuscript from draft to page masters and is a helpful portrait of a day in the life of a technical editor.

A discussion of the professional life of the technical editor would be incomplete without mentioning Mary Fran Buehler's work on editorial function and the levels-of-edit concept, as discussed in "Controlled Flexibility in Technical Editing" (1977), which briefly sketches the on-the-job activities of the technical editor. Buehler is also co-author, with Robert Van Buren, of *The Levels of Edit* (1980). Van Buren and Buehler acknowledge that technical editing is "a rather inconsistently defined endeavor" (p. 1). Using the levels-of-edit approach, however, the authors define the scope and responsibilities of the technical editor.

Journals published by professional societies provide a continuing source of information about the technical writing profession. The Society for Technical Communication is the major organization representing the interests and concerns of technical writers and editors and all other individuals (including technical illustrators and audio-video specialists) involved in the communication of technical data. The Society's quarterly publication,

Technical Communication, features articles on subjects of interest to its members, as well as book reviews, editorials, Society news, and correspondence. The Society's bi-monthly newsletter, *Intercom*, also keeps members informed of professional activities and developments in the technical communication field; *Intercom* is supplemented by newsletters published by regional chapters.

Another quarterly publication of interest to professional technical communicators is the *IEEE Transactions on Professional Communication*, published by the IEEE Professional Communication Society, a division of the Institute of Electrical and Electronics Engineers dedicated to improving the quality of technical communication. Each issue will typically address a particular topic, such as writing proposals, developing useful graphics, or enhancing communication of technical information to non-technical audiences.

The American Business Communication Association's *Journal of Business Communications* and its sister publication, the *ABCA Bulletin*, primarily address the needs and concerns of the business or managerial communicator as well as the teacher of business communication. However, both journals do publish some articles, as well as announcements of meetings, seminars, and research opportunities, that will interest the technical writer or editor.

The *Journal of Technical Writing and Communication* (*JTWC*) serves as a forum for academic and practicing professionals alike. The *JTWC* prints both speculative and practical papers that often exemplify the interdisciplinary nature of the technical communication profession. Book reviews, profiles of noteworthy professionals, and announcements of conferences and other professional activities are also included.

Teachers of technical communication may find useful information concerning curriculum development, classroom activities, and general pedagogical issues in *The Technical Writing Teacher*, published by the Association of Teachers of Technical Writing.

Professional Status

The professional status of the technical writing specialist has been the subject of several surveys. The more comprehensive of these studies were done some time ago; the remainder are limited to special segments of the profession and represent a biased sample. Thus, it is difficult to extrapolate more than a very general profile of the practicing technical writer. Nonetheless, these studies provide a fair indication of the personal, educational, and employment characteristics of the communications professional.

A survey of the educational background of technical writers in the aerospace industry conducted by Gerard J. Ennis (1966) showed that formal training tended to be balanced between technical and communications disciplines. A far more comprehensive study of 1,474 companies and government agencies, done in 1966 by Vernon M. Root ("Technical Publications Job Patterns and Knowledge Requirements"[1968]), revealed that employers of technical writers preferred college graduates with communications skills.

The only readily available comprehensive profile of the technical communicator is Austin C. Farrell's "A Membership Profile of the Society for Technical Communication" (1971), based on information supplied by the 1,874 respondents to a 1970 mail survey of the STC membership. According to Farrell, the average age of respondents was 44 years; 50 percent were between the ages of 38 and 52. One-third were classified as editors, 26 percent as writers, and 17 percent as managers or supervisors. The salary received by 41 percent of the respondents ranged between $10,000 and $16,000; 68 percent were employed in private industry and 17 percent by government; manufacturing and engineering firms employed 46 percent. Perhaps the most interesting revelation of Farrell's study concerns education. Technical writers were found to come from very diverse disciplines. Only 24 percent were trained as engineers, and only 15 percent had degrees in English; 11 percent held journalism degrees, 9 percent had degrees in science, and the remainder held degrees in a variety of disciplines.

Louis Perica's "Profile of Respondents to Advertisements for Technical Communicators" (1974) contrasts the composite profiles of respondents to newspaper advertisements for senior and junior level positions. On the basis of this limited sample, he finds that the typical applicant for a senior level position was male, currently employed and with more than ten years' experience in the field, and held a degree in English or journalism. The typical applicant for a junior position was female, unemployed, and a recent college graduate lacking relevant experience.

Perica's results might lead to the assumption that women are inadequately prepared for technical writing positions. A study by Harriet L. Duzet, "The Status of Women in Communications" (1974), offers a much more optimistic picture, although neither Perica's nor Duzet's surveys are wide enough in scope to be truly representative. Duzet surveyed female registrants at the 20th ITCC conference; she found that position titles varied widely, although most respondents were involved in the preparation of reports and manuals. Most held undergraduate, and many held graduate, degrees, primarily in English, journalism, or science. Forty percent reported salaries ranging from $15,000 to nearly $20,000 a year. However, despite finding that women technical communicators were well educated, well paid, and generally satisfied in their work, Duzet also found continuing evidence that women remained disadvantaged relative to their male colleagues.

In "Technical Writer Profile" (1979), K. Clark Davis reports results of a 1978 questionnaire sent to members of the Association for Computing Machinery's Special Interest Group on Documentation. Most respondents (80 percent) were between 21 and 39 years of age; most (86 percent) held bachelor's degrees, primarily in English, other humanities, engineering, or computer science. Salaries ranged from $15,000 to $20,000 for 39 percent of those responding; women tended to receive lower salaries than men. However, the validity of Clark's results is qualified by its limitation to a specialized group and by a small percentage of responses.

Students majoring in technical communications have also been the subjects of study by at least two researchers. Maryan Schall, in "Profile of the Technical Communication Student" (1976), profiles the technical communications student at the University of Minnesota. "Profiles of 1981 Communication Students," a broader study performed by Earl E. McDowell and colleagues (1982), reports the results of a 1981 survey of the job goals and expectations of students enrolled in technical communication programs in a representative sampling of U.S. colleges and universities. The study provides a profile of the background, education, and self-assessed personal attributes of future technical writing professionals.

Career Guidance and Preparation

A large body of literature addresses the qualifications, education, and career development of the technical communicator. Most of this material falls under the general heading of career guidance material produced by private individuals or government agencies.

The Encyclopedia of Careers and Vocational Guidance (1978) discusses the definition and history of the technical writing profession, the nature of the work, educational requirements, and means of entry and advancement in the field. It provides earnings summaries and projects an optimistic employment outlook, based especially on three important developments: the ever-increasing volume and complexity of scientific and technical data; the need for cooperative sharing of process and assembly data among organizations involved in coordinated manufacturing endeavors; and, finally, the current expansion of joint research efforts by business, government, and industry.

General descriptions of the technical writing profession and the educational and personal requirements for success in the field can be found in two helpful books, *Your Future in Technical and Science Writing* (1972) and *Opportunities in Technical Communications* (1980). Both works are designed to assist the young adult in planning a career in technical writing; both insist on the importance of a solid engineering or scientific background and stress that college or university coursework in communication should support a basically technical education.

Emerson Clarke and Vernon Root's *Your Future in Technical and Science Writing* (1972) offers a comprehensive description of the educational requirements, professional responsibilities, and employment opportunities for technical writers in engineering, the biological sciences, and science journalism. The authors distinguish between the *technical writer*, who is generally trained in science and engineering and writes to an exclusively professional audience, and the *science writer*, whose training as a journalist enables him to effectively communicate scientific and technical information to a general readership. A strong point of Clarke and Root's book is their analysis of the relation of the technical writer to the engineering professions according to the type of documents produced. The writer may work (a) in direct support of engineering, writing or editing instruction manuals, parts documentation, specifications, and assisting in data management; (b) in general support of engineering, responsible for reports, proposals, software, technical advertising, and industrial audiovisuals; or (c) for general publication, as an editor for technical and trade publications, scientific journals, or in technical book publication. The writer trained in the biological sciences may work as a medical writer or editor for professional journals, in pharmaceutical writing, or in the growing field of medical electronics; a preparation in the biological sciences can also lead to employment in agricultural writing.

Less emphasis is given to the science writer. The authors devote one chapter to science writing and publishing in journalism. They stress that journalism should be the science writer's primary course of study. Chapters are also devoted to the situation of the female technical writer and to a listing of the professional organizations of interest to the technical medical, business, or science writer.

Your Future in Technical and Science Writing covers a wide range of topics of interest to the aspiring technical writer and supplies practical, solid advice. It is limited by its date, and, as a consequence, it is not fully representative of present opportunities, particularly in the fields of computer science and microelectronics.

Jay R. Gould and Wayne A. Losano's *Opportunities in Technical Communications* covers much of the same territory as does Clarke and Root's book, although it places less emphasis on describing the day-to-day tasks and publications of the technical writer and editor, and it offers more concrete information on education and training. Originally published in 1964 as *Opportunities in Technical Writing Today*, this very useful book has been consistently updated to reflect changes in the technical communications profession; another edition is scheduled for release in late 1983.

Gould and Losano begin with an overview of the technical writing profession, coupled with a list of the qualities and characteristics the technical writer or editor should possess. Chapters cover the kinds of documents the technical writer produces, the sorts of institutions and organizations that employ technical writers, the nature of medical and business writing, and practical employment advice. Students planning an academic program leading to employment as a technical writer will find the list of colleges and universities offering technical writing programs and short courses especially helpful in career planning. Up-to-date information on academic programs can also be found in the Society for Technical Communication's *Academic Programs in Technical Communication* (1982). Like Clarke and Root, Gould and Losano provide a list of the professional organizations in the technical writing field.

Both *Your Future in Technical and Science Writing* and *Opportunities in Technical Communications* contain practical information that should prove helpful not only to the young adult, but also to the advanced college student or other individual considering a career as a technical writer. Teachers of technical writing with little or no on-the-job experience will also benefit from the detailed description of the technical writer's working conditions and duties.

Of related interest is Alice Sins's *Women in Communications* (1979), which is in the same series of career guidance books as *Opportunities in Technical Communications*. *Women in Communications* examines technical writing as one of many communications-related professions offering opportunities for women.

Francis W. Weeks's paper, "Employment Perspective" (1976) unfortunately does not supply the synoptic overview its title promises. On the basis of informal telephone interviews with five Illinois employers of writers, Weeks concludes that hiring is serendipitous.

Some material is available on careers in technical communication addressed to more specialized audiences. Writing to the high school industrial arts students, Clint McGirr describes in "Careers for the 70's in Technical Writing" (1974) what a technical writer does and stresses the importance of qualities such as verbal skills, organizational ability, and visual form perception. In "The Information Industry" (1972) Alun Jones discusses opportunities for physics graduates to work as science writers. "Chemists Can Use Their Skills in Many Jobs Outside the Laboratory" (1977), a survey of employment opportunities for non-laboratory chemists, lists science writing as one option among others. Finally, Andrew D. Turnbull in "Technical Writing in the Computer Industry" (1981) suggests that Ph.D.s in English might look to the computer industry for employment as technical writers.

A number of U.S. government publications provide information about careers in technical communication and related fields, most notably the 1982 *Occupational Outlook Handbook* (*OOH*). This work contains a short but comprehensive description of the technical writing profession.

Technical writers put scientific and technical information into readily understandable language. They research, write, and edit technical materials and also may produce publications or sales or audiovisual materials. Technical writers use their knowledge of a technical subject area—laser beams or pharmacology, for example—along with their command of language and versatility of style to convey information in a way that is helpful to people who need it—scientists, engineers, technicians, mechanics and repairers, managers, sales representatives, and the general public. In addition to clarifying technical information, technical writers often use their writing skills in marketing, advertising, and public relations work (p. 232).

According to the *OOH*, approximately 25,000 technical writers and editors were employed in 1980; of these, 1,700 worked for the U.S. government. The greatest number of technical writing employment opportunities were clustered in California, Texas, and the Northeast. In 1980 the average annual starting salary for a technical writer in industry was $15,200; experienced technical writers commanded from $17,000 to $25,000, while salaries for technical editors ranged from $21,000 to $31,000. Demand for technical writers is expected to grow throughout the 1980s with the growth of technical and scientific information and increased spending for research and development. However, the *OOH* cautions that expansion of technical writing opportunities is closely tied to R&D expenditures; any reduction in R&D funding would be expected to affect the demand for technical writers.

Information on the career opportunities in technical communication can also be found in *Communications Occupations* (1979), reprinted from the 1980–81 *OOH*, and *Communications-Related Occupations* (1978), reprinted from the 1978–79 *OOH*.

Other career guidance material published by the U.S. government include *Exploring Careers—Performing Arts, Design, and Communications Occupations* (1979) and *Exploring Writing Careers* (1976). Both of these works are intended primarily for a junior or senior high school reader. *Exploring Careers* includes a very brief job description, emphasizing that the aspiring technical writer should obtain a college degree with courses in technical and scientific subjects as well as writing, editing, and publication production experience. *Exploring Writing Careers* has brief sections on technical and scientific writing and a chapter on editing careers; appendices include a glossary of writing and publishing terminology, a list of writing occupations, and a list of relevant professional organizations.

The Cincinnati Public Schools includes a discussion of the personal qualifications and educational background required of a technical writer in its *Exploring Careers in Writing for the Market* (1973). Part of a Career Development series for grades 9 through 12, Cincinnati's *Exploring Careers* is comparable in content to U.S. government publications of similar titles.

Conclusion

The foregoing essay should be taken provisionally. As a young profession, technical writing is still in a process of self-definition. Furthermore, it is a profession tied to and particularly sensitive to technological developments, most notably, at present, to developments in the electronics and computer fields. These changes will affect both the content and the production of technical documents. The literature on the professional aspects of technical communication will no doubt continue to reflect these changes.

References

Academic Programs in Technical Communication. Washington, D.C.: Society for Technical Communication, 1982.

Buehler, Mary Fran. "Controlled Flexibility in Technical Editing: The Levels-of-Edit Concept at JPL." *Tech Comm*, 24, No. 1 (1977) 1–4.

"Chemists Can Use Their Skills in Many Jobs Outside the Laboratory." *Chem Eng News*, 55, No. 43 (1977), 29–36.

Clarke, Emerson, and Vernon Root. *Your Future in Technical and Science Writing*. New York: Richards Rosen, 1972.

Clements, Wallace, and Robert G. Waite. *Guide for Beginning Technical Editors*. Livermore, Calif.: Lawrence Livermore Laboratories, 1979.

Cogan, Eugene A. *For the Technical Communicator: Pursuing Professional Identity and Maturity*. Professional Paper No. 8–74. Alexandria, Va.: Human Resources Research, 1974.

Communications Occupations. Washington, D.C.: U.S. Department of Labor, 1979.

Communications-Related Occupations. Washington, D.C.: U.S. Department of Labor, 1978.

Conners, Robert J. "The Rise of Technical Writing Instruction in America." *J Tech Writ Comm*, 12 (1982), 329–52.

Davis, K. Clark. "Technical Writer Profile." *Tech Comm*, 26 No. 3 (1979), 3.

Dillingham, J. W. "*Technical* Writing vs. Technical *Writing*." Annual Conference of College Composition and Communication, Dallas, 26–28 Mar. 1981. ERIC ED 204 788.

Duzet, Harriet L. "The Status of Women in Communications." *Proceedings of the 21st International Technical Communication Conference*. Washington, D.C.: STC, 1974, pp. 153–56.

The Encyclopedia of Careers and Vocational Guidance. Vol. II: *Careers and Occupations*. Chicago: J. C. Ferguson, 1978.

Ennis, Gerard J. "Survey of Technical Writers in the Aerospace Industry." *STWP Rev* 13, No. 2 (1966), 10–13.

Exploring Careers in Writing for the Market. Cincinnati, Ohio: Cincinnati Public Schools, 1973. ERIC ED 106 590.

Exploring Careers—Performing Arts, Design, and Communications Occupations. Washington, D.C.: U.S. Department of Labor, 1979.

Exploring Writing Careers. Washington, D.C.: U.S. GPO, 1976.

Farrell, Austin C. "A Membership Profile of the Society for Technical Communication." *Tech Comm*, 18, No. 4 (1971), 4–8.

Gould, J. R., and Wayne A. Losano. *Opportunities in Technical Communications*. Skokie, Ill.: VGM Career, 1980.

Jones, Alun. "The Information Industry: Science Writing." *Physics Educ*, 7 (1972), 333–34.

Jordan, Stello, ed. *Handbook of Technical Writing Practices*. 2 vols. New York: Wiley, 1971.

Kindilien, Carlin T. *Technical Writing and Communications*. Waterford, Conn.: Prentice-Hall, 1963.

McDowell, Earl E., Joanne Frissell, and Victoria M. Winkler. "Profiles of 1981 Technical Communication Students." *Tech Comm*, 29, No. 2 (1982), 11–18.

McGirr, Clint. "Careers for the 70's in Technical Writing." *Indus Educ*, 63, No. 7 (1974), 26–27.

Occupational Outlook Handbook. Washington, D.C.: U.S. Department of Labor, 1982.

Paul, Lois. "Tech Writers Addressing New Audience." *Computerworld*, 16, No. 46 (1982), 8.

———. "Tech Writers Changing 'Retread' Image." *Computerworld*, 16, No. 46 (1982), 1, 8.

Perica, Louis. "Profile of Respondents to Advertisements for Technical Communicators." *Tech Comm*, 21, No. 1, (1974), 14–16.

Root, Vernon M. "Technical Publications Job Patterns and Knowledge Requirements." *Tech Comm*, 15, No. 3, (1968), 5–12.

Schall, Maryan. "Profile of the Technical Communication Student at the University of Minnesota." *Tech Comm*, 23, No. 3 (1976), 2–6.

Sins, Alice. *Women in Communications*. Skokie, Ill.: VGM Career, 1979.

Skowron, Walter A. "Job Classifications." In *Handbook of Technical Writing Practices*. Ed. Stello Jordan. New York: Wiley, 1971, pp. 1073–1100.

Turnbull, Andrew D. "Technical Writing in the Computer Industry: Job Opportunities for Ph.D.'s." *ADE Bul*, No. 67 (1981), 26–30.

Van Buren, Robert, and Mary Fran Buehler. *The Levels of Edit*. JPL Publication 80–1. Pasadena, Calif.: Jet Propulsion Laboratory, 1980. NAS 1.12/7 80-1.

Weeks, Francis W. "Employment Perspective—Business and Technical Writing." *Proceedings of a Seminar on Career Trends in Communication*. Silver Spring, Md.: Council of Communication Societies, 1976, pp. 22–25. ERIC ED 140 823.

Weil, B. H., ed. *Technical Editing*. Westport, Conn.: Greenwood, 1975.

Whitesell, Carl F., Jr. "Role and Scope of Technical Writing Activities." In *Handbook of Technical Writing Practices*. Ed. Stello Jordan. New York: Wiley, 1971, II, 1029–70.

Zook, Lola M. "Editing and the Editor: Views and Values." *Tech Comm*, 28, No. 4 (1981), 5–9.

———, ed. *Technical Editing: Principles and Practices*. Washington, D.C.: STC, 1975.

Author Index

Subject Index

abstract, 97, 300
abstraction, 368–70. *See also* computers
advertising, direct mail, 317
Aristotle, 3, 121–22
associationism, 132
audience, 13, 25, 137–38; adaptation, 180–83, 360, 364–66; analysis, 163–91, 328, 387–89; and computers, 365; historical importance, 165; style in, 328; rhetorical emphasis on, 164; and structure of messages, 52–58; and teaching, 171–72, 180–83; textbooks, 172; writer's awareness of, 166

Bacon, Sir Francis, 28, 29, 121, 122, 125, 128
business writing, 27, 313–337; collection letters, 322; cover letters, 319–21, 335; form letters, 320, 324; letters of application, 335–36; letters of complaint, 322–23; management letters, 319; persuasive letters, 324; sales letters, 317–18; teaching of 325–26; textbooks on, 326. *See also* memoranda; resumés; writing, technical and scientific

channels, 58–62, 72. *See also* audience
Cicero, 28, 121–22
cognitive theory, 175, 359

cohesion, 175, 226
communication: attributes, 49; channels, 58–62; defined, 39; effective, 50; environment, 69; evolution of, 40; feedback, 68–69, models, 41–48; scientific and technical, 14, 15, 359; situation, 167–70; sources, 48; theory of, and technical communication, 39–83. *See also* audience
composing process, 122, 195
composition, 123
computers, 353–80; as audience, 171–72, 365; cognition, 364, 372, 374; cultural implications of, 355–58; and cybernetics, 363; ethical implications, 359; graphics, 371; implementation design, 365; mode, 370; and sentence structure, 175; tools, 367. *See also* abstraction; information networks; linearization; parsing
contingency theory, 71
correspondence, business, 313–49. *See also* business writing
criticism, literary, 170
culture, 4–6, 7. *See also* computers

dialectic, 3, 118
decision-making, 143–46
discourse, 142–167; modes of 9, 194–95, 200–201, 209, 210, 212; theories of, 163, 168

About the Contributors

MARILYN BARNES-OSTRANDER is a graduate student in technical communication at Rennselaer Polytechnic Institute.

GEORGE A. BARNETT is Associate Professor of Communication at the State University of New York at Buffalo where he teaches courses in systems theory, organizational communication, and intercultural communication. He has published numerous articles and books in political, organizational, intercultural, and technical communication.

WILLIAM L. BENZON teaches at Rensselaer Polytechnic Institute in the Department of Language, Literature, and Communication. He teaches literature, linguistics, and writing. He has published articles on literature, on discourse theory, and on technical communication. In 1981 he was a NASA Summer Faculty Fellow.

GLENN J. BROADHEAD is Associate Professor of English at Iowa State University where he teaches courses in composition and in business and technical writing. His published work includes articles on sentence structure, style, argumentation, "real-world" composing and revising processes, and the rhetoric of conversation.

BERTIE E. FEARING is Associate Professor of English at East Carolina University where she is Co-director of the Undergraduate and Graduate Programs in Technical and Professional Writing. She is Senior Editor of *Teaching English in the Two-Year College*, Associate Editor of *Technical Communication*, and author of several journal articles. She has recently co-authored a book entitled *Teaching Technical Writing in the Secondary School*.

CAROLINE R. GOFORTH teaches English at Clemson University. She has published articles in composition and in children's literature. A former newspaper editor, she is also a freelance writer whose general-interest articles and short stories have appeared in publications for children and for adults.

MARK P. HASELKORN is Assistant Professor of English at Louisiana State

University where he teaches courses in technical communication and linguistics. He is the author of articles on technical writing, computers and language, and formal semantics.

SUSAN HILLIGOSS is Assistant Professor of English at Clemson University where she teaches courses in business writing, technical writing, and medieval literature.

CAROL HUGHES is a graduate student in technical communication at Rensselaer Polytechnic Institute.

DEBRA JOURNET is Assistant Professor of English and Director of Technical and Professional Communication at Louisiana State University where she teaches courses in technical writing and in modern British literature. She has published several articles about rhetoric and science and is the co-author of *Readings for Technical Writers*.

MICHAEL L. KEENE is Assistant Professor of English at the University of Tennessee, Knoxville, where his major responsibility is the creation and supervision of the university's technical communication program. Author of a number of articles on mental processes in language use, his current research interest is the demographics of the technical writing community and its role in the information economy. He has authored the revised eighth edition of W. Paul Jones's *Writing Scientific Papers and Reports*.

ROBERT SCOTT KELLNER is Assistant Professor of English at Texas A&M University where he teaches undergraduate and graduate courses in technical writing and literature. He was a technical writer for the U.S. Navy, IBM Corporation, and Honeywell. He has written numerous award-winning articles on writing and literature and is the author of *Understanding the Media* and *Technical Writing*.

JULIE LEPICK KLING is a technical writer in software documentation, specializing in user interface design and online documentation at Data General Corporation. She is the author of *Opportunities in Computer Science Careers* and co-author of *Readings for Technical Writers*.

CAROLYN R. MILLER is Associate Professor of English at North Carolina State University where she directs the program in writing-editing and teaches courses in editing, technical communication, and rhetoric. Her research interests and publications are in the areas of rhetorical theory and the rhetoric of science and technology. She is Co-editor of *New Essays in Technical and Scientific Communication*.

MARY HURLEY MORAN is Assistant Professor of English at Clemson University where she has coordinated the Writing Laboratory. She has published essays in composition and twentieth-century British literature, and she is the author of *Margaret Drabble: Existing Within Structures*.

MICHAEL G. MORAN is Assistant Professor of English at Clemson University where he has directed the Composition and Rhetoric Program. Since completing a Post-doctoral Fellowship in Composition at the University of Kansas, his main research interests have been in rhetorical invention and the rhetoric of scientific writing. He has published essays in composition theory and pedagogy, technical communication, and business writing and is Co-editor of *Research in Composition and Rhetoric*.

ANTHONY O'KEEFFE teaches in the technical writing program and in the undergraduate writing lab at Louisiana State University.

PHILIP M. RUBENS is Associate Professor of Technical Communication and Graphics at Rensselaer Polytechnic Institute where he currently directs the Technical Writers' Institute. He is a former member of the Board of Directors of the Society for Technical Communication. He has published widely in communications, ethics, and literary studies. At present he is co-editing a book on word processing in the classroom.

RUSSELL RUTTER is Associate Professor of English at Illinois State University where he serves as Coordinator of Technical Writing and as Director of Professional Practice in English. He teaches courses in technical writing and has published articles on technical writing theory and pedagogy, as well as a textbook, *Writing Professional Reports*, which he co-authored with Karl E. Gwiasda.

JUDITH P. STANTON is Assistant Professor of English at Clemson University where she teaches technical writing. Her interests include the computer and technical communication, medical writing, and editing.

VICTORIA M. WINKLER is Associate Professor of Rhetoric at the University of Minnesota at Minneapolis-St. Paul. She has contributed essays to several anthologies on technical writing and is the Editor of *The Technical Writing Teacher*.